Political Studies from Spatial Perspectives

Anglo-American Essays on Political Geography

Edited by

Alan D. Burnett
Department of Geography, Portsmouth Polytechnic

and

Peter J. Taylor
Department of Geography, University of Newcastle-upon-Tyne

JOHN WILEY & SONS
Chichester • New York • Brisbane • Toronto

British Library Cataloguing in Publication Data:
Political studies from spatial perspectives.
  1. Geography, Political
  I. Burnett, Alan D.
  II. Taylor, Peter J.
  327.101'1   JC319   80-41384

ISBN 0 471 27909 9
ISBN 0 471 27910 2 Pbk

Typeset by Photo-Graphics, Yarcombe, Honiton, Devon
Printed by Pitmans of Bath

Contents

Preface

This book originated from an Anglo-American seminar held under the auspices of the Political Geography Working Party at the annual conference of the Institute of British Geographers at Lancaster University, January 1980. The 16 papers given at the seminar and the interest which was shown in them was such as to convince us that they would constitute the basis of a useful book. Subsequently we were offered, and indeed solicited, additional papers from colleagues who are teaching and researching political and human geography in North American and British universities.

The scope of the text therefore was largely dictated by the current research interests of our contributors. Apart from the introductory sections provided by ourselves the book comprises over 20 original papers — theoretical, thematic, and empirical. The diversity of approach and topic is, we believe, a reflection of the pluralism of contemporary political geography and indeed the social sciences. We make no apology for the fact that the text has 'turned out' more theoretical, political, adisciplinary than other books in political geography. It includes studies of what the state does as well as its spatial structure, and investigates political systems at all levels and in different parts of the world.

While eschewing the adjective 'modern' from its title we nonetheless believe that the book as a whole covers both contemporary theoretical advances (often stimulated by other social sciences) and recent research developments. As such it should be of value to those undertaking research into political aspects of human geography and spatial aspects of political studies at all levels of the academic hierarchy. It should also be useful to students in all but introductory courses. We hope that it will point to key research directions in a revitalized political geography in the 1980s and fruitful collaboration between American and British social scientists from whatever disciplinary background but who are interested in the interface between politics and geography.

Clearly the set of papers could have been presented in a number of different ways. The organization structure we have adopted is based on both deductive-inductive and scale continuums. In our introduction to Part One this organization is outlined and justified as part of our general discussion of the book and its place in developments in political geography. This is followed by specific reviews of these developments on either side of the Atlantic. In Part Two, a series of theoretical paradigms for political geography as a whole are outlined and evaluated. Part Three comprises a number of major themes which have in the past, or might in the future, constitute foci for political geographical analysis. Although the papers in this section show considerable variation in the extent to which they are deductive and/or inductive, they have a common aim to provide research agendas. A series of empirically based studies are included in the final section. Although these are on very different topics they share a concern for detailed investigation of specific cases albeit from a variety of theoretical stances.

A scale dimension has also guided the ordering of chapters in the second, third, and fourth parts of the book. An attempt has been made to start with local-level studies and progress through to the international scale. While many readers may only be interested in specific chapters or parts of the text, those who do choose to read the book as a whole will hopefully find that their task is made both easier and more fruitful by the structure we have adopted.

Our editorial role has been relatively limited. In our introductions we have tried to avoid value-judgments, preferring that the contributions are judged on their merits. We have merely sought to identify salient features and links between the contributed chapters in our introductions to each section. Nor have we attempted to mould them around any (spurious) theme. We hope that none of our contributors are upset by the placing of their articles in the book or that their chapters have suffered from the minor changes to title, content, or style that we have taken the liberty to make in the interests of standardization as well as overall length and coherence.

Our warm thanks are due to all our contributors for submitting their manuscripts in such good shape and good time. We trust that their papers will be as widely read as part of this book as they would had they been published in an American or British journal.

We would like to thank the Institute of British Geographers for helping to finance several of our American colleagues to come to the original seminar and the IBG Political Study Working Party under whose auspices this work was started. We are also indebted to Celia Bird and her colleagues at Wileys; to our families, and to all our academic colleagues and typists who have advised and assisted us. We are only too pleased to share any credit for the production of this volume with all involved in it.

About the Contributors

JOHN AGNEW (Department of Geography, 343 H.B. Crouse Hall, Syracuse University, Syracuse, New York 13210). Obtained his PhD from Ohio State University. He has published articles on residential segregation, locational conflict, political regionalism, and is editor of *Innovation Research and Public Policy* (1980).

J. CLARK ARCHER (Department of Geography, Dartmouth College, Hanover, New Hampshire 03755). Educated at Indiana University and received his PhD from the University of Iowa. He is engaged on the Urban and Regional Studies Programme at Dartmouth College. His earlier research was on residential structure and electoral geography; recently he has been investigating federal expenditures. He is currently working (with Peter Taylor) on a historical study of American presidential elections.

JOHN A. BROHMAN (Department of Geography, University of California, Los Angeles, California 90024). He has studied at the University of Western Ontario, and Carleton University, Ottawa. He specializes in studies of the developing countries and has travelled widely in Southern Africa.

STANLEY BRUNN (Department of Geography, University of Kentucky, Lexington, Kentucky 40506). Formerly at Michigan State University, and is now chairman of the Geography Department of Kentucky. Author of *Geography and Politics in America* (1974) and co-author of *The Geography of Laws and the Administration of Justice* (1978), he has written numerous articles on voting in American elections and referenda, and federal policies and expenditure. Has recently published the results of a survey of residents' attitudes towards the Three Mile Island nuclear power station. Co-organizer of the AAG Political Geography Speciality Group.

ALAN BURNETT (Department of Geography, Lion Terrace, Portsmouth Polytechnic, Portsmouth PO1 3HE). Was educated at the University of Durham and Indiana University, and is principal lecturer at Portsmouth Polytechnic. His research interests include political participation and resource allocation in British cities, and residential structure in state socialist societies.

GORDON L. CLARK (John F. Kennedy School of Government, Harvard University, Cambridge, Mass. 02138). Formerly of the Department of Geography at McMaster University where he worked (with Michael Dear) on developing Marxist theories of the state for geographical research. He has related interests in regional disparities and environmental impacts, and is now assistant professor in government at Harvard.

MICHAEL DEAR (Department of Geography, McMaster University, 1280 Main Street, West Hamilton, Ontario L854KI). Is associate professor at McMaster. He has published papers on Marxist geography, locational conflict, and community-based mental health care. He is co-editor of *Urbanization and Urban Planning in Capitalist Society* (1980).

DEREK HALL (Department of Geography and History, Sunderland Polytechnic, Chester Road, Sunderland SR13 3SD). Obtained his PhD from the University of London, writing a thesis on community and social areas for neighbourhood councils. He has travelled widely in developing and socialist countries, and is currently writing a book on spatial aspects of urban community development policy in India. He is a senior lecturer at Sunderland Polytechnic.

JOHN W. HOUSE (School of Geography, University of Oxford, Mansfield Road, Oxford OX1 3TB). Since 1974 has been the Halford Mackinder professor of geography at the University of Oxford. Was formerly professor of geography at the University of Newcastle upon Tyne and has published many articles on applied and political geography in the context of North East England and Western Europe. He is author of *France: An Applied Geography* (1978) and editor of *The UK Space: Resources, Environment and the Future* (1977).

RAY HUDSON (Department of Geography, University of Durham, Science Laboratories, South Road, Durham DH13LE). Obtained his PhD from the University of Bristol. He has published on a wide range of aspects in human geography including regional development — with particular reference to the north-east of England — environmental images, land use and women at work. He is co-editor of *Regions in Crisis: New Directions in European Regional Theory* (1980) and co-author of *The Use of Land* (1980).

RON JOHNSTON (Department of Geography, The University, Sheffield S10 2TN). Is professor of geography at the University of Sheffield and has also taught in Australia, New Zealand, and Canada. He is the author of numerous articles on voting, campaigning, government expenditure, and other aspects of political and human geography. He is co-editor of *Geography and the Urban Environment,* co-author of *The Geography of Elections* (1979), and author of *Political, Electoral and Spatial Systems* (1979). He is currently working on studies of European elections and locational conflict and American courts.

ANDREW KIRBY (Department of Geography, University of Reading, Whiteknights, Reading RG6 2AB). Obtained his PhD from the University of Newcastle-upon-Tyne where he investigated urban housing markets and the distribution and use of public facilities. He has published articles on managerialism and municipal services, and is author of *Education Health and Housing* (1979) and co-editor of *Resources and Planning* (1979).

DAVID B. KNIGHT (Department of Geography, Loeb Building, Carleton University, Ottawa KIS5B6). Received his PhD from the University of Chicago and is currently associate professor and chairman of the Department of Geography at Carleton University. He is a specialist in political and cultural-historical geography, and is also interested in the role of territoriality in conflict. He is author of *A Capital for Canada* (1977).

ANTHONY LEMON (School of Geography, University of Oxford, Mansfield Road, Oxford OX1 3TB). Is fellow and tutor in geography at Mansfield College, Oxford and is a specialist on the political geography of Southern Africa. He has taught at the Universities of Natal and Rhodesia, and during 1979 undertook research at Rhodes University in South Africa. He has published on politics and settlement in Southern Africa and is author of *Apartheid: Geography of Separation* (1976).

JULIAN V. MINGHI (Department of Geography, University of South Carolina, Columbia, South Carolina 29208). Is now chairman of the Department of Geography at the University of South Carolina, after teaching for many years at the University of British Columbia. He is co-editor of *The Structure of Political Geography* (1969) and has published articles on the political geography of boundaries and conflict in the Pacific North-West and Alpine Europe. He is co-organiser of the AAG Speciality Group in Political Geography.

JOHN V. O'LOUGHLIN (Department of Geography, 220 Davenport Hall, University of Illinois, Urbana, Illinois 61801). Was educated at University College, Dublin, and received his PhD from Pennsylvania State University. His research interests include the electoral geography of minority groups, electoral bias, urban social geography, and comparative voting behaviour. During 1978-79 he was visiting professor at the Geographical Institute of the University of Dusseldorf.

RONAN PADDISON (Department of Geography, University of Glasgow, Glasgow G12 8QQ). Obtained his PhD from the University of Aberdeen, and has taught at the University of Dublin. He has published articles on electoral bias, town and country planning, and jurisdictional boundaries. He is convenor of a SSRC seminar series on urban politics and is editing a forthcoming edition of *Antipode* on urban political geography.

DAVID REYNOLDS (Department of Geography, University of Iowa, Iowa City, Iowa 52242). Has worked for several years on spatial aspects of local elections and theoretical aspects of public choice issues. He is co-editor of *Locational Approaches to Power and Conflict* (1974). He has taught at Indiana University and is professor in the Department of Geography at Iowa where he is also associated with the Institute of Urban and Regional Research.

GWYN ROWLEY (Department of Geography, The University, Sheffield SI0 2TN). Is senior lecturer in the Department of Geography at the University of Sheffield. He has written articles on central place theory in Wales, squatter settlements in Latin America, skid rows in North America, and, in political geography, has specialized in electoral studies, and conflict in the Middle East.

ROBERT SACK (Department of Geography, University of Wisconsin, Madison, Wisconsin 53706). During the academic year 1979-80 was at the University of Leicester, but is professor of geography at the University of Wisconsin. His major research contributions have been on developing and clarifying the spatial logic underlying geographical studies. He is author of a forth-coming book on territoriality.

PETER TAYLOR (Department of Geography, University of Newcastle-upon-Tyne, Newcastle-upon-Tyne NE1 7RU). Is lecturer and associate director of the Centre for Urban and Regional Studies. He has taught at the universities of Iowa, Alberta, and more recently, at Clark University and Dartmouth College. He has contributed numerous articles on the spatial organization of British and American elections, and is author of *Quantitative Methods in Geography* (1977), co-author of *The Geography of Elections* (1979), and *Seats, Votes and the Spatial Organisation of Elections* (1979).

COLIN WILLIAMS (Department of Geography, North Staffordshire Polytechnic, Beaconside, Stafford ST1 8AD). Obtained his PhD from the University of Wales for a thesis on language decline and nationalist resurgence in Wales. He has taught in Sweden, Canada, and the United States, and published articles on regional political movements in Western Europe and Quebec.

Part I

Introductions

Introduction

The title of this volume has been carefully chosen to reflect the views of the editors and to match the discussion and contributions to the seminar from which this set of essays emanated. *Political Studies from Spatial Perspectives* is intended to imply that we should finally halt the search for a separate 'political geography' and turn our energies instead towards contributing our particular perspectives to research on politics. The collection of essays presented below do not represent an addition to some core of geographical knowledge such as regional synthesis or abstract spatial modelling but rather they are a set of ideas produced by geographers but concerning political aspects of society. Hence they qualify as *political studies* irrespective of the work in this field by specialist political scientists. In this way political geography can be ranked alongside political sociology (Lipset, 1959; Lipset and Bendix, 1966; Greer and Orleans, 1964) and the new political economy (Mitchell, 1967). In the latter two cases techniques and ideas from other social sciences have been applied to political studies to produce quite distinctive contributions. We hope that this volume illustrates a similar effort on the part of political geographers employing their techniques and ideas which we describe simply as spatial perspectives.

Of course political geography has a much longer pedigree than either political sociology which emerged in the 1950s or the new political economy of the 1960s. In contrast, political geography has been a bulwark of traditional geographical studies for over half a century. Geography's isolation from other social science in the mid-twentieth century is found in an extreme form in its political branch. Isolationism in geography was a reaction to the

3

embarrassment of environmental determinism (Wrigley, 1965). The uniqueness of geography was formulated by Richard Hartshorne (1939) who gave all geographers the task of describing areal differentiation on the earth's surface. Within political geography even more embarrassment was felt concerning rash generalizations of geopolitics in Hitler's Germany (Soja, 1974). Hartshorne, as the leading political geographer of his generation, used political geography to illustrate how unique appreciation of (political) areal differentiation could be employed in systematic studies (Hartshorne, 1954). A position was reached whereby political geography achieved parity with the rest of geography in an isolated discipline. Since the 1950s human geographers have made huge strides in breaking down this isolation and entering the realms of social science (Johnston, 1979a). Political geography as a whole did not follow this path and hence finished up being isolated *within* human geography (Taylor, 1977, 1979). This accounts for the low esteem of the subdiscipline as reflected in the numerous derogatory terms used by various authorities and comically brought together at the end of Minghi's essay below.

Of course there have been numerous attempts to break out of this isolationism since the 1950s but they have not been completely successful, especially in the realm of teaching. Textbooks change by title and author but the same old topics reappear to suggest that vestiges of the old traditionalism are deeply steeped within the geographical body-politic. The dilemma between the old and the new can be seen in most recent publications. The most determined effort to break the isolation came in 1969 with Kasperson and Minghi's readings in *The Structure of Political Geography* where fifteen of the forty contributions were by non-geographers. Nevertheless in 1975 two new textbooks appeared, both called *Modern Political Geography* (Bergman, 1975 and Muir, 1975), and although both played explicit lip-service to systems analysis they clearly had more in common with traditional 'old-style' political geography than with the rest of 'modern' human geography. We trust that this book will mark the point when political geographers stop worrying about being modern. Hence the need to specify a definition of political geography in clear and simple terms: political geography is no more and no less than political studies carried out by geographers using the techniques and ideas associated with their spatial perspectives. The goal of such researches, like all political studies, involves an understanding of those aspects of society which are commonly designated 'political'. A single ultimate goal is shared with all social science — to understand society whether using the tools and ideas of geography or politics, economics, or ' sociology. We see no reason to elaborate a more comprehensive definition.

Such a loose definition inevitably encompasses a wide variety of ideas, themes, and approaches under the umbrella of political geography. This volume of essays illustrates this diversity. For those readers who prefer a neat compartmentalization of knowledge this book will be a profound disappointment. As we have indicated, political geography has had enough trouble getting out of one straight-jacket (state area, population, administrative areas, capital cities, frontiers and boundaries, etc., etc.) without us attempting to impose any new framework. Hence we interpret the variety within this volume as a major plus: it is a really healthy sign that political geographers disagree with each other on fundamental issues. Political geography, like other political studies, is at last beginning to reflect the conflicts within the politics it analyses.

One potential problem of the variety emanating from recent political geography is the possibility of a dichotomy arising between old and new. It is easy to see how this can happen given the unusual history described above. In fact in a recent review of four political geography books published in 1979 Archer (1980) points out how they all omit any reference to the major political geographers of the past. Clearly new political geography can be accused of emulating the myopic vision of their predecessors by cutting off all links with the past. In fact the basic criticism of the old approaches was not just in terms of the way they treated their material but also what they left out of consideration. Ignoring topics of relevance in the past is no advance on past geographers' failure to bring their materials up to date. The variety to be found in this volume does not make this mistake. Popular past theories — global political patterns, boundaries, and political territoriality — are to be found alongside new theories ranging from local state through to world politics in the twenty-first century. All are equally contributions by geographers towards political studies.

The deepest divisions among our papers do not reflect this old/new dichotomy, however, but relate to the basic political assumptions underlying the papers. A minority of the papers are built upon the Marxist tradition in social science which has come to be known as political economy. This is the broad 'classical' idea of political economy, not to be confused with the narrow application of economic concepts to political studies of the 'new' political economy, referred to previously. To ease comparison we will follow Lewis and Melville (1978) and term the former 'critical social theory', leaving the other papers in this volume (including the new political economy papers) to be denoted as either developing, or being based upon, traditional social theory. This is the most fundamental difference within the variety of papers in this collection. Differences range through all levels of epistemology from assumptions concerning the basic units of action through to means of evaluation theoretically and empirically. The most obvious difference is that traditional theory accepts the broad outlines of our current society and generally works to improve it through reform, whereas critical theory attempts to go beyond 'appearances' and finds 'hidden' structural conditions inhibiting any 'piecemeal social engineering'. This dichotomy will become readily apparent when we discuss individual papers below.

One problem that does arise from the variety before us as editors is how to organize the essays for the reader. Several possibilities suggested themselves; for instance by topic or geographical scale or alternatively by political assumptions or approach. We have chosen to classify each essay by its essential purpose. Hence there are four parts headed 'Introductions', 'Orientations', 'Agendas' and 'Applications'. The first section is self-explanatory and consists of two papers to cover Britain and North America respectively. These will be discussed below. It will be useful at this point if we briefly indicate distinctions between the other three sections, although each section does have its own introduction where definitions and contents are more fully elaborated.

Papers classified as presenting *orientations* towards political geography are those having essentially general themes suggesting ways in which researches should advance on a fairly broad front. They are all statements of how the authors would like to see a future political geography. As such they exemplify the variety within the book. In contrast the *agendas* deal with more specific topics and provide helpful ways of proceeding in research on these topics. These include literature reviews, development of specific models, and more general discussions of themes on which we may expect future political geography research. Finally the *applications* are identified as having a fundamental empirical purpose to their papers. These may range from particular case-studies through to empirical illustration of theoretical arguments.

We readily admit at this early stage that classification of the papers was not as straightforward as the above discussion implies. Several papers could be arguably allocated to more than one category because all attempt to be more than simple orientations, agendas, or applications. Nevertheless we feel that this organization does reflect the flavour of the offerings we have collected together, in that rather than separating out contrasting viewpoints they are placed alongside one another for comparative purposes.

This volume is about Anglo-American perspectives on political geography and hence we start with two contributions that review developments in both areas. What is presented are two very different essays. British political geography has produced no major work of international significance since Mackinder. Hence Johnston's review is very critical of post-Mackinder political geography in Britain. The essay reflects Johnston's (1979a) wider interests in the recent developments of thought in human geography as a whole and he illustrates the way political geography has lagged behind the rest of human geography as we have briefly described above. Johnston's (1971) research background is in urban geography and his interests in political geography originally derived from his work on public policy and electoral research at the urban scale. Hence Johnston's (1979b) political geography writings have no antecedents within pre-1970 political geography which for him merely represents a backwater by-passed by the rest of human geography. The message is that political geography should start afresh, drawing techniques and ideas from other modern political studies.

Minghi's review of North American geography is much more conciliatory. He has taken the opportunity to consider the changes that have occurred in political geography since the publication of his (and Kasperson's) *The Structure of Political Geography*. The hopes of the editors of that volume are briefly discussed and the recent literature is reviewed to see whether those hopes have been fulfilled. In some cases (e.g. electoral geography) the answer is yes, in others (e.g. environmental conflicts) the answer is no. Minghi's review is far less critical, not just because it takes cognizance of only recent publications but also because it is written by someone more fully in the political geography tradition than Johnson (e.g. Minghi, 1963). Hence the 'old' versus the 'new' is not evident in this review which to some degree reflects the greater achievements of traditional North American political geography. (In the Kasperson and Minghi reader only two of the forty contributions are by British geographers — Mackinder and John House, who is a contributor to this volume.) Nevertheless it is of interest to note that in the books of one of the most influential modern political geographers in North America, Kevin Cox (1973, 1979), the big names of the past — Whittlesey, Hartshorne, and Jones — are again ignored. On the basis of his preface to the 1979 book we may speculate that a Cox review of the last decade of North American political geography would be less conciliatory and more in the style of Johnston.

Minghi's essay records his hopes as co-editor, a decade ago, of what was to become a benchmark book against which political geographies of the 1970s were to be compared — generally unfavourably. As editors of this volume of twenty-two original essays involving eleven contributors from Britain and twelve from North America we are naturally equally ambitious. We believe that we can fairly claim to have put together a representative cross-section of current work in political geography, despite our personal biases, so that we are presenting a 'state of the art' statement *circa* 1980. For readers outside political geography, either in other geographies·or other political studies, this book represents a guide to what passes for political geography at this time. For researchers in political geography their interest will inevitably focus upon a limited number of the papers which are consistent with their personal perspective, and we hope that the many ideas and the comprehensive sets of references accompanying the individual papers prove instructive. The real challenge of this volume is to the teachers of political geography, however. Can this set of essays form the textbook for an intermediate or advanced course in the subject? Clearly it is no formal text with ideas presented in an ordered, progressive sequence. And yet, as we have argued above, the lack of a one-dimensional pattern of thought is the very strength of this volume. This is not a book of facts and simple cross-national comparisons; it is about contrasting ideas and approaches. The teacher is provided with material to encourage debate and discussion. The task will be a more difficult one, but we think a more rewarding one, as political geography is finally opened up to the conflicts endemic to the realm of the social sciences.

References and bibliography

Archer, J. C. (1980). 'Political geography' (Progress Report), *Progress in Human Geography*, **4** (2), 255-64.

Bergman, E. F. (1975). *Modern Political Geography* (Wm. Brown, Dubuque, Iowa).

Cox, K. R. (1973). *Conflict, Power and Politics in the City: A Geographic View* (McGraw Hill, New York).

Cox, K. R. (1979). *Location and Public Problems. A Political Geography of the Contemporary World* (Maaroufa, Chicago).

Greer, S., and Orleans, P. (1964). 'Political sociology'. In Faris, R. E. L. (ed.), *Handbook of Modern Sociology*, pp. 805-35 (Rand McNally, Chicago).

Hartshorne, R. (1939). *The Native of Geography* (AAG, Washington DC).

Hartshorne, R. (1954). 'Political geography'. In James, P. E., and Jones, C. F. (eds.), *American Geography: Inventory and Prospect*, pp. 167-225 (Syracuse University Press, New York).

Johnston, R. J. (1971). *Urban Residential Patterns* (Bell, London).

Johnston, R. J. (1979a). *Geography and Geographers* (Edward Arnold, London).

Johnston, R. J. (1979b). *Political, Electoral and Spatial Systems* (Oxford University Press, Oxford).

Kasperson, R. E. and Minghi, J. V. (eds.) (1969). *The Structure of Political Geography* (Aldine, Chicago).

Lewis, J. and Melville, B. (1978). 'The politics of epistemology in regional science'. In Bates, P. W. J. (ed.), *Theory and Method in Urban and Regional Analysis,* pp. 82-99 (Pion, London).

Lipset, S. M. (1959). 'Political sociology'. In Merton, R. K. *et al.* (eds.), *Sociology To-day,* pp. 82-95 (Basic Books, New York).

Lipset, S. M. and Bendix, R. (1966). 'The field of political sociology'. In Coser, L. A. (ed.), *Political Sociology,* pp. 1-23 (Harper & Row, New York).

Minghi, J. V. (1963). 'Boundary studies in political geography', *Annals of the Association of American Geographers,* **53,** 407-28.

Mitchell, W. C. (1967). 'The shape of political theory to come: from political sociology to political economy', *The American Behavioral Scientist,* **11,** 8-37.

Muir, R. (1975). *Modern Political Geography* (Macmillan, London).

Soja, E. W. (1974). 'A paradigm for the geographical analysis of political systems'. In Cox, K. R., Reynolds, D. R., and Rokkan, S. (eds.), *Locational Approaches to Power and Conflict,* pp. 43-72 (Sage, Beverley Hills).

Taylor, P. J. (1977). 'Political geography' (Progress Report), *Progress in Human Geography,* **1,** 130-5.

Taylor, P. J. (1979). 'Political geography' (Progress Report), *Progress in Human Geography,* **3,** 139-42.

Wrigley, E.A. (1965). 'Changes in the philosophy of geography'. In Chorley, R. J., and Haggett, P. (eds.), *Frontiers in Geographical Teaching,* pp. 3-24 (Methuen, London).

Political studies from spatial perspectives
Edited by A.D. Burnett and P.J. Taylor
© 1981 John Wiley & Sons Ltd

_____*1*__

British political geography since Mackinder: a critical review

R. J. Johnston

Any review such as this must recognize that subdisciplines do not exist independently of the larger discipline, although the trends in the two may be far from parallel. Most scholars only enter a sub-discipline, such as political geography, after they have been socialized into the discipline as a whole, and they bring the ideology of scientific work learned in the latter to bear on their specialized studies. With time, new ideologies may be introduced to the discipline at large and thus into the subdiscipline; occasionally, members of the subdiscipline may be responsible for the ideological changes. Some of the ideological changes may bypass the subdiscipline, however; either nobody attempts to introduce them or the established interests in the subdiscipline are such as to repel any invasion from without.

A review of the literature of political geography in Britain, therefore, requires setting it within the framework of disciplinary trends as a whole (Johnston, 1979a). Over the last four decades these have involved the introduction of three 'new' approaches, which have gained sufficient support to make a substantial contribution to the geographical literature. The baseline for such changes is the regional approach, which focused on the unique characteristics and 'personality' of vaguely defined areas and, as a remnant of the previous environmental determinism phase in geographical writing, emphasized the importance of the physical environment as the basic influence on man's occupance of the earth. This was followed by the quantitatively based spatial science, aiming at the derivation of geographical generalizations based on man's reactions to the 'frictions of distance'; in turn, this was challenged by a behaviourist approach, increasingly emphasizing the unique elements of man's interaction with his physical and social environments, and a 'radical/structural' approach, which advocated studying geographical phenomena in the context of the political-economic constraints that circumscribe human activity.

A review of what has been written within political geography in recent decades suggests that this has indeed been a frequently bypassed subdiscipline; one which is not widely represented at present in curricula at universities and polytechnics (Muir, 1976). The bulk of its writing remains in the regionalism mould, and the works of the American Hartshorne in the 1930s are still the guiding light for many writers. Some political geographers are concerned that quantification has passed them by, and have tried to suggest the use of statistical procedures in their work (Prescott, 1972; Muir, 1975, uses a number of relatively naive statistical measures). The behaviourist approach has received less attention; only Muir, 1975, allocates much space to it in recent texts and, as Taylor (1977) has pointed out, most of those who have studied political issues within the 'radical/structural' approach would not consider themselves as political geographers (in large part because their approach is a holistic one, which is unable to separate political, economic, and social factors).

A consequence of the recent history of political geography in Britain, as outlined in the previous paragraph, is its overemphasis on the unique features of individual places and its lack of concern with relevant theory, especially the theory necessary to understand the actors involved in political behaviour. It is this lack of concern, and the poverty of understanding which follows from it, that will be traced in the present review.[1]

Beginnings

British political geography has lacked a doyen, a major scholarly figure who has dominated the subdiscipline for a considerable period and whose writings have provided the basis on which others build. (This is in part true only. As pointed out earlier, to many British political geographers the doyen has been an American, Hartshorne. This review is concerned with British political geography only, however.) If one goes back 50 years or more, such a doyen can be identified in Mackinder, whose geopolitical ideas, first published in 1904, were the base for much deterministic thinking in political geography (Mackinder, 1904, 1919). They still receive treatment in political geography texts (e.g. Muir, 1975, pp.

192-8). Most attention here is on the post Second World War literature, however, on which Mackinder's influence was generally slight.

Although not widely referenced, perhaps because it was published in a short-lived, non-geographical journal, a paper by East (1937) provides a useful foundation on which to build a discussion of the content of British political geography. His discourse on 'The nature of political geography' is set within his definition of the whole field of human geography: 'the study of the man-made features of the present countryside in their relation to the physical background' (p. 266). This contains traces of environmental determinism, which come through in a statement that:

> It is a fact of some geographical interest that the great states of the past and present were or are located within the temperate latitudes of the northern hemisphere.... The climatic factor, together with other factors, notably the disposition and physique of the land areas, was doubtless important in conditioning a favourable stage for political development (p. 275).

(He does qualify this, however, with the question 'But was climate the dominant factor?', which he does not answer directly.) East's attempts at a definition for political geography follow:

> ...the proper function of political geography is the study of the geographical results of political differentiation. That the visible landscape is modified by the results of state and inter-state activities is a matter of common observation and experience (p. 263).

> ...political geography is distinguishable from other branches of geography only in its subject matter and in its specific objectives.... Whereas the regional geographer has for his objective the discovery and description of the distinct components of a physical and human landscape... the political geographer... analyses geographically the human and physical texture of political territories (p. 267).

Thus the state is a particular type of region, and

> the geographer is able to show by careful observation, analysis and cartographical technique, many facts of inter-relationship,

which, for the better understanding of present day politics...
it is important not to ignore (p. 260).

The topics which East then proposes as proper for political-
geographical study include: the mismatch between political
territories and 'natural regions'; the existence of nations within
states (as particular internal regions); frontiers and boundaries as
geographical expressions, and their relationships with physical
features; the roles of routes and capital cities in the integration of
political territories; and the growing concern with the political
geography of maritime territory. All of these appear and reappear in
the literature of the next 40 years.
    The prime focus of political geography, East contends, is the
state.

> Whatever else it is,... a state... is additionally and inevitably
> a geographical expression.... States, like physiographic
> regions, have their origins, histories, individualities and
> relationships: it is these which we have to investigate and to
> explain (p. 270).

Such investigation and explanation requires 'an appeal to history'
(p. 271) — just, presumably, as explanation of physiographic regions
requires an appeal to geology. But in common with much of the
literature that follows, the true nature of the state is never
discussed. There is a paragraph (p. 271) on the territorial formation
of states, but no discussion of why states have existed for many
centuries. It is for this reason that the political geography of East,
and most of those who have written since, is apolitical.

The post-war decades

Virtually all of the political geography published in the 1940s,
1950s, and 1960s sits within the ideological and substantive
framework provided by East. Much of it was presented in book form
— relatively few research papers were published, and almost all of
these are set in the same mould: it is the books which receive
greatest attention here.
    The state is one form of region, according to East, and several
texts have been published with the term 'political' in their title for
which the main use of the state is as an organizing framework for
the sequence of chapters. This is a characteristic of the text by
Pounds (1947) — *An Historical and Political Geography of Europe* —

much of which is 'traditional regional geography' presented state by state. The overtones of environmental determinism are strong: 'The history of Russia... can be understood only in the light of its geography' (p. 162); 'The history of Russia is written in her rivers' (p. 167); 'The soil of Novgarod and Pskov was glacial and poor; and grain was imported from Suzdal, and in this way probably began the supremacy of Moscow' (p. 166) (see also Fisher, 1950, pp. 16-17.) There are chapters on imperialism, however, in which the true role of the state is hinted at: 'Overseas possessions were intended to supplement the resources and increase the wealth of the colonial power' (p. 379); an economic function to which a strategic one was later added. But although 'Much of Africa was opened up by trading companies, whose motive was private gain' (p. 393), and who cloaked this motive with moralistic paternalism, the link between private gain and the state is never forged. The state is an organism 'necessarily subject to the natural processes of growth, maturity and decay' (p. 518), in part controlled or guided in its development by geographical factors (p. 521). Pounds recognizes the crucial role of other factors — men and the state-idea — but never develops them. The state exists: its growth can be traced and its territorial disputes charted (Pounds, 1969, p. 117), but its function in human affairs is not questioned.

One of the few attempts to write a 'political geography' during these decades was by Moodie (1949); its title — *Geography behind Politics* — indicates that it is built on the foundation provided by East (the editor of the series in which the book appeared). Thus Moodie begins by pointing out the lack of conformity between states and natural regions (p. 7) and identifying the two main foci of political geography: 'First, and of fundamental importance, is the analysis of the relationships between community and physical environment' (p. 7) (it is of interest that he uses the term community, but this appears to be fortuitous) and:

> The second basic consideration... is that States are subject to change.... Perhaps the chief result is an increasing aware-ness of the relationships between communities and their environments (p. 10)
>
> ...the political geographer is concerned with the observation, recording and analysis of the changes which have already taken place (p. 12).

Thus political geographers are very much like other human geographers in their concern for regions; the only difference is that the political geographer's region — the state territory — is defined for him.

The substantive chapters of Moodie's book all illustrate these general themes. That on the evolution of the state has strong environmental overtones although, like East, he makes passing reference to the role of group organization and military skill in state expansion and, like Pounds, allocates a few paragraphs to economic imperialism. More important, however, is the dichotomy between nation and state and the frequent mismatch betwen natural region (nation) and political region (state).

Environmental issues are writ large in the chapter on the internal structure of the state and the relationships between states are set in the same framework: 'the relation between physical conditions and human activities on a global scale... which find expression in the foreign policies of the constituent state' (p. 59). In discussing imperialism, economic considerations are quoted, but the role of the state is not tackled directly, and the chapter concludes:

> the outcome of this rapidly expanding awareness of the pattern of the earth's surface is a realization that the global physical environment has the quality of orderliness which the present arrangement of States appears to lack (p. 71).

(Is this a plea for matching the two?) Frontiers and boundaries are then investigated as elements of the mismatch, with especial reference to Moodie's (1945) own detailed study of the Italo-Yugoslav boundary, which traces frontier conflicts in an inter-regional marchland and concludes, after a brief mention of topics such as terrorism and anti-religious practices, that 'It may be argued that such activities and controversial matters have no place in a book of this description' (Moodie, 1945, p. 226). (Political geography should not study political action!) Moodie then considers communications and demographic topics in the final chapters of his text. His conclusion shifts the focus somewhat from the physical environment to aspects of human decision-making (much as Pounds suggested in his, 1947, text). Thus:

> The State represents the results of human efforts to bring order out of chaos in a restricted area... man... is primarily respon-sible for the changes which have been stressed repeatedly in preceding chapters (p. 165),

but, like so many political geographers before and since, Moodie makes no attempt to understand man and the state. (What order? In whose interests?)

Two themes highlighted by Moodie dominate much of the other writing of the decades under discussion here: the boundaries of the state in their physical context; and the state as a region within which to study processes of change in human affairs. Both are represented in a series of books of essays. The first of these to appear — *The Changing Map of Asia* — has gone through several editions (beginning with East and Spate, 1950). The latest issue (East, *et al.*, 1971) continues its tradition of analysis:

> The political geographer, concerned as he is primarily with place and space relations, cannot ignore the human realities which give uniqueness to the many Asian societies and condition their politics.... Some review of the historical and social factors is therefore necessary for the disentangling of the more important interlaced patterns (East *et al.*, 1971, p. 9).

Thus economic motives are sometimes stressed and the role of elites in nation-building highlighted. But, as always with this literature, the role of, even need for, the state is weakly treated: there is even a chapter subtitle (p. 515) 'Relations with China: the separation of economics from politics'. Leadership is identified as crucial, but not in terms of personalities and motives, and a statement on p. 651 suggests that 'financial, commercial, and political interests' are somehow separable. Perhaps the major feature of this book is the relative downgrading of the naive environmental determinism characteristic of earlier times.

The Changing World (East and Moodie, 1956), not surprisingly, is cast in the same mould. Its traditional stance is illustrated by a prefatory statement that 'The exposition of political geography requires many maps' (p. vi) and the editors' introduction 'The World Background' begins with a section entitled 'The physical setting'. Moodie himself is still deterministic with statements such as 'The terrain of Western Europe was appropriate to the growth of nations' (p. 47).

The book is a large one (1039 pages) and difficult to categorize or generalize from. In general, the authors take the state as a given entity, and personify it. It is a region, to be treated as such, with the same mystic organic qualities as a 'natural region'. There are hints of a realization that the state is a human creation, to meet particular needs, although much of the book is traditional regional description. Whittlesey (not a British geographer) provides useful political insights on the USA, however; East identifies economic interests in Russian imperialism; Spate (p. 472) points to the important role of interest groups; Harrison-Church indicates the element of prestige in the scramble for Africa (though fails to note who is impressed!); James hints at the role of legitimation in the development of the 'state idea'; Keith Buchanan writes of 'The Ideological Background of Development' and of bitter racial antagonisms in South Africa; and W. B. Fisher hints at class conflict in the Middle East. But these are minor highlights in a morass of atheoretical description. (Atheoretical by default, of course, since all academic work has a theoretical base, however implicit and subconscious.) Such political geography could almost be described as current affairs with maps and historical background.

A third book — *Essays in Political Geography* (Fisher, 1968) — is largely composed of case-studies of one type of political change — decolonization. Many of these deal with boundary conflicts, providing detailed descriptions of the course of events but little basis for generalization. Each case is a unique event in time and place, or so it seems. (And perhaps it is, but can the event be understood not only as a unique but also as a singular phenomenon?)

This concern with case-studies of particular (singular?) events is highlighted in Prescott's (1965) book *The Geography of Frontiers and Boundaries* (also published in the series edited by East). His rationale for such work is that:

> Boundaries and frontiers are elements of the landscape which mark either the *de facto* or *de jure* limits of political sovereignty, which is one quality of areal differentiation. They are therefore objects of interest to both political geographers and regional geographers studying areas within which they occur. There are two aspects of boundary and frontier studies which are of interest to geographers.... First, the position and character of any boundary or frontier is the resultant of the interaction of many factors, some of which are geographical, and best studied by geographers. Second any boundary or frontier... is capable of influencing the landscape of which it is a part and the development and policies of the separated states. This aspect is also a legitimate field of geographic inquiry (pp. 28-9).

Within this framework the presentation is clear and concise. But the links between people, territory, and state, and thus the disputes over frontiers and boundaries, are not explored, and this perhaps explains the relative insignificance of the study of boundaries within states (as well as a misunderstanding — p. 101 — of the crucial fiscal roles of such boundaries in some states). A revision of the book (Prescott, 1978) retains the format and framework; the extra chapter on maritime boundaries is particularly weak in ignoring the basis for territorial claims in the oceans.

Prescott (1975) has also produced a book on the political geography of the oceans, which in format and type of content is very similar to his other books. According to his introduction:

> Political geographers are interested in the oceans because states claim sovereignty over parts of them, because states use portions of the oceans during their commercial and strategic activities, and because these claims and activities involve states in some measure of conflict and cooperation (p. 24).

As in his other works, Prescott claims that geographers should focus their attention on variations between states in their demands on the oceans (the regional geography of the oceans) and on the geographical consequences of these variations. His discussions of such topics as claims to territorial seas, continental shelves, and fishing zones, are set in a thin theoretical matrix which identifies the conflicts over marine and submarine resources, but the prime focus is on morphological aspects of boundary definition and delimitation and on detailed case-studies of particulars. The link between state and commercial interests is hardly identified; as with all Prescott's writings, form very much triumphs over process.

Few studies of frontiers and boundaries have attempted to forge the link between people, territory, and state, and thus to enlighten the conflict between states which occurs where they meet. Empiricism and exceptionalism have dominated, and the few attempts at generalization (such as House's chapter in the present volume) are founded on weak inductive bases. One who did introduce the role of the individual and what one might call the 'stuff of politics', in a study of the Jugoslav Kosmet border region (Wilkinson, 1955), included an investigation of the role of cartography in the solution of the disputes (Wilkinson, 1955). As he put it:

> All powers, both great and small, imperialistic and nationalistic, discerned the importance of plotting exactly that interpretation on the ethnography of Macedonia which might best extend their influence in the area and so prepare the way for establishment of local hegemony, or Near Eastern ascendancy, as the case might be (p. 6).

Such maps 'reflect the evils and the merits of their age' (p. 324) and in this context Wilkinson refers to the influential maps produced by a geographer, Cvijic, whose 'choice of criteria was [apparently] motivated by political considerations' (p. 176); the result

> was by no means the product of well balanced and impartial scholarship. Like many of the other ethnographic maps of the Balkans, its ideas were dictated both by the march of events and by the patriotic outlook of its author (p. 180).

(Interestingly, this critique of Cvijic's work is not referred to in Freeman's brief biography (1967) of 'A reluctant political geographer'. Nor does Prescott (1965, 1978) refer to this piece of work by Wilkinson.)

This lack of concern with the people-territory-state links in Prescott's work on frontiers and boundaries also characterizes his more general treatment in *The Geography of State Policies* (Prescott, 1968). The bitty introductory chapter on 'Aims and concepts' — in which he indicates a continued acceptance of Hartshorne's definition of political geography — argues that one should not equate governments with states, but nowhere builds on this fundamental point. Three aspects of policy are identified as relevant topics for the political geographer: those in which geographical factors influence the policy decision; those in which geographical factors influence policy operation; and those which have an impact on the cultural landscape. Every policy comprises four qualities: motive, method, subject, and area of operation (p. 14). Three motives are relevant to the political geographer — defence, development, and administration/organization: unfortunately, Prescott does not define these terms, especially development, and assumes that what is good for the state (an undefined entity) is good for its population.

Prescott's substantive chapters begin with one on global policies, with a focus on *geopolitik*. He concludes that what happens in one place affects what happens in others, that interdisciplinary cooperation is needed, and that:

> In the case of political geography the greatest benefit would seem to flow from theoretical studies... and studies which present the significance to policy-making of geographical factors (p. 51).

(On p. 19, Prescott *appears* to say that 'laws or general principles' are not possible in political geography!) On 'Policies for the defence of the state', the lack of any definition of the state and the interests it represents stands out, a criticism which also applies to the chapter on 'Administrative policies' where 'the promotion of the state's welfare' (p.115) is similarly problematic. Similarly, in 'Policies for the development of the state', no reason is given for governments being interested in either depressed areas or areas with potential for expansion; the issue of legitimation and its link to electoral geography is ignored. The book is a catalogue of policies in which there is apparently some geographical element, but it presents no comprehensive treatment of its object of study — the state.

These general criticisms of the books by East, Moodie, Prescott, and others apply to another published in the late 1960s, Crone's (1967) *Background to Political Geography.* Much of this book, like some of its predecessors, simply uses political divisions as convenient 'regions' about which to present information. To Crone, as to those writing before him, political geography deals with 'men organized in political units' and 'those facts of the natural environment, as they are distributed over the earth's surface, which are significant for political activity' (p. 16). Crone does realize, however, that:

> the State represents the balance between a number of interests pursued by the active sections of the community.... There is likely to be, however, one overriding consideration, the continued functioning, or the very existence, of the state (p. 18),

although this leads to the rather weak conclusion that 'the primary purpose of the state is to exist' (p. 18).

Probably the most original piece of political geography written during this period was Gottmann's (1973) series of lectures on *The Significance of Territory.* [2] As he expressed it: 'territory appears as a material, spatial notion establishing links between politics, people, and the natural setting' (p. ix)'; and 'The concept of territory appears in this study as a psychosomatic device and its evolution as closely related to the human striving for security, opportunity, and happiness' (p. x). The role of territory as providing a haven of security is repeatedly expressed, and forges some of the links which are missing from other political geographies. But Gottmann fails to develop an understanding of why national or state territories are created: states, nations, and communities evolve, for reasons largely uncharted.

> Territorial sovereignty is an indispensable attribute of independent nations; the territory is the very basis on which national existence rests, the 'sacred soil' in whose defense true

citizens will be prepared to give their lives. The concept is one
of self-preservation, but also one of preserving the community's
way of life, the right to self-government, freedom, and whatever
opportunity a free people is entitled to (p. 15).

But what creates a community and a nation? What (or who) defines
the entitlements of a free people and the duties of a true citizen? It
is in not answering such questions, in not tackling the forces which
create a 'national identity', that eventually Gottmann fails to
provide a complete political geography, despite the much deeper
insights that he provides.

   After security is achieved, Gottmann argues, the goal of the state
is 'internal happiness' (p. 86). Thus the state becomes involved in
the economy, in its support for mercantilist expansion, and states
are created to provide the means to the desired happiness: 'Those
who sought political independence or a democratic form of
government were also aiming at the free control of the resources in
their territory' (p. 82). This nationalism, when it succeeded in
providing both security and wealth, led to the welfare state.

> Once security was assured and economic opportunity ex-
> panded, more people asked for more participation in the
> common wealth. They would not have dreamt of it, had their
> daily routine been merely one of struggling for physical safety.
> Having provided protection, governments had to start providing
> participation, more sharing out by an elite, more sharing in for
> the mass (pp. 92-3).

This was because of nationalism:

> Nationalism has been basically concerned with the people
> belonging to the national community: it wants to give these
> people as good a life as possible.... Little by little central
> governments took responsibility for services to the mass of the
> people.... These measures were not adopted in most cases to
> honor any socialist doctrine but rather to lessen tensions from
> which manufacturers and the economy suffered, to remove
> threats to survival, to increase the labor force and improve the
> performance (with the health) of the average worker. While
> working toward more economic security, for the multitude,
> these laws also favored the efficiency of industry as desired
> by the employers (pp. 99-101).

Something of the conflict with which the state has to contend
(hinted at by Crone) is involved here, but Gottmann is no different

from most other post-war British political geographers in omitting to consider the conflict which is basic not just to the state but to any element of a class-based, capitalist society.

Territory is the basis for the good life, according to Gottman; if a nation's supply is insufficient, it must seek more. Hence the concept of *Lebensraum,* part of the *geopolitik* which political geographers seek avidly to avoid, despite its importance to an understanding of the people-territory-state linkage. Indeed, such is the reluctance to discuss this topic and its military and ideological implications that no political geographers refer to Dickinson's (1943) outline of *The German Lebensraum.* Similarly, although many political geographers allocate space to multinational organizations (the successors to *Lebensraum* policies?), the political bases of these are not delved into: Blacksell (1977), for example, does not ask why the USA insisted on the OECD to guide Western European recovery and subtitles his chapter on EFTA 'An apolitical approach to integration.'

Two recent texts

While the work just reviewed was being undertaken, human geography as a whole was subject to a number of major changes in its orientation, one of which at least probably merits the term revolution. The latter, by far the most important in numerical terms, began in the 1950s in the USA; its impact was widespread in Britain by the mid-1960s. Philosophically it involved a reorientation of geographical work away from the exceptionalist view of the uniqueness of places and towards the logical positivist view of science as the derivation of laws and generalizations. Within geography, these laws were to be about spatial organization of society, not the interrelationships between man and the natural environment; their derivation was to involve the use of mathematical and statistical procedures. A strong behaviourist theme characterized this new work: initially it was deductive in its formulation, based on naive notions of economic man, but it later incorporated a more inductive stance.

Little attempt was made to introduce this new approach to political geography, especially in the United Kingdom. Even in the United States, it was only in electoral geography — notably the work of Kevin Cox — that positivism was introduced. Thus political geography remained, according to Brian Berry (1968), a 'moribund backwater'. His description stung political geographers. The two texts to be reviewed here undoubtedly were not a direct reply to

Berry, but both combined defence against his attack with a mild, generally ineffective, attempt to incorporate some of the new ways of thinking. (Prescott (1972, p. xiii), for example, states that 'Electoral geography has been specially considered, because there appear to be dangers that the latest fashions in the field will distort the subject'.)

The first of these texts was by Prescott (1972), who began by reiterating his faith in Hartshorne's definition of political geography as the study of areal differences and similarities in political character; unfortunately he still fails to define political character, despite his call for more links with political science — 'a view which I have persistently supported' (p. 1). Indeed, his own definition reiterates the statements in his earlier books:

> Political geographers are... concerned with the geographical consequence of... political decisions and actions, the geographical factors which were considered during the making of any decision, and the role of any geographical factors which influenced the outcome of political actions (p. 2).

There can be little dispute with this as it stands. My main criticism concerns method. Prescott never defines the nature of politics as a decision-making process (there is no discussion in the book, for example, of public participation, except via elections); he lists (p. 5) the geographical factors which influence politics, failing to realize that many of those factors are themselves political outcomes.

Prescott's second chapter is entitled 'Methods of political geographers'. Their use, he claims, should be in the pursuit of 'total explanation', but his discussion, which lacks any definition of crucial concepts such as the state, does not point very far in that direction. Much of the chapter is a trivial discussion of what topics political geographers might study by quantitative means, which indicates a shallow comprehension of the nature of geography's 'quantitative revolution'. The 'comparative method' is the approved procedure for producing insight and useful generalization, always remembering that 'Obviously the two cases being compared must be neither identical nor completely different; it is essential that there should be both common and distinctive elements'! (p. 39); without any guiding theory, it is not clear how the cases could be selected.

Chapter three reconsiders 'Frontiers and boundaries', which contains little that is new except a suggestion that Losch might provide a useful supplementation to the study of gun-running. It is followed by a chapter on 'Electoral geography' which attacks the behaviourist and quantitative approaches (the latter, at least, based on an apparent lack of understanding) and largely reiterates his earlier claim (Prescott, 1959) that electoral geography is a particular form of regional geography (see Johnston, 1980b). The final chapter (of 11 pages) deals with 'Political geography and public policy', which applies the three concerns of political geographers (see the above quote from p. 2) to the study of policy. Thus: 'The aim of political geographers who study policy formation is to determine the importance of geographical factors in the process' (p. 98), which hardly proposes any fertile links with political science.

Apart from the reactions to quantification and developments in electoral geography, therefore, there is little that is new in Prescott's text; it simply summarizes his earlier statements. Muir's (1975) book, on the other hand, does attempt to assimilate some of the changes in geographical philosophy and methodology, even though he sticks to Hartshorne's definition (p. 2) and is often naive and trivial in his attempts to be 'with it'. In general, he too fails to tackle the major theoretical issues surrounding the state and its link to territory and people:

> The elements of statehood are population, territory, sovereignty and government, and the state derives its political-geographical personality from the interplay of these variables within the wider environment of the international system (p. 28).

If these four variables, plus the wider environment, are to be defined (or assumed!) exogenously, this leaves little for the political geographer to study except mere particulars. (This comes through clearly in 'Parts' — not chapters — on 'Political process, perception and decision-making' and 'Political process and the state'. Sovereignty in the eighteenth century was vested in the monarch, we are told; by whom? and why?) The state exists — as East concluded — and its existence does not appear to be problematic. Its political base in class conflict is never investigated and the local state is tackled as if it were a totally apolitical entity, something whose only function is to be 'efficient' (another ambiguous and undefined term; efficient for whom? See also the chapter by Douglas in Fisher, 1968.) Freeman's (1968) book on *Geography and Regional Administration* recognizes that there is more to the local state than efficiency: 'Local government... has to keep a balance between a wide range of conflicting issues in the community' (p. 11); and the impacts of these on individuals, plus their political and other reactions, are crucial (Freeman, 1968, p. 186). In general, however, Muir, like Prescott, prefers to avoid the conflict which is the basis of political geography and, despite his avant garde attempts: 'Although Muir, like many political geographers before him, talks of political processes he does not adequately deal with the essence of such processes, the use and non-use of political power' (Taylor, 1977, p. 130), let alone with the acquisition of power.

Neither Muir nor Prescott effectively countered the attacks on political geography with a vigorous defence of the traditional (Hartshorne's and East's) view, or provided a solid base for the re-emergence of political geography from its moribund backwater. Their efforts compare unfavourably with the recent editions of a text by a British emigré (Pounds, 1972), even though that book too leaves much to be desired in the problematic area of the theory of the state.

The contemporary scene

The general tenor of this review is clearly both negative and pessimistic. British political geographers have not only failed to grasp the import of changes within the wider discipline of human geography; they have also totally neglected to consider the real status of the central element in their discussions — the state. With regard to the quantitative/positivist trend, for example, the few studies conducted by political geographers were quantitatively naive, whereas those involving work by non-political geographers were politically naive (Johnston, 1981). The prospect for any change would seem bleak.

This last conclusion is bolstered by reference to a publication entitled *Teaching Political Geography* (Jenkins and McEvoy, 1977). This contains the materials presented at a similarly entitled session held at the annual conference of the Institute of British Geographers in January 1977. Thirteen outlines of degree-level courses in political geography were displayed and formed the basis of a discussion session, led by four speakers. The outlines show an eclectic approach, differing widely in conceptual structure and content; much of the latter is of inherent interest, relating to a range of current issues. There is, however, little evidence in the outlines that the fundamental issues relating to the nature of politics were being tackled, and this comes through in the transcript of the speakers' presentations and the discussions. The problematic of the state is not presented, and only Taylor discusses the related issue of ideology. British political geography, as currently taught, seems largely concerned with discussion of current public policy issues, with some theoretical links to either Hartshorne or systems analysis (whether political systems *a la* Easton or spatial systems *a la* Haggett). The approaches are not entirely apolitical, but no conflict-based theory of politics informs the analyses.

That political geography remains largely apolitical is illustrated by the several editions of Cole's *Geography of World Affairs*. The first edition (Cole, 1959) was very largely set in the tradition of East, Moodie, and Pounds: a general introductory section on maps, population and resource distributions, and the spread of European influence, was followed by a series of regional studies, in which states and groups of states were used as the framework for a presentation of historical and factual material. (As Cole admits, Mackinder's work strongly influenced his regional division of the world for the second section.) The aim of the book, (according to the inside cover) was 'to help the reader who is not a specialist in geography to find his way about the world and to provide him with facts about... the more important countries in it'. The latest edition (1979) — the fifth — still has the same general objective, expressed by the publisher as: 'it would be difficult to name a better guide to have lying beside the newspaper or on the television set'. The format is considerably changed (Mackinder has been downgraded, there is much more attention to problems such as the population/ resources equation and the development gap, and quantification is strongly represented), but although Cole recognizes both the need to study 'disputes and conflicts *between* states' (1979, p. 60) and that 'internal problems of countries are clearly or apparently related to external relations' (p. 126), his recognition that 'The sovereign states of the world have not been designed "from above" to give them some uniformity or to make them fit under- lying cultural features' (p. 60), does not lead him to tackle the origin and nature of the state. The reader of this stimulating and highly informative book is left unaided in his attempts to explain the patterns so admirably described.

Is there any prospect for change? Two sets of evidence allow for some optimism. The first is provided by some of the other chapters in this book, which illustrate that there are geographers (who may call themselves political geographers) who are tackling the fundamental problems which their predecessors ignored. The second is the increasing volume of literature with its origins in electoral geography. As Taylor (1978) has pointed out, 'elections are a positivist's dream' (p. 153) and it is possible to do no more than analyse spatial variations in election results within the areal differentiation/regionalism paradigm (Prescott, 1959), updated by the modern procedures of spatial analysis. But the recent work has not fallen into this trap. The positivist work has been set in the context of both the legitimation of the state (Johnston, 1980b) and the political context of voting decisions (Taylor and Johnston, 1979). Detailed statistical analysis has identified the partisan content of electoral districting (Gudgin and Taylor, 1979), and the geography of voting has been associated with the geography of political decision-making (Johnston, 1979b). Thus the growing recognition of the need to understand the *raison d'être* of the state, the integration of electoral and political geography, and the study of public policy as a part of state decision-making all suggest that work in the next decades will be better informed theoretically than that of the last decades, which can only improve the understanding provided by descriptive studies.

Conclusions

In a recent paper, Muir (1976) has claimed that 'the contemporary climate of geographical opinion augurs well for the future of political geography' (p. 200). He is aware that:

> The greatest weakness of modern political geography concerns its theoretical basis; too many notions which have become entrenched as fundamental political-geographical concepts remain ambiguous, subjective and improperly tested (p. 199),

but the notions that he identified are not the fundamental ones if we are to achieve the 'total explanation' that Prescott desires. Indeed, to follow the blueprints put forward by Muir and Prescott will ensure certain failure in that enterprise.

Such failure will come about because political geographers will continue to ignore the crucial question for any study of political phenomena: 'what is the state?'.[3] Without an answer to this question, which involves either developing or adopting a theory of the state, much political geography must continue to display the poverty of empiricism, historicism, and exceptionalism. Some of it may be well-informed writing on issues of current affairs (or on certain aspects of history) and its detailed morphological studies will provide illustrations of the realization of conflict. But without a theory of the state — what it is, how it has come about, what it does and why, how it relates to class conflict, and so on — the sub-discipline will never escape the moribund backwater that some have relegated it to. At present, too many political geographers accept the existence of the state, personify it, do not recognize that it is constantly changing, equate it with government, and assume that the state's interests are those of the entire population of its territory.

Political geographers in Britain have focused their attention very much on the external relations of the state, at the expense of internal relations and the links between the nation-state (or sovereign state) and the local state. According to Pounds (1972, p. vii):

> People act politically every day of their lives, and their actions are no less susceptible of political analysis than those of the decision-makers in the nations' capitals.

Muir (1976, p. 200) apparently disagrees with this, in saying:

> A potential source of danger to political geography may lie in attempts to circumscribe its area of study and direct its development into a few currently popular, relevant but specialized fields such as electoral geography, urban political systems or the provision of field services,

which is in opposition to Hall's (1974) call for

> The new style of urban political geographer, for that is what he seems destined to become, will be concerned with the values, the organization, and the access to power of groups.... He will study how different agents in the decision process... interact, how they form alliances and coalitions, how they bargain, promise or threaten each other to obtain objectives (p. 51).

What the traditional British political geographers have ignored, therefore, is the politics which is the stuff of everyday life, so that, as Taylor (1977) points out, most of the interesting political geography is now being written by others. Regarding electoral geography, for example, there is a failure to see the important links between this and legitimation (Johnston, 1980b), nation-building (Taylor, 1979; Taylor and Johnston, 1979, Chapter 3), and the spatial pattern of political activity (Johnston, 1979b). But without such efforts to link people, state, and territory, and to recognize that conflict (in much of the world, class conflict) is the infrastructure of social and economic existence, political geography can never aspire to a high standing in the halls of geographical academe.

Notes

1. The original paper presented at the seminar was a polemical piece —
   Political Geography without Politics — which is being published elsewhere (Johnston, 1980a). It began with the statement: 'The main theme
   of this paper is a contention which will be treated as an axiom'; the
   main aim of the present paper is to justify that contention.
2. Gottmann is, of course, French by training and has spent much time in
   the United States. He is treated here as a British political geographer by
   virtue of his holding a chair at Oxford. Such a decision is as arbitrary as
   that to include Prescott as a British political geographer — he was
   trained in Britain and his books have been published in Britain, but he
   has only held academic posts outside Britain; Pounds, on the other
   hand, has been classified as an American political geographer, because
   his text *Political Geography* (1972) was published there. The general
   tone of Pounds' writing is the same as Prescott's, with a focus on
   morphological consequences of political activity, but his presentation
   is less naive with respect, for example, to colonialism and decision
   makers.
3. In the original seminar paper I argued that politics is concerned with a
   particular form of conflict (conflict being an endemic characteristic of
   society); thus political geography, I claim, is the study of those social
   and economic conflicts which focus on the state.

References and bibliography

Berry, B. J. L. (1968). Review. *Geographical Review,* **58,** 450-1.
Blacksell, M. (1977). *Post-War Europe: A Political Geography* (Dawson,
    Folkestone).
Cole, J. P. (1959) *Geography of World Affairs* (Penguin Books, Harmondsworth;
    5th edn., 1979).
Crone, G. R. (1967). *Background to Political Geography* (Museum Press,
    London).
Dickinson, R. E. (1943). *The German Lebensraum* (Penguin Books,
    Harmondsworth).
East, W. G., (1937) 'The nature of political geography', *Politica,* **2,** 259-86.
East, W. G., and Moodie, A. E. (eds.) (1956). *This Changing World* (Harrap,
    London).
East, W. G., and Spate, O. H. K. (eds.) (1950). *The Changing Map of Asia*
    (Methuen, London).
East, W. G., Spate, O. H. K., and Fisher, C. A. (1971). *The Changing Map of
    Asia* (Methuen, London).
Fisher, C. A. (1950). 'The expansion of Japan: a study in oriental geopolitics',
    Geographical Journal, **115,** 1-19.
Fisher, C. A. (ed.) (1968). *Essays in Political Geography* (Methuen, London).
·Freeman, T. W. (1967). *The Geographer's Craft* (Manchester University Press,
    Manchester).
Freeman, T. W. (1968). *Geography and Regional Administration* (Hutchinson,
    London).

Gottmann, J. (1973). *The Significance of Territory* (The University Press of Virginia, Charlottesville).

Gudgin, G., and Taylor, P. J. (1979). *Seats, Votes and the Spatial Organization of Elections* (Pion Ltd, London).

Hall, P. (1974). 'The new political geography', *Transactions of the Institute of British Geographers*, **63**, 48-52.

Jenkins, A. and McEvoy, D. (eds.) (1977). *Teaching Political Geography* (Oxford Polytechnic Discussion Papers in Geography, No. 7, Oxford).

Johnston, R. J. (1979a). *Geography and Geographers* (Edward Arnold, London).

Johnston, R. J. (1979b). *Political, Electoral and Spatial Systems* (Oxford University Press, Oxford).

Johnston, R.J. (1980a). 'Political geography without politics', *Progress in Human Geography*, **4**, 439-446.

Johnston, R. J. (1980b). 'Political geography and electoral geography', *Australian Geographical Studies*, **18**, 37-50.

Johnston, R. J. (1981). 'Political geography'. In Bennett, R. J., and Wrigley, N. (eds.), *Quantitative Geography in Britain: Review and Prospect* (Routledge & Kegan Paul, London).

Mackinder, H. J. (1904). 'The geographical pivot of history', *Geographical Journal*, **23**, 421-37.

Mackinder, H. J. (1919). *Democratic Ideals and Reality* (Holt, Rinehart & Winston, New York).

Moodie, A. E. (1945). *The Italo-Yugoslav Boundary* (George Philip, London).

Moodie, A. E. (1949). *Geography behind Politics* (Hutchinson, London).

Muir, R. (1975). *Modern Political Geography* (Macmillan, London).

Muir, R. (1976). 'Political geography: dead duck or phoenix?', *Area*, **8**, 195-200.

Pounds, N. J. G. (1947). *An Historical and Political Geography of Europe* (Harrap, London).

Pounds, N. J. G. (1969). *Eastern Europe* (Longmans, London).

Pounds, N. J. G. (1972). *Political Geography* (McGraw Hill, New York).

Prescott, J. R. V. (1959). 'The function and methods of electoral geography'. *Annals of the Association of American Geographers*, **49**, 296-304.

Prescott, J. R. V. (1965). *The Geography of Frontiers and Boundaries* (Hutchinson, London).

Prescott, J. R. V. (1968). *The Geography of State Policies* (Hutchinson, London).

Prescott, J. R. V. (1972). *Political Geography* (Methuen, London).

Prescott, J. R. V. (1975). *The Political Geography of the Oceans* (David & Charles, Newton Abbot).

Prescott, J. R. V. (1978). *Boundaries and Frontiers* (Croom Helm, London).

Taylor, P. J. (1977). 'Political geography', *Progress in Human Geography*, **1**, 130-5.

Taylor, P. J. (1978). 'Political geography'. *Progress in Human Geography*, **2**, 153-62.

Taylor, P. J. (1979). 'Political geography'. *Progress in Human Geography*, **3**, 139-42.

Taylor, P. J. and Johnston, R. J. (1979). *Geography of Elections* (Penguin Books, Harmondsworth).

Wilkinson, H. R. (1951). *Maps and Politics* (University of Liverpool Press, Liverpool).

Wilkinson, H. R. (1955). 'The Jugoslav Kosmet', *Transactions and Papers, Institute of British Geographers*, **21**, 171-93.

Political studies from spatial perspectives
Edited by A.D. Burnett and P.J. Taylor
© 1981 John Wiley & Sons Ltd

_2__

Recent developments in political geographical research in North America

Julian V. Minghi

Background

A decade ago Roger Kasperson and I collaborated in publishing a text-reader in political geography with the rather pretentious subtitle 'Theory and Applications', an idea I hasten to add which did not originate with the authors but came from the rather fertile brain of Norton Ginsburg of Chicago who was serving as academic editor for Aldine at the time (Kasperson and Minghi, 1969).

As we took stock of our discipline from the perspective of the late 1960s we looked back with a degree of dissatisfaction both at the lack of any adequate representation in contemporary political geography textbooks of the growing research trends in the sub-discipline, and at the relative paucity of research being undertaken by so-called political geographers compared to those in other sub-fields of human geography, many of which had made great strides during the 1960s. We particularly wished to demonstrate that research in political geography could be integrated with the rest of the geography field. Both of us felt strongly the need to give students a clear perspective on the heritage of past political-geographical ideas, and, on that foundation, we rather boldly suggested restructuring the approach to political geography through the four major categories of structure, process, behaviour and environment. We wanted to give a sense of purpose and order to our subdiscipline by bringing it more into line with contemporary trends in geography as a whole and also with other social sciences. In short, we very much hoped that the claim on the dust-jacket would come true — 'a theoretical contribution that will influence the nature and scope of the field and help shape future research'.

David Reynolds, in the least flattering yet most penetrating and scholarly review of the Kasperson and Minghi book, submitted that there simply had not been enough non-descriptive research published in political geography to justify a text-reader and hence the volume was premature (Reynolds, 1970). Reynolds did, however, see some 'recent encouraging signs' to suggest that the paucity problem would soon be rectified. In another review Bryan Massam reflected similar sentiments about the prematurity but did predict a promising future for the book heralding a new era in which Carl Sauer's 'wayward child' of the 1920s would 'surely develop into a mature and respectable adult' (Massam, 1970). Even co-editor, Alan Burnett, in a review, felt 'quite certain' about the great value the book would be to students of political geography in the 1970s (Burnett, 1971).

The introduction to each major part in the book ended with a short section entitled 'Future Research Needs', in which we reversed our perspective from the immediate past towards the decade to come. It may well be a useful exercise at this point to re-state these 'needs' identified at the outset of the decade and to assess against them the actual research trends since.

A greater degree of emphasis on the functional attributes of structure was needed, including more perceptual and behavioural studies of capitals and boundaries. Even the traditional political-geographical concern with global structure model-building held future research potential with increased use of comparative data and the application of factor analysis and cognitive spatial models.

The processes of integration, disintegration, sovereignty transfer, and growth and development — all of central concern for theory-building in other social sciences in the 1960s — demanded greater attention from the political geographer, especially in reference to the newly independent third world.

In the behavioural area, a most pressing need existed for an enlargement of both the volume and scope of research. Electoral geography represented by studies simply relating areal voting aggregates to social environment seemed to have little to offer. Future research on voting behaviour needed to focus on spatial causation, more elaborate pattern analysis, and the relationships with the spatial political system. Nor should future behavioural research, we felt, be restricted to electoral themes. Conflict behaviour at all scales presented some very likely research opportunities, from crime and urban violence to national and international problems. And lastly, opportunities for political geography research in environmental problems seemed positively boundless for the 1970s.

Research developments

So what has happened over the past decade in North American political geography? The brief answer is 'quite a lot'. Many of the future research needs identified in 1969 have, in fact, been met. The most impressive area of research effort has been in voting studies, with an increased emphasis on the behavioural approach and even including such topics as electoral campaigning (see for example, Minghi and Rumley, 1978). The scale at which research effort has been concentrated has been overwhelmingly urban and metropolitan, and the emphasis has been on problems of contemporary societal relevance. On the other hand, little has been accomplished in following structural-functional approaches, and political-geographical approaches to research on environmental problems have not blossomed as expected. Another theme, insurgency, included enthusiastically and rather proudly as a new topic under core area-related research in the Kasperson-Minghi book, seems to have faded completely as an active research topic following the American curtailment of involvement in Vietnam and the advent of relative peace in America's major inner cities.

Early in the decade came the landmark and oft-cited Cohen and Rosenthal article suggesting a systems analysis model in which political processes and spatial attributes were linked (Cohen and Rosenthal, 1971). While this normative elaboration on Whittlesey's descriptive law-landscape theme has obviously been widely used in political geography courses on both sides of the Atlantic, the model itself does not seem to have led to any significant research contributions.

The 1970s have seen the rise of awareness among North American geographers of the applicability of their expertise in contributing directly not only to the better understanding of, but also to actual solutions to, public issues. This renewed interest in the applied side of the discipline has also had its impact in political geography. Perhaps the best illustration in the United States is the work of Richard Morrill who, working with the federal courts in Washington State, was responsible for drawing up the redistricting plan adopted for that State's legislature (Morrill, 1973). After 18 months of research and deliberation, the Legislature could not settle on a reapportionment plan. The House and Senate had each passed a partisan plan drastically different from the other, and compromise seemed impossible. Morrill was appointed as 'Special Master' by the Federal District Court in Seattle, an unprecedented event for a geographer. After reviewing theoretical and practical criteria and methodologies for re-districting, Morrill compared **the** two partisan plans against these criteria (constitutional, political, and geographical), and then presented his own plan which was accepted and is now in effect.

In Canada, the very real and continuing threat to confederation of a secessionist Quebec has attracted much attention from social scientists including a political geographer, Andrew Burghardt (Burghardt, 1971). He draws the historical analogy with the post-1867 Austro-Hungarian Dual Monarchy. Ontario (Austria) will continue to dominate the economic structure. Quebec (Hungary) will become too centralized with the over-dominance of Montreal (Budapest) in which an insistence on unilingualism and on greater autonomy will create problems throughout Canada (the Austrian States). Burghardt elaborates on the likely impact of future secession in an incisive analysis. Given subsequent events in Quebec and with the rise to power of the Parti Quebecois, the secession of Quebec from Canada has gone beyond an interesting academic hypothesis and may well become a reality in the 1980s.

The three major American textbooks of the decade most certainly do not reflect the weaknesses found in their predecessors of the 1960s (Brunn, 1974; Bergman, 1975; and Cox, 1979). They not only gave adequate representation to contemporary research trends and interests but each, in its own way, makes a real contribution to the discipline. Focusing exclusively on the American scene and generously illustrated with maps, Stanley Brunn's book breaks new ground. Fully half the book is given over to the theme of political behaviour in space, integrating with spatial perception and organization such political science themes as identification and attitudes, elites, recruitment, and decision-making. Continuing under a general theme of 'Patterns and Organization', Brunn covers such topics as geography and the law, political cultures, electoral geography, government programmes, and politics and the environment. A valuable and innovative dimension is added to the literature with a section on the future, including a proposal for a new federal system with fewer states, each based on a major metropolitan core. Brunn expects the United States, by the year 2000, to demonstrate several interrelated characteristics which add up to a considerable challenge to its political-geographical structure. These characteristics include the erosion of boundaries, the emergence of city-states, the rise of new political cultures, the reorientation of voting patterns, centralized government and planning, and the politicalization of the environment. These in turn will lead to irresistible pressures for reorganization of the federal system. Sixteen new states are suggested, as is an entirely new territorial base for reallocation of

Senate seats. Brunn is not alone in such prognostications (Pearcy, 1973) and it is good to see the 'alternative futures' theme — one of growing research interest in geography and among other social scientists — make its mark in political geography (Minghi, 1981).

Edward Bergman tried with considerable success not only to include material on America but also to give ideas and perspectives for understanding on a world-wide basis the complexities of the challenge to traditional political-territorial arrangements. Bergman includes a particularly innovative section on local and regional organization in which school districting and racial problems, and metropolitan area allocation-location models are discussed. Yet this American micro-scale treatment is balanced by a more macro-scale future-oriented section on the international political system. Contrary to Brunn, however, Bergman — as has already been noted elsewhere (Minghi, 1976) — fails to recognize political geography's most recent 'growth area', electoral geography.

With a 1979 publication date and a subtitle of 'a political geography of the contemporary world', Kevin Cox's book must command the attention of anyone attempting to assess research trends over the past decade. Dissatisfied with the lack of coherence in political geography, with the neglect of the urban scale and the irrelevance to pressing societal problems of much political-geographical writing, Cox organizes the field around the basic concepts of location and residential quality, the geography of private income, and location and politics — all at three distinct levels: the international, the intranational, and the metropolitan. Hence, rather than discussing such topics as capital-city location, the function of boundaries, gerrymandering or irredentism, Cox develops around the above concepts a group of integrative ideas: the notion of welfare geography, the role of individual location processes, the role of governments as locators, and the role of the judicial context, so crucially important in the United States. Inevitably locational conflict, competition, and resultant disparities and inequities become the recurring themes. Thus the book is somewhat polemical in the tradition of its publisher, the Maaroufa Press, and points to a potentially radical change of focus for the discipline in the 1980s, offering, as it does, a solid conceptual base in locational terms to investigate problems from the local through to the international scale. Cox regards the book as a stepping stone, describing the surface features of locational politics and suggesting directions for a deeper understanding into the structural forces. Recently Peter Taylor has suggested that Rokkan's formulations identifying four process of political integration — penetration, standardization, participation, and redistribution — offer a promising opportunity for the political geographer to focus on the salient aspects of the modern welfare state (Taylor, 1979 and Rokkan, 1975). There is some parallel here with Cox's approach.

It may be that locational conflict as political geography will not be the wave of future research but the coherence, the relevance of society's major concerns, and the long-sought-after scale integration provided by the Cox approach are together a direct challenge to political geography's conventional wisdom and hence will inevitably make the book a hard act to follow. Let us hope that Cox's dissatisfaction with past approaches to our subdiscipline has led to a work which will inspire even more and better research effort over the next decade than that which followed the Kasperson and Minghi opus over the past ten years — an opus which itself was born out of frustration and dissatisfaction with the past.

Cox's book is a logical outcome of a series of publications exploring similar themes begun a decade before with the publication of a group of papers presented at a special session on politics and geography at the 1969 meetings of the American Political Science Association (Cox et al., 1974). Cox and Reynolds in an opening chapter set out basic theoretical and empirical imperatives for developing locational approaches to politics, and developed concepts for analysing political systems as allocational systems, managing locational conflicts between individuals and groups (Cox and Reynolds, 1974). Reynolds later extends this 'conflict' theme by assessing strategies based on a 'spatial contagion' concept for explaining the locational patterns of election returns — the conflict among political candidates for the support of the voters (Reynolds, 1974). More recently at a special session on political-geographical research developments, David Reynolds has introduced the concept of collective decision-making (Reynolds, 1979). In a paper, later expanded for inclusion in this volume, Reynolds tackles the question of 'social choice' and its applicability to political geography. He does not present a complete theory of social choice but he does invite political geographers to follow up on his speculations and to contribute to developing a social choice theory by investigating the linkages between (a) individually held concepts of procedural justice in collective decision-making tasks in reference to 'spatially impure' public goods, and (b) the conceptions of distributive justice (fairness) resulting from these collective decisions.

From the late 1950s onwards there was, as a result of the 1956 Interstate Highways Act, a spate of urban freeway building. Frequently, the siting of such highways raised locational conflicts between government and urban citizens. In a study of such a conflict, Seley and Wolpert made a major contribution to urban political geography by introducing the concept of 'purposeful ambiguity' (Seley and Wolpert, 1974). By use of a simulation model, they show that such a strategy of ambiguity followed by policy-makers in locating noxious public facilities can work better under a certain set of behavioural and locational circumstances. Hence the implications of this research are crucial for developing any community policy of retaliation agaist these ambiguity strategies.

One traditional but hitherto minor area of research focus in American political geography has been the oceans or the high seas. Despite the appearance of a book specifically on this theme (Prescott, 1975) there seems, as yet, to be no real growth of research interest on this topic, although very recently an article on this problem by The Geographer and a colleague at the State Department has appeared which may lead to renewed interest in what should be a 'growth area' for the 1980s (Hodgson and Smith, 1979). These authors closely examine the implications of the recent extension to 200 nautical miles of national marine jurisdiction. It will, for example, force every single coastal state eventually to negotiate jurisdictional limits over marine space with at least one neighbour. Recent agreements and disagreements over marine space delimitation are discussed, as are the various Law of the Sea and Continental Shelf conventions. Two particular North Sea cases recently adjudicated and arbitrated are analysed to provide evidence for general future implications of the 200-mile extension. These two geographers with the US Department of State have brought into new focus an old research theme in American political geography. It is likely that, with rising concern about possible conflict between coastal states over the last two decades of this century, we will see a sharp increase in research activity among political geographers in maritime problems.

A word needs to be said about the 'official' aspects of the sub-discipline in America. Political geography has been well represented in the activities of the Association of American Geographers. At each national meeting, and at most regional division meetings, lively paper-sessions on political-geographical themes have been standard features of the 1970s. At least six works in the AAG Resource Paper series have been on political themes during the 1970s, including papers on political organization (Soja, 1971), administrative systems (Massam, 1972), metropolitan neighbourhood conflict (Wolpert *et al.*, 1972), advocacy planning (Kasperson and Breitbart, 1973), land-use control (Platt, 1976), and crime (Georges, 1978). These Resource Papers are widely distributed to the membership and normally become required reading in graduate seminars. Hence in providing both the stimulation for finding research topics and the exposure to methodological application, these papers tend to have a long-term positive effect on research activity.

Furthermore the Association, as part of the implementation of recommendations made by its Long-Range Planning Committee, is currently setting up a series of 25 'specialty' groups. One of these will be a political geography group for which its co-chairmen, Stanley Brunn and the author, significantly had no trouble in far exceeding the required number of petition-signers and in attracting an enthusiastic overflow attendance for its initial meeting in Philadelphia in April 1979. The aims of the specialty group are to promote participation of members with diverse research and teaching interests in political geography; to promote the exchange of ideas at national and divisional meetings, conferences and symposia, through papers, special sessions and workshops; to produce periodically a newsletter describing completed and ongoing research activity of members, faculty exchange, forthcoming meetings, and potential grant sources. Even moderate success in achieving these aims over the next decade would ensure a healthy climate for political-geographical research.

Final word

One thing at least is clear. Our field continues unabated with its tradition of attracting a colourful if gratuitous outside comment and internal reaction to it. What other subdiscipline has had its progress (or lack of it) critically reviewed so often and what other can claim a history of metaphorical eloquence giving rise to such a tempting mixture? Will Sauer's wayward child drown in Berry's moribund backwater (Berry, 1969), be trapped and de-energized in Prescott's dangerous swamp (Prescott, 1972, p. 40), or experience transfiguration to dead duck only to be reincarnated as a Phoenix à la Muir? (Muir, 1976). Perhaps we should plan to gather again to consider the answer a decade from now, by which time an entirely new collection of inspired metaphors will no doubt have sprouted.

Acknowledgement

The author wishes to thank the Institute of International Studies, University of South Carolina for its support for the original presentation and in the subsequent preparation of this paper.

References

Bergman, E. F. (1975). *Modern Political Geography* (Wm. Brown, Dubuque, Iowa).

Berry, B. J. (1969). Review of Russett, B. M., *International Regions and the International System,* in *Geographical Review,* **59,** 450.

Brunn, S. D. (1974). *Geography and Politics in America* (Harper & Row, New York).

Burghardt, A. F. (1971). 'Quebec separatism and the future of Canada'. In Gentilcore, R. L., (ed.), *Geographical Approaches to Canadian Problems,* pp. 229-35 (Prentice-Hall, Scarborough, Ont.).

Burnett, A. (1971). 'Relative merit', review of Kasperson, R. E., and Minghi, J. V., *The Structure of Political Geography,* in *Pacific Viewpoint,* **12,** 95-7.

Cohen, S. B., and Rosenthal, L. D. (1971). 'A geographical model for political systems analysis', *Geographical Review,* **61,** 5-31.

Cox, K. R. (1979). *Location and Public Problems: A Political Geography of the Contemporary World* (Maaroufa, Chicago).

Cox, K. R., and Reynolds, D. R. (1974). 'Locational approaches to power and conflict', in Cox, K. R., Reynolds, D. R., and Rokkan, S. (eds.), *Locational Approaches to Power and Conflict,* pp. 19-41 (Wiley, New York).

Cox, K. R., Reynolds, D. R., and Rokkan, S. (eds.). (1974). *Locational Approaches to Power and Conflict* (Wiley, New York).

Georges, D. E. (1978). *The Geography of Crime and Violence: A Spatial and Ecological Perspective.* Resource Paper No. 78-1 (AAG, Washington).

Hodgson, R. D., and Smith, R. W. (1979). 'Boundary issues created by extended national marine jurisdiction', *Geographical Review,* **69,** 423-33.

Kasperson, R. E., and Breibart, M. (1973). *Participation, Decentralization, and Advocacy Planning.* Resource Paper No. 25 (AAG, Washington).

Kasperson, R. E., and Minghi, J. V. (1969). *The Structure of Political Geography* (Aldine, Chicago).

Massam, B. H. (1970). Review of Kasperson, R. E., and Minghi, J. V., *The Structure of Political Geography,* in *Canadian Geographer,* **14,** 187-9.

Massam, B. H. (1972). *The Spatial Structure of Administrative Systems.* Resource Paper No. 12 (AAG, Washington).

Minghi, J. V. (1976). Review of Bergman, E. F., *Modern Political Geography,* in *Professional Geographer,* **28,** 211-12.

Minghi, J. V. (1981 expected). 'Politics', in Louder, D., Rooney, J. R., and Zelinsky, W. (eds.), *This Remarkable Continent: An Atlas of North American Cultures and Society* (Texas A&M University Press, College Station, Texas).

Minghi, J. V., and Rumley, D. (1978). 'Toward a geography of campaigning: some evidence from a provincial election in Vancouver, B.C.', *Canadian Geographer,* **22,** 145-62.

Morrill, R. L. (1973). 'Ideal and reality in reapportionment', *Annals of the Association of American Geographers,* **63,** 463-77.

Muir, R. (1976). 'Political geography: dead duck or phoenix?', *Area,* **8,** 195-200.

Pearcy, G. E. (1973). *A Thirty-Eight State USA* (Plycon, Fullerton).

Platt, R. H. (1976). *Land Use Control: Interface of Law and Geography.* Resource Paper No. 75-1 (AAG, Washington).

Prescott, J. R. V. (1972). *Political Geography* (Methuen, London).

Prescott, J. R. V. (1975). *The Political Geography of the Oceans.* (David and Charles, Newton Abbot).

Reynolds, D. R. (1970). Review of Kasperson, R. E., and Minghi, J. V., *The Structure of Political Geography,* in *Geographical Analysis* (April), 199-202.

Reynolds, D. R. (1974). 'Spatial contagion in political influence processes', in Cox, K. R., Reynolds, D. R., and Rokkan, S. (eds.), *Locational Approaches to Power and Conflict,* pp. 233-73 (Wiley, New York).

Reynolds, D. R. (1979). 'The geography of social choice', Paper presented to the Annual Meeting, Association of American Geographers, Philadelphia.

Rokkan, S. (1975). 'Dimensions of state formulation and nation building: a possible paradigm for research on variations within Europe', in Tilly, C. (ed.), *The Formation of Nation States,* pp. 562-600 (Princeton University Press, Princeton).

Seley, J., and Wolpert, J. (1974). 'A strategy of ambiguity in locational conflicts', in Cox, K. R., Reynolds, D. R., and Rokkan, S. (eds.), *Locational Approaches to Power and Conflict,* pp. 275-300 (Wiley, New York).

Soja, E. W. (1971). *The Political Organization of Space.* Resource Paper No. 8 (AAG, Washington).

Taylor, P. J. (1979). 'Progress report on political geography', *Progress in Human Geography,* **3,** 139-42.

Wolpert, J., Mumphrey, A., and Seley, J. (1972). *Metropolitan Neighborhoods: Participation and Conflict Over Change.* Resource Paper No. 16 (AAG, Washington).

Part II

Orientations

Introduction

This section of the book most clearly illustrates the current variety of approaches in political geography. This is as we would expect since the papers allocated to this section are those concerned with more general themes; they discuss what the authors believe to be fundamental issues confronting political geography as it enters the 1980s. The importance of delineating orientations in political geography to explicitly elucidate the purpose of alternative approaches can be illustrated by considering the strange case of electoral geography. The geography of elections is usually traced back to the work of Siegfried (1913), Kareil (1916) and Sauer (1918) but its history is one of sporadic papers with no overall structure and purpose (Taylor and Johnston, 1979). In 1959 Prescott tried to link such study to Hartshorne's areal differentiation approach but to little effect. In the 1960s and 1970s there was an expansion of electoral studies by geographers (Taylor, 1978) but it seemed to be heading in no coherent or particular direction. Hence electoral geography had the peculiar distinction of being rejected by political geographers (Crone, 1967; Muir, 1975) and so became isolated within geography's own isolate! This situation is now changing as political geographers become more concerned for the political role of the state so that elections can become a relevant topic within a new orientation (Taylor, 1978; Johnston, 1979). In this way electoral geography has come to be integrated, finally, within a political geography framework (Johnston, 1980). It is hoped that the explicit recognition of alternative orientations in this section will go some way to preventing aimless repetitions of the electoral geography story.

The new orientation that electoral geography has been integrated into involves analysing the state and its operation using a systems approach (Johnston, 1979). Interestingly enough this orientation is not represented by the papers in this section. This is probably the most surprising feature of this section, if not of the whole volume. The essays of this collection represent a reasonable cross-section of Anglo-American political geography including several authors who have previously applied systems thinking to their work, and yet in 1980 this dominant orientation of the late 1960s and 1970s is conspicuous by its absence. Perhaps it is simply that all that can be said by political geographers about a systems approach has been said, so that the approach is firmly part of our battery of ideas. Alternatively it may be that it has been tried, applied, and found to be wanting. As editors we found the omission of this topic from our orientations set of papers so intriguing that we felt a brief discussion of the matter was warranted before we introduce the papers that do appear in the section.

The systems approach entered geography as part of the breakdown of the discipline's isolation discussed in the introduction to Part One. In 1963 Edward Ackerman in his presidential address to the American Association of Geographers urged his colleagues to reorder their researches into a systems framework. Three years later the *Ad Hoc* Committee on Geography under Ackerman's chairmanship expounded this viewpoint in *The Science of Geography* (NAS-NRC, 1965) where political geography was explicitly discussed in these terms. Political geographers were expected to study political *systems* within their *territorial* jurisdictions. In fact the committee reinterpreted the earlier works of Whittlesey, Hartshorne, Gottman, and Jones in a systems framework so that they are able to comment in their conclusions that

> Political geographers have been accustomed to thinking in terms of systems and system relationships almost from the beginning of their field (Ratzel). Thus a system framework... will be easily understood by the political geographer, and his work easily adapted to it. (NAS—NRC, 1965, p. 51).

The prediction was well justified by events.

There are three basic types of system thinking that have applied to political geography, and they can be ordered from the very general to the specifically political. The most general applications involve invoking the original general systems theory of von Bertalanffy (1951), and Hall and Fagen (1956), which was claimed to apply to all phenomena from physical systems through biological systems to social systems. This set of ideas was introduced into geography by Ackerman (1963) and Haggett (1965) and when applied to political geography consisted of rewriting the past work in systems terminology. This was the approach of the *Ad Hoc* Committee as noted previously, but it has been most rigorously appied by Cohen and Rosenthal (1971). They essentially codified Whittlesey's (1939) pioneer ideas in terms of systems methodology. Despite some use of this work in teaching (Jenkins and McEvoy, 1977), it has not really been influential for political geography research.

The second use of systems in political geography has involved use of Talcott Parsons' (1951) concept of the social system. Bergman's (1975) textbook includes a first chapter describing Parsons' four prime operations of a social system — pattern maintenance, adaptation, integration and goal attainment — but does not apply them subsequently in the rest of the book. Parsons' approach has been applied in political geography, however indirectly, throught the work of Stein Rokkan (1970). Rokkan's work on the bases of political parties consists of interpretation of Parsons' integration subsystem, although this point is not explicitly developed in the use made of Rokkan's ideas in political geography (Taylor and Johnston, 1979).

By far the most common application of systems in political geography has involved use of David Easton's (1953, 1965a, b) concept of the political system. Some of Easton's work has been directly reproduced in a set of readings for political geographers (Jackson and Samuels, 1974, pp. 1-40 and 345-60), and he gets numerous citations in Kasperson and Minghi (1969) and other textbooks (e.g. Bergman, 1975; Muir, 1975) as well as being used as the basis for research formulation and presentation (e.g. Kasperson, 1969 and Whitney, 1969). Nevertheless like the other two forms of systems work, the research gains from this perspective can, with hindsight, be seen to have been disappointing. Sometimes, systems ideas are poorly integrated into the discussion — Muir (1975) describes the approach in an appendix — and it is even sometimes described but then not applied (Douglas, 1973). In fact its major role has been a heuristic one (Burnett, 1974) for ordering an argument or linking together ideas but providing little or no further insights to the problem at hand. This pedagogic role is exemplified by the theoretical papers in Cox *et al.* (1974). Cox and Reynolds (1974) present a neat diagram describing 'the political system in a locational context' (p. 30) and Soja (1974) offers a diagram of 'a paradigm for the locational analysis of political systems' (p. 48). Both are useful ways of organizing ideas but they do not really go any further. Perhaps the major application and substantive use of this approach is to be found in Johnston's (1979) *Political, Electoral and Spatial Systems,* but again the major interest of this work is not so much the fact that 'systems' are prominent, but more generally the integration of several modern themes (including electoral geography) in political geography into a coherent scheme as previously discussed. After a while heuristic devices consisting of boxes and arrows seem less exciting than when first discovered, so that there is less interest in writing yet more papers on systems approaches. Hence our orientation papers contain no discussion of the topic.

One final point concerning the systems approach may also have contributed to its fall in popularity. The critical, neo-Marxist political economy framework allows no place for the sort of abstraction found in systems work. Despite attempts by Johnston (1979) to encompass class conflicts into his work, the systems approach is overtly descriptive of appearances and ultimately views society as tending towards an equilibrium state. The alternative offered by critical social theory will become apparent as we now come to introduce the papers that are found in this orientation section.

In his detailed discussion of territory and territoriality in the first essay, Robert Sack covers what to many political geographers are the fundamental concepts in political geography. The *Ad Hoc* Committee (NAS-NRC, 1965), for instance, proclaimed that: 'Political geography's consistent concern with the expression of the sense of territoriality in man makes it one of the foremost keys to the spatial behaviour of human society' (p. 50), and in Kasperson and Minghi's (1969) readings 'territoriality and hierarchy' have a section devoted to them. Nevertheless Sack's essay breaks new ground as he shows how these topics can be interpreted as central to any political-geographical understanding. Sack has been working for some years on drawing links between human actions and spatial relations (e.g. Sack, 1972). In his scheme territoriality is a type of human action involving control over specified geographical areas. The implications of this for political geography can be appreciated when it is realized that this behaviour may be applied to such diverse topics as differential access to resources, reification of power, and processes of divide-and-rule using hierarchical territories. Sack illustrates his arguments by using simple everyday situations rather than well-known political-geographical themes, but clearly his analysis can be related to the topics covered by Burnett and Honey in the agendas section and the applications of Paddison, Williams, and Rowley. This is clearly one area where a modern behavioural approach can add significantly to our ways of looking at both past and recent topics in political geography.

The next two papers, by Archer and Reynolds, develop previous work which attempts to draw out the spatial implications of the public choice paradigm (the new political economy) for political geography (Cox, 1973; Hall, 1974; Cox and Reynolds, 1974). These two authors have previously worked together to attempt to formulate a distinctive electoral geography (Reynolds and Archer, 1969) (which O'Loughlin follows up in his paper in the applications section), and this has been developed into consideration of relations of voting to policy (Archer and Reynolds, 1976). In their papers here it is the policy theme which is developed as they search for a theoretical framework in which to assess public policy. Archer presents a thorough overview where the salient aspects of the public choice paradigm are discussed and fully referenced. It is particularly interesting that Archer is able to conclude with a supporting quotation from Walter Christaller, the founder of theoretical economic geography, highlighting the neo-classical economic concepts that underlie this approach.

Reynolds' paper is much more specific in that he identifies the lack of theory as the primary deficiency of political geography and then sets himself the task of beginning to right the situation. He illustrates the rigour that this public choice approach can supply in terms of defining problems and paradoxes and pointing the way to solutions. He lists seven questions of 'central concern' to the paradigm and then assesses alternative approaches to answering them within this framework. His preferred approach consists of 'procedural fairness' within a constitutional choice framework so that the task of 'more political geographers' in the 1980s should be to investigate 'the underlying logic of systems of social choice'.

The public choice approach tends to promote minimal collective action as the world is seen through the eyes of individual consumers. In stark contrast the paper by Clark and the other critical-theoretical papers in this volume argue that the individual can only be adequately modelled within the structure of the social formation of his or her society. Gordon Clark is most well known to political geographers for his review of theories of the state with Michael Dear (Dear and Clark, 1978) who contributes the first paper to the agendas section. Their discussion of different theories of the state is augmented in Clark's paper here by specifically focusing on the role of democracy and its treatment in traditional theory. Many writers have noted how democracy is a key concept of legitimation in the capitalist state (e.g. Miliband, 1969). It is perhaps ironic that 'western' states tend to see themselves as defenders of democracy while eastern-bloc states invariably include 'democracy' in their official titles. This, of course, reflects different interpretations of the term democracy and as Macpherson (1965) points out the western view is best termed liberal-democracy, to distinguish it from other theories which do not place so much emphasis upon individual actions. A general criticism of liberal-democracy has been briefly outlined by Blackburn (1969), and Clark specifically develops criticisms of interest in political geography. In particular he discusses the most influential 'spatial' argument in the public choice paradigm, Tiebout's (1956) notion that citizens vote with their feet according to their preference for a specific bundle of taxes and services among competitive local government areas. The problem is, of course, that many of the people who are dependent on public services cannot in fact move to the jurisdiction 'of their choice' (Stanyer, 1980). Clark's criticism is, however, more fundamental. He argues that Tiebout's model does not fit the reality of democratic politics in a capitalist society where ideology, economic inequalities, and class conflict are pervasive elements. The implication is that if liberal-democracy does not operate at this most local level of the state hierarchy where authority is most accessible, then development of theory within this framework is either naive or mystifying.

The final two papers in this section involve studies at a much greater geographical scale, but once again they express contrasting sets of theoretical assumptions. Brunn applies futuristic methodology to the traditional political geography theme of global geopolitics. This involves applying knowledge of international relations, technology, resources, and economic and social trends to produce a variety of scenarios for the twenty-first century. Some of the scenarios involve discussion of topics of traditional interest in geography (regional powers, mini-states, regionalism within states, time-space convergence) plus treatment of more recent themes (a new international political order, sovereignty of the oceans, transnational corporations). A very comprehensive bibliography, which includes Brunn's earlier work applying this methodology to the scale of the individual country (USA), makes this contribution an ideal starting point for debate in the classroom, and research.

The time dimension is also dominant in the final paper of this section by Taylor, but here it is represented historically in the description of the evolution of the dynamically changing world economy. An argument is presented which frees political geography from both its past and present concentration on the state as object of analysis to be replaced by the over-arching capitalist world economy. One consequence of this new orientation is to place the North versus South (core-periphery) economic conflict at the centre of the world stage at the expense of the cold-war East versus West political conflict. Mackinder and traditional global political geography can then be seen to fall neatly into the framework of the neoconservatives (Ajami, 1978). The emphasis upon North versus South in this paper is a consequence of the materialistic basis of the paper which it shares with the other critical-theoretical papers in the agendas (Dear) and applications (Hudson).

References and bibliography

Ackerman, E. A. (1963). 'Where is a research frontier?', *Annals of the Association of American Geographers,* **53,** 429-40.

Ajami, F. (1978). 'The global logic of the neoconservatives', *World Politics,* **30,** 450-68.

Archer, J. C., and Reynolds, D. R. (1976). 'Locational logrolling and citizen support of municipal bond proposals: the example of St. Louis', *Public Choice,* **27,** 21-40.

Bergman, E. F. (1975). *Modern Political Geography* (Wm. Brown, Dubuque, Iowa).

Bertalanffy, L. Von. (1951). 'An outline of general systems theory', *British Journal of the Philosophy of Science,* **1,** 134-65.

Blackburn, R. (1969). 'A brief guide to bourgeois ideology', in Cockburn, A., and Blackburn, R. (eds.), *Student Power,* pp. 163-213 (Penguin, London).

Burnett, A. D. (1974). 'A systems approach to the geographical study of public policy'. Paper given at symposium on Geography and Public Policy. Institute of British Geographers, Norwich.

Cohen, S. B., and Rosenthal, L. D (1971). 'A geographical model for political systems analysis', *Geographical Review,* **61,** 5-31.

Cox, K. R. (1973). *Conflict, Power and Politics in the City: A Geographic View* (McGraw Hill, New York).

Cox, K. R., Reynolds, D. R., and Rokkan, S. (eds.), (1974). *Locational Approaches to Power and Conflict* (Sage, Beverley Hills).

Cox, K. R., and Reynolds, D. R. (1974). 'Locational approaches to power and conflict', in Cox, K. R., Reynolds, D. R., and Rokkan, S. (eds.), *Locational Approaches to Power and Conflict,* pp. 19-41 (Sage, Beverley Hills).

Crone, G. R. (1967). *Background to Political Geography* (Heinemann, London).

Dear, M. and Clark, G. (1978). 'The state and geographic process: a critical review', *Environment and Planning A,* **10,** 173-83.

Douglas, V. N. H. (1973). 'Politics', in Dawson, A. H., and Doornkamp, J. (eds.), *Evaluating the Human Environment,* pp. 160-75 (Methuen, London).

Easton, D. (1953). *The Political System* (Knopf, New York).

Easton, D. (1965a). *A Framework for Political Analysis* (Prentice Hall, Englewood Cliffs, NJ).

Easton, D. (1965b). *A Systems Analysis of Political Life* (Wiley, New York).

Haggett, P. (1965). *Locational Analysis in Human Geography* (Edward Arnold, London).

Hall, A. D. and Fagen, R. E. (1956). 'Definition of system', *General Systems Yearbook,* **1,** 18-28.

Hall, P. (1974). 'The new political geography', *Transactions of the Institute of British Geographers,* **63,** 48-52.

Jackson, W. A. D., and Samuels, M. S. (eds.) (1974). *Political Geographical Relationships* (2nd ed.) (Prentice Hall, Englewood Cliffs, NJ).

Jenkins, A., and McEvoy, D. (eds.), (1977). *Teaching Political Geography* (Oxford Polytechnic. Discussion Papers in Geography, 7, Oxford).

Johnston, R. J. (1979). *Political, Electoral and Spatial Systems* (Oxford University Press, London).

Johnston, R. J. (1980). 'Electoral geography and political geography', *Australian Geographical Studies,* **11,** 35-50.

Kareil, E. (1916). 'Geographical influences in British elections', *Geographical Review,* **6,** 419-32.

Kasperson, R. E. (1969). 'Environmental stress and the municipal political system: the Brockton water crisis of 1961-1966', in Kasperson, R. E. and Minghi, J. V. (eds.), *The Structure of Political Geography,* pp. 481-97 (Aldine, Chicago).

Kasperson, R. E. and Minghi, J. V. (eds.) (1969). *The Structure of Political Geography* (Aldine, Chicago).

Macpherson, C. B. (1965). *The Real World of Democracy* (Oxford University Press, London).

Miliband, R. (1969). *The State in Capitalist Society* (Weidenfeld & Nicholson, London).

Muir, R. (1975). *Modern Political Geography* (Macmillan, London).

NAS-NRC (1975). *The Science of Geography* (National Academy of Sciences and National Research Council, Washington, DC).

Parsons, T. (1951). *The Social System* (Free Press of Glencoe, Illinois).

Reynolds, D. R., and Archer, J. C. (1969). 'An inquiry into the spatial basis of electoral geography', *Discussion Paper,* 11 (Department of Geography, University of Iowa, Iowa City).

Rokkan, S. (1970). *Citizens, Elections, Parties* (McKay, New York).

Sack, R. D. (1972). 'Geography, geometry and explanation', *Annals of the Association of American Geographers,* **62,** 439-52.

Sauer, C. O. (1918). 'Geography and the gerrymander', *American Political Science Review,* **12,** 403-26.

Siegfried, A. (1913). *Tableau Politique de la France de l'Ouest* (Colin, Paris).

Soja, E. W. (1974). 'A paradigm for the geographical analysis of political systems', in Cox, K. R., Reynolds, D. R., and Rokkan, S. (eds.), *Locational Approaches to Power and Conflict,* pp. 43-72 (Sage, Beverley Hills).

Stanyer, J. (1980). 'The Logic of Metropolitan Local Government', paper given at SSRC seminar on urban politics, Exeter.

Taylor, P. J. (1978). 'Political geography' (Progress Report). *Progress in Human Geography,* **2,** 153-62.

Taylor, P. J. and Johnston, R. J. (1979). *Geography of Elections* (Penguin, London).

Tiebout, C. M. (1956). 'A pure theory of local expenditures', *Journal of Political Economy,* **64,** 416-24.

Whitney, J. B. R. (1969). *China — Area Administration and Nation Building.* Department of Geography, University of Chicago, Research Paper 123 (Chicago).

Whittlesey, D. (1939). *The Earth and the State: A Study in Political Geography* (Holt, New York).

Political studies from spatial perspectives
Edited by A.D. Burnett and P.J. Taylor
© 1981 John Wiley & Sons Ltd

_3_

Territorial bases of power

Robert D. Sack

Introduction

One of geography's two major perspectives is the study of places and spatial relations. The other is man's relationship to nature. Both are interrelated in the study of landscape and its areal differentiation. A geographic approach to such systematic disciplines as economics, sociology, anthropology, and political science means approaching their subject-matter from either or both perspectives. Our interest here is in exploring the spatial perspective and its application to political behaviour in the field of political geography.

From a spatial analysis perspective, the scope of political geography is the analysis of the spatial properties and relationships among political events and activities on the earth's surface. Putting aside the problems of defining political events and activities (which is a thorny problem for political science) the nature of political geography depends on what is meant by spatial analysis. This paper will consider two related issues on the matter. First it will show that the traditional idea of spatial analysis in geography, even if generously portrayed, concentrates on only one of the two essential roles which physical space and spatial relations play in human actions — that of *action by contact;* whereas it has neglected or ignored the second essential role — that of *territoriality.* The same of course is true of political geography. Neglecting territoriality seriously limits geography's effectiveness and cripples the field of political geography, for here more than anywhere else we find territoriality an explicit and socially recognized form of behaviour. We do not contend that political geography is the study of territoriality, for we find it in all realms of life. Rather we believe it is especially important and visible in the realms of politics and power, and has to form a prominent part of political geography.

The second issue is making clear what we mean by territoriality and its functions. This is a vast topic. In this short a space we can offer only a sketch of what territoriality is and its import for both political geography and spatial analysis. A more extended analysis of territoriality and its historical forms is under way by the author in a book, *Territoriality*.

Definition and domain of territoriality

Action by contact

Physical space and time are inextricably linked with the existence of things and their interactions. Things have location and extension in space and time. For something to influence or affect another there must be some degree of contact. The influence or effect involves transmitting energy from one to the other in space. Contact can be *direct* in that they touch, or *indirect* and *circuitous* in that the energy is carried by agents or media connecting the two. Either direct or indirect contact in space must exist between interacting objects. Things must be spatially accessible. Take for example the positioning of people in normal conversation. While they are not in direct contact — they are not touching — they are in contact because the sounds they make, as energy, are being transmitted by the expansion and compression of the air molecules between them. If they are too far apart for a face-to-face talk, they could have a conversation by telephone. This would make them in contact, but more indirectly and circuitously. If they did not have access to a telephone, or if there were a three-foot glass partition between them when face-to-face, there would be no contact and hence no conversation.

If we do not push the meanings of concepts such as 'space', 'things, and 'interactions' too far, the above provides a brief (but reasonable) description of the principle of *action by contact* (whether direct or indirect contact) which is the core of the idea of *causality* in our practical everyday considerations, as well as in the social and physical sciences concerned with actions on the earth's surface. The principle outlines only a very basic condition which we expect physical space to fulfil. It does not specify the actual spatial arrangements and configurations of interacting things. For instance the distance between people engaged in normal face-to-face conversations varies considerably according to their culture, age, sex, and degree of familiarity, as well as to the condition of the air between them. Such details and specifics would be addressed in generalizations, hypotheses, or laws covering particular interactions — if such generalizations were to be developed. But even without them our confidence in the idea of action by contact would not be shaken. We would still believe that face-to-face conversations among people would be possible because of the energy transmitted by the expansion and compression of air molecules, and that the ease and even the possibility of conversation would be affected by the quality of air and other intervening substances. Certainly conversations would not occur in a vacuum.

Our point here is not to challenge the concept of action by contact and its role in causality, for by and large it is a reasonable supposition for actions on the earth's surface. Rather we will employ it as a principle of cause and effect, and point out that there is a large class of actions in which space seems to play yet another role in causality. We will refer to this class as *territoriality*.

Territoriality

Territoriality neither dispenses with action by contact nor violates it. Rather it extends the particulars of action by contact to the point where a new principle relating space and action seems to emerge; and, which, in turn, affects the details of action by contact. We will define territoriality in very general terms to point to its role as a principle of space in causality. We will use the term to mean *the attempt to affect, influence, or control actions and interactions (of people, things and relationships, etc.) by asserting and attempting to enforce control over a specific geographical area*. This area is the territory. Territoriality makes the territory appear to be filled with power, influence, authority, or sovereignty. Territoriality can either include or exclude actions from the territory; and the purposes of territoriality can be either good or bad, just or unjust. Territories can be any scale; the room, the house, the street, the factory, the school, the city, the state, the medieval manor, are all examples of territory, whereas the circumscription of a distribution or a process as in the geographical areas called the corn belt, the south, or central place hinterlands, are not territories. They are descriptions of locations, not assertions of control with implied sanctions for transgressions.

Our purpose is to develop a definition that is sensitive and flexible enough to help distinguish territoriality from non-territoriality and to help explain the many forms territories take.

Because the word has come to mean so many things, it may have been wise either to select another term or to coin a new one. But no simple alternative comes to mind which does not itself create problems about connotations. Nor is there another term which points to the kind of behaviour we wish to analyse. We will therefore continue to use the term territoriality and rely on the context to differentiate our meaning of the term from other meanings.

Our definition of territoriality could apply to both human and animal behaviour but our discussion will concentrate on human *territoriality* almost exclusively. We use 'could' because there is some question about whether the definition uses terms which refer to uniquely human relationships. This is especially the case for the term 'area'. Although it is used in practically every definition of territoriality in the biological literature, area and space in general are particularly abstract concepts and may be peculiar to human language and experience. Whereas many animals act as though they were defending area, they may not have had the idea in mind. We could skirt the issue by cumbersomely describing their behaviour less abstractly, avoiding the term area or space, by referring to the particular actions and reactions of the animal to things in space. We can refer to the need of an animal to smell its own scent and use this need to explain its periodic spraying — the extension of the scent conforming to its most recurrent movements. Whether we need to do this depends on how much conceptual and symbolic ability we think animals possess. We can be sure, though, that for humans the concepts area, territory, and space do have meaning and can be communicated.

To illustrate the way in which human beings use space territorially, and how this differs from simple action by contact, let us suppose a father is home minding the children. He finds them in his study doodling on his note cards, upsetting piles of books, and ripping up manuscripts. The father can have a face-to-face, heart-to-heart talk with the children, telling them not to touch these books, note cards, and manuscripts. He might even spank them. In either case, the father is attempting to control the actions of his children directly, by contact, and in a way that is directed towards specific categories of things such as books, note cards, and manuscripts.

But there is another alternative. The father could hope to control the actions of his children regarding books, manuscripts, and note cards without telling them not to touch just these kinds of things. He could do this by telling his children that they may not go into his study without him; that the study is off limits. This is an example of *territoriality* because it is an attempt to control actions (of children) by asserting control over an area (the study). Of course asserting that the study is off limits, as well as enforcing the assertion, require that the information be transmitted to the children and that their behaviour be monitored. Hence it employs direct contact. But the assertion is no longer specific to the things in the place; rather it is specific to the place itself. In this way, territoriality uses action by contact to make it appear as though the control of space controls cause and effect. It is an alternative, and an extremely important one, to the non-territorial use of action by contact.

While the particular actions of the father in one case are an example of either territoriality or non-territoriality, there is a considerable interdependence between the two. Not only does territoriality depend on the principle of action by contact, and in turn help determine the particulars of the principle, but in our example, the non-territorial action of talking to the children, and of disciplining them, takes place in the context of territories. There is the house, the land it occupies, the municipality, the state, and so on; and the powers and authorities that people have in each. We may select a non-territorial activity because we know it can be backed up by a territorial action and *vice-versa*. Similarly a particular structure like a room may be territorial at one time, as in the second strategy of the father, while non-territorial at another, as in the rooms of a deserted house; in which case they simply are objects.

Sometimes it may not be clear whether an action is territorial or not. We find this to be the case in social distance, *personal space* or 'social force fields' (McBride, quoted in N. Peterson, 1977). The concept is used to refer to the 'volume' of air or space which we surround ourselves with, and within which we do not permit others unless they be our intimates. The average distance of three feet in normal conversation is one component of this volume. Just as the distance of three feet depends on a variety of things such as age, sex, culture, the medium surrounding us, and the kind of con-versations we will undertake, so too does the rest of the volume. The point is that our personal interactions arrange themselves so that this volume is more or less maintained. When it is not — when people are too close or too far — we feel uncomfortable. We may assume that others have the same feelings about positioning and use this distance to communicate. If we feel hostile we may shorten the distance, if we feel aloof we may lengthen it. While it is reasonable to talk about this distance and volume, it is not clearly territorial because we do not make explicit and direct pronouncements about controlling the area or volume and we do not state the consequence of trespass. Moreover the components of the distance and volume are so closely related to particular actions that we can affect them more by making direct reference to them than by making reference to spatial relations. For instance the three-foot distance of normal conversation is due to a preference for combinations of sensori-stimuli of certain intensities. If one or several of these do not occur in the proper quantity and quality we may make reference directly to these stimuli instead of to the distance. Rather than ask someone to step back we may ask them to speak more softly.

Personal space can be made more explicitly territorial. Take for instance the designing of a factory and layout of the assembly line. The architect's drawings may designate a working area around each seat or place on the assembly line. This often conforms to the range of motions the individual worker will perform at his tasks and to the general 'personal space' that we assume people want and need. Once a basic element of factory design, the supervisors, the foremen and workers alike will think of such areas, although they be 'invisible' and personal, as more or less explicit, instituted, and enforcible — hence as territories.

While some territories, like the house, are embedded in others, like the state, some are explicitly part of a hierarchy of territories. The territories of the local municipalities, the counties, the states, and the nations are a case in point. So too are the hierarchies of areas within the office, the shop, the factory, and even the house. In all of these cases, certain geographical areas, as territories, are used to control actions and interactions by either excluding or including them within the territory. Not only do territories vary according to the kinds of actions they include or exclude, but also according to the intensity of control and to the degree to which they organize the actions within their domain. The organizations can be so specific, that not only is the location of an individual restricted in space but the individual's bodily motions may be stipulated and controlled, making it appear as though territoriality penetrates the body, compartmentalizing and reorganizing its parts and correcting them to tools and machines of the work place. For example, the work areas in factories are territories which not only contain the worker's body, but also place the worker and the instruments of work in a specific spatial relationship determining the orientation of the body and the movements of the limbs for extended periods of time. Similarly giving a letter to a typist in an office means that for the job to get done the typist will be in a specified place and orientation and the words on the page dictate the relative position of the hands and fingers. In such cases the body appears as an appendage to the machine and the *territory* helps stipulate and enforce their connection.

Previous work on territoriality

All of these examples are contemporary. We could equally well have selected past territorial organizations but our intention here is to present familiar situations to illustrate what we mean by territoriality and to suggest its importance and ubiquity. It is remarkable that the phenomenon has been neglected by geographers. Because their interests have been concentrated primarily on the principle of action by contact and its specific forms in particular circumstances, what we have called territoriality has been lost in the background of *ceteris paribus* assumptions. For instance Central Place Theory explores the spatial relationships between rural populations and marketing centres. The theory discusses the number of goods and services, the distribution of the rural population and their needs, and the existence of transportation facilities. Territoriality arises explicitly only in the 'administrative principle' which tries to make the boundaries of hierarchical central places nested instead of overlapping. What is unproblematical within the theory is the fact that the places exist within some kind of political entity with sovereignty over the area, that the populace agree to abide by laws assigning particular functions to areas or parcels of land, that land can be bought and sold, that transportation routes are public, and so on. Just the slightest alteration of one of these suppositions and the analysis is altered dramatically.

Political geography, more than any other area, has sensed the significance of *territoriality* but, with the exception of Soja (1971), has not had a sustained and systematic analysis of its role and function. In fact much of political geography is defined in terms of the spatial analysis which has ignored *territoriality* even at the state level. Hence we find the emphasis on voting behaviour, electoral geography, the effects of boundaries on interactions, the morphology of the state, rather than on the role and function of territory. Even when the political *territory* is considered it is approached by and large from the viewpoint of spatial analysis. That political geography more than any other area contains something different about space has attracted some to the idea that political geography is potentially central to the geographical discipline. From our viewpoint it is the sense that *territoriality* is different from other kinds of actions in space and that political-geographical units are explicit *territorial* organizations that has drawn this interest.

The neglect of *territoriality* by geography is easier to understand when we consider the way in which it has been approached by other fields. The definitions of territoriality have been narrow and most of the examples are from animal behaviour. There are the well-documented studies of territoriality in Song Sparrows, in Field Crickets, in Three-Spined Sticklebacks, in the Uganda Kob, to mention a few of the many species referred to in the literature (Stokes, 1974). There has not, however, been a general statement which satisfactorily comprehends the variety of examples and which can be extended to human action. (In fact territoriality has been used to refer to any process of spatial distancing and arrangements in animals.) Even clearly territorial actions like private property and political jurisdictions are only occasionally and begrudgingly considered territorial. And when they are analysed as territorial activities the result is polemical and sensational rather than scholarly and analytical.

Most definitions of territoriality have taken the obvious aspect of territoriality — the control of area — and made it the most essential issue, often the only aspect of the definition. For instance Howard (1920) uses it to mean 'any defended area'; Pitelka (1959) refers to it as 'an exclusive area, not merely a defended one', and Wilson (1975) defines it as 'an area occupied more or less exclusively by an animal or group of animals by means of repulsion through overt defense or advertisement'. In Ardrey's (1969) work the emphasis on area is so strong that it becomes not only an object which is recognized and defended instinctively but a driving force. While the definition we offered also is about the control of area, the concept area, as we said, can be replaced by particular actions in space which the animal or person employs to create barriers to interactions. Moreover when the term area is retained for both animals and man, it must be taken to mean area in a *relational* sense. Earth space is not empty and empty space is a conception, an abstraction, requiring a fair degree of intellectual sophistication with symbolic forms. Hence control of space *per se* can hardly be an instinct. It is unlikely to be a conception in animals, and while conceivable by man it is not attainable. Rather it is control of an area of things that is sometimes attained. Things and relationships in space are controlled and this is what we mean by *relational* space. A fish does not act territorially out of water. It is the volume of water that counts (and with the ayu it is shallow, not deep water — Chapman, 1966), just as it is the quality of air that matters in our spatial arrangements in conversations.

Granted then that we are not to take the idea of area or space to mean empty space, the definition of territoriality as the control of area still leaves us without a purpose. Why act territorially? When researchers have addressed this question their answers have been in terms of specific needs or functions which territoriality is supposed to provide. Thus it is argued that territoriality is a means of providing food, mates, population control, relief from stress, and of expressing sexual dominance; and in Ardrey's (1969) terms, of providing security, stimulation, and identity, which he considers basic needs or instincts. Indeed, these are all possible functions which can be provided by territoriality; but are they provided by all instances of territoriality, and for all species, and all together? And does this exhaust the list?

Most importantly, it leaves the question at this stage, keeping the answer within the realms of correlation between territoriality and particular things or functions which then often become part of the definition. It does not ask what there is about the control of area that allows it to produce these functions. More generally, it does not underscore the fact that territoriality is a strategy; that is, only one of two possible means of control, the other being non-territorial. That it is a strategy is demonstrated by the empirical evidence. Territories, even in animals, change in size and even disappear, depending on the distribution of material to defend or exclude (Dyson-Hudson and Alden-Smith (1975), p. 23). Even the way territoriality is expressed or communicated varies according to the source of danger or competition. Conspecifics require one form of warning; other creatures another.

That territoriality is a strategy is abundantly clear in human behaviour. The forms territoriality takes, and the possible things it can provide for humans, are so numerous and complex that applying the older definitions and searching for particular functions have so overwhelmed students of human behaviour as to make some despair of ever defining the concept adequately — and of finding its instances in human actions (Crook, 1973). Even Ardrey (1969), who makes the most persistent claim that people are territorial, nevertheless has to deal with much of human territoriality as a thwarted instinct or drive.

Approach

The details about specific functions are exactly what we want to know. But the best way is to step back from the details to develop an understanding of the general potential functions which territoriality, as a relationship between space and causality, can provide. Potentials are made actual and given import by the social and economic conditions at particular times. Yet the occurrence of territoriality and the specific forms it takes cannot be understood unless we have some idea of the most general advantages which it can offer and which are not as easily available with non-territorial control.

Clearly the definition of territoriality itself does not reveal these potentials. Nor does the particular association of territoriality with the provision of food, sex, status, etc. An Iroquois long house, a medieval monastery, and a modern factory are all very different kinds of organizations providing different functions, but they are also all examples of hierarchical territories. The general functions we are searching for would help us see not only that these are hierarchical territories but why in each case territorial organizations were used differently.

In conventional terms a good concept ought to be defined clearly enough so that instances of it can be observed and described. This we hope is the case with our definition of territoriality; but concepts should also be significant in that they should be connected to other concepts in laws or generalizations. That is, knowing instances of one kind of thing (e.g. territoriality) we then should be led to know that instances of another kind of thing will be associated with it (e.g. particular functions). This connection would disclose an empirical association or relationship. The stronger this relationship, and the more interlocking it becomes with other relationships, the more significance we attach to it. Generalizations in a sense disclose the structure of relationships which the facts — represented by the concepts — enter into. This structure, sometimes in the form of a theory, is the significant context and gives the concept meaning or import.

Generalizations can vary in their degrees of levels of generality and comprehensiveness. A generalization about carbon and oxygen combining to form CO_2 is more particular than theories of the atom and chemical bonding. These can help us understand why CO_2 occurs, as well as outline the potentials for bondings between carbon and the other elements. Generalizations with broader ranges and scope help place the more specialized ones in perspective. If the latter can be subsumed by the former, or if the broader generalizations are part of a theory so that the specialized generalizations can be derived from them, we not only have more confidence in the specialized relationships, but we can also understand more about the structure they disclose. In other words they become more significant. Most of the work on territoriality has concentrated on the narrower relationships as though exploring the nature of carbon by looking only at its actual combinations with other elements and by ignoring a deeper and broader context about bondings and atomic structures.

Potential functions

Our problem is to determine how, why, and under what conditions, a person or group uses a *territorial* rather than, or in addition to, a non-territorial strategy to control other people, things, and relationships. The answer will be in terms of a series of functions which territoriality has the potential to provide under very general conditions — ones which might obtain in practically any society. These potentials involve different disciplines and perspectives, covering the economic, political, and personal levels both for those in control and for those being controlled. The following discussion of tendencies or potentials covers most of the important functions but is not exhaustive; nor are the tendencies independent — some can be combined to form contradictory potentials. Historical contexts draw upon different combinations to form their own *territorial* organizations and give these tendencies their import. (How this is done is beyond the scope of this paper.)

Territoriality, by definition, is about control. Hence one of its primary functional advantages must be that it can make control easier. This is indeed the case, as we shall see; but first we must turn to two other functions which practically all forms of *territoriality* provide and upon which the function of *territorial* control depends. These are *classification* and *communication.*

Territoriality involves a form of classification which is extremely efficient under certain circumstances. Territoriality classifies at least in part by area, rather than by type. These two forms of classification according to Piaget exhaust the alternatives. He calls classification by area *infralogical* and classification by type *logical,* without intending to mean that the one is superior or more advanced than the other (Piaget and Inhelder, 1956). Classification by area means that something belongs to a class at least in part because of its geographical location in an area. When we say that anything in this area or room is ours, or is off limits to you, we are classifying or assigning the things to a category such as ours or not yours — according to its location in space. We need not stipulate the kinds of things in the place that are ours or not yours. Anything and everything can fall within that category provided it is in this area. By contrast the other kind of classification — by type — would mean that things would have to be defined sufficiently clearly in terms of characteristics other than by their location to be able to identify them or determine if a fact is indeed an instance of them. For example if the territory is the study, the categories would be books, papers, desk, chair, pencils, typewriter, and so on, and these would be defined clearly enough so that instances of them would or could be identified. But even for the study, the possibility of classifying by type or kind, so that all of the things that one wants to claim or protect are included and clearly stipulated, would require a great deal of time and effort. In fact we may never really be able to do it if we also consider relationships among things that we would prefer not to happen, or if we consider that the content of the place changes. For instance, although it may be clear that nothing in the study is to be touched, we may not have made it clear that nothing new is to be brought into the study. If the areas are larger and more complex the problem of classification becomes more acute. Thus territoriality avoids at least in part the necessity of enumeration and classification by kind, and may be the only means of asserting control if we cannot enumerate all of the significant factors and relationships. This is especially true in political affairs where a part of political activities is its concern with novel conditions and relationships.

Classification by area is essential when we consider the problems of communicating to others the list of things we need to control. This problem occurs immediately if we know that the person to whom this is to be communicated cannot understand the categories or the relationships. We encounter this most acutely with young children. We often say 'don't touch this or that', and find that the child may obey in terms of the particular things pointed to but may not be able to generalize and apply the direction to the appropriate categories. To avoid such mistakes we place things we don't want touched in an area beyond the reach or control of the child. In fact the younger the child the more we rely on *territorial* circumscription to protect it. Only when the child comes to understand categories and relationships are these territorial restrictions lifted, but then to be replaced by other kinds of territorial restraints as in the school, the church, athletic games, place of work, and so on.

Territoriality is easy to communicate because it requires only one kind of marker or sign — the boundary. The territorial boundary in fact is the only symbolic form which combines direction in space and a statement about possession or exclusion (road signs and other directional signs do not indicate possession). Its simplicity for communication may be why territoriality is often used in animal behaviour.

In addition to efficiently classifying and communicating, territoriality can be the most efficient strategy for enforcing control, if the distribution in space and time of the resources or things to be controlled fall somewhere between ubiquity and unpredictability (Dyson-Hudson and Alden-Smith, 1975). For instance models of animal foraging have shown that territoriality is more efficient when food is distributed uniformly in space and predictably in time, while non-territorial actions are more suitable for the converse situation. The same has been shown to hold in selected cases of humans; e.g. the Basin Plateau Indians, the Northern Ojibwa Indians and the Karamojong of East Africa. Here territoriality occurred especially when resources were both predictable and dense in space and time (Dyson-Hudson and Alden-Smith, 1975).

We should bear in mind that territoriality provides differential access to resources either by preventing things from outside the territory having access to things within, or by preventing things within from having access to things without, or both. (The latter can also mean preventing things from escaping, because the desire to escape depends on the relative availability of things outside.) For example a herding society might pen in its cattle during the night to protect them from predators (i.e. to prevent things from coming in) and/or to keep the cattle together (to prevent the cattle from going out or wandering off to find more desirable environments). If the society also practised cultivation, the more desirable things for the cattle may be the fields. Penning the animals in would prevent them from grazing in the fields (hence protect the fields from the cattle and keep the cattle together). But if the cattle were to be provided with constant attention they would have no need or opportunity to wander off and graze elsewhere; hence there would be no need to constrain them.

As the activities of a group become more numerous and complex so too do their territories. The interrelationships among the territorial units and the activities they enclose may be so complicated that it is virtually impossible to unpack all of the reasons for controlling the activities territorially. When this happens the territoriality appears as a general, neutral, and essential means by which a place is made, or a space cleared and maintained, for things to exist. Societies make this place-clearing function explicit and permanent in the concept of *property*. The many controls over things distributed in space (as the interplay between preventing things without the territory having access to things within, and preventing things within having access to things without) become condensed to the view that *things need space to exist*. In fact they do need space in the sense that they are located and extended, but the need is territorial only when there are certain kinds of competitions for things (in space). Moreover it is not a competition for space that occurs among things and systems but rather a competition for things and relationships in space.

The discussion of territorial classification, communication, and control made reference to both the principle of action by contact and to the use of symbols and conceptualizations about spatial relationships. The functions of territoriality that follow will rely even more on references to conceptualization and symbolization. The degree that such matters are more the domain of man than animals determines how much of the following pertains only to one or to both.

Among the primary symbolic consequences of territoriality is that it provides a *reification* of power. Power and influence are not always as tangible as are streams and mountains, roads and houses. Moreover, power and the like are often potentialities. Territoriality makes potentials explicit and real by making them 'visible'.

Besides reifying power, territorial units act as a *mould* for the spatial properties of events. A family may have its members geographically dispersed. Yet their locations are assigned to the 'official' place of residence of head of household. The influence and authority of a city, although spreading far and wide, is 'legally' assigned to its political boundaries. The territory, moreover, becomes the object to which other attributes are assigned, as when the political territory is also the location of the wealth, health, and religion of its citizens and to the unit receiving federal support. There are cases where assigning facts to territories is not simply convenient. It is the only possible way of describing their location. For instance in democracies, ballots are secret and hence we cannot determine the location of particular votes beyond the scale of the district in which the votes were tallied. If a district voted 60% liberal and 40% conservative we can guess where the liberals and conservatives live, but, because the votes are secret, we cannot know for sure. Similarly census tract material is often presented in aggregate units by territories to ensure the anonymity and privacy of individuals.

Territoriality can (be used intentionally or unintentionally to) *obfuscate* the relationship between controller and controlled, as when we say 'it is the law of the land', or 'you may not do this here'. Legal and conventional assignments of behaviour to territories are so complex and yet so important and well-understood in the well-socialized individual that he often takes such assignments for granted. When in a restaurant he may not be conscious of the numerous customary and legal constraints on his actions, just as he is unaware of the different constraints that apply as soon as he leaves the restaurant and enters the streets (Goffman, 1963). Even if he becomes aware of them he may not know who established the rules, sanctioned them, and benefited by them.

Territoriality can be used (intentionally or unintentionally) to obfuscate by claiming that a territory should control a process which it can not. This happens when local political units are given responsibility for the control of poverty or education which are too complex and geographically extensive for them to encompass. Yet the act of assigning responsibility to the local units may appear to be a step towards solving the problems (Dear, 1981).

Such assignments bring up the problem of *mismatches* between things, systems, etc., and territory. Things may be too large, too small, too many, or at the wrong time for a particular territory. This leads to the need for new places to store things, for new things, and new things for new places. For instance, a house is subdivided into rooms with special functions which 'require' special furniture in turn. We may order a rug for the living room that is too large, or we may have a dining-room set from another house but no dining room in this one. The set of course cannot go into the bedrooms for that is the place for beds, etc. If we sell the house the furniture must be moved or stored. Hence the need for storage and warehouses. New kinds of rooms can be added and these 'need' new kinds of furniture.

Conceptually, territoriality is a container for specific things, events, and relationships. When these are not present the territory is 'empty'. Territoriality in fact creates the idea of a socially *empty space*. Take the parcel of land in the city which has no buildings on it. It is an empty lot, though it is not physically empty for there may be grass and soil on it. It is an empty lot because it is devoid of socially or economically valuable artifacts. But even as an empty lot it has value because of the possible things and relationships that can occur there. It is a thing of value to be bought and sold and held for speculation. In this respect *territoriality conceptually separates space from things* and then recombines them as an assignment of things to places and places to things. This assignment or recombination makes it appear as though there is a problem of which facts to place where, or of facts without places and places without facts.

To consider how territoriality can lead to the idea of a socially empty space or place, imagine a group of people in the wilderness who get together in a clearing to set up a projection screen and chairs to watch a motion picture. When the picture is over, the screen and chairs are folded up and put away along with the projector, and the clearing where this took place is once again a clearing. But it is not thought of as empty space. In contrast imagine the more familiar situation of a picture theatre in the city showing the same film. In this case there is a building having specifiable exits and entrances and containing a screen, a projector, and seats. The theatre is licensed to show only films and one goes there only to see films. If there is a picture showing, and no-one is in the theatre, the seats are 'empty' or the theatre is 'empty', even though there are still things in it. If the seats are taken, the theatre is full.

This conceptual separation and recombination of space (as territory) and things or processes that can go into it, problematizes the relationships between things and space. No longer is it simply a fact that things are in space, but also a duty, a right, a privilege, and a problem that things are there. Ironically the very advantage of classification by area which territoriality provides aggravates the problem of mismatching things and territory. Territoriality provides the advantage of setting up barriers to cause and effect without us having either to enunciate or know completely the things, and the cause and effect chains, to be controlled. But this advantage can create unforeseen consequences of control and problems of regional coordination. In politics, for instance, local areas are given the right to control aspects of land use through zoning. While specific activities may be prevented from locating in an area, zoning may also simply transfer the problems or undesirable activities elsewhere, and the elsewhere may be close enough to the zoned territory so that it still affects it negatively (hence the problems of regional externalities). To coordinate these actions of the local units we need a hierarchy of territories which in turn creates further problems of territorial definition and control. The possible mismatches between things or processes and territories is further aggravated by the fact that political territories especially, but territories in general, often involve enormous emotional and physical investments. Once they are established it becomes difficult, if not impossible, to alter their boundaries even when the processes they were designed once to contain are clearly no longer within the territory.

All of these functions and issues are found even more forcefully in hierarchical territorial organizations, and these also create new combinations and tendencies. The tendency of territoriality to reify and define the spatial properties of facts becomes more complex with hierarchies of territories wherein an activity may be defined at only one level and yet have impact on several. Part of the national defence appropriations goes to weapons systems; but at the time the appropriations are made, the particular manufacturers and their locations have not been determined. Therefore the nation is committing itself to an action which will have unforeseen local impact. The opposite is also true as in zoning, where local areas make decisions the consequences of which can be felt at the national level. The point is that the use of *hierarchies makes it possible for things to be geographically specified at one level but not at another.* This differentiation in turn can be used to segment actions and decisions into stages in space-time, as when the national policy is the one to be discussed in detail first and the local impacts are to be ironed out later, after the decisions at the national level have been taken. Siting of nuclear power plants, and disposing of waste, comes to the local authorities after a national energy policy has been adopted. It is the *territorial hierarchy that helps make an action in space divisible into scales and temporal stages.*

Territoriality in general, and hierarchical territorial organization in particular, circumscribe our knowledge and our responsibilities, the more so as we go down the hierarchy. If such hierarchies are part of a social organization there needs to be a bureaucracy to manage, control, and integrate this partitioning — hence the greater the responsibility up the hierarchy. Before the factory system, the craftsman owned his own tools and produced a product from beginning to end. The assembly-line worker in the hierarchical factory is involved with only one small part of a product and does not know the entire production system. This circumscription of knowledge and responsibility into parts and the concomitant need to coordinate and integrate the parts makes *hierarchical territorial organization,* in a negative sense, *a means of dividing and conquering* a social process; and in a neutral or positive sense, *an entailment of complexity and bureaucracy.*

The association of hierarchical territoriality with bureaucracy is reinforced by the fact that generally, as one goes up the hierarchy, the range of control over the bottom increases, while detailed knowledge of the bottom decreases. Territoriality can help accomplish this dual function because it can screen information by classifying and assigning responsibilities and tasks, and yet be accurate about delimitations, and scopes of responsibility. The association of territoriality with bureaucracy is also strengthened by the fact that complex organizations need to separate activities into short-term and long-term ones and to assign each to a specific subsystem or level. As we have seen, hierarchical territorial organizations can provide such a division of responsibility. The lowest levels concentrate on short-term and repetitive actions while the largest territorial units — the whole — are responsible for integrating the parts and planning for long-range actions. The relationship between bureaucracy and complex organizations on the one hand and territorial hierarchies on the other is so close that the latter may be indispensable for the former.

Conclusion

There are other functions which territoriality has the potential to perform, but by and large they are extensions and combinations of the ones we have mentioned. And of these, we must remind ourselves that it is the particular historical context which determines which ones will be employed and what their import will be. The relationship between historical context and import is not one way. Although the major forms of social influence and control, as outlined for instance in the functional relationship between the forces and relations of production, utilize territoriality and help determine its functional import, the territorial organizations themselves will also exert their own influence on these forces — not a determinant one, but in many cases a significant one. Exploring the major historical forms of social-economic organizations with these territorial functions in mind may help us understand more about the role of territoriality in such organizations as the modern state and its subdivisions, and in the factory, school, asylum, hospital and their origins in capitalism; the feudal manor and city; the classical city-state. (But as we noted before such explorations are beyond the scope of this paper.) Furthermore territoriality adds another dimension to spatial analysis, explicitly addressing the areas which traditional spatial analysis either took for granted or assumed away, and which political geography has raised explicitly (in the form of the national territory) but analysed only indirectly and unsystematically.

Acknowledgements

I am grateful to the International Exchange of Scholars for awarding me a Fulbright Hayes senior research fellowship (1979-1980) to the University of Leicester, Department of Geography and to the members of that department for a stimulating year during which this paper was conceived and written.

References

Ardrey, R. (1969). *The Territorial Imperative* (Collins, London).
Chapman, D. (1966). 'Food and space as regulation of salmonid populations in streams', *American Naturalist,* **100,** 395-456.
Crook, J. (1973). 'The nature of territorial aggression', in Montagu, A. (ed.), *Man and Aggression* (Oxford University Press, London).
Dear, M. (1981). 'A theory of the local state', in this volume.

Dyson-Hudson, R., and Alden-Smith, E. (1975). 'Human territoriality: an ecological reassessment', *American Anthropologist,* **80,** 21-41.

Goffman, E. (1963). *Behaviour in public places* (Free Press, New York).

Howard, H. (1920). *Territory in Bird Life* (Atheneum, New York).

Peterson, N. (1977). 'Hunter-gatherer territoriality', *American Anthropologist,* **82,** 53-60.

Piaget, J., and Inhelder, B. (1956). *The Child's Conception of Space* (Routledge & Kegan Paul, London).

Pitelka, F. (1959). 'Numbers, breeding schedule and territoriality in pectorial sandpipers of North America', *Conder,* **20,** 233-64.

Soja, E. (1971). *The Political Organization of Space* (Association of American Geographers, Commission on College Geography, Washington, DC).

Stokes, A. (ed.) (1974). *Territory* (P. A. Dowden, Hutchinson & Ross, New York).

Wilson, E. (1975). *Sociobiology* (Harvard University Press, Cambridge, Mass.).

Political studies from spatial perspectives
Edited by A.D. Burnett and P.J. Taylor
© 1981 John Wiley & Sons Ltd

_____4__

Public choice paradigms in political geography

J. Clarke Archer

Introduction

Public choice theory concerns such matters as voting behaviour, representation, party politics, bureaucratic decision-making, and so on. The basic behavioural postulate employed is that political man is an 'egoistic, rational, utility maximizer' (Mueller, 1979, p. 1). This postulate has been more common in economics than in political science, though by no means unknown in the latter field. Thus, the public choice paradigm, as it is coming to be known in social science inquiry, can be defined as the application of economics methodology to the empirical domain of political science. The purpose of this essay is to selectively review the outcome of this merger of the techniques of analysis of one field with the subject domain of another, and to consider whether the results may be used to seek insights into the political organization of space.

   Recent writings in political geography within the United States by such authors as Cox, Reynolds, and others reveal the use of novel concepts, categories, and methods of analysis more reminiscent of contemporary work in public choice than of traditional work in political geography (Cox, 1973, 1979; Honey, 1976b; Lea, 1979; Papageorgiou, 1979; Reynolds, 1976; Reynolds, 1980; Thrall and Casetti, 1978). An essential aspect of the appeal of the public choice framework to these American political geographers is that it offers an ingredient essential to the systematic investigation of the relationship between political processes and the geographical landscape. Specifically, the public choice framework provides a general theory of the state, an answer, in other words, to the question 'what does government do?' The typical public choice response is that government exists in order to make collective choices about the provision of public good (Reynolds, this volume). Although this answer and the theory of the state which it embodies may not be all-encompassing, it is turning out to be surprisingly broad. Yet, because it is exclusive of certain aspects of political life as popularly considered, it is also reminiscent of the premise which Christaller once adopted and which his and others' investigations proved seminal in urban geographic theory, that 'The chief profession — or characteristic — of a town is to be the center of a region' (Christaller, 1966, p. 16). This comparison is apt since the basic contribution which Christaller made to the geography of towns is precisely that contemplated in the application of public choice constructs to the geography of states, namely the use of rational analysis based upon the precept of utility-maximizing behaviour. Whether the premise that the chief profession of government is to allocate public goods will prove as rewarding is as yet partly unseen, but there are strong parallels in method and objective between Christaller's effort to create a 'theory of location of urban trades and institutions' and current efforts to create a theory of location of democratic political institutions grounded in public choice.

Public choice

The public choice framework has roots in modern welfare economics and has acquired a variety of labels in the literature, including 'the economic theory of politics' (Backhaus, 1978, p. 5); 'the economics of democracy' (Sheldon, 1976, p. lx), and 'the theory of governmental decision' (Tullock, 1972, p. 323). Seminal works include Downs' *An Economic Theory of Democracy* (1957) which explored two-party competition in representative democracy; Buchanan and Tullock's *The Calculus of Consent* (1962) which examined the formation of democratic constitutions from an individual viewpoint; and Olson's *The Logic of Collective Action* (1965) which considered group interests as a public good. A useful survey of the subject is by Mueller (1976) and a sometimes lively discussion of economics' foray into the sphere of political science is by Tullock (1972). His 'modest proposal' to reorganize social science into economics on the one hand, and everything else on the other, is intentionally annoying, but his argument is interesting. Tullock's *The Vote Motive* (1976) provides an accessible introduction.

A readable general survey of democratic political theory and of empirical findings which reflect upon the theory is Pennock's recent *Democratic Political Theory* (1979). This source is useful, in part because it places public choice, which Pennock refers to as 'radical' or 'methodological' individualism, within a perspective which is broader than that usually encountered in standard works on the subject. It is also couched in the language of political science rather than of economics. Like any field whose boundaries are encroached upon, political science has been sometimes hostile to public choice, but this is changing, as evidenced by Moon's recent observation that 'in political science we have few well-articulated research programs rooted in clearly worked-out models of man. Indeed, it might be argued that there is really only one; the rational choice model of human behavior' (Moon, 1975, p. 195). Moon goes on to examine work by Downs, among others, and suggests that the public choice framework 'has long been fundamental, in economics, and it is attracting increasing interest in the other social sciences; in sociology it goes under the name of "exchange theory"' (Moon, 1975, p. 195).

Public choice theory developed largely within the past two or three decades, and although the Public Choice Society now consists of economists and political scientists in about equal numbers (Tullock, 1976, p. 3), the original impetus sprang from issues arising within the field of economics. While there is not to be an attempt to review here what has become a very large literature, certain issues deserve discussion. Doing so will illustrate how an economics of politics has emerged upon an individualistically oriented philosophical foundation. Buchanan's *The Limits of Liberty* (1975) more fully develops several of the ideas which follow here.

From a welfare economic point of view, there are at least two reasons for the existence of political institutions. First, a private market in which individuals can improve their respective positions through voluntary exchange requires collective acknowledgment and perhaps enforcement of property rights. Otherwise, 'A can choose to steal B's corn, rather than give up his cattle for it; B can do likewise' (Mueller, 1976, p. 397). Thus, 'Economic exhange among persons is facilitated by mutual agreement on defined rights' (Buchanan, 1975, p. 18). This provides the basis for what Buchanan labels the protective role of government. A second justification for government is that certain goods and services are not optimally provided through private exchange; these include so-called 'public goods'. Public goods establish a basis for what Buchanan labels the productive role of government. This role is to generate a supply and to ascertain an allocation of goods and services which cannot be distributed privately but which citizens collectively view as needed for their general welfare.

Other justifications exist for collective allocation in a market setting. One of these is market failure in the presence of externalities. An externality is said to exist when individuals not party to an exchange are affected by it. Such affects can be positive (desirable) or negative (undesirable) from the standpoint of third-party recipients. A typical empirical example of externalities can be found in the over-exploitation of common pool resources. One frequent proposal is to 'internalize' responsibility through the creation of previously non-existent property rights as a way of inducing publicly beneficial private behaviour. Current trends towards extending national jurisdiction over once non-territorial seas are sometimes justified in these terms, for example. Another way of handling externalities is for affected parties to become organized into an inclusive group in order to implement an exchange of public goods (Buchanan, 1975, p. 38). To provide an example, consider a firm in a specific location producing consumer goods sold throughout a large region as well as a noxious discharge into a local stream. Residents along the stream suffer damages but their interests are not reflected in buyer-seller exchanges between the firm and its clients. If the impact of the discharge is regarded by stream-side residents as worth expending resources to remedy then collective action may achieve an efficient outcome (Buchanan, 1975, p. 38; Bish, 1973, pp. 18-25).

Two points involving this example deserve discussion. First, the impact upon third parties might have been positive. If the firm needed better-quality water than that directly available from the stream and removed existing impurities before using it in a manufacturing process which added no new ones, then the costs of improving the stream could pass on to the outside consumers. This would yield a positive externality for stream-side residents. This is doubtless a rarer case than the first, but could also yield a suboptimal outcome in a welfare economic sense since stream-side residents might be willing to compensate the firm to produce even cleaner water as a by-product.

The second point is that efficiency is apt to be construed as Pareto efficiency. Pareto optimality is reached when no-one can be made better off without making another worse off given the limited resources which are available, a standard of judgement equivalent to a democratic rule of unanimity (Buchanan, 1975, p. 38). Thus, private market exchanges are in effect unanimous consent agreements between buyers and sellers with the former obtaining higher utility and the latter profit as a result of exchange. Pareto-relevant externalities are therefore those for which affected parties are willing to employ their own resources in an effort to alter the outcome, a point sometimes overlooked in the geographical literature (Bish, 1973).

A common distinction in welfare economics is between allocation as the domain of the market under the Pareto criterion and distribution as the responsibility of government using politically determined criteria (Buchanan, 1975, p. 51). The will of the majority is sometimes mentioned although this is not always explicit. If this is not the case, then it is likely that the Pareto criterion is assumed in order to analytically separate distributional and allocational issues. As a result, as the formal welfare economic literature often applies the Pareto principle to market processes, the formal public choice literature often attempts to do the same to political processes. The rationale is to avoid problems attendant to an interpersonal comparison of utility. Pennock, citing Arrow, clarifies this:

> The problem, it would appear, is the difficulty, if not impossi-bility, of formulating a general rule describing what we do when we make these comparisons. Kenneth Arrow himself, protagonist of the modern welfare economics, which eschews interpersonal comparison, has this to say: 'The principle of extended sympathy as a basis for interpersonal comparisons seems basic to many of the welfare judgments made in ordinary practice. But it is not easy to see how to construct a theory of social choice from the principle.' In short, the radical individualist [i.e. public choice theorist] sacrifices some realism for a greater degree of rigor.... [R]adical individualism is, in the strictest sense of the term, a 'model,' not simply a theory. (Pennock, 1979, p. 186).

The significance of the Pareto criterion is thus that it enables political behaviour to be modelled as a form of voluntary action. Quite often the resulting models focus upon the allocation of public goods.

Public goods

Public goods theory can be traced to an origin in a brief, yet influential, essay by Samuelson on 'The Pure Theory of Public Expenditure' (1954), which distinguished between public and private goods. Since then a very large literature has developed on the basis of this distinction (e.g. Samuelson, 1955; Samuelson, 1969; Musgrave, 1959; Head, 1974; Loehr and Sandler, 1978; Buchanan, 1975). While Samuelson specified two, more recent literature sometimes acknowledges three, properties of public goods. These are non-rivalness, non-exclusion, and non-rejectability (Head, 1974, pp. 263-4; Lea, 1979, pp. 218-19; Goldin, 1977, pp. 53-71). Non-rivalness, sometimes referred to as jointness in supply or non-congestability, means that once a good (or service) is supplied to one, it is supplied to all relevant individuals. An example is a public road network. In the case of a pure public good, the marginal costs of supplying additional consumers are zero once it becomes available. Hence, it is efficient to supply it free of charge to additional consumers since a marginal use of scarce resources is not involved. Whether actual goods in fact achieve this condition is a matter of controversy (e.g. Goldin, 1977); some, such as a highway before the point of congestion, appear to come quite close. Non-exclusion, sometimes labelled jointness in consumption or non-packageability, involves the presumption that once a good becomes available to one relevant individual, others cannot be prevented from consuming it. Defence is a commonly cited example: once a level of defence effort is established, it becomes freely available to all within a jurisdiction. A pure public good would be perfectly joint in both supply and in consumption. Impure public goods meet these criteria in varying degrees. A roadway, for example, requires the purchase of a private good (automobile), exhibits congestion above a certain level (marginal social costs become non-zero), and can be packaged (tolls).

Jointness in consumption poses the problem of 'free ridership'. On the one hand, if public goods are supplied privately, additional consumers cannot be made to pay to obtain them. On the other, if public goods are supplied publicly, voter-taxpayers may be tempted to conceal their preferences in order to avoid an appropriate level benefit tax. This underscores a frequently mentioned problem of preference revelation in joint consumption which has attracted a great deal of attention in the literature (e.g. Tideman and Tullock, 1977). The free rider problem is not limited to the case of individuals, it may also involve collectivities. A notion that suburban municipalities draw upon central city facilities without compensation, for instance, has sparked controversy (e.g. Reynolds, 1975, 1976). The weight of empirical evidence on the matter is by no means clear (Johnston, 1979, pp. 41-4).

There is an obverse to the free rider problem. This involves the third characteristic of a public good which is often ignored in literature concerned with market failure. In particular, some public goods are not merely freely available to all who would desire to consume them, they are non-rejectable by those who would prefer not to do so. This yields problems of 'forced ridership' (Loehr and Sandler, 1978); 'political externality' (Buchanan and Tullock, 1962); and 'non-market failure' (Wolf, 1979). Forced ridership at least means that there are individuals receiving a desired public good at a level other than that which they would freely choose, and may also mean the consumption of goods which are not desired at all. Loehr and Sandler (1978) provide a pertinent example:

> A pacifist... must pay the same tax price charged for defense as any other individual, his negative marginal evaluation not withstanding. The true cost to the economy of providing defense in this case must include the welfare losses falling upon all relevant 'forced riders' (pp. 27-8).

Political externalities arise because budget levels and public goods mixes are selected by collectivities rather than individuals. If these are chosen with less than unanimous consent, then some individuals will receive more public goods, and pay higher taxes, than they otherwise would prefer; the opposite condition may characterize other members of the collectivity. Buchanan and Tullock explored this in their *Calculus of Consent* (1962) and concluded that utility-maximizing individuals must balance, under uncertainty, expected political externalities against expected decision-making costs in consenting to collective authority. A unanimity requirement (Pareto criterion) may yield infinite decision-making costs because of strategic bargaining. At the other end of the democratic scale, majority rule can produce an essentially utilitarian outcome in which the preferences of the median voter are decisive (Mueller, 1976, pp. 408-10). In this case, half minus one see a government budget as excessive and half minus one see it as deficient.

As a sidelight, there is a fairly large literature on spatial models of party competition. Unfortunately, these deal with competition in (often) one-dimensional political space. Downs' *An Economic Theory of Democracy* (1957) which examined the application of duopolistic competition theory to the American two-party system, is a good example. Interestingly, such work can be traced to an origin in Hotelling's article on 'Stability in competition' (1929) which gave rise to the familiar vendor-on-the-beach illustration used in economic geography. As Mueller put it in his review of public choice, 'Hotelling's article could be regarded as *the* pioneering contribution in public choice' (1976, p. 408). This article might also be regarded as *the* pioneering contribution in research on the space-economy as well.

Public goods in geography

The concept of public goods has broad potential application in political geography. Indeed, it may even be a concept which can be applied in a scale-independent manner because it can be conceptually linked to the notion of the region. This would fulfil an appeal recently made by Cox in *Location and Public Problems* (1979, p. vii). It should be cautioned, however, that the concept is an abstraction which may prove as elusive in empirical application as Christaller's concept of a central function. As a theoretical construct, however, it has potentially rich possibilities which are beginning to be explored with increasing vigour (e.g. Cox, 1973; Reynolds, 1975, 1976, 1981; Reynolds and Honey, 1978; Thrall, 1979; Papageorgiou, 1979, 1978; Bigman and ReVelle, 1978). Lea offers a good, though compact, review of the literature in his study of 'Welfare theory, public goods, and public facility location' (1979).

Probably the first to introduce the concept of public goods into geography was Teitz (1968) who pointed at an almost total neglect of public facilities in economic and geographical location theory. Important advances have since been made, especially in the application of computational location-allocation models to public facility location problems (e.g. Rushton, 1979; Scott, 1971; Lea, 1973). Most of the models involve identification of a spatial median, or point of minimum aggregate travel. This, of course, relates to the Hotelling problem. It would be interesting to explore opportunities to extend location-allocation models by drawing from the literature on spatial competition among parties or vice-versa;Mueller (1976) provides citations.

The article by Teitz (1968) made several important points. One was that a normative theory of public facility location, unlike one of private facility location, would require a foundation relating to public budgets. As a result, 'public location theory may bear a relationship to conventional location theory similar to that between the expenditure side of public finance or welfare economics and conventional economic theory' (p. 413). He also noticed the problem that public facilities are in the vexing situation of being able to influence their own level of 'demand' since such facilities offer public goods in the sense of provision, but often require consumption of private goods to achieve access. Travel costs, therefore, represent an implicit price. The Tietz article, however, was more in the mainstream of conventional economic geography than of public choice political geography in two respects. First, although he acknowledged earlier work by Tiebout (1956) on multi-jurisdictional local governments, he posited a single governmental authority. Second, while he acknowledged 'the absence of a social welfare function' (p. 417), he avoided issues concerning voter preference aggregation to arrive at a socially preferred state. Thus, problems of free riders, forced riders, etc. were kept outside of his purview. The problem of making collective decisions in the absence of a social welfare function is central in the concerns of public choice theory.

Tiebout's article on 'A pure theory of local expenditures' (1956) used the Samuelsonian concept of public goods to demonstrate that multi-jurisdictional local government offers, under certain assumptions about freedom of migration, an escape from the collective choice problems of free ridership and forced ridership (although these were not his terms). As mentioned earlier if collective decisions are made on a public budget level and a mixture of public goods to be supplied under a less than unanimous voting rule, then political externalities are likely. However, if multiple jurisdictions exist, then consumer-voter-taxpayers can express their preferences either within jurisdictions through their ballots or between jurisdictions with their feet. This, 'in part, solves the public choice problem by significantly limiting its scope' (Mueller, 1976, p. 412). This is the economist's perspective and has resulted in theoretical efforts to retain the logic but eliminate the geographical context within a quite parallel Theory of Clubs (Buchanan, 1965). From a different perspective, that the voting-with-the-feet hypothesis is consistent with empirical observations dealing with urban settlements — individuals do in fact sort themselves geographically by taste (Yeates and Garner, 1976) — and the logic of the connection between preference revelation by voting and by moving suggests that a public choice theory of the political-space-economy is highly plausible. As the Tiebout hypothesis makes clear, voting with the feet is, in theory as in speech, a democratic institution. Buchanan and Tullock's *Calculus of Consent* might provide a starting point, with the addition of a geographical dimension, for such a theory. An alternative beginning point might be Rawls' *Theory of Justice* (1971), from which Reynolds (1980) draws in investigating 'The geography of social choice' in order to avoid some of the limitations of the Pareto criterion.

One issue has so far been slighted, although it was mentioned at the outset of the discussion on geographical applications of public goods; namely that the public goods concept may be, in a sense, scale-free in that it might be applied at several levels of political-geographical investigation. So far geographical research predicated upon the concept of public goods has been restricted to the urban-metropolitan scale. Yet, just as goods can be arrayed along a scale from completely partitionable (private) to completely collective (public), they also can be arrayed on a scale from completely local, even family level, to completely international (Loehr and Sandler, 1978, pp. 17-18). They also fit very nicely with the notion of regions, even nation-states as regions. Indeed, the *raison d'être* of a state might be seen as the provision of public goods to its citizens. Thrall and Casetti (1978) stipulate this to be the case of 'democratic governments, local and otherwise' (p. 319).

Public goods theory is just beginning to be examined at an international scale, and alas, not by geographers (e.g. Schneider, 1979; Loehr and Sandler, 1978). A recent essay on 'Analyzing international externalities: the case of the law of the sea negotiations' (Amacher and Tollison, 1978), for example, is amazingly parallel to the essay by Ostrom *et al.* (1961) on an urban scale, in both logic and conclusions. Furthermore, Hirschman (1978) has recently extended the thesis of *Exit, Voice, and Loyalty* (1970) to the nation-state with interesting implications. Essentially it is a variation on the Tiebout model:

> It is possible to visualize a state system in which, in spite of close contact and free movement of people and capital, exit would never assume threatening proportions because each country would supply its citizens with a different assortment of public goods.... Different countries would then 'specialize' in power, wealth, growth, equity, peacefulness, the observance of human rights, and so on.... [But,] the foregoing 'polyphonic' solution to the problem is perhaps too beautiful to be real (Hirshman, 1978, p. 106).

Research on the interface of political geography and public choice

So far discussion has been conducted largely on a conceptual level. This has been in keeping with the objective of examining precepts contained in the public choice paradigm. Empirical patterns, however, also deserve attention. These are relevant in two ways. First, there is the question of empirically testing propositions involving the rational man hypothesis of the public choice paradigm within geographical contexts. Second, there is the question of using public choice constructs to illuminate existing observations regarding political-geographical patterns. That such questions are poseable reflects the possibility that an empirical-deductive research process heretofore much more characteristic of economic than of political geography may emerge. An extensive examination of empirical relevancy is beyond the scope of this essay, however, so that several examples must suffice for illustrative purposes. These are drawn from the American context at local, state, and national scales.

At local scale there is an abundance of evidence that the rational man hypothesis of the public choice paradigm has empirical research potential in a geographically relevant fashion. Reynolds' study of 'Progress toward achieving efficient and responsive spatial-political systems in urban America' (1976), for example, provides much to support the notion that such public choice constructs as those of public goods and the voting-with-the-feet hypothesis can be used to illuminate empirical patterns, specifically those of Detroit, Los Angeles, and St Louis, as well as to provide a foundation for policy relevant recommendations. The intellectual lineage of his research is obvious from his bibliographic citations, which include such previously discussed writers as Arrow, Ostrom, Tiebout, and Tullock.

Urban scale research running in the opposite direction, intended to test public choice precepts in a geographical context, is somewhat more difficult to find; nevertheless, there are examples. Archer and Reynolds (1976) examined a bond referendum to test the rational voter hypothesis with considerable empirical support being found. From a geographical point of view, the findings indicated that voter self-interest can be a statistically viable hypothesis in interpreting geographical patterns of electoral behaviour. From a public choice standpoint, the setting, which involved explicit publicity about the geographical pattern of expected benefit incidence, eliminated ambiguities often present in empirical test of the rational voter model.

The scale of the US state has been conspicuous for its neglect by American political geographers in recent years. This is a pity since others have pointed to the utility of the regional concept in accounting for geographical variations in the politics of various states (e.g. Sharkansky, 1970b; Elazar, 1972). Work by Brunn (1974) offers a counter-example to this charge of neglect by political geographers, although explicit links to a public choice paradigm are mainly absent. There are undoubtedly unexploited opportunities at this scale. The 'policy analysis' literature in political science can be used to exemplify the point (e.g. Dye, 1966; Sharkansky, 1970a). A major aim of this literature has been to explain policy variations among American states, generally operationalized via public expenditures across functional categories, through the use of political variables such as party competitiveness, party control, or administrative organization, and through the use of environmental variables such as urbanization, ethnic character, or income level. Environmental variables are commonly viewed as measures of local needs and local resources.

A usual finding has been that the bulk of statistical explanation rests upon the environmental variables rather than upon the political variables (Dye, 1966). Needless to say, such results have not been viewed with equanimity by political scientists and a subliterature has developed attempting to counter them by pointing towards technical deficiencies in procedure or by noting the strong interdependencies in the system being investigated. Political culture, for example, sometimes has been suggested as an absent intermediary concept perhaps underlying both patterns of the environment and those of the polity, as well as the observed policy variation between states (e.g. Elazar, 1972). The possibility of resorting to a geographically interpreted public goods theory seems at least plausible and the voting-with-the-feet hypothesis appears potentially germane. Indeed, it would seem this hypothesis might well be employed to argue that the typical empirical outcome of policy analysis research is as it should be; namely, that there is little policy variation among states left to be accounted for after the effects of environmental variation have been taken into consideration. The rationale could be as follows:

The US Constitution constrains states from imposing limitations upon interstate trade or mobility. This is one requisite for the operation of a Tiebout-style process. States are, therefore, in competition for potentially mobile citizens, including their human and non-human capital resources. This is perhaps best illustrated by citing research into the interregional movement of industrial plant and equipment (*President's National Urban Policy Report,* 1978), but the point would seem to be more generally relevant. Thus, a competitive process yields a situation in which states are minimally variable in their policy determinations because of the possibility that residents may vote with their feet within the context of constitutionally established freedom of mobility. If this hypothesis is true, then the missing ingredients in the policy analysis literature are a rational actor construct and a geographical perspective. With these, what seems paradoxical becomes, or at least appears to become, highly transparent.

To be sure, such an explanation begs attention to further issues. For instance, there is the possibility that geographical externalities may be created in the process. In particular, a state's tax base is, in an exclusion sense, a public good. Mobility of citizens and their resources, therefore, poses the possibility that positive geographical externalities may be bestowed upon recipient locations and that negative geographical externalities may fall upon sending locations as citizens vote with their feet to improve their individual welfare. Unless mechanisms exist to compensate third-party losses, in this case those of stayers — to use the language of current geographical migration theory, such mobility might create an outcome which is inconsistent with the Pareto criterion. There could be, however, beneficial impacts in the form of a reduction in political externalities. Within a federal system, compensation via intergovernmental transfers can serve to collectively minimize fiscal externalities while allowing individual choices to reduce political externalities. Such an argument partially parallels several which Cox develops in *Location and Public Problems* (1979). However, his stress is more often upon equity than upon efficiency so that negative spillovers tend to receive the greatest emphasis. Despite these additional issues, the point remains that invoking a framework involving the political-space-economy would seem to provide an explanation for what the policy analysis literature finds difficult to explain.

American, as well as other, political geographers have recently evidenced increasing interest in political-geographical patterns at the federal scale (e.g. Archer, 1979, 1980; Brunn, 1974; Johnston, 1979a, 1979b). Although this is merely an emerging trend, opportunities once again seem available. Archer (1980), for instance, examined empirical evidence relating to popular voting for incumbent US Representatives and the geographical distribution of federal outlays. The existence of relationships between these appears essential to conventional rationalistic models of the US Congress (e.g. Mayhew, 1974). The modesty, even elusiveness, of the statistical relationships encountered, therefore, suggests that simple assumptions about voter rationality, and by extension about the motivations and the behaviour of Representatives, deserve more careful examination. Johnston (1978) has reached similar conclusions regarding the campaign-expenditure patterns of candidates and parties. These examples provide evidence that research interest in essentially political-geographical issues such as the geographical distribution of votes and expenditures can uncover findings of potential interest outside geography.

Conclusion

The seeming assertion of the title that there is a 'public choice paradigm in political geography' is perhaps too strong. For one thing, there are those who may well be suspicious of the neoclassical economic formulations in the background of the public choice paradigm as it now exists in economics and elsewhere; this is inferrable from recent statements that these same assumptions in economic geography deserve greater attention and scrutiny (e.g. Harvey, 1973; King and Clark, 1978). However, some with an interest along the interface between economics, politics, and space are clearly willing to adopt a positive stance on the matter; in Lea's recent phrasing: 'a general welfare theory must be formally articulated before it may be properly evaluated (and perhaps rejected)' (Lea, 1979, p. 218).

Another point to be raised against an assertion that there now exists a 'public choice paradigm' in political geography is that there may be no paradigm at all in a field so small and diverse in practitioner interest. However, this condition may be subject to change. For one thing, geographical research into political processes is clearly on the upswing, as befits a sector of the economy which allocates and distributes a large fraction of economic, as well as other, resources. There is also an apparent convergence of concern taking place, as well as of precept and technique, between American political and American economic geography. This will probably strengthen both. The result may be a general political-space-economy theory as several works consulted for this essay suggest by their tone and their content. If so, this would be fitting tribute to Christaller who once observed that:

> A theoretical political-geography is just as possible and may be as approximately 'exact' as a theoretical economic-geography although the rationality of action which is easily accessible in an exact understanding falls to the background... with the help of the understanding method it is, however, also possible to obtain laws, rational schemes and tendencies (Christaller, 1966, p. 83).

Within the context of an external milieu in which values are allocated in relation to the preferences of consumer-taxpayer-voters through market and democratic processes, 'laws, rational schemes and tendencies' are likely to be discoverable through an 'understanding method' predicated upon public goods, ballots, and spatial mobility.

References and bibliography

Amacher, R. C., and Tollison, R. D. (1978). 'Analyzing international exter-
    nalities: the case of the law of the sea negotiations', in Loehr, W., and
    Sandler, T. (eds.), *Public Goods and Public Policy*, pp. 191-206 (Sage,
    Beverley Hills).

Archer, J. C. (1979). 'Incrementalism and federal outlays among states',
    Geographical Perspectives (forthcoming).

Archer, J. C. (1980). 'Congressional incumbent reelection success and
    federal outlays distribution: a test of the electoral connection hypo-
    thesis', *Environment and Planning* (forthcoming).

Archer, J. C., and Reynolds, D. R. (1976). 'Locational logrolling and citizen
    support of municipal bond proposals: the example of St. Louis', *Public
    Choice*, **27**, 21-40.

Arrow, K. F. (1963). *Social Choice and Individual Value*, 2nd edn. (Wiley,
    London).

Backhaus, J. (1978). 'Pareto on public choice', *Public Choice*, **33**, 5-17.

Bigman, D., and ReVelle, C. (1978). 'The theory of welfare considerations in
    public facility location problems', *Geographical Analysis*, **10**, 229-40.

Bish, R. L. (1973). *The Public Economy of Metropolitan Areas* (Markham,
    Chicago).

Brunn, S. D. (1974). *Geography and Politics in America* (Harper & Row, New
    York).

Buchanan, J. M. (1965). 'An economic Theory of Clubs', *Economica*, **32**, 1-14.

Buchanan, J. M. (1975). *The Limits of Liberty* (University of Chicago Press,
    Chicago).

Buchanan, J. M., and Tullock, G. (1962). *The Calculus of Consent* (University
    of Michigan Press, Ann Arbor).

Christaller, W. (1966). *Central Places in Southern Germany* (Prentice-Hall,
    Englewood Cliffs, NJ).

Cox, K. R. (1969). 'The voting decision in a spatial context', in Board, C.,
    Chorley, R. J., and Haggett, P. (eds.), *Progress in Geography*, vol. 1,
    pp. 81-117 (Edward Arnold, London).

Cox, K. R. (1973). *Conflict, Power and Politics in the City* (McGraw-Hill, New
    York).

Cox, K. R. (1979). *Location and Public Problems* (Maaroufa Press, Chicago).

Downs, A. (1957). *An Economic Theory of Democracy* (Harper & Row, New
    York).

Dye, T. R. (1966). *Politics, Economics and the Public* (Rand McNally, New
    York).

Elazar, D. J. (1972). *American Federalism: A View From the States*, 2nd edn.
    (Thomas R. Crowell, New York).

Goldin, K. D. (1977). 'Equal access vs. selective access: a critique of public
    goods theory', *Public Choice*, **29**, 53-72.

Hartshorne, R. (1950). 'The functional approach in political geography',
    Annals of the Association of American Geographers 40. Reprinted (1969)
    in Kasperson, R. E., and Minghi, J. V. (eds.), pp. 34-49 (Aldine, Chicago).

Harvey, D. (1973). *Social Justice and The City* (Johns Hopkins University
    Press, Baltimore, Maryland).

Head, J. G. (1974). *Public Goods and Public Welfare* (North Carolina, Duke
    University Press, Durham, North Carolina).

Hirschman, A. O. (1970). *Exit, Voice, and Loyalty* (Harvard University Press, Cambridge, Mass.).

Hirschman, A. O. (1978). 'Exit, voice, and the state', *World Politics*, **31**, 90-107.

Honey, R. (1976a). 'Metropolitan Governance', in Adams, J. S. (ed.), *Urban Policymaking and Metropolitan Dynamics*, pp. 425-62 (Ballinger, Cambridge, Mass.).

Honey, R. (1976b). 'Conflicting problems in the political organization of space', *Annals of Regional Science*, **10**, 45-60.

Honey, R. (1978). 'Locational equity and tax base sharing'. Paper presented to Association of American Geographers Annual Meeting, New Orleans, Louisiana.

Hotelling, H. (1929). 'Stability in competition', *Economic Journal*, **39**, 41-57.

Johnston, R. J. (1978). 'Campaign spending and votes: a reconsideration', *Public Choice*, **33**, 83-92.

Johnston, R. J. (1979a). *Political, Electoral and Spatial Systems* (Oxford University Press, Oxford).

Johnston, R. J. (1979b). 'Governmental influences in the human geography of developed countries', *Geography*, **64**, 1-11.

King, L. J., and Clark, G. L. (1978). 'Government policy and regional development', *Progress in Human Geography*, **2**, 1-16.

Lea, A. C. (1973). *Location-Allocation Systems: An Annotated Bibliography.* Discussion Paper 13 (Department of Geography, University of Toronto, Toronto).

Lea, A. C. (1979). 'Welfare theory, public goods and public facility location', *Geographical Analysis*, **11**, 217-39.

Loehr, W., and Sandler, T. (eds.) (1978). *Public Goods and Public Policy* (Beverley Hills, California).

Mayhew, D. R. (1974). *Congress: The Electoral Connection* (Yale University Press, New Haven, Conn.).

Moon, J. D. (1975). 'The logic of political inquiry: a synthesis of opposed perspectives', in Greenstein, F. I., and Polsby, N. W. (eds.), *Political Science: Scope and Theory*, pp. 131-228 (Addison-Wesley, Reading, Mass.).

Mueller, D. C. (1976). 'Public choice: a survey', *Journal of Economic Literature*, **54**, 395-433.

Mueller, D. C. (1979). *Public Choice* (Cambridge University Press, Cambridge).

Musgrave, R. A. (1959). *The Theory of Public Finance* (McGraw Hill, New York).

Olson, M. (1965). *The Logic of Collective Action* (Schocken Books, New York).

Ostrom, V. Tiebout, C. M., and Warren, R. (1961). 'The organization of government in metropolitan areas', *American Political Science Review*, **55**, 831-42.

Papageorgiou, G. J. (1977). 'Fundamental problems of theoretical planning', *Environment and Planning*, **9**, 1329-56.

Papageorgiou, G. J. (1979). 'Spatial externalities I, II', *Annals of The Association of American Geographers*, **68**, 465-92.

Pennock, J. R. (1979). *Democratic Political Theory* (Princeton University Press, Princeton, NJ).

President's National Urban Policy Report (1978) (US Department of Housing and Urban Development, Washington, DC).

Rawls, J. (1971). *A Theory of Justice* (Harvard University Press, Cambridge, Mass.).

Reynolds, D. R. (1974). 'Spatial contagion in political influence processes', in Cox, K., Reynolds, D. R., and Rokkan, S. (eds.), *Locational Approaches to Power and Conflict,* pp. 233-74 (Halsted, New York).

Reynolds, D. R. (1975). 'Metropolitan governance and service delivery in the United States'. Paper presented to Joint Hungarian Academy of Sciences-Association of American Geographers Seminar, Budapest, Hungary.

Reynolds, D. R. (1976). 'Progress toward achieving efficient and responsible spatial-political systems in urban America', in Adams, J. S. (ed.), *Urban Policymaking and Metropolitan Dynamics,* pp. 463-538 (Ballinger, Cambridge, Mass.).

Reynolds, D. R. (1981). 'The geography of social choice', in Burnett, A., and Taylor, P. (eds.), *Political Studies from Spatial Perspectives* (Wiley, Chichester).

Reynolds, D. R., and Honey, R. (1978). 'Conflict in the location of salutory facilities', in Cox, K. R. (ed.), *Urbanization and Conflict in Market Societies,* pp. 144-60 (Maaroufa, Chicago).

Rushton, G. (1979). *Optimal Location of Facilities* (Compress, Wentworth, New Hampshire).

Samuelson, P. A. (1954). 'The pure theory of public expenditure', *Review of Economics and Statistics,* **36,** 387-9.

Samuelson, P. A. (1955). 'Diagrammatic exposition of a theory of public expenditure', *Review of Economics and Statistics,* **37,** 350-6.

Samuelson, P. A. (1969). 'Pure theory of public expenditure and taxation', in Margolis, J., and Guitton, H. (eds.), *Public Economics* pp. 98-123 (St Martin's Press, New York).

Schneider, J. (1979). *World Public Order of the Environment* (University of Toronto Press, Toronto).

Scott, A. J. (1971). *Combinatorial Programming, Spatial Analysis and Planning* (Methuen, London).

Sharkansky, I. (ed.) (1970a). *Policy Analysis in Political Science* (Markham, Chicago).

Sharkansky, I. (1970b). 'Regionalism, economic status, and the public policies of American states', in Sharkansky, I. (ed.), *Policy Analysis in Political Science,* pp. 186-206 (Markham, Chicago).

Sheldon, A. (1976). 'Preface', in Tullock, G. (ed.), *The Vote Motive,* pp. ix-xiii (Institute of Economic Affairs, London).

Teitz, M. B. (1968). 'Toward a theory of urban public facility location', *Papers and Proceedings of the Regional Science Association,* **31,** 35-44; reprinted (1971) in Bourne, L. S. (ed.), *Internal Structure of the City,* pp. 411-20 (Oxford University Press, Oxford).

Thrall, G. I. (1979). 'Public goods and the derivation of land value assessment schedules within a spatial equilibrium setting', *Geographical Analysis,* **11,** 23-35.

Thrall, G. I. and Casetti, E. (1978). 'Local public goods and spatial equilibrium in an ideal urban centre', *Canadian Geographer,* **22,** 319-33.

Tideman, T. N. and Tullock, G. (1977). 'Some limitations of demand-revealing processes: a comment', *Public Choice,* **29,** 125-8.

Tiebout, C. M. (1956). 'A pure theory of local expenditures', *Journal of Political Economy,* **64,** 416-24.

Tullock, G. (1972). 'Economic imperialism', in Buchanan, J. M., and Tollison, R. B. (eds.), *Theory of Public Choice,* pp. 317-29 (University of Michigan Press, Ann Arbor).
Tullock, G. (1976). *The Vote Motive* (Institute of Economic Affairs, London).
Wolf, C. (1979). 'A theory of non-market failures', *Public Interest,* **55,** 114-33.
Yeates, M. and Garner, B. (1976). *The North American City,* 2nd edn. (Harper & Row, New York).

Political studies from spatial perspectives
Edited by A.D. Burnett and P.J. Taylor
© 1981 John Wiley & Sons Ltd

5

The geography of social choice

David R. Reynolds

Political geography is theory-deficient. Like any subfield of social science, its future vitality is dependent on the ability of its practitioners to develop theory which is rich both in concept and in application.

Political geographers, despite their long-standing interest in the ways in which regions, particularly nation-states, are organized politically, have tended to eschew attempts to develop general theoretical frameworks that could inform their empirical analysis of particular regions. This is not to say that political geographers have been atheoretical; merely that they have been consumers rather than producers of theory. For example, most have implicitly accepted some generalized 'theory of the state' (at least to the extent of identifying particular *functions* performed by the state), however ill-articulated, and then have attempted to discern the particular institutional and cultural patterns that have been adopted/adapted in carrying out the function. The most widely accepted 'theory of the state' appears to be the view that the state exists to facilitate territorial and societal integration. Hartshorne (1950), for example, in one of political geography's more important methodological statements, asserted that the 'fundamental purpose of any state... is to bring all the varied territorial parts, the diverse regions of the state-area, into a single organized unit' (p. 104). More recently, Soja (1971) has echoed much the same theme.

The research area described in this paper also accepts a general 'theory of the state'. Instead of viewing the state as an agent of integration, states or, more specifically, governments are said to exist in order to make social (collective) choices pertaining to the provision of economic goods and services which in consumption possess the properties of what economists refer to as public goods. To accept this view, however, is not to imply that this particular 'theory of the state' constitutes a well-developed theory or that it is more or less 'fundamental', or in some other sense superior to alternative perspectives. It does happen to be better developed than the societal integration perspective but considerably more theoretical elaboration is necessary. The research identified, although emphasizing the geographical aspects of the ways in which regions are or could be organized politically, can be viewed as at the conceptual interface of political and economic geography and public-choice economics.

Need for theories of social choice

The need for theories of social choice is widely recognized in economics (Arrow, 1963; Head, 1974; Mueller, 1973; Sen, 1970), political science (Haefele, 1973; Taylor, 1976), sociology (Coleman, 1966), and in modern political philosophy (Nozick, 1974; Rawls, 1971) but appears to have gone largely unrecognized in geography until quite recently (see, for example, Papageorgiou, 1977). One reason why such theories are necessary is that modern economies are exceedingly complex both in their operations and in their geographies; without theory the complex of political-economic reality is difficult to comprehend. In western nation states public expenditures are large, growing rapidly and, since they are lumpily distributed over space, have a significant impact on the over-all level and geography of well-being.

Are present political institutions well suited to, and capable of, making the social choices confronting societies in the modern world? Some think not. Clealy, theory capable of informing us of generally desirable institutional change would be 'useful' theory. In the US most local governments, many state governments, and occasionally the federal government, periodically attempt reform in their institutions of social choice, but, at present, there is no generally accepted body of theory capable of providing policy guidance. For example, many cities attempt to expand their jurisdictional boundaries in anticipation of subsequent urban expansion. Should they be permitted to do so? We have no good answers to such questions. Good answers call for normative theory with well-grounded positive underpinnings.

Public goods

It was suggested earlier that one conception of the state was as a system or set of systems for making social choices pertaining to the provision of public goods. But what are public goods?

In the original formulations of Samuelson (1954) and Musgrave (1959), the concept of *pure* public good is regarded as an extreme polar case to be set against the logically equally extreme category of a *private good* around which so much neoclassical economic theory revolves. Unlike private goods whose consumption is tailored to the individual economic demands of consumers and can be allocated via a price (or market) system, a pure public good is one which must be consumed in equal amounts by all members in a specific 'public'. Such a good has two main properties. The first is *joint supply*, in the special sense that, if any of the good or service is supplied to one person, equal quantities of identical quality can be made available to other persons in the group without limit at no additional cost. The second is *impossibility of exclusion*, whereby if the good or service is supplied to one person in the public, it cannot feasibly be withheld from any other person in the same public wishing to consume it. Pure public goods may or may not exist, depending upon how the public or publics is (are) defined. When the 'public' is identified as all residents of a nation-state, national defence and the legal system are typically cited as examples of pure public goods (but even here their 'pureness' is controvertible). Importantly, however, there are also few purely private goods; most real goods or services lie between these two polar extremes. Even the humble private good of dandelion eradication from individual lawns provides some benefits to the owners of other lawns in the neighbourhood and perhaps even to passers-by.

Goods and services lying in the two-dimensional space between pure public goods and pure private goods can be referred to as *impure public goods*. An example is the service provided by a fire station — which in some institutional settings can be made exclusive on a subscription basis; also additional costs of use are zero, provided several fires in the area served by the station do not occur at dispersed locations simultaneously. The joint supply or externality aspect of impure public goods generally has a strong spatial component. For example, benefits of fire protection provided through a fire station decrease with distance from the station. As Lea (1976) has pointed out, impurities due to space, despite their pervasiveness, have been much neglected in the economics literature.

Pure public goods and other goods (services) possessing strong elements of one or both of the two major public good characteristics typically will not be provided through private market systems or through individual initiative alone. 'Market failure' can be attributed to the 'impossibility-of-exclusion' characteristic: each individual realizing he does not need to contribute any of his resources in order to consume the good, if it is provided (say by someone else), fails to contribute; hence, the good is not provided at all. This has been referred to as the 'free-rider problem'. Similarly this characteristic of public goods also engenders the so-called 'preference revelation problem': each individual fails to state his true preferences for the good lest he be burdened with more of the cost. As Samuelson (1954) puts it:

> ...no decentralized pricing system can serve to determine optimally these levels of collective consumption... one could imagine every person in the community being indoctrinated to behave like a 'parametric decentralized bureaucrat' who reveals his preferences by signalling in response to price parameters of Lagrangean multipliers, to questionnaires, or to other devices. but... by departing from his indoctrinated rules, any one person can hope to snatch some selfish benefit in a way not possible under the self-policing competitive pricing of private goods.... It is in the selfish interest of each person to give false signals, to pretend to have less interest in a given collective consumption activity than he really has (p. 388).

The joint supply characteristic of public goods creates additional difficulties for market provison. If marginal costs of additional consumption (not production) are zero (as they are under extreme jointness), then the theory of the (private) firm suggests that additional consumption should not be excluded and prices charged for this additional consumption should also be zero. Clearly, a private firm charging zero prices cannot be viable. Furthermore, for efficient provision (in the Paretian sense) a firm serving consumers with different preferences for the public good must engage in differential pricing. This requirement follows from the fact that different consumers must be brought into utility-maximizing equilibrium at the same level of consumption.

Quite clearly, if the 'real world' can be characterized as populated by utility-maximizing individuals with 'demands' for goods and services with the properties of public goods and the relevant 'publics' are large, the prediction is that, in the absence of collective action which coerces all individuals to contribute to the provision of a public good, the good will either not be provided at all or at grossly suboptimal levels.

Unfortunately, market failure leads to no presumption of government success. In fact much of the recent literature suggests that governments can be as unsuccessful as private markets unless institutions of collective (social) choice are effective in determining individuals' marginal evaluations of public good outputs and in aggregating them into service provision and taxation policy. Whereas there may be no theoretical reason to presume that individuals fail to possess preferences for public goods, the expectation from public goods theory remains: individuals have an economic incentive to conceal them or to reveal them inaccurately. However, it is still clear that somehow promoting 'adequate', if not optimal, provision of public goods is widely held as one of the appropriate economic functions of government.

Social choice

If public goods create provision problems in market systems, they also create difficulties for governmental systems. No two people ever completely agree about public goods — in short, the assumption of complete preference homogeneity, so typical in much of the economic and location theory literature, is fictional. Therefore, at least mild forms of conflict are endemic in reaching collective decisions about public goods and, as argued above, no public goods will be provided, or at least provided at adequate levels, in the absence of collective action.

Although collective action need not entail formal governments as we commonly think of them, some sort of political entity possessing a means of making collective (social) choices is clearly necessary. This is true regardless of which decisions are left to private market decision making (unless all of them are) and which are deemed public. In a very real way even the issue of private or public provision is a social choice (recall that a public good is defined in terms of its characteristics in consumption; not in production). As long as there is a presumption that at least some socially important decisions are not made on an individual basis then some machinery must be set up to make them collectively (Haefele, 1973, p. 93). The possible existence of public goods provides the sufficiency of this presumption.

There appear to be at least seven questions of central concern in social choice. Phrased normatively, these are:

1. What goods and services should be provided collectively?
2. How should the collectivity(ies) (perhaps, benefit regions) be
    defined? If the answer is territorially, then what should be the
    sizes (areal extent and population) of jurisdictions?
3. Where should the facilities through which public goods will be
    provided (delivered) be located?
4. How should the issues (including levels and mixes of public
    goods) for decision be framed?
5. By whom and through what structures and processes should
    they be made? Are some of the structures territorial? If so,
    what should the spatial arrangement of jurisdictions be?
6. How should the expenses of implementing social choices be
    borne?
7. By what means should the social choices be implemented?

These questions could also be phrased positively. If so phrased
and answered for a particular society or region, one would have a
reasonably complete analytical description of that society's or
region's mechanisms of social choice. Upon reflection it is equally
obvious that different societies have worked out different answers
to such questions, usually through processes of historical accretion.
There are, however, some important communalities across societies
and many of these are inherently geographical. For example, in the
modern nation state, many, if not most, of its subordinate collective
decision making units are defined territorially. Systems of
delegation and representation with a territorial basis are universal
in western democracies; and most social choices in all nation-states
are implemented through territorially defined administrative units;
and so on. In brief, geographically structured systems of social
choice have been decisively elected in the modern state. But do
such decisions have more than history to recommend them? Is there
an underlying logic to what Soja (1971) and others have called the
political organization of space; particularly — is there, or could
there be, a logic entailing the concepts of impure public goods and
social choice? The approach taken in the remainder of this paper
focuses on the 'could there be' aspect of this question in that it is
highly speculative and abstract. It argues not for the development
of purely positive or purely normative theory but for the
development of theories which can be described as *positive at the
margin* — theories that do not describe/explain the particular
spatial structures of social choice that exist in reality but, instead,
that identify those spatial structures of social choice which would
be chosen by all or almost all in a region *if such structures were*

within the realm of choice. Such a theory, in the context discussed here, is one of constitutional choice.

Two lines of inquiry

There are roughly two general lines of inquiry extant in the literature which appear relevant in addressing the central questions of social choice. Both appear to provide useful bases for subsequent development by economic and political geographers. Indeed, it might even be argued that these lines of inquiry are largely dead-ended without geographical analysis and elaboration. Both approaches are derivatives of modern (neoclassical) economics and are based on four primary assumptions: (1) scarcity; (2) methodological individualism (the basic unit of analysis is the individual); (3) self-interest (not necessarily narrowly construed in a hedonistic manner and with respect to economic and political goals); (4) individual rationality. These assumptions lead to a view of social choice which necessarily is concerned, at least to some extent, with the workings of political systems in somehow translating or aggregating individual preferences into public outputs. Analysis is directed at forging a logical nexus between these, rather than establishing linkages through detailed empirical analysis. As Fromm (1955) has put it, such empirical analysis would be difficult indeed: 'Between the act of voting and the most momentous high-level political decisions is a connection which is mysterious. One cannot say that there is none at all, nor can one say that the final decision is an outcome of the voter's will' (p. 191).

The first approach, usually referred to as 'fiscal federalism' in the public finance literature, assumes a particular institutional-political context (i.e. provides answers to some of the central issues of social choice exogenously) and then seeks to determine how a system of multi-level jurisdictions should be structured from the point of view of ensuring an optimal supply of an explicit array of public goods. In perspective it is closely related to modern welfare economics. The second approach assumes only the existence of a minimal state which fixes the initial definition of human and property rights and the enforcement of sanctions against violations of these rights, posits the existence of public goods, and then attempts to identify the properties of social choice institutions (including their spatial organization) within which utility-maximizing individuals would prefer public goods decision making to take place. In perspective, this approach, although 'economic', is in the tradition of the contractarian theories of the state.

It is thought that the second approach, with its more explicit focus on preference heterogeneity and social conflict, will hold greater interest for political geographers and hence this approach is emphasized below. The first approach appears to be attracting the attention of theoretical economic geographers (see for example, Lea, 1976, 1978; Papageorgiou, 1977, 1978; Thrall, 1979) and hence good discussions of it already appear in the geographical literature. Attention to it here will be brief and somewhat critical.

Fiscal-federalism approach

The 'fiscal-federalism' approach (perhaps best described in Head, 1974, chap. 12) argues that the degree to which effective decision making power should be delegated to subnational jurisdictions (i.e. to regional and/or local governments) should depend primarily on the possible advantages to be derived in terms of preference revelation. Such advantages, it is argued, can be quite significant in the instance of public goods for which preferences are highly clustered in space, either locally or regionally, but are areally inhomogeneous at larger geographical scales. In short, this approach maintains that the spatial organization, of a system for collective decision making should reflect the geography of public goods preferences to the maximum extent consistent with efficiency in service delivery.

There are some problems with this 'fiscal federalist' type of approach — not the least of which is that there may be no good reason to expect economically rational individuals to 'contract-into' such a system even if one were to come within their purview of choice. Furthermore, for this approach to be useful from a policy perspective, the following two generalizations must hold:

1. that the severity of the preference-relevation or free-rider problem within a jurisdiction is a decreasing function of the degree of preference homogeneity within it; and
2. that the severity of the preference-relevation problem is an *increasing* function of jurisdictional size (both areally and in terms of population).

At least for the geographer, these are inherently interesting empirical questions, but they remain untested. For such testing, the accurate measurement of preferences is clearly essential. Unfortunately, there appear to be few, if any, reliable procedures capable of this measurement task. Even the so-called Clarke-tax (Tideman and Tulloch, 1976) mentioned so frequently in the public choice work offers at best only a partial solution to this problem.

Constitutional choice approach

'Economic' approach

The second approach can be characterized as one of constitutional choice wherein the choice confronting individuals is among the rules, procedures, and structures through which subsequent social choices will be made when it is known that, once selected, they will remain in being over an indeterminately long sequence of social choices. A rational person cannot be expected to be drawn voluntarily into making constitutional choices unless he is highly uncertain as to what his own position will be at any particular moment in the post-constitutional sequence (Brennan and Buchanan, 1977). As the economist Mueller (1977) has put it:

> Indeed, it is usually only when collective decisions extend into the future, that contracts and other indications of formal agreement are needed. An exchange of goods could be written as a contract obliging each individual to part with his good, and specifying the present as the point of time. When exchange is immediate a formal contract is typically unnecessary. When it is not, a contract may be required to ensure each party that the other will provide the specified good at the stipulated point of time. A contract is unnecessary for immediate two person exchange because each is certain, or nearly so, of the outcome.... It is the uncertainties inherent in many decisions requiring collective action or future consequences, which requires formal collective decision processes (p. 227).

In the context of public goods, uncertainties can be grouped into two categories: (1) uncertainty over what one's own subsequent preferences will be because of uncertainty about future 'state of the world', and (2) uncertainty over the behaviour of other individuals (Radner, 1968).

The economic theory of constitutions has been pioneered by Buchanan and Tullock (1962). Their approach, unlike that of 'fiscal federalism', purports to avoid any necessity for preference measurement. Instead, it highlights the possibility that governmental provision of goods and services entails an additional set of costs not encountered in the market economy: the costs of reaching collective decisions, and the costs imposed on those disagreeing with the collective decision (what might be called 'political externality costs'). In their analysis, they argue that the rational person considers these costs in his choices of public goods constitutions and in evaluating proposed constitutional changes in existing governments.

Buchanan and Tullock's argument has received scant attention and appears never to have been subjected to empirical scrutiny. Part of the reason is that at the constitutional level of decision making uncertainty may be sufficiently great to render the concept of political externality irrelevant in the decision calculus. Although their theory is ambiguous, one interpretation of it is that the rational individual attempts to determine the magnitudes of the allocation of goods and costs he expects to receive under all feasible constitutional structures. The more goods, at the least cost, a particular constitutional arrangement yields him the better he likes it. Where *his* choice of constitutions will be decisive (i.e. whatever constitution he favours is *certain* to be implemented) he chooses *under conditions of certainty* and bases his preference on a simple comparison of the amounts of utility each alternative constitution would yield to him. Under more typical conditions of uncertainty, he attempts to choose constitutions on the basis of *expected utilities* reflecting the relevant probabilistic considerations (the probability a constitution will be adopted and implemented, if he chooses it; the probabilities of various constitutions yielding him certain allocations).

However, questions arise as to whether it is possible for a person, however rational, to calculate the relevant *expected utilities* and whether all other rational men will calculate the same or similar expected utilities. (In Buchanan and Tullock's theory, constitutions must be agreed upon unanimously.) For the economically rational individual to perform such calculations, it must be possible:

1. to enumerate the possible allocational and distributional outcomes (defined in terms of his receipt of public goods) from the operation of all feasible constitutional arrangements for making collective decisions;
2. to evaluate the utility associated with each outcome; and
3. to estimate the probability with which each of the outcomes can or will occur.

Although the enumeration of possible outcomes and the evaluation of their associated utilities pose some problems, it appears reasonable that these tasks can be accomplished without much difficulty by the rational individual — indeed these acts approach the definition of economic rationality itself. However, in the absence of knowledge of the public good preferences of others there is no rational objective basis for assigning the requisite probabilities to allocational and distributional outcomes. What should constitute the calculus of the rational individual in this (highly realistic) situation? Should he accept the 'principle of insufficient reason' and assume that all feasible outcomes are equiprobable and then simply select the constitutional arrangement which maximizes the sum of the probabilities times the utilities? There is something quite disquieting about this approach, particularly if it is likely that almost any outcome can arise from the operation of almost any feasible constitution (even dictators can be benevolent). It suggests that the rational individual should be indifferent in his choice of constitutions, since within limits they all could yield the same expected utility! One possible solution to this dilemma is for the individual to invest at least some resources in ascertaining the public good preferences of others. However, this takes us back to the problem of estimating such preferences — to precisely what Buchanan and Tullock's theory attempts to avoid and points to the possible deficiency of purely economic theory as a guide for the political organization of space — its basic dependence on the satisfactory measurement of preferences for public goods and services — preferences which are likely to be resistant to direct measurement and which are only imperfectly revealed in overt behaviour.

Even if we could assume that individuals could attach probabilistic estimates to their own future preferences and to those of others, there appears to be no reason to expect that all, or even almost all, persons would arrive at the same or similar estimates. Hence, we are left without theoretical guidance regarding constitutional decison making. At least part of the difficulty with Buchanan and Tullock's framework is that it fails to more fully exploit the properties of public goods — those goods and services over which social choices must be made.

Public goods and procedural justice

The approach to constitutional choice proposed here is not to devise methods by which estimates of public good preferences can be made with a modicum of accuracy and then attempt to identify the locational and other correlates of such estimates, but to depart from the thicket of individual cost-benefit perspectives and attempt to develop a geographically relevant theory in which such estimation is logically irrelevant. It is argued that utility-maximizing individuals with uncertain preferences for public goods are naturally and logically drawn from their own myopic utility calculations and drawn to principles of procedural justice in choices of their institutions and structures of social choice and in choices regarding changes in such institutions and structures.

Scenario 1
Let us begin analysis by examining a problem in the social choice of a public good that, at first sight, appears not to be one of constitutional choice (since the requisite uncertainty appears absent). The problem is very simple but it highlights social choice difficulties that arise over the geographical impurities typically associated with the provision of public goods as well as suggesting that a concept of procedural justice or fairness may be adhered to in certain public goods contexts.

Define a *local public good* as any economic good provided from a fixed location which, at points of consumption, exhibits considerable jointness and non-excludability; the amount of the good available for joint consumption, however, is some decreasing function of location *vis-à-vis* the point of supply (the public facility). The provision of fire protection can be thought of as an example.

Consider a region populated by economically rational individuals, with similar but not identical incomes, tastes, and preferences who, motivated solely by their individual self-interests, wish to be supplied with a local public good (say fire protection). For the sake of simplicity, also assume that the preferences of these individuals and the technology available to them are such that only one public facility (fire station) can be located in the region and that once it is located it cannot feasibly be moved. Given only these assumptions, it is clear that each person would prefer that the facility (station) be located in close proximity to his residence, but it is equally clear that this is impossible. Is there some location or locational principle that would be unanimously chosen by persons in the region?

One potential facility location which might be argued for by an 'outside observer' and perhaps also by those residing near the 'centre' of the region is the 'point of minimum aggregate travel'. However, this would surely not command the support of those on the periphery and they like anyone else hold veto power over the decision. The likelihood of agreement on a single location is at least in part a function of the distance decay of the benefits of the good out from the facility (in the case of fire protection, it is a function of travel time). If the nature of this 'spatial impurity' was such that the welfare of every person in the region would be improved, irrespective of where the facility was located and yet benefits could still be presumed to decay with distance, everyone in the region would have an economic incentive to agree to some location. Nevertheless, the cost of bargaining could be sufficiently great for the persons involved to entertain the thought of institutionalizing this social choice, say by unanimously agreeing to select someone to make the choice for the region as a whole. But who could be unanimously selected? Only someone (or some process) who (which) was unequivocally viewed as unbiased or fair — perhaps some highly respected 'senior citizen' who had little to gain personally.

Note the general characteristics of this scenario: the certainty that everyone wished to be near the facility led to social conflict, which in turn rendered the likelihood of providing the good small, or if a location could be agreed upon, the cost, in terms of decision-making (and lost opportunity costs), could be sufficiently great to result in net welfare losses to some. For those familiar with game theory, it can be seen that the example has properties of a 'prisoner's dilemma' in an N-person, positive-sum game. The solution is to institutionalize some procedure that could be construed as fair to all and not simply a procedure that was 'less costly' (in the sense of that proposed in the theory of Buchanan and Tullock). For example, there are a large number of other 'democratic' procedures which are candidates for choice — e.g. any voting rule requiring less than unanimity. Why would a simple voting rule, say majority rule, not be preferred? Because, even ignoring the problems of how locations upon which to vote might be proposed, majority rule would ensure that a more or less central location be chosen (provided, of course, that the population was evenly distributed in the region) — a bias from the perspective of those on the periphery because it occurred as the result of the utility-maximizing calculations of only a geographically defined subset of the region's population.

Scenario 2

Now, consider a generalization of this scenario to the choice of a constitution constraining the social choice of public goods that must be made on a continuing basis. Imagine a minimal state which guarantees basic human and property rights and enforces them over its territory. The state is populated by persons who are viewed as social equals. All are economically rational and there are no basic cleavages along class, income, or any other lines existing in the state. However, no other public goods are provided. Assume that some subset of the population has (or develops) an interest in providing a public good. Given the externality fields associated with the jointness-in-supply characteristic of most public goods, it is reasonable to suggest that such a subset will be geographically definable; i.e. if a public good is provided, there will be a potential benefit region associated with it. (The potential benefit region of the public good associated with the installation of pollution control devices at specific sites in an air shed is an example.) Assume further that the number of persons in the subset is large and heterogeneous in terms of income, tastes, etc., and that there are no institutional barriers to the creation of 'local governments' for the purpose of providing public goods except that public goods constitutions must be agreed to unanimously by those who will subsequently be coerced into contributing resources for supplying the good.

Any individual in this subset may be sure of his own preferences for the public good (this will be questioned in more detail below), but he is very uncertain of anybody else's preferences. Recall that there are no market-type mechanisms or as yet formal political mechanisms for the revelation of preferences. Initially then, being self-interested he might wish to propose a constitution that ensures that his tax-price and receipt of the public good are such that he reaches a 'high' indifference curve on his preference map. Ideally, of course, he would prefer any constitution that ensures some provision of the public good at a tax-price to him of zero. But equally surely everybody else would have similar preferences — with the result that there could be agreement on the constitution, but an empty one in that there would be no provision of the good. Realizing this, our rational individual might propose a constitution which ensures that his tax-price would be low compared to those of other members — that is, he would attempt to be a 'partial-payment' rider — but, again, all others would behave similarly with the result that all would know they would end up on lower indifference curves than intended. Somewhere in these hypothetical deliberations, he might flirt with the idea of proposing a constitution which would lead to a Wicksellian solution, whereby members of the subset were assessed tax-prices proportional to their individual benefits (Wicksell, 1964) but, failing in his attempt at identifying a constitution that would ensure the accurate revelation of preferences, this would be a brief flirtation.

From this scenario, it is clear that there will be no unanimous agreement on a public goods constitution (or one even approaching relative unanimity) as long as there is the significant hint of differential advantage to potentially indefinable individuals in its provisions. Ironically, self-interest ensures that narrow (myopic) self-interest must be suppressed if any of the good is to be provided. In this more general case, constitutional agreement appears possible only if there is assurance:

1. that all will expect long-run benefits from the provision of the good;
2. that the total costs of public good provision will be allocated among group members in a manner which is viewed by all as 'fair', 'just' or 'equitable' (benefit taxation in a public goods context could not be so viewed);
3. that the procedures and structures employed by government in determining the public good output can also be considered by all as 'fair', 'just' or 'equitable'; and
4. that for a given level of output the total costs are as low as possible (i.e. that the relevant factor inputs are combined in a maximally efficient manner).

Condition 1 simply assures that there is a meaningful collectivity or public, while the remaining three conditions appear to be minimal constraints the rational, self-interested individual would place on his basic institutions of social choice before he would willingly agree to allow them to coerce him into contributing to the provision of public goods. Interestingly, of these only the fourth is an efficiency condition and here the efficiency is 'efficiency in production'; not in an overall allocational sense. Condition 2 embodies at least weak notions of distributive justice. Public goods, under the assumptions employed, cannot be provided to achieve some specific distributive goal primarily because of the impossibility of forging unanimous (or near unanimous) agreement on an appropriate goal or goals at the constitutional stage of decision-making, otherwise a form of the preference revelation problem is again encountered. However, if the distribution of income in the subset is viewed as sufficiently unequal to lead the relatively 'poor' not to expect long-run benefits from the provision of a public good, then some form of progressive taxation is one means of helping to ensure agreement on a constitution. Alternatively, all may agree that it is desirable to redistribute income *in some manner* through the provision of public goods, but the only *certain* way to achieve redistribution may be through 'just taxation' based on 'ability to pay'.

The third condition is clearly one of procedural justice. As in the first scenario, any decision making procedure (e.g. representative government with majority voting) operating through a structure (e.g. single-member, territorial constituencies) must be adjudged as unbiased in that the actual distributional consequences of post-constitutional social choices cannot be consistently weighted to the advantage of any group. From a geographical perspective this may imply that a constitution which is viewed as unfair in a large group may be viewed as fair in a smaller group. For example, in a geographically extensive group, a constitution embodying a system of representative government in which representatives are all elected from a single constituency coincident with the territory occupied by the group may be viewed as unjust (persons from more heavily populated regions would be thought over-represented), whereas in a smaller (again territorially defined) group such a constitution could well be viewed as just. The justice of any constitution, then, is not dependent on the specific magnitudes of expected individual benefits of public good provision *per se,* but upon whether the operation of the constitution reinforces already extant cleavages in the group or is likely to lead to new ones.

Scenario 3
Finally, consider a simple modification of the second scenario. Instead of presuming that the individual is certain of his own preferences, assume that he is *completely uncertain* of his preferences for a public good, yet realizes that under some future conditions he would be supportive of formal collective action to provide it. Such uncertainty could be the result of a lack of previous experience in consuming the public good. Would he rationally support the creation of a formal public goods constitution (or constitutions)? The answer to this, to my view, is a qualified yes. Not knowing his own preferences, yet having an interest in public goods (at least latent interest since they have the potential of improving his welfare), it is rational to invest some resources in reducing uncertainty. Conceptually, the reduction of uncertainty itself can be viewed as a public good and hence it is rational to explore the possibility of identifying social choice mechanisms (constitutions) appropriate to the task. One mechanism is to choose persons who are charged with providing information about public goods, including exploring alternative production technologies, identifying 'alternative futures', etc. Such persons might be referred to as public goods entrepreneurs (if selected through a competitive mechanism) or as mobilizers of latent groups (to borrow some terminology from Olson, 1965). Much the same arguments as before would lead to conclusions about the constitutional agreement similar (or identical) to those

identified in conditions 1-3 above. Here, it can be argued that issues of procedural justice will loom even larger in constitutional choice. Also, social choice mechanisms resembling those of representative government are more easily envisioned as being within the purview of choice. However, the question remains as to whether these public goods entrepreneurs would also be constitutionally entitled to render actual social choices pertaining to public goods. There may be distinct economies in so doing, but analysis of this more complicated situation is beyond the scope of this paper.

Geography of social choice: conclusions

Is there a geography of social choice pertaining to public goods? Yes, and it is surely a complicated one. Could there be an underlying logic to the ways in which modern nation-states are organized spatially for making public goods choices? Yes, but analysis would be essentially historical, shrouded by an incomplete record, and unlikely to provide any direct guidance in pointing to generally desirable institutional change. Is there an underlying logic to systems of social choice which 'could be'? Yes, and it is precisely this type of investigation that more political geographers should consider.

The approach taken in this paper has been abstract, loosely deductive and, hence, almost entirely speculative. Clearly, it needs to be made more rigorous theoretically than has been the case here. However, in so far as the properties of public goods are understood by the average citizen, and to the extent that he is self-interested and economically rational, the speculations discussed here suggest no necessary incompatibility between the individual's goal of utility maximization, and the norm of social justice at the level of constitutional choice. Indeed, it has been argued that the problem of public good provision places a person in a decisional setting analogous to Rawls' 'veil of ignorance' (Rawls, 1971). For Rawls, his 'veil' is purely a theoretical construct having no experiential referent, but in a world with public goods at least partial 'veils of ignorance' arise empirically.

If the arguments of this paper are well founded, it suggests that rational persons with an interest in a public good must evolve or develop some concept of procedural justice if a public good is to be provided through joint consent rather than imposed by some 'higher authority' or by some more powerful group. It is in their self-interest to do so. This is not to suggest that any of the actual institutions of social choice found in the modern nation state are in any way the results of the types of hypothetical deliberations discussed earlier. Surely few if any are. But in contemplating governmental reform at the local, regional, and state levels, as so many of us as political geographers are asked to do, it appears that we might begin to explore more fully, not simply the likely distributional outcomes of decisions made in the post-reform governments, but also the procedural fairness of such reforms. This is not to imply that the likely output decisions of governments are irrelevant in a person's decision of whether to support or oppose a particular 'reform', but merely that people may possess relatively well-defined views of social justice in social choice contexts. This leads to the possibility that for the average individual with an interest in receiving a public good there is no sharp conceptual separation between social choice processes and the outcomes of such processes. Indeed, for an outcome to be considered fair, it may be necessary that it can be fairly arrived at.

Clearly, no full-blown normative theory of social choice has been presented nor is any likely to be developed in the near future. Political geographers can, however, contribute to the development of such a theory. One place to begin is by exploring the linkages, if any, between individually held conceptions of procedural justice in simple, yet conflict-riven, collective decision-making tasks involving a spatially impure public good, and their conceptions of distributive justice (fairness in terms of who gets what) in the same context. Specifically, one would wish to ascertain whether and in what social and spatial contexts (1) geographically based procedures (e.g. a territorial system of interest representation) dominate those with another basis; (2) large jurisdictions are preferred to smaller ones; and (3) procedural preferences are (or are not) traded off against distributional preferences. These are, of course, empirical questions but these (and many more) must be addressed if a theory of social choice is to be 'positive at the margin'.

References and bibliography

Arrow, K. (1963). *Social Choice and Individual Values* (Wiley, New York).
Brennan, G., and Buchanan, J. M. (1977). 'Towards a tax constitution for Leviathan', *Journal of Public Economics*, **8**, 255-73.
Buchanan, J. M. (1959). 'Positive economics, welfare economics, and political economy,' *Journal of Law and Economics*, **2**, 124-38.
Buchanan, J. M., and Tullock, G. (1962). *The Calculus of Consent* (University of Michigan Press, Ann Arbor).

Coleman, J. S. (1966). 'Foundations for a theory of collective decisions', *American Journal of Sociology*, **71**, 615-27.

Fromm, E. (1955). *The Sane Society* (Holt, Rinehart & Winston, New York).

Haefele, E. T. (1973). *Representative Government and Environmental Management* (The Johns Hopkins University Press, Baltimore).

Hartshorne, R. (1950). 'The functional approach in political geography', *Annals of the Association of American Geographers*, **40**, 95-130.

Head, J. G. (1974). *Public Goods and Public Welfare* (Duke University Press, Durham, NC).

Lea, A. C. (1976). 'Aspects of a theory of the public space economy' (University of Toronto, mimeo).

Lea, A. C. (1978). 'Interjurisdictional spillovers and efficient public good provision'. Paper presented to the Annual Meeting of the Association of American Geographers, New Orleans, 12 April.

Mueller, D. C. (1973). 'Constitutional democracy and social welfare', *Quarterly Journal of Economics*, **87**, 60-80.

Mueller, D. C. (1977). 'Allocation, redistribution, and collective choice', *Public Finance*, **32**, 225-41.

Musgrave, R. A. (1959). *The Theory of Public Finance* (McGraw-Hill, New York).

Nozick, R. (1974). *Anarchy, State, and Utopia* (Basic Books, New York).

Olson, M. (1965). *The Logic of Collective Action* (Harvard University Press, Cambridge, Mass.).

Papageorgiou, G. J. (1977). 'Fundamental problems of theoretical planning', *Environment and Planning*, **9**, 1329-56.

Papageorgiou, G. J. (1978). 'Spatial externalities: I — Theory, II — Applications', *Annals of the Association of American Geographers*, **68**, 465-92.

Radner, R. (1968). 'Competitive equilibrium under uncertainty', *Econometrica*, **36**, 31-58.

Rawls, J. (1971). *A Theory of Justice* (Harvard University Press, Cambridge, Mass.).

Reynolds, D. R., and Honey, R. (1978). 'Conflict in the location of salutary public facilities', in Cox, K. R. (ed.), *Urbanization and Conflict in Market Societies*, pp. 144-60 (Maaroufa Press, Chicago).

Samuelson, P. A. (1954). 'The pure theory of public expenditure', *Review of Economics and Statistics*, **36**, 387-9.

Sen, A. K. (1970). *Collective Choice and Social Welfare* (Holden-Day, San Francisco).

Soja, E. W. (1971). *The Political Organization of Space*, Association of American Geographers: Commission on College Geography. Resource Paper No. 8 (Washington, DC).

Taylor, M. (1976). *Anarchy and Cooperation* (Wiley, New York).

Thrall, G. I. (1979). 'Public goods and the derivation of land value assessment schedules within a spatial equilibrium setting', *Geographical Analysis*, **11**, 23-5.

Tideman, T. N., and Tullock, G. (1976). 'A new and superior process for making social choices', *Journal of Political Economy*, **84**, 1145-59.

Wicksell, K. (1964). 'A new principle of just taxation', in Musgrave, R. A., and Peacock, A. T. (eds.), *Classics in the Theory of Public Finance*, pp. 72-118 (Macmillan, London).

Political studies from spatial perspectives
Edited by A.D. Burnett and P.J. Taylor
© 1981 John Wiley & Sons Ltd

6

Democracy and the capitalist state: towards a critique of the Tiebout hypothesis

Gordon L. Clark

Introduction

Research on the provision of local public goods has neglected the institution providing those goods: the local state. Few studies have analysed how and why local governments function. In the North American context the major reason for this neglect is the dominance of Tiebout's (1956) model of democracy, public choice, and competition between local governments. The concern for establishing rules of public intervention in providing local goods and services has provided by default the *raison d'être* of the local state. Interest in geography with the related issues of citizen participation, interest groups and conflict over the provision of local public goods reflects a general agreement, albeit often implicit, with Tiebout's model.

The Tiebout model abstracts and ignores many issues that do not readily fit within its structure. For example, the interdependence between different spatial scales of the state is often ignored in the literature (Dear, 1981). Questions of the local state's relative dependency or independence from the national state do not readily fit the democratic model of the local state. However, the degree of relative independence of the local state is a fundamental issue since a local state that is morally and fiscally independent may be able to refuse the directives (class or otherwise) of the national state and be open to the control of local interest groups opposed to national state objectives. A completely dependent local state, on the other hand, may simply mirror the objectives and the class

111

biases of the national state. The notions of dependency and independence imply a fundamental determining role for democracy: a role which is intimately related to the spatial and structural interdependencies of the capitalist system itself (Clark, 1980).

While democracy is the basic organizing principle of the liberal theory of the state, Marxists have generally ignored the issue. Marxist theorists have been unequivocal in their rejection of the possibility of a true democracy in capitalism (Poulantzas, 1973). It is argued that capitalist democracy is a sham: a means of manipulating and subverting the true aspirations of the people. According to Reich and Edwards (1978) to take democratic bourgeois politics seriously diverts attention from the more significant issues of class exploitation and alienation. While it is accepted that 'politics is important', many Marxist critiques reduce the elements of social and political struggle to either an insignificant issue or a class-related problem (Miliband, 1977). This collapses the significance of legitimate social and political interests of different segments of society through a claim that 'all would be solved through the imposition of a class-less society'.

There are many difficulties with such Marxist interpretations of democracy. With respect to the role of democracy in capitalism, the dismissal of bourgeois politics as irrelevant and facile has led many theorists to reject all advances of the working class. Thus political actions that wrought an improvement in working conditions, the reduction and regulation of work hours, and improved health and medical benefits (to cite only a few examples) are often ridiculed. Further, the neglect of democracy has meant that no serious challenge has been made to the authority of models, such as Tiebout's, which dominate orthodox theory of the spatial arrangement of government.

In this paper the relationship between democracy and the state is analysed from a radical perspective. Three issues are central to this analysis: the role of democracy with respect to the capitalist state; ideology and legitimization of the national state through the democratic process; and consequently, where the local state draws its own legitimacy and degree of independence. The emphasis upon democracy, ideology, and the legitimization of different spatial scales of the state is argued to be a necessary first step in the development of a more general theory of the local state. Following Scott and Roweis (1977) this paper is directed towards formalizing, in a non-eclectic manner, the democratic-capitalist structural relationships within which the spatial organization of the state is situated.

Modern democracy and the organization of government

Modern political scientists define democracy as a process or procedure. Accordingly democracy is defined as a political system in which elections decide the competition for power and policies (Dahl, 1956). A set of conditions have to be met in order to have legitimate democracy. First, all citizens, regardless of socioeconomic identity or status, must have the right to vote for those who would best express voters' opinions. Second, such votes must be equally weighted, and, third, represent the true opinion of the voter formed in a completely free environment. A free environment in this sense is one where there is no coercion as to the 'right' opinion, as well as a full awareness of all possible alternative options. Fourth, in a collective sense the numerical majority must rule although, fifthly, majority decisions must not limit minority rights (Downs, 1957).

The modern theory of democracy is not concerned with the socioeconomic structure of society. Rather it is a theory concerned with defining the proper method or means for the resolution of social conflict. By definition the democratic method is argued to necessarily result in democratic outcomes. Analogous is Rawls' (1971, p. 80) pure procedural justice conceptualization which 'obtains when there is no independent criterion for the right result; instead there is a correct or fair procedure such that the outcome is likewise correct or fair, whatever it is, provided that the procedure has been properly followed'. Democracy is argued by many modern theorists to be one such pure procedural method (see Cave, 1978). Democracy is not necessarily defined on moral or social grounds, as perhaps commonly supposed; rather democracy is defined in terms of the system of voting.

Dahl (1956) amongst many other orthodox writers on democracy, has argued that as in the *laissez-faire* economic market, votes are market signals. They represent the ultimate test of consumer choice and preference. The choice between competing leaders and elites is argued to be based upon two interrelated criteria: policies and potential outputs. Votes are taken as the true expression of rational self-interest on behalf of the majority of the population (Pateman, 1970). Control over leaders and elites is exercised periodically through elections with the ultimate sanction being the loss of elected office. Political participation for the majority of voters is argued to be simply and solely for the choice of the elite decision-makers through the exercise of their vote. Dahl (1956) also argued that the theory of democracy is a function of, and implicitly, a description of, current political methods. In the empirical tradition the theory is claimed to be positivistic and value-free. However as Pateman (1979) has remarked, this claim would appear to be invalid on two grounds. First, the process of theory-building is itself selective of the full range of facts and dimensions of society. Concepts themselves are derivative from the dominant ideology. Second, selectivity itself is the cornerstone of normative theory-building. Thus the modern theory of democracy is prescriptive in that a particular type of system is implied, as well as the standards by which democratic practice ought to be judged by. Modern theories of democracy are ideological and have a particular view of society.

Three assumptions can be identified as being central to democratic theory that illustrate this proposition. First, modern democratic theory is prefaced upon an assumption of equal opportunity or access to power. Access is a precondition for Rawlsian pure procedural justice. Power, however, is rather narrowly defined. Macpherson (1973) noted that the concept of power in such theories is often defined as the right to exercise the vote. Few theorists have been concerned to analyse either the distribution of economic power in society or the assumption that the 'ends' of democratic decision-making match the 'means'. In essence modern theorists of democracy ignore the basic inequalities of capitalism. Second, and interrelated with this issue, is the assumption that the distribution of income and class power are assumed to be unimportant. Dahl (1956) goes further by claiming that recognition of such differences would lead to widespread and unjustified instability in the political process. He argued that only certain segments of society participate and typically only for their own narrow self-interest. Consequently economic equality and biased class or group distributions are argued to be separable from the political system. In the economic system individuals are assumed to be rewarded according to their marginal product, not according to the political power they hold.

Third, the process of voting is itself a logical extension of the assumption of rational self-interest and implicitly principles of utilitarianism. Society is thought to be composed of individual political decision-making units who know their own utility functions; rationally choose the party or elite that best express their utility, and are able to differentiate between different levels of their own utility (Harsanyi, 1977). Although these conditions may not hold in all circumstances it is the inherent tendency towards such decision-making that is the crucial factor for modern theorists of democracy.

The research agenda for Dahl and others is the product of these assumptions and is more often than not an analysis of the voting process *per se*. For example major research themes have been the defining of optimal arrangements of voting; analysing equilibrium tendencies of the system; voter apathy and the so-called aberrant or perverse non-optimizing behaviour of some social groups. Geographers have by and large accepted this form of democratic theory as the premise for studying the spatial pattern of voting, elections, and the organization of local government. Many have concentrated upon the adequacy of electoral boundaries as well as voting biases that may be a product of location and not direct rational self-interest. Local government expenditures and functions are often seen as a special case of democracy theory and orthodox public finance economics (Downs, 1957). In this context writers such as Papageorgiou (1978) have emphasized that the existence of local government is a product of consumer preferences, market supply, and competing opportunities.

In a landmark study of North American local government Ostrom *et al.* (1961) argued that the principal objective of metropolitan government is the provision of public goods and services. These authors identified three reasons for the public rather than private provision of certain goods at the local level:

1. public goods may be provided as a means of controlling spatial externalities or spillover effects;
2. public goods may be provided at a particular level because the market cannot; and
3. public goods may be provided as a means of maintaining certain desired collective (moral, political or otherwise) preferences of the local community.

Obvious examples of local public goods are police and fire protection, as well as local welfare services. Their contribution was to shift concern from the simple provisions of the public goods to the question of the appropriate spatial organization of the provision of public goods. This was accomplished by invoking modern democratic theory. Local residents were assumed to locate and exercise their vote according to their preferences for public goods and services. Consumer attributes (family size, income, stage in the life-cycle, etc.) and the maximization of their utility functions were assumed to be the determinants of consumer preferences and location decisions. Given a wide range of choice in possible local government (assuming that employment location is unimportant) then consumers will locate and vote according to their demand for particular sets of public goods.

According to this model local governments seek to continue their existence (particularly in the short run) through serving voter preferences. Thus local governments compete for voter (consumer) support on the basis of public goods provision as well as according to the level of taxes and service delivery efficiency. This theory is dependent upon a number of assumptions. First, that consumers (or voters) are mobile and have full knowledge of competing alternative local governments and their own preferences; second, that there exist a large number of alternative communities; and third, that votes are cast and recorded in the manner of pure procedural democracy.

The first assumption is necessary to establish the principle that consumers (voters) are rational and maximize their individual utility functions. Related is the concept that rational self-interest can be aggregated to a particular spatial scale. This, then, is the mechanism for creating a particular spatial allocation of public goods. It should be emphasized that voting, as in the analysis of the democratic method, is argued to be solely the function of individual interests. The spatial pattern of social justice is assumed to be irrelevant as a voting criterion although consumers (voters) have preferences related to their incomes.

The second assumption was derived by Ostrom *et al.* from the economics of markets and from organization literature. In essence, choice is a fundamental condition for the true expression of consumer preferences. A large number of communities also implies that no one local government is able to control the 'market'. That is, without the possibility of consumers being able to move to another jurisdiction, the system would tend to ossify — become unrepresentative and restrict public good choices by consumers. The obvious parallel to this particular conceptualization is the neoclassical economic theory of perfect competition amongst atomistic firms.

The concept of democracy is used in this model of local government as a procedural voting method. Rawls (1971) argued that given a just voting or allocative procedure, then the outcome is likewise fair. Since political and social issues are decided in common and according to individual preferences for local public goods then the distribution of welfare and allocation of public goods amongst social groups within a spatial jurisdiction implies a local social welfare function. The 'ends' or 'social outcomes' are the results of the democratic method, not inputs to democratic decision-making. Similarly, the Tiebout model implies that the existence of inequalities in economic power does not determine a certain distributive pattern amongst local governments.

Thus the neoclassical theory of the spatial organization of government is intertwined with the modern theory of democracy. Both theories are inherently normative and abstract, implying a particular conception of the purpose of government as well as the notion of how individual decisions are made and expressed. The legacy for geography and the empirical studies of governments, and policies and electoral politics, is then all too predictable. Concern for boundary problems (the mismatch between local goods provision and the political constituency); efficiency versus equity in spatial public goods allocation; and conflict over public policy outcomes are all implicitly based on a rather narrow and idealized conception of the democratic process.

Democracy and the capitalist state

Many writers have designed critiques of the theoretical and empirical foundations of modern democratic theory. Within economics criticism has often focused upon the notions of utilitarianism implicit in individual choice models such as Downs' (1957). This has often broadened into a full-scale attack on the very foundations of neoclassical economics (Bowles and Gintis, 1978). Within sociology, attention has been drawn to the lack of adequate recognition of the socialization processes and group interdynamics inherent in political conflict. Critics from political science have argued that equating political processes to economic systems is totally inadequate. They have argued that the analogy is so stripped of reality as to be completely irrelevant. Worse still, some theorists have argued that the interest of political scientists in elegant theories of democracy has diverted political science from the more significant problems (Pateman, 1970). It is not intended here to repeat the wide criticisms from these disciplines concerning the modern theory of democracy. Rather a narrow set of the total possible themes are highlighted and serve to introduce the reader to the latter and more substantive critique of liberal democracy *vis-à-vis* the capitalist state.

Downs (1957) was concerned with the implications of uncertainty and inadequate information in affecting rational decision-making. The analogy in economics is that less than perfect information can collapse market equilibrium solutions as false trading may occur because of inadequate information of true market prices. In voting, a similar problem is implied. Voters may not know the true policies of competing parties while parties may mistake true voter preferences. Barry (1978) provided a detailed analysis of these problems of voting through an analogous examination of the theory of spatial market competition. In the absence of information costs it is argued that competing political parties will tend towards the 'centre' of the political spectrum (the political spectrum can be thought of as analogous to the straight-line distance between competing retail outlets in Hotelling's problem). Lack of adequate information could create, however, as in spatial economics, problems of political monopoly and disequilibrium solutions.

At the heart of this analysis is the negation of political ideology as a legitimate, identifiable, and non-divisible political attribute of individuals and groups. Ideology for Downs and others is a problem of inadequate knowledge or of irrationality in decision-making. Ideology is seen as a screen or impediment to the expression of true voter preferences and implies less than optimal solutions for the allocation of government outputs *vis-à-vis* voter preferences. A means of circumventing this problem is to place ideologies on a continuum (presumably left to right) and assume that ideology is marginally divisible — that is, a voter could move along the continuum, as in fact could governments in their search for the majority of consumer votes. For Downs the problems argued to be inherent in ideology would and should disappear as voters come to realize their own self-interests. This theory is, after all, one of individual utility-maximization. The conception of divisible ideologies and revealed true voter preferences is prefaced upon an implicit assumption of what society is like. Basically there are no classes that have a distinct and mirrored image of themselves simultaneously both in the political and economic arenas. That is, although economic inequality may exist, this is presumed to be separable from the sharing and distribution of political power. The obvious instrument that may be invoked to support this contention is the one-man, one-vote voting process. However, there is a stronger assumption often unacknowledged in this process. Macpherson (1973) argued that Downs assumed a particular political process whereby

> the politically important demands of each individual are diverse and are shared with varied and shifting combinations of other individuals none of which combinations can be expected to be a numerical majority (except perhaps momentarily).

Downs then claimed two 'conditions'. First, that individuals view politics as '...a matter of discussion which is conducted from a common premises [of evaluation]...', and second, individual preferences are the market signals for government.

It is apparent that individual political preferences exist; however, it is only under very special circumstances that these preferences are likely to swamp class interests as well. Macpherson (1977) argued that class interests are likely to be swamped when distributive outcomes are related to ever-expending (or growing) aggregate welfare. Thus governments of growing economies are able to increase welfare for lower economic groups from a growing 'pie', not redistribute a given stock of wealth. Thus the political reality of capitalist economies is two-tiered. At a superficial level it is simply the modern democratic version; at the heart of political reality, however, is class identification — a tension between economic inequality, group identification, and the political expression of one class interest over others. Voters have social and ideological agendas, the result of class identification, work-place or interest-group affiliation.

These arguments raise a fundamental issue and point of disagreement with the Downsian and Tiebout models. The abstraction and negation of ideology, class, and economic inequality as vital and inherent mechanisms of political decision-making enforces a rigid and very narrow view of human nature and political institutions. It is implicitly assumed that a 'party' is a group of single-minded individuals with a common goal: the maximization of votes at the next election. The existence of a permanent capitalist state and governmental system is totally ignored.

Marx aptly dismissed the supposed neutrality of the capitalist state by arguing that: '[t]he executive of the modern state is but a committee for managing the common affairs of the whole bourgeoisie' (see Dear and Clark, 1978). This statement has been picked up by many theorists and some have argued that in conjunction with Lenin's pamphlet on the *State and Revolution* it represents an operational theory of the capitalist state. However, it has become recognized that it is hardly an adequate hypothesis for understanding the genesis of state actions, let alone as a basis for theoretical development (Clark, 1979). A number of rather different approaches have been developed including, for example, the instrumentalist approach (Miliband, 1969); the structuralist approach, most closely identified with Poulantzas (1973); and the more recent German 'derivative' state theories which attempt to link the nature of state's functions to the issues of capital accumulation and exploitation (Clark and Dear, 1980).

Whatever the differences between these groups, and there are many (see Poulantzas, 1976) there is broad agreement on the following theoretical principles of the Marxist theory of the state. First, it is agreed that the capitalist state is an intrinsic element of the class structure of society. As such, class conflict and political struggle is a functional aspect of its existence. Second, the state operates to protect the hegemony of the ruling class through ideological and legitimization functions as well as through providing the economic structures and means of accumulation. Third, the capitalist state attempts to diffuse class conflict and control dissent through a variety of coercive functions, although incidentally, its own position within such conflict may actually paralyse action (Clark, 1980). The capitalist state exists within the democratic fabric of society yet its role cannot even be hinted at in modern democratic theory. This is because democratic practice is assumed to be equivalent to the theoretical requirements of democracy. Further, as Downs and Tiebout ignore class, class conflict, and ideology in their analyses, they also inevitably ignore the product of capitalist class society: the state.

It should be acknowledged that disagreement with the modern theory of democracy is in part related to the paradigm of inquiry central to this paper. Those elements central to any critical analysis of capitalist democracy, class conflict, the mode of production, ideology, and the state are missing from Downs and Tiebout. Thus the level of disagreement is with their basic assumptions of society, not necessarily with the analysis given those assumptions. Second, the modern theory of democracy was intended to be abstract and not necessarily related to one particular historical context. Much like neoclassical economics it was conceived to deal with particular and idealized problems.

Capitalism and the practice of democracy

How democracy should be organized in practice is subject to a set of operational principles (see Bobbio, 1978a, 1978b). First, direct representation is generally taken as the preferable mode of voter representation rather than the more common practice of indirect representation. Not only should voters have the right to elect whoever best represents their interests, voters should also have the right to terminate their representatives' mandate at any time. This means more than electing a representative for a fixed term: voters must be able to 'fire' their representative at a moment's notice. Direct representation is not typical of most capitalist countries. Rather indirect representation is the key principle, whereby voters exercise their right at regularly scheduled intervals (up to 5 years).

Second, formal authority and responsibility for the actions of voter representatives should be held by the voters themselves. By this it is meant that control and the responsibility of control of collective actions must be in the arena of direct citizen power. In practice there is a division between the ability to elect an official to a position of power and the ability to exercise control over the position of power itself. Thus, no matter what degree of electoral control over the individual official a society may have, if authority for particular functions is delegated then power becomes divorced from those democratic rules that may characterize other forms of societal organization.

Third, democratic organizations should be decentralized so that form and functions are directly related to the structure of voter organization. Abstractly, this implies that voter representatives should be organized in a spatial-horizontal manner. This would preserve the immediacy and directness of voter responsibility and control. This is related to the issue of delegated authority and means that separation often exists between the democratic caucus and society (voters) and how the state institutions are in fact controlled and run.

In an ideological context capitalist democracy both disenfranchises direct control and enables the perpetuation and legitimization of the state. Separation between authority and control may lead to the practice of democracy being relatively weak. The lack of an adequate mechanism to influence directly political systems raises the possibility of political repression. Under these circumstances it is no longer clear how control over elected representatives, let alone those who exercise delegated authority, can reasonably function (Arrow, 1974).

The separation between the political control process and its institutional representation (the state) has a number of consequences. First, it creates an illusion of control. The dominant ideology is expressed in terms of the rules of democracy, not its actual organization. This encourages the illusion of a political process directed by the people in direct control of the state (Wright, 1978). Not only does this allow repression by the capitalist state for its own interests to be represented as the actions of the democratic process, but it also provides the rationale for the state's perpetuation. The state as a relatively autonomous entity becomes a bureaucracy and power relation with its own agenda.

Second, as a result of indirect representation, responsibility for the control of the state resides in the parliamentary arena. However, even as the people may have very little power over their representatives, the parliament may also be relatively powerless to control the state's operation. Reason for this is to be found in, again, the separation of control from responsibility and its expression in bureaucrats who are delegated authority by reason of their positions in the hierarchy. It is not simply the individual bureaucrat who is at issue, rather it is in inherent power vested in the state by the praxis of democracy. As a consequence of democratic ideology, the parliament is taken to be in control, yet if the state were to act against the majority the government may be defeated. This would leave the state intact (physically and ideologically) and diffuse revolt through the democratic process.

Third, inherent in these notions of separability is the possibility of the converse happening. That is, it is not clear that the state could stop one party from identifying itself with the state structure. In fact, it may be in the interest of a political party to appear as synonymous with the state. Consequently, the state could be drawn into the political arena, identified with one party and possibly destroyed against its own wishes. The capitalist state in this context may well have its own motivations but also be part of an ongoing political process where desired political outcomes may be out of its control.

The links between class conflict, democracy, and the state may be more complex. Democracy could function to diffuse class conflict by channelling dissent through the party structure which may be unsympathetic to issues that threaten political stability. Democracy may also serve as a 'screen'; a means of diluting popular dissent by invoking the rules of democracy. In this manner democracy may function as many of its critics would suggest: a minor 'game' which dominates the popular imagination by reason of its innate legitimacy and societal acceptance. This aspect may be reinforced by tendencies towards homogeneity in social organization and structure. For example, the process of simplification inherent in capitalist ideology may result in having individuals appear as objects or commodities. The result is a negation of social complexity and the rise of a one-dimensional (Marcusian) mass society. The legitimacy of class-based democratic politics is seriously questioned. Three implications follow from this argument.

First, the ideological conception of a mass society encourages an acceptance of consensus-based politics. The rights of individuals and groups are considered subservient to the national interest. This serves to reinforce the power of the state by questioning the rights of groups to participate in democracy. Changes promoted by one group are considered undemocratic since they are seen as promoted by a 'small' and 'unrepresentative' segment of society.

Second, as the capitalist state becomes more complex and institutionalized it must account for the diversity of society dismissed through the democratic process. In essence, the state becomes a substitute for society through the provision of social goods to different segments of society. There are a number of advantages for the state in such an arrangement. As the state comes to represent society it also becomes the representative of legitimate policy options That is, the state is legitimized through its own actions and diversity. The threat of democratic interference by the parliamentary wing is also lessened as society tends to a more conservative arrangement of politics. There are disadvantages, however, and these relate to the state's inability to directly determine political outcomes. Social conflict disenfranchised through the 'mass society' may focus on different components of the states' actions. This can involve a simple neighbourhood problem as well as direct class conflict. The latter aspect is particularly important since class conflict may be focused on the immediate sources of antagonisms and not mediated through the democratic process.

Third, as the state comes to reflect the diversity of society its structure may become more complex and bureaucratic. It must take on more and more functions as the free market conception of society gains more ideological power. These functions may be simple democratic and/or class-related. Further, the very number of such functions and their often contradictory nature may lead to a paralysis of action.

These issues can be taken one step further. While simplification is an ongoing process, democracy holds the possibility of a very real class-related threat for the state. It is possible that a democratic party could represent explicitly a particular class interest. This would result in a direct attack on the state through the democratic process. Although there would still remain a division between the state and the parliament in terms of authority and its derivation, an inevitable crisis would occur with the state existing outside the democratic arena and with political parties being unable to affect their power upon the state's structure.

In summary, the relationship between democracy and the state is more complex than supposed both by modern political theorists and even Marxists. In terms of ordinary bourgeois politics, the state is protected against direct attack because of democratic rules of responsibility and authority. Yet democracy and the trend towards social homogenization holds also a threat of crisis, stagnation, and powerlessness for the state. At the heart of the issue is the degree of identification that special-interest groups may have with specific and often contradictory state programmes. In this respect capitalist democracy is clearly different from fascism. In terms of class politics, the state may in fact be extremely vulnerable if the democratic political process becomes polarized over class-related antagonisms. The separability of organizational democracy between responsibility and control may create a direct conflict between the parliamentary wing and the state structures. Furthermore, such political polarization will inevitably focus on those functions of the state that have particular class origins or biases.

The spatial organization of the state

The practice of democracy and the functions of the capitalist state are important determinants of the spatial arrangement of the state. Centralization, indirect representation, and relative autonomy are key determinants of the interrelationship between democracy and the state. To anticipate the argument concerning the spatial structure of the state, in this section it is argued that the local state is potentially the most democratic element in the total state structure. However, in contrast to the Tiebout model's assumption, in many capitalist countries the local state is the least powerful element (responsibility, authority, and fiscal capacity) compared to higher tiers of the state's structure. The reasons for this outcome are to be found in the imperatives of separation between authority, responsibility, and control.

The beginning of democracy for the United States was at the local level. The local state was the embodiment of the local democratic process. Not only were representatives directly elected, they were also held to be directly responsible for the operation and control of the local state's functions. The parliament was typically an assembly of the town's population. Decisions were taken through a direct involvement of voters according to the principles of democracy, rather than the organizational rules typical of latter-day national state structures. There are, of course, inherent conservative tendencies in such a system. In particular, as each locality tended to be independent of others the conception of societal responsibility was also very limited. The early local state was an abstraction from societal complexity and could be hardly appropriate for social organization today.

The collapse of the independence of the local state can be linked to the development of capitalism and the concomitant spatial integration of the national economy. As integration has progressed, power has become centralized in the organization of the state.

Democratic practice has become more like those organizational principles noted earlier than the theoretical notions of democracy. Separation between authority/responsibility and power to control has become a dominant feature of capitalist society. As the states' structure has become more spatially centralized and hierarchical, so too has the spatial pattern of economic activity. These tendencies are one part of the more general process of capitalist development and it is not the intention here to review the massive literature on this topic.

While the complexity and extent of the spatial economy necessitated a shift of organizational responsibility from the local level to the national state arena, the flexibility of the local state has also shrunk. In particular, its democratic character has been circumvented by the vesting of authority and control for the states' functions at the national level. The local state is now dependent upon the higher tiers for ideological legitimacy: The 'national interest' has become dominant over the 'local interest'. Social integration, like economic integration, has tended toward a spatial and cultural homogeneity. In essence the conception of mass society and the atomistic individual is a negation of spatial and social complexity.

The local state may be more democratic than higher tiers of the state structure. The reasons for this could be found in its origins as well as its particular locational character. In many cases the local state is small and less complex simply because it reflects the social structures of very limited area. The avenues to power in such a system are more distinct and accessible. Elected officials are more closely tied to the administration of the local state as well as being identified as both responsible and in conrol of the state. The separability between control and authority/responsibility may not be as distinct in practice or in ideological terms. However, it could be argued that it is controlled from higher tiers of the state because of distinctly democratic character. Two reasons can be advanced to support this notion.

First, as noted above, the local state is dependent upon the higher tiers of the state for fiscal support. Even if decisions were taken democratically at the local level against general state interests, the local level has little fiscal power to enact its own decisions (again in contrast to Tiebout's model). Further, the national state has coercive power to regiment local decisions through its fiscal and moral levers. Not only can power be applied to local bourgeois political or self-interest issues, but also to conditions where a class may 'capture' a local component of the national state. In essence, the local states' democratic character is ultimately subordinate to the undemocratic separation between responsibility and control at the national level.

Second, the nature of the local state's functions reflect its vulnerability to local democratic pressures. In particular, local flexibility in the provision of functions is very limited, both with respect to the extent of provision of any one function and with the choice of the functions themselves. Again the national state is able to circumvent local democratic forces by tying fiscal support to a particular level of public service provision. Local functions are also determined at the national level. Although infrastructure provision is a significant element for the reproduction of the capitalist economy and is provided by the local state, its character is determined exogenously.

While the local state is potentially a vulnerable democratic element in the total state structure, its dependence upon higher tiers limits the impact of democratic forces. It is possible that conflicts could still occur between the local and national state, and these conflicts could be distinctly class-related in character. The local state could be a useful base for political groups to attack the nationstate (much the same way as the democratic process could be used to attack the state in general, as noted above). However, the local state has a number of advantages for the nationstate as well. The local state can be used to disperse politically contentious issues. It may be able to deflect dissent by breaking up organized political groups into very small and spatially isolated sections. At the same time it may be able to maintain control of such functions through its fiscal links to the local state. The national state may also be able to use the local state as a means of manipulating the space economy, not only in terms of the location of infrastructure but also in terms of the spatial redistribution of surplus value. Thus, patterns of uneven development are facilitated through the very organizational structure of the state system.

In summary, the local state is often the battleground between local democratic, as well as class-related politics, and the functional necessities of the spatial economy. The linkage between responsibility and control is more clearly articulated at this level of the state than at the national level. As such, direct representation as opposed to a separation between responsibility and control often characterizes the local state. However, the organizational and ideological constraints imposed upon the local state tend to minimize the impact that democratic politics could have on the local and national capitalist system. The possibility exists that different levels of the state could be in conflict with one another as the democratic nature of the local state allows for political dissidents to gain control. Here are, in fact, the conditions for political self-determination through separation. On the other hand, such a revolt at the local level has to contend with the various coercive tools of the national state as well as the ideological legitimacy of the national democratic structure.

Conclusions

Democracy is a vital element in the continued existence and reproduction of the capitalist state. Democracy could also be a significant revolutionary threat to the state. However, capitalist democracy is typically a tool enabling the continued hegemony of the ruling class. The principal reasons for this are to be found in its organizational principles and the practice of indirect representation. In other words, the separation between responsibility and control creates a situation whereby the state may act as an autonomous and independent body; independent, that is, from direct intervention by the enfranchised corpus of voters. It is clear as well that the state depends on the democratic idealization of society and its implications of authority and popular control. Legitimization of the state's form and functions cannot be divorced from democracy, rather they are interrelated and this remains a central difference between fascism and capitalism. Force, repression, or even the direct participation of the ruling class in the democratic process is not necessary or sufficient to maintain the state's legitimacy. On the other hand, if the state was shown to be antagonistic to popular aspirations for change, reform or restructuring of class relationships, then its relative autonomy could become the focus for popular democratic action. The hierarchical concentration of the state of both form and function is indicative of ongoing processes within capitalism that encourage abstraction and simplification of class and social relationships. The ideology of democracy is one component in this process: basically the rejection of legitimate group interests and social conflicts; the imposition of a one-dimensional view of social interactions and a negation of the role of the individual in voicing dissent. The local state, the original basis for democracy, has become disenfranchised in the development of capitalism. Although its democratic features have been preserved relative to the national state, its own legitimacy is dependent upon the national state. Through the social-political and spatial integration of the national economy power has become centralized and hierarchical. The local state's functions, although important in the reproduction of capital, are predetermined at the centre; it has little ability to reorder priorities let alone internally attack the class nature of the state itself. It is precisely because of the democratic nature of the local state that it is so controlled and dependent. In these terms, it is clear that the Tiebout hypothesis is totally inadequate as an explanation of the reality of the organization and functions of the local state. How democracy is viewed as functioning in capitalism is the central issue for analysing the actions of the local state. Moreover once democracy is viewed in relation to the state, the Tiebout hypothesis can be shown to be both incomplete and overly simplistic.

References and bibliography

Arrow, K. J. (1974). *The Limits of Organization* (W. W. Norton, New York).

Barry, B. (1978). *Sociologists, Economists and Democracy,* rev. edn. (University of Chicago Press, Chicago).

Bobbio, N. (1978a). 'Are there alternatives to representative democracy?', *Telos,* **35,** 17-30.

Bobbio, N. (1978b). 'Why democracy?' *Telos,* **36,** 45-54.

Bowles, S., and Gintis, H. (1978). 'The invisible fist: have capitalism and democracy reached a parting of the ways?', *American Economic Review,* **68,** 358-63.

Cave, N. S. (1978). 'Participation and policy', *Ethics,* **88,** 316-37.

Clark, G. L. (1979). 'Democracy and the capitalist state: towards a critique of the Tiebout hypothesis'. Discussion Paper 79-8, Department of City and Regional Planning, Harvard University, Cambridge.

Clark, G. L. (1980). 'Capitalism and regional disparities', *Annals of the Association of American Geographers,* **70,** 213-29.

Clark, G. L., and Dear, M. (1980). 'The state in capitalism and the capitalist state', in Dear, M., and Scott, A.J. (eds.), *Urbanization and Urban Planning in Capitalist Societies* (Methuen, London).

Dahl, R. A. (1956). *Preface to Democratic Theory* (Chicago University Press, Chicago).

Dahl, R. A. (1966). 'Further reflections on the "Elitist Theory of Democracy"', *American Political Science Review,* **60,** 296-306.

Dear, M. (1981). 'A theory of the local state', in this volume.

Dear, M., and Clark, G. L. (1978). 'The state and geographic process: a critical review', *Environment and Planning A,* **10,** 173-83.

Downs, A. (1957). *An Economic Theory of Democracy* (Harper & Row, New York).

Harsanyi, J. C. (1977). *Rational Behaviour and Bargaining Equilibrium in Games and Social Situations* (Cambridge University Press, Cambridge).

Holloway, J., and Picciotto, S. (1978) (eds.) *State and Capital: A Marxist Debate* (Edward Arnold, London).

Macpherson, C. B. (1973). *Democratic Theory: Essays in Retrieval* (Oxford University Press, Oxford).

Macpherson, C. B. (1977). *The Life and Times of Liberal Democracy* (Oxford University Press, Oxford).

Miliband, R. (1969). *The State in Capitalist Society* (Weidenfeld and Nicolson, London).

Miliband, R. (1977). *Marxism and Politics* (Oxford University Press, Oxford).

Ostrom, V., Tiebout, C. M., and Warren, R. (1961). 'The organization of government in metropolitan areas: a theoretical inquiry', *American Political Science Review,* **55,** 831-42.

Papageorgiou, G. J. (1978). 'Political aspects of social justice and physical planning in an abstract city', *Geographical Analysis,* **10,** 373-85.

Pateman, C. (1970). *Participation and Democratic Theory* (Cambridge University Press, Cambridge).

Pateman, C. (1979). *The Problem of Political Obligation: A Critical Analysis of Liberal Theory* (Wiley, Chichester).

Poulantzas, N. (1973). *Political Power and Social Classes* (New Left Books, London).

Poulantzas, N. (1976). 'The capitalist state: a reply to Miliband and Laclau', *New Left Review,* **95,** 63-83.

Rawls, J. (1971). *A Theory of Justice* (Harvard University Press, Cambridge).

Reich, M., and Edwards, R. (1978). 'Political parties and class conflict in the Unites States', *Socialist Review,* **8,** 37-57.

Scott, A. J., and Roweis, S. (1977). 'Urban planning in theory and practice: a reappraisal', *Environment and Planning A,* **9,** 1097-119.

Tiebout, C. M. (1956). 'A pure theory of local expenditures', *Journal of Political Economy,* **64,** 416-24.

Wright, E.O. (1978). *Class, Crisis and the State* (New Left Books, London).

Political studies from spatial perspectives
Edited by A.D. Burnett and P.J. Taylor
© 1981 John Wiley & Sons Ltd

_7_

Geopolitics in a shrinking world: a political geography of the twenty-first century

Stanley D. Brunn

From the present time forth, in the post-Columbian age, we shall again have to deal with a closed political system, and none the less that it will be one of world-wide scope.

(Sir Halford J. Mackinder, 1904)

An increasing number of political events and decisions that occur in the world every day can be considered to have extraterritorial and global significance. The occurrence of such events and the impress of political decision-making are reflected both in the ways political spaces are organized and reorganized and how individuals behave, interact in, and perceive their own and other spaces. Regional and world maps of political organization, activity, interaction, and influence at any point in time reveal a constant state of dynamism. Hardly a year passes without some boundary- and name-changes as well as new political leaders and locations of military conflict.

While a given map may illustrate a specific pattern, such as parties to a defence treaty or purchasers of military weapons, it is understood that there are underlying spatial and political processes operating to produce what is often depicted as a static pattern and considered a state of equilibrium. Temporal and spatial dynamics represent constants in the global geopolitical structure and in international relations; constants that comprise part of the ever-changing dynamic equilibrium. In a global political arena characterized by instant news coverage of events anywhere, international communications networks, and greater global interest in international events, struggles for political legitimacy and authority by competing groups are anticipated as are new responsibilities for national and world political bodies. As internal and external changes of a geopolitical nature occur within individual countries, regions, and the world, the equilibrating forces that are responsible for some degree of global order themselves are being altered. At issue in this thesis is the identification of a number of futuristic events, forces, and processes and their effect on creating and maintaining dynamic equilibria or disequilibria in the future.

Examinations of the temporal and spatial changes in the political order of an individual country, or the world for that matter, are familiar topics of political geography inquiry (Kasperson and Minghi, 1969). Geographers have investigated international boundary changes, expanding and retreating frontiers, the evolution of nation-states and colonial empires, and the successes and failures of federations and alliances. Research for the most part on change has examined a previous time in a country's or region's development or has explained the present by looking backwards, i.e., back-casting. What has been lacking is a forward-looking description and analysis of what patterns and processes might occur and integrating these components into futuristic models or scenarios. It is the purpose of this paper to focus on a promising and profitable area of scholarly inquiry, i.e. the interfaces between political geography and future studies. The discussion below is divided into three parts. First, a framework for studying the geography of the future and especially political geography is explored. Precedence exists within geography for conducting such research, especially in human geography (Hall, 1963; Bird, 1969; Berry, 1970; Chisholm et al., 1970; Chojnicki, 1970; Curry, 1970; Garrison, 1970, 1972; Gerasimov, 1970; Wise, 1970; Zelinsky, 1970; Ryan, 1971; Abler et al., 1972, 1975; Cook, 1972; Bourne et al., 1974; Johnson, 1974; Haggett, 1975; Henderson and Voiland, 1975; Hurst, 1977; Klee, 1975; Brunn, 1976; Austin and Gunter, 1977; Dutt and Costa, 1977; Dury, 1977; Janiskee, 1977, 1978; Phillips and Brunn, 1978; Austin, 1979; Brunn and Wheeler, 1980). Second, a review of pertinent literature that focuses on geopolitical futures is presented; this review illustrates the diversity of scholarly topics that are commanding attention. Third, a number of geopolitical scenarios likely to be characteristic of the late twentieth and early twenty-first centuries are developed. The topics and problems identified merit the attention and discussion of political geographers interested in conducting futuristic political geography research and for including such materials in the classroom (Padbury and Wilkins, 1972; *Symposium...*, 1975; Kauffman, 1976a, 1976b; McHale, 1976; Cornish, 1977; Ferkiss, 1977; Linstone, 1977; World

Future Society, 1978; Roysdon and Misticelli, 1978; Fowles, 1978; Kierstead *et al.,* 1979). Many useful references for budding and initiated futurists are found in issues of *The Futurist, Futures, Futuribles, Alternative Futures, 2000 avenir* and the Worldwatch papers published by the Worldwatch Institute, Washington, DC.

Political geography and the future

As geographers and other social scientists are beginning to conduct more future-oriented scholarly research, several caveats seem worthy of comment regarding the serious study of geopolitical and political futures. First, the forecasting of political geographic patterns, and even projecting the future state of an ultimate geopolitical equilibrium, as well as specific processes and events does not merely entail an extrapolation of the present. There are doubtless many events and processes of future geographies and histories occurring now, as there will be in subsequent decades, that will be unanticipated and unexpected, both in individual countries and the world. However, the unexpected is not totally unpredictable given careful thought and an atmosphere where realistic and alternative futures are proposed, scrutinized, and appreciated. The US defeat in Vietnam, the openness of post-Mao China, the growing political significance of Islamic countries, the Soviet invasion of Afghanistan, the political clout of OPEC, and the proliferation of nuclear weapons seem likely to represent turning points in global history for the 1980s and beyond. Second, the future will call for an understanding of long-range geographical, economic, social, political, and technological forecasts. Transdisciplinary concepts, paradigms, and models will be sought. Third, it is important to become familiar with and utilize futuristic methods of inquiry for research and teaching (Traub, 1979). The Delphi approach, cross-impact matrices, linkage trees, simulations, and scenarios are seen as possibilities. Fourth, it is probably more important in writing and instructing about the future that we raise legitimate questions rather than attempt to provide answers to them. That is, to 'think the unthinkable' may become a more important component of futuristic geographic inquiry than presenting orderly, logical, and persuasive arguments for specific regional or global futures or the state of world order and disorder. The specific forecasting of a single event may be incorrect at some point (1984 or 2001) but insightful views of broad patterns and processes will lend themselves to productive inquiry.

At this time in human history there is a need to investigate possible and potential future worlds and to consider alternative solutions to global economic, social, and political problems and orders. In looking at future worlds it is important to focus on the likelihood of certain specific events, patterns, and processes occurring whether they relate to transnational corporations, international terrorism, Third World politics, ocean law, or social revolutions. In our analyses of forecasting regional and global political futures, some events and processes will occur while others will not. Likewise some futuristic equilibrating forces can be identified; an understanding of such forces is helpful in studying the newly created imbalances that will exist.

In all likelihood political worlds and global geopolitical order in the twenty-first century will bear some resemblance to the present. Probably many of the major current political issues will continue well beyond AD 2000 such as the need to avoid complete annihilation, the protection of universal human rights, and equitable representation in international bodies. The issue of scale, that is, global geopolitics, as it affects an awareness of solutions to global political problems may be the most important issue to command the attention of the world community of nations and regions in the next century. To the extent that it is recognized and understood will also possibly affect the degree of world order. It is important in studying the present geopolitical worlds and considering the future to identify and seek to interpret possible spatial and political patterns and processes. As we critically assess futures we are also improving the art and science of geographical prediction and forecasting, themes largely ignored in political geography research to date, and most other areas of human geography save economic geography. Also as we improve forecasting techniques and methods we will contribute respect to scholarly inquiry into futures in government policy, basic research, and in the classroom.

The state of research on geopolitical futures

Studying political geographies of the future, while not a major thread in the discipline's heritage, is not completely without precedence. We can recall the significance of and controversy generated by Mackinder's 1904 address on 'The geographical pivot of history' before the Royal Geographical Society in London (Mackinder, 1904). Some of the events and processes that influence Mackinder's thought have been examined by Blouet (1973, 1976); also the content of some essays in *Compass of the World* and

New Compass of the World edited by Weigert *et al.* (1947, 1949) outline the geopolitical significance of frontiers and boundary changes in post-world-war Europe and Asia, circumpolar areas, and strategic areas *vis-à-vis* an expanding air transport system. Spykman's (1944) *The Geography of Peace* also conveys in map and textual form ideas about political and military security.

After nearly two decades of limited political geography research focusing on the future, futuristic research began to enter our professional journals and texts during the 1970s. The paucity of studies previously may be attributed to some geographers thinking such research was unscholarly or impossible, or that projects and futuristic thinking would be ammunition for professional ridicule and scorn. Recent works include mine on some features of the political geography of the United States at 2000 and a political reorganization of the country to reflect a highly mobile urban-oriented society (Brunn, 1970, 1972, 1973, 1974, 1975, 1977). The political reorganization theme was also addressed by G. Etzel Pearcy, formerly The Geographer, Department of State (Pearcy, 1973). Additional studies containing a futuristic theme were Burghardt's (1971) study on Quebec's role in Canada's future, Honey's (1976) statement on internal boundary changes in England, Breton's (1976) discussion on the changing political map of South Africa, Senfleben's (1976) article on conflicting sovereignty claims in the South China Sea, Johnston and Hunt's (1977) brief statement on inequity problems in the EEC's Council of Ministers, Sanguin's (1977) discussion on the frontiers of air and outer space, and Smil's (1977) use of the Delphi approach to examine China's future.

Political geographers are not alone among social scientists in their research on the interfaces between politics and the future. Political scientists, sociologists, and economists are beginning to conduct studies on specific regions or countries and are using specific futuristic techniques to examine particular processes (Molnar, 1971; Mushkat, 1973; Castañeda, 1974; Sewell, 1974; Gilpin, 1975; Cox, 1976; Frisch, 1976; Hy, 1976; Lall, 1976; Solem, 1976; Bozeman, 1977; Deutsch, 1977; Groom, 1977; Dror, 1978; Interfutures, 1979). Among those studies that geographers would find of interest are the following: those that focus on growth and economic development issues in Third World countries and elsewhere (Tugwell, 1971; Seynes, 1972; Castañeda, 1974), political disorder and crises (Dror, 1974; Weil, 1974; Weiss, 1975; Deutsch, 1976; Gray, 1976; Bell, 1977; Hamilton, 1977; McIntyre, 1979; Smernoff, 1979), defence and disarmament (Culver, 1976; Curnow *et al.*, 1976, Hansen, 1978), mini-states, and issues of governance (Shriner, 1973; Toffler, 1975a, 1975b; Baker, 1976; Wood *et al.*,

1978). Individual countries have also been examined (Kahn, 1970; Kahn *et al.,* 1979; Wilson, 1972; Horvik, 1973; Hoadley, 1975; Mishan, 1975; Kennet, 1976; Kim and Halpern, 1977; Koslow, 1977; Cleron, 1978; Shaw and Mouton, 1978; Syed Kechik Foundation, 1978), regions including Latin America and North America (Wolfgang, 1973; van Dam 1978; Feldman, 1979), and the Pacific Ocean (Macrae, 1975). Opinion surveys conducted suggest additional research possibilities by geographers and others investigating the optimism and pessimism of the public *vis-à-vis* specific events and problems (Remy and Nathan, 1974; Avison and Nettler, 1976).

   While political geography of the future as a research frontier is only beginning to become visible in the discipline, there have been few attempts to construct futuristic maps of a country or a part of the world (Christy and Herfindahl, 1968; Brunn, 1972, 1974, 1975; Capone and Ryan, 1973; Djilas, 1974; Knight, 1975; McHale and McHale, 1976b; de Blij and Glassner, 1980). The reluctance on the part of any student of political geography to delineate futuristic processes and patterns within a country or continent is somewhat expected since professional peers may question the credibility and audacity of the individual geographer. The public, on the other hand, may perceive these futuristic maps as eventual realities. Nevertheless, geographers and others conducting futuristic research need to be encouraged to project political patterns and processes on maps, both to stimulate discussion and debate among colleagues and students, not to mention the public, and to lend support to further research on realistic futures.

Geopolitical scenarios on the twenty-first century

An examination and understanding of future political geographies in part rest on completed studies treating political behaviour, international relations, social and economic development, and those interpreting the short- and long-term significance of contemporary events and processes. There is no shortage of diversity of opinion and interpretation about the state of current and future political worlds. This diversity applies whether one is treating the world, a particular region, or a given country (Gordon, 1965; Jungk and Galtung, 1969; McHale, 1969; McHale and McHale, 1976a; Meadows *et al.,* 1972; *Seventeen Prospective Essays,* 1972; Toffler, 1972; Kothari, 1974; Mesarovic and Pestel, 1974; Rose, 1975; Falk, 1975; Harman, 1976; Rogers, 1976; Stavrianos, 1976; Theobold, 1976; Tinbergen, 1976; N. Brown, 1977; Brown, 1978; Freeman and

Jahoda, 1978; Kahn *et al.*, 1976, 1979; Kahn and Pepper, 1979; Ways, 1979). The individual or team assessing political geographies of the future must possess some degree of imagination, creativity, flexibility of thought, as well as exercise critical judgement and insight into the presents and futures of economic and social worlds. In the preparation and development of this paper, I have relied on the writings and concepts of a number of social scientists and social critics, many referenced above. In some cases there was substantial agreement on geopolitical futures; in others the views were widely divergent. No single study specifically has treated significant characteristics, problem areas, and political processes of the world next century.

Ten major scenarios of the global political geography of the twenty-first century are advanced and examined below. They are: (1) the influences of emerging regional powers, (2) the demands of a new international political order, (3) the destinies of mini-states in a macropower world, (4) the exploitation and sovereignty of oceans and outer space, (5) the reorganization of political spaces, (6) the renaissance of regionalism, (7) transnational corporations as the new corporate states or neo-imperialists, (8) adjusting to the realities of a four-dimensional world (time-space convergence), (9) government and governments redefined, and (10) apocalypse: Gardens of Eden or Armageddons. The scenarios described and themes discussed under these ten headings are not meant to be mutually exclusive. Rather the ideas and topics are meant to provide a framework for further discussion and research.

The influences of emerging regional powers

The formal if not symbolic end of European colonialism and US and Soviet expansionism in the developing world during the past two decades left a vacuum into which selected rich and powerful Third World countries have begun to exercise a strong influence over the politics and economies of their region. Wars of liberation or independence from the British, French, Dutch, Spanish, and Portuguese led to the termination of colonialism and a new political order in which prominent Latin American, African, and Asian countries within these continents have begun to exercise dominance rather than that by an outside foreign power. The emerging regional powers have several underlying similarities: large land areas, large populations and GNPs, higher rates of literacy that their neighbours, diverse and prosperous economies (agriculture, minerals, industries, etc.) for the most part, and larger and better-equipped armed forces than their neighbours. Brazil in South

America, Mexico in Central America, Venezuela in the Caribbean, Nigeria in West Africa, South Africa in southern Africa, Egypt in North Africa, Saudi Arabia and Iran in the Middle East, India in South Asia, and Indonesia in Southeast Asia are examples of emerging regional powers. Not infrequently there are rivalries among countries striving for political, military, and economic hegemony; Libya and Egypt in North Africa, Pakistan and India in South Asia, Iran and Saudi Arabia in the Persian or Arabian Gulf, and Brazil and Argentina in South America are examples. Many emerging regional powers occupy strategic military and economic areas that are important to major superpowers, hence the high levels of military and economic assistance accorded these Third World countries. The geopolitical significance of these powers in the developing world will become apparent in global international relations and conflicts and in internal political, military, and economic affairs in Latin America, Africa, and Asia. These powers have the resources, technology, and diplomacy to steer their region's economy and politics to their liking via extending development loans and credit to their friends for specific projects, supporting guerilla movements or terrorist activities in rivalling nations, and threatening smaller and weaker neighbours with economic or military blackmail. 'As Brazil goes, so goes the rest of Latin America', is almost an unspoken policy among European and North American powers. Within South America, the Brazilianization of the continent is recognized by wary neighbours who see Amazon development and settlement schemes, the perimeter road network, and the acquisition of nuclear technology as threats to their own internal economy and security. Similar political dominance is recognized by neighbours of Nigeria, Iran, and Indonesia among others. The polycentric geopolitical worlds of the next century will doubtless see the emerging regional powers as significant (possibly more so) in global politics as the US, USSR, China, Japan, France, and the United Kingdom.

The demands of a new international political order

A term that will probably achieve equal significance in global politics of the twenty-first century, as the new economic order (NEO) currently holds, is one that addresses the political priorities of the developing world. The Third, Fourth, and Fifth Worlds, while not homogeneous in culture history, economic assets, political ideologies, or military capabilities, are beginning to demand a greater stake in global decision-making and in their own destinies. Members included within the Group of 77 (now more than 120 developing nations) who address world issues in the United Nations General Assembly, United Nations-sponsored conferences relating to the Law of the Sea, Trade and Development, Food, etc. and in the North-South dialogue are pressing for a recognition of their problems by the global community, and expecially by the traditional global powers. If much of the nineteenth century was dominated by European colonial powers and the twentieth century by the US and USSR, the next century may see the Third World countries dominating the global political arena. The priorities of the developing countries include satisfying basic human needs, coping with rising debts and higher energy costs, as well as demanding respect for self-determination. A major objective of the NEO is to support changes in the economic policies of developed countries that would facilitate their entry into the global economies. Governments in the developing world, which have three-quarters of the world's population but less than one-third of the world's income, are gradually realizing that much of the energy supplies, industrial raw materials, and cash crops they produce are consumed in the rich worlds. That is, the rich worlds depend on the poor worlds for their affluence and continued economic satisfaction and growth. The transfer of economic power into political power among the LDCs is best exemplified by the success of the 14-member OPEC cartel; price hikes and embargoes influence global politics and monetary systems. Similar cartels have been proposed by the major producers of fibres, luxury foods, and strategic industrial minerals in the developing world. The new political order of next century will represent conflicting ideologies and philosophies but will be in agreement on policies designed to improve their political and economic standing as well as their own human condition. In spite of general agreement there may be differences in outlook and policy among the few resource-rich and the many resource-poor. Members of the new political order (NPO) will become more politically astute and aware of their role in international politics; these influences are likely to be felt by garnering support for their stances and votes in the United Nations and by identifying basic human needs as a major funding priority over stockpiling military weapons. The NPO may also be the catalyst to influence either the proliferation or the curtailment of nuclear weapons. Members of the NPO may also favour the following: economic sanctions against countries in the developed world not in support of their political views, less stringent international migration laws, a reorganized world body to give the LDCs greater influence, proposals for a global redistribution of income (reduce the widening rich-poor gaps), and armed conflict against countries insensitive to their economic problems and their violations of self-government and of human rights. Whether the NPO will function as a tightly knit organization or a collection of loosely coordinated leagues and alliances in the future is less significant than the recognition that its influences will be felt increasingly world-wide.

The destinies of mini-states in a macropower world

Serious questions arise when examining the economic and political futures of totally or partially autonomous political units that are small in area and population or large in area but small in population. There are nearly four score mini-states, most in the West Indies, Pacific Ocean, and Africa; a few also exist in Europe (Vatican City, Andorra, and San Marino) and Asia (Sikkim, Bhutan, Singapore, and Brunei). In a political world carved up for the most part since 1500 by competitive expansionist economies and governments, the viability of mini-states remains as one of the dominating legacies of that period in human history. Mini-states run the gamut from those that owed their existence to transoceanic and circum-continental refuelling stops and plantation estates (St Helena, Mauritius, Fiji, and Barbados), strategic locations (Bahrein, Malta, Singapore, and Macao) or valuable mineral economies (Trinidad, Kuwait, New Caledonia, and Nauru). The sprinkling of handkerchief-size states in West Africa, the Arabian peninsula, the island states in the West Indies and Pacific Ocean, and coastal and insular mini-states in Asia and Latin America remain as vestiges of colonial systems whose formal organization no longer exists. The need for retaining many of these postage-stamp-sized possessions ceased with new means of communications and transportation, new strategic weapons, and alternative food and mineral sources. In many cases the small and distant island and mainland possessions became economic and political deadweights, hence the reason some European countries supported self-government. While formal political independence is achieved, economic dependence often remains to the same extent as prior to internal self-government. The futures of mini-states and mini-possessions vary. Some may be absorbed (peacefully or via aggression) by nationalist-hungry neighbours who have legal claims to said territories; Belize by Guatemala, Timor by Indonesia, the Falkland Islands by Argentina, and Macao and Hong Kong by China are cases in point. Others may retain their political and economic autonomy, as have Leichtenstein, Andorra, and San Marino, by orienting their economies to tourism (Jamaica, Bermuda, and French Polynesia), satellite-tracking (Fiji), oceanographic research (Malta), and defence systems of major superpowers (Diego Garcia in the Indian Ocean and Samoa in the Pacific). Still other mini-states may retain some economic and political viability by merging with other mini-states into loose economic and political federations. It bears mention that to date internal squabbles and rivalries among members of the now defunct West Indian, Malaysia, East Africa, and Rhodesian Federations contributed to their demise. Two future issues that will need addressing regarding mini-states in the twenty-first century are:

(a) their representation and voting weight (one country-one vote or a vote proportional to their total population) in inter-national assemblies; and
(b) their ability to alienate and embarrass major powers and receive world attention.

During the past two decades internal political events within Cuba, Anguilla, Timor, Gibraltar, and South Yemen have commanded the attention of one or more major powers.

The exploitation and sovereignty of oceans and outer space

The demand for new supplies of industrial raw materials, energy supplies, and foods by developed and developing nations has stimulated increased activity and interest in the world's oceans and continental shelves. Major fishing nations are searching for potentially valuable grounds in areas considered of little importance currently as well as perfecting technologies to catch fish at greater depths. Nations with sophisticated ocean-mining technologies are intensifying their search for minerals on continental shelves, in circumpolar areas, and in the high seas. The potential wealth of oceans is reflected in their present political significance. Disputes over ocean claims have been raised in the Indian Ocean, Antarctic waters, Barents Sea, Mediterranean Sea, and South China Sea in the 1970s. Nations with short and long coastlines have extended economic zones up to 200 miles, or more in some cases, both to stake claims to actual or potential valuable resources and to halt the unwelcome intrusion of other greedy nations. During the past decade ocean spaces have begun to be delimited much like continents were in previous centuries. Nations unilaterally established limits, sometimes at great variance with those of their neighbours. The politics of the world's oceans and seas, as discussed in Law of the Sea conferences and elsewhere, involve questions that will not be resolved quickly. These include whether the world's oceans are 'a part of the common heritage of all mankind' like outer space or whether they can be divided and subdivided by states with coastlines. Do land-locked and shelf-locked countries have any rights to mining or fishing the world's oceans and receiving monetary benefits from them? Is it realistic and legal to delimit a 200-mile economic zone around uninhabited islands in the Pacific Ocean or around floating cities (possibly some in the future) or a human-made island that serves as a satellite-tracking station or oil-drilling platform? Who decides what nations shall use international straits and what materials (foods, nuclear materials, petroleum, etc.) shall be transported through them? Who should and can insure that the oceans' environments are not destroyed or upset ecologically by careless mining technologies, overfishing, industrial and oil tanker pollution, and the clandestine burial of toxic substances and nuclear wastes? A related ticklish international issue is whether the Antarctic treaty, due for expiration in 1991, will be renewed or the continent will become a vast frontier for nationalistic land- and mineral-grabbing. Outer space frontiers will become politically significant both from a security-military standpoint and the eventual mining of asteroids and planetary surfaces. Although treaties exist that call for the peaceful exploration of outer space, there is no treaty at present to prevent the secret launching of killer satellites and the placing of deadly weapons on other planets or their moons. Many of the questions regarding ownership, use, protection, and regulation of oceans and outer space in the future were raised in previous centuries about land areas.

The reorganization of political spaces

The world's political map that displays the number and actual delimitation of independent, quasi-independent, and dependent states and territories changes from century to century. Changes in name, size, and boundaries result from the settlement of national and regional conflicts, the emergence of new ideologies, and the dissolution or establishments of cultural and economic ties with other political units. There is no more likelihood the world's political maps at 2000, 2030, or 2080 will be like that for 1980 than the present is like that for 1950 or 1920. Above we have already identified some of the major forces that will operate, and events that may occur, next century to change the present political map. These include the dominating influences of emerging regional powers in the developing world, the demise of some mini-states, and the partitioning of the world's oceans. Other changes that will result in the reorganization of the world's political spaces stem from nationalistic groups seeking greater autonomy, some nations forming loose or tightly-knit alliances and federations, and urban-oriented administrative structures to replace outdated agrarian political and economic systems. The impact of integrated telecommunications, satellite, and computer systems, all discussed below in greater detail, will profoundly affect the form, scale, and frequency of regional and global transactions. The growing recognition among large and small, strong and weak governments, that the world community is urbanized and integrated via instant communications may usher in political organizations of space based on humane justice, greater economic and political integration, and humane administrative efficiency. Under such proposals cities and metropolitan areas will achieve greater significance, even in traditionally agrarian societies, and international boundaries that were once barriers to economic and social intercourse will become more functional than formal.

The renaissance of regionalism

A persistent thread in international politics during the last half of the twentieth century, both in developing and developed countries, is the growing importance of regionalism. Regional interests and concerns are being raised at the same time as there are efforts to centralize and consolidate decision-making. Within a number of countries, cultures and groups unintentionally or deliberately excluded from the existing government's economic and social policies are seeking greater political representation (or autonomy) and territorial control over their own destinies. While the bonds are often strongly cultural and nationalistic, they are also regional. Examples where regionalism is emerging or had been recognized as a contemporary political issue include Canada (Native Americans in the Northwest Territories and French-speaking Quebec), France (Brittany), United Kingdom (Scotland and Wales), Spain (Basque provinces), and Australia (Western Australia). Within the United States there is some support for greater regional autonomy (even statehood) in the Upper Great Lakes, northern California, and Puerto Rico. Regionalism translated into nationalism has been important in developing countries including West and East Pakistan (now Bangladesh), India (the unsettled Kashmir issue), Nigeria (Biafra, non-existent), and Spanish Sahara (also non-existent); the issue remains important in Ethiopia (Eritrea and Ogaden provinces) and Iran (Kurdish areas). A prime example of a nation of people without formal political autonomy is the Palestinians. Support for greater political autonomy may assume non-violent postures (Quebec, Scotland, etc.) or violent terrorist activities (Spain and elsewhere). In the future regionalism may transcend international boundaries providing there is agreement on the religious or political ideologies. Examples may be Islamic-oriented governments in North Africa and the Middle East, pan-African solidarity movements among West and East African governments, and a federation of associated states in mainland Southeast Asia. Partly in response to the growing recognition of regional cultures and economic disparities, governments are implementing internal administrative reorganizations to reflect regional concerns. Canada, US, France, UK, Nigeria, Brazil, China, and the USSR are examples where the administrative structures have been reorganized.

Transnational corporations as the new corporate states or neo-imperialists

The future political order of the next century will have to consider the impact and influence of transnational or multinational corporations. These giant and wealthy American, Japanese, French, British, and West German conglomerates with annual sales exceeding that of many individual European and Latin American countries, or the combined GNPs of several dozen African countries, are continental and global political forces that need to be reckoned with before 2000 as well as beyond. Their vast land and industrial holdings and global networks of affiliates and subsidiaries, which almost make the future world a 'company town', are more extensive than the political and economic strength of most nation-states. The political forces shaping the planetary human destinies of the next century may be the richest, most powerful, and most influential transnational corporations. While these conglomerates promote global interdependence by their ease in transferring credit, capital, and personnel anywhere, and by their ease in introducing new technologies and products, they also have a seamy side. Their not infrequent single devotion to profit, their disregard for inhumane technologies and the values and social well-being of the host population, their lack of a conservation ethic, their elusive legal structure and subtle, and sometimes blatant political bribery, are all perceived as shortcomings. The modern transnational corporation is considered by its harshest critics as perpetuating similar external economies and the kinds of paternalism reminiscent of colonial powers. These same critics see the exploitative, corrupt, and illegal practices of some corporations illustrative of a twenty-first century kind of imperialism where the corporation headquartered in New York City, Paris, London, Tokyo, or Brussels exerts a greater influence on global economic development priorities, accepted international codes of conduct, voting in international conferences, and short-range military postures than many 'independent' nation-states in the developed and developing worlds. The subtle and intricate nature of these corporations' economic and political networks, plus the allegiances individuals are attaching to them rather than nation-states or cultures, can promote much good and bad in future international relations.

Adjusting to the realities of a four-dimensional world (time-space convergence)

The introduction of aircraft, orbiting satellites, ICBM systems, and instant global contact via telephone and television has altered our perception and organization of space. The two-dimensional local and continental worlds of the past have been replaced by the three-dimensional world where outer space and ocean depths are significant in global political and military actions. The juxtaposing or converging of time and space, that is, the vast reductions in the amount of time required to communicate or be transported short and long distances, is contributing to a 'world of points', and even one point, in which all locations and distances between them are relative. Time-space convergence in an absolute sense defines places that are equally easy to communicate with, regardless of distance between the sender and receiver. In such a context the significance of international land and ocean boundaries, that were actual or perceived as barriers, is reduced. Furthermore, in a 'world without borders' political and cultural isolation, whether voluntary or involuntary, becomes outdated. No location can remain 'closed' from ever-expanding international airline networks, television cameras, and international ballistic missile systems. Superpowers, mini-states, inaccessible continental interiors, democratic and totalitarian states are exposed to seeing-eye resource and military satellites, orbiting weapons, powerful radio transmitters, communications' pirates and journalists who can report almost anything from anywhere at any time. An awareness of the third- and fourth-dimensional worlds contributes to instant news coverage and analysis of both good and bad events, information overload, little news filtering, and ad hocracy forms of decision-making. For some individuals and governments the adjustments bring future shock, that is, too much change in too short a time, or a premature arrival of the future. In a political sense the political spaces and forms of government established at a time of little cultural interaction and political cooperation, as well as slow land transportation and little formal communication, become unwieldy with the diffusion of high-speed technologies. On a balance sheet there will be problems that accompany instant, rapid, and inexpensive contact with close and distant locations in the twenty-first century. Advantages, however, exist as well. These include a recognition that most pressing human problems (food, population growth, housing, employment, and environmental deterioration) are not geographically unique; rather they have global dimensions. The world's governments also need to fashion agreements on those pressing issues facing all humankind, whether halting the production and spread of nuclear weapons, devoting more resources to meeting basic human needs, or supporting the demilitarization of ocean floors, space colonies, and planets. United Nations conferences in New York City, Geneva, and other world cities including Nairobi, Singapore, and Buenos Aires represent examples of the 'world city' concept, where representatives from more than 150 countries meet at the same time and in the same room to discuss and debate global concerns that affect traditional friends and foes. Many a nation's international and internal political and economic relations, which have been structured by pre-twentieth-century transportation and communications systems, will face a severe test as they confront the realities of rapidly shrinking global communities. Eighteenth-century time-zones, as one example, will have to be scrapped in the twenty-first century (if not before) and be replaced by fewer (or only one) zones to accommodate rapid transportation and communication contact among global neighbours. Smooth and humane transitions to three- and four-dimensional worlds are seldom achieved easily as remnants of harsh totalitarian governments and insulated pre-industrial economies exist. The choices are whether global interdependence and understanding can and will replace isolation and independence.

Government and governments redefined

The definitions, structures, and responsibilities of governments on local and international levels at any point in time depend on historical antecedents, countervailing powers and influences, and the government's ability and willingness to adjust to contemporary and future worlds. In a world being characterized by instant global communications, a growing recognition of planetary human priorities, social inequities, and new centres of global and regional power, the erosion of land boundaries and the nation-state, and the acceptance of more centralized planning schemes, we find the ways governments are structured and the rights of citizens themselves are being redefined. Among the pressing issues facing traditionally and newly defined democracies are how to weigh and interpret public opinion in a more complex technology-oriented society as well as how to define freedom, privacy, individualism, responsibility, and the public good. It is possible in some democracies that individual civil liberties will be replaced by a greater concern for group rights. Special-interest groups petitioning for greater legal and economic rights and protection, whether they be minorities, women, the elderly, or disabled, are cases in point. Will or can the advances anticipated in telecommunications, information collecting and processing, and geographical surveillance, as well as the ease in manipulating public opinion, lead to a technocratic society in which complex machines and inhumane computerized games, not humans, decide where to allocate financial and human resources, where the individual must live and work to satisfy a redefined larger public good, and how to resolve ticklish and controversial political crises at home and abroad? Will Alvin Toffler's concept of anticipatory democracy become a trademark of governments having heterogeneous societies that are bombarded by high-speed change? In the case of traditionally and voluntarily closed societies, the questions raised will be somewhat different, viz., how long will it be possible to insulate a citizenry from the global airwaves and pictures which transcend their borders? Will strong centralized and dictatorial governments, whether in the Second, Third, Fourth, or Fifth Worlds, be able to adjust without severe social internal conflicts and strains into new political worlds where the politically disenfranchised minorities, women, youth, poor, and emerging middle classes will demand greater rights, representation, and protection? What new ideologies might emerge in the twenty-first century and what will be their political impacts on the developed and developing worlds? Nationalism in some areas might be replaced by regionalism as the important vehicle for political solidarity and organization. Examples in the next century might include Pan-African ideologies that cross national boundaries, secular Islamic movements in North Africa and the Middle East, a North Atlantic Community, and a loose North American federation. Loose and tight Sino-US, Sino-Third World, US-Latin America, Europe-Africa, and USSR-Third World pacts are also possible. A critical question is the faces which

Soviet and Chinese Marxism, West European democracies, and the democratic, socialist, and totalitarian governments in the Third World will assume. Perhaps some new appealing ideologies will emerge that will facilitate the opening of closed societies. New citizen controls may also be imposed on those traditionally open societies. Governments may assume new forms and functions as new special-interest groups, new policy issues, and the realities of global inter-dependence become integrated into the decision-making machinery. Regional and international policy bodies will be confronted with some new problems including the implementation of equitable voting formulas in international bodies, the assessment of international income taxes for global development, the formation of food, energy, and information banks, the guaranteed protection of universal human rights, the monitoring of environmental quality, and the implementation of ways to prevent international terrorism and the proliferation of nuclear weapons.

Apocalypse: gardens of Eden or Armageddons

A final topic that merits treatment in a global context is the state of conflict and global equilibrium in the twenty-first century. Those same issues have been raised by seers and scholars each century with some believing enduring peace is at hand and others predicting increased armed conflict and global imbalances. Even though 'end of the world' queries have been raised previously, the fact that global inter-dependency and shrinking worlds are recognized by more governments and citizens as contemporary realities helps legitimize concern about future global security. Mackinder (1942), in his postscript to an examination of the changing political geographies, recognized that advances in communication were changing the definitions of 'friends and neighbours' in a global context. At issue is whether a world community, however defined, that is cognizant of the fragility of international human relations and the capacity for complete annihilation by a growing number of nations, is more likely to usher in a more balanced world where conflict resolution exists or whether prolonged and increased hostility and aggression will exist. On the one hand the potentials for some ultimate homeostatis exist. Large weapons caches by the major superpowers seem to serve as deterrents to conflict. Also agreements aimed at reducing the stockpiling of arms and limiting the sale and use of nuclear and biological weapons raise the hope that equilibriating forces may prevent global holocausts. The reluctance of the major powers to engage directly in military conflicts (more 'wars' of words), their willingness to fight surrogate wars rather than become directly involved, and the use of the United Nations as a platform to air differences also lend credence to the view that world wars are becoming passé and a future state of dynamic equilibrium is predictable. In regard to the issue of war itself, questions are even raised at a global scale about wars themselves, that is, why have wars and what is a nation fighting for? To counter that optimism, there are the harsh realities that suggest the world's future state may experience more disequilibria than currently. Military budgets are increasing for almost all nations (large and small, powerful and weak), more nuclear weapons are being manufactured and stockpiled, nuclear technology is being made easily available, and new generations of more sophisticated weapons (lasers, heat sensor weapons, etc.) are being developed for deployment from ocean floors and outer space. The rise in international terrorism is another reality that powerful and weak governments are having to confront. These realities suggest that destructive regional and global conflict, even complete annihilation, are more than a remote possibility. If such are indeed the realities the imbalances would upset any attempt to fashion equilibrating forces or an ultimate equilibrium where conflicts would be resolved. Not all wars or conflict in the future will necessarily involve military conflict, although such are real possibilities in very large countries (USSR for example) where large ethnic minorities at their periphery are under-represented in national decision-making. The politics of food, energy, and fresh water — that is, basic necessities — are destined to be more important in maintaining global stability and survival in the future than aggressive countries grabbing pieces of real estate or strategic land sites for military superiority. Covet wars might break out, from the poor countries desiring some of what the rich have. Terrorists and guerrilla groups within countries may demand food and energy supplies in the future more than military arms, comrades, or money. Conflicts may emerge over the global dissemination of foreign technologies and values in traditionally oriented societies. Technology wars may also be waged on a small scale using the weather or unmanned weapons. Struggles for liberation against oppressive totalitarian regimes, dynasties, and dictators-for-life will possibly continue for several more decades until politically disenfranchised groups have some representation in national and local governments. Beyond planet earth, computer, space, and 'star' wars may occur between the earth's superpowers over favoured sites for orbiting space colonies or colonies on the moon and elsewhere. The same reasons that inhumane wars occurred in the past, among them greed, superpatriotism, and machismo, will be why extraterrestrial wars will exist probably in some forms in the future. While it is difficult to eliminate tensions, conflict, and military skirmishes completely in any region at any point in time, the major question that needs to be answered is whether the policies and senses of the world's governments will be used to promote more peaceful or destructive worlds. The degree to which equilibrating forces succeed over those that increase planetary imbalances will determine whether conflict resolution and some ultimate homeostatis will characterize the twenty-first century.

Summary

This paper has investigated a number of geopolitical scenarios likely to be characteristic of the global political order in the twenty-first century. Selected events, problems, and processes have been identified with the developed and developing worlds. Predicting and forecasting the likelihood of specific political events, not to mention processes and problems, is always fraught with some degree of danger because of the element of uncertainty that operates in defining equilibria and disequilibria. In spite of these hurdles there is a need for political geographers to utilize their training and insights into contemporary worlds and orders and to suggest possible future geopolitical worlds. The successes we reap in predicting components of those worlds will aid in understanding the significance of present and short-term processes as well as those likely to occur in the distant future. The extent to which global interdependence, time-space convergence, transnational corporations, regionalism, and Third World politics are understood within a geopolitical context will determine whether equilibrating forces or imbalances will become the trademarks of the twenty-first century.

References and bibliography

Abler, R. *et al.* (1972). *Spatial Organization: The Geographer's View of the World* (Prentice-Hall, Englewood Cliffs, NJ).
Abler, R. *et al.* (1975). *Human Geography in a Shrinking World* (Duxbury, North Scituate, Mass).
Austin, C. M. (1979). 'Future-oriented geography: an exciting prospect', *Journal of Geography,* **78,** 142-6.
Austin, C. M. and Gunter, J. D. (1977). 'Incorporating a futures perspective in geographic education', *Bulletin of the Illinois Geographical Society,* **19,** 61-74.

Avison, W. R. and Nettler, G. (1976). 'World views and crystal balls', *Futures*, **8**, 11-21.

Baker, D. (1976). 'The states experiment with anticipatory democracy', *Futurist*, **10**, 262-71.

Bell, D. (1977). 'The future world disorder: the structural context of crises', *Foreign Policy*, **27**, 525-30.

Berry, B. J. L. (1970). 'The geography of the United States in the year 2000', *Transactions of the Institute of British Geographers*, **51**, 21-53.

Bird, J. (1969). 'Forecasting and geography', *Geographical Journal*, **145**, 69-72.

Blouet, B. W. (1973). 'The maritime origins of Mackinder's Heartland Thesis', *Rocky Mountain Geographical Journal*, **2**, 6-11.

Blouet, B. W. (1976). 'Halford Mackinder's Heartland Thesis: formative influences', *Rocky Mountain Geographical Journal*, **5**, 2-6.

Bourne, L. S. *et al.* (1974). *Urban Futures of Central Canada: Perspectives on Forecasting Urban Growth and Form* (University of Toronto Press, Toronto).

Bozeman, B. (1977). 'Epistemology and future studies: how do we know what we cannot know'? *Public Administration Review*, **37**, 544-9.

Breton, R. (1976). 'La mise en place d'une nouvelle carte politique de l'Afrique du Sud', *Information Géographique*, **40**, 237-40.

Brown, L. (1978). *The Twenty-Ninth Day* (Norton, New York).

Brown, N. (1977). *The Future Global Challenge: A Predictive Study of World Scarcity, 1977-1990* (Crane and Russak, New York and Royal United Services Institute, London).

Brunn, S. D. (1970). 'A political geography of the future', First Conference on the Geography of the Future, University of Western Ontario, London (unpublished manuscript).

Brunn, S. D. (1972). 'Political reorganization of the United States; a future perspective', International Conference on Building Regions for the Future, University of Montreal (unpublished paper).

Brunn, S. D. (1973). 'Geography and politics of the United States in the year 2000', *Journal of Geography*, **72**, 42-9.

Brunn, S. D. (1974). 'Political geography of the future', in *Geography and Politics in America*, pp. 139-54 (Harper & Row, New York).

Brunn, S. D. (1975). 'Political reorganization of the United States', *Notes de Documentation de Recherche, Département de Géographie, Université Laval*, **6**, 139-54.

Brunn, S. D. (1976). 'The geography of the future: a neglected segment in world regional courses', *Professional Geographer*, **28**, 400-1.

Brunn, S. D. (1977). 'Geopolitics in a shrinking world', Southeast Division and Middle Atlantic division, Ass. Amer. Geog., Annual Meeting (unpublished paper).

Brunn, S. D. and Wheeler, J. O. (eds.) (1980). *The American Metropolitan System: Present and Future* (Wiley, New York and Edward Arnold, London).

Burghardt, A. (1971). 'Quebec separatism and the future of Canada', in Gentilcore, R. L. (ed.), *Geographical Approaches to Canadian Problems*, pp. 229-35 (Prentice-Hall, Scarborough, Ont.).

Capone, D. L. and Ryan, A. F. (1973). 'The regional sea: a theoretical division of the Gulf of Mexico and the Caribbean Sea', *Transactions of the Miami Geographical Society*, **3**, 1-9.

Castañeda, J. (1974). 'El mundo futuro y los cambios en las instituciones póliticas internacionales', *Folio Intern.*, **15**, 1-12.

Chisholm, R. D. *et al.* (1970). *Regional Forecasting* (Butterworth, London).

Chojnicki, Z. (1970 supplement). 'Prediction in economic geography', *Economic Geography,* **46,** 213-22.

Christy, F. T. Jr., and Herfindahl, H. (1968). *A Hypothetical Division of the Sea Floor* (University of Rhode Island, Law of Sea Institute, Kingston).

Cleron, J. P. (1978). *Saudi Arabia 2000: A Strategy for Growth* (St Martin's Press, New York).

Cook, E. (1972). 'Energy sources for the future', *Futurist,* **6,** 142-52.

Cornish, E. (1977). *The Study of the Future: An Introduction to the Art and Science of Understanding and Shaping Tomorrow's World* (World Future Society, Washington, DC).

Cox, R. W. (1976). 'On thinking about future world order', *World Politics,* **28,** 175-96.

Culver, J. J. (1976). 'Foreign Affairs and national defense in the year 2000', *Public Administration Review,* **36,** 599-602.

Curnow, R. *et al.* (1976). 'General and complete disarmament: a systems analysis approach', *Futures,* **8,** 384-96.

Curry, L. (1970 supplement). 'Univariate spatial forecasting', *Economic Geography,* **46,** 241-58.

Daedalus, Journal of the American Academy of Arts and Science, *Towards the Year 2000: Work in Progress,* Summer 1967.

de Blij, H. J. (1973). *Systematic Political Geography* (Wiley, New York).

de Blij, H. J., and Glassner, M. (1980). *Systematic Political Geography* (Wiley, New York).

Deutsch, K. W. (1976). 'Towards an interdisciplinary model of world stability and change: some intellectual preconditions', *Journal of Peace Research,* **2,** 1-14.

Deutsch, K. W. (1977). 'Some prospects for the future', *Journal of International Affairs,* **31,** 315-26.

Djilas, M. (1974). 'A world atlas for 2024', *Saturday Review/World* (24 August), pp. 25-31.

Dror, Y. (1974). 'War, violence, and future studies', *Futures,* **6,** 2-3.

Dror, Y. (1978). 'Idéia politológica dos estudos do futuro, futuro alternativos e ação presente', *Revista Ciencia Politica,* **21,** 97-114.

Dury, G. H. (1977). 'Likely hurricane damage by the year 2000', *Professional Geographer,* **29,** 254-8.

Dutt, A. K. and Costa, F. J. (1977). 'Spatial patterns and design policies for future American cities', *Journal of Geography,* **76,** 24-7.

Falk, R. (1975). *A Study of Future Worlds* (Macmillan, Free Press, New York).

Feldman, E. S. (ed.) (1979). *The Future of North America: Canada, The United States, and Quebec Nationalism* (Harvard University, Cambridge, Mass.).

Ferkiss, V. C. (1977). *Futurology: Promise, Performance, and Prospects,* (Sage Beverley Hills).

Foreign Policy Association (1968). *Toward the Year 2018* (Cowles, New York).

Fowles, J. (ed.) (1978). *Handbook of Futures Research* (Greenwood Press, Westport, Conn.).

Freeman, C. and Jahoda, M. (eds.) (1978). *World Futures: The Great Debate* (Martin Robertson, London, and Universe Books, New York).

Frisch, A. (1976). 'Futurologie et politique', *Res Publica,* **18,** 115-30.

Garrison, W. L. (1970). 'Future geographies', in Chorley, R. (ed.). *Directions in Geography,* pp. 219-35 (Methuen, London).

Garrison, W. L. (1972). *Future Knowledge* (University of Iowa, Department of Geography, Iowa City).

Gerasimov, I. P. (1970). 'Futurology in Soviet geography', *Soviet Geography: Reviews and Transactions,* **11,** 521-7.

Gilpin, R. (1975). 'Three models of the future', *International Organization,* **29,** 37-62.

Gordon, T. J. (1965). *The Future* (St Martin's Press, New York).

Gray, C. S. (1976). 'From disarmament, to arms control, to ... what'? *Futures,* **8,** 525-30.

Groom, A. J. R. (1977). 'After 1984: ten disturbing trends', *Osterreichische Zeitscrift für Assenpolitik,* **17,** 116-31.

Haggett, P. (1975). 'Worlds present, worlds future', in *Geography: A Modern Synthesis,* pp. 545-72 (Harper & Row, New York).

Hall, P. (1963). *London: 2000* (Faber & Faber, London).

Hamilton, C. M. P. (1977). 'Terrorism: its ethical implications for the future', *Futurist,* **11,** 351-4.

Harman, W. (1976). *an Incomplete Guide to the Future* (San Francisco Book Co., San Francisco).

Hansen, R. E. (1978). 'Freedom of passage in the high seas of space', *Atlantic Communications Quarterly,* **16,** 345-57.

Henderson, F. M., and Voiland, M. P. Jr., (1975). 'Some possible effects of energy shortages in residential preferences', *Professional Geographer,* **27,** 323-6.

Hoadley, J. S. (1975). *The Future of Portuguese Timor: Dilemmas and Opportunities* (Institute of Southeast Asian Studies, Singapore).

Honey, R. (1976). 'England's new county map', *Professional Geographer,* **28,** 50-6.

Horvik, T. (1973). 'Norvège 1990: l'avenir d'une petite nation', *Analyse et Prévision,* **16,** 341-72.

Hurst. M. E. E. (1977). 'The city and the future', in *I Came To the City,* pp. 292-354 (Houghton-Mifflin, Boston).

Hy, R. (1976). 'Futures research and policy studies', *Policy Studies Journal,* **4,** 416-18.

Interfutures (1979). *Facing the Future: Mastering the Probable and Managing the Unpredictable* (OECD, Paris).

Janiskee, R. L. (1977). 'Further comment on future-oriented materials in world regional geography courses', *Professional Geographer,* **29,** 410.

Janiskee, R. L. (1978). 'Futuristics and geographic education', World Future Society, Annual Meeting, Education Section, Houston.

Johnson, R. J. and Hunt, A. J. (1977). 'Voting power in the E.E.C.'s Council of Ministers: an essay on method in political geography', *Geoforum,* **8,** 1-9.

Johnson, W. A. (1974). 'The future as a learning exercise in geography', *Journal of Geography,* **73,** 59-63.

Jungk, R., and Galtung, J. (eds.) (1969). *Mankind 2000* (Brazilier, New York).

Kahn, H. (1970). *The Emerging Japanese Superstate: Challenge and Response* (Prentice-Hall, Englewood-Cliffs, NJ).

Kahn, H. *et al.* (1976). *The Next 200 Years* (Morrow, New York).

Kahn, H. *et al.* (1979). *World Economic Development: 1979 and Beyond* (Westview, Boulder, Co.).

Kahn, H. and Pepper, T. (1979). *The Japanese Challenge* (Crowell, New York).

Kasperson, R. E. and Minghi, J. V. (eds.). (1969). *The Structure of Political Geography* (Aldine, Chicago).

Kauffman, D. L. (1976a). *Futurism and Future Studies* (National Education Association, Washington, DC).

Kauffman, D. L. (1976b). *Teaching the Future: A Guide for Future-Oriented Education* (ETC Pub., Palm Springs, Ca.).

Kennet, W. (ed.) (1976). *The Futures of Europe* (Cambridge University Press, New York).

Kierstead, F. *et al.* (1979). *Educational Futures: Sourcebook* (World Future Society, Washington, DC).

Kim, Y. C. and Halpern, A. M. (1977). *The Future of the Korean Peninsula* (Praeger, New York).

Klee, G. A. (1975). 'Future studies in geography', *Journal of Geography,* **73,** 59-63.

Knight, D. B. (1975). 'Maps as constraints or springboards to imaginative thought: future maps of Canada', *Bulletin of the Association of Canadian Map Librarians,* **18,** 1-9.

Koslow, L. E. (ed.) (1977). *The Future of Mexico* (Arizona State University Press, Tempe, Az.).

Kothari, R. (1974). *Footsteps into the Future* (Macmillan, Free Press, New York).

Lall, A. (1976). 'The future world order', *India Quarterly,* **32,** 226-30.

Linstone, H. A. (ed.) (1977). *Futures Research: New Directions* (Addison-Wesley, Reading, Mass.).

Mackinder, Sir H. J. (1904). 'The geographical pivot of history', *Geographical Journal,* **23,** 421-37.

Mackinder, Sir H. J. (1942). *Democratic Ideals and Reality* (Holt, New York).

Macrae, N. (1975). 'Pacific century, 1975-2075'? *Atlantic Communications Quarterly,* **13,** 220-5.

Mayer, H. M. (1969). 'The future of cities: governmental coordination and planning', *Journal of Geography,* **68,** 518-26.

McHale, J. (1969). *the Future of the Future* (Brazilier, New York).

McHale, J., and McHale, M. (1976a). *Future Studies: An International Survey* (UNITAR, New York).

McHale, J., and Mc Hale, M. (1976b). 'World trends and alternative futures', in *The United Nations and the Future,* p. 98 (UNITAR, New York).

McIntyre, J. J. (ed.) (1979). 'The prospects for conflict (1980-2000)', in *The Future of Conflict, The Seminar Series of the National Security Affairs Institute, 1978-1979,* pp. 31-58 (National Defense University Press, Washington, DC).

Meadows, D. *et al.* (1972). *Limits to Growth* (New American Library, New York).

Mesarovic, M., and Pestel, E. (1974). *Mankind at the Turning Point* (New American Library, New York).

Mishan, E. J. (1975). 'Vues d'avenir', *L'Afrique et l'Asie Modernes,* **105,** 3-26.

Molnar, T. (1971). 'Zur Gesellschaft der Zukunft', *Schweizerische Monatshef.,* **51,** 393-8.

Mushkat, M. (1973). 'Politik and Zukunftsforschung', *Zeitschrift Politik,* **20,** 97-108.

Padbury, P. and Wilkins, D. (1972). *The Future: A Bibliography of Issues and Forecasting Techniques* (Council of Planning Librarians, No. 279, Monticello, Il.).

Pearcey, G. E. (1973). *A Thirty-Eight State U.S.A.* (Plycon, Fullerton, Ca.).

Phillips, P. D. and Brunn, S. D. (1978). 'Slow growth: a new epoch of American metropolitan evolution', *Geographical Review,* **68,** 274-92.

Remy, R. C. and Nathan, J. A. (1974). 'The future of political systems; what young people think', *Futures,* **6,** 463-76.

Rogers, P. (ed.) (1976). *Future Resources and World Development* (Plenum, New York).

Rose, S. (1975). *Future Facts* (Simon & Schuster, New York).

Roysdon, C. and Misticelli, J. (1978). *Futures Resources: A Library Guide for Clairvoyants* (Council of Planning Librarians, No. 1472, Monticello, Il.).

Ryan, B. (1971). 'Geography of futurology', *Australian Geographer,* **11,** 510-21.

Sanguin, A. -L. (1977). 'Géographie politique: espace aérien et cosmos', *Annales de Géographie,* **82,** 257-78.

Schumacher, E. (1973). *Small is Beautiful* (Harper & Row, New York).

Senfleben, W. (1976). 'Political geography of the South China Sea', *Philippines Geographical Journal,* **20,** 163-75.

Seventeen Prospective Essays. (1972) (Nijhoff, The Hague).

Sewell, J. P. (1974). 'Shapes of the world to come', *World Politics,* **26,** 592-603.

Seynes, P. de (1972). 'Prospects for a future whole world', *International Organization,* **26,** 1-17.

Shaw, T. M. and Mouton, D. (1978). 'The Futures of Africa', African Studies Association Meeting, Annual Meeting, Baltimore.

Shriner, R. D. (1973). 'Governance problems in the world of the future', *Public Administration Review,* **33,** 449-55.

Smernoff, B. J. (1979). 'The new faces of conflict; some implications of the military innovation process for 1980-2000', in McIntyre, J. J. (ed.), *The Future of Conflict: The Seminar Series of the National Security Affairs Institute, 1978-1979',* pp. 89-112. (National Defense University Press, Washington, DC).

Smil, V. (1977). 'China's future: a Delphi forecast', *Futures,* **9,** 474-89.

Solem, E. (1976). 'Future applications of political science', *Journal of International Affairs,* **31,** 315-26.

Spykman, N. J. (1944). *The Geography of the Peace* (Harcourt, Brace, New York).

Stavrianos, L. S. (1976). *The Promise of the Coming Dark Age* (Freeman, San Francisco).

Syed Kechik Foundation (1978). *Malaysia 2001* (Banyan Pte. Ltd, Singapore).

Symposium on the Future as an Academic Discipline (1975) (Elsevier, Amsterdam and New York).

Theobold, R. (1976). *An Alternative Future for America's Third Century* (Swallow Press, Chicago).

Tinbergen, J. (1976). *RIO: Reshaping International Order* (Dutton, New York).

Toffler, A. (1976). *Future Shock* (Random House, New York).

Toffler, A. (1972). *The Futurists* (Random House, New York).

Toffler, A. (1975a). 'A future for parliaments', *Futures,* **7,** 182-3.

Toffler, A. (1975b). 'What is anticipatory democracy'? *Futurist,* **9,** 224-9.

Traub, J. (1979). 'Futurology: the rise of the predicting profession', *Saturday Review* (December), 24-32.

Tugwell, F. (1971). 'L'ordre international et l'avenir du sous-développement', *Analyse et Prévision,* **12,** 1329-58; 1493-1506.

van Dam, A. (1978). 'El futuro de América Latina', *Revue de Politique Internationale,* **155,** 181-90.

Underwood, R. (1977). *The Future of Scotland* (Croom Helm, London).

Ways, M. (ed.) (1979). *The Future of Business: Global Issues in the 80s and 90s* (Pergamon, New York).

Weigert, H. W. *et al.* (1947). *Compass of the World* (Macmillan, New York).

Weigert, H. W. *et al.* (1949). *New Compass of the World* (Macmillan, New York).

Weil, H. C. (1974). 'Domestic and international violence: a forecasting approach', *Futures,* **6,** 477-85.

Weiss, T. G. (1975). 'The tradition of philosophical anarchism and future directions in foreign policy', *Journal of Peace Research,* **12,** 1-18.

Wilson, R. G. (1972). *The Future of Singapore* (Oxford, New York and London).

Wise, M. J. (1970). 'The geographical environment of the future', *Advancement of Science,* **26,** 429-37.

Wolfgang, M. E. (ed.) (1973). 'The future society: aspects of America in the year 2000', *Annals of the American Academy of Political and Social Science,* **408,** entire issue.

Wood, F. B. *et al.* (1978). 'Video conferencing via satellite: opening government to the people', *Futurist,* **12,** 321-6.

World Future Society (1978). *The Future: A Guide to Information Sources* (World Future Society, Washington, DC).

Zelinsky, W. (1970 supplement). 'Beyond the exponentials: the role of geography in the great transition', *Economic Geography,* **46,** 495-535.

Political studies from spatial perspectives
Edited by A.D. Burnett and P.J. Taylor

_8_

Political geography and the world-economy

Peter J. Taylor

This paper presents an argument for the reorientation of political geography in both theory and practice. It is a skeleton argument stripped, for the most part, of all caveats and provisos that would make it intellectually respectable. It is not that the argument is particularly difficult, it is rather that it is highly controversial within its own system of thought so that my application of it to political geography within a short paper is necessarily basic and elementary, and possible naive. All that is hoped for is that the paper may stimulate interest to form the basic framework for a more political geography.

The controversial argument is that of Wallerstein, and the system of thought within which it lies is Marxism. It is by no means conventional Marxism and incorporates many features that will appeal to researchers of other persuasions. Put simply Wallerstein asserts that the study of countries or states in social science should be replaced by the study of the world-economy of which states are merely interrelated parts. Such an argument should be of direct interest to geography generally and political geography in particular. We will introduce the debate by looking at geography in general and its perennial problem of deciding its object of analysis in the first section. In the next section Wallerstein's framework is described as a solution and the debate surrounding his ideas is briefly outlined. In the final section there is an attempt to apply these ideas to part of the subject-matter that political geographers have been concerned with.

The problem of object of analysis in geography

It is often claimed that the geographer's development of the
concept of a region came out of dissatisfaction with the political
state as a unit for geographical description (Hartshorne, 1939).
Concern for the object of analysis has been sharpened by the recent
positive school where it was conclusively shown that literally any
'findings' can be generated by manipulation of the boundaries of
the units of analysis (Openshaw, 1977). This is hardly a satisfactory
situation and the general reaction of the minority of geographers
who have not ignored the problem has been to utilize units of
analysis that are in some sense systems or subsystems — for
instance the definition of urban areas as daily urban systems
(Coombes *et al.*, 1978). Such areally defined 'objects' do not meet
all of Chapman's (1977) criteria for meaningful objects but are
generally preferable to the more arbitrary alternatives. He
advocates that geographers end their search for relevant areal units
and concentrate their activities on studying the objects of other
social sciences (households, firms, etc.) in their spatial context. One
such object widely studied in the social sciences is also areally
defined, however. The modern state is precisely delimited within its
territory and in many ways 'behaves' through its government and
hence qualifies as a 'meaningful' object of analysis. There is
certainly a trend within geography for a return to studies at this
scale, as the 'state' has been rediscovered largely through the
efforts of the radical school of geographers.

The state as object of analysis

The state has been used as a basic unit of analysis in all of the social
sciences, both in their theory and their empirical studies. In much
theory the state is implicitly hiding behind concern for particular
'systems'. In economics, economic systems are typically defined as
national economies, and in sociology the social system alluded to is
inevitably a society within a country (usually USA). Of course in
political science the state is more explicitly found in theory where
political systems with, for instance, problems of integration and
with political parties as actors, are all 'naturally' considered in the
context of the political unit. In geography 'systems of cities' are
normally viewed in a national context and the resulting national
rank-size rules are explained in systems terms. Of course political
geographers have most of their heritage vested at this scale.

Each of the above traditions of studying the state as a unit of
analysis has developed into a comparative sphere. Here the use of

the state becomes explicit. Attempts at comparative analysis usually produce some classification of states often involving some 'dynamic' notion of sequencing. Hence studying economic systems has spawned the very popular idea of stages of economic growth with each country climbing the ladder to prosperity, as it were. In the social-anthropological field societies within countries are seen as 'modernizing' as they throw off inhibiting 'traditional' attributes and progressively join the club of modern societies. Studies of political systems are replete with classifications although they no longer inevitably assume progression to liberal-democracy. In geography the increasing 'complexity' of national urban systems determines where they lie on a continuum from primate city to fully integrated rank-size rule. It is, of course, the exceptions to this 'rule' in 'advanced' countries, notably Britain and France, which suggests that even complex urban systems may not be 'systems' after all as their capital cities have to reply upon much more than the state's territory to sustain them.

Criticism 1   States as mobilization of bias

The fact that a large number of decisions and activities are carried out at the scale of the state unit does not make that unit in any sense 'natural' and hence correct. All organization, including the spatial organization of the earth's surface into about 150 sovereign states represents, as Schattschneider (1959) puts it 'mobilization of bias'. This is explicit in the spatial organization of elections by gerrymanderers but it is no less true of all other spatial organization. The boundaries surrounding states are man-made, and reflect and are sustained by specific distributions of power between different groups. To accept such spatial units as given and then to base theory and analysis around them is to take sides, to bias findings in favour of those groups best served by the current spatial organization.

Let us briefly expand this assertion. In any conflict situation we can expect those with less power (potential losers) to attempt to extend the scope of the conflict in order to change around the distribution of power. Conversely those with more power (potential winners) will attempt to restrict the conflict at the scale of which they are winning. This pattern of simple strategy will underlie all forms of conflict. In a judicial context losers at a district court may continue to appeal 'upwards' to a state's supreme court or perhaps even to the International Court at The Hague. In the liberal-democracies extensions of the suffrage seem to have followed a pattern of opportunism of parties extending the scope of elections in this way (e.g. Disraeli extending suffrage to the urban working class to counter the power of the Liberal Party and their industrialist support in the cities). In a spatial context locational conflicts at a neighbourhood scale may be resolved at a local, urban, or state level and we expect a different mix of interests to be represented at each scale with potentially alternative outcomes (e.g. road inquiries, airport inquiries, etc.).

Where does the state fit into this strategy model? It represents a scale of operation at which a series of conflicts have been resolved in favour of particularly powerful groups. The fact that these spatial units seem 'natural' merely reflects the power of these state-building or nation-building groups to mould our way of thinking. Molotch (1976) has recently described the city as a 'growth machine'. This has historically been much more true of the state which actually had its origin in Europe in defeating city mercantilism. States could mobilize more taxes, produce larger armies at their larger scale, and hence apply similar but grander mercantile policies. It is the examples of these early European mercantilist states that are emulated in the rest of the world. Today competition for growth, although occurring between cities and between regions within states, is primarily about conflict between states. This requires governments to produce environments conducive to business (i.e. investment) confidence at a level consistent with profitability. The current pattern of spatial organization of 150 states may actually be less to the advantage of the states and their governing class than it is for transnational corporations who may divide and rule.

This argument leads on to two separate themes. First the need for an explicit theory of the state to guide our discussion of the topic. Second a theory of organization that transcends the state and can incorporate other actors, notably transnational companies. Development of the former will depend upon the structure derived for the latter need, which is the major theme of this paper.

Criticism 2   Interdependence between states

The basic criticism of comparative studies of states is that they treat states as separate entities and hence avoid or neglect the vital interactions between states. Sri Lanka is not in a position similar to England at some point in the past — when England was at the bottom of the 'ladder' there was nobody above them. The alternative perspective is that of dependency: Sri Lanka's tea-based economy is dependent upon events beyond the state's control in the richer countries. Since 1974 dependency has given way to interdependency as a catchphrase that incorporates western dependence on the OPEC countries.

It is of course no accident that new developments along these lines have come from economists from the poorer countries (Frank, 1969). This argument is now well known in geography, thanks to the expositions of Brookfield (1975) and de Souze and Porter (1974) (geographers with Third World interests), and so I do not need to develop it here. In fact the Wallerstein approach I introduce below is directly derivative of this dependency school and hence their arguments will occur in the next section. Just one topic is of note here. Comparative studies of economic growth and social modernization have come under severe criticism, but this does not seem to have occurred to the same degree for comparative studies of political systems. Comparative politics is still going strong without any emphasis on the interdependency which seems so necessary in the economic and social spheres. I hope to show in the final section how comparative political study of state institutions such as political parties do require what has come to be known as the world-economy approach.

The world-economy as solution

Let us begin by saying what the world-economy approach is not. Several recent textbooks in political and welfare geography have utilized geographical scale as organizing principles (Johnston, 1973; Coates *et al*, 1977; Smith, 1979; Cox, 1979). This involves description and explanation of patterns at three scales: urban, national, and international. In Cox's work he is explicitly trying to find an approach that can be equally well applied at all three scales. In the present argument we are not advocating the international scale as one of several geographical scales of analysis, but rather we argue that it is the basic determining scale of study so that other analyses at other scales can only be fully understood within the context of the world-economy.

Wallerstein's approach to social change

Like his adversaries in the fields of economic growth and modernization Wallerstein is primarily interested in social change. The change he is concerned with is structural change — 'the great watersheds of mankind'. It is this interest that has prompted him to ask the question 'what is the appropriate object of study in such an exercise?' His answer is that, in the modern world, structures can only be comprehended at the scale of the modern world-economy. Wallerstein has set himself the task of compiling the evolution of this structure in four volumes, only the first of which is currently available (Wallerstein, 1974a). Nevertheless he has written enough about his whole scheme in separate essays (especially 1974b and 1976) which have been brought together into a single volume of readings (Wallerstein, 1979) for us to outline the rudiments of his contribution.

Wallerstein identifies three basic types of society based upon different modes of production. The simplest is the reciprocal-lineage mode based upon exchange between producers in small mini-systems. World-systems cover larger spaces and times than mini-systems. There are two such examples — world-empires and world-economies. The former is based upon a redistributive-tributary mode of production where an agrarian class of producers supports a non-producing group. Superstructures upon this base may very from true empires such as the Roman to more decentralized systems such as European feudalism. World-economies are based upon a market mode of production which Wallerstein identifies as capitalist. There is no overarching political structure and redistribution is via the market based on the profit motive.

Each of the above 'systems' is identified by the existence of an ongoing division of labour. Such entities constitute the object of social science. Whereas there have been 'countless' mini-systems covering small areas and few generations, world-systems are relatively rarer. There have been large numbers of world-empires since Neolithic times which have normally dominated typically fragile and short-lived world-economies. Since approximately 1500, however, a European world-economy has survived and become an ongoing capital-expanding system operating around two basic inequalities. A class inequality of bourgeois versus proletarian and a spatial inequality of core versus periphery. The interweaving of these two processes of exploitation has enabled the system to respond to pressures and crises 'by rearranging spatial hierarchies without significantly impairing class hierarchies' (Wallerstein, 1976) in its continual drive for expansion both geographically and technologically. In geographical terms it has absorbed all contemporary world-empires and residual mini-systems to cover the whole surface of the earth. Hence in the modern world there is only *one* entity in which to study social change — the modern world capitalist economy; the ultimate solution to the geographer's problem of object of study.

The structure and evolution of the world economy

It is claimed that Wallerstein's thesis heralds the return of history to social science (Goldfrank, 1978) and so it is important to understand the evolving structure of the system. The key period is the long sixteenth century (1450-1640) when the European world-economy began as an expanding capitalist system and survived. By the end of this period it had a definite geographical structure of three zones — core, semi-periphery, and periphery. The former had come to rest in northwest Europe covering England, the Low Countries and northern France, the semi-periphery included declining Mediterranean Europe while the periphery consisted of eastern Europe and the colonized areas of the Americas. These three zones are identified as a spatial division of labour, each zone functioning as an interdependent element of the world-system largely based upon agricultural production. In the core classical capitalism was emerging with wage-labour, in the periphery there was coerced cash crop production (in eastern Europe) and slavery (New World) while in the semi-periphery sharecropping became the typical mode of labour control. Hence there had developed by 1640 a spatial structure whereby surplus value was appropriated not only by an owner from a producer but also by core areas from semi-periphery and periphery (and semi-periphery from periphery).

The emergence of the world capitalist system was followed by a long recession (1650-1730) where the decline in surplus for appropriation allowed only one core state to survive. This is the mercantilist era leading to the pre-industrial English supremacy. This consolidation phase for agricultural capitalism was followed by the emergence of industrial capitalism and the expansion of the world-economy to cover the whole world in the nineteenth century with the incorporation of Asia and Africa. The twentieth century has seen a second consolidation phase but this time technological and geographical expansion have meant a vast increase in surplus for appropriation allowing more states to achieve core location in the spatial division of labour as British hegemony has given way to American leadership of world capitalism.

The nature of this way of organizing our ideas can be seen in the way capitalism is viewed as originating several different processes in different parts of the spatial hierarchy. In the core the processes of economic growth and development dominate. In the periphery on the other hand the processes of underdevelopment occur. This directly follows Frank's (1969) analysis where he explains that Chile's underdevelopment is *not* due to feudal resistance to progressive capitalism but rather is a direct result of four centuries of capitalism in the periphery. In Wallerstein's world-economy feudal-like structures are part of the capitalist spatial division of labour. Hence he uses arguments similar to Frank's to explain the decline of eastern Europe relative to western Europe in the sixteenth century. The Polish state and bourgeois decline as they become incorporated into the world-economy through the Baltic grain trade. They become part of the periphery and hence suffer processes of underdevelopment. This type of argument has been described by Harvey (1975) as 'a single-faceted development out of Marx' so we must next turn to its criticism.

Criticism and debate

Wallerstein's *The Modern World System* has made a major impact upon a large segment of social science. An American sociologist has referred to it as 'stunning' and 'a visionary work' (Hechter, 1975) and an English historian admits to finding the 'heroic and impressive achievement' both 'exhilarating and satisfying' (Thirsk, 1977). A new journal dedicated to developing Wallerstein's perspective, *Review*, was launched in 1977 and the following year was marked by Volume I of the *Political Economy of the World System Annuals*. Not all reviewers and commentators have been so sympathetic, however, and we must recognize that, particularly within Marxist circles, Wallerstein's thesis on the world-economy is highly controversial. There are numerous criticisms of varying importance to be found in, for example, Skocpol (1977) but the most systematic critique is that of Brenner (1977).

Brenner's fundamental criticism is that what Wallerstein is describing between 1450 and 1640 is *not* capitalism. Whereas capitalism does involve production for profit in the market it does not follow that such production must inevitably be capitalist. Historically the crucial characteristic of capitalism has been its ability to develop vast increases in the productivity of labour by means of technical innovation. This is only possible under conditions of free labour being bought in the market as a commodity. It is this class-structured system of production which lies behind economic development and defines the capitalist mode of production. Wallerstein's emphasis on market forces alone is thus denigrated as 'Neo-Smithian Marxism'.

Brenner's return to traditional Marxist conceptions of capitalism has several important implications. Although he concedes that underdevelopment is the result of capitalist expansion on a world scale, he does not see it as a necessary corollary that the core in its turn should have developed as a result of the existence of a world-economy. Rather the phenomenal economic growth of northwest Europe during the industrial revolution is seen as emanating from the class relations within that part of the world and not in its relations with other parts of the world. This approach provides several interpretations that are directly counter to Wallerstein's ideas. Historically, for instance, European mercantilism and the absolute monarchies are seen as the last years of 'feudalism' (Anderson, 1974; Hetcher, 1977) rather than the early expression of 'core behaviour' in a world-economy. Geographically, of course, capitalism is seen as still penetrating pre-capitalist modes of production in the world today rather than being a single world capitalist economy.

Superficially this debate comes down to a choice between the emphasis on exchange or production as the determining quality of capitalism. Although Wallerstein seems to predict criticism such as Brenner's he does not provide a good rebuttal of this classical Marxist criticism. It seems we will have to wait for volume 3 of his world-economy history project before we see how he is able to 'handle' the industrial revolution within his scheme. Fortunately Frank (1978) has directly confronted the issues raised above and provides the beginnings of a resolution. Frank argues for dealing with world-economy and local modes of production simultaneously in concrete analyses of particular situations. In this way the evolution of the world-economy is the result of, and depends upon, local modes of production which are themselves determined by the place of the actors in the world-economy. The similarities between under-development processes described by Wallerstein for the sixteenth century to similar processes under capitalism in the nineteenth and twentieth century leads me to prefer to interpret the early period as agricultural capitalism rather than the final throes of an expanding feudalism. To define capitalism purely in terms of core development processes does smack of Euro-centricism (Blaut, 1975).

For further justification of, and implications of, the world-economy approach reference should be made to Wallerstein (1978), and Hopkins (1977a, b, 1978, 1979) and Frobel *et al.* (1977). For the origins of these ideas within theories of imperialism see Baran (1957), Barratt Brown (1974) and Blaut (1975).

Application to political geography

Wallerstein's world-economy approach presents an opportunity for political geographers to return to the global scale of analysis without paying any homage to Mackinder. Whereas Mackinder points towards East versus West conflict (the basis of his enduring popularity) and hence intra-core conflict, the Wallerstein approach places the North versus South conflict at the centre of the stage. The change of spatial orientation is a direct result of the social theories being used: Wallerstein's approach is deeply embedded in the economic base of the global situation whereas Mackinder-type approaches only consider the workings of the political superstructure. Modelski (1978) has shown how intra-core conflict may be modelled as competition for global economic monopoly rights.

The acceptance of the Marxist economic perspective does not preclude analysis of the politics but it does constrain interpretation of the politics. Despite Wallerstein's explicit rejection of the state as the prime unit of analysis, states do feature prominently as 'actors' in his world-system. By considering states within the wider economic structure explanations of the wide variety of state forms and behaviours have been shown to be possible — Frank (1978) is particularly good on this theme. This is clearly the 'stuff' of much political geography, ancient and modern. The point is that unlike the Mackinder-Cohen tradition, Wallerstein does not offer one scale of political analysis but a framework through, which all political activities may be viewed.

The culmination of our arguments is that studies in political geography, whether they be historical concerning political boundaries or functional concerning urban policy-making, should be set within the world-economy approach. Obviously not all topics in political geography can be so treated in this section. By way of illustration therefore I have taken the work of Stein Rokkan as recently discussed in political geography (Taylor and Johnston, 1979; Taylor, 1979) and have attempted to set this within a world economy framework.

The European state system

The similarities between the ideas of Wallerstein and Rokkan stem from the fact that they both derive spatial structural explanations. For the period when Wallerstein is identifying the emergence of a European world-economy, Rokkan describes the development of the European state-system. Of course Wallerstein has much to say about the rise of strong western Europe states as part of his world-economy and hence we can relate his ideas directly to Rokkan's.

Rokkan (1975) produces a geopolitical map of Europe based upon three spatial variables. First there is distance north from the cultural centre of Rome with its imperial tradition which becomes reflected in a Protestant north and Catholic south. Second, distance east and west from the central spine of Europe (the trading centres running from north Italy through Switzerland up the Rhine to the Low Countries, with its developing city-state/federation tradition) is employed. In the early modern period strong centralized states evolve to the west of the 'city-state Europe' leaving the vestiges of empire to the east. Finally, within the states of the west the core-periphery pattern is vital in early state-building processes.

The economic dimension of Rokkan's structure revolves around city-state Europe. While this may be adequate for the earliest stages of state development, the dominance of the Atlantic states after 1500 is the basis of the whole evolution of the European world-economy described by Wallerstein. This spatial economic reorientation finds no direct expression in Rokkan's framework. In fact the anomalies of the work are the direct result of this failure. The most obvious example is the strength of Catholicism in eastern Europe where it reaches the Baltic in Poland. In Rokkan's scheme, since Catholicism is to be related to the north-south dimension, Poland becomes part of southern Europe! The key locational characteristic of Poland is not its relative distance from Rome but its position in the world-economy. The peripheralization of eastern Europe and the resulting rise to dominance of the rural landowning class are the circumstances for the counter-Reformation (Wallerstein, 1974a). A similar argument relates to the Iberian decline to semi-periphery status.

The most important dimension in Rokkan's scheme is the east-west one, not because of medieval city-state structure but because it measures levels of capitalist penetration from northwest Europe. Western Europe experiences state-formation within the 'first agricultural world-economy' confirmed by the treaties of 1648 (Gottman, 1973) whereas eastern Europe experiences nation-formation within the second industrial world-economy experienced as waves of nationalism mobilized first in Germany, then through the three eastern empires of Austria, Turkey, and Russia confirmed as nation-states in 1919 (Nairn, 1977).

Cleavages and parties within states

Rokkan's work is particularly strong in the way in which he shows how conflicts are resolved and reflected in party political structures within European states (Rokkan, 1970). Once again, however, recourse to a world-economy context forces vital improvements.

Rokkan (1975) identifies four stages in the changing nature of the state based upon the experience of northwest Europe. The first stage relates to the internal core-periphery pattern, the process being 'penetration' leading to the 'territorial state' typified by mercantilist fiscal policies and absolute monarchies. The second process is standardization (religion and language) or nation-building leading to the nation-state which is culturally homogeneous. The third process is participation as more citizens obtain the franchise leading to the democratic state with competitive political parties. Finally the process of redistribution leads to the welfare state that has evolved in western Europe in the twentieth century.

The first two stages have been experiences by states throughout the world. In eastern Europe the two stages collapse as one under the theory of national self-determination in 1919 where state and nation were supposed to coincide. In much of the rest of the world penetration was a colonial process and standardization is an ongoing process of the post-independent era. It is when we reach the third stage that we are unable to extrapolate beyond western Europe. The emergence of political parties in Europe coincides with the conflict over the commodity market between industrial and agricultural interests. Competition between these two groups led to the increases in the franchise to produce the democratic state. The policies pursued, however, can only be interpreted in the light of each country's position in the world economy. This can be illustrated using examples from the nineteenth century. In the core country industrial interests dominate and will favour free trade: the classic party of free trade are the British Liberals. In the semi-periphery the industrial interest favours protection (from the core) and hence the Republican Party of the USA (and German Liberals) are classic protectionists defeating agricultural free-traders (Democrats in the South, Junkers in Russia) (Robinson, 1978). In the periphery the dominant agricultural landowner class generally favours free trade to sell its goods to the core and hence operates to peripheralize its own country. In Latin America the nineteenth-century successes of 'Europe' parties over 'America' parties made the continent economically part of the 'informal' British Empire (Frank, 1978).

Hence stage three in Rokkan's model can lead to a democratic state in core and advanced semi-periphery as part of the rise of industrial over agricultural interests, but in the periphery stage three is the dependent state under the rural-landowners hegemony. It is this division between democratic economic core states and dependent periphery states that enables the former to develop into a welfare state. In the conflict over the labour market in the core, labour and social democratic parties have been able to win some of the world surplus for their own supporters. Where this is not possible in the poorer semi-periphery or periphery, success of communist parties has resulted in 'withdrawal' from the world-economy, as in the case of Russia in 1917 and China in 1949. Such protectionist state policy is, in Wallerstein's scheme, merely latter-day mercantilism — the standard structural response to prevent peripheralization whose origins go back to early English policy (against the Dutch) followed by other later successes such as those of the USA and Germany discussed above.

Concluding remarks

As has been previously pointed out, the world-economy approach purports to be all-embracing in its implications rather than a framework for analysis at one particular scale. Hence it may be useful to conclude this short paper by briefly commenting on its application at the two other scales commonly used in political geography — the state and the urban area.

We have downgraded the state as object of study in this paper but this should not be read as implying any lessening of the need for political geographers to be explicit in the theory of the state which they employ (Dear and Clark, 1978). Rather the world-economy approach leads the researcher away from an instrumentalist definition towards a structural theory of the state (Block, 1978) or even to the state derivation school (von Braumuhl, 1978). As Block points out, taking a more historical perspective leads to certain problems in the instrumentalist case — it is easy to identify the class (national) heroes when a country is 'rising' in the world-economy but the equivalent 'villains' during a state's relative decline are not usually identified. As major units within the world-economy states cannot be ignored and in fact are closely integrated in the development of Wallerstein's ideas on global spatial structure.

The opposite situation obtains concerning urban areas. Despite the increasing interest in urban problems by Marxist scholars in recent years (Harvey, 1973; Tabb and Sawers, 1978; Castells, 1977) the linking of this work through the state to the world-economy has not been fully articulated. This problem has directly concerned Pahl (1979) where he denigrates emphasis on local issues surrounding urban deprivation as 'the fallacy of misplaced geographical concreteness' although he does go on to remark that a theory 'that the world capitalist crisis is responsible for everything

from dirty streets to the closure of teacher-training colleges is...
inadequate' (*ibid.* p. 42). It seems to me that linking the three
geographical scales of global economy, nation-state and urban area
can be a profitable task for political geography because it unites
interests from both old and new political geography in a relevant
exercise in understanding our world (Taylor, 1980).

References and bibliography

Anderson, P. (1974). *Lineages of the Absolute State* (New Left Books, London).
Baran, P. A. (1957). *The Political Economy of Growth* (Monthly R.P., New
    York).
Barratt Brown, M. (1974). *The Economics of Imperialism* (Penguin, London).
Blaut, J. M. (1975). 'Imperialism: the Marxist theory and its evolution',
    Antipode, 7(1), 1-19.
Block, F. (1978). 'Marxist theories of the state in world systems analysis' in
    Kaplan, B. (ed.), *Social Change in the Capitalist World Economy,*
    pp. 27-38 (Sage, Beverley Hills).
von Braumuhl, C. (1978). 'On the analysis of the bourgeois national state
    within the world market context', in Holloway, J., and Picciotta, S.
    (eds.), *State and Capital: a Marxist Debate,* pp. 160-77. (Edward Arnold,
    London).
Brenner, R. (1977). 'The origins of capitalist development: a critique of neo-
    Smithian Marxism', *New Left Review,* **104,** 28-92.
Brookfield, H. (1975). *Interdependent Development* (Methuen, London).
Castells, M. (1977). *The Urban Question* (Edward Arnold, London).
Chapman, G. P. (1977). *Human and Environmental Systems* (Academic Press,
    London).
Coates, B. E., Johnston, R.J., and Knox, P. L. (1977). *Geography and Inequality*
    (Oxford University Press, London).
Coombes, M. G., Dixon, J. S., Goddard, J. B., Openshaw, S., and Taylor, P. J.
    (1978). 'Towards a more rational consideration of census areal units:
    daily urban systems in Britain', *Environment and Planning, A,* **10,** 1174-85.
Cox, K. R. (1979). *Location and Public Problems* (Maaroufa, Chicago).
Dear, M., and Clark, G. L. (1978). 'The state and geographic process: a critical
    review', *Environment and Planning, A,* **10,** 173-83.
Frank, A. G. (1969). *Capitalism and Underdevelopment in Latin America*
    (Monthly R. P., New York).
Frank, A. G. (1978). *Dependent Accumulation and Under-Development*
    (Macmillan, New York).
Frobel, F., Heinrichs, J., and Kreye, O. (1977). 'The tendency towards a new
    international division of labour', *Review,* **1,** 73-88.
Goldfrank, W. L. (1978). 'Introduction: bringing history back in', in Goldfrank,
    W. L. (ed.), *The World System of Capitalism* (Sage, Beverley Hills). 9-19.
Gottman, J. (1973). *The Significance of Territory* (University of Virginia Press,
    Richmond).
Hartshorne, R. (1939). *The Nature of Geography* (AAG, Washington, DC).
Harvey, D. (1975). 'The geography of capitalist accumulation: A reconstruc-
    tion of the Marxian theory.' *Antipode,* 7(2), 9-21.

Hechter, M. (1975). 'Review essay: *The Modern World System'*, *Contemporary Sociology*, **4**, 217-22.

Hechter, M. (1977). 'Review essay: *Lineages of the Capitalist State'*, *American Journal of Sociology*, **82**, 1057-74.

Hopkins, T. K. (1977a). 'Notes on class analysis and the world system', *Review*, **1**, 67-72.

Hopkins, T. K. (1977b). 'Patterns of development of the modern world-system', *Review*, **1**, 111-45.

Hopkins, T. K. (1978). 'World system analysis: methodological issues', in Kaplan, B. H. (ed.), *Social Change in the Capitalist World Economy*, pp. 199-218 (Sage, Beverley Hills).

Hopkins, T. K. (1979). 'The study of the capitalist world economy: some introductory considerations', in Goldfrank, W. L. (ed.), *The World-System of Capitalism* (Sage: Beverley Hills).

Johnston, R. J. (1973). *Spatial Structures* (Methuen, London).

Modelski, G. (1978). 'The long cycle of global politics and the nation state', *Comparative Studies in History and Sociology*, **20**, 214-35.

Molotch, H. (1976). 'The city as a growth machine: toward a political economy of place', *American Journal of Sociology*, **82**, 309-55.

Nairn, T. (1977). *The Break-up of Britain* (New Left Books, London).

Openshaw, S. (1977). 'A geographical solution to scale and aggregation problems in region-building, partitioning and spatial modelling', *Transactions of the Institute of British Geographers*, NS **2**, 459-72.

Pahl, R. E. (1979). 'Socio-political factors in resource allocation', in Herbert, D. T., and Smith, D. M. (eds.), *Social Problems and the City*, pp. 33-46 (Oxford University Press, London).

Robinson, R. (1978). 'Political transformation in Germany and the United States', in Kaplan, B. (ed.), *Social Change in the Capitalist World Economy*, pp. 39-74 (Sage, Beverley Hills).

Rokkan, S. (1970). *Citizens, Elections, Parties* (Free Press, New York).

Rokkan, S. (1975). 'Dimensions of state formation and nation-building: a possible paradigm for research on variations within Europe', in Tilley, C. (ed.), *The Formation of Nation States in Western Europe*, pp. 318-65 (Princeton University Press, New Jersey).

Schattschneider, E. E. (1959). *The Semi-Sovereign People* (Dryden, Hinsdale, Ill.).

Skocpol, T. (1977). 'Wallerstein's world capitalist system: a theoretical and historical critique', *American Journal of Sociology*, **82**, 1075-90.

Smith, D. M. (1979) *Where the Grass is Greener* (Penguin, London).

de Souza, A. R., and Porter, P. W. (1974). *The Underdevelopment and Modernization of the Third World* (AAG, Washington, DC).

Tabb, W. K., and Sawers, L. (1978). *Marxism and the Metropolis* (Oxford University Press, New York).

Taylor, P. J. (1979). 'Political geography' (Progress Report), *Progress in Human Geography*, **3**(1), 139-42.

Taylor, P. J. (1980). 'A materialistic framework for political geography', *Seminar Paper No. 37*, Department of Geography, University of Newcastle-upon-Tyne.

Taylor, P. J., and Johnston, R. J. (1979). *Geography of Elections* (Penguin, London).

Thirsk, J. (1977). 'Economic and social development on a European world scale', *American Journal of Sociology*, **82**, 1097-1102.

Wallerstein, I. (1974a). *The Modern World System* (Academic Press, New York).

Wallerstein, I. (1974b). 'The rise and future demise of the capitalist world system: concepts for comparative analysis', *Comparative Studies in History and Sociology,* **16,** 387-418.

Wallerstein, I. (1976). 'A world-system perspective on the social sciences', *British Journal of Sociology,* **27,** 345-54.

Wallerstein, I. (1978). 'World system analysis: theoretical and interpretative issues', in Kaplan, B. (ed.), *Social Change in the Capitalist World Economy,* pp. 219-36 (Sage, Beverley Hills).

Wallerstein, I. (1979). *The Capitalist World Economy* (Cambridge University Press, London).

Part III

Agendas

Introduction

A series of alternative paradigms for political geography were introduced in the previous section of the book. There are also theoretical contributions in this part, notably by Agnew and Dear, but they are more specific in that they are applicable to certain aspects of research within the broader field of political geography. These 'middle-range' theories are essential if future studies are to attain sufficient depth of analysis to contribute substantially to political studies generally. The aim of this section of the book is to present papers which we think indicate important future research agendas for political geography in the 1980s. Clearly the formulation, adaptation, and elaboration of theoretical frameworks such as those by Agnew and Dear are major tasks to be accomplished.

By way of contrast a highly empirical research agenda is suggested by Burnett, following his review of the literature on the causes, characteristics, and consequences of local political outputs in British and North American cities. Likewise House favours a more inductive approach to model-building and provides an analytical framework with which to study the interface between policies and spatial interaction in international frontier zones. While House and Burnett deal with topics of both past and recent concern in political geography, Kirby and Hall are introducing themes which have not been systematically studied by geographers — planning inquiries and propaganda — respectively. There are, of course, other political topics which have barely been touched by geographers (Burnett, 1978); for example, spatial aspects of the recruitment and role of political actors (Pederson, 1975; Fenno, 1977).

Thus however diverse the papers in this section are in scope and method, they represent, in their own ways, definite signposts for future research. It is evident that the directions they give us as to which topics should be studied, and how, are far from uniform. No doubt the coming decade will see a pluralist political geography emerge in which a variety of theories and themes will be explored. The papers in this section thus reflect current preoccupations, but they also indicate future lines of inquiry for geographers concerned with political issues, and other social scientists interested in spatial dimensions of politics.

Half the chapters are concerned with political systems and their jurisdictional structure at the *intra-state* level. The functions and form of municipal government (the local state) are being investigated. Like Clark in the previous section (in his critique of the Tiebout thesis) Honey's paper is concerned with the principles of jurisdictional area determination and change. In this respect although British and American systems have common antecedents they differ greatly in character and propensity to be reformed. On the one hand localism and independence are enshrined in the United States and the *status quo* is buttressed by 'Tiebout' arguments. Meanwhile, in Britain in the 1970s, central government control and dominant 'efficiency' considerations made for wholesale structural reorganization. As Honey shows the Victorian system was deemed (though rarely proved) to be ineffective. The conventional wisdom of the day was that new authorities should have larger areas — but what sort of areas? A range of cohesive sociogeographical areas based on spatial behaviour *and* beliefs were dutifully delimited by geographers, who rightly urged that the new counties and districts should not merely comprise arbitrary 'chunks' of population. At the end of the day a Conservative government introduced a system and set of areas which bore only a slight resemblance to those previously recommended. The political and bureaucratic implications of these changes are only now being analysed in depth (Dearlove, 1979; Sharpe, 1980).

The chapter by Dear represents an addition to the growing Marxist literature on the local state (Flynn, 1978; Saunders, 1979, 1980; Tabb and Sawers, 1978). As Herbert (1979) has suggested this approach represents a significant level of explanation. It may well be that the role that local authorities play in resolving conflicts (at public inquiries) and allocating resources in the form of social investment and consumption, are *also* subject to managerial control and citizen pressure.

As has already been noted in the earlier reviews of British and American political geography, the topics of political/territorial structure (boundaries) and integration (regionalism/secession) are well established. However spatial aspects of conflict and cooperation over international boundaries have often been treated descriptively in the past, and the model introduced by House attempts to remedy this deficiency. The insights provided by the theoretical approaches to regional movements discussed by Agnew (and also Williams in the next section of the book) should not obscure the merits of the introductory essays written by Kasperson and Minghi (1969), or more recent 'centre-periphery' studies (Gottmann, 1980).

It is arguable that propaganda is a ubiquitous ingredient in politics. Some might say that paradigms advocated in the earlier sections of this book have a propagandist flavour! Certainly many of the themes discussed in this and the next section involve conflict and sometimes coercion, and not surprisingly, the forms of propaganda classified by Hall are frequently employed by the contestants.

However divergent the following chapters are in approach and theme their authors appear to share a common dissatisfaction with the scope and/or method of past political geography. In differing ways they indicate research opportunities in theoretical and empirical studies both of political areas and spatial aspects of political processes. Having established some salient links between the papers for this part of the book there remains the task of highlighting major features of the individual contributions.

There has been a substantial debate in the 1970s on the validity of Marxist analysis in social sciences (Dunleavy, 1980). Dear and Clarke have made a significant contribution to the question of the efficacy of Marxist analysis in human geography (1978). They have queried assumptions and aired geographical implications in a refreshingly non-polemical fashion. In the previous section Clarke questioned the nature of local democracy in western states and found the Tiebout model unrealistic. In his paper in this section Dear further elaborates a theory of the local state. He argues that in being forced to support private capital accumulation in its social investment policies *and* at the same time to legitimize the system by acceding to demands from labour in the form of social consumption policies, the local state inevitably faces difficulties if not crisis. The relative unfamiliarity of this approach with its 'alien' jargon should not blind geographers to the insights to be gained from its use. Dear singles out electoral politics and planning as appropriate subjects to be thus examined. The local state in western capitalist countries differs from its counterparts in state socialist societies. Comparative studies of the two situations might illuminate these contrasts in terms of such aspects as role, spatial policies, and management (Lewis and Sternheimer, 1979).

An interest in urban political participation has led Burnett to study the spatial distribution of public services and other local outputs. This is a topic which North American geographers (and political scientists) have studied for some time now (Massam, 1974). The range of studies cited and scrutinized display enormous diversity in terms of the explanatory and distributional models on which they are based. As far as who *does* get what, and where, it seems that many *American* findings confirm that spatial variations do exist in the form of *unpatterned inequality* between neighbour- hoods and jurisdictions differing in racial and class compo- sition. Such unequality may be as much a factor of the 'neutral' bureaucratic rules adopted by the agencies responsible for service delivery as overt discrimination or political clout. Many *British* studies have focused on the extent to which local expenditure is redistributed socially and spatially. Resources are not always allocated on the basis of need, and indeed there is evidence that in some cases the 'inverse care rule' applies (Pinch, 1980; Lambert *et al.,* 1980). Burnett is clearly impressed by the research methodologies and findings of urban service delivery studies conducted by American political scientists. He urges that alternative paradigms should be used eclectically in the sort of future research which he is advocating.

Kirby's research interests also include the impact of public service and facilities on social well-being. Perhaps the well-known planning ethos of Reading University's Geography Department has encouraged an interest in public inquiries which have become a familiar part of the British political scene in the post-war period. At such inquiries local government officials present and attempt to justify their plans, and the public who may be (adversely) affected by such proposals have an opportunity to explain their objections. Although such inquiries have a quasi-legal flavour, the reports and recommendations of the inspectors who adjudicate are not always accepted by Ministers. As Kirby indicates, a great deal has been written about the participants and the arguments (propaganda) they employ as well as the outcomes (Benyon, 1978). One of the most perceptive comments on public inquiries — from a politician's perspective — was that provided by the late John Mackintosh, Scottish Labour MP (Mackintosh, 1974). As Kirby notes, locational conflicts which are at the heart of such inquiries have represented a mainstream concern in urban political geography in the 1970s (P. Hall, 1974). The political theories outlined by Kirby should be helpful in making sense of what is happening on such occasions even if they do not always allow an accurate forecast of eventual outcomes or guide us in objectively assessing the environmental

impacts and spatial costs and benefits of the public proposal at
stake (Bale, 1978). Still there can be little disagreement with the
idea that public inquiries represent a rich research lode *and*
valuable teaching laboratory.

Reference has already been made to the difference between
American and British local government. The sharply contrasted
approaches are amply illustrated by Honey. Many earlier
geographical studies of jurisdictional change failed to specify why
such areas should conform to patterns of everyday life — in terms
of *either* behaviour or beliefs (Burnett, 1974). Honey has performed
a valuable task of clarifying the theoretical principles *behind* the
proposals. He outlines the six major proposals made to reform the
structure of local government in England in terms of their
antecedents, organizing principles, and consistency between
professed goals and actual areas proposed. Perhaps because he was
an 'outsider' from abroad, he was able to secure the confidence of
key (normally tight-lipped) British politicians and officials involved
in the process in both England and Scotland (Honey, 1976). While it
is unlikely that any major jurisdictional change will be forthcoming
in the near future on either side of the Atlantic, nonetheless the
applied behavioural and deductive research strategy adopted
might well be applied to proposed changes in administrative areas,
for example, in the British health service and special-purpose
districts (Stetzer, 1971).

Honey and Agnew share a research interest in locational conflict,
and the latter has studied the political geography of public housing
estates on both sides of the Atlantic. Political regionalisation is a
topic which geographers have traditionally made an exclusively
empirical contribution, although neither geographers nor other
social scientists have entirely disregarded either structural or
behavioural theories (Prescott, 1968; Mayer, 1968; Lijphart, 1975).
The differences between structural and dialectical theories are
explained by Agnew. The author favours the latter with its emphasis
on process and actors in 'concrete situations'. The incidence of
political regionalist movements in western Europe and Canada, he
believes, is less satisfactorily explained by structural theories such
as Hechter's internal colonialist model. This particular theory is
also considered by Williams in the final section of the book.

National boundary lines and frontier zones, albeit peripheral
features of states, have been popular topics within traditional
political geography. The Mexican-United States boundary has
attracted its fair share of studies in the past (Burnett, 1966; Dillman,
1970; Hill, 1970; and Price, 1973). Today — thankfully — fighting
has been replaced by 'fidgeting' over this and international

boundaries in many parts of the world. The tension management model provided by House is an overdue yet timely aid to the comparative analysis of problematic, yet relatively peaceful, frontiers. The author is concerned to structure the relationship between the spatial flow of transactions of various sorts across boundaries and government policies of the states involved. The model he has formulated is complex but it is carefully illustrated with reference to a boundary which, for the United States at least, is a major irritant in the form of illegal immigration and drug-smuggling. There can be little doubt that the model can usefully be applied and adopted to frontiers of whatever status and scale, for example, in the case of maritime political control. It is an applied study (like much of House's work) in the sense that a clear understanding of the spatial dynamics of frontier interaction may help policy-makers comprehend the geographical basis for conflict, and thus, if it suits them, pursue cooperative policies.

D. R. Hall's earlier publications were concerned with urban community and social area analysis and neighbourhood councils (Hall, 1977). More recently his research interests have broadened in scope and field of study. His paper on the geography of propaganda is evidence of an impressive width of reading and travel. As the author points out 'cartographic' propaganda, i.e. the use of a map in transmitting a message, is not limited to public agencies. In fact in recent years commercial, often international, companies — airlines, banks or property developers — have resorted to advertisements in which maps play a central role.

The purpose of Hall's paper is to differentiate and illustrate different modes of propaganda. He proposes a four-fold typology — graphics, numerics, semantics, and technologies (this particular form possessing a strong resemblance to the symbolic outputs noted previously by Burnett). Certainly in many of the theories and topics which are or might be pursued in modern political geography, for example, campaigning, locational conflict, and futurology (1984 and all that), propaganda plays an important part. Future research might investigate what types of propaganda are employed by whom, when, where, and to what effect. Whether such studies can and should be carried out 'objectively' is a moot point.

References and Bibliography

Bale, J. (1978). 'Externality gradients', *Area,* **10,** 344-6.
Benyon, J. (1968). 'Some political implications of airport location: the case of Edinburgh Airport', *Public Administration,* **56,** 439-56.

Bristow, J. L. (1972). 'The criterion for local government reorganisation and local authority autonomy', *Policy and Politics,* **1**(2), 143-62.

Burnett, A. D. (1966). 'The political geography of the Imperial and Mexicali Valleys' (unpublished MA thesis, University of Indiana).

Burnett, A. D. (1974). *Hampshire, the Facts of Geography and the Local Government Act.* Portsmouth Papers 1 (Department of Geography, Portsmouth Polytechnic).

Burnett, A. D. (1978). 'Political geography: dead duck or phoenix — a reply', *Area,* **9**(2), 209-11.

Dear, M. J., and Clark, G. (1978). 'The state and geographic process: a critical review', *Environment and Planning, A,* **9,** 137-47.

Dearlove, J. (1979). *The Reorganisation of British Local Government* (Cambridge University Press, Cambridge).

Dillman, C. D. (1970). 'Recent developments in Mexico's national boundary programme', *Professional Geographer,* **22**(5), 243-8.

Dunleavy, P. (1980). *Urban Political Analysis* (Macmillan, London).

Fenno, R.F. Jr. (1977). 'U.S. House members and their constituencies', *American Political Science Review,* **71**(3), 883-917.

Flynn, R. (1978). 'State planning: a review and critique of some recent Marxist writings', *Public Administration Bulletin,* **28,** 4-17.

Gottman, J. (1980). *Centre and Periphery: Spatial Variations in Politics* (Wiley, Chichester).

Hall, D. R. (1977). 'Applied social area analysis: defining and evaluating areas for neighbourhood councils', *Geoforum,* **8**(5/6), 277-311.

Hall, P. (1974). 'The new political geography', *Transactions of the Institute of British Geographers,* **63,** 41-52.

Hansen, N. (1977). 'Border regions: a critique of spatial theory and a European case study', *Annals of Regional Science,* **11**(1), 1-15.

Herbert, D.T. (1979). 'Introduction: geographical perspectives and urban problems', in Herbert, D. T., and Smith, D. M. (eds.), *Social Problems and the City* (Oxford University Press, Oxford).

Hill, J.E. (1970). 'El Chamizal: a century old boundary dispute', *Geographical Review,* **60,** 510-22.

Honey, R. (1976). 'Efficiency with humanity: geographical issues in Scotland's local government reform', *Scottish Geographical Magazine,* **92** 109-20.

Kasparson, R. E. and Minghi, J. V. (1969). *The Structure of Political Geography* (Aldine, Chicago).

Lambert, C., Penny, J., and Webster, B. (1980). 'The impact of services in the inner city: the case of housing improvements' (unpublished paper, Institute of Local Government Studies, University of Birmingham).

Lewis, C. W., and Sternheimer, S. (1979). *Soviet Urban Management: with comparisons to the United States* (Praeger, New York).

Lijphart, A. (1975). Review article: 'The Northern Ireland problem: cases, theories and solutions', *British Journal of Political Science,* **5,** 83-106.

Mackintosh, J. (1974). 'The politician's view of public participation' (unpublished paper given to a seminar on public participation, University of Edinburgh).

Massam, B. (1974). 'Political geography and the provision of public services', in Board, C., Chorley, R. J., Haggett, P., and Stoddart, D. R. (eds.), *Progress in Geography,* vol. 6, pp. 179-211 (Edward Arnold, London).

Mayer, K. B. (1968). 'The Jura problem: ethnic conflict in Switzerland', *Social Research,* **35,** 707-40.

Pederson, M. N. (1975). 'The geographical matrix of parliamentary representation: a spatial model of parliamentary recruitment', *European Journal of Political Research,* **3,** 1-21.

Pinch, S. (1980). 'Spatial aspects of local service provision' (unpublished paper given to SSRC seminar on urban politics, University of Exeter).

Prescott, J.R.V. (1968). *The Geography of State Policies* (Hutchinson, London).

Price, J. A. (1973). *Tijuana: Urbanism in a Border Culture* (Notre Dame Press, Paris).

Saunders, P. (1979). *Urban Politics: a Sociological Interpretation* (Hutchinson, London).

Saunders, P. (1980). 'Local government and the state', *New Society* (March), 550-1.

Sharpe, L.J. (1980). 'Managing the metropolitan area: the case of London' (unpublished paper given at SSRC seminar on urban politics, University of Exeter).

Stanyer, J. (1980). 'The logic of metropolitan local government' (unpublished paper given at SSRC seminar on urban politics, University of Exeter).

Stetzer, D.F. (1971). *Special Districts in Cook County: Towards a Geography of Local Government* (Department of Geography, University of Chicago).

Tabb, W.K. and Sawers, L. (1978) *Marxism and the Metropolis* (Oxford University Press, Oxford).

Political studies from spatial perspectives
Edited by A.D. Burnett and P.J. Taylor
© 1981 John Wiley & Sons Ltd

9

A theory of the
local state

Michael Dear

Introduction

The derivation of a theory of the local state poses considerable conceptual and analytical challenges. What exactly is the 'local state'? Is it simply an extension of the national, or federal state? To what extent are its form and function distinguishable from the national state? And how are the activities of urban and regional planning and spatial process linked to the local states? Until recently, very little attention has been paid to these questions in geographical research. However, analysts are now taking up the challenge posed by the issue of the local state. Some pertinent themes were explored in the review by Dear and Clark (1978), while Fincher (1979) and Kirby (1979) have begun more explicit analyses of local state activities.

Traditional theories of the local state, in North America at least, have tended to support decentralization of political authority. In keeping with the liberal democratic tradition, emphasis has been placed upon local control and local self-determination. Consequently debate has typically focused upon the tenable range of government functions, and the scale at which these functions are allocated. The *efficiency* of a decentralized system of local governments is the most typical operational criterion in these studies (e.g. Ostrom *et al.*, 1961).

More recently, attention has been focused upon the dual nature of the government system: as a *symbolic* input-output system structured around electoral politics; and as a *substantive* input-output system, involving massive investment in infrastructure and public goods and services (Offe, 1974). This viewpoint has been extensively developed in the Marxist literature. The state's role in

the social formation is to provide support for various social groups:
namely the conditions for accumulation for capital; the
reproduction of the labour force through welfare outputs, ideology,
and repression; and direct investment in the economic
infrastructure. However, these descriptions of the capitalist state
have generally not considered the significance of the local state *per
se*.

In this brief essay, a tentative outline of a theory of the local
state is developed. First, a general review of the capitalist state is
presented, in order to lay the foundations for our discussions.
Secondly, the functions of the local state are examined, including
reference to the pattern of state expenditure in Canada. Thirdly, the
form of the local state is defined, emphasizing its links with the
central state. And finally, the practical consequences of the spatial
organization of local states are explored with reference to two
major research themes.

It is important to emphasize that there can be no formal
conclusions at the end of this essentially exploratory paper. I am
guided in the analysis by two epistemological principles. First, there
is a need to delve below the 'level of appearances' in state
organization to the 'social reality' underlying and causing those
appearances. Secondly, this paper aims at 'discourse', in the sense
of Hindess and Hirst (1977, pp. 7-8), as '...the construction of
problems for analysis and solutions to them by means of concepts'.
As such, there is no closure in this debate, merely the construction
of a hierarchical set of explanations which are themselves subject
to further reconstruction and analysis.

The capitalist state

The role of the state in spatial process and spatial pattern has been
curiously neglected. Contemporary mainstream political science
has tended to focus on the *functions* of the state in any given
society. Typically, the state is viewed as an input-output system,
responding to a set of constituency pressures in support of the
wider social fabric (cf. Easton, 1965). More penetrating analyses of
the political system have explored the structure of power and
dominance in state functions. These include the Marxist-oriented
analyses of Miliband (1973) *inter alia*. Other recent studies have
turned attention to the *form* of the capitalist state, i.e. how different
social organizations give rise to different state structures (Holloway
and Picciotto, 1978).

I have argued elsewhere that most conventional analyses of the state's role tend to fall into four categories (Clark and Dear, 1978). The state is identified alternately as: (1) a *supplier* of public goods and services; (2) a *regulator and facilitator* of the operation of the market economy; (3) a *social engineer* in the sense of intervening in the economy to achieve its own policy objectives; and (4) *an arbiter* between competing social groups or classes. The typically functionalist viewpoints emphasize (respectively) the allocation, stabilization, distribution, and arbitration roles of the state.

The more recent analysis of state form has derived from the Marxist tradition. Although the classical Marxist texts provide no sustained theoretical analysis of the state, they do provide the basis for these contemporary extensions of the theory of the capitalist state (Jessop, 1977). Three extensions have been particularly prominent: (1) the *instrumentalist* approach, in which the links between the ruling class and the state elite are systematized (e.g. Miliband, 1973); (2) the *structuralist* approach, which views the state as an embedded element of the capitalist social structure (Poulantzas, 1969); and (3) an *ideological* perspective which places emphasis on the 'mystification' function of the state in moulding a collective national consciousness and in diverting attention from class exploitation and control (cf. Gold *et al.*, 1975).

Serious criticism has since been directed at these analytical categories. For example, Offe and Ronge (1975) have drawn attention to the empiricist bias of the instrumental approach, and the ahistoricism of the structuralists who fail to account for the evolution of the contemporary state. Out of these criticisms, a major new debate has developed in the German literature. This has been summarized in English by Holloway and Picciotto (1978) as the *state derivation debate*. This debate begins with a simple question: Why do social relations in capitalism take *separable* forms of political and economic relations? More specifically:

> Why does the dominance of a class not continue... [as] the subordination... of one part of the population to another part? Why does it take on the form of official state domination? ...why is not the mechanism of state constraint created as a private mechanism of the dominant class? Why is it dis-associated from the dominant class — taking the form of an impersonal mechanism... isolated from society? (Pashukanis, quoted in Holloway and Picciotto, 1978, pp. 18-19).

Needless to say, a number of alternative theories are employed to answer these questions (Holloway and Picciotto, 1978, chap. 1). In arguing for a *materialist* theory of the state, Hirsch (1978) notes that the specific form of the state derives directly from the social relations of domination in capitalism. The exploitative nature of these relations is hidden by the constituting of separable political and economic spheres. Hence, state domination abstracts the coercive relations of force from the immediate production processes. State intervention becomes a response to the political repercussions of the emergent crises of capitalism, as manifest especially in crises of rationality and legitimation (Habermas, 1976). In its support of the capitalist system, the state provides (1) for the conditions for accumulation, including the necessary infrastructural support: and (2) for the welfare of the labour force, as well as (where necessary) for ideological and repressive control of labour. Under these circumstances, there is no necessity for state intervention always to be in the interests of capital. Instead, state intervention is better interpreted as 'crisis-management' in response to the changing balance of class forces (Offe, 1976).

In summary, a materialist theory of the capitalist state suggests that the precise *form* of the state may be derived from the stage of development of the relevant mode of production, and in relationship to other modes in the international order (cf. Therborn, 1978). The form of the state may change as conditions of capital accumulation change. State *functions* are determined by the political repercussions of crises in accumulation and by the overriding need to ensure the reproduction of the system of social relations. The separation of the economic and the political spheres obscures the purpose of state intervention, but places new importance on the ideological and repressive functions of the state. The state plays a vital role in convincing the ruled of the legitimacy of the rulers. This is achieved via a state apparatus by which demands (inputs) are translated into administrative decisions (outputs), and hence, crises of rationality and legitimacy are avoided.

The functions of the local state

The logic of the materialist theory suggests that it ought to be possible to derive the form of the local state from a set of social relations. However, I would prefer to defer this exploration until the next section. First, it is useful to determine some of the empirical dimensions of the local state's operations. What are the characteristics of the local state, as manifest in its functions? Can we identify the relevant external appearance of the object which we wish to explain?

For operational purposes, a 'local state' may be defined as any government entity having a political and spatial jurisdiction at less than a national scale, and having the authority to raise revenues from, and make expenditures on behalf of, its territorial electorate. The local state may therefore take many forms, and there may exist more than one type of local state in any nation. For instance, in Canada there exist provincial and municipal local states below the central or federal state.

Three broad categories of state 'output' have been recognized: (1) social investment, in the production-related sectors of the social formation (including infrastructure); (2) social consumption, with emphasis on the maintenance and reproduction of the labour force; and (3) military, police, and other expenses designed to protect the social formation from disruption (O'Connor, 1973). Although local state expenditures occur in all three categories, Broadbent (1977, pp. 132-7) argues that the local state acts far more in the social consumption sector, especially as direct provider of services. He notes three important local state interventions in the local economy, all of which support the productive and reproductive components of the social formation. These interventions are (1) employment of labour; (2) purchaser and provider of goods and services; and (3) capital construction.

In pursuit of these enterprises, local states have been involved in steadily rising expenditures. In Canada expenditures by provincial and local municipalities have been increasing rapidly during the past two decades. For example, provincial revenues and expenditures have risen from 40% and 52% of federal revenues and expenditures in 1950, to 96% and 91% respectively by 1976. At the same time, local municipal revenues and expenditures have increased from 27% and 39% of federal levels, to 43 and 41% respectively (Table 9.1). About one-quarter of federal expenditures, one-third of provincial expenditures, and three-quarters of local expenditures are on the provision of goods and services. However, two other major financial commitments are worth comment: inter-jurisdictional transfer payments, and interest payment on the public debt. The integration of various levels of state operation is evident in the system of inter-jurisdictional transfer payments (Table 9.2). Federal payments to other levels of government have doubled since 1950, while provincial transfers have almost tripled. Payments by local municipalities to other levels of government are minimal. During the same period provincial revenues from other government sources have remained relatively constant, but local municipalities' revenues from other governments have doubled. A final important dimension of government budgets is the increase in

Table 9.1   Canadian government revenues and expenditures, 1950-76 (selected year; millions of dollars)

Year	Federal Revenue	Federal Expenditure	Provincial Revenue $	Provincial Revenue As percentage of federal	Provincial Expenditure $	Provincial Expenditure As percentage of federal	Local Revenue $	Local Revenue As percentage of federal	Local Expenditure $	Local Expenditure As percentage of federal
1950	3,020	2,370	1,226	40	1,230	52	821	27	913	39
1955	5,008	4,806	1,842	37	1,814	38	1,407	28	1,677	35
1960	6,517	6,746	3,319	51	3,532	52	2,599	40	2,827	42
1965	9,095	8,551	6,328	70	6,328	74	4,160	46	4,527	53
1970	15,528	15,262	13,895	89	14,124	92	7,630	49	8,100	53
1975	31,316	35,278	29,522	94	31,007	88	13,097	44	14,224	40
1976	35,246	38,862	33,840	96	35,526	91	15,144	43	16,170	41

Source: Canada Department of Finance *Economic Review*, May 1977; reference tables 50, 53, 54, and 57

Table 9.2   Inter-governmental transfer payments Canadian Federal, provincial, and local governments 1950-76 (selected years) as percentage of total expenditures revenue

Year	Federal transfers	Provincial		Local	
		Revenues from other governments	Expenditures to other governments	Revenues from other governments	Expenditures to other governments
1950	10.6	21.3	13.9	21.0	1.2
1955	9.4	25.2	18.0	23.7	1.3
1960	14.0	29.5	20.2	28.7	0.6
1965	16.7	21.8	40.5	36.4	0.8
1970	22.3	24.1	38.3	41.8	0.8
1975	21.6	25.6	36.1	48.3	0.5
1976	21.9	24.7	34.8	47.4	0.5

Source: As Table 9.1.

Table 9.3   Canadian government public debt interest, 1950-76 (selected years)

Year	Total interest ($ million)	As percentage of total interest		
		Federal	Provincial	Local
1950	544	78	14	8
1955	664	73	14	13
1960	1093	69	13	18
1965	1656	64	16	20
1970	3216	58	24	19
1975	6287	56	29	15
1976	7898	57	30	13

Source: As Table 9.1.

interest paid on the public debt at various state levels (Table 9.3). In 1950, out of a total interest payment of $544 million, 78% was paid by the Federal government, 14% by provincial governments, and 8% by local municipal governments. By 1976, these proportions had altered to 57%, 30% and 13% respectively.

In her study of the local state, Cockburn (1977) argues that the state and its several institutions function to serve the interests of capital, and that the local state is simply an extension of the central state. This viewpoint is apparently supported by Kirby (1979) and Broadbent (1977, p. 128): 'The whole system of local states... is nevertheless part of the national state.' A logic is thus established linking capital to the central state and, by extension, to the local state. Local states are increasingly in competition with one another and with other levels of government for scarce capital resources. This competition is itself an important dynamic in the movement of capital and is, therefore, a potentially important unifying factor linking different levels of state operations in a common objective — the maintenance of capitalist social relations. If O'Connor's argument that the public debt is a 'tightening of the grip of capital on the state' is accurate, then the increased public debt of local states is evidence of the effective penetration of capital interests below the level of the central state. Fincher (1979, pp. 362-76) has also shown how, in Boston, the local state has increasingly cooperated with large-scale corporate capital in dominating the pattern of city development. This, of course, is part of the local state's wider function of facilitating capital accumulation.

According to Cockburn (1977, pp. 51-2) while the central state predominantly contributes to capitalist *production,* the local state essentially contributes to capitalist *reproduction.* The general requirements of social reproduction involve the perpetuation of two key sets of social relations: the means of production, and the relations of production (Althusser, 1971). The latter requires the use of ideology, coercion, and repression, as well as cultural aspects of reproduction (including school, electoral politics, and the church). One of the major purposes of this system of 'extended reproduction' is the reproduction of the labour power necessary for the capitalist mode of production. Cockburn (1977, pp. 158-63) suggests that analysis of the local state involves an investigation of three particular forms of reproduction: (1) the point of *collective reproduction,* where we are 'clients' of state services; (2) the point of *employment in reproduction,* where we are the work-force of the local state; and (3) the point of *privatized reproduction,* i.e. our family life. Hence, increasing local state expenditures on social consumption is an effective way of coopting and thereby controlling, the population.

In summary, this brief examination of the functions of the local state tends to confirm its implication in the maintenance of capitalist social relations, especially through the flow of capital and expenditures on social consumption. The relative emphasis placed by Cockburn and others on the reproductive aspects of the local state function warrants further investigation. It may merely appear that the local state's concern is primarily in this sector because it is at the local level that expenditure outcomes are most visible. The responsibility for production and reproduction decisions may remain with the central state. Hence, we shall need to examine the interrelationships between central and local states before accounting for the functions (and, ultimately, the form) of the local state.

The form of the local state

Central state — local state interrelationships

A materialist view of the state, which views the state as deriving from a specific set of social relations, does not provide an automatic explanation for the form (or even the necessity) of a local state. Why should a smaller-scale replica of the central state institutions be necessary? Is the replica exactly equivalent? If not, what are the reasons for the formal differences?

The key to the answers to these questions lies in the relationship between the central state and the local state. There are four dimensions in this relationship: (1) the interrelationships between the various levels of state and their respective levels in the economy; (2) the fiscal crises which derive from the local state-local economy interface; (3) the adjustment of state functions amongst the various levels of government; and (4) the increasing demands for political decentralization as technological and managerial centralization occurs. Let us examine these dimensions in more detail.

The relationships between the local state and the local economy tend to be ambiguous. The local state derives revenue from its own jurisdiction, and is therefore relatively autonomous yet answerable to local economic pressures. At the same time the local state receives an increasing proportion of its funds from central sources, thus curtailing local discretion and autonomy. Hence, as Broadbent (1977, chap. 4) has argued, the local state-local economy 'system' is much more open than the relatively closed system of central state and national economy. Yet it is obvious that local state flexibility is constrained by the imperatives of central state operations. For example, the reform of local government in England and Wales was stimulated by the central government because of the depressed condition of the British economy (Cockburn, 1977). More importantly, while central state debts are externally owed, the increasing local state debts are owed to the central government. The local state need not be acting as an agent of the central state before being answerable to its strong guiding hand (Broadbent, 1977, p. 138). In short, the main stabilizing influences in the central and local economies are felt through the relatively constant injection of central state funds. The local state acts only indirectly to maintain a crisis-free local economy.

One effect of these structural arrangements is to exacerbate the fiscal crisis of the local state. The genesis of the fiscal crisis of the state, and its concentration in urban areas, has been well documented in, respectively, O'Connor (1973) and Alcaly and Mermelstein (1977). In brief, local states have lacked the authority to deal with imbalances in the local economy which derived from the continued decentralization of economic activity (including residential construction) beyond their jurisdictions. These imbalances have led to a crisis in legitimacy and rationality which, according to Habermas (1976), rival the local accumulation crises. Thic lack of integration between local economy and local state jurisdiction is a major difference between local and central states. It is a significant difference in the formal structure of the two levels of government, and it generates major tensions between those levels. The most significant outcome of this tension is the constant call for a reallocation of state functions amongst various levels of government.

The issue of centralization and decentralization of state authority has a long tradition in political analyses (cf. Wolfe, 1977). North American ideology argues for maximum feasible decentralization of political discretion subject to the needs of efficiency, control, and local self-determination (e.g. Ostrom *et al.,* 1961). More pragmatically, Cockburn (1977, chap. 4) has referred to the constant reallocation of state functions amongst various state levels as an effort to unload 'knotty problems' to adjacent state tiers (see also Friedland *et al.,* 1977). Thus, one level of government may take care to dissociate itself from the unpleasant consequences of its actions by ensuring that another level will 'reap the whirlwind'. According to Hirsch (1980), this represents a purposeful 'conflict-diversification' strategy, which shifts the effects of a structural crisis to community and local levels. The local state lacks the authority and jurisdiction to attack the local crisis, which is controlled at the central level in capital's interest. The financial, rationality, and legitimacy crises are *regionalized,* thus temporarily removing the burden from the central state, and implicating the local state in the genesis of the crises.

Two opposing trends seem to capture the essence of the operations of the advanced capitalist economies. On the one hand, there is an increasing centralization of technological and managerial skills in both large corporate and large state-administered agencies. On the other hand, there is an increasing demand for political decentralization, as the interventionist role of the central state is rejected and the plea for local autonomy is advanced. The net effect of these two trends is to force an increased 'politicization' of the structure of capitalist social relations (Carillo, 1977; Offe, 1976). As the political and economic spheres in capitalism become fully integrated, the tension between local and central states becomes a structural feature which is vital to the maintenance of the social order.

Local state and social reproduction

Most state intervention may be viewed as a long-term strategy of crisis-avoidance in order to facilitate the reproduction of the social relations of capitalism. These strategies place emphasis on system stability instead of on reform (Offe, 1976). According to Roweis (1980), the dominant mode of state operation in late capitalism is the *pre-politics processing of political information*. This mainly involves preparatory work by complex state bureaux in order to forestall political disputes, and is typically achieved through citizen participation, commissions of inquiry, etc. The pre-politics processing of information is an important method of social control, and is best regarded as part of the 'ideological hegemony' of the state.

Liberal democratic traditions have always insisted on the consent of those being governed. In early capitalism, such consent was easily achieved (Wolfe, 1977). However, in a complex advanced capitalism, a much firmer state-induced ideological hegemony is necessary for the survival of the social order (Gramsci, 1971). This hegemony includes the traditional socializing agencies of the church and education, as well as the family and (more recently) the helping professions (Lasch, 1977). For present purposes it is more important to observe that the local state is strongly implicated in ideological hegemony. This occurs in many ways.

Most fundamentally, the decentralization of certain powers to the local level implies that conflicts over state outputs (rationality crises) are most likely to be focused at the local level. This may occur irrespective of the actual responsibility for a given state output, because it is at the local level that the output becomes manifest. If state efforts fail to coopt and control the population through expenditures on social consumption, then the state requires defensive mechanisms to avert conflict. Hence, in its own efforts at crisis-avoidance the local state may develop citizen participation channels in order to reduce uncertainty by learning the demands of its electorate. Local state decisions are thereby legitimized and facilitated. As Cockburn (1977, chap. 6) has pointed out, an important ancillary benefit of social consumption expenditures is that they tend to isolate social pathologies in the individual, the family, or the community, rather than in the wider social formation (see also Gaylin et al., 1978). Community action for improvement of social conditions is thus directed not at deficiencies in the mode of production, but in its product. Similarly, problems in urban and regional planning policies are typically blamed on the planning machinery, and not attributed to structural contradictions in the social formation. Fincher (1979, chaps 5 and 6) provides evidence of the local state's conflict regulation through the selective response to various community-based interest groups.

Two vital elements in achieving state ideological hegemony are electoral politics and the state bureaucracy. The issue of politics will be discussed fully in the following section. Here, attention is focused on the bureaucracy or civil services, which may be the most significant cooptive mechanism in contemporary capitalism (Boggs, after Gramsci, 1976). It has often been said that 'real power' lies with the civil service, but the separation of political and executive powers has been rejected by others, given the commonality between the two (Poulantzas, 1973). What does seem consistently important is the *proliferation of responsible state or quasi-state decision agents*. These may be viewed as direct attempts to obfuscate the system of authority and control in capitalist social relations, both vertically (across various state levels), and horizontally (between various local state jurisdictions and different, though ideologically related, branches of the political and executive authorities). The local state bureaucracy plays an integral, supportive role in this obfuscation (cf. Cockburn, 1977).

In summary, the system of local states is an integral component of capitalist social relations. As well as being an agent of production of goods and services through delegation of central state authority, the local state also acts to reproduce the system of social relations. It does so by containing and deflecting social conflict; in addition, it has a primary ideological role in ensuring social reproduction. Local state operations cannot be separated from those of the central state. However, the local state possesses a unique structural relationship with local and national economies, and its form and functions are demonstrably different from the central state. In particular, the way in which the local state is spatially constituted separates it formally from the central state. Hence, it would be appropriate if we now focused on the spatial component of the local state's operation.

The political geography of the local state

An essential component of the research agenda in political geography is the politics of the local state. In his analysis Kirby (1979, p. 30) isolates two primary variables: the *source* of public policy; and the *scale* at which it operates. This is consistent with the theoretical viewpoint presented here. In practical terms, two aspects of local state form and function require the urgent attention of political geographers: urban and regional planning policies, and electoral politics. Needless to say, an extensive literature already exists in both areas. However, a local state viewpoint of these topics provoke new and challenging questions.

Urban and regional planning

In his study of planning and profit in the urban economy, Broadbent (1977, p. 141) suggests that it is '...through land-use planning that the local state intervenes in the major internal market of the city — the land market — and helps to smooth the way for market forces to operate'. Planning is thus *responding* to the impetus of the market, helping to reduce the 'anarchy' of the land market as well as redistributing values therein. The local state is implicated through planning in the creation of intra- and inter-regional disparities and of the horizontal pattern of inequality which is increasingly the driving force for social change (Offe, 1976, p. 417).

The conditions under which planning is activated vary as capitalist society evolves through time, and as it encounters new political imperatives. At each stage, planning enters the scene in the form of an indispensable, but always restrained, instrument for overcoming specific predicaments of the social formation. However, because it is so limited in its range of operation, planning also emerges as a social phenomenon that compounds the overall problems of capitalist urbanization. Since the political collectivity cannot transcend the structures of civil society, it can never secure decisive control over the development of the urban system. Urban planning interventions are, by their very nature, remedial measures generated as reactive responses to land development pathologies. Planners are frequently able to control the symptoms of these pathologies, but they can never abolish the capitalist logic that produces them. Thus, each time that planners intervene to correct a given predicament, so the whole system is carried forward to a new stage of structural complexity, in which new predicaments begin to manifest themselves. These, in turn, call for yet further rounds of collective intervention, and so on, in repetitive sequence.

The state is thus caught up in a constantly escalating spiral of interventions. The more it acts, the more it must continue to act. There can be no practical possibility of withdrawing from this process, except through risking a resurgence of those very predicaments that made intervention necessary in the first place. It therefore seems safe to assume that planning, whatever its specific content, will continue to penetrate into all layers of urban life. This process, however, carries with it severe political penalties. As the state increasingly mediates the process of production and development of urban space, so does it visibly modify the distribution of material benefits and cost accruing to various individuals and groups. The more the state intervenes in the urban system, the greater is the likelihood that different social groups and fractions will contest the legitimacy of its decisions. Planning as a whole becomes progressively invaded by political controversies and dilemmas. These are as much related to geographical and territorial divisions of interest (neighbourhoods, suburban versus central city alliances) as they are to strict class lines. In the contemporary city, political conflicts based on class are permeated and frequently submerged by conflicts based on spatial aggregates (cf. Castells, 1976). In these conflicts, the role of planning as an instrument for regulating society becomes increasingly apparent; the ideological confusions and distractions (such as mainstream planning theory) that surround the activity of planning slowly disappear, as they are confronted with a reality which is increasingly inexplicable in terms of the received wisdom; urban planning experiences the same crisis of legitimation that haunts the state as a whole in capitalist society; and planning emerges as one more administrative function within a state apparatus that is rooted in the logic of capitalist society. (Further elaboration of these arguments is presented in Dear and Scott, 1980.)

Electoral politics

Electoral politics have long held a fascination for geographers. The variety of issues which have engaged their attention include the effect of spatial proximity and gerrymandering on voting outcomes, and the optimal size and shape of electoral districts. However, in his thorough review of these contributions, Johnston (1979) points out their almost exclusive concentration on the 'level of appearances' in patterns of electoral behaviour. The social reality underlying this structure is rarely questioned. However, a materialist view of the local state must immediately provoke more structural research on the nature of politics (cf. Miliband, 1977). As Cockburn argues (1977, p. 94) electoral politics is one of the 'bulwarks' of capitalism; the party system and elections themselves are part of the mechanism by which the state achieves its ideological hegemony. Electoral politics are simultaneously a way of containing and channelling social conflict and of obtaining the consent of the governed. The partition of class-based conflict into a conflict based on spatial units (as in urban social movements) consolidates the role of electoral politics and, incidentally, intensifies horizontal inequalities as more powerful territories induce greater concessions from central and local state organizations.

The importance of electoral politics in the state's ideological hegemony is, of course, consistent with Gramsci's view of the 'primacy of politics' (Boggs, 1976, chap. 5). The concrete meaning of politics, for Gramsci, was its role in enlisting the energies of the populace — in support either of the *status quo* or of social change. Given the increasing complexity of civil society, and its increasing penetration by the state, Gramsci argued that it was essential to place the state in the context of the wider social 'ensemble of relations' (in which it was neither an epiphenomenon nor an all-powerful catalyst). The limits and functions of electoral politics may then be interpreted in a clearer perspective.

Concluding comment

In this paper I have attempted to outline a theory of the local state. There is little research on this topic, and still less consensus amongst researchers. My purpose has been to initiate a 'discourse', and hence this essay has proceeded via the establishment of a series of concepts and categories which stand to be refuted and reconstructed. Although I have paid scant attention to empirical reality, I have tried to avoid the sort of abstract reductionism which would create an impregnable theoretical position (cf. Pahl, 1977). The main elements of a theory of the local state may be tentatively outlined as follows:

1. A materialist theory of the capitalist state derives the *form* of the state from the stage of development attained by the specific mode of production. The *functions* of the state are, in turn, determined by the political repercussions induced by crises in accumulation, and the need to ensure the reproduction of social relations.
2. The separation of the economic and political spheres of society ensures the consent of the ruled, and emphasizes the ideological and repressive (control) functions of the state.

3. The functions of the local state are to act as an input-output
   mechanism providing services in response to local demands
   according to central state-constituted constraints. These
   functions include employment, provision of goods and
   services, and capital construction.
4. The local state has been effectively penetrated by capital
   interests, and is itself an important catalyst in the movement
   of capital.
5. The tension between central and local states is a structural
   necessity of capitalist social relations. The links between local
   state and local economy are tenuous. The significance of the
   degree of control retained by the central state is manifest in
   the fiscal crises of cities. One consequence is the continuous
   reallocation of state functions and responsibilities among
   various levels of government. Crises are thus regionalized, and
   the local state is implicated, in a mystifying way, in the
   genesis of the crisis. An increasing demand for political
   decentralization is felt as technological and managerial skills
   are progressively centralized.
6. The local state is vital to the reproduction of the social
   formation, in its role in crisis-avoidance and the pre-politics
   processing of political information. The local state is a
   primary agent of ideological hegemony; it facilitates the
   locating of social pathologies at the level of the individual,
   family, or community.
7. The proliferation of state and quasi-state agencies obfuscates
   the structure of power and control both vertically (through
   various state levels) and horizontally (across different
   jurisdictions and their political and executive arms).
8. Local state form and function cannot be separated from those
   of the central state. However, the local state has a distinctive
   spatial and functional constitution. In spatial terms, two
   aspects are worth particular research attention: urban and
   regional planning policies and outcomes; and the limits and
   functions of electoral politics.

Acknowledgement

The helpful comments of Gordon Clark and Tim Wills are gratefully
acknowledged.

References and Bibliography

Alcaly, R. E. and Mermelstein, D. (eds.) (1977). *The Fiscal Crisis of American Cities* (Vintage Books, New York).

Althusser, L. (1971). *Lenin and Philosophy and Other Essays* (New Left Books, London).

Boggs, C. (1976). *Gramsci's Marxism* (Pluto Press. London).

Broadbent, T. A. (1977). *Planning and Profit in the Urban Economy* (Methuen, London).

Carrillo, S. (1977). *Eurocommunism and the State,* (Lawrence & Wishart, London).

Castells, M. (1976). 'Theory and ideology in urban sociology', in Pickvance, C.G. (ed.), *Urban Sociology: Critical Essays* (London: Tavistock Publications), pp. 60-84.

Clark, G., and Dear, M. (1978). 'The state in capitalism and the capitalist state', Department of City and Regional Planning Discussion Paper, Harvard University. Reprinted in Dear, M., Scott, A. J. (eds.) (1980) *Urbanization and Urban Planning in Capitalist Society* (Methuen, London).

Cockburn, C. (1977). *The Local State* (Pluto Press, London).

Dear, M., and Clark, G. (1978). 'The state and geographical process: a critical review', *Environment and Planning, A,* **10,** 173-83.

Dear, M., and Scott, A. J. (eds.) (1980) *Urbanization and Urban Planning in Capitalist Society* (Methuen, London).

Easton, D. (1965). *A Systems Analysis of Political Life* (Wiley, New York).

Fincher, R. (1979). 'The local state and the urban built environment: the case of Boston in late capitalism' (unpublished PhD dissertation, Department of Geography, Clark University, Worcester, Mass.).

Friedland, R., Piven, F.F., and Alford, R.R. (1977). 'Political conflict, urban structure and the fiscal crisis', *International Journal of Urban and Regional Research,* **1,** 447-71.

Gaylin, W., Glasser, I., Marcus, S., and Rothman, D. (1978). *Doing Good: The Limits of Benevolence* (Pantheon, New York).

Gold, D. A., Lo, C. Y. H., and Wright, E. O. (1975). 'Recent developments in Marxist theories of the capitalist state', *Monthly Review,* **27**(5), 29-43; **27**(6), 36-51.

Gramsci, A. (1971). *Selections from the Prison Notebooks* (International Publishers, New York).

Habermas, J. (1976). 'Problems of legitimation in late capitalism', in Connerton, P. (ed.), *Critical Sociology* (Penguin Books, Harmondsworth).

Hindess, B., and Hirst, P. (1977). *Mode of Production and Social Formation* (Macmillan, London).

Hirsch, J. (1978). 'The state apparatus and social reproduction: elements of theory of the bourgeois state', in Holloway, J., and Picciotto, S. (eds.), (1978). *State and Capital: A Marxist Debate,* pp. 116-36 (Edward Arnold, London).

Hirsch, J. (1980). 'The apparatus of the state, the reproduction of capital, and urban conflicts', in Dear, M., and Scott, A. J. (eds.), *Urbanization and Urban Planning in Capitalist Society* (Methuen, London).

Holloway, J. and Picciotto, S. (eds.) (1978). *State and Capital: A Marxist Debate* (Edward Arnold, London).

Jessop, R. (1977). 'Recent theories of the capitalist state', *Cambridge Journal of Economics*, **1,** 353-74.

Johnston, R.J. (1979). *Political, Electoral and Spatial Systems* (Oxford, Clarendon Press).

Kirby, A. (1979). 'Towards an understanding of the local state', Reading Geographical Papers No. 70 (University of Reading, England).

Lasch, C. (1979). *Haven in a Heartless World: The Family Besieged* (Harper, New York).

Miliband, R. (1973). *The State in Capitalist Society* (Basic Books, New York).

Miliband, R. (1977). *Marxism and Politics* (Oxford University Press, Oxford).

O'Connor, J. (1973). *The Fiscal Crisis of the State* (St Martin's Press, New York).

Offe, C. (1974). 'Structural problems of the capitalist state'; in von Beyme, K. (ed.), *German Political Studies,* Vol. 1 (Sage, London).

Offe, C. (1976). 'Political authority and class structures', in Connerton, P. (ed.), *Critical Sociology* (Penguin, Harmondsworth).

Offe, C., and Ronge, V. (1975). 'Theses on the theory of the state', *New German Critique,* **6,** 137-47.

Ostrom, V., Tiebout, C., and Warren, R. (1961). 'The organization of government in metropolitan areas', *American Political Science Review,* **55,** 831-42.

Pahl, R. (1977). 'Stratification, the relations between states and urban and regional development', *International Journal of Urban and Regional Research,* **1,** 6-18.

Poulantzas, N. (1969). 'The problem of the capitalist state', *New Left Review,* **58,** 67-78.

Poulantzas, N. (1973). *Political Power and Social Classes* (New Left Books, London).

Roweis, S. (1980) 'Urban planning in early and late capitalist society', in Dear, M., and Scott, A. J. (eds.), *Urbanization and Urban Planning in Capitalist Society* (Methuen, London).

Therborn, G. (1978). *What Does the Ruling Class Do When It Rules?* (New Left Books, London).

Wolfe, A. (1977). *The Limits of Legitimacy: Political Contradictions of Contemporary Capitalism* (The Free Press, New York).

Political studies from spatial perspectives
Edited by A.D. Burnett and P.J. Taylor
© 1981 John Wiley & Sons Ltd

_____ _10__

The distribution of local political outputs and outcomes in British and North American cities: a review and research agenda

Alan D. Burnett

Urban political geography

Spatial aspects of urban political systems have been extensively studied by social scientists during the 1970s. Amongst geographers there has been a tendency to concentrate on the input side of local urban politics. Thus electoral geography has flourished and there have been many excellent studies of voting behaviour (Rumley and Minghi, 1977; Wolfe and Burghardt, 1978; Taylor and Johnston, 1979). Other modes of political participation such as campaigning (Minghi and Rumley, 1978) and individual and collective contacting and demand-making (Wall, 1974; P. D. Lowe, 1977; Margolis, 1977; Burnett, 1978) have also been researched. Jurisdictional and electoral areas have also been the subject of many applied studies (Chisholm, 1974; Honey, 1976; Hall, 1977; Stetzer, 1971; Gudgin and Taylor, 1979). Political processes such as locational conflict have been amply researched both in North American and British cities (Janelle and Millward, 1976; Blowers, 1974; Cox, 1978b; Dear and Long, 1978; Ley and Mercer, 1980) and there is an extensive literature on the optimum location of public facilities (Mumphrey and Wolpert, 1973; Hodge and Gattrell, 1976; Hodgart, 1978; Bigman and Revelle, 1978). Geographers have made an important conceptual and empirical contribution to these topics in which they share an interest with political and other social sciences. It is true, of course, that many of these studies have been undertaken by geographers who profess no exclusive allegiance to political geography _per se_.

The 1970s have also been characterized by a continuing debate on the merits of alternative theoretical approaches in urban politics and geography. Most of the major initiatives in this respect have come from outside geography (Elkin, 1974; Dunleavy, 1977, 1980; Saunders, 1979), or from urban geographers who have sought to adapt theories in an attempt to understand patterns, processes, and problems in the contemporary Western city. Clearly urban/political geographers, political scientists, urban sociologists, and specialists in public and social administration have a lot to learn from each other (Burnett, 1979b). They share an interest in the topics already noted and also the subject being discussed in this paper — namely the distribution of local political outputs and outcomes in North American and British cities.

The distribution of outputs

Like much of systems' terminology the concepts of political output and outcome have been widely and variously used. Despite valiant attempts to cut through this conceptual confusion (Webster, 1977) there is no universal agreement over definition and differentiation of these and related terms in the field of comparative public policy analysis. Here outputs will be defined as the authoritative decisions and actions of public authorities and the resources, expenditure, services and facilities, and regulations associated with them. Outcomes are the consequences and impacts of these outputs on those who are affected by them.

What we are concerned with therefore is *who gets what, how, when and where* by way of public proposals, plans, and policies; what type, level, and quality of services are provided by municipal governments and other public agencies, and where they are distributed; with allocational patterns of expenditure and staff; with variation in the speed and quality of bureaucratic responses to contacts and demands, and locational decisions influencing the distribution of salutary, noxious, and hybrid facilities. Also in an era of 'stagflation' in Western capitalist economies with the distribution of cutbacks, closures, and contracting services (McTighe, 1978).

Typologies of political outputs are numerous. Easton (1965) proposed a four-fold division — extractive, regulative, allocative, and symbolic. Froman (1967) characterized policies as areal and segmental. Services have been classified in terms of exclusion, divisibility, choice, and mode of delivery (Ostrom, 1974; Webster et al., 1979) and as either place-specific or outreach-type (Wolch, 1979).

A major focus for urban output research is distributional. Variations in terms of, for example, services allocated, taxes demanded, judicial sentences handed down, and promises made between groups and areas. At one end of the scale are studies which focus on international, nationwide *inter-city* variations and, at the other end, research concentrates on the distribution of outputs between individuals, classes, racial/ethnic, and other groups, and often neighbourhoods *within* cities. A few comparative studies have analysed a number of cities or jurisdictions within a given metropolitan area.

While describing and mapping outputs is itself a worthwhile task it is only the start. Causes are to be found and consequences estimated.

Alternative paradigms

As has already been suggested, apart from a few notable exceptions like David Harvey, it is mainly other social scientists who have given a lead in formulating theoretical approaches to explain the spatial allocation of public resources. Explanations may be sought in the environment, political structure, processes and actors, and the structure of society. Three major, possibly competing, approaches may be identified, all of which incorporate a spatial element in them. First, there is the systems paradigm in its 'mainstream' or modified form (Morgan and Kirkpatrick, 1972). Many inter-authority output (especially expenditure) studies have tested associational relationships statistically between policy outputs and a whole range of variables in the political system and/or its environment. This *ecological-system* approach has been critically evaluated in terms of the independent variables employed, the level of explanation and the neglect of linkages offered (Munns, 1975; Coulter, 1972). Others such as Zisk (1972) have focused on the political processes whereby environmental demands and support are converted into outputs.

The second major approach is widely used in intra-authority studies and can be subsumed under the title of the 'managerialist-bureaucratic bargaining' model (Jones and Kaufman, 1974; Pahl, 1979; Elkin, 1974; Lewis, 1975b; Kirby, 1979b). Here the emphasis is placed on the. interaction between managers-gatekeepers-bureaucrats and the organizations in which they operate. Lastly there is the *political economy* perspective which suggests that urban problems and the responses to them (by the local state) should be approached by means of Marxist analysis (Cockburn,

1977; Dear and Clarke, 1978; Flynn, 1978; Friedland, 1979). Thus 'determinant' studies vary considerably in their approach and there is discernible divergence in both theory and practice. At the risk of academic indigestion it may be desirable for geographers to choose eclectically from the different modes or levels of analysis and explanation (Herbert, 1979). It has been suggested, for example, that the choice should depend on the scale and type of analysis; specific distributional decisions being best explained in terms of interactions between and within public agencies, and broad patterns of resource allocation in terms of the overall economic, social, and geographical characteristics of jurisdictions and societies (Newton and Sharpe, 1977; Pinch, 1980a).

Definition of outcomes

Turning to outcomes, there seems at least to be a measure of agreement as to what is meant by the term. The impacts of political outputs can be both immediate and long-term, direct or indirect (spatial externalities), intended and unintended. Public decisions and actions affect the amenity, accessibility, real income, life chances, and well-being of urban citizens as individuals, members of groups, or neighbourhood residents. They can be measured 'objectively' or 'subjectively' (Lovrich and Taylor, 1976; Stipak, 1979). Because of variations in the interests, needs, and preferences of different groups/areas there are considerable problems of measuring spatial variations in terms of equity, fairness, and territorial justice. It has been suggested that social indicators research can illuminate some of the difficulties which have arisen in evaluating urban outcomes (Knox, 1979).

Existing reviews

It seems to have been mainly political scientists who have taken on the onerous task of attempting to synthesize the vast literature in this field (Newton, 1976; Fenton and Chamberlayne, 1969; Gray, 1975; Rhodes, 1975; Newton and Sharpe, 1977; Webster, 1977). Geographical reviews have been limited in number and restricted in scope.

Newton's review of community performance

The scores of comparative studies of British local authorities' outputs undertaken in the 1960s and 1970s have been summarized by Newton (1976). Variation between local authorities (often county boroughs) in terms of how budgets were divided between services and how 'efficiently' they were provided was typically explained with reference to environmental characteristics such as population size, change, and density; age structure; educational attainment; social class; housing conditions; and size and type of tax-base. Political variables commonly used as explanatory variables included voter turnout, party control, and competition. Even the strongest variables did not explain statistically most or even much of inter-authority variance in how much was spent and on what. Studies of the significance of size were largely inconclusive — a finding which was ignored by the conventional wisdom of the day that 'big was beautiful'. Party control was found to be an important factor in costly and politicized services such as education, housing, and personal services — with Labour Party-controlled authorities spending more on those services than Conservative councils.

Pinch's overview

These last results were in part replicated in research conducted in London. Pinch analysed variation between the 32 London boroughs in terms of need for, and provision of, housing, health, and welfare services (Pinch, 1976, 1978, 1979, 1980a). Apart from the intrinsic merits of Pinch's research in terms of methodology, and the significance of his findings for policy-makers he has also provided a four-fold classification of geographical studies of provision of urban services. These are:

1. elementary descriptions of spending and staffing levels between or within authorities;
2. studies which relate levels of provision to need, i.e. 'territorial justice';
3. explanatory studies which regress environmental/political influences with levels of resource allocation; and
4. studies which attempt all three of these tasks.

The same author has also provided a list of the range of possible explanatory variables for comparative or case studies. It is suggested that the following factors may be significant in determining public outputs — needs, local political control, political marginality or competitiveness, local authority size, resources or local wealth, costs, attitudes of professional staff, case-workers and reception staff, intelligence and research capacity, local demand (use), pressure groups, central government, financial problems, staff availability, substitute (private) provision, coordination and planning, and personalities (Pinch, 1980a). The first five factors are variables which have frequently been examined in regression-based studies. It is possible that much of the unexplained variation in local authorities' service provision can be accounted for by the remaining factors (Pinch, 1980b).

A rich contribution

A recent American review which is worthy of note is that provided by Richard Rich (1979). It is concerned with service distribution — the package of services and their spatial allocation. He highlights four features which characterize empirical research in different American cities:

1. most studies have concentrated on obtaining measures of policy outputs and have neglected outcomes;
2. variations between jurisdictions *within* metropolitan areas have not been researched;
3. 'arbitrary' neighbourhoods have been used as the basis of measuring distributions and the needs of their inhabitants and if and how they are satisfied through private services; and
4. equality has been measured only at a given point in time.

Summarizing the findings in Oakland (Levy *et al.*, 1974), San Antonio (Lineberry, 1977), and other American cities (Jones *et al.*, 1977, 1979; Mladenka and Hill, 1977, *inter alia*), Rich concludes that there are no glaring and systematic inequalities for every service in every city. Nor are municipal services consistently manipulated by the rich to the advantage of the poor. Location and environment, rather than political favouritism or racial discrimination, are significant sources of variation between neighbourhoods. But variation in the built environment or socioeconomic composition of neighbourhoods are not themselves determinants of service distribution unless perceived needs and demands emanating from them are evaluated as significant in terms of bureaucratic rules and regulations of the agencies involved (Jones and Kaufman, 1974). A degree of equality does exist in the distribution of such services as libraries, public housing inspections, education, police patrolling, street lighting, and recreational provision; but measured against a backcloth of vast disparities in income, educational attainment, and amenity is this significant? The author concludes that future research should concentrate on outcomes, metropolitan-wide distributions, the influence of neighbourhood organizations, the role of private provision, and equity rather than equality as a measure of observed distributions across neighbourhoods which are meaningful social and political units.

Scope of the present review

It would be foolish to confine a review of recent output and outcome research in North American and British cities only to the work of geographers, because many distributional studies have been undertaken by other social scientists and, as can be seen in the References, are published in multidisciplinary journals. Comparable research has also been done outside the North Atlantic area, for example, in socialist cities (Nelson, 1977; Oliver, 1968; French and Hamilton, 1979; Fuchs and Demko, 1979) and elsewhere (Cornelius, 1974; Cohen, 1974; Walker, 1979; Aiken and Depre, 1980). This review will, however, be selective and cover only British and North American studies, notably those which are either *recent, representative,* or *restricted* (in circulation).

British studies

Grant's highway policy study

The changing urban highway policies of three English county boroughs (Southampton, Nottingham, and Portsmouth) have been analysed (Grant, 1977). Traditionally 'needs, resources, and dispositions' were assumed to be significant determinants in urban policy-making (Boaden, 1971). Grant's explanation was framed in terms of the interaction of three sets of participants — technical, political, and community actors. Two sets of factors explained the different policies adopted in these three cities — those which *enabled* a policy change to occur, i.e. Conservative to Labour Party control, existence of a strong protest group which opposed new road construction, and a change in key professional actors (city engineer). In Nottingham all these conditions were fulfilled and complete policy reversal occurred. In Southampton and Portsmouth this was not the case. A second set of factors also influenced the final outputs. They included the ratio of the members of the incoming Labour regime who were 'uncommitted' or represented affected wards or both, the existence of several varied pressure groups opposing road building, and the size of the highway schemes.

Grant's explanations may not be entirely convincing in that important political and bureaucratic processes were largely ignored. Nonetheless the research is significant in that it represents a transition between the ecological inter-city studies of the late 1960s and early 1970s and the more process-orientated work to follow.

Newton's central place theory

Local government outputs in England and Wales are currently being carried out by Newton and Sharpe, who have investigated the links between central place theory, city types, and public expenditures in England and Wales. Cities can be viewed in terms of their role and function in the national urban system rather than their population characteristics. A city's position in the urban hierarchy is likely to affect its public expenditure in two ways. First, higher-order central places provide large and specialized municipal facilities and services. Secondly, the higher the city's position in the urban hierarchy the greater the use made of its public services by those living outside it. Thus 'additional' road construction and repairs, public transport, refuse collection, public health facilities, police, and cultural services are required. Having ranked county boroughs according to existing geographical classifications and variables derived from them, such as the proportion of rates derived from office and commercial property, commuter flows, and retail turnover per capita, the author regressed these with expenditures on different services and total expenditure levels. The results indicate significant relationships between some variables; for example, the amount of commercial property having a close bearing on spending on education, libraries, police, highways; and total expenditure and population flows having a fairly close relationship with parks and planning spending. A unified model is formulated which specifies these relationships. One significant finding is that centrality does not appear to be as important a determinant of urban expenditure in Britain as in the United States or in Belgium (Aiken and Depre, 1980). One possible explanation for this may be the relative absence of jurisdictional fragmentation in the United Kingdom. The location, economy, and place in the urban hierarchy may be the key to understanding a city's package of public expenditure (Newton, 1980).

Difficult-to-let housing and dental provision in Northern England

A series of applied studies have been published on the allocation of public provision and its impacts, by Taylor and his colleagues, in

Newcastle-upon-Tyne (Bradley *et al.*, 1976; Kirby, 1979d; Taylor, 1979). 'Difficult-to-let', 'difficult-to-live in', and sometimes 'difficult-to-get-out-of' housing stock is a ubiquitous feature of British cities. Unpopular, often stygmatized, council estates — whatever their age, location, and design — are a problem for housing managers and tenants. Taylor rejects sale or demolition as a solution. On the basis of a detailed study of the peripheral Killingworth estate and its allocation system, he suggests a socially just allocation-transfer procedure whereby all tenants will first occupy the 'worst' (high-rise) accommodation for an agreed limited period before filtering upward to have access to more popular dwellings.

A notable attempt to untangle the causal links between accessibility to public facilities, attitudes towards them, and use of them by different socioeconomic groups, and relative well-being has also been conducted in Newcastle. It found that those areas with poorest provision and longest journeys to a dentist were also ones with the highest rates of dental decay.

The haves and have-nots of Havant

The suburban borough of Havant in southeast Hampshire comprises several non-contiguous and distinctive districts, as well as both post-war private and public (Portsmouth overspill) estates. Indices of both the supply and demand/need for indoor recreational provision between wards and districts within the borough were calculated, and an equitable allocation of new facilities was proposed (Moon, 1980). This was compared to the proposed distribution of municipal multi-purpose sports centres being planned by the local council, and the differences between the two patterns accounted for by political and administrative factors. It was found that need was determined by local councillors on the subjective basis, and electoral considerations, and pressure from local neighbourhood organizations played a significant part in influencing which districts should be allocated new facilities and where they should be sited.

Fire services in Leeds

An investigation into spatial imbalance costs and benefits of one local government service has been undertaken in Leeds (A. P. Smith *et al.*, 1977). The city was divided into 39 zones. First each zonal contribution to the cost of city fire services on the basis of estimated rates and taxes paid was calculated and mapped — the largest contribution occurring in outer zones in the northern sector.

Then the records of the fire service were investigated to identify the pattern of its activity, and the cost was calculated for each zone. As expenditure was highly skewed — being concentrated in the central and inner-city areas — it appeared that considerable imbalance existed in fire service revenue and expenditure. Inner-city residents are in receipt of a positive subsidy from peripheral zones and, in general, local authorities may be seen to be performing a redistributive function through the financing and delivery of this particular service at least.

Political participation and response in Portsmouth

If British studies of individual and group political participation between elections are scarce (Wall, 1974; P. D. Lowe, 1977; S. Lowe, 1977), then research which investigates the causes *and* consequences of political participation is even rarer. Neighbourhood organizations and protest groups in Portsmouth in the late 1970s were concerned with a variety of issues, including the location of public facilities and quantity of service delivery (Burnett, 1978 and forthcoming). Which sort of groups demanded what, *where,* how, to whom, and to what effect has been investigated. Protests, petitions and pressure were at least partly responsible for public service 'noxious' facilities being relocated and salutary facilities being kept open; staff being increased; resources being spent or saved, and existing land-use retained. Neither political clout nor media support were any guarantee of success. Politicians and officials were certainly more prone to accede to public service demands when the costs and commitments entailed in so doing were not too onerous.

   K. Cole (1979) has also investigated the distribution of individual contacts in the same city. He found that numerous complaints were received by the city's Environmental Health Department and were automatically followed up with an inspection. Depending on the circumstances, action was taken to abate the nuisance, be it in the form of foreign bodies in food, dampness, or rats. Housing complaints and the resulting resource allocation were found to be concentrated in older, inner-city areas.

Knox in Scotland

This finding is reinforced by a study of the intra-urban ecology of primary medical care in the four major Scottish cities of Glasgow, Edinburgh, Aberdeen, and Dundee (Knox, 1978). Knox is concerned with the externalities associated with the location of public facilities — in this case doctors' surgeries — for different socioeconomic groups in different urban zones. The social ecology of general practitioners' surgeries is shown for the four cities. It is characterized by the following features:

1. surgeries are not located with CBDs but adjacent to them, often in deprived inner-city areas;
2. few surgeries are to be found in post-war peripheral areas (private or public).

The four cities vary in the degree to which under-doctored or over-doctored areas correspond to the worst- and best-off neighbourhoods respectively. In terms of community health outcomes the author concludes that most under-doctored areas of the cities seem to be the type normally associated with above-average rates of morbidity and with high rates of infant and perinatal mortality. A careful revision of public policy relating to the location of premises of family doctors in the NHS is proposed.

Methodological advances in the Midlands

Lastly, in this selective review of British research, attention should be paid to Webster and colleagues at the Institute of Local Government Studies at the University of Birmingham. Much of this research has been conducted in conjunction with the local authorities concerned and sponsored by the Department of the Environment. The first study to be undertaken was on experimental analysis of area expenditure in Coventry. The conceptual and technical problems encountered, and the results, have been published in two papers (Webster and Stewart, 1975; Randall et al., 1973). Expenditures incurred in three municipal services — home helps, branch libraries, and maternal/child health clinics — were calculated on the basis of cost per head of population for the electoral wards and planning districts of the city. Disparities were identified in terms of resources allocated to these different types of services, but perhaps even more significantly general problems relating to the measurement of outcomes were clarified and methodological difficulties solved, such as how to assign costs to areas for different types of services.

In 1977 Webster delivered a thoughtful review paper — which drew heavily on American work — in which the previous research in the United Kingdom and United States was outlined and suggestions made as to how the mechanisms determining service distributions should be studied. These mechanisms, it was postulated, encompass the whole range of policy decisions, professional standards, allocation rules, departmental practices, and procedures. They were said to be responsible for inequitable distribution of outcomes in relation to need. Empirical research into mechanisms and outputs is currently being undertaken in Walsall (Webster *et al.*, 1979; C. Lambert *et al.*, 1980), with particular reference to the impact of local authority services on the inner city — an urban zone which represents a current preoccupation on both sides of the Atlantic (D. M. Smith, 1979a).

Overall empirical research into the distribution of political outputs in British cities is limited, although there are a considerable number of studies which have been restricted in service or city covered. In the capital, in addition to Pinch's analysis of the variation in housing, health, and welfare provision between London boroughs, there is Lewis's study of health and social services in four London boroughs (1975a). Most other studies are service- and city-specific (Bassett and Hauser, 1975; Bassett and Short, 1980; Elcock, 1979; Gray, 1976; Hooper, 1978; J. Lambert *et al.*, 1978; S. Lowe, 1977; Schofield, 1978; Simmie and Hale, 1978b; Allen, 1979). While these empirical studies vary in scope and methodology, together they represent substantial evidence that urban public resources are not equally allocated as between classes and/or areas.

Translantic research

Comparative studies of urban political outputs which are based on the United Kingdom *and* the United States are rare. One such is Glassberg's research on the links between voting behaviour and 'neighbourhood-orientated' capital spending decisions (Glassberg, 1973). A model of 'continuous feedback' is presented in which the voting behaviour of the electorate and spending patterns of office-holders influence each other. It is tested

1. in New York Mayoral elections and a geographical analysis of expenditure on neighbourhood serving facilities; and
2. in London to see if the spatial results of elections to the Borough of Greenwich and the ILEA were mutually linked to the pattern of school construction and housing respectively.

Results showed that while power changed hands in the two study areas the spatial distribution of resources did not, as predicted, alter to any great extent. In New York there was a weak relationship between capital budgeting patterns and voting behaviour, while in

London there was none. Explanations offered by the author for these overall and differential results include:

1. the different styles of urban politics in the two cities — the American officials openly admitting to the 'politics' of neighbourhood facilities and the British strenuously denying such a possibility;
2. the stability of the budgeting process and the time lag between project planning and construction which reduced the potential in part of 'short-term' changes in political control; and
3. technical measures of need playing a crucial role in the allocational process.

Glassberg concludes by speculating as to the consequences of political participation (voting), the lack of links between voting behaviour, and capital budgeting.

North American research

Much of the output and outcome research in Britain, particularly the studies which have analysed variations in expenditure and service provision between and within cities, has been inspired by comparable work in political science and to a lesser extent geography on the western side of the Atlantic. Notwithstanding the important theoretical, empirical, and applied contribution of geographers on such topics as locational conflict and the optimum location for public facilities, it is 'spatially aware' political scientists who seem to have made the running in inter- and intra-city research. Regarding the latter body of research, as a recent review has suggested, there has been an explosion of interest in the study of urban service production and delivery, much of which has focused on the distribution of services to identifiable groups (Goldenberg, 1979). Who gains and who loses as a consequence of delivery practices is the question that these studies have asked.

Discrimination in maze

A focus on discrimination in the financing, delivery, and distribution of public services within metropolitan areas has been a feature of American studies. One recent book synthesizes the findings of such studies (Dimond *et al.*, 1979). The authors discuss discrimination in relation to a hypothetical metropolitan area —

'Maze' — and discuss its jurisdictional structure, racial and class composition, pattern of public service financing, and delivery. Maze is fragmented into the following government units — Shantytown, Central City, Industrial Grime, Exclusive Point, Blacktown, Poortown, Suburbia and Sprawl. The population and fiscal character of these units may be readily surmised. Service levels are shown by dollars spent per capita; resource inputs (teachers, firemen, and library books per capita, and police response time); outcomes (reading level and property losses) and user satisfaction for such services as education, sanitation, public health, police, fire, public transport, streets, dispute resolution, leisure, parks and recreation, and finance administration. Individual services and the total package of benefits is charted by jurisdiction and social area. In a series of appendices the 'real' statistics are provided for the Detroit-centred southeast Michigan area. The study also outlines the mechanism of discriminations evident and opportunities for redressing the situation through legislation.

Oakland outputs

Undoubtedly the pioneering study in the early 1970s into the distribution of local services in urban America was a Californian study of local educational, library, and street provision in Oakland (Levy *et al.*, 1974). Despite its title, the book is about outputs (as defined in this paper), i.e. what local municipal agencies allocate by way of dollars, facilities, and personnel across income/racial groups, and not about outcomes such as variation in educational attainment, incidence of street potholes, and borrowing/literacy rates. Unequal allocations of agency resources are largely explained in terms of neutral-sounding bureaucratic routines. In *school* budgeting personnel were assigned on an equal student-per-teacher ratio basis except that schools in poor areas were given more teachers. However, more experienced and better-trained teachers preferred to teach in richer neighbourhoods and, since they were allowed to transfer freely, total teacher salaries followed a U-shaped distribution: middle-income neighbourhood schools having fewer resources than poorer areas with many teachers and rich areas with highly paid teachers. Library budget allocations were based on circulation, and because the poor used library books less frequently than others they got the worst deal — a J-shaped distribution. This process is termed, by the authors, the 'Adam Smith rule', because areas of higher demand get more resources. The priorities of state, county, bureaucracies, and public utility companies explain the allocation of investments in road construction and street repairs. The rich, 'Waspish' Uplands get newer roads and quick repairs and also derive greater benefit from the commuter freeways built through the poor black flatlands adjoining San Francisco Bay.

Another merit of this research is the systematic evidence that is provided in terms of the effect of rules governing distributional decision-making and the subsequent allocations of agency resources. A useful and — in the context of other American political studies of service distribution — unique feature of this book is the detail that is provided of the residential structure and composition of Oakland's neighbourhoods. Comparable studies by Jones and his colleagues in Detroit (1977 and 1979), Mladenka and Hill (1977 and 1978) in Houston, and Lineberry in San Antonio (1977b), for all the statistical sophistication of their analysis do not treat us to so much as a map of the neighbourhoods in their respective study cities.

Environmental services in Detroit

The publications of Jones and his co-workers have made a major theoretical and empirical contribution to the study of the local bureaucratic outputs. They have modelled the links between the character of neighbourhoods and their needs and demands, the agencies responsible for allocating resources, and levels of services (Jones and Kaufman, 1974). They have also provided a wealth of detail on how environmental services are distributed in Detroit and why (Jones *et al.*, 1977, 1979), and performed a useful service in summarizing the overall results of comparable research. They suggested that in large American cities no clear cumulative pattern of service distribution emerges regardless of region. In fact the specific pattern identified may vary depending on which service is studied and which output indicator is used. On the other hand, despite the fact that it seems resources are virtually never distributed equally, and neighbourhood variation is the rule, nonetheless (unlike certain small southern towns) there is no strong evidence that the 'underclass hypothesis' is true: namely that the poor, powerless, and minority groups consistently receive less than an equal share of the benefits of city public services. A corollary of this is, of course, that despite their greater 'needs' they do not consistently enjoy any positive discrimination in terms of the allocation of resources despite a whole range of federal programmes designed with that goal in mind (Cole, 1974).

Nivola in Boston

A recent study of housing inspection in Boston by Nivola replicates
many of these conclusions, but it also contains empirical findings
which are somewhat unique (Nivola, 1978, 1979). In this case the
quality of response by housing inspection agencies to complaints is
measured by the speed of official reaction and the likelihood of a
building code violation being issued. In general, of the nine Boston
neighbourhoods studied, white lower middle-class neighbourhoods
do better than do the three black slums or wealthy white areas
(including Beacon Hill). The reasons cannot be attributed to any
political factor — party control or neighbourhood organizational
activity. Nor are local differences in housing conditions a sufficient
explanation for observed variations. The answer, according to
Nivola, lies in a collection of mundane administrative factors which
reflect the nature of the service being provided and the
organization — lack of central control — of the department
concerned. The perceptions of the officials who are given
significant discretion in what they do — and where — is also
significant. The slums are given up in despair — they are liable to
be 'torched' anyway; beats there include dark hallways, stairwells,
hidden passages and yards, rat-infested basements and the
innermost living quarters of sometimes desperate individuals. In
such areas as Roxbury and North Dorchester a concern for safety
means that delays are caused when police escorts have to be
arranged and officials are allowed to go home at 3 p.m. (before the
schools get out). In contrast, well-heeled districts are perceived as
less deserving and more likely to win subsequent actions. They tend
to be neglected partly because a more visible role might stimulate
an onslaught of demands for more or better inspections. In the
meantime, 'cooperative' white working-class areas are getting
quicker responses to their complaints by way of inspections and
more legal actions. Even if little strong evidence is provided in
terms of these 'bureaucratic' explanatory factors, the study does
offer some useful insights into decision rules and the goals and
perceptions and spatial activities of housing inspectors.

The influence of pressure groups

So far as the influence of neighbourhood organizations on the
distribution of policy outputs was examined at all in the studies
outlined above, it was found to be of minor significance, certainly
when compared to other modes of political participation such as
individual contacting and even voting. However, there is a

substantial body of literature which is specifically concerned with urban pressure groups, the demands they make and the responsiveness of policy-makers to them. The empirical work of P. D. Schumaker and his co-researchers may be singled out to exemplify this sort of enquiry (Schumaker, 1975; Schumaker and Billeaux, 1978; Getter and Schumaker, 1978). On the basis of analysis of questionnaires sent to officials representing different agencies in 51 cities, Schumaker concludes that it is not the environmental or political character of the cities themselves which are important influences in determining whether or not groups are represented in city bureaucracies or have their demands met. It depends far more on the tactics employed, the amount of support they enjoyed from the media and other pressure groups. The zero-sumness of demands, and whether they are 'public or private regarding', was also significant. Urban officials from a variety of service agencies — housing, health, environmental protection, community development, welfare, schools, and police — responded positively to the demands of selected groups. While it is true to say that this research tells us more about participation in American cities than outputs and outcomes, nonetheless it provides some evidence that policy-makers are responsive to citizen demands. It is regrettable that, unlike Cornelius (1974), no indication is given as to what services are influenced, how, and in which cities.

Rat control in Newark

By way of contrast, there is Margolis' detailed study of the activities of the Bureau of Pest and Rodent Control in Newark (Margolis, 1977). The function of this agency is to improve neighbourhood sanitation and eliminate rats in that city. The relative quality of sanitation did not explain the level of rat complaints, and some of the most insanitary areas which the author surveyed did not make a high volume of complaints to the bureau. Overall the agency had an unsuccessful record of achievement in eliminating rats. Its costs could hardly be justified on its long-term results, and the author concludes that such problems faced most by slum-dwellers could only be solved by a massive programme of economic assistance and house-building.

The ethnography of fire stations

Locational studies of public facilities are, of course, well established in American geographical literature. A recent trend

towards examining outcomes is apparent. Seley (1979) has framed
an ethnographical approach to the study of fire stations and
service. His claim is that insights into aspects of location,
community support and use, and service delivery can be gained
from such a perspective. Location-allocation models are based on
the assumption that facility siting decisions are all important in
terms of efficiency and equity. This assumption is refuted on the
basis that response times are not the only, or necessarily the most
important, consideration. Social aspects of fire house (station) life
may be more significant in terms of effectiveness than their
location. The service operates in such a way that there is a
temporal/spatial progression from busy inner-city stations to those
in quieter, suburban middle-class areas evident in the careers of
firemen. The fire-prone ghettos get the more enthusiastic
(sometimes experienced) staff while those firemen wishing a quiet
life nearer retirement tend to gravitate to less busy stations.
Wherever they are located fire stations are very definitely social
centres for the staff based on them and their colleagues, and they
could perform a similar function, it is suggested, for neighbouring
residents. The author concludes that when fire stations are being
relocated and services reorganized these social implications should
be taken into account if fires are to be prevented and be extin-
guished quickly whenever they do occur.

The distribution of discharged mental health patients

Another service which has attracted geographical analysis is mental
health. Spatial aspects of policies have been analysed as well as
locational aspects of such facilities as hospitals, hostels, and after-
care clinics (Wolpert et al., 1975; Wolpert and Wolpert, 1976; Dear,
1977; C. J. Smith and Hanham, 1980). In recent years in the United
States many of the mentally disabled have been released from
institutionalized care into the community. The distributional
consequences (outcomes) of this policy in terms of the benefits and
burdens placed on ex-patients and recipient areas alike have been
examined. There is a tendency for such 'dependent' groups to end
up concentrated in low-income inner-city areas. Such segregation
may be desirable in that the appropriate services may also be so
concentrated. But are these sorts of areas the most suitable? A
more equitable dispersed placement policy may be preferable, and
an assignment model is proposed to achieve a 'better' pattern of
medical and social outcomes than the present 'dumping' practice.
Wolpert and Wolpert (1976) make several recommendations which
they believe would make the release process more humane and

effective both for those suffering from mental illness and the communities from which they come and to which they are being returned.

Major trends

Thus far this review has indicated the sort of research being done in human geography and related disciplines. What overall trends and patterns can be discerned?

First, much of the research is *adisciplinary* in so far as evidently all manner of social scientists are interested in who gets what urban public resources, how, why, *and* where. It may be that geographers tend to concentrate on public goods which have a fixed location, and political scientists focus on patterns of expenditure and service delivery. It does not seem to be the case any more that researchers from different backgrounds are concerned to demonstrate the importance of particular disciplinary explanations in which they have a 'vested interest'. If anything, the reverse is true. Thus we see British political scientists concentrating on 'geographical' factors (Newton, 1979, 1980), and Americans focusing on 'non-political' bureaucratic processes (Jones and Kaufman, 1974; Nivola, 1978). Geographers meanwhile are decrying area-based explanations in favour of conflict theory and political economy.

Secondly, although the overall scope of recent research is impressive — inter-/intra-authority, theoretical/empirical, aggregate/individual, expenditures/facility location, quality/quantity of services, outputs/outcomes, statistical/behavioural — it is nonetheless highly diffuse and uneven. There seems to be a general trend towards concentrating on patterns of public allocations *within* metropolitan areas/cities. Greater weight is increasingly being attached to political and administrative *explanations*. A clear understanding is thus required of the decisions and actions of key actors, the organizations in which they operate, and the spatial, economic, and other influences which constrain them.

As far as any 'international division of labour' is concerned, it appears that there is some common ground between American and British geographers and other social scientists. Emphasis has been firmly placed on output studies, and there is a trend towards theoretical pluralism and divergence on both sides of the Atlantic. The recent spate of American studies of service distribution has not yet, however, been matched in Britain or Canada. Lastly, the scope for further comparative and case-studies would seem to be immense despite the rapid expansion of urban public policy research. Some useful research agendas have recently been formulated (Rich, 1979; Wolch, 1979). However, this chapter will conclude by mapping out some possible future lines of enquiry.

Future research

Notwithstanding notable contributions by Kirby (1979b, c) and Saunders (1979), one of the most urgent tasks for human geographers and other social scientists must be to operationalize alternative *explanatory paradigms*. Commending these approaches is relatively simple, but putting them into practice is not always attempted, or successfully accomplished. As Dear and Clarke (1978) have indicated, the relative merits and demerits of managerial and Marxist approaches need to be demonstrated empirically. If public sector decisions and the patterns of resource allocations they produce are to be fully understood then individuals, organizations, *and* how they are influenced by larger structural forces or conflicts have to be analysed.

As has already been noted, there have been relatively few comparative studies of urban expenditure or service provision which have looked at both North American and British cities. Agnew (1978) investigated the differing attitudes of homeowners in Drayton and Leicester towards locating public housing estates nearby. More controversy was reported in American cities by housing managers partly, it would seem, because the home is seen as primarily an investment. There is evidence in the United Kingdom that municipal and/or pressure by residents can influence if and where council estates are built, especially in peripheral green-field sites. However, further research is clearly required on how British and North American cities differ in their size, socioeconomic composition, spatial structure, political culture, local government system, and if and how these contrasts are reflected in the distribution of housing or any other aspect of public provision.

Specific explanatory variables - such as those listed by Pinch (1980a) remain to be studied in depth. For example, as Rich (1979) has pointed out, the role of neighbourhood organizations has been neglected. There is only limited systematic evidence if and how citizen participation between elections or neighbourhood decent-ralization increases attentiveness and responsiveness to neigh-bourhood needs and affects the allocation of municipal goods and services (Cosgrove *et al.*, 1978; Hambleton, 1978). Certainly there is a dearth of studies in British and Canadian cities on the consequences of individual contacting and collective demand-making (Ley, 1974). While the spatial consequences of decision rules of municipal bureaucracies are known in the United States, this is not the case in Britain. In inter-authority studies causal relationships between location, jurisdictional structure, economic base (in addition to rank in the urban hierarchy), and size and shape of municipal expenditures are required. Important regional differences in the urban systems in the United States are evident (Adams, 1979; Clark, 1976b).

Although diffusion studies are well established in human geography, apart from the studies of Agnew *et al.* (1978) and Bingham (1978), there do not seem to have been many attempts to investigate spatial aspects of the process of the adoption and implementation of policy innovations by local authorities. In recent years, for example, British urban authorities have gradually stopped building high-rise blocks of flats, replaced rank-order council house allocation procedures with computer-based points systems, and now indicate roadworks with battery-operated, rather than paraffin, lamps. Temporal and spatial trends in the diffusion of paracme and innovation of such urban features can be identified, and the significant explanatory processes and factors investigated.

Another imbalance which exists in output studies is the evident concentration on *allocative* outputs. Imporant though expenditure and the provision of services and facilities are in influencing social/spatial welfare and the built environment, nonetheless this does not mean that regulative, symbolic, and extractive decisions and actions should be avoided. There are some studies of urban courts (Eisenstein and Jacob, 1974; Davidson, 1977; Johnston, forthcoming) but not of spatial distribution of sentences by local (magistrates) courts — for example, custodial sentences, fines, and community/probation orders. Likewise, it would be interesting to see if 'symbolic' output distributions in the form of promises and visits, for example, corresponded to those of more tangible goods and services.

The politics, but not the geography, of municipal revenue and budgeting have been investigated in the United States (Meltsner, 1971) and the United Kingdom. Variations in local taxation, fines, and other forms of extractive outputs could also be examined (Thrall, 1979; Talarchek and Agnew, 1979; Levin, 1978). With their expertise in the measurement of spatial externalities, urban geographers should be in a good position to analyse 'benefit structures' (Mollenkopf, 1979). That is, policies, organizations, and services/facilities would be viewed in terms of who benefits, how and where; and who pays, how and where. Temporal/spatial consistencies may be identified which may result from the incremental nature of urban policy-making.

Notwithstanding the difficulties of data collection, it would be a feasible if painstaking task to document in detail the output distribution for individual cities and/or authorities. As Dimond *et al.* (1978) have noted, although the number of studies of service provision is great, surprisingly little information on the level, variety, and quality of public services is available to identifiable neighbourhoods within particular jurisdictions or comparable neighbourhoods in different jurisdictions and cities. American studies discussed above, and in particular those in Oakland and San Antonio, have pointed the way in this respect. In the United Kingdom the work of Pinch in London on the mismatch between need and provision, and Kirby in Newcastle on class-specific and location-specific deprivation may be singled out as pioneering efforts of this type. Measuring and mapping variations in the quality and quantity of such services as *housing* repairs, inspections and grants; police patrols and prosecutions; planning permissions and orders; street cleaning, lighting and patching is not necessarily a menial task. Similarly, plotting the location of facilities such as allotments, adventure playgrounds, bus stops, car parks, cemeteries, community centres, council and civic offices, family planning clinics, gypsy sites, health centres, hospitals, hostels, libraries, nurseries, parks, post offices, police stations, prisons, schools, sports centres, surgeries, taxi ranks, and WCs, can be revealing (Burnett, 1979a). The distribution of outputs can be shown in imaginative ways, for example, by constructing 'spending and activity surfaces', analysing spatial domains (Rondinelli, 1978), identifying 'service-rich areas' (Wolch, 1979) and surplus/deficit areas in relation to need (Bassett and Hauser, 1975). Such studies of the 'minutiae' of municipal services might be considered to be too trivial in an era of theory-building, but Bunge has shown that street-level expeditions can be revealing and evolutionary. It is unlikely that other social scientists have the inclination and expertise to map such distributions and the 'neutral' or 'malevolent' processes which are responsible for them.

Catalogues of what is spent, located, and provided where is merely the first step. More important is to see how policies and procedures affect the lives of urban citizens — particularly those individuals and groups who depend on them — the elderly, the impoverished, and the most 'necessitous'. Urban outcomes for specific services have been and are being studied in numerous American cities, Mayer (1980). In British cities current research projects known to the author include investigations into 'local-specific' and 'class-specific' deprivation in health provision in Reading, public provision in inner-city Walsall, and the distribution of bureaucratic responses, service delivery, facilities, and expenditure in south east Hampshire. Where British researchers focus on the mismatch between needs and resources and territorial injustice, Americans are primarily concerned with spatial inequality and discrimination. Perhaps fresh insights could be gained from an exchange of approach and methodology.

There are also possibilities for such research at the micro scale. Individuals and neighbourhoods are affected by public decisions and actions positively or negatively; intentionally or unintentionally; directly or indirectly; and there is scope for small-scale studies of the impacts of a whole range of public policies and provision. Here 'hard data' can be collected from the census, municipal minutes and appendices, local newspapers, and by observation survey methods employed to find out more about the views of local people about the location of facilities (Smith and Hanham, 1980), their use or non-use of services, and consequences for their well-being and real income.

Applied urban political geography need not be restricted to jurisdictional and electoral or optimum location studies, useful though they are. There is ample scope for politicians and officials who make distributional decisions to be advised and enlightened about the social and spatial consequences of their actions; but explanations must be carefully considered if prescriptions are to be offered to alleviate or eliminate inequality in outputs and inequity in outcomes. There is ample evidence that political and other social scientists are taking a keen interest in the study of urban service distributions (Rich, forthcoming). Whatever North American and British geographers have on their research agendas in the 1980s, it would be a pity if distributional studies of outputs and outcomes were to be omitted.

Acknowledgements

I would like to acknowledge the helpful comments on an earlier draft of this paper by John Agnew, Keith Cole, Robert Hanham, Dilys Hill, Graham Moon, and Stephen Pinch.

References and bibliography

Aberbach, J. D., and Walker, J. L. (1972). 'Citizen desires, policy outcomes and community control', *Urban Affairs Quarterly*, **8**, 55-75.

Adams, B., Okeley, J., McGraw, D., and Smith, D. (1975). 'Gypsies: current policies and practices', *Journal of Social Policy*, **4**, 129-50.

Adams, J. (1976). *Urban Policymaking and Metropolitan Dynamics*, (Ballinger, Cambridge, Mass.).

Adams, J. (1979). 'A geographical basis for urban public policy', *Professional Geographer*, **31**(2), 135-45.

Agnew, J. (1976). 'Public policy and the spatial form of the city: a case study of public housing location' (unpublished PhD thesis, Ohio State University).

Agnew, J. (1978). 'Market relations and locational conflict in cross-national perspective', in Cox, K. R. (ed.), *Urbanisation and Conflict in Market Societies*, pp. 128-44 (Methuen, London).

Agnew, J., Brown, L.A., and Herr, J.P. (1978). 'The community innovation process. A conceptualization and empirical analysis', *Urban Affairs Quarterly*, **14**(1), 3-30.

Aiken, M., and Depre, R. (1980). 'Policy and politics in Belgian cities', *Policy and Politics*, **8**(1), 73-107.

Allen, R. (1979). 'Area analysis of resources in South Glamorgan', in Davis, E. M. (ed.), *Research and Intelligence: papers delivered at the Annual Conference 1978*, pp. 219-35 (INLOGOV, University of Birmingham).

Alt, J. E. (1977). 'Politics and expenditure models', *Policy and Politics*, **5**(3), 83-92.

Antunes, G., and Plumlee, J. (1977). 'The distribution of an urban public service ethnicity, socio-economic status, and bureaucracy as determinants of the quality of neighbourhood streets', *Urban Affairs Quarterly*, **12**, 312-32.

Arnstein, S. R. (1969). 'A ladder of citizen participation', *Journal of the American Institute of Planners*, **35**(4), 216-24.

Austin, C. M. (1974). 'The evaluation of urban public facility location: an alternative to cost-benefit analysis', *Geographical Analysis*, **6**(2), 135-46.

Bardach, E. (1976). 'Policy termination as a political process', *Policy Sciences*, **7**, 123-31.

Barton, A. H. *et al.* (1977). *Decentralizing City Government: an evaluation of the New York city district manager experiment* (Lexington Books, Lexington).

Bassett, K., and Hauser, D. (1975). 'Public policy and spatial structure', in Peel, R., Chisholm, M., and Haggett, P. (eds.), *Processes in Human and Physical Geography: Bristol Essays*, pp. 20-66 (Heinemann, London).

Bassett, K., and Short, J. (1980). 'Patterns of building society and local authority lending in the 1970s', *Environment and Planning, A*, **12**(3), 279-301.

Batley, R., and Edwards, J. (1975). *The Politics of Positive Discrimination* (Tavistock, London).

Behn, R. D. (1978). 'Closing a government facility', *Public Administration Review*, **38**, 332-8.

Behn, R. D., and Bardach, E. (1976). 'Policy termination as a political process', *Policy Sciences*, **7**(2), 126-7.

Benson, C., and Lund, P. B. (1969). *Neighbourhood Distribution of Local Public Services* (Institute of Government Studies, University of California, Berkeley).

Benyon, J. (1978). 'Some implications of airport location: the case of Edinburgh Airport', *Public Administration*, **56**, 439-56.

Bigman, D., and Revelle, C. (1978). 'The theory of welfare considerations in public facility location problems', *Geographical Analysis,* **10**(3), 229-40.

Bingham, R. D. (1978). 'Innovation, bureaucracy and public policy: a study of innovation adoption by local government', *Western Political Quarterly,* **31**(2), 179-205.

Block, P. B. (1974). *Equality in the Distribution of Policing Services: A Case Study of Washington, DC* (Urban Institute, Washington, DC).

Bloom, H. S., Brown, H. J., and Jackson, J. E. (1975). 'Residential location and local public services', in Jansen, J. E. (ed.), *Public Needs and Private Wants in Metropolitan Areas,* (Ballinger, Cambridge, Mass.).

Blowers, A. (1974). 'Land ownership and the public interest: the case of Operation Leapfrog', *Town and Country Planning,* **42,** 499-503.

Boaden, N. T. (1971). *Urban Policy Making* (Cambridge University Press, Cambridge).

Boaden, N. T., and Alford, R. R. (1969). 'Sources of diversity in English local government decisions', *Public Administration,* **47**(2), 203-23.

Boots, A. J., Dawson, G., Silverman, W., and Hatry, H. P. (1972). *Inequality in Local Government Services: A Case Study of Neighbourhood Roads* (Urban Institute, Washington, DC).

Bourne, L. S. (1976). 'Urban structure and land-use decisions', *Annals of the Association of American Geographers,* **66**(4), 531-47.

Bradley, J. E., Kirby, A. M., and Taylor, P. J. (1976). *Distance Decay and Tooth Decay: A Socio Dental Study of School-Children in the Newcastle Area Health Authority* (Seminar Paper 31, Department of Geography, University of Newcastle).

Bruce, A. (1974). 'Facilities required near home', *Built Environment,* **3**(4), 290-1.

Bunge, W. W. (1971). *Fitzgerald: Geography of a Revolution* (Schenkman, Cambridge, Mass.).

Bunge, W. W. (1977). 'The politics of reproduction: a second front', *Antipode,* **9**(1), 66-76.

Burnett, A. D. (1976). 'Legislating for neighbourhood councils', *Local Government Studies,* **2**(4), 31-8.

Burnett, A. D. (1978). 'Political demands and public services: geographical aspects of petitioning and protesting over Portsmouth's public services' (Portsmouth Polytechnic, Discussion Paper).

Burnett, A. D. (1979a) (ed.). *An Everyday Atlas of Portsmouth* (Portsmouth City Council).

Burnett, A. D. (1979b). 'The study of spatial aspects of urban political systems' (unpublished paper given at SSRC seminar in Urban Politics, University of Warwick, September).

Burnett, A. D. (forthcoming). 'Protesting and petitioning in Portsmouth', in Cox, K. R., and Johnston, R. J. (eds.), *Conflict, Politics and the Urban Scene* (Longmans, London).

Burnett, A. D., and Hamilton, F. E. I. (1979b). 'Social processes and residential structure', in French, R. A., and Hamilton, F. E. I. (eds.), *The Socialist City: Spatial Structure and Urban Policy* (Wiley, Chichester), pp. 263-304.

Butler, E. W. (1977). 'Government and services', *The Urban Crisis: Problems and Prospects in America,* chap. 7, pp. 103-21 (Goodyear, Santa Monica).

Carney, J. G. (1972). 'Urban public goods: positivist and radical positions', *Area,* **4**(3), 175-7.

Chisholm, M. (1974). 'The reformation of local government in England', in Peel, R. J., Chisholm, M., and Haggett, P. (eds.), *Processes in Human and Physical Geography,* pp. 305-19 (Heinemann, London).

Cho, Y. H. (1967). 'The effect of local government systems on local policy outcomes in the U.S.', *Public Administration Review,* **27**(1), 31-8.

Clark, T. N. (1976a) (ed.) 'Citizen preferences and urban public policymaking: models, measures and uses', *Policy and Politics,* **4**(4).

Clark, T. N. (1976b). 'Cities differ... but how and why? Inputs to National urban policy from research on decisionmaking in 51 American Municipalities' (unpublished report).

Cockburn, C. (1977). *The Local State* (Pluto Press, London).

Cohen, M. A. (1974). *Urban Policy and Political Conflict in Africa* (University of Chicago Press, Chicago).

Cole, K. (1979). *Individual Demand Making in an Urban Environment: Some Geographical Considerations* (Research Seminar Series, Department of Geography, Portsmouth Polytechnic).

Cole, R. L. (1974). *Citizen participation and the urban policy process.* (Lexington Books, Lexington, Mass.).

Cornelius, W.A. (1974). 'Urbanisation and political demand-making: political participation among the migrant poor in Latin American cities', *American Political Science Review,* **68**, 1125-46.

Cosgrove, D. F., Sheldon, H. N., Masterton, M. P., and Masterman, E. M. (1978). 'Community councils research projects interim reports', *Central Research Unit, Scottish Office,* Part 1, Appendix A, 128-31, and Part 2, Appendix B.

Coulter, P. B. (1972). 'Comparative community politics and public policy: problems in theory and research', in Morgan, D. R., and Kirkpatrick, S. A. (eds.), *Urban Political Analysis: a systems approach,* pp. 370-83 (Free Press, New York).

Cox, A. W. (1979). 'Administrative inertia and inner-city politics', *Public Administration Bulletin,* **29**, 2-18.

Cox, K. R. (1973). *Conflict, Power and Politics in the City: a Geographic View* (McGraw Hill, New York).

Cox, K. R. (1978a). 'The politics of exclusion in the United States' (unpublished paper, IBG Conference Paper, Hull University).

Cox, K. R. (1978b) (ed.) *Urbanisation and Conflict in Market Societies* (Methuen, London).

Cox, K. R. (1978c). 'Local interests and urban political process in market societies', in Cox, K. R. (ed.), *Urbanization and Conflict in Market Societies,* pp. 94-110 (Methuen, London).

Cox, W. H. (1976). *Cities: the Public Dimension* (Pelican, London).

Crenson, M. A. (1978). 'Social networks and political processes in urban neighbourhoods', *American Journal of Political Science,* **22**(3), 578-94.

Cupps, D. S. (1977). 'Emerging problems of citizen participation', *Public Administrative Review,* **37**(5), 478-87.

Currie, L. (1976). 'Attitudes of users and non-users towards public facilities and services' (unpublished Master's thesis, McMaster University, Ottawa).

Danziger, J. N. (1976). 'Twenty-six outputs in search of a taxonomy', *Policy and Politics,* **3**, 201-12.

Darke, J., and Walker, R. (eds.), (1979). *Who Needs Housing?* (Papermac, Macmillan, London).

Davidson, R. N. (1977). 'Spatial bias in court sentencing' (unpublished paper given to IBG Urban Studies Group, University of Leicester).

Davies, B. (1977). 'Social service studies and the explanation of policy outcomes', *Policy and Politics* (special issue on urban policy in Britain — influences, processes and impacts), **5**(3), 41-60.

Dear, M. J. (1976). 'Spatial externalities and locational conflict', in Massey, D., and Batey, P. (eds.), *London Papers in regional Science Alternative Frameworks for Analysis*, pp. 152-67. (Pion, London).

Dear, M. J. (1977). 'Psychiatric patients and the inner-city', Annals of the Association of American Geographers, **67**(4), 588-94.

Dear, M. J. (1978). 'Planning for mental health care: a reconsideration of public facility location theory', *International Regional Science Review*, **3**(2), 93-111.

Dear, M. J., and Clark, G. (1978). 'The state and geographic process: a critical review', *Environment and Planning, A,* **10**(2), 173-85.

Dear, M. J., Fincher, R., and Currie, L. (1977). 'Measuring the external effects of public programmes', *Environment and Planning, A,* **9**, 137-47.

Dear, M. J., and Long, J. (1978). 'Community strategies in locational conflict', in Cox, K. R. (ed.), *Urbanisation and Conflict in Market Societies*, chap. 5, pp. 113-28.

Dearlove, J. (1973). *The Politics of Policy in Local Government* (Cambridge University Press, Cambridge).

Dearlove, J. (1979). *The Reorganisation of Local Government* (Cambridge University Press, London).

De Vise, P. (1973). 'Misused and misplaced hospitals and doctors: a locational analysis of the urban health care crisis', *Commission on College Geography Research Paper No. 22* (Association of American Geographers, Washington, DC).

Dimond, P. R., Chamberlain, C., and Hillyard, W. (1979). *A Dilemma of Local Government: Discrimination in the Provision of Public Services* Lexington Books, Lexington, Mass.).

Downs, G. W., Jnr. (1976). *Bureaucracy, Innovation and Public Policy,* (Lexington Books, Lexington, Mass.).

Duncan, S. S. (1974). 'Cosmetic planning or social engineering', *Area,* **6**(4), 259-60.

Dunleavy, P. (1977). 'Protest and quiescence in urban politics: a critique of some pluralist and structuralist myths', *International Journal of Urban and Regional Research,* **1**(2).

Dunleavy, P. (1980). *Urban Political Analysis* (Macmillan, London).

Easton, D. (1965). *A Systems Analysis of Political Life* (Wiley, New York).

Edwards, T., and Batley, R. (1979). *The Politics of Positive Discrimination* (Tavistock, London).

Eisenstein, J., and Jacob, H. (1974). 'Measuring performance and outputs of urban criminal courts', *Social Science Quarterly,* **54**(4), 713-25.

Elcock, H. (1979). 'Politicians, organisations and the public — the provision of gypsy sites', *Local Government Studies,* **5**(3), 43-54.

Elkin, S. L. (1974). 'Comparative urban politics and inter-organisational behaviour', *Policy and Politics,* **2**(4), 289-308.

Eulau, H., and Eyestone, R. (1968). 'Policy maps of city councils and policy outcomes: a developmental analysis', *American Political Science Review,* **62,** 124-43.

Eyles, J. (1978). 'Social geography and the study of the capitalist city', *Tijdschrift voor Economische en Sociale Geografie,* **69**(5), 296-305.

Fenton, J. H., and Chamberlayne, P. W. (1969). 'The literature dealing with the relationship between political processes, socio-economic conditions and policies in American States', *Politics,* **1,** 388-404.

Fisk, D. M., and Winnie, R. E. (1974). 'Output measurement in urban government. Current status and likely prospects', *Social Science Quarterly,* **54**(4), 725-41.

Flynn, R. (1978). 'State planning: a review and critique of some recent marxist writings', *Public Administration Bulletin,* No. 28, 4-17.

Forest, R., Lloyd, J., Rogers, N., and Williams, P. (1979). 'The inner-city: in search of the problem', *Geoforum,* **10,** 109-16.

French, R. A. and Hamilton, F. E. I. (eds.) (1979). *The Socialist City: Spatial Structure and Urban Policy* (Wiley, Chichester).

Friedland, R. (ed.) (1979). 'State intervention and the social wage', *International Journal of Health Services,* **9**(2), 191-206.

Friedland, R., Piven, F. F., and Alford, R. R. (1977). 'Political conflict, urban structure and the fiscal crisis', *International Journal of Urban and Regional Research,* **1**(3), 447-73.

Froman, L. A. (1967). 'An analysis of public policies in cities', *Journal of Politics,* **29**(1), 94-108.

Fuchs, R. J., and Demko, G. J. (1979). 'Geographic inequality under socialism', *Annals of the Association of American Geographers* **69**(2), 304-18.

Getter, R. W., and Schumaker, P. D. (1978). 'Contextual bases of responsiveness to citizen preferences and group demands', *Policy and Politics,* **6,** 249-79.

Glassberg, A. (1973). 'The linkage between urban policy outputs and voting behaviour: New York and London', *British Journal of Political Science,* **3,** 341-61.

Goldenberg, E. N. (1979). 'Evaluating municipal services', *Public Administration Review,* **39**(1), 94-8.

Goldsmith, M. J., and Rhodes, R. A. W. (eds.) (1978). 'New trends in local government research', special issue of *Public Administration Bulletin,* No. 28.

Goodwin, R. E. (1977). 'Symbolic rewards: being bought off cheaply', *Political Studies,* **25**(3), 383-96.

Grant, J. A. (1977). *The Politics of Urban Transport Planning* (Earth Resources Research Publication, London).

Gray, A. (1975). 'The study of public policy in local government: some reflections for British political science', *Public Administration Bulletin,* No. 18, 13-24.

Gray, F. (1976). 'The selection and allocation of council housing', *Transactions of the Institute of British Geographers,* NS **1,** 34-46.

Greenwood, R., Hinings, C. R., and Ranson, S. (1977). 'The politics of the budgetary process in English local government', *Political Studies,* **25**(1), 25-47.

Gudgin, G., and Taylor, P. J. (1978). *Votes, Seats and the Spatial Organisation of Elections* (Pion, London).

Gyford, J. (1976). *Local Politics in Britain* (Croom Helm, London).

Hall, D. R. (1977). 'Applied social area analysis: defining and evaluating areas for urban neighbourhood councils, *Geoforum,* **8**(5/6), 277-311.

Hambleton, R. (1978). *Policy Planning and Local Government* (Hutchinson, London).

Hammett, C. (1979). 'Area based explanations: a critical appraisal', in Herbert, D. T., and Smith D. M. (eds.), *Social Problems and the City,* pp. 244-57 (Oxford University Press, Oxford).

Harries, K. D., and Brun, S. D. (1978). *The Geography of Laws and Justice* (Praeger, New York).

Harrop, K. J. (1979). 'The development of structure and influences of externality fields on residential location on Tyneside' (unpublished PhD thesis, University of Newcastle).

Harvey, D. (1978). 'Labor, capital and class struggle around the built environment in advanced capitalist societies', in Cox, K. R. (ed.), *Urbanisation and Conflict in Market Societies,* pp. 9-37 (Methuen, London).

Hawley, W. D., and Lipsky, M. (1976). *Theoretical Perspectives on Urban Politics* (Prentice Hall, Englewood Cliffs, New Jersey).

Heclo, H. H. (1972). Review Article: 'Policy analysis', *British Journal of Political Science,* **2,** 83-108.

Herbert, D. T. (1979). 'Introduction: geographical perspectives and urban problems', in Herbert, D. T., and Smith, D. M. (eds.), *Social Problems and the City,* pp. 1-8 (Oxford University Press, Oxford).

Hill, R. C. (1978). 'Fiscal collapse and political struggle in decaying capital cities in the United States', in Tabb, W. K., and Sawers, L. (eds.), *Marxism and the Metropolis,* pp. 213-40 (Oxford University Press, New York).

Hodgart, R. L. (1978). 'Optimizing access to public services: a review of problems, models and methods of locating central facilities', *Progress in Human Geography,* **2**(1), 17-48.

Hodge, D. and Gattrell, A. (1976). 'Spatial constraint and the location of urban public facilities', *Environment and Planning, A,* **8,** 215-30.

Homenuck, H. P. M. (1970). 'Intra-urban locational patterns of civic decision-making power: a case study of Calgary 1948-68', *Proceedings of the Canadian Association of Geographers,* 149-56.

Honey, R. (1976). 'Conflicting problems in the political organisation of space', *Annals of Regional Science,* **10**(1), 45-61.

Honey, R., and Reynolds, D. R. (1977). 'Conflict in the location of salutary facilities', in Cox, K. R. (ed.), *Urbanisation and Conflict in Market Societies,* pp. 144-62 (Methuen, London).

Hooper, A. (1978). 'Political economy of housing in Britain', *Journal of Urban and Regional Research,* **2**(1), 175-87.

Huckfeldt, R. R. (1979). 'Political participation and the neighbourhood social context', *American Journal of Political Science,* **23**(3), 579-92.

Jackman, R. (1978). 'Local expenditure and local discretion', *Centre for Environmental Studies Review,* **4,** 63-73.

Jacob, H. (1972). 'Contact with government agencies: a preliminary analysis of the distribution of government services', *Mid West Journal of Political Science,* **16,** 123-46.

Janelle, D. G., and Millward, H. A. (1976). 'Locational conflict patterns and urban ecological structure', *Tijdschrift voor Economische en Sociale Geografie,* **67**(2), 102-14.

Johnston, R. J. (1977). 'Environment, elections and expenditure', *Regional Studies,* **11**(6), 383-94.

Johnston, R. J. (1979). *Political, Electoral and Spatial Systems* (Oxford University Press, Oxford).

Johnston, R. J. (forthcoming). 'The courts as the focus for neighbourhood conflict', in Johnston, R. J. and Cox, K. R. (eds.), *Conflict, Politics and the Urban Scene* (Longmans, London).

Jones, B. D. (1977). 'Distributional considerations in models of urban government service provision', *Urban Affairs Quarterly,* **12**, 291-312.

Jones, B. D., and Kaufman, C. (1974). 'The distribution of urban public services: a preliminary model', *Administration and Society,* **6**, 337-60.

Jones, B. D., Greenberg, J. R., Kaufman, C., and Drew, J. (1977). 'Bureaucratic response to citizen initiated contacts', *American Political Science Review,* **71**, 148-65.

Jones, B. D., Greenberg, J. R., Kaufman, C., and Drew, J. (1979). 'Service delivery rules and the distribution of local services: three Detroit bureaucracies', *Journal of Politics,* **40**(2), 332-68.

King, R. (1974). 'Social class, educational attainment and provision: a L.E.A. study', *Policy and Politics,* **3**(1), 17-35.

Kirby, A. M. (1979a). 'Public resource allocation: spatial inputs and social outcomes', in Goodall, B., and Kirby, A. M. (eds.), *Resources and Planning,* pp. 343-60. (Pergamon Press, Oxford).

Kirby, A. M. (1979b). 'Managerialism': a view of local authority housing', *Public Administration Bulletin,* No. 30, pp. 47-60.

Kirby, A. M. (1979c). *Towards an Understanding of the Local State,* Geographical papers, No. 70 (Department of Geography, University of Reading).

Kirby, A. M. (1979d). *Education Health and Housing. An Empirical Investigation of Resource Accessibility* (Saxon House, Farnborough).

Klein, R. (1976). 'The politics of public expenditure: American theory and British practice', *British Journal of Political Science,* **6**, 401-32.

Knox, P. L. (1978). 'The intra urban ecology of primary medical care: patterns of accessibility and their policy implications', *Environment and Planning, A,* **10**, 415-35.

Knox, P. L. (1979). 'Subjective social indicators and urban social policy: a review', *Policy and Politics,* **7**(3), 299-309.

Lambert, C., Penny, J., and Webster, B. (1980). *The Impact of Services on the Inner City: the Case of Housing Improvement* (Institute of Local Government Studies, University of Birmingham).

Lambert, J., Paris, C., and Blackaby, R. (1978). *Housing Policy and the State: Allocation, Access and Control* (Macmillan, London).

Levin, M. A. (1977). *Urban Policies and the Criminal Courts* (University of Chicago Press, Chicago).

Levin, M. A. (1978). 'Urban politics and political economy: the politics of the property tax', *Policy Sciences,* **9**(2), 237-47.

Levy, F. S., Meltsner, A. J. and Wildavsky, A. (1974). *Urban Outcomes: Schools, Streets and Libaries* (University of California Press, Berkeley).

Lewis, J. (1975a). 'The local authority health and social services in four London boroughs: an examination of the forces of variation' (unpublished University of London PhD Thesis).

Lewis, J. (1975b). 'Variations in service provision: politics at the lay-professional interface', in Young, K. (ed.), *Essays on the Study of Urban Politics,* pp. 52-77 (Macmillan, London).

Lewis, N. (1976). 'Council house allocation: problems of discretion and control', *Public Administration,* **54,** 147-60.

Ley, D. (ed.)(1974). *Community Participation and the Spatial Order of the City* (Tantulus, Vancouver).

Ley, D., and Mercer, J. (1980) 'Locational conflict and the politics of consumption', *Economic Geography,* **56,** 89-109.

Lineberry, R. L. (1977b). *Equality and Public Policy* (Sage, Beverley Hills).

Lineberry, R. L., and Sharkansky, I. (1974). *Urban Politics and Public Policy* (Harper & Row, New York).

Lineberry, R. L., and Welch, R. E. (1974). 'Who get's what: measuring the distribution of urban public services', *Social Science Quarterly,* **54,** 700-12.

Lord, D. T. (1975). 'School busing and white abandonment of public schools', *South Eastern Geographer,* **15**(2), 81-92.

Lovrich, N. P., and Taylor, G. T., Jnr. (1976). 'Neighbourhood evaluation of local government services: a citizen survey approach', *Urban Affairs Quarterly,* **12**(2), 197-222.

Lowe, P. D. (1977). 'Amenity and equity: a review of local environmental pressure groups in Britain', *Environment and Planning, A,* **9,** 35-59.

Lowe, S. (1977). 'Community groups and local politics', in Darke, R., and Walker, R. (eds.), *Local Government and the Public,* pp. 123-42 (Leonard Hill).

Lowry, M. (1973). 'Schools in transition', *Annals of the Association of American Geographers,* Seminar Paper, **63,** 17-80.

Lucy, W. H., Gilbert, D., and Birkhead, G. S. (1977). 'Equity in local service distribution', *Public Administration Review,* **51**(6), 687-97.

McKay, D. H., and Cox, A. W. (1979). *The Politics of Urban Change* (Croom Helm, London).

McTighe, J. J. (1978). 'Management strategies to deal with shrinking resources', *Public Administrations Review,* **39**(1), 86-91.

Margolis, R. (1977). 'Ratfields, neighbourhood sanitation and rat complaints in Newark, New Jersey', *Geographical Review,* **67**(2), 221-32.

Markunsen, A. R. (1978). 'Class and urban social expenditure: a marxist theory of metropolitan government', in Tabb, W. K., and Sawers, L. (eds.), *Marxism and the Metropolis,* pp. 90-112 (Oxford University Press, New York).

Massam, B. H. (1974). 'Political geography and the provision of public services', *Progress in Human Geography,* **6,** 179-210.

Massam, B. H. (1975). *Location and Space in Social Administration* (Edward Arnold, London).

Massotti, L. H., and Bowen, D. R. (1965), 'Communities and budgets: the sociology of municipal expenditures', *Urban Affairs Quarterly,* **1,** 39-58.

Massotti, L. H., and Lineberry, R. L. (eds.) (1976). *The New Urban Politics* (Ballinger, Cambridge, Mass.).

Mayer, J. D. (1980). 'Response time and its significance in medical emergencies', *Geographical Review,* **70,** 79-87.

Meltsner, A. J. (1971). *The Politics of City Revenue* (California University Press, Berkeley).

Mercer, J., and Barnett, J. R. (1975). 'Spatial modifications to models of the urban policy process', in Lineberry, R. L., and Massotti, L. H. (eds.), *The New Urban Politics,* pp. 3-9 (Lexington Books, Lexington, Mass.).

Minghi, J. V. and Rumley, D. (1978). 'Towards a geography of campaigning: some evidence from a provincial election in Vancouver B.C.', *Canadian Geographer*, **22**(2), 145-62.

Mladenka, K. R. (1977). 'Citizen demand and bureaucratic response: direct dialling democracy in a major American city', *Urban Affairs Quarterly*, **12**(3), 273-90.

Mladenka, K. R., and Hill, K. Q. (1977). 'The distribution of benefits in an urban environment: parks and libraries in Houston', *Urban Affairs Quarterly*, **13**(1), 73-94.

Mladenka, K. R., and Hill, K. Q. (1978). 'The distribution of urban police services', *Journal of Politics*, **40**, 112-33.

Mollenkopf, J. (1979). 'Untangling the logics of urban service bureaucracies: the strange case of the San Francisco municipal railway', *International Journal of Health Services*, **9**(2), 225-69.

Moon, G. (1980). 'Distributing indoor recreation facilities in suburban local authority areas' (unpublished Research Seminar Paper, Department of Geography, Portsmouth Polytechnic).

Morgan, D. R., and Kirkpatrick, S. A. (1972). *Urban Political Analysis: A Systems Approach* (Free Press, New York).

Mumphrey, A. J., and Wolpert, J. (1973). 'Equity considerations and concessions in the siting of public facilities', *Economic Geography*, **49**, 109-21.

Munns, J. M. (1975). 'The environment, politics and policy literature: a critique and reformulation', *Western Political Quarterly*, **28**, 646-67.

Murphy, T. R., and Warren, C. R. (1974). *Organising Public Services in Metropolitan America* (Heath, Lexington).

Nelson, K. (1975a). 'Social class, political structure and public goods in American urban politics', *Urban Affairs Quarterly*, **11**, 241-64.

Newton, K. (1975b). 'Community politics and decision making: the American experience and its lessons', in Young, K. (ed.), *Essays on the Study of Urban Politics*, pp. 1-24 (Macmillan, London).

Newton, K. (1976). 'Community performance in Britain', *Current Sociology*, **26**, 49-86.

Newton, K. (1979). 'Central place theory and local expenditure in Britain' (unpublished IPSA Conference Paper, Moscow).

Newton, K. (1980). 'Cities and their services' (unpublished paper given at SSRC Seminar in Urban Politics, Exeter).

Newton, K., and Sharpe, L. J. (1977). 'Local outputs research: some reflections and proposals', *Policy and Politics*, **5**, 61-82.

Nivola, P. S. (1978). 'Distributing a municipal service: a case study of housing inspection', *Journal of Politics*, **40**, 59-81.

Nivola, P. S. (1979). *The Urban Service Problem* (Lexington Books, Lexington, Mass.).

O'Hare, M. (1977). 'Not on my door you don't: facility siting and the strategic importance of compensation', *Public Policy*, **25**(4), 407-58.

Oliver, J. H. (1968). 'Citizen demands and the soviet political system', *American Political Science Review*, **63**, 465-75.

Ostrom, E. (1974). 'Exclusion, choice and divisibility: factors affecting the measurement of urban agency output and impact', *Social Science Quarterly*, **54**(4), 691-700.

Pahl, R. E. (1979). 'Socio-political factors in resource allocation', in Herbert, D. T., and Smith, D. M. (eds.), *Social Problems and the City*, pp. 33-41 (Oxford University Press, Oxford).

Paris, C., and Lambert, J. (1978). 'Housing problems and the state: the case of Birmingham, England', in Herbert, D. T., and Johnston, R. J. (eds.), *Geography and the Urban Environment,* Vol. II, pp. 227-58 (John Wiley, Chichester).

Perry, J. L., and Kraemer, K. L. (1978). 'Innovation attributes, policy intervention and the diffusion of computer applications among local governments', *Political Sciences,* **9**, 176-206.

Phillips, D. R. (1979). 'Public attitudes to general practitioner services: a reflection of an inverse care law in intra-urban primary medical care', *Environment and Planning, A,* **11**, 815-24.

Pickvance, C. G. (1977). 'Marxist approaches to the study of urban politics', *International Journal of Urban and Regional Research,* **1**(2), 218-55.

Pinch, S. P. (1976). 'The geography of local authority housing, health and welfare resource allocation in London 1965-73' (unpublished PhD Thesis, University of London).

Pinch, S. P. (1978). 'Patterns of local authority housing allocation in Greater London between 1966-1973: an inter-borough analysis', *Transactions of the Institute of British Geographers,* **3**(1), 35-54.

Pinch, S. (1979). 'Territorial justice in the city: a case study of social services for the elderly in Greater London', in Herbert, D. T. and Smith, D. M. (eds.), *Social Problems and the City,* pp. 201-19 (Oxford University Press, Oxford).

Pinch, S. P. (1980a). 'Local authority provision for the elderly: an overview and case study of London', in Herbert, D. T., and Johnston, R. J. (eds.), *Geography and the Urban Environment,* p. 3 (Wiley, Chichester).

Pinch, S. P. (1980b). 'Spatial aspects of local service provision'. (Paper presented to SSRC Urban Politics Seminar, Exeter).

Price, D., and Cummings, A. (1977). *Family Planning Clinics in London,* Working Paper 2 (Central London Polytechnic).

Prottas, J. M. (1978). 'The power of the street-level bureaucrat in public service bureaucracies', *Urban Affairs Quarterly,* **13**(3), 285-312.

Pyle, D. (1976). 'Aspects of resource allocation by local education authorities', *Social and Economic Administration,* **10**(2), 106-21.

Rakoff, S. H., and Schaefer, G. F. (1970). 'Politics, policy and political science: theoretical alternatives', *Politics and Society,* 1, 51-77.

Randall, G. W., Lomas, K. W., and Newton, T. (1973). 'Area distribution of resources in Coventry', *Local Government Finance,* **77**, 396-400.

Rhodes, R. A. W. (1975). 'The Lost World of British local politics', *Local Government Studies,* **1**(3), 39-59.

Ribbins, P. M., and Brown, R. J. (1979). 'Policymaking in English local government: the case of secondary school reorganisation', *Public Administration,* **57**, 187-203.

Rich, R. C. (1979). 'Neglected issues in the study of urban service distributions: a research agenda', *Urban Studies,* **16**, 143-56.

Rich, R. C. (ed.) (forthcoming). 'New approaches to the study of urban service distributions.' Special issue of the *Policy Studies Journal, Analyzing Inequality in Urban Services,* and *Causes and Effects of Inequality in Urban Services* (Lexington Books, Lexington, Mass.).

Rondinelli, D. A. (1978). 'Policy Coordination in Metropolitan Area: an ecological perspective', *Administration and Society,* **10**, 203-33.

Salamon, L. S. (1977). 'Urban politics, policy, case studies and political theory', *Public Administration Review,* **37**, 418-28.

Saunders, P. (1979). *Urban Politics: a Sociological Approach* (Hutchinson, London).

Schofield, J. A. (1978). 'Determinants of urban services expenditures — fire and social services', *Local Government Studies*, **4**, 65-80.

Schumaker, P. D. (1975). 'Policy responsiveness to protest group demands', *Journal of Politics*, **34**(2), 489-521.

Schumaker, P. D., and Billeaux, D. M. (1978). 'Group representation in local bureaucracies', *Administration and Society*, **10**(3), 285-316.

Seley, J. E. (1979). 'A comparison of technical and ethnographic approaches to the study of fire services', *Economic Geography*, **55**, 36-51.

Shin, D. C. (1977). 'The quality of municipal services: concepts, measures and results', *Social Indicators Research*, **4**, 218-35.

Shonick, W. (1979). 'The public hospital and its local ecology in the United States. Some relationships between the plight of the public hospital and the plight of the cities', *International Journal of Health Services*, **9**(3), 359-96.

Short, J. R., and Bassett, K. (1978). 'Housing action areas: an evaluation', *Area*, **10**(2), 153-7.

Sibley, D. (1977). 'Classification and control in local government: a case study of gypsies in Hull', *Town Planning Review*, **49**(3).

Simmie, J. M., and Hale, D. J. (1978a). 'Urban self management in Yugoslavia', *Regional Studies*, **12**, 701-12.

Simmie, J. M., and Hale, D. J. (1978b). 'The distributional effects of ownership and control of land-use in Oxford', *Urban Studies*, **15**, 9-21.

Smith, C. J., and Hanham, R. Q. (forthcoming). 'Any place but here! Mental health facilities as noxious neighbours', *Professional Geographer*.

Smith, D. M. (1975). *Human Geography: a Welfare Approach* (Edward Arnold, London).

Smith, D. M. (1979a). 'Inner City deprivation: problems and policies in advanced capitalist countries', *Geoforum*, **10**, 297-310.

Smith, D. M. (1979b). *Where the Grass is Greener* (Pelican, London).

Smith, G. C. (1976). 'The responses of residents and policy-makers to urban environmental hazards', *Area*, **8**(4), 279-83.

Smith, A. P., Whitehead, P. J., and Matchett, R. L. (1977). 'The utilization of services', in Wilson, A. G., Rees, P. H., and Lugh, C. M. (eds.), *Models of Cities and Regions*, pp. 323-404 (Wiley, Chichester).

Stetzer, D. F. (1971). *Special Districts in Cook Country: Towards a Geography of Local Government* (Department of Geography, University of Chicago).

Stipak, B. (1979). 'Citizen satisfaction with urban services', *Public Administration Review*, **39**(1), 46-53.

Tabb, W. K., and Sawers, L. (eds.) (1978). *Marxism and the Metropolis* (Oxford University Press, Oxford).

Talarchek, G. M., and Agnew, J. A. (1979). 'The pattern of property tax exemptions in a metropolitan fiscal setting', *Professional Geographer*, **31**(3), 284-91.

Taylor, P. J. (1979). '"Difficult-to-let", "difficult-to-live-in", and sometimes "difficult-to-get-out-of": an essay on the provision of council housing, with special reference to Killingworth', *Environment and Planning, A*, **11**(2), 1305-1320.

Taylor, P. J. and Johnston, R. J. (1979). *The Geography of Elections* (Penguin, Harmondsworth).

Thrall, G. I. (1979). 'A geographic criterion for identifying property tax assessment inequity', *Professional Geographer,* **31**(3), 278-83.

Walker, S. R. (1979). 'Educational services in Sydney: some spatial variations', *Australian Geographical Studies,* **17**(2), 175-92.

Wall, G. (1974). 'Complaints concerning air pollution in Sheffield', *Area,* **6**, 6-8.

Webster, B. A. (1977). 'Distributional impacts of local government policy' (unpublished Conference Paper, IBG Study Group, Leicester).

Webster, B. A. and Stewart, J. D. (1975). 'The area analysis of resources', *Policy and Politics,* **3**(1).

Webster, B. A., Lambert, C., and Penny, J. (1979). *The Impact of Local Authority Services on the Inner-city* (Interim Report, INLOGOV, University of Birmingham).

White, A. N. (1979). 'Accessibility and public facility location', *Economic Geography,* **55**, 18-35.

Wolch, J. R. (1979). 'Residential location and the provision of human services: some directions for geographic research', *Professional Geographer,* **31**(3), 271-7.

Wolfe, J. S., and Burghardt, A. F. (1978). 'The neighbourhood effect in a local election,' *Canadian Geographer,* **22**(4), 298-305.

Wolpert, J., Dear, M., and Crawford, R. (1975). 'Satellite mental health facilities', *Annals of the Association of American Geographers,* **65**, 24-35.

Wolpert, J., and Wolpert, E. R. (1976). 'The relocation of released mental hospital patients into residential communities', *Policy Sciences,* **71**, 31-51.

Young, K. (ed.) (1975). *Essays on the Study of Urban Politics* (Macmillan, London).

Young, K., and Kramer, J. (1978). *Strategy and Conflict in Metropolitan Housing, Suburbia versus the G.L.C., 1965-1975* (Heinemann, London).

Zisk, B. H. (1972). 'Local interest politics and municipal outputs', in Hahn, H. (ed.), *People and Politics in Urban Societies,* pp. 231-54.

Political studies from spatial perspectives
Edited by A.D. Burnett and P.J. Taylor
© 1981 John Wiley & Sons Ltd

_____ *11*__

Planning inquiries as a research issue

Andrew Kirby

Introduction

In a recent review of political geography Taylor (1979) has commented upon the failure of the subject to deal with the role of the state in modern society. In this paper I want to examine a particular aspect of the state's involvement in the planning process, namely the public inquiry.

In general, analyses of phenomena such as the urban renewal process, the construction of major trunk roads, the siting of airports and the location of hazards such as nuclear power stations have concentrated upon either the protagonists, the technical aspects of locational analysis, or the outcomes. Castells (1978), for example has discussed the political tensions that may create urban social movements where urban renewal is scheduled, whilst Self (1975) has analysed in depth the quantitative bases upon which such planning decisions are based. Few researchers have, however, concentrated upon the public inquiry, that formal occasion upon which the individual is able to involve himself or herself in the decision-making process. As I shall argue below, this lacuna has caused us to overlook a perspective upon the activities of the state and the important political tensions that stem from these activities.

Parenthetically, it should at this juncture be pointed out that the rest of the paper is expressed in the context of British experience: namely, a planning process in which the right of opposition is guaranteed, with a formal inquiry providing a venue for neighbourhood protest. The American experience is a different one; as Wolpert *et al.* (1972) state, 'the public hearing, as now structured, acts as an arena for contest, a therapeutic device for "letting off steam". It is not a vehicle for deliberation'. Due to the weakness of this system, an alternative tradition has come to typify American plan-making; this is the explicitly political activity of advocacy planning, in which different interest groups and localities draw upon different professionals in order to produce alternative plans. Superficially, it may appear that advocacy planning bears some similarities to the British tradition (i.e. the presentation of alternative views). However, the political nature of this process is very different: Goodman, for example describes it as a 'plurastic mechanism' (1972, p. 213). As we shall see, the British case is to be understood in the context of conflict, albeit within a very formal setting.

Planning inquiries

The remarks that follow are predicated on the assumption that the scale of the state's involvement in society is growing — not necessarily in all contexts, but most notably in terms of what has been termed *meta-planning* (Allison, 1975). Through the various agencies that deal with issues such as energy, transport, and land-use planning, government (and local government) is responsible for placing on the landscape a large number of negative externalities. In the last decade a new generation of such 'nuisances' has proliferated in both the UK and the USA, and in many instances planning inquiries have revealed the detailed deliberations involved in their location. In Britain the Roskill Commission, created to site the Third London Airport, constituted one of the largest exercises in spatial analysis ever undertaken, whilst the decade closed with a surrogate debate on the country's nuclear future, undertaken under the auspices of a local land-use planning inquiry at Windscale (Breach, 1978; Hall, 1980). Energy has also figured in the deliberations over the Vale of Belvoir coal resources, though in this instance the intrusion is visual rather than radioactive or aural (Hills and Cope, 1979). Throughout the decade a series of local inquiries has also highlighted the extent of both the national road-building programme and neighbourhood opposition; the motorway has been hyperbolically described as 'the greatest threat to the interests of this nation in all its history' (Tyme, 1978, p. 1).

The importance of these developments lies in the fact that the state has now replaced private industry as a source of large negative externalities (following a long period of anti-pollution legislation), and that this antisocial activity has prompted a political response. At one level this manifests itself in the formation of ecological parties; such groups, with very similar platforms on issues like 'nukes', have sprung up across Europe and America. A more interesting development in this context is the creation of ephemeral political organizations, based upon *spatial* rather than ideological cleavages. Using the distinction observed by Stephenson (1979), we may identify protest or conflict groups with *direct* and *indirect* spatial links. In the latter case groups emerge with an interest in a specific issue and an associated location (e.g. the Save the Redwoods (of California) League). In the direct case, traditional political cleavages at a particular location are suppressed in the face of some threatened externality, and spatially based political opposition results. (Interestingly, this of course represents a return to the historical bases of political development; this spatial legacy remains in our constituency system of elections, which sits uneasily alongside the ideological party divisions.)

These spatially based conflict groups may be very short-lived or particularly well organized. There is evidence that if the threat is large enough, 'normal' political cleavages within a neighbourhood can be suppressed for some time (although other factors are important here; see below). Furthermore, cooperation within a particular location may precede conflict with a nearby district, as is caricatured in Figure 11.1. These spatial conflicts (or 'salami

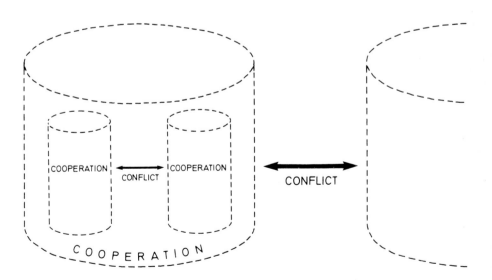

FIGURE 11.1 Locational conflict and cooperation at different spatial scales

politics') are particularly evident in the case of road constructions, where localities attempt to divert the motorway away from their area and towards another district. An interesting example of this is found in the deliberations surrounding the construction of a trunk road in Yorkshire, England; one locally based protest group has recently reported another protest group to the Minority Rights Group of the United Nations in Geneva for alleged misconduct during the period preceding the public inquiry (this is examined in greater depth in Kirby, 1980).

This mention of the inquiry procedure reminds us that this is the venue at which these conflicts are expressed, and as far as the state is concerned, also the means of conflict resolution. It thus provides a context within which to examine both issues: local conflicts and state intervention.

A political theory

Political science has not provided geography with many sources of inspiration. The limited number of exceptions includes the work of researchers such as Kendall and Stuart, which has been developed in electoral studies (Gudgin and Taylor, 1979) and Anthony Downs, whose spatial theory of party competition is utilized by Johnston (1979). Much of the material which deals with the analysis of government and policy remains unreferenced, despite the fact that the topics covered are of common interest to both subjects (see, for example, McKay and Cox on inner city strategies, 1978). This is particularly true in the present context, and both Budge and Allison have advanced the understanding of public inquiries (Allison, 1975; Budge, 1978).

Allison identifies within British planning a strong utilitarian element, which he characterizes as being 'want-regarding'. This is in contrast to many conservation groups, who are essentially 'ideal-regarding'. This produces a basic tension within both the planning process and planning inquiries: 'the arguments even of appellants who value conservation on ideal grounds have to be cast in utilitarian form if they are to have any chance of winning'. Moreover, the currency of want-regarding is a precise definition of wants: 'one must be able to talk authoritatively about what people want or rather (since different wants conflict) which decision will optimise the wants of most people. This puts a premium on technical approaches to optimisation, such as cost-benefit analysis' (Budge, 1978, p. 440). This is clearly unsatisfactory for several reasons: because technical responses to problems cannot be easily manipulated by lay observers; because 'ideal' issues cannot be readily converted to monetary terms; and because techniques like cost-benefit analysis are partial and ignore distributional effects between individuals and groups (Broadbent, 1977; Smith, 1977).

Allison's argument has been extended by Budge to include a formal representation of the relationships between administrators and appellants at inquiries. Basing his model on that of Downs, he identifies a continuum extending between want — and ideal — regarding views. In this schema, the appellants to an inquiry become the equivalents of political parties, and the inspector(s) become the counterparts of the voters. Consequently those overseeing inquiries will agree with those who express a case that is nearest to their own views, which dictates that the appellants will tailor their case (or political outlook) to the want-regarding stance of the administrators.

The Allison/Budge representation of what occurs at a planning inquiry is a useful method of approaching the protagonists and their behaviour. It is, however, only a partial representation, as Budge observes:

> the main substantive point on which both the models can be faulted is on their arbitrary assumption that arguments are the only determining factor in planning decisions. If other factors such as the size, nature and location of pressure groups determine outcomes, the models of arguments become irrelevant to planning decisions (1978, p. 447).

Politics, planning, and community

As Budge suggests, we need to develop our understanding of the inquiry process further. To achieve this, it is useful to distinguish more clearly the protagonists, and in the following discussion I draw on the typology outlined by Batty (1979), which differentiates between the planning system, the political system, and the community.

This typology has several advantages, but the most useful is that it redefines the planning inquiry as a three-sided affair, in which the planning system and the community compete within a political context. If we return to our remarks concerning externalities, we can see the planning system producing proposals that threaten particular groups and particular locations. The latter then are placed in conflict with the planning system, and both are in competition to achieve a particular political outcome.

This view has several implications, not least of which is a rejection of the view that the community is closely linked with the planning system via participative exercises. (It also redefines the traditional view of planning *vis-à-vis* the state.) More importantly, it allows us to develop an alternative explanation for success or failure by the community at the inquiry; this is based upon Dahrendorf's concept of *authority*. The major weakness of the Allison/Budge model is that it does not account for those instances in which appellants are successful, whereas an emphasis upon an ability to access authority (in the context of a situation such as a public inquiry) provides this.

According to Dahrendorf (1959), 'authority is a universal element of social structure. In this sense, it is more general than for example property, or even status' (p. 168). Furthermore, 'a clear line can at least in theory be drawn between those who participate in its exercise in given associations and those who are subject to the authoritative commands of others' (p. 170). Authority is here presented therefore as a cumulative issue, with some individuals generally being able to access it, and others unable. This is crucial at the stage at which a location is threatened by the planning process; in some instances conflict will produce a conflict group which will challenge authority. In other cases 'oppression and deprivation may reach a point at which militant conflict motivation gives way to apathy and lethargy' (p. 217).

Groups defined in relation to authority provide some insight into those who suffer in, for example, the urban renewal process; i.e. the neighbourhoods that are incapable of having their views incorporated into the planning proposals. In contrast, other locations may unite successfully against a spatial threat, if they have the ability to manipulate the inquiry system and even to involve themselves directly in the political arena. This was particularly true, for example, of opposition to the location of the Third London Airport in the high-status agricultural county of Buckinghamshire, which was particularly successful: using Dahrendorf's interpretation, the abilities of the local population and the economic threat coincided to allow a strong 'community' to emerge: 'dominant groups are correspondingly not so likely to be as involved in the defence of their authority unless their high socio-economic status is simultaneously involved' (p. 218). Indeed so strong was this spatially based cleavage that it interfered with more traditional patterns of support at a subsequent election (Perman, 1973).

Limitations

This outline is a simplification of several issues; 'community' for example is a term that should only be used with care, whilst Dahrendorf's work is not without criticism, although this is for the most part relatively unconvincing (Giddens, 1973). A more serious problem is the precise definition of the social model within which the components are thought to operate. A clear distinction is made for instance between the state (as planner) and the political system; this separates, say, the Department of Transport on the one hand (which is proposing a road construction) from the Secretary of State for the Environment, who ultimately reaches a decision via the inquiry inspector's advice. Such a distinction may not be possible. Similarly, it may be necessary to distinguish the activities of the state and different local government units, despite the fact that the latter can also function as planning authorities in their own right: in some instances, local authorities may actually become opponents to the state's plans at an inquiry, whilst in other instances they represent the source of the planning initiative.

For these reasons therefore the outline presented here may be only a partial representation. Nonetheless the limitations focus attention back on planning inquiries as particularly rich sources of material for an understanding of political-geographical and planning issues.

Conclusions

To summarize, this brief paper has suggested that spatial tensions constitute an addition to 'normal' political cleavages. Frequently these tensions emerge as a result of the planning process, which is increasingly responsible for the location of major negative externalities upon the landscape. Rather than simply regarding these spatial conflicts as local expressions of hostility to the state, it is useful instead to focus upon planning inquiries, which reveal more of the issues involved. A study of inquiries can be approached via an extension of Downs' spatial model, but here a threefold typology of planning system, community, and political system has been utilized, and Dahrendorf's notion of authority is used to account for the relative success or failure of different conflict groups. These formulations leave unresolved some questions, particularly in relation to the nature of the state and the role of planning; nonetheless this approach suggests itself as a rewarding line of inquiry.

References and bibliography

Allison, L. (1975). *Environmental Planning, a Political and Philosophical Analysis* (Allen & Unwin, London).

Batty, M. (1979). 'On planning processes', in Goodall, B. and Kirby, A. M. (eds.), *Resources and Planning*, pp. 17-50 (Pergamon Press, Oxford).

Breach, I. (1978). *Windscale Fallout* (Penguin, Harmondsworth).

Broadbent, T. A. (1977). *Planning and Profit in the Urban Economy* (Methuen, London).

Budge, I. (1978). 'Representations of political argument: applications within meta-planning', *Political Studies*, **XXVI**(4), 439-49.

Castells, M. (1978). *City, Class and Power* (Macmillan, London).

Dahrendorf, R. (1959). *Class and Class Conflicts in Industrial Societies* (Routledge & Kegan Paul, London).

Giddens, A. (1973). *The Class Structure of the Advanced Societies* (Hutchinson, London).

Goodman, R. (1974). *After the Planners* (Penguin, Harmondsworth).

Gudgin, G., and Taylor, P. J. (1979). *Seats, Votes and the Spatial Organisation of Elections* (Pion, London).

Hall, P. G. (1980). *Great Planning Disasters* (Weidenfeld & Nicolson, London).

Hills, P., and Cope, D. (1979). 'Energy and the built environment', *The Planner* (December), 172-4.

Johnston, R. J. (1979). *Political, Electoral and Spatial Systems* (Oxford University Press, Oxford).

Kirby, A. M. (1980). *'Space and Society'*, mimeo, University of Reading.

McKay, D. H. and Cox, A. W. (1979). *The Politics of Urban Change* (Croom Helm, London).

Perman, D. (1973). *Cublington: Blueprint for Resistance* (Bodley Head, Oxford).

Self, P. (1975). *Econocrats and the Policy·Process* (Macmillan, London).

Smith, D. M. (1977). *Human Geography: a Welfare Approach* (Edward Arnold, London).

Stephenson, L. (1979). 'Towards spatial understanding of environmentally-based voluntary groups', *Geoforum*, **10**, 195-201.

Taylor, P. J. (1979). 'Political geography', *Progress in Human Geography*, **3**(1), 139-41.

Tyme, J. (1978). *Motorways versus Democracy* (Macmillan, London).

Wolpert, J., Mumphrey, A., and Seley, J. (1972). 'Metropolitan neighbourhoods: participation and conflict over change', *Resource Paper* 16 (Commission on College Geography, AAAG, Washington, DC).

Political studies from spatial perspectives
Edited by A.D. Burnett and P.J. Taylor
© 1981 John Wiley & Sons Ltd

_____ *12*__

Alternative approaches to local government change

Rex Honey

The title of this paper is a conscious *double entendre*. As a glance at the titles in this volume (let alone familiarity with recent literature) will show, academics study local government change from a number of perspectives. I want to deal briefly with some of these alternative approaches. Alternatives also exist in the ways societies actually deal with local government change. The bulk of my paper will focus on the alternative proposals for local government change in England during the past decade. The proposals are analysed in terms of the process that generated them, the organizing principles behind them, and the consistency of the professed goals of each proposal with the actual jurisdictional structure proposed. The paper will conclude with a section contrasting England's experience with local government change in the United States.

Academic approaches

Several interesting pieces, many of them by geographers, have appeared in the literature on jurisdictional issues during the past few years. A number of literary threads can be identified. Some authors regard local government jurisdictional issues as essentially questions of optimizing the production and delivery of public goods. One set of authors takes a new-classical approach; Lea (1979) and Papageorgiou (1977) appear to fall in this category. They present interesting, creative analyses; but their methods have formidable operational problems. They pay scant attention to the ways in which jurisdictional issues are actually decided, in particular ignoring the fact that local government does many things besides provide goods — set policy and provide a focus of attention, for example.

Another group which pursues normative goals is that working with public choice theory, e.g. the work of Reynolds and his colleagues. The geographical use of public choice theory has largely shown what would result from some specified set of ideal behaviours given environmental situations. Again, the work is revealing and intellectually challenging, yet the links between actual jurisdictional decisions and public choice theory remain for the most part tenuous at best. Reynolds' claim (1981) that his formulation is 'positive at the margin' is encouraging, even if yet to be illustrated.

Marxist geographers also have their views of jurisdictional change. Nartowicz (1979) has reviewed the issues of metropolitan fragmentation from a Marxist perspective. Much of what he has to say has a ring of truth. Dearlove (1979) likewise takes a Marxist view of England's local government reorganization. Unfortunately, as with most Marxist 'analyses', Nartowicz and Dearlove are long on charges and short on evidence. The fault appears to be with a predetermined model of causes and forces rather than a vigorous analysis of the validity of Marxist premises in particular situations. Their topics are well chosen; their methodology too constricted.

Social justice (without the limiting Marxist baggage) is the chief interest of another group of geographers interested in jurisdictional issues. Morrill (1974) and his colleagues (1977) have evidenced such a concern for some time. Shelley (1979) provides an interesting spatial interpretation of Rawls (1971) — one that arguably is quite different from the economic optimization approach of the neoclassicists or public choice theorists.

Collectively these approaches are interesting intellectual puzzles. We can change an assumption or two and deduce the outcome; we can apply the same behavioural assumptions in different environments. Of what utility, however, is knowledge about hypothetical, abstract, unrealistic societies and the ways they affect jurisdictional change? Surely there is an infinite number of such hypothetical societies. What do we learn about societies that actually exist (even about possible changes in societies that exist) from such abstractions? If the assumptions are reasonable and the logic sound, we certainly can learn something. Yet what we can learn is very limited unless tied closely to empirical evidence. The strictly deductive approach can indeed lead to laws, but they will probably be laws with no domain.

More promising, in terms of advancing knowledge about how the world actually operates is a combination of observation, synthesis, analysis — the conventional hypothetico-deductive approach. Normative models, with their ideal worlds, will have little utility if they fail to capture the processes actually operating in a society. Positive models, i.e. models capturing the processes extant in a society, have the advantage of helping us understand what the society is like as well as giving us the requisite information for changing the society so that desirable ends can be met. In terms of jurisdictional change, we accomplish this understanding more by looking at the way societies make their decisions than through tenuously linked deductions. We can — and should — examine the antecedent conditions for change, i.e. the environment in which the change occurs. We can — and should — examine the political process of change, emphasizing especially the organizing principles espoused and applied by the various actors in the decision-making process. We can — and should — analyze outcomes, both in terms of correspondence with avowed principles and in terms of achieving social objectives.

The next section of this paper is an illustration of this research method, applied to the local government reorganization which was implemented in England in 1974. The emphasis is on the people involved in the decision-making process, their perceptions of problems and solutions, and the match between their stated principles and their proposals.

Jurisdictional change in England

The political organization of space responds to principles different from those governing the economic and social organization of space. Political space is absolute with monopolistic powers and discrete, well-defined boundaries. The fluidity of economic and social space on one hand, and the rigidity of political space on the other, lead to obsolescence of political space. Governmental units appropriate at one time may serve a society poorly when patterns of economic and social interaction change. Consider, for example, the impacts of transportation improvements on a set of jurisdictions delimiting communities. By changing the scale of communities, transport improvements may render jurisdictions obsolete. Consequently, jurisdictions may fail to achieve the goals for which they were designed, and pressure for governmental reform may arise.

If reform is desired, how should jurisdictions be organized spatially? The task may be divided into three problems: identifying the objectives the jurisdictions are to fulfil; devising organizing principles so that objectives may be met; and applying the principles, again in order to meet objectives (Figure 12.1).

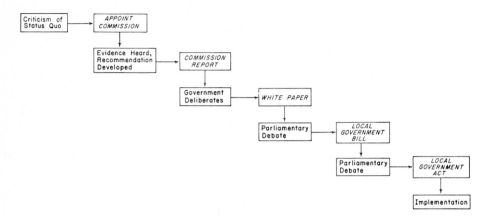

FIGURE 12.1   Conceptual model of jurisdictional organization

Democratic local government may be expected to fulfil numerous potential objectives. In addition, political sovereignty may be paramount. The spatial implications of these jurisdictional objectives are likely to be in conflict (Honey, 1976a). Hence a system designed to provide efficient police protection may have a different spatial solution from one maximizing educational effectiveness or environmental quality.

Assuming that consensus on objectives is obtained, these goals must then be translated into organizing principles so that jurisdictions may be delimited and duties assigned consistent with the objectives. Those principles most often cited easily lead to two approaches (Honey, 1976b). One has a functional orientation, asking the appropriate size for a governmental unit providing a specific service, then designating units of that size. The other has a systematic orientation, asking how the society in question is organized spatially, then defining a *de jure* organization matching the *de facto* one.

Whichever approach is taken, four major variables are manipulated in the design of a jurisdictional system. One of these is the number of levels in a governmental system, i.e. the number of steps in the jurisdictional hierarchy. Hypothetically, this number can range from one (national government only) to separate jurisdictions for each governmental activity. The former would permit coordination by placing all public activity under unified control. The latter would permit the provision of services by authorities tailored for specific functional requirements. This necessitates a trade-off between functional requirements of individual services and coordination of related services. A second variable is the number (and therefore size) of authorities at each level in a governmental system. Varying the number of authorities permits enlarging or reducing the units in accordance with organizing principles. The third and fourth variables are the assignment of territory and duties to each governmental unit. The functional approach solves the former after determining the latter. The systematic approach determines appropriate areas, then assigns appropriate functions.

Given the range of objectives and potential organizing principles, it is not possible to manipulate the four variables to define an *a priori* optimal system. Jurisdictions are appropriate only in terms of specified objectives and principles. If a set of jurisdictions is indeed based on an identifiable set of principles, then it should differ spatially from jurisdictions based on another set. Similarly, the process of jurisdicitonal delimitation must influence the results. The order of the steps — i.e. are functional or systematic requirements solved first? — and the exercise of political power are bound to influence the product.

When a society does reorganize local government, how does it treat the spatial problems? Do alternative objectives and principles really influence proposals? England's local government reform provides a case-study to address these questions. The English experience is doubly interesting. Not only was reform actually accomplished, but several alternative proposals, based on different principles, were also considered.

When a new local government system began operation in England in 1974, it culminated an 8-year reform process and replaced a system established at the end of the nineteenth century. The new system emerged from deliberate consideration and identification of objectives and organizing principles (Figure 12.2). Thanks to a dissenting member of the Royal Commission on Local Government in England, and to a change of governments in the middle of the reform, several distinct reform proposals came forth: that of the Royal Commission (1967) majority, Derek Senior's *Memorandum of Dissent (1969);* the Labour Government's White Paper (1971); the Conservative Government's White Paper; the Local Government Bill; and finally, the Local Government Act. Those proposing reform had somewhat different objectives and substantially different organizing principles. Consequently, what they proposed as solutions to England's jurisdictional problems differed markedly.

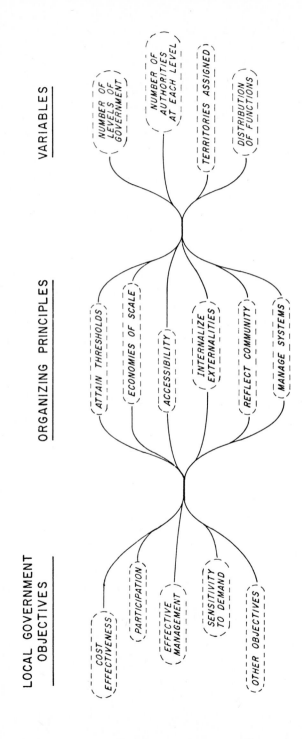

FIGURE 12.2 England's local government reform process

The Victorian system

The spatial problem plaguing England's local government system stemmed primarily from the fact that the system was designed at the end of one era to serve another. The Victorian system came into being in 1888 to serve the England of its day, not the motorized, egalitarian England to come. The hallmark of Victorian local government was the division between town and country — the England of the country squire and that of the dark, satanic mill. Counties were the chief organs of local government. They were divided into districts which dealt with local considerations. The larger cities qualified for county borough status and in effect seceded from their surrounding counties. A county borough was a unitary authority performing both district and county services.

As the twentieth century advanced, changes in English life far outpaced jurisdictional changes. Much of what ailed English local government was spatial, and calls for reorganization arose. Robson (1968) cited 'three principal defects' in the Victorian system:

1. local authorities were often too small 'to provide an adequate base for existing municipal services';
2. division between counties and county boroughs generated needless conflict; and
3. fragmentation precluded 'effective performance of services requiring large areas of administration or planning'.

In other words, Robson argued that English local government failed to reach service thresholds and internalize externalities. Robson's views diffused sufficiently for restructuring to begin in the early 1960s with the reorganization of local government in Greater London.

Redcliffe-Maud Commission

The Government took the first step toward reforming local government in the rest of England in 1966 when it appointed the Royal Commission on Local Government in England (Redcliffe-Maud Commission). The 11 member commission was warranted (1969):

> ...to consider the structure of Local Government in England, outside Greater London, in relation to its existing functions; and to make recommendations for authorities and

boundaries, and for functions and their divisions, having regard to the size and character of areas in which these can be most effectively exercised and the need to sustain a viable system of local democracy.

Within these broad guidelines of effective services and viable local democracy, as well as the constraint of existing local government services, the commission was authorized to study extensively and recommend radical steps. Consistent with its warrant and research findings, the commission cited four objectives: to be efficient in the provision of a wide range of tasks; to attract and maintain citizen interest; to develop sufficient strength to be effective; and to be adaptable to social and economic change (Royal Commission, 1966).

To accomplish its objectives, the commission argued, local government should: correspond to the patterns of society; be cost-effective; and be democratically viable. The commission laid out several general principles for achieving these goals. In particular it stressed three: to bracket related services under unified control for improved efficiency and effectiveness; to require a threshold minimum of 250,000 and accessibility maximum of 1,000,000 for what the British call personal services (education, social services); and to internalize externalities, both in determining the size of areas for environmental services and in delimiting areas meeting the threshold requirement for personal services. The commission employed both functional and systematic organizing principles, and it chose the coordinating advantages of grouping services over the flexibility advantages of separating them. The county borough, with its advantages of functional coordination, became the model of the proposed system (Sharp, 1975; Hill, 1975). The commission was confident that county borough performance was not dependent on high density and small area, so it felt justified in spreading unitary authorities to the rest of England. The 250,000 threshold was a compromise. Experts from the central government testified that even larger authorities were needed, but research found economies of scale difficult to substantiate (Sharp, 1975).

The Redcliffe-Maud Commission did not want to erase Victorian boundaries completely. The boundaries were of historical significance; in some cases Saxon. In addition, historical identity could engender that common interest between citizen and public official that the commission felt essential for good government. Consequently, the commission sought change only where it felt the reasons for doing so were compelling.

Jurisdictions Assigned

Having set the rules, the Royal Commission began to design its new system. Its paramount principle was size: 250,000 people. To find appropriate areas meeting the threshold, the commission looked to patterns of interaction. Examining data on commuting, population change, shopping, communication, and transportation, the commission identified zones of indifference between cities. Where areas of urban influence were discrete (and populations above 250,000), city regions formed the basis of proposed authorities. In some areas, however, the commission found the city region approach wanting. In the Lake District and southwest, the city region principle would have required authorities with very large areas and little internal affinity. In other areas, e.g., Lancashire and Yorkshire, several cities compete with none pre-eminent.

In only three areas — Merseyside (Liverpool), Greater Manchester, and the West Midlands (Birmingham) — did the Redcliffe-Maude Commission apply its accessibility maximum of 1,000,000 residents and propose a two-level system. The commission felt that in these areas the population internalized by eliminating externalities was too large for authorities discharging personal services. For environmental services, such as transportation planning, and overspill housing, the commission proposed metropolitan counties. It proposed assignment of personal services to districts with at least 250,000 people. The commission considered but rejected two tiers in several other areas — and in fact proposed three unitary counties above the 1,000,000 population constraint.

In all, the commission proposed 58 unitary authorities. Some were essentially the old county plus county borough enclaves. Others were city regions paying scant attention to old county boundaries. The commission proposed to partition some counties and amalgamate several others. Figure 12.3 shows the extent to which the commission's plan called for change at the county level. It offered 58 unitary authorities, three metropolitan counties, and 20 metropolitan districts, reducing the number of authorities by over 90%.

Senior's dissent

The Redcliffe-Maud proposal was a radical departure from the Victorian jurisdictions. The commission proposed authorities with more resources, fewer externalities, and better service

coordination. When published in 1969, the commission report
advanced to the government along with a *Memorandum of Dissent*
that was even more radical (Senior, 1969). Derek Senior
fundamentally disagreed with his Royal Commission colleagues on
the way to design a new local government system. The Redcliffe-
Maud strategy was to define the functional requirements and then
find interaction areas consistent with functional needs. Senior
preferred to work the other way, discovering patterns of daily life
and fitting government to them. While his colleagues were trying to
establish the scale requirements of the personal services, Senior
was mapping England's city regions. He used a multivariate
approach — commuting, shopping, bus services, newspapers, and
more — and in fact his colleagues used his findings but only after
defining the functional requirements. Senior (1969) saw the problem
of organizing a local government system as:

> ...simply a matter of picking... the rung in the urban hierarchy
> that yields a unit population of the right order of size... What
> we are concerned with is 'community in terms of people's
> actual behavior' — the objective community of interest which
> binds together the people who participate in a self-contained
> complex of social and economic activities based on a single
> centre.

   Senior thought that the Royal Commission pushed the coordination
and threshold arguments too hard. He agreed that environmental
and personal services should be grouped, but he thought it folly to
force both groups together. He felt that the area necessary for
effective planning was too large for the operation of social services.
Senior also argued that it made no sense to attain a threshold by
amalgamating rural counties merely to increase numbers. Loss in
accessibility, he felt, would offset gains in administrative
efficiency. The problem of low density would not simply disappear
because jurisdictions were enlarged. Senior proposed large
jurisdictions because they would internalize externalities, not
because they would reach what he regarded as misleading
thresholds. Senior proposed 35 regions to be subdivided into 148
districts. In his own mind, the areas defined themselves. If areas of
strong daily contact were territorially extensive and high in
population, his proposal reflected that. For small city regions, he
proposed small authorities. In fact, Senior proposed 50 districts
with more people than his smallest proposed region — because that
was the way life was organized. He did not truncate big city regions
merely to keep population down, nor did he force sparsely

populated areas together just to obtain a large population. Senior ignored historical boundaries, as a glance at Figure 12.4 will confirm. He did not think something as important as local government should be a captive of the past.

Labour's White Paper

Early in 1970, the Labour Government published a white paper outlining its intent to legislate on the Redcliffe-Maud model. In the most consequential change from the commission's proposal, Labour added another pair of two-tier metropolitan authorities, tentatively accepting the remaining unitary authorities and the commission's three metropolitan counties. In the only other change of consequence, Labour moved some powers (particularly education) from metropolitan districts to metropolitan counties.

Conservative proposals

The Conservatives won the 1970 election, quashing Labour's (and Redcliffe-Maud's) reform. In 1971 the Conservatives published a White Paper outlining their intended reform. It cited objectives similar to the Royal Commission's, but the organizing principles and proposed structure differed markedly. The White Paper stressed objectives similar to those of its predecessors: strengthen local government so that power could be exercised locally; bring local government jurisdictions into correspondence with 'the pattern of life and work in modern society'; and increase efficiency and effectiveness by creating local authorities 'large enough in size, population, and resources to meet administrative needs'. In terms of organizing principles, the Conservatives

1. accepted the 250,000 population threshold for many but not all services;
2. concurred on the 1,000,000 maximum for such functions as education and personal services;
3. dismissed the unitary principles;
4. rejected the city region as a general jurisdictional model;
5. embraced the retention of historic county boundaries.

The Conservatives recommended a dual two-tier local government system. Throughout most of the country, counties about the 250,000 threshold were designed to provide most services. Districts ranging upwards from 75,000 would handle local concerns. The six

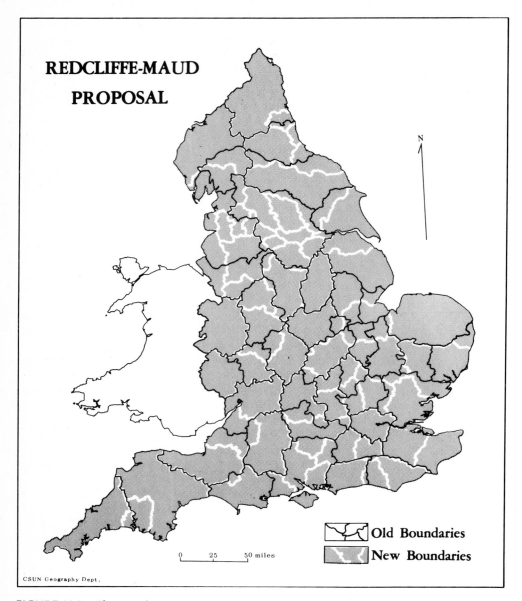

FIGURE 12.3   The Royal Commission majority's proposals and the Victorian counties

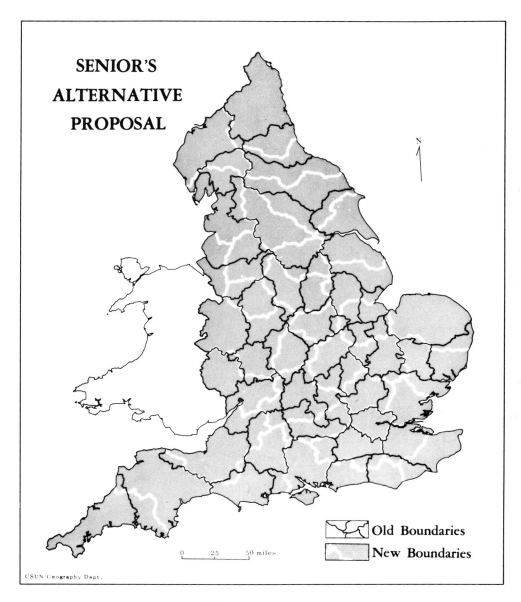

FIGURE 12.4   Senior's regions and the Victorian counties

largest metropolitan areas were to have districts of 250,000 or more
providing most services. Metropolitan counties were to discharge
those environmental services requiring area-wide management.
Thus authorities at the Royal Commission's threshold level were to
be paramount in the Conservative reform.

The Conservatives' proposed reform looked much more like the
Victorian county map than did either Royal Commission proposal
(Figure 12.5). Their assignment procedure was to retain those
counties meeting the threshold, amalgamate those short of the
threshold, adjust boundaries where anomalies clearly impeded
good management, and create a handful of new counties where
urban growth had most strongly altered social geography.
Jurisdictionally, the biggest changes in the reform were elimination
of county boroughs and reduction of the number of districts,
boundaries of which were to be set by a boundary commission. The
White Paper proposed 44 counties, a reduction of one. The creation
of urban-based counties almost offset the elimination of the most
lightly populated rural counties.

Most demonstrative reaction to the White Paper dealt with the
metropolitan counties (Senior, 1975; Sharp, 1975; Hall, 1975). Some
members of the Royal Commission lamented the demise of the
unitary principle, but most criticism attached to the bricks and
mortar metropolitan definitions. Redcliffe-Maud and Senior had
recommended metropolitan authorities extending into the
countryside so that adequate space for planning and management
would be available. The Conservatives trimmed the metropolitan
counties severely. They disputed the purported benefits of city
region management, questioned the value of internalizing
externalities, and doubted alleged affinity among urban, suburban,
and rural dwellers. They defended the trimmed metropolitan areas
on two bases:

1. it kept apart local residents with different life styles, values
   and needs; and
2. it helped contain sprawl.

The former was based in effect on the public choice argument —
different publics should be able to make different choices (Walker,
1975). The latter was based on the argument that open space could
be more easily retained if the decision to expand were removed
from central city domination.

The Conservatives refined their White Paper into a Local
Government Bill by the end of 1971. Where the Bill deviated from
the White Paper the change was usually in the direction of less

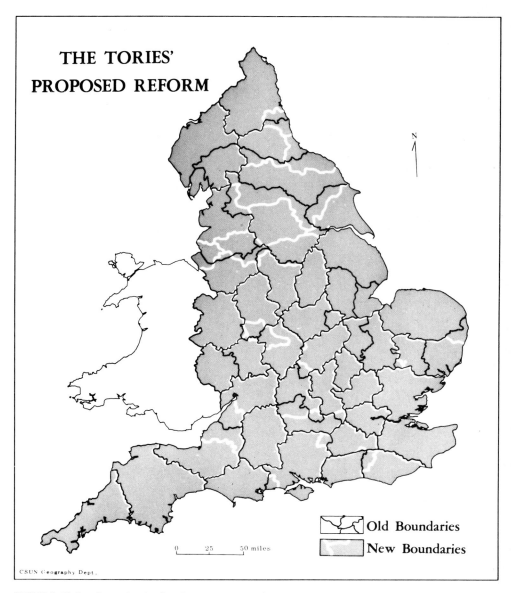

FIGURE 12.5   Counties in the Conservative White Paper and the Victorian counties

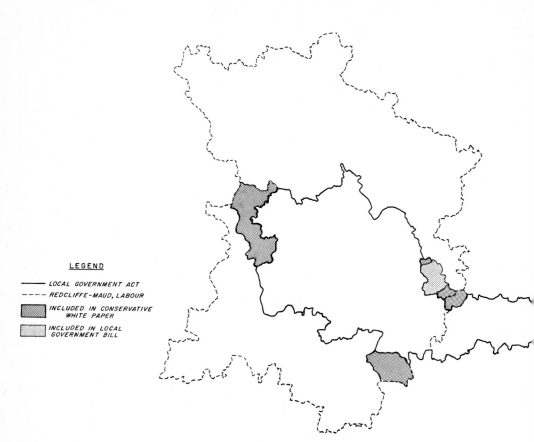

FIGURE 12.6   Alternative proposals for the West Midlands (Greater Birmingham)

rather than more reform. The Bill further trimmed the metropolitan counties, for instance, and eliminated a number of boundary 'corrections'. Critics argued that the changes made a mockery of the reform. Chipping away at the metropolitan counties meant retaining externalities. The Local Government Bill replaced battles between county boroughs and counties with battles between metropolitan counties and their neighbours (Figure 12.6).

The trend toward the *status quo* continued as the Bill travelled through Parliament. The Isle of Wight escaped amalgamation with Hampshire even though it fell far below the threshold population, and several districts were returned from metropolitan counties to their original counties. The Local Government Act passed Parliament in 1972, and the new local government system became operational in 1974 (Figure 12.7).

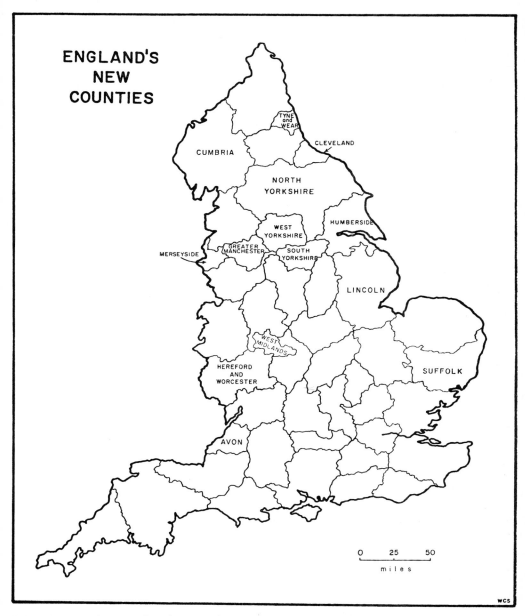

FIGURE 12.7   Counties legislated in the Local Government Act

Objectives, principles, and form

Had Labour won the 1970 election, the outcome of England's local
government reform would have been greatly different. This is not to
say that Labour would have enacted reform based on its White
Paper, because that does not follow. The important point is that the
form of the new system emerged from organizing principles
tempered by political expediency. The differences in form of the
official proposals show how the pattern of political organization
follows from the principles applied in the organization process. The
adequacy of the various proposals may be gauged by measuring the
extent to which the proposals followed their own organizing
principles — and by the extent to which they addressed the
problems necessitating reform in the first place.

Adequate size

Proponents of reform consistently cited the small size of many
authorities as one of England's jurisdictional ills. The consensus was
that the society and its public services had outgrown many
Victorian authorities. When the Royal Commission was
deliberating, over 1000 districts still operated, and over 100 of them
had fewer than 5000 inhabitants. With the exception of Senior, the
official proposals cited a population threshold of 250,000 as the
minimum for authorities responsible for personal services. With
the threshold as the criterion, the severity of inadequate size in the
Victorian structure and the extent to which the official proposals
remedied this inadequacy may be measured by calculating the
threshold gap. For each jurisdiction or proposed jurisdiction, the
threshold gap is the amount the population falls below the
threshold, in this case 250,000. The threshold gap for each proposal
is the sum of the individual threshold gaps for all jurisdictions with
populations below the threshold. An alternative measure is to sum
the populations living in those jurisdictions failing to meet the
threshold (Table 12.1). Ironically, only Senior's regions met the
threshold in all instances. Senior chose to assign responsibility high
up the urban hierarchy, so the authorities he proposed met
functional standards even though he assigned areas more on
externality rather than functional grounds.

   Advocates of a population threshold used it as a guide, deviating
from it when other considerations intervened. Redcliffe-Maud
proposed five counties and four metropolitan districts with sub-
threshold populations. The latter were all growing suburban
districts which were expected to reach the threshold through

Table 12.1 Threshold gap and population in sub-threshold authorities

	Victorian jurisdictions	Redcliffe-Maud	Senior	Labour	Conservative White Paper	Local government Bill	Local government Bill
Threshold gap (000s)							
Counties	820	163	0	65	0	0	140
Districts**	7728	145	0	243	285	331	583
Total	8548	308	0	308	285	331	723
Number and percentage of sub-threshold authorities							
Counties	9/20	5/09	0	3/06	0	0	1/02
Districts**	65/82	4/20	0	6/22	11/29	8/26	14/39
Total	74/60	9/12	0	9/12	11/15	8/11	15/20
Population in sub-threshold authorities							
Counties	1180	1087	0	685	0	0	110
Districts**	7433	855	0	1257	2465	1919	2916
Total	8613	1942	0	1942	2465	1919	3026

* Threshold gap is the sum of number of people an authority is below 250,000 for all authorities with fewer than 250,000 people.
** Metropolitan districts except for the Victorian jurisdictions where county boroughs are used.

metropolitan growth. One of the counties was expected to grow, too, so only three of the commission's proposals really contravened the threshold principle. Thus, the commission eased the threshold requirement rather than create unnecessary externalities. Labour's application of the threshold requirement differed from the commission's only in the switch of two authorities from county to metropolitan district status.

The Conservative proposals differed from the commission's more markedly. They applied the threshold much less vigorously in the metropolitan districts than the counties — in part perhaps because another tier of authority stood over them, but equally plausibly because they were largely Labour strongholds. Subsequent Conservative proposals had increasing threshold gaps, with the Bill having more than the White Paper and the Act having more than the Bill. Nevertheless, the Conservatives held to their threshold in their proposed counties, so it was a seriously applied criterion, even if one that could be eased in the metropolitan districts.

Internalizing externalities

The inability of the Victorian system to deal with circulation was one of the major justifications cited in the calls for local government reform (Robson, 1968). Management was difficult not only because counties and county boroughs were divided but also because many metropolitan areas possessed several county boroughs and more than one county. In short, there were externality problems. Internalization of externalities may be regarded as:

1. a measure of each proposal's success at matching jurisdictions to actual patterns of daily life; and
2. a measure of the importance of internalizing externalities to those responsible for the proposal.

One measure of internalization is the extent to which the population within commuting fields was placed within a single county. If jurisdictions encompass whole commuting fields, management of commuting is simplified, as is the provision of goods affecting commuting, such as the location of public housing development. One test of the adequacy of the official proposals at internalizing commuting is the population in, and number of, 'misallocated' districts. A district was misallocated if it and its chief commuting designation were assigned to different counties. Commuting externalities for each of the six official proposals were

Table 12.2   Commuting externalities

A.   Misallocated districts* (percentages in parentheses)

	Metropolitan ring**	Outer ring***	Total
Redcliffe-Maud	18 (0.03)	95 (0.24)	113 (0.12)
Senior	9 (0.02)	29 (0.07)	38 (0.04)
Labour	10 (0.02)	88 (0.22)	98 (0.11)
Conservative White Paper	45 (0.09)	92 (0.23)	137 (0.15)
Local government Bill	53 (0.10)	96 (0.24)	149 (0.16)
Local government Act	55 (0.11)	102 (0.26)	157 (0.17)

*A district is misallocated if assigned to a county different from the one containing the district's chief commuting destination.
**The metropolitan ring includes those districts with at least 15% of their work-force commuting to an employment centre, and with no more commuters going to any other centre.
***The outer ring is composed of districts with less than 15% of their work-force commuting to a centre, but more workers commuting to that centre than any other centre.

B.   Significance of the results*

Paired Fisher-Irwin tests were used to see if the success of the proposals at allocating districts differed significantly. Each proposal was in turn used as a control and regarded as the mean of a normal distribution of all possible allocations that could be made under that proposal's assignment rules. The other proposals were tested to see if their results could be part of the same distribution. Capital letters indicate that two proposals differed at the 0.01 level of significance; lower case letters indicate that they differed at the 0.05 level. M indicates significant differences in the metropolitan ring, O in the outer ring.

	Test					
Control	Redcliffe-Maud	Senior	Labour	Conservative White Paper	Bill	Act
Redcliffe-Maud		O		M	M	M
Senior	m O		O	M O	M O	M O
Labour	m		O	M	M	M
Conservative White Paper	M	M O	M			
Conservative Bill	M	M O	M			
Conservative Act	M	M O	M			

*Each proposal was treated as a sample of all possible assignments which each proposal author would have made in applying the organizing principles.

Source: Hodges, J. L., and Lehmann, E. L., *Basic Concepts of Probability and Statistics* (San Francisco: Holden-Day, 1964).

calculated from commuting data in the 1971 census. The cores of England's 110 Metropolitan Economic Labour Areas served as the commuting destinations. Two levels of the commuting field were utilized: a metropolitan ring composed of districts with at least 15% of their work-force commuting to a destination (and with no more commuters going to a different destination); and an outer ring composed of areas with less than 15% commuting to a destination but with more commuting to that destination than any other destination.

Senior's proposed jurisdictions most successfully internalized commuting, as was expected given his strategy (Table 12.2). His proposal was particularly sensitive to the heavier commuting of the metropolitan ring. Senior used non-commuting interaction data in delimiting his jurisdictions, or he would have had no commuting externalities.

Labour and Redcliffe-Maud were more sensitive to externalities than the Conservatives but less sensitive than Senior — a predictable result given the organizing principles employed by each group. Redcliffe-Maud and Labour eased the threshold requirement when it conflicted with its heavier commuting. Statistically, Labour's metropolitan ring externalities were not significantly greater than Senior's; Redcliffe-Maud's were significantly worse at a 0.05 level of confidence but not at 0.01. Labour and Redcliffe-Maud did not pursue the externalities argument into the outer ring with such vigour. Their misallocations in the outer ring were significantly better than the Conservatives. Labour had fewer commuting externalities than Redcliffe-Maud because it preferred the two-tier metropolitan structure in West Yorkshire. This brought an area with heavy cross-commuting under one county — and would have provided more clear-cut authority to manage transport in the region.

The Conservatives did not weigh the internalization of externalities as an important criterion, particularly in the metropolitan areas where they preferred to separate urban and suburban interests. In lightly populated areas the Conservatives could reach the threshold only by including several commuting fields; otherwise their externality figures would have been even larger.

Population-distance trade-off

Despite their fervour for overcoming the deficiencies of the Victorian jursidictions those authoring the official proposals strove to prevent local government from becoming too large and inaccessible. Redcliffe-Maud proposed two measures for keeping government accessible:

1. The 1,000,000 maximum for authorities providing personal services; and
2. local councils, primarily of an advisory nature, to work with county officials.

Labour in its proposal concurred. Senior and the Conservatives, of course, proposed district authorities to assure local decisions. In addition, the Conservatives argued against having large counties that would bring people with very different interests together. They used a public-choice-type argument to limit the metropolitan counties to the continuously developed area. The Conservatives stressed functional requirements — threshold and accessibility — and downplayed the internalization of externalities.

The Conservatives alone systematically traded-off population and distance (Table 12.3). Redcliffe-Maud's and Labour's proposals exhibit no discernible relationship between population and accessibility, even when several different measures are calculated. Senior's proposal exhibits a slight positive relationship — distance and population rising together. The three Conservative formulations — White Paper, Bill, and Act — all show a statistically significantly inverse relationship between population and distance,

Table 12.3   Trading accessibility for population or resources

Correlation	R-M	Sr.	Lab.	Cons. W.P.	Bill	Act
Population and maximum distance*	0.03	0.13	0.03	−0.39**	−0.46**	−0.33***
Population and maximum distance squared	−0.03	0.13	−0.02	−0.36***	−0.41**	−0.33***
Gross rateable value and maximum distance	0.03	0.07	−0.02	−0.41**	−0.50**	
Gross rateable value and maximum distance squared	−0.06	0.07	−0.07	−0.38***	−0.46**	
Population and inverse of distance	−0.14	−0.11	−0.12	0.45**	0.52**	0.28
Population and log of distance	0.09	0.12	0.08	−0.43**	−0.50**	−0.32***

R-M = Redcliffe-Maud; Sr. = Senior; Lab. = Labour; Cons. W.P. = Conservative White Paper.

*From administrative centre to most distant point in each proposed county.
**Significant at 0.01 level.
***Significant at 0.05 level.

as expected. The Conservative approach to jurisdictional design —
using one or more whole old counties to form new ones with at
least 250,000 people — increases the likelihood of a significant
inverse relationship because it requires bringing large areas with
sparse populations together in a single jurisdiction. The approach
also means that correlation coefficients are only moderate because
counties with large populations are not divided. The Local
Government Bill has a stronger relationship between population
and distance than the Conservative White Paper, largely because of
the reductions in the sizes of the metropolitan counties.
Consequently, the highly populated metropolitan counties are left
with small areas. Many of the suburban counties are brought in line
with the trade-off, too. They wind up with moderately large
populations and moderately small areas. Amendments changed the
bill as it passed through Parliament. Consequently, the Local
Government Act bears the stamp of the Conservative's population-
distance trade-off with moderation.

Historical considerations

Another area of contention among the reform participants was the
importance of historical boundaries. Senior thought they interfered
with effective local government, so he paid little attention to them.
Redcliffe-Maud and Labour retained them when they did not
interfere strongly with the chief organizing principles. For the
Conservatives, retention of historical boundaries was an organizing
principle — to be sacrificed only when the weight of the other
principles stood heavily on the side of change. Opening
Parliamentary debate on the Conservative White Paper, Peter
Walker said he had 'wherever possible taken note of historic
boundaries and only changed them where there were good planning
reasons for altering them'. A glance at Figures 12.3-12.5 and 12.7
shows how far the official proposals deviated from the old
boundaries. The Conservative White Paper followed the Victorian
boundaries 'closely', and the Local Government Bill deviated even
less. Most of the amendments in the Local Government Act
retained rather than changed Victorian boundaries. The
Conservatives kept more of the old counties intact, and they
proposed more new counties based on a single old county (Table
12.4). In short, the Conservatives did not feel that the arguments for
change were strong enough to warrant wholesale redrawing of
England's county map. They agreed to two major kinds of change
— new counties for the metropolitan areas and new districts for the
whole country — but they resisted change elsewhere.

Table 12.4 Relationship between Victorian counties and proposed counties

Relationship		R-M	Senr.	Lab.	Cons. W.P.	Bill	Act
A.	Number of old counties proposed for each new county						
	1	22	2	17	17	20	22
	2	26	8	26	18	14	16
	3	7	7	7	7	9	7
	4	5	11	5	2	1	
	5		4				
	6						
	7	1	2	1			
	8		1				
	Mean	2.00	3.57	2.09	1.82	1.76	1.67
B.	Number of new counties proposed for each old county						
	1	5	2	5	22	22	25
	2	23	21	23	13	18	15
	3	10	13	10	7	2	2
	4	3	6	4	1	1	1
	5	2	2	2	1	1	1
	6		1		1	1	1
	7	1		1			
	8						
	9	1					
	Mean	2.76	2.71	2.64	1.96	1.84	1.82

Abbreviations as in Table 12.3.

Form, process, and political space

England's local government reform illustrates how the form of a jurisdictional system follows from the organizing principles applied in design, ameliorated by political compromise. The six official proposals exhibit spatial properties consistent with their organizing principles. Senior's city regions best internalized externalities. The Conservatives' functional emphasis led to trade-offs between population and distance. The Royal Commission and Labour, using interaction data to define jurisdictions meeting functional criteria, stood between Senior and the Conservatives. Amendments reduced correspondence between the Conservatives' principles and their legislated product. The reform also offered a caution to work from principles to form, rather than the other way around, in explaining results. Senior's total satisfaction of the threshold requirement, for example, might induce one to infer incorrectly that he among the reform authors espoused the threshold requirement most strongly. He merely achieved the threshold — pursuit of which he rejected — in the process of applying his interaction criteria.

The reform experience does show the potential conflict among spatial problems in jurisdictional organization. Senior directly, Redcliffe-Maud and Labour more obliquely, sought to internalize externalities. All the proposals sought to achieve accessibility; all but Senior stressed a threshold. The Conservatives preferred homogeneous jurisdictions in the public choice mould. Each proposal had to weigh objectives. While a hidden agenda may have really prompted actual decisions, the form of each proposal was consistent with the proposals espoused. Differences flowed from the selection and weighting of those principles. The dissatisfaction of many long-time proponents of reform results from the final design of the new system by individuals less enamoured with change. It was a conservative as well as a Conservative reform.

The American approach

Jurisdictional change in the United States is fundamentally different from that of Britain despite a common heritage and democratic character. Americans and Britons both developed their major traditions of local democracy, i.e., determine and execute policies locally, after American independence. Consequently they followed divergent lines of development including actual jurisdictional structures, citizen expectations, and rules for change.

Democratic traditions

Britain's government is much more centralized than that of the United States, and this is but one of a number of differences between the two in democratic traditions. Britain's national government controls local government very closely in terms of budget and policies; the US federal government is essentially limited to inducements, the individual states holding real power. Only in the 1970s in fact did even the states begin to control local authority (city, county, school districts) expenditures severely.

Budgetary control flies in the face of home rule, an important tradition in American democracy. Equivalent to the royal charters which gave some British cities extensive powers, home rule is the possession of independent power to govern over a range of decisions without having to obtain specific permission from the state. Generally larger and older American cities have home rule charters — and would give them up only with great reluctance. The states, in turn, have been willing to allow the home rule cities to keep their powers as long as the states do not have to assume the cities' responsibilities. Unfortunately, suburbanization has reduced the ability of home rule cities to solve their problems, partly because they do not have jurisdiction over the requisite areas, partly because resources as well as people have moved to the suburbs.

Couple suburbanization — and the proliferation of incorporated municipalities — with the mobility of Americans, and another difference between British and American democratic traditions emerges: Americans are much more likely to follow the Tiebout (1956) dictum of voting with their feet. When dissatisfied with their local authorities, Americans (or more properly, those Americans who can afford to do so) tend to move more readily than Britons. Moving reduces pressure to change local government.

Decision-making structure

Perhaps more fundamentally affecting pressure to change local government is the labyrinth of decisions required to effect such change in the US. The systems of checks and balances not only require concordance among branches of government, but local government change in the US generally requires agreement among those affected with broad veto powers for anyone in opposition. By contrast, Britain's local government reorganizations required neither the assent of local authorities nor the formal vote of the citizens affected. Seldom is power exercised so simply in the US. Change as fundamental as that in Britain would generally require positive votes by the residents of several constituencies (each counted separately), and approval of local government officials. Such fundamental change is likely to remove some advantages now held by some municipalities, e.g. tax advantages, so opposition is likely to arise — and this opposition generally can stop reorganization.

Many changes in the American jurisdictional system have occurred in the last two decades. A layer of regional planning organizations, for example, has developed. Federal inducements, especially funds, spawned the planning organizations. Real power, especially over policies and budgets, is retained by cities and counties which are often ill-designed to handle contemporary problems, especially when resources and problems are concentrated in different authorities. The federal carrot-and-stick approach is successful only where problems are not severe, vested interests not jeopardized. As long as unanimity is required, difficult problems are beyond attack.

Societal problems

The justification for Britain's local government reorganizations included arguments that the Victorian jurisdictions were inappropriate for contemporary Britain. One might argue with as much power that American jurisdictions are poorly designed for meeting the problems of contemporary America. Likewise, the problems facing the two societies are different, so the jurisdictional structures appropriate may be different — and the types and degrees of opposition may be different.

Issues of racial segregation are much more serious in the US than in Britain, for example. In each country, wealth (and fiscal strength) is concentrated more in the suburbs than the central city, but in the US racial segregation compounds the division. Where metropolitan governments have emerged, one frequent factor is that whites have been able to maintain their political control over what were becoming predominantly black central cities. This is true of Indianapolis, Nashville, and Jacksonville, for example. Suburban financial interests are thus able to maintain hegemony over their central business district investments.

More typically suburban voters refuse amalgamation with impoverished central cities, e.g. the referenda of Cleveland and St Louis. Even without race as an issue, the fiscal disparity among municipalities is an inducement for many to oppose far-reaching reorganization. Generally the highest disparities in fiscal strength are actually among suburbs rather than between the suburbs and central city, but this does not reduce the fiscal incentive to oppose reorganization.

In short, the American experience of jurisdiction change differs from Britain's because the decision-making structure makes change more difficult, democratic traditions place more emphasis on local autonomy, and the racial divisions within the society are greater.

Conclusion

The student of jurisdictional change may choose among several alternative approaches, each with a potential for contributing to knowledge. One approach, the one followed here, is to analyse the change by examining the behaviour of those involved in the decision-making process, and by examining the institutional constraints on choice. England's local government reform stemmed from perceived inadequacies of the Victorian jurisdictional system. The reformers cited idealistic organizing principles. The eventual reform proposals emerged from the application of the principles preferred by those designing the proposals to the circumstances they found in England. The data analysed in the paper show that those proposing reform differed in their applications of principles even if their statements of principle were similar. The product of the reform experience is as much a function of political history — the Conservatives rather than Labour held power at the critical time — as public preferences or expert opinion. The institutional constraints and institutional behaviour, then, were crucial to the establishment of the new jurisdictional system. The form of the jurisdictional organization, in short, follows from the process of jurisdictional change, especially the behaviour of the actors involved within their limits of choice.

References and bibliography

Advisory Committee on Intergovernmental Relations (1963). *Performance of Urban Functions: Local and Areawide* (Report M-21, Washington, DC).

Braun, C. L. (1975). Principal, Local Government Directorate, Department of the Environment, England. Personal interview.

Burnett, P. (1979). Comments during special session on radical critique of behavioural geography. Annual Meeting of the West Lakes Division, Association of American Geographers, 12 October.

Chisholm, M. (1975). Member, Local Government Boundary Commission for England. Personal interview.

Conservative Government White Paper (1971). 'Local Government in England'. (HMSO, Cmnd. 4584, London).

Dearlove, J. (1979). *The Reorganization of British Local Government: Old Orthodoxies and a Political Perspective* (Cambridge University Press, Cambridge).

Dent, D. (1975). Member, Royal Commission's Intelligence Unit. Personal interview.

Hall, P. (1975). Consultant to the Labour Government. Personal interview.

Hill, Sir F. (1975). Member, Royal Commission on Local Government in England, 1966-69. Personal interview.

Hodges, J. L., and Lehmann, E. L. (1964). *Basic Concepts of Probability and Statistics* (Holden-Day, San Francisco).

Honey, R. (1976a). 'Conflicting problems in the political organization of space', *Annals of Regional Science*, **10**, 45-60.

Honey, R. (1976b). 'Metropolitan governance: transformation of political space', in Adams, J. S. (ed.), *Urban Policymaking and Metropolitan Dynamics*, pp. 425-62 (Ballinger, New York).

Labour Government White Paper (1971). 'Reform of Local Government in England' (HMSO, Cmnd. 4276, London).

Lea, A. C. (1979). 'Welfare theory, public goods, and public facility location', *Geographical Analysis,* **11,** 217-39.

Longland, Sir J. (1975). Member, Royal Commission on Local Government in England, 1966-69. Personal interview.

Marshall, A. H. (1975). Member, Royal Commission on Local Government in England, 1966-69. Personal interview.

Morrill, R. (1974). 'Efficiency and equity aspects of optimum location models', *Antipode,* **6,** 41-6.

Morrill, R., and Symons, J. G. (1977). 'Efficiency and equity aspects of optimum location', *Geographical Analysis,* **9,** 215-25.

Mursell, Sir P. (1975). Member, Royal Commission on Local Government in England, 1966-69. Personal interview.

Nartowicz, F. Z. (1979). 'Alternative approaches to metropolitan fragmentation'. Paper presented at Annual Meeting of the Association of American Geographers, 24 April.

Papageorgiou, G. J. (1977). 'Fundamental problems of theoretical planning', *Environment and Planning, A,* **9,** 1329-56.

Rawls, J. (1971). *A Theory of Justice* (Belknap Press, Cambridge, Mass.).

Redcliffe-Maud, Lord (1975). Chairman, Royal Commission on Local Government in England, 1966-69. Personal interview.

Reynolds, D. R. (1979). 'The geography of social choice'. This volume chapter 5 above.

Reynolds, D. R., and Archer, J. C. (1976). 'Locational logrolling and citizen support of municipal bond proposals', *Public Choice,* **27,** 21-39.

Reynolds, D. R., and Honey, R. (1978). 'Conflict in the location of salutary public facilities', in Cox, K. R. (ed.), *Urbanization and Conflict in Marketing Societies,* pp. 144-60 (Maaroufa, Chicago).

Robson, W. A. (1968). *Local Government in Crisis.* (Allen & Unwin, London).

Royal Commission on Local Government in England, 1966-69 (1969). *Report* (HMSO, Cmnd. 4040, London).

Senior, D. (1969). *Memorandum of Dissent* (HMSO, Cmnd. 4040-1, London).

Senior, D. (1975). Member, Royal Commission on Local Government in England, 1966-69. Personal interview.

Sharp, Lady E. (1975). Member, Royal Commission on Local Government in England, 1966-69. Personal interview.

Sharpe, L. J. (1975). Director, Royal Commission's Intelligence Unit. Personal interview.

Shelley, F. M. (1979). 'Locational procedures for public goods under a Rawlsian system of social justice', Discussion Paper No. 30, Department of Geography, The University of Iowa, Iowa City, Iowa.

Staff, P. W. (1975). Principal, Local Government Directorate, Department of the Environment, England. Personal interview.

Tiebout, C. M. (1956). 'A pure theory of local expenditure', *Journal of Political Economy,* **64,** 416-24.

Vince, S. (1975). Member, Royal Commission's Intelligence Unit. Personal interview.

Walker, Rt Hon. P. (1975). Secretary for the Environment when the legislation was proposed and passed. Personal interview.

_____ *13*__

Structural and dialectical theories of political regionalism

John A. Agnew

An important controversy in the philosophy of social science concerns the extent to which human behaviour is determined by factors outside the control of human agency — ecological factors, occupational structures, age structures etc. — and the extent to which these structures are the product of human agency. At one extreme is a *structural* position which maintains that structures are uniquely determining and evolve without the action of concrete individuals (e.g. Durkheim, Althusser) and at the other a *voluntarist* position which posits that there are no limits to the exercise of moral choice or the operation of critical rationality (e.g. Sartre, Popper). Of course, one can argue that both these positions are not only extreme but also incorrect. The adoption of what can be called a dialectical perspective offers a way out (Murphy, 1971; Bourdieu, 1973; Cosgrove, 1978; Burman, 1979). According to this position, human behaviour is viewed as both determined *and* determining, '...a web of possibilities for agents, whose nature is both active and structured, to make choices and pursue strategies within given limits, which in consequence expand and contract over time' (Lukes, 1977, p. 29). It is with the conflict between the dialectical position and the structural viewpoint in a specific context of interest to geographers and other scientists that this paper is concerned.

A widely accepted structural theory of social and political change holds that the processes of industrialization and modernization, while they may initially disrupt 'traditional' societies and exacerbate ethnic conflict, in the long run erode the significance of ethnic identifications and commitments (Kautsky,

1972). As a consequence political conflict becomes inexorably defined in terms of class and socioeconomic status. Lipset and Rokkan, for example, argue that:

> The National Revolution forced ever-widening circles of the territorial population to choose sides in conflicts over values and cultural identities. The Industrial Revolution also triggered a variety of cultural counter-movements, but in the longer run tended to cut across the value communities within the nation and to force the enfranchised citizenry to choose sides in terms of their economic interest, their shares in the increased wealth generated through the spread of new technologies and the widening markets (Lipset and Rokkan, 1967, pp. 18-19).

However, the recent political successes of regionally based nationalist movements in some of the world's most 'modernized' societies, most notably Canada, the United Kingdom, and Belgium, have indicated the need to revise or abandon this thesis of social and political change.

This paper presents and contrasts two different theoretical approaches to explaining what is termed here 'political regionalism': the politics of regional 'nationalism' and incipient separatism within multinational states. Political regionalism, then, includes both sectionalist and separatist political tendencies with the former giving way to the latter when cultural and territorial loyalties are conjoined. The first approach, labelled the 'structural', subsumes several perspectives: the uneven development, internal colonialism, and ethnic competition schools of thought. These have arisen as a reaction to the perceived failure of the modernization thesis and are argued for most forcefully by, respectively, Nairn (1977), Hechter (1975), and Ragin (1979). They all see political regionalism arising as a *direct* result of objective social forces (structures) but stress different structures in their explanations. In terms of reasoning they do not differ from the structural determinism of the modernization thesis and available writing by political geographers on the geographically structured (core-periphery) basis to political integration and separatism (e.g. Hartshorne, 1950; Whebell, 1973). In this paper Hechter's study serves as a major example of the structural approach.

The second theory, referred to as the 'dialectical', is proposed here as an alternative to the presently dominant structural approach. Its focus is upon exploring the roots of political action in relation to the contexts in which political regionalism has arisen.

'Action' and 'structure' are both key words rather than one or the other.

The major objective of the paper is to suggest the relative superiority of dialectical theorizing in explaining political regionalism as manifested in recent Western European and North American experience. To this end the paper is organized in the following manner: first, the structural theories of political regionalism are described; second, a dialectical theory is proposed; third, the two types of theory are compared in empirical and philosophical terms; fourth, and finally, some tentative conclusions are offered.

Structural theories of political regionalism

In some recent research Hechter (1975) has proposed a theory of 'internal colonialism' according to which states, such as the United Kingdom, are both built and 'integrated' by a process of domination by a central or core ethnic group (also see Havens and Flinn, 1970). Peripheral areas are permanently disadvantaged or exploited, and their local cultures are subject to systematic assault by the dominant group. Cultural differences do not disappear, however, and in certain circumstances, such as a decline in the core group's power, they may lead to agitation and the rise of separatist politics in peripheral areas.

In an attempt to demonstrate this theory, Hechter takes electoral data for the period 1885-1966 and, using percentage Conservative vote as his dependent variable, tries to predict areas of pro- and anti-Conservative sentiment in Britain and Northern Ireland using a variety of economic and cultural variables. The whole empirical procedure, however, revolves around the assumption that in the 'Celtic Fringe' a vote against the Conservatives is *an anti-English vote*. Voting for Labour, Liberal, or other candidates no longer has any positive content. In peripheral areas such as central Scotland and south Wales, where the Labour Party has enjoyed fervent working-class support, voting is clearly not an entirely negative activity (see Ragin, 1977). Hechter claims, however, to have shown a persisting anti-English sentiment or 'peripheral sectionalism', which he equates with a latent separatism, in large parts of Wales and Scotland.

Whatever the merits of Hechter's empiricism, his theory deserves serious treatment partly because it has received favourable reviews and is serving as the basis for further research and partly because it represents an increasingly popular mode of theorizing about political regionalism (e.g. Scott, 1976; S. H. Williams, 1977; Verdery, 1976; Hechter and Levi, 1979; Reece, 1979; McRobert, 1979). This theorizing is *structural* because it sees a particular type of political behaviour arising ineluctably as a *direct* result of ethnic mobilization in the face of internal colonialism. The structural conditions determine the human reaction. Consequently, the theory provides a set of rules indicating the causal links between the objective condition of cultural-economic domination and the subjective reaction of political regionalism *wherever it might occur.* In this respect Hechter's theory is no different from the other structural theories mentioned earlier. The only difference lies in the specific structures which are held to be determining. For instance, Nairn (1975, 1977) traces nationalism directly to the operation of the global capitalism economy (also see Sloan, 1979). Nairn writes: 'The real origins of nationalism are located not in the folk, nor in the individual's repressed passion for some sort of wholeness or identity, but in the machinery of world political economy' (1975, p. 8). Finally, Ragin (1979) sees political regionalism arising from a competition between ethnic groups for the same rewards and resources which in turn has resulted from the growing interconnectedness of the previously economically and territorially separate groups. This is a structural perspective insofar as both ethnic identity and political action are seen as determined by ecological processes and constraints (also see Barth, 1969; Hannan, 1979).

A dialectical theory of political regionalism

Although not denying the reality of objective conditions, such as those specified by 'internal colonialism', we should be careful not to reify an explanatory scheme such that everything is explained before there is anything to explain. In particular, if one ignores the dialectical relationship between objective structures and human behaviour then one is condemned to reduce all behaviour to a logical formula: 'objective' structural conditions *cause* predictable and specific human behaviour. In so doing theory is severed from the lives of people 'reflecting on the crises in their communication, the conflicts of principles in their moral existence, and the clash of concepts in their efforts to articulate the actual context of their human lives' (Schrag, 1975, p. 30). Yet, it is striking in the context of political regionalism that rather than being overwhelmingly and strongly committed to a nationalist consciousness, as the Hechter theory would predict, the peoples of many 'peripheries' and 'fringes' are ambivalent in their political commitments. Further, some do not even care about politics even at the most politicized times in the most politicized places (e.g. Fitzpatrick, 1978, p. 113, on Ireland 1910-21).

I have previously attempted to show, in the context of northwest Scotland (Agnew, 1980), that people have a variety of cultural, territorial, and class interests which they must see as compatible and reinforcing for political regionalism, as indicated by electoral support for anti-establishment (Labour?) or separatist candidates, to indicate a strategy of political independence or separation rather than strategy for pursuing limited goals such as obtaining greater recognition of some interest from the central government, protesting the failures of the orthodox political parties (also see Mackintosh, 1977; Miller *et al.*, 1977) or protesting against distant bureaucracy. Bernard (1978) has made a similar observation with respect to Quebec. We should not accept *a priori* that a vote for a 'separatist', or against some other, political party indicates a deep-seated allegiance to a political regionalism generated by internal colonialism or some other structural recipe. People must be allowed to define their own interests and strategies by themselves and in communication with others (Bourdieu, 1977).

Ambivalence in political consciousness is not unique to the populations of geographically peripheral or ethnically distinct areas (e.g. Mann, 1970; Zolberg, 1976; Sennett and Cobb, 1972). Rather, people in general have contradictory political commitments, man versus party, class versus culture, territory versus class, which intersect in different ways in different 'situational contexts' reflecting the different configurations of objective conditions and their histories in these places and the interpretations people put on these. A dialectical theory of political regionalism, then, identifies the nature and relationships of political commitments for particular groups and relates these to underlying objective conditions and definitions of interest, i.e. it is *process-oriented*. It argues that people act politically by pursuing 'symbolic' and 'material' interests, which may or may not be compatible, defined by them in reference to their situational contexts. In agreement with the position of Marx in the *Theses on Feuerbach*, dialectical theorizing insists that political regionalism results from human choice and action under conditions of structural constraint yet sees the basis of this outcome as the pursuit of socially defined interests, ones arrived at through social interaction and communication, rather than the expression of a 'collective idea' (Billig, 1976; Applebaum, 1978). 'Practical reason' serving symbolic and material interests deriving from local situations is at the heart of dialectical theorizing; and practical reason is the application of human powers of reasoning to pursue interests defined in everyday life (Fay, 1978).

Comparing the theories

Empirical evidence

A major component of Hechter's internal colonialism theory is the necessary link between cultural-economic domination and reactive political regionalism. Yet there are examples of political regionalism arising in peripheral areas other than those where one might most expect it, given this theory. In Spain, for instance, political regionalism is much more a feature of Catalonia and the Basque Provinces than it is of Galicia. Yet. Galicia has a lower standard of living than both of these regions and a language as distinct from Castilian Spanish as that of Catalonia (Linz and de Miguel, 1966). The critical issue in the Galician case has been the close political and social ties that the region has maintained since the Civil War with powerful elements in the Franco regime. In Catalonia and the Basque Provinces, however, although there are many differences between them, civil war traditions, local employment opportunities, and local traditions of political and social activism *combine* to produce an alienation from the Spain of Madrid (Linz, 1964; Ortega y Gasset, 1937; Brenan, 1943). In particular, they have not provided many recruits to high national office or the judiciary (Linz and de Miguel, 1966). Consequently, local elites have been deflected into local political activities and flirtation with separatist politics (more generally, see Gourevitch, 1979).

The lesson of the Spanish example is that regional environments provide different objective conditions in which different sets of interests are defined. And these are not simply a direct reflection of levels of economic development. They involve historical attachments and contemporary interpretations of material and symbolic deprivation. Political regionalism as a strategy for political independence arises when local ethnic/regional interests prevail or are compatible with other interests and there is some organization, a political movement or party, which can engage in elections and other political activities such as demonstrations and acts of terrorism. This last point is of some importance. Even with reinforcing cleavages and interests which crystallize in favour of regional 'nationalism' there can be little prospect for a successful separatism without a clearly defined and supportable political movement. It is through such an organization and its leadership that a regional population can be educated as to its grievances, informed about a noble and unique past, and made aware of separation's benefits. However favourable the objective conditions but without a rhetoric and a suitable organization to represent it, political regionalism will never have an unambiguous means of representation and focus of loyalty (see Desbarats, 1976; Harvie, 1977; Mitchison, 1978; Brand, 1978).

Certain other conditions are also important in creating an environment for the possible expression of a regional political consciousness. These include an intelligentsia prepared to propagandize and act on behalf of ethnic/regional rather than other commitments (Gellner, 1969; Smith, 1971, 1977, 1979; Khleif, 1978, pp. 107-8; Ragin, 1979, p. 633; Williams, 1979) and political party and electoral systems that allow for the growth and *stimulation* of new voting and general political habits (Duverger, 1964; Pinard, 1975; Taylor and Johnston, 1979). The presence or absence of sympathetic business interests may also be important for funding and support of regional political movements (Dalyell, 1977). There are, therefore, critical constraints upon the growth of political regionalism which differ in their impact and consequent effects from regional context to regional context, depending upon how local elites and populations evaluate and react to them.

Another important feature of the structural type of theory in addition to its structure-behaviour determinism is its monolithic image of political consciousness. It postulates a political consciousness dominated by local ethnic identity. Although such a consciousness surely does exist for some people it is only when other commitments have declined in significance or are seen as compatible with a nationalist or ethnic/regional consciousness. Moreover, such a consciousness should not be confused with reactions against centralized bureaucracy and 'other entities on a scale beyond human relations' (Osmond, 1978). This may in fact be the overriding commitment behind the rise of the Scottish National Party to electoral prominence in the years 1966-76. At the very least this is an hypothesis that deserves investigation before we *infer* a deep-seated ethnic identity as *the* cause of this Scottish political regionalism merely because our theory tells us this is so (Hobsbawm, 1977).

The fragmented political consciousness of individuals living in some areas presently experiencing an upsurge in political regionalism is attested to be a variety of research, and indicates the care which must be taken in invariably viewing the successes of apparently 'anti-core groups' or of separatist political parties as manifestations of a dominant commitment to local ethnic/regional interests. For instance, some recent social psychological research suggests that Welshmen regard an ability to speak the local language as the fundamental dimension of Welshness (Giles *et al.,* 1977). Yet, most Welshmen are not Welsh-speaking and, consequently, feel culturally inconsistent. Moreover, in reactions to English accents English-speaking Welshmen offer social class rather than ethnic evaluations of speakers (Bourhis *et al.,* 1973). Most Welshmen, then, appear to have self-images which have separable ethnic and class components. Research with French Canadian subjects, however, indicates that cultural and class interests and sentiments are not separable and competing but merged and compatible. French Canadians apparently feel relatively deprived in comparison with English Canadians (Yackley and Lambert, 1971) and also have strong cultural and linguistic affiliations (Taylor *et al.,* 1973). The French Canadian consciousness, then, is less fragmented than that of the Welsh. The fact that the Welsh have no *resident* dominant reference group equivalent to that which French Canadians have in the English Canadians of Montreal may account for this difference (Laponce, 1978). 'English' and 'middle class' may be synonymous in French Canada to an extent that is not the case in Wales.

The lesson of the Welsh and French Canadian examples is that political consciousness is not invariably monolithic. People have interests internalized as commitments which may or may not be compatible. In French Canada there are empirical grounds for suggesting that these commitments are compatible, whereas in Wales as a whole there are no such grounds. Over a variety of regions, then, we can recognize degrees to which political regionalism represents a deep-seated local ethnic consciousness and degrees to which it is epiphenomenal, produced by some strategy of protest against centralized bureaucracy or strategy to serve local economic interests, independent of any cultural concerns or ethnic identity (Hobsbawm, 1971, 1977).

By way of conclusion for this section, even a cursory empirical survey suggests that:

1. political regionalism (as the pursuit of 'national' independence) is linked to regional environments in complex ways not accounted for by a simple cultural-economic domination theory, or other structural theory; and
2. political regionalism, as manifested by electoral behaviour, can be deep-seated or epiphenomenal.

If the former, then political consciousness is more monolithic and 'ethnic' in tone, if the latter, then it is more fragmented. Depending on the nature of the consciousness we can characterize political regionalism as representing (a) political independence, or (b) other strategies of political action on the part of local inhabitants.

Philosophical issues

The two types of theory, the structural and the dialectical, can be regarded as respectively 'fitting' and 'guiding' approaches to understanding political regionalism. In the former case political behaviour is treated as a mechanical reaction to directly determining and antecedent structures. With the latter such structural and successional causality is abandoned for a theory which does not rely on causes external to human action but which builds understanding from the position of actors in concrete situations. This is not to advocate an intentionalist as opposed to a causalist account of behaviour. Rather the causes of behaviour are seen to include reasons (Toulmin, 1970; Fay, 1978). Moreover, and this is even more critical, people are also viewed as having *causal power*. They can act for their reasons. But the efficacy of a given individual's causal power is severely circumscribed by the contemporary *relative distribution* of causal powers (some people are more free to act than others and/or can block the actions of others) and the uses to which previous generations put their powers, i.e. *in toto* the structural constraints on individual action. The goal of a dialectical theory is to demarcate the social psychological processes which link objective conditions and human action in such a way as to see how people define the interests and settle on the strategies which produce their political behaviour. The theory guides us into searching for and identifying the specific processes that are involved.

The essential difference between the structural and the dialectical theories is clearly expressed by the anthropologist Bourdieu when he writes of kinship relationships that:

> To treat kin relationships as something people *make,* and with *which* they *do,* something, is not merely to substitute a 'functionalist' for a 'structuralist' interpretation, as current taxonomies would lead one to believe; it is radically to question the implicit theory of practice which causes the anthropological tradition to see kin relationships 'in the form of an object or an intuition', as Marx put it, rather than in the form of the practices which produce, reproduce, and use them

by reference to necessarily practical functions. The same is true, *a fortiori,* of official relationships: it is only when one records these relationships as a *fait accompli, post festum,* as the anthropologist does when he draws up a genealogy, that one can forget that they are the product of strategies (conscious and unconscious) oriented towards the satisfaction of material and symbolic interests and organized by reference to a determinate set of economic and social conditions (Bourdieu, 1977, pp. 34-5).

The dialectical theory is not then merely the old 'behavioural' approach dressed up in nineteenth-century jargon. It involves recognizing real structural constraints as well as emphasizing the role of human agency in creating and remaking these constraints. In the present context the slogan of the dialectical approach is that today's 'revolutionary' political regionalism *can be* tomorrow's constraining orthodoxy and, given our limited knowledge of intentions and desires, may not *mean* what we think it does for involved populations even now. A task of research is to fathom shifts in the meaning and expectations of political regionalism as they occur in specific contexts.

The major failings of the structural theories of political regionalism correspond to the major strengths of the dialectical. The first of these lies in the reification of the term 'political regionalism' necessitated by the *a priori* claim to universality implicit in any structural theory (the nominalist fallacy). Political regionalism is seen as something-in-itself as it is defined in the theory rather than as a label for a variety of political expressions to be examined and compared. In the dialectical theory 'political regionalism' is regarded as meaningful only in its situational or regional contexts even though many contexts appear to be similar. Evaluation of the theory's major elements (e.g. contradictory political commitments, the effects of specific structural constraints) is by means of comparative analysis.

A second major problem with structural theories is their assumption of a direct, one-way causal relationship between structures, such as class, culture, territory, and political behaviour. But where do these structures come from? And, more specifically, do human minds mediate and process the structural effects or, as is apparently implied, is there a simple mechanical reaction of behaviour from structure? The precise position of structural theorists with respect to these points is unclear. However the major difference between structural and dialectical theories appears to lie in what is regarded as a satisfactory explanation by their respective proponents. For the structural theorist a correlation between a structure and a behaviour is sufficient explanation of that behaviour. But the dialectical theorist does not accept this 'successional' view of causality. Rather, he adopts a 'generative' perspective which requires the investigation of all possible links (in both directions) between structure and behaviour (see Keat and Urry, 1975). In the present context this suggests that a dialectical theory focuses on the social organization of political regionalism, what it means to and does for people, as much as the structural settings in which it emerges (see Wenger, 1978; Fishman, 1977). At the risk of repetition, this is not to say that behaviour is cause-less and hence inexplicable or mysterious, but to emphasize that many actions have compelling reasons rather than compulsive external causes.

In the final analysis, however, preferences for a theory of political regionalism, or any other phenomenon involving human behaviour, depend upon one's acceptance or denial of the place of the human subject in history. If one agrees with the denial of the thinking/acting subject and displaces the concrete historical, then one will see dialectical theorizing as a form of idealism and the structural as a preferable trans-historical and 'scientific' position. This, of course, is the central issue in contemporary disputes among anthropologists, Marxists and Marxologists (e.g. Sahlins, 1976; Thompson, 1978; Kolakowski, 1978).

Conclusion

In this paper two approaches to explaining political regionalism have been presented and contrasted. Particular stress has been placed on querying the dominant one: the structural. On both philosophical and empirical grounds another theory, a dialectical one, has been proposed as superior. In particular dialectical theorizing focuses on process rather than structure in searching for processual regularities rather than fitting structural rules. For geographers there may be some utility in comparing the argument of this paper to that of those writings which questioned the 'Davisian Geomorphic Cycle'. In that case there was also a structural theory being imposed on reality and lending itself to easy classroom exposition. The imperative behind this paper is that political geography must travel the same route as geomorphology in its retreat from structural determinism in order to treat *process* and consequently approach understanding of the real causes of what has been labelled 'political regionalism'.

References and bibliography

Agnew, J. A. (1980). 'Political regionalism and Scottish nationalism in Gaelic
    Scotland', *Canadian Review of Studies in Nationalism* (forthcoming).
Applebaum, R. P. (1978). 'Marxist method: structural constraints and social
    praxis', *American Sociologist,* **13,** 73-81.
Barth, F. (1969). *Ethnic Groups and Boundaries* (Little Brown, Boston).
Bernard, A. (1978). *What Does Quebec Want?* (James Lorimer, Toronto).
Billig, M. (1976). *Social Psychology and Intergroup Relations* (Academic
    Press, London).
Bourdieu, P. (1973). 'The three forms of theoretical knowledge', *Social
    Science Information,* **12,** 53-80.
Bourdieu, P. (1977). *Outline of a Theory of Practice* (Cambridge University
    Press, Cambridge).
Bourhis, R. Y., Gils, H., and Tajfel, H. (1973). 'Language as a determinant of
    Welsh identity', *European Journal of Social Psychology,* **3,** 447-60.
Brand, J. (1978). *The National Movement in Scotland* (Routledge & Kegan
    Paul, London).
Brenan, G. (1943). *The Spanish Labyrinth* (Cambridge University Press,
    Cambridge).
Burman, P. (1979). 'Variations on a dialectical theme', *Philosophy of the
    Social Sciences,* **9,** 357-75.
Cosgrove, D. (1978). 'Place, landscape and the dialectics of cultural
    geography', *Canadian Geographer,* **22**(1), 66-72.
Dalyell, T. (1977). *Devolution: The End of Britain?* (Jonathan Cape, London).
Desbarats, P. (1976). *Rene: A Canadian in Search of a Country* (McClelland &
    Stewart, Toronto).
Duverger, M. (1964). *Political Parties: Their Organization and Activity in the
    Modern State* (Methuen, London).
Fay, B. (1978). 'Practical reasoning, rationality and the explanation of
    intentional action', *Journal of the Theory of Social Behaviour,* **8**(1),
    77-101.
Fishman, J. A. (1977). 'Language and ethnicity', in Giles, H. (ed.), *Language,
    Ethnicity and Intergroup Relations,* pp. 15-57 (Academic Press,
    London).
Fitzpatrick, D. (1978). 'The geography of Irish nationalism, 1910-1921', *Past
    and Present,* **78,** 113-44.
Gellner, E. (1969). *Thought and Change* (University of Chicago Press,
    Chicago).
Giles, H., Taylor D. M., and Bourhis, R. Y. (1977). 'Dimensions of Welsh
    identity', *European Journal of Social Psychology,* **7,** 165-74.
Gourevitch, P. A. (1979). 'The reemergence of "peripheral nationalism":
    some comparative speculations on the spatial distribution of political
    leadership and economic growth', *Comparative Studies in Society and
    History,* **21,** 303-22.
Hannan, M. (1979). 'The dynamics of ethnic boundaries in modern states', in
    Hannan, M., and Meyer, J. (eds.), *National Development and the
    World System: Educational, Economic and Political Change, 1950-1970*
    (University of Chicago Press, Chicago).
Hartshorne, R. (1950). 'The functional approach to political geography',
    Annals of the Association of American Geographers, **40,** 95-130.

Harvie, C. (1977). *Scotland and Nationalism: Scottish Society and Politics 1707-1977* (George Allen & Unwin, London).

Havens, A. E., and Flinn, W. L. (1970). *Internal Colonialism and Structural Change in Colombia* (Praeger, New York).

Hechter, M. (1975). *Internal Colonialism: The Celtic Fringe in British National Development, 1536-1966* (University of California Press, Berkeley).

Hechter, M., and Levi, M. (1979). 'The comparative analysis of ethnoregional movements', *Ethnography and Racial Studies*, **2,** 260-74.

Hobsbawm, E. J. (1971). *Mouvements nationaux d'indépendences et classes populaires aux XIX et XX siécles* (Paris).

Hobsbawm, E. J. (1977), 'Some reflections on "The break-up of Britain"', *New Left Review*, **105,** 3-23.

Kautsky, J. H. (1972). *The Political Consequences of Modernization* (Wiley, New York).

Keat, R., and Urry, J. (1975). *Social Theory as Science* (Routledge & Kegan Paul, London).

Khleif, B. (1978). 'Ethnic awakening in the First World: the case of Wales', in Williams, G. (ed.), *Social and Cultural Change in Contemporary Wales*, pp. 102-19 (Routledge & Kegan Paul, London).

Kolakowski, L. (1978). *Main Currents of Marxism*, 3 vols. (Clarendon Press, Oxford).

Laponce, J. A. (1978). 'The city center as a factor of national disintegration: the case of Montreal'. Paper prepared for the 1978 Canadian Political Science Association Meetings, London, Canada.

Linz, J. J. (1964). 'An authoritarian regime: Spain', in Allardt, E., and Littman, Y. (eds.), *Cleavages, Ideologies, and Party Systems: Contributions to Comparative Political Sociology,* (Westermark Society, Helsinki).

Linz, J. J. (1970). 'An authoritarian regime: Spain', in E. Allardt and S. Rokkan (eds.), *Mass Politics*, pp. 251-83 (Free Press, New York).

Linz, J. J., and de Miguel, A. (1966). 'Within-nation differences and comparisons: the eight Spains', in Merritt, R. L., and Rokkan, S. (eds.), *Comparing Nations: The Uses of Quantitative Data in Cross-National Research,* (Yale University Press, New Haven).

Lipset, S. M., and Rokkan, S. (1967). 'Cleavage structures, party systems and voter alignments', in Lipset, S. M., and Rokkan, S. (eds.), *Party Systems and Voter Alignments*, pp. 3-64 (Free Press, New York).

Lukes, S. (1977). *Essays in Social Theory* (Macmillan, London).

Mackintosh, J. (1977). 'Is Labour facing catastrophe?' *Encounter* (January), pp. 47-54.

Mann, M. (1970). 'The social cohesion of liberal democracy', *American Sociology Review*, **35,** 423-39.

McRobert, K. (1979). 'Internal colonialism: the case of Quebec', *Ethnography and Racial Studies*, **3,** 293-318.

Miller, W. L., Sarlvik, B., Crewe, T., and Alt, J. (1977). 'The connection between SNP voting and the demand for Scottish self-government', *European Journal of Political Research*, **5,** 86-102.

Mitchison, R. (1978). 'Patriotism and national identity in eighteenth century Scotland', in Moody, T. W. (ed.), *Nationality and the Pursuit of National Independence* (Appletree Press for the Irish Committee of Historical Sciences, Belfast).

Murphy, R. F. (1971). *The Dialectics of Social Life: Alarms and Excursions in Anthropological Theory* (Basic Books, New York).

Nairn, T. (1975). 'The modern Janus', *New Left Review,* **94.**

Nairn, T. (1977). *The Break-up of Britain* (New Left Books, London).

Ortega y Gasset, J. (1937). *Invertebrate Spain* (Norton, New York).

Osmond, J. (1978). *Creative Conflict: The Politics of Welsh Devolution* (Routledge & Kegan Paul, London).

Pinard, M. (1975). *The Rise of a Third Party: A Study in Crisis Politics* (McGill-Queens University Press, Montreal).

Ragin, C. (1977). 'Class, status, and "reactive ethnic cleavages": the social bases of political regionalism', *American Sociological Review,* **42,** 438-50.

Ragin, C. (1979). 'Ethnic political mobilization: the Welsh case', *American Sociological Review,* **44,** 619-34.

Reece, J. (1979). 'Internal colonialism: the case of Brittany', *Ethnography and Racial Studies,* **3,** 275-92.

Sahlins, M. (1976). *Culture and Practical Reason* (University of Chicago Press, Chicago).

Schrag, C. O. (1975). 'Praxis and structure: conflicting models in the science of man', *Journal of the British Society for Phenomenology,* **6,** 23-31.

Scott, J. (1976). 'Extended review', *Sociology Review* (February), 187-92.

Sennett, R., and Cobb, J. (1972). *The Hidden Injuries of Class* (Random House, New York).

Sloan, W. N. (1979). 'Ethnicity of imperialism? A review article', *Comparative Studies in Society and History,* **21** 113-25.

Smith, A. D. (1971). *Theories of Nationalism* (Duckworth, London).

Smith, A. D. (1977). 'Neo-classicist and romantic elements in the emergence of nationalist conceptions' in Smith, A. D. (ed.), *Nationalist Movements,* pp. 1-30 (St Martin's Press, New York).

Smith, A. D. (1979). 'Towards a theory of ethnic separatism', *Ethnography and Racial Studies,* **2,** 21-37.

Taylor, D. M., Bassili, J. N. and Aboud, F. E. (1973). 'Dimensions of ethnic identity: an example from Quebec', *Journal of Social Psychology,* **89,** 185-92.

Taylor, P. J., and Johnston, R. J. (1979). *Geography of Elections* (Penguin, Harmondsworth).

Thompson, E. P. (1978). *The Poverty of Theory and Other Essays* (Merlin Press, London).

Toulmin, S. (1970). 'Reasons and causes', in Borger, R., and Cioffi, F. (ed.), *Explanation in the Behavioural Sciences,* pp. 1-26 (Cambridge University Press, Cambridge).

Verdery, K. (1976). 'Ethnicity and local systems: the religious organization of Welshness', in Smith, C. A. (ed.), *Regional Analysis,* vol. II: *Social Systems,* pp. 191-228 (Academic Press, New York).

Wenger, G. C. (1978). 'Ethnicity and social organization in north-east Wales', in Williams, G. (ed.), *Social and Cultural Change in Contemporary Wales,* pp. 120-32 (Routledge & Kegan Paul, London).

Whebell, C. F. J. (1973). 'A model of territorial separatism', *Proceedings of the Association of American Geographers,* **5,** 95-8.

Williams, C. H. (1979). 'Ethnic resurgence in the periphery'. *Area,* **11**(4), 279-83.

Williams, S. W. (1977). 'Internal colonialism, core-periphery contacts and devolution: an integrative comment', *Area,* **9,** 272-8.

Yackley, A., and Lambert, W. E. (1971). 'Inter-ethnic group competition and levels of aspiration', *Canadian Journal of Behavioural Science,* **3,** 135-47.

Zolberg, A. (1976). 'Culture, territory, class: ethnicity demystified'. Paper presented at the Xth World Congress, International Political Science Association, Edinburgh, Scotland.

Political studies from spatial perspectives
Edited by A.D. Burnett and P.J. Taylor
© 1981 John Wiley & Sons Ltd

_____ *14*__

Frontier studies:
an applied approach

J. W. House

Though the study of frontiers is one of the most traditional in
political geography (Minghi, 1963; Guichonnet and Raffestin, 1974;
Sanguin, 1976) it has suffered, perhaps more than most branches,
from the somewhat exceptionalist position to which the subject has
become increasingly relegated. Arising from an empirical study of
the United States-Mexican border on the Rio Grande (House,
forthcoming (a)), the paper explores a methodology which draws
upon contemporary thinking, both in general geography and the
cognate disciplines of international relations and political science.
In the light of this experience some tentative observations are
advanced on likely directions of progress in this field of political
geography.

The framework of the study defines an applied political geography.
As elsewhere in applied geography (House, 1976) there are
similarities with the purposes and methodology of general
geography, but also additional distinct and deliberate differences.
The differences relate to: an operational stance, perhaps on
occasion involving service to a client; the development of models
with some predictive content; a greater requirement for both
precision and priority concern for the implications of subjectivity in
any analysis; and a fuller integration with the contributions by
specialists in related disciplines. Hitherto, applied geography has
been focused primarily on urban or regional planning, on resource
management or environmental problems. In adding a deliberate
political dimension to environment, economy, and society not only
is the field unpredictably widened, but methodological rigour risks
becoming lost in a maelstrom of ideology, opinions, or even
emotions. For this reason the method advanced is empirically
based, building a progressively coherent framework towards theory

and principle, rather than attempting the deductively reverse order of reasoning.

The focus in the study is upon the dynamics of change within a potential conflict situation, rather than being limited to a functionalist exploration of relationships in the present, as the summation of evolution from an historic past. Alternatively put, the perspective is on tension management within a field of forces, forces which are economic, social, cultural, as well as political in their manifestation. Apart from the well-known 'unified field theory' (Jones, 1954), with its incorporation of a 'power' variable, there have been regrettably few attempts by political geographers to produce behavioural models of an operational character. Political scientists and, more particularly, students of international relations, have moved further in that direction, but in somewhat abstract and structuralist rather than in spatial terms. Nevertheless, such contributions offer an analytical context, within which the genesis, impact, and spatial differentiation of political change can be prospectively advanced. There are broadly three alternative approaches in international relations (Frankel, 1973a, p. 28): the study of power, of social communication (cybernetics), and an analysis in systems terms.

The study of power interaction interprets conflict as a general social process (Boulding, 1962), with negative (dissociative) and positive (associative) aspects, more realistically than the amorphous concept of centrifugal-centripetal forces balance used by earlier political geographers (Hartshorne, 1950). The social communications model (Deutsch, 1963) analyses the flow of communications among actors as the basic process in international relations, balancing adaptive behaviour with a refusal to adapt or to take heed. The systems-analytical method (Kaplan, 1967) offers the same exciting possibilities and yet has aroused no less misgivings in political science than in geography (Bull, 1966; Knorr and Rosenau, 1969). Though limited in explanatory power its comprehensive nature is useful in organizational terms, for formulating hypotheses from complex data (Frankel, 1973b, p. 41). In political geography, it further offers perhaps the most useful thinking framework for the scale-level problem, with nested levels of analysis: the international system; the state; the province; and local or peripheral (the frontier). Surprisingly, the study of the functional relationships or linkages within this hierarchy is one of the most neglected at the heart of political geography. This is no less true in frontier studies than in electoral geography (Stokes, 1965; Woolstencroft, forthcoming). Finally, the 'linkage' approach, drawn from international relations research (Frankel, 1973b, p. 42), is a more limited but valuable way of studying recurrent sequences of behaviour that originate in one system (scale-level) and are reacted to in another. This input-output interpretation also permits the integrative study of domestic politics and foreign policy (Rosenau, 1969), by regarding each sphere as a system in interaction. Such a specific examination of actual transaction flows adds depth to the more abstract systems-analytical approach, but even so it still affords only a partial introduction to the underlying adaptive or maladaptive behaviour of states.

An operational model for frontier studies

Hitherto, some variant of the centre (core)-periphery model has been the most characteristic in frontier studies, though many such studies have remained empirical in character rather than seeking for valid generalizations. The centre-periphery model was perhaps at its most useful when the focus in political geography rested on the nation-state, the time perspective was long, and the interpretation primarily descriptive rather than analytical. It is difficult to adapt the centre-periphery model for the operational needs of today, when the focus has shifted to regulation of the international system and to the behavioural interactions of states in relation to specific, often dramatic, events or slow, incremental policy changes. Moreover, the need for a more operational model is underlined by the wide range of frontier problems in the contemporary world. The more violent confrontational situations come readily to mind, but as significant are the less tension-ridden, but characteristically asymmetrical, relationships between almost all pairs of states. On a more positive note, the trend towards supranational cooperation, first in Europe (West and East) and, more recently, diffusing elsewhere, has caused a creative revaluation in the significance of frontiers. There are, indeed, some encouraging signs for the creation of transnational frontier regions as a manner of furthering international cooperation (Guichonnet and Raffestin, 1974, pp. 147-233).

An operational model for the study of frontiers has to be constructed from as complete as possible a picture of total cross-frontier transaction flows, of goods, people, capital, and services (public and private). These flows then need to be aggregated and, as far as possible, integrated progressively in terms of structure (Figure 14.1), space (Figure 14.2) and time. The resulting flow patterns must next be interpreted within a framework of perceptions, policies, and politics, all of which are in their turn to be differentiated by

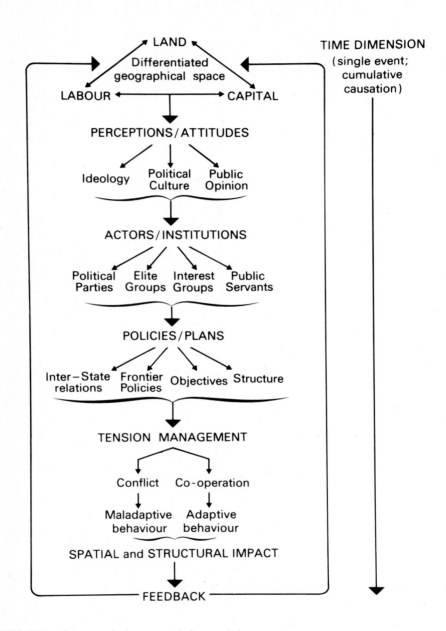

FIGURE 14.1   Structural elements of the model

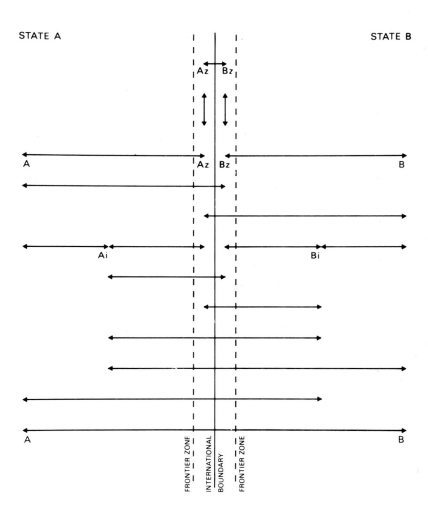

FIGURE 14.2   Spatial elements of the model

structure, space, and time. Inevitably, there is overlapping within the flux of transactions, their linkages, and among the reasons postulated for their characteristics, trends, manipulation, and the resulting impact of decisions once reached.

Central to a geographical investigation of the cross-frontier transaction flows is their spatial manifestation. Figure 14.2 disaggregates the flows by distance and direction of interaction, distinguishing: centre (core) of one state (A) to centre of an adjacent state (B); centre (A, B) to periphery (Az, Bz), the frontier zones, including also the periphery of the adjacent state (Az to B, Bz to A); regional centre (Ai, Bi) to core, regional centre and periphery within each state; and frontier zone interaction (Az-Bz), both cross-frontier and, laterally, within the same frontier zone. The frontier zone is to be defined either statutorily, where there is a treaty or operational definition in depth, or conceptually in terms of some measurable or perceived distance-decay effect from the boundary line. Such a distance-decay effect might be postulated in theoretical terms (Loesch, 1954, pp. 196-210; Gendarme, 1970) but it is very difficult to define on the ground. Included in such an effect must be the spatial incidence of 'spread' and 'backwash' effects across international boundaries, arising from the aggravation of inequalities in the course of differential development on either side (Myrdal, 1957).

The model outlined is based on an analysis of total transaction flows across the United States-Mexican boundary on the Rio Grande (House, forthcoming (a)) but it is suggested that its principles may be tested for any cross-frontier set of relationships, whether within or between capitalist, socialist, or developing countries. Basic to the model is the underlying concept of asymmetrical relationships, whether real or perceived, and the policies and politics bearing upon attempts to maintain, change, adjust to or adapt such relationships. The framework is in a limited sense power-political, more evidently concerned with social, economic, and political communication, and specifically related to a linkages interpretation of systems analysis. When the model is fully constructed, and at present it is only partially so (House, forthcoming (b)), it may be possible to feed in particular events, intentions, policy changes, and variable rates of change, and to assess — as a result — the spatial origins, influences, and the impact of decisions upon the transaction flows and their milieu. Indeed, it must never be forgotten that the complex differentiation of geographical space is a fundamental, if disguised, ingredient in the model. It influences and complicates any attempt at a more abstract, systems understanding of the political environment, and also qualifies application of the findings in particular discrete areas.

A note on the United States-Mexican case study

Any general validity of the model postulated must be viewed in the context of the specific study from which it has emerged. Hence a brief picture of the United States-Mexican borderland on the Rio Grande is outlined.

The social and economic gradients across this frontier are perhaps the most extreme in the world, even though the US border zone ranks as a depressed area in the national economy and the Mexican border zone is not one of the outstanding problem areas of that country. During more than a century since establishment of the boundary (1848) the United States has dominated in the frontier zones. Social and economic gradients across the border have steepened steadily and the Mexican side has become ever more dependent. Such an entrenched pattern of unequal development has been reflected in a troubled history of frontier relationships, until very recent times. During the twentieth century Mexican nationalism has become more powerful and US assets have been expropriated, but the 1944 Boundary Waters agreement brought in a period of closer collaboration. Problems of sovereignty over the riverain tracts of the Rio Grande have been solved to the advantage of Mexico, accommodation has been reached on compensation for pollution by salinity of Colorado river waters reaching Mexico. Boundary jurisdiction in the territorial sea remains in dispute, but fishing rights in the Gulf of Mexico have been agreed.

The boundary of Spanish speech, surnames, and cultural affinity lies to the north of the present international boundary (the 'critical' boundary for Mexicans, to use Boulding's terminology (1962, p. 265)). On either side of the boundary there are depressed areas with a multitude of economic and social problems. Both the USA (EDA designation, 1966) and Mexico (1961 Border development, 1966 PRONAF, programmes) have implemented aid policies for their respective frontier zones. Mexican workers in large numbers cross into the USA, the vast proportion of them illegally. United States industry has established 'off-shore' border plants (maquiladoras) on the Mexican side, with Mexican government support, to make up products which must then be exported 100%. American investment in land, property, and urban utilities is limited by Mexican decree but is, and has long been, substantial. In frontier retailing and wholesaling there is an intricate pattern of flows, favouring the US

Table 14.1 An input-output model of frontier transactional flows (linkages)

Structural	Spatial					
	Local (periphery)		Regional (intermediate)		National (core)	
	Mexico Az	USA Bz	Mexico Ai	USA Bi	Mexico A	USA B
Economic and social						
Labour						
daily, weekly	out– commuters	in– commuters				
seasonal	out– migration	in– migration	out–	in–	out–	in–
Semi-permanent	out– migration	in– migration	out–	in–	out–	in–
illegal (rising rapidly)	out– 'safety valve'	in– concentration	out– 'safety valve'	in– diffusion	out– distance decay	in– diffusion
executive/professional	selective out–	selective in–; managers out–	out–	in–	out–	in–; managers out
	(maximum movement in this zone)					

Capital						
exports	natural resources; high labour content	higher value manufacturer, consumer goods	as Az	as Bz	as Az	as Bz
factory investment	'offshore' plants from US	competition with Az	US investment limited	source of 'offshore' plants	as Ai	as Bi
investments	US investment latent resources	savings from Az	US investment limited	nil	as Ai	as Bi
retailing/wholesaling	selective US purchases	major Mexican purchases	distance decay to c. 100 miles	distance decay very marked	negligible	negligible
tourism/recreation	exploit culture, scenery, cheapness	high-quality items	as Az	as Bz	selected major sites	diffused
illegal	smuggling; drugs out; crime; vice; prostitution, etc.	smuggling; arms, electronics, durables	concentration from region	diffusion into US region	concentration from nation	diffusion into nation
Land						
natural resources ⎰ farmland ⎱ second homes	purchases by US citizens	no interaction	as Az	as Bz	as Az	as Bz

[Time dimension:
Shifts in volume, direction, distance of flows and interaction]
e.g. *impact* of devaluation of peso 1976

Table 14.1   contd.

| Structural | Spatial | | | | | |
| | Local (periphery) | | Regional (intermediate) | | National (core) | |
	Mexico Az	USA Bz	Mexico Ai	USA Bi	Mexico A	USA B
Perceptions (attitudes)						
Ideology						
sense of history	oppression, dependency, unequal treaties	expanding frontier, development	as Az	as Bz	as Az	as Bz but more remote
mythology	'Aztlan'	Texas Rangers	heroic past as Az	Imperial Texas as Bz	national symbols as	national symbols as
stereotypes	greaser wet-back	gringo	as Az	as Bz	as Az	as Bz but less significant
value system/beliefs	'Mexicanness'; catholic; heroes; Spanish-Indian; peasant base	WASP; 'chicano'; urban dominant	as Az	as Bz, diffused	as Az	as Bz but more diverse
Political culture	authoritarian tradition; male-dominated	democratic; male-dominated	as Az	as Bz, diffused	as Az	as Bz but more diverse
Public opinion	less influential; manipulated; continuity of tradition	strong media influences; prejudiced on Az	as Az	as Bz	as Az	as Bz

Time dimension:

Shifts in attitudes, opinions, re-calibrated by changing events, manipulation. Momentum of continuity often strong]

Actors/institutions

Political parties	PRI	Democratic. 'Raza Unida' small	PRI	mainly Democratic	PRI	Democratic-Republican
Elite groups	political; bureaucratic; landed; industrial	political; landed; professional; entre-preneurial	as Az	as Bz	as Az	as Bz
Interest groups	peasants; workers; middle class	unions; farmers; middle class, including environ-mentalists	as Az	as Bz	as Az	more diverse and regionally based

Public servants (Key sectors)

Administration	Municipio	County	Border States	Texas	Mexican Federal	US Federal
Planning	Border Programme 1961; PRONAF 1966	EDA	contributions to National Plan	State Planning	National Development Plan	Federal Agencies
Health	higher disease incidence; less medical provision	better, more expensive provision	as Az	as Bz	as Az	as Bz

Table 14.1   contd.

	Spatial					
	Local (periphery)		Regional (intermediate)		National (core)	
	Mexico Az	USA Bz	Mexico Ai	USA Bi	Mexico A	USA B
Structural						
Public servants (Key sectors) — continued						
Education	less priority on intellectual development 'obedient-passive-affiliative'	stronger pressures to develop; active; individualist	as Az	as Bz	as Az	as Bz
Utilities	less provision	more provision	as Az	as Bz	as Az	as Bz
[Time dimension: Shifts in quantum and balance of functions and powers]						

Policies/plans

Scale level

	Local (periphery)		Regional (intermediate)		National (core)	
inter-state relationships	cooperation in environmental health, frontier passage, and local rights issues		limited interaction at regional (state) level		treaty provisions on major issues. Border Commission but largely inoperative	
policies on the frontier	protection; stimulation	cooperation; protection; exploitation of Az	no special policies	state planning bodies for distressed areas	Border Programme 1961; PRONAF 1966	SW Border Commission 1976-9

Objectives			central planning	market forces	central planning	market forces
development	urban growth; industrialization	growth points; polarization	central planning	market forces	central planning	market forces
well-being/social justice	municipal aid	municipal aid	limited state programmes	limited state programmes		anti-poverty programmes; urban programmes
environmental integrity	cooperation on water pollution	air and water controls	state policies but limited	state policies, advisory		standards for pollution management
Structure						
urban	municipal sector planning	land-use zoning	—	zoning	—	Federal agencies, e.g. HUD
rural	demographic pressures	rural depopulation	provincial policies	state advisory	sector programmes including 'ejido'	Federal agencies
regional	—	—	—	—	Border Programme PRONAF	SW Border Commission

[Time dimension:
Policy shifts in focus, objectives, priorities, efficiency-equity ratio]

Table 14.1 contd.

	Spatial					
	Local (periphery)		Regional (intermediate)		National (core)	
Structural	Mexico Az	USA Bz	Mexico Ai	USA Bi	Mexico A	USA B
Tension management						
conflict	crime, vice; dependency; exploitation; deprivation; curbs on out-migration; human rights of migrants in USA	illegal migrants; labour market; effects on 'chicanos'; labour unions; drugs traffic	dependency; exploitation; deprivation; oil and gas exports	illegal migrants; drugs traffic	dependency; exploitation; deprivation; oil and gas exports	illegal migrants; drugs traffic; political character of Mexico (Cuba, COMECON)
cooperation (conflict resolution)	town to town on environment, health, labour market, crime, frontier passage		bilateral but limited negotiation (health, veterinary); border policing, little cooperation		Presidential meetings (infrequent) Border Commission (inoperative) Boundary Waters Commission (effective)	
Behavioural response						
adaptive or entropic (system-merging)	*By Mexico* – Control/suppression of illegal drugs traffic, illegal migrants; freer access to Mexican market for US goods, investments; fuller allegiance by Mexico to Pan-Americanism, and abandonment of 'non-alignment'; accommodation on oil and gas exports to USA. *By USA* – Increased quota for legal migrants: 'human rights' charter/amnesty for illegal migrants; more open acces for Mexican goods in US market; economic aid from US without political strings. *Within Mexico and USA* – More stable equilibrium between decentralization of powers and functions (to state and local levels) and more effective funding, aid and planning from the federal centres.					

maladaptive or negentropic
(system-sustaining, i.e. divisive
at all levels)

By Mexico – Restrictions on US access to Mexican markets; breaking off negotiations on oil and gas exports; more active policy links with Cuba/COMECON.

By USA – Continuing restrictions on Mexican exports; no action on 'human rights' for illegal migrants or the raising of legal immigrant quotas; continuance of 'neo-colonialist' exploitation tactics.

Internally – neglect of the frontier zone problems of underdevelopment and social pathology; withdrawal of functions and powers from local and regional levels; policies of economic autarchy, damaging frontier zone trade.

border cities, in spite of a 50% devaluation of the peso in 1976. Tourism is two-way, but the Mexican border cities in particular have reaped major financial benefits. With traditionally large garrisons in US border towns, vice has been a major growth industry across the border in Mexico. Illegal flows of narcotics into the USA have now reached dramatic proportions, whilst there is an illegal arms trade in reverse.

Given such remarkable contrasts between development and underdevelopment across the frontier, and the resultant major concentration of social pathologies in the frontier zone, cross-frontier cooperation has seemed imperative. Yet inter-state relations have been sensitive and intermittent, from the periodic meetings of the two Presidents to the establishment of Commissions to study common problems, but with little effect as yet. On the other hand, the border towns on both sides have developed cooperation in industrial promotion, anti-pollution measures, infrastructure harmonization, and welfare provision. The recent major oil discoveries in Mexico, and their possible linkage to the US market, threaten a major revaluation of cross-frontier relationships.

Elements of the model

Table 14.1 outlines a schematic input-output application of the model to United States-Mexican frontier relations on the Rio Grande. The columns indicate the sequential structural elements of transactions and their context (Figure 14.1), the rows the variable distance and direction of spatial linkages (Figure 14.2). The time dimension is incorporated at each stage in the structural interpretation; it should also be envisaged in the diffusion process linking local, regional, and national levels of spatial interaction. The model might be used as a general thinking framework for the totality of inter-state relations at various structural and spatial scale-levels, or for the interpretation of particular events or intended actions and their likely spatial or structural outcome. In its present incomplete formulation it is being used to integrate a complexity of social, economic, cultural, and political data as a coherent basis for understanding United States-Mexican frontier interaction, primarily within the frontier zone itself (House, forthcoming (b)). One clear indication from Table 14.1 is the considerable extent to which the problems of the frontier zone are an aggravated microcosm of the general social, economic, cultural, and political issues dominating relations between the two states.

Another general point is the difficulty of identifying and differentiating transactions, perceptions, and many of the actors at the regional and national, as compared with the local (frontier, periphery) level. Though the administrative definitions of regional and national are clear, and relate to state (province) and Federal units on both sides of the boundary, the distance-decay effect of frontier problems into the interior, and the degree of significance of issues like illegal migration, the drugs traffic or trade provisions, at the higher scale-levels, are difficult to evaluate independently. Nevertheless, since frontier problems are not treated by local decisions alone, some appreciation of the regional and national levels of policy-making on the frontiers is essential, though at present more problematical for assessment.

The operation of the model first defines the geographically differentiated economic and social realities. These are derived from the flux of transactions and the problems these represent, at different spatial scale-levels, to the decision-takers on their side of the boundary. The problems are then interpreted within the framework of perceptions/attitudes, which are likely to condition subsequent actions, and also may colour the interpretation of and reaction to initiatives by the other party. The assessment of the roles of actors/institutions is the operational' background to implementation through policies or plans. These may or may not be consciously directed to tension management of cross-frontier problems, but even if not they are unlikely to be without either indirect or induced effects in inter-state relations. The overall assessment of these relations may thus be incorporated within a tension-management analysis, balancing overall adaptive-maladaptive tendencies with the outcome of particular events, policies or intentions. Thereafter, there are spatial and structural impacts, which feed back, both to the differentiated geographical space and the land-labour-capital relationships, which are then modified in their turn.

A critique of the model

The analysis of the findings on the United States-Mexican frontier will be fully presented elsewhere (House, forthcoming (a)). It remains to point out some of the problems brought to light in preparing the model, and to comment on its general utility for frontier studies. The initial and unsurprising problem, common to all transnational studies, was the lack of a comparable database for the two countries. This shortcoming covered not only the range and

volume of data, but also the spatial units and the time intervals for
which data were available. Though this may be inescapable in most
cases, it is important that for supranational bodies at least (e.g. EEC,
COMECON), there should be a priority for harmonization of
statistical sources (Szalai and Petrella, 1977).

The analysis of economic and social transaction flows in the
model most closely approximates to an economist's appreciation
and contains the fullest range of measurable parameters. In turn, it
rests upon the firmest, differentiated geographical foundation. The
problems are principally those of adequacy of data collection,
particularly on the illegal transactions involving labour migrants,
smuggling, crime, vice, and other social pathologies. On present
evidence the economic and social data will not bear the kind of
sophisticated statistical analysis which is already well established
in studies of social justice or social areas in the city (multivariate
procedures; indices of segregation). Inevitably and early, value-
judgments filter in, and any investigator of this type of material
feeds in a third-party view alongside those to be derived from the
frontier-participant nations. It may be that the model outlined
should be calibrated independently by the three parties, to detect
the different mental maps or national perceptions. But, of course,
the two frontier-nations also contain a wide diversity of internal
perceptions/attitudes, actors on stage, and thus domestic
differences too may need to be resolved.

Indeed, the greatest difficulty in preparing the model lies in the
section on perceptions/attitudes. Though behavioural approaches
in geography have progressed considerably there is little evidence
of their application to some of the more intractable problems of
political geography, with nothing comparable in frontier studies to
the behavioural contributions to electoral geography. One line of
possible advance is indicated by cross-cultural studies, to
determine the differences between the values and characteristics
of, say, the Mexican and American cultures (Diaz-Guerrero, 1978).
Such a psychological interpretation, based on interviews and
widespread sample testing, is even so only the first step to
understanding interpersonal and group interactions between
Mexicans and Americans, within and across social classes, ages, and
sexes, in social as well as economic and political situations. Diffusion
from one culture into another is also clearly involved, in the
understanding of both acculturation and culture shock, with their
inevitable contribution to the problems of tension management.
Long-held and deeply entrenched cultural 'mores' often show
surprising continuity in political behaviour and are in many cases
little-understood motivations in international affairs (e.g. the

contemporary Sino-Soviet disputes). An alternative avenue lies in the exploration of the mental maps of decision-takers, the actors on the political stage, scanning their operational environment (Henrikson). Drawing on the work of behavioural geographers, among others, Henrikson distinguishes between image-plans and behaviour-spaces. The image-plans are the conscious visual and logical (abstract) concepts or designs that policy-makers impose upon or discern in the world. Behaviour-space is the sensed geographical environment, within which political actors and public opinion function at different spatial levels. National-space parallels national-perspective on world, national, regional, or local affairs and problems. Image-plans are the guidelines for strategy, behaviour-spaces for local initiatives and particular transactions. In markedly asymmetrical relationships among states, as between the United States and Mexico, image-plans and behaviour-spaces are likely to be sharply differentiated in the minds of the two parties. Moreover, if a decision-taker in one country imaginatively seeks to place himself in his neighbour's position, he does not really enter his adversary's mental map at all, whilst remaining somewhat of a prisoner within his own. This reinforces the merits of common research on frontier problems from both sides of an international boundary, and adds some justification to the originality of a third-party view.

Both the basic data and an adequate geographical methodology seem lacking for a full behavioural understanding of within- and cross-frontier relationships. For this reason gaming simulation or the application of game theory may have a part to play, as has recently been shown in political science (Harsanyi, 1969; Rapoport, 1974). This is so both for general interaction between states, at the different scale-levels, and also for particular transactions. The simulation attempted may, in time, be either mathematical, keyed in to a full systems-analytical framework in the frontier model (not at present possible), or as scenario-writing and empirical modification with much less complex, though inevitably more subjective, ground-rules, as in war-gaming. Simulation relates also to the growing interdisciplinary field of policy studies, in which political geographers should surely have a more distinctive part to play. Policy studies too are concerned with transactional flows, linkages, and a systems approach to structural and spatial understanding of the genesis and outcome of political decision-making.

The policies and plans section of the model is more clear-cut, with more data and documentation available. The spatial units, functions, and powers are identifiable and the declared policy objectives may be traced, largely through legislation, and in its ultimate spatial and structural outcomes. Inevitably, policy objectives are mixed and not always identifiable, plans miscarry or may have unintended effects or be ineffective, but there is an underlying rationale, and sufficient parameters of achievement are measurable to evaluate success or failure in general terms.

The final phase of the model is perhaps the most speculative, but it is important for two reasons: as the meeting-place with political scientists and scholars in international relations, and for testing the operational validity of the model. The framework for the study of tension management seeks to test for the balance/imbalance between conflict and cooperation at the three different scale-levels within and between each country. The conflict tensions may have distinctions in degree rather than in kind within each country, but very marked, even potentially violent, differences between the United States and Mexico at the present time. Cross-frontier cooperation at all scale-levels needs to be stimulated, since it is for the most part mutually beneficial, though more limited and generalized in character with distance from the borderlands. The spatial origins, nature, and impacts of the tensions (positive and negative) are the major novel contributions the political geographer has to make at this end-stage, in a field already well-tenanted by political scientists and students of international relations.

The indicative behavioural responses illustrate possible ways, again both negative and positive of feeding back transactions into the model, to trace their impacts on the frontier situation in all its complexities (Figure 14.1). In practice, such clear-cut policy changes are rarer than the disjointed incrementalism, and tardy graduated responses which all too often pass for policy in the international fields. On the other hand, when major policy changes do occur it is important to be able to trace their spatial and structural implications. Indeed, if the embryonic operational model outlined is ever to fulfil its intended function, in concert with the findings of other disciplines, it must also be capable of evaluating the spatial and structural effects of alternative options for policy in the future, and, equally, the likely outcomes of changing perceptions/ attitudes on the balance of power among the diverse actors on the political stages. An ambitious and daunting task, but one political geographers must progress towards, if we are to shift our focus from the armchair effectively into the political arena.

A postscript: some theoretical implications

Though the type of operational model outlined is intended for practical application in a wide variety of situations it may be related also to the testing of theories and their refinement. There is no single comprehensive theory for frontier studies, but rather a spectrum of relevant parts of theories. Conflict theory (Boulding, 1962) is one dynamic framework, whilst the cybernetic theory of social communications (Deutsch, 1978) offers a more creative and constructive alternative for the assessment of tensions and their management. In the composition and working of the model both structuralist and dialectical theories (Agnew, 1981) are utilized, and by implication are thereby capable of being both tested and refined. Pluralist decision-maker theory is the framework for the 'actors/institutions' and 'policies/plans' segments of the model, with the theory of public choice an underlying paradigm for the analysis of objectives and trade-offs in the management of conflict and cooperation. Among theories of economic development that of cumulative causation (Myrdal, 1957) is perhaps the most relevant to the study of markedly asymmetrical cross-frontier relationships. Game theory (Harsanyi, 1969; Rapoport, 1974) offers a great potential for the modelling and simulation of the interaction resulting from particular international transaction flows. Within particular spatial theories that of the centre and periphery relationships still holds pride of place, though as a contemporary intellectual framework in frontier studies the example used here demonstrates its manifest shortcomings in operational use.

If the links between theories and empirical realities are to be more effectively forged it can but be by working both deductively from above and inductively from below. It is to the latter approach that the operational model outlined offers a contribution. Empirical realities inevitably constrain the contribution to theory, just as the prior adaptation of ideological premises or postures limits the effectiveness of some theories in their relevance to the real world which it is sought either to explain or to improve.

References

Agnew, J. A. (1981). 'Structural and dialectical theories of political regionalism', chap. 13 in this volume.

Boulding, K. E. (1962). *Conflict and Defense: a General Theory* (Harper & Row, New York).

Bull, H. (1966). 'International theory: the case for a classical approach', *World Politics*, **XVIII**(3), 361-77.

Deutsch, K. (1963). *Nerves of Government* (Free Press, New York).

Deutsch, K. (1978). *The Analysis of International Relations,* 2nd edn. (Prentice Hall, Englewood Cliffs, NJ).

Diaz-Guerrero, R. (1978). 'Mexicans and Americans: two worlds, one border… and one observer', in Ross, S. R. (ed.) *Views across the Border,* pp. 283-307 (University of New Mexico Press, Albuquerque).

Frankel, J. (1973a). *International Politics* (Penguin, Harmondsworth).

Frankel, J. (1973b). *Contemporary International Theory and the Behaviour of States* (Oxford University Press, Oxford).

Gendarme, R. (1970). 'Les problèmes économiques des régions frontalières européennes' in *Les Régions frontalières à l'heure du Marché Commun,* pp. 175-205 (Institut d'Etudes Européennes; Presses Universitaires de Bruxelles, Brussels).

Guichonnet, P., and Raffestin, C. (1974). *La Géographie des Frontières* (Presses Universitaires de France, Paris).

Harsanyi, J. C. (1969). 'Game theory and the analysis of international conflict', in Rosenau, J. N. (ed.), *International Politics and Foreign Policy,* pp. 370-9 (Free Press, New York).

Hartshorne, R. (1950). 'The functional approach in political geography', *Annals of the Association of American Geographers,* **40,** 95-130.

Henrikson, A. K. (forthcoming). 'The geographical "mental maps" of American foreign policy makers', *International Political Science Review.*

House, J. W. (1976). 'Applied geography in Britain', in Clarke, J. I., and Pinchemel, P. (eds.) *Human Geography in Britain and France,* pp. 45-50 (SSRC, London).

House, J. W. (forthcoming (a)). *The Rio Grande Frontier: a Study in Development and Social Pathology* (Oxford University Press, Oxford).

House, J. W. (forthcoming (b)). 'The frontier zone: a conceptual problem for policy-makers', *International Political Science Review.*

Jones, S. B. (1954). 'A unified theory of political geography', *Annals of the Association of American Geographers,* **44,** 111-23.

Kaplan, M. A. (1967). *System and Process in International Politics* (Wiley, New York).

Knorr, K., and Rosenau, J. N. (eds.) (1969). *Contending Approaches to International Politics* (Princeton University Press, Princeton).

Loesch, A. (1954). *The Economics of Location,* translated by W. H. Woglom from *Die räumliche Ordnung der Wirtschaft,* (1940), pp. 196-210 (Yale University Press, New Haven).

Minghi, J. V. (1963). 'Boundary studies in political geography: a review article', *Annals of the Association of Amrican Geographers,* **53**(3), 407-28.

Myrdal, G. (1957). *Economic Theory and Under-developed Regions* (Duckworth, London).

Rapoport, A. (ed.) (1974). *Game Theory as a Theory of Conflict Resolution* (D. Reidel, Dordrecht).

Rosenau, J. N. (ed.) (1969). *International Politics and Foreign Policy* (Free Press, New York).

Sanguin, A. -L. (1976). *Géographie politique: Bibliographie internationale* (Presses de l'Université de Québec, Montreal).

Stokes, D. E. (1965). 'A variance components model of political effects', in Claunch, J. M. (ed.), *Mathematical Applications in Political Science,* pp. 61-95 (Southern Methodist University Press, Dallas).

Szalai, A., and Petrella, E. (eds.) (1977). *Cross-national Comparative Survey Research: Theory and Practice* (Pergamon, Oxford).

Woolstencroft, R. P. (forthcoming). 'Models of electoral geography: a critique and a proposal', *International Political Science Review.*

Political studies from spatial perspectives
Edited by A.D. Burnett and P.J. Taylor
© 1981 John Wiley & Sons Ltd

_____ 15__

A geographical approach to propaganda

Derek R. Hall

Propaganda

The noun 'propaganda' is derived from the New Latin — *Congregatio de propaganda fide* — the congregation for propagating the faith, an organization established by Pope Gregory XV. Webster's (1973) dictionary definition of the word includes: 'the spreading of ideas, information or rumour for the purpose of helping or injuring an institution, a cause, or a person; ideas, facts or allegations spread deliberately to further one's cause or to damage an opposing cause; or a public action having such an effect'.

As such, propaganda may be seen to pervade all aspects of public life. It is needed by organizations with political, administrative, and economic functions: political parties, the state, and manufacturers. Because individual attitudes are potentially so diverse and contradictory, political, administrative, and economic activity, complicated further by the technical nature of many matters which are outside the scope of everyday public awareness, cannot afford to follow public opinion: it must lead that opinion.

Ellul (1965) therefore suggested that propaganda fulfils two functions: not only does it help to obtain public compliance, but it can also be used to provoke otherwise acquiescent groups into making demands for actions which were going to be carried out anyway. The secret for success or failure of propaganda is thus suggested to lie in its ability to satisfy the unconscious need of the individual to whom it is addressed. It may be readily accepted by allowing greater 'participation'; participation in the sense of hiding individual incapacities to form judgments by presenting elementary explanations and conveying bridging signals to each isolated individual within the group. In this way, propaganda is the

313

'inevitable result of the various components of the technological society and plays so central a role in the life of that society that no economic or political development can take place without the influence of its great power' (Ellul, 1965, p. 160).

Propaganda geography

Political geographers have always been aware of the existence of propaganda. Indeed, it might almost be said that the discipline's rise and subsequent relative demise during the first half of this century was largely due to the geopolitical propaganda use to which the discipline was subjected (e.g. see A. R. Hall, 1955).

A post-war cloud-cuckoo ethos of attempted 'objectivity' and 'value-free' studies was gradually rendered unfashionable by declared ideological stances and by the use of such methodological vehicles as conflict theory. This trend was helped on its way by the often crass utterances perpetrated by certain (usually 'regional') geographers in their self-declared 'value-free' assessments of politically influenced spatial phenomena. Pahl (1967), while not the first (e.g. see also Kirk, 1963; Connell, 1971), was certainly one of the more articulate observers in reminding us that:

> seemingly every generation is obliged to rewrite the past in terms of its own values and ideologies... in geography controversial aspects of economic development and regional planning are played down... The geographer, as any other social scientist, cannot avoid being socialized into a specific culture — or, more accurately, sub-culture — at a particular period of time... By the material he chooses to teach from the research problems he investigates, certain attitudes about the nature of society become incorporated into a pattern of thought, a system of values, which may or may not be made explicit (Pahl, 1967, pp. 217, 219, 220).

Irrespective of whether we are Marxist or fascist, or, fashionably, just claiming to be such (Peet, 1978; but see also Muir, 1978), or somewhere in between, we all implicitly disseminate propaganda, however innocuous, by virtue of our own value systems, whether singularly or widely held (Watson, 1977). The present writer therefore, appreciates, wryly, the irony of his quest for a geography of propaganda being itself vested with strong value-judgments.

A geography of propaganda

The remainder of this paper briefly surveys some aspects of propaganda, at varying structural levels, which the writer considers to be susceptible to geographical analysis. This exploration attempts to suggest that the practitioners of political geography might gain further insights into the interrelationships between space and politics by developing an analytical framework for the recognition of propaganda as an often powerful force in shaping spatial relationships, and examining the motives, both stated and hidden, behind such processes.

As a first faltering step, four categories of spatially based propaganda are here outlined.

Graphics

The manipulation of maps, diagrams, graphs, etc., is traditionally the most familiar form of propaganda to, and by, geographers. Maps, in addition to straightforward navigation, are employed to increase the accuracy of a person's perception of reality. While this is undertaken in two stages — the measurement of elements of spatial information cartographically represented, and the conception of spatial organization of those elements (Board and Taylor, 1977) — it is the first stage which is directly assaulted by propagandist manipulation. The misplaced faith put into the veracity of data depicted on maps (Wright, 1942) has long rendered the cartographic art open to abuse (Lobeck, 1956; Thrower, 1972), such that: 'the map becomes a psychological force instead of a scientific tool' (Quam, 1943, p. 21). One may briefly note some of the components of cartographic propaganda.

(a) Symbolic elaboration
The German geopoliticians laid great emphasis on the use of appropriate symbols in creating 'suggestive' maps. As Speier (1941) has shown, a wide range of techniques to elaborate such symbols are available for propagandist manipulation: size (e.g. for a reducing effect, the psycho-physical power function of proportional area and volume symbols); colour (e.g. the use of 'advancing' red); design (e.g. arrows; pictograms, which can convey a unidimensional quality in two dimensions, and by representing size with area can produce apparent geometric growth out of arithmetic increases); class intervals (e.g. geometric rather than arithmetic; 16 systems are available — see Evans, 1977) etc. A propaganda atlas prepared at the Geopolitical Institute in Munich

and distributed in the United States in an effort to forestall that country's entry into the Second World War (Wirsing *et al.*, 1941) presented a whole range of symbolic exaggerations and misrepresentations aimed primarily at Britain. For example, strong smooth lines were employed to suggest stable, natural, and friendly boundaries, while broken, irregular lines denoted weakness, disunity, or hostility.

(b) Cartographic distortion
This term can usefully subsume the cartographic manipulation of boundaries, areas, names and projections for propagandist purposes. Certainly, while any one projection may accurately reflect some of the qualities of distance, shape, relative area, and direction, it will not be able to accurately represent them all. Thus by choosing a projection which appears to accurately portray spatial relationships, but which distorts the one key dimension, the propagandist has a powerful weapon at his disposal. Under such circumstances, cartography can be seen as the complementary tool of semantic propaganda and gerrymandering (see below). Quam (1943), for example, pointed to the use of the Mercator projection by German geopoliticians firstly to cartographically reveal the desirability of an alliance with the Soviet Union, and later, to spread fear of the 'Bolshevik menace'.

More recently, Mazrui (1979, p. 619) in his inaugural Reith Lecture, has pointed to the Mercator's diminution effect on the size of Africa, a doubly humiliating prospect since he claims that this projection is used in the majority of (colonial vintage?) maps in African schools. This 'ethnocentrism of the Western cartographer' is seen to symbolize, by its cartographic ordering of north and south ('an accident of the history of science'; but see Hodgkiss, 1977), the dominance of the northern hemisphere ('up') over the underdeveloped south ('down').

Cartographic distortion often involves a rewriting of history (e.g. ignoring or over-emphasizing boundaries that may have once existed and which could act as justification for uncomfortable irridentist claims). Such distortion is complemented and 'authorized' by 'historical' texts from similar sources (e.g. Lyons, 1977).

(c) Cartographic precedent
Maps may be used for establishing precedents and conveying 'authorized' images of 'reality' in advance of that reality, usually precluding the possibilities of alternative strategies. Once affirmed cartographically, an obligation may follow to pursue particular

objectives. Many of Britain's local authority plans may be seen in this light, with bureaucrats setting down their conventional wisdoms (e.g. high-rise local authority housing) on maps whose very existence may be subsequently treated as the authority for enactment of the appropriate policy. Such authority may have followed an exercise in public 'participation', from which, because of the often conflicting public needs and aspirations voiced, bureaucrats can claim that their own conventional wisdoms (which would have been applied in any case) appositely articulate 'the public's wish' (e.g. see Wraith and Lamb, 1971).

Numerics

'... it would be easy to show, by stating the figures for fuel consumption and saying nothing about the temperature, that everyone in Central Africa is suffering from cold' (Orwell, 1939/1970, p. 418).

Here defined as the spatial use or misuse of quantitative information for explicit or implicit propaganda purposes, three categories of numerics can be suggested for further consideration.

(a) Obfuscation

A familiar ploy used by a wide range of bureaucrats at all levels, obfuscation can arise through the omission, rearrangement, or incomparability of published quantitative data. In a wide range of developing societies, planned economies, and fascist dictatorships, it often takes the form of masking, in absolute terms, base points from which present (e.g. growth) figures are projected. In the case of Albania, where there are, theoretically at least, annual compilations of national statistics — 'Vjetari Statistikor i RPSH' (latterly RSPSH), production/growth data are usually presented in one of three ways: as a percentage increase/decrease over a previously (proportionately) recorded figure; as a percentage increase/decrease in relation to a base year (usually pre-war); or as a percentage of a particular sector's production/growth for any given period.

In this way absolute figures are avoided and any reliable base with which to compare other statistics is precluded. Indeed, such information is often conveyed in comparative pictogram form, thus adding a further distorting dimension. Albania's case is additionally obscured by the fact that apparently little information is even made available to the United Nations, so that when Albania does publish statistics in absolute figures, usually for internal consumption, they often radically differ from estimates published in UN Yearbooks.

The writer has come across, for example, divergencies in figures for hydroelectric power production of over 3500% (Hall, 1975).

Bailey (1975) has referred to a 'bamboozle effect' whereby those controlling information largely required to be disseminated to the public, employ a wide range of 'sophisticated' quantitative techniques, technical jargon, and imagery to obscure the actual content of the information to be transmitted. Such a phenomenon is not unknown, for example, in relation to local planning inquiries or meetings for formal 'public participation'. The public may not be the only ones to be 'bamboozled', however. Local councillors, or even government ministers, with relatively little time and limited expertise in technical affairs, and presented with weighty technical documents by their officers over which relatively rapid political decisions may need to be made, may themselves feel, and be, 'bamboozled'. Some geographers might also recognize a familiar role here.

(b) Over-'estimation' and under-'estimation'

These processes may be seen to operate in a wide variety of contexts. In 'democratic' societies over-'estimation' and optimism in relation to a wide range of phenomena may characterize the utterances of politicians during election campaign periods. Decision-makers in planned economies may over-'estimate' plan figures in order to present an image of optimism or may under-'estimate' in order that the completion of plan periods may witness an overfulfilment of norms which can then be pointed to as reflecting high efficiency/morale/level of ideological consciousness etc. Under-'estimation' of figures, and indeed the absence of any published data at all, is often revealed in aspects of socioeconomic life which might reflect a negative, or at least unwelcome image of society, such as crime (e.g. Clinard, 1978), disease, poverty, and emigration. (Of course this may reflect the inadequacy of a data-collecting and collating system as much as any conscious desire for suppression, although the two may not be totally unrelated.) Thus, for example, in the Soviet Union crime figures are not published. Yet we are told that (typically?) in an old district of Moscow with a population of 7,000: 'There are perhaps fifty people who demand constant attention on the part of the district militiamen' (Tsfasman, 1979, p. 13).

In India the caste system officially does not exist, and the enumeration of population in categories of caste status has not been undertaken in national censuses since 1921. Yet the caste system remains as one of the most pernicious forces shaping Indian social, economic, and political life today (e.g. see Hall, forthcoming).

(c) Selectivity

Complementing some of the previous comments on under-'estimation' and non-recording, various interest groups within a society — even geographers — may filter spatial information in order to bias response or otherwise achieve a desired propagandist effect. As Brooks (1977) has said in the context of the Polish geographer: 'what he writes may well be the truth, and nothing but the truth. But it is likely to be not the whole truth' (p. 21). This could equally well apply to western multinational drug companies marketing their wares in the 'Third World', to Afrikaaner nationalists when explaining the 'independence' of the Transkei, or of 'Democratic' Ulster Unionists in referring to themselves as 'loyalists'.

Those British geographers whose interest in patterns of crime and criminals has largely rested with the more spatially amenable 'working-class' crimes can here be harangued (Herbert, 1979; see also Murray and Boal, 1979). As successive sociological analyses have shown (e.g. Spencer, 1968; Geis and Meier, 1977):

> financial losses to society in a single case of white-collar business crime may well equal the total amount involved in thousands of larcenies and burglaries... a double standard of justice exists when illegal behavior among the lower or working classes is viewed with strong disapproval and is prosecuted readily, while illegal behavior among business and banking interests, for example, is defined as nothing more malevolent than shrewd business and financial practice (Clinard, 1978, p. 83).

This largely reflects the fact that: 'criminal definitions are applied by the segments of society that have the power to shape the enforcement and administration of criminal law' (Quinney, 1970, p. 18).

Thus the geography of (working-class) crime may be seen to merely perpetuate and buttress propaganda-based myths established by vested interest groups. Inevitably, as with many aspects of propaganda geography, one can plead that data are simply not available, or at least not available within a suitable spatial frame, for adequate employment in a wider analysis (e.g. see Kettle, 1979). Police records only relate to reported crimes, vis-à-vis total crimes committed; the vigour of reports is notoriously inconsistent. Arrests and prosecutions are subject to a wide range of dynamic factors, from police strength and the attitude of chief constables, to jury vetting procedures and car-ownership patterns amongst magistrates.

Returning to the problem of spatial frameworks, despite its importance in political geography, the gerrymandering of unit boundaries has not perhaps received as much attention as it might warrant, political geographers having been over-concerned with the nature and classification of boundaries rather than with the values and propaganda motives underlying their establishment (Prescott (1959) being one of the relative few exceptions).

Semantics

For present purposes, semantics is defined as the explicit or implicit propaganda use of lexical items in a spatial context. The concept can be further subdivided into three related categories.

(a) Spatial nomenclature
The use/misuse of place/area names for purposes which are not always wholly altruistic, would appear to be particularly prevalent in irridentist situations where territorial claims and counter-claims, cultural diversity, and historical interdigitations have lent particularly strong symbolic value to the use of certain spatial nomenclature.

Let us consider the word 'Ulster' in this context. Until Irish partition in 1921, Ulster was one of the country's four traditional provinces (along with Leinster, Munster and Connacht). In the plebiscite prior to Irish partition, however, only six of the province of Ulster's nine counties voted in the majority to remain within the United Kingdom. (Although in 1925 the Irish Boundary Commission recommended transferring, on cultural grounds, parts of County Armagh and County Down, together with the town of Newry, to the Irish Free State; but these findings were suppressed by all three governments concerned (Hand, 1970). An inaccurate report was, however, published in the *Morning Post* of 7 November 1925 (Andrews, 1960; Freeman, 1965)).

Thus 'Northern Ireland' only consists of six of Ulster's nine counties. Of interest to the propaganda (as opposed to the propagandist) geographer, therefore, is the spatial significance of the nature and source of the value systems lying behind the use of 'Ulster' (or, conversely, of 'Northern Ireland'). Does its use imply that 'Northern Ireland' should be larger than it is, or should be independent? More comprehensively, can the use of 'Ulster' be interpreted as reflecting the desire for a reversion to a situation when Ireland was: (a) united — with implications for nationalists for a future united independent Ireland; or (b) a British dominion — and thus used by 'loyalists' to imply that British rule should again prevail over all four provinces?

Certainly the term 'Ulster' is a potentially emotive spatial term in an overtly emotive situation. In this context, further grist to the propaganda geographer's mill can be found in two relatively recent publications — *Ulster! Violations of Human Rights in Northern Ireland* (Mikhalyov et al., 1977) and *Ulster and the German Solution* (Sheane, 1978). The latter suggests that the use of 'Ulster', at least by Irish nationalists, reflects the fact that 'Northern Ireland' was a term bestowed upon the six counties by the British government, thereby tending to be identified more with Protestantism. Sheane also suggests that Catholics regard present-day Ulster in terms of a wider, pre-partition Irish province. (Where does that leave the propaganda role of 'Northern Ireland'?)

The value systems behind the use of 'Israel'/'Palestine' have, of course, even wider implications. The incipient irridentism between Austria and Italy regarding a piece of territory straddling the Brenner Pass, however, perhaps reveals one of the best examples of contemporary spatially based semantic propaganda. The same piece of territory is invoked in both the German and Italian languages as being implicitly linked to, and interrelated with, the relative core areas of Austria and Italy respectively. Thus to Austrians the 'Sud Tirol' is inextricably tied to the North Tyrol and the motherland, while for Italians the 'Alto Adige' is naturally complementary to the lower Adige valley and an intrinsic part of northern Italy (see also Minghi, 1963).

Within our British shores we can find in the English (not British) language topographic terms which may be interpreted as implicitly propagandist — English Channel (but a French arm), Straits of Dover (but Pas de Calais), Irish Sea, St George's Channel (between Ireland and Wales!) How far do such value-laden labels affect our perceptual structuring of reality, especially if buttressed by the media (e.g. the 'fog in Channel; Continent cut off' syndrome).

The theme of alternative names bearing differing interpretations but used for the same place/area/phenomenon occurs time and again. An examination of the nature, causes, and consequences of the use of such spatial nomenclature is surely of relevance to the political geographer. What are the implicit value-judgments lying behind such uses as that, for example, of the *Daily Telegraph,* which, until the recent revolution there, insisted on referring to Iran as 'Persia'? How far is the widespread erroneous reference to the

Soviet Union as 'Russia' a subliminal (or otherwise) rejection of
Soviet ideology? Visual symbolism would appear to provide at least
a clue. The Persian cat was once a favourite symbol for national
portrayal in newspaper cartoons; 'Iran' possesses no such
zoological imagery. On the other hand, the Russian bear persists,
although at the time of writing the Soviets are reflecting their own
self-image through the cuddly, peace-loving Olympic bear Mischa.
Certainly such animal symbolism provides clues as to the way
nations are seen by others and how they see themselves (White,
1980), or at least, how they would like to be seen. By contrast, the
roar of the Great British imperial lion has given way to such
farcical, self-mocking symbols as World Cup Willie: 'World Cup
Willie, the ultimate vulgarisation of the British lion, represents a
kind of agnosticism: a refusal to take anything — other than the
World Cup — very seriously' (White, 1980, p. 116).

The post-war propagandist spatial terminology associated with
the two German states still awaits adequate analysis (at least in
English; although see Pounds (1962, 1963), Scholler (1963), Mellor
(1978)). In the (East) German Democratic Republic, for example, it
has been claimed that the word 'Germany' is now never used by the
media (Anon, 1979). Only the initials of the two states — DDR and
BRD — are employed.

A second form of propagandist spatial nomenclature has often
been invoked by newly independent ex-colonial states wishing to
symbolize their new self-recognition and emergence from a
subjugated past. A number have assumed names which have either
reflected the nature and strength of the ruling (though not
necessarily majority) ethnic group, or which embody and thereby
transmit to the present former glories when (part of) the
contemporary state area was a powerful military, economic, or
cultural force. In this way the names of Botswana and Lesotho,
Ghana, Mali, and Benin have appeared on the post-independence
map of Africa. Indeed, in the slow climb out of the age of colonial
imperialism, 'Namibia' and 'Zimbabwe' have appeared to act as
important symbols of aspiration and cultural legacy for the peoples
of southern Africa.

Yet the question needs to be asked as to the extent to which such
semantic symbols do accurately reflect a people's (or indeed
peoples') loyalties and associations. Closer to home, at a somewhat
more mundane level, have the names of reorganized local
government units developed a functional significance in attracting
people's allegiances? What proportion of Sunderland residents
associate with 'Tyne and Wear'; and what of the 'Thamesdown'
community spirit?

(b) Spatial processes
The names attributed to certain spatially expressed processes may be value-laden, far from unequivocal in meaning, and may be misleadingly applied to static situations, falsely implying, through that application, a dynamic process. Thus 'community', an extremely evasive term to define (e.g. Hillery, 1955; Hall, 1978) may often be thought of as representing a specified area within which 'successful' interaction is presumed to engender a self-defined 'community spirit'. It may, however, be misused by the media and such vested interests as new town corporations and estate agents, or by residents whose homes are threatened by demolition, simply as a description of where people live, being synonymous with 'place' or 'settlement', while falsely implying the existence of 'successful' interaction. Cresswell (1974) refers to this as propaganda, and cites other everyday words which are similarly abused. 'Slum', he points out, does not appear in the Housing Act, 1954, which enumerates the criteria for defining a dwelling as unfit: 'Yet it is effective for groups attempting to make out a case of housing neglect or for a local authority that wishes to clear an area to use the label "slum" rather than the more neutral term "unfit"' (Cresswell, 1974, p. 9) (see also Kirby, 1979; Dennis, 1970, 1972; Davies, 1972; Ungerson, 1971).

A further 'code word' (Alonso, 1970) suggested is 'home', which, like 'community' and 'slum' is used: 'to persuade, engender support, provoke a response or allay criticism... part of the means by which individuals and institutions attempt to exert control over each other' (Cresswell, 1974, p. 10).

On a wider scale, the use of 'development'/'underdevelopment'/ 'separate development'/'homeland', etc. may be seen in similar propagandist terms, while the conjoining of 'community' and 'development' never fails to obfuscate reality and promote ideological confusion; and what of the terms 'participation', 'immigration', and 'full employment'? The somewhat pejorative term 'Third World' particularly suffers from ethnocentrically based assumptions of 'objectivity' and 'neutrality'.

(c) Spatial associations
Diachronic studies of the changing semantics associated with the tortuous twists of fate in international relations would reveal a richly interwoven fabric of time, space, and propaganda; where ideology and pragmatism, as point and counterpoint, build up an historical palimpsest of propaganda, reducing and increasing space friction according to circumstance.

One may note, for example, various blocs' use of specific terms for their (often transient) perceived friends and foes. Thus, 'fraternal' (e.g. the Czechoslovak people's feelings towards their Soviet 'liberators'), 'freedom-loving' (e.g. Albanians), 'people's democracies' can be lined up against 'hegemonism', 'social imperialism', 'revisionism', 'colonialism', 'fascism', etc., all such code words being placed on a sliding scale of perceived relationships 'scientifically' assessed and labelled accordingly. But that is not to admit to any semantic precision. Western lexicographers have been no less shamefaced in their linguistic perfidy — 'iron curtain', 'bamboo curtain', 'totalitarian', 'command economy', 'free world', 'free market', 'liberty', 'democracy', etc. Time, space, and metaphorical wind direction often appear to be the only salient factors in the choice of specific terms from the ubiquitous sliding scale of 'patriot'-'freedom fighter'-'guerilla'-'terrorist'.

> The words *democracy, socialism, freedom, patriotic, realistic, justice,* have each of them several different meanings which cannot be reconciled with one another… [but]… It is almost universally felt that when we call a country democratic we are praising it: consequently the defenders of every kind of regime claim that it is a democracy… Other words used in variable meanings, in most cases more or less dishonestly, are: *class, totalitarian, science, progressive, reactionary, bourgeois, equality* (Orwell, 1946/1970, p. 162).

Technologics

This term is meant to subsume the area of use/misuse of technology (in its widest sense) for propaganda purposes, especially where such use appears relatively irrelevant to, or is unable to be easily supported by, the society within which it is generated. Three categories may be discussed.

(a) Propaganda projects

Prestige industrial and technological schemes have been undertaken by a large number of societies either to symbolize independence and to reflect upon themselves aspects of 'modernization' and 'self-sufficiency', or to pursue a stated ideological goal (neither of which, of course, need be mutually exclusive).

In the first case, newly independent ex-colonial states set out to reflect their new political fortunes by building such prestige projects as steel plants, HEP schemes, and aluminium smelters, often at a scale out of all proportion to the country's needs, at a cost difficult to support within that society, and with little heed paid to any form of regional rationalization or division of specialization with neighbouring states. One may cite Nkrumah's Volta River aluminium and HEP schemes, Nasser's Great Aswan Dam, and Argentina's San Nicholas iron and steel plant.

Sparkling new capital cities, often in stark contrast to, and out of all proportion with, indigenous settlement forms, and typically employing western planners and architects, have provided a further form of propagandist technology for developing societies — Brasilia, Islamabad, and Chandigarh (Panjabi, 1958) being prime examples.

Other projects (real or imaginary) in this category might include Nkrumah's Black Star Line shipping fleet for Ghana, Amin's Ugandan space programme, India's nuclear programme, Concorde, and various states' willingness to host the monumentally costly Olympic Games.

In terms of pursuing stated ideologies, the well-documented, so-called 'adoptive' industrial location decisions of East European socialist societies have seen the pursuit of ideologically inspired locational goals which may: overrule 'expert' advice regarding scale, structure of location; minimize or ignore constraints threatening economic or technological success; represent measures to open bottlenecks or break vicious poverty circles; act as a 'technical demonstration effect' against an apathetic peasantry or the church; show a poor perception of significant environmental conditions (Hamilton, 1971). Examples include the 'poorly' sited steel plants of Eisenhüttenstadt (German Democratic Republic) and Kosice (Czechoslovakia), located in relatively remote areas away from raw materials and major markets, but heralded as examples of a spatial equalization policy to reduce regional, ethnic, and urban-rural differentials.

(b) Propaganda infrastructure

In an attempt to present a 'good face' to the outside world, a society may go to great lengths to impress foreign visitors. On the one hand foreign dignitaries may enjoy the experience of arriving at a modern, well-equipped airport, being chauffeured in a curtained Rolls or Mercedes along multi-lane highways to impressive hotels and government buildings, and back again, without even catching fleeting glimpses of the impoverishment, neglect, repression, or persecution which may exist within such a society. This blinkering effect may be further buttressed by the benign images of society promoted by specially equipped public relations organizations (either governmental departments or companies hired by the authorities).

On a somewhat wider, if similar plane, foreign tourism may be stimulated (for economic as well as propaganda reasons), but may be so organized and infrastructurally prescribed that visitors return home from the host country with only a very contained, and, in the absence of evidence to the contrary, optimistic conception of the society 'visited'. Filtering may take place at a number of levels to ensure this. The restrictive selection of prescribed tourist sites and areas, routes between them, accommodation, transport, information and 'guidance', time spent, numerical size and even currency used, is a strong weapon for a state desperate to present a favourable face. Indeed, preliminary filter processes may well occur before the tourist has even begun his/her journey to the holiday utopia. Most states, from Albania to the United States, employ a proscriptive visa system to eliminate undesirables at an early stage. The former country perhaps applies some of the most draconian restrictions. As noted elsewhere (Hall and Howlett, 1976), while one can only enter Albania as part of an organized group, on a group visa, citizens of the USA, USSR (and now China?), and Yugoslavia (and formerly also Greece and Portugal), as well as all journalists, are summarily excluded, while the barber and tailor at Rinas airport, Tiranë, ensure that incoming visitors conform (at their own additional expense) to the sartorial requirements of the People's Socialist Republic before stepping out onto Albanian soil proper.

In his splenetic interpretation of China in the mid-1970s, Leys (1979) devotes a large section of his book to the apparently manipulated nature of foreigners' travel there. The ever-present guides are seen as *modi operandi* of double-think (or is it treble-think?):

> In the end, it is that feeling of being a perpetual source of problems for your escort — who is so friendly and full of goodwill — which may be the most powerful brake on the foreign traveller's longings for more freedom of movement... under the conditions in which foreign residents and visitors now live in the People's Republic of China, it is impossible to write anything but frivolities (Leys, 1979, pp. 72, xiv).

One should also add, of course, that such governments as those of the USSR, South Africa, Zimbabwe-Rhodesia, Israel, Egypt, Chile, and Argentina have all encouraged foreign visitors while at times simultaneously imposing severe spatial restrictions on their movement.

(c) Propaganda communications

Variously disseminated books, leaflets, newspapers, photographs, radio and television broadcasts (especially in time of war; e.g. see Balfour, 1979), all provide specific interpretations of reality. From the same sources, however, such interpretations may need to be different, or at least presented in modified terms for the different audiences of the outside world as well as the home market; or need to be aimed at a specific portion of a given market. For example, since 1960, Chinese radio propaganda against the Soviet Union has been vigorously aimed at the provinces and the countryside, apparently to stimulate non-Russian nationalism and separatist tendencies in Soviet Asia (Lisann, 1975).

In relation to Soviet broadcasting (a value-free *Pravda?*), the Tashkent earthquake of April 1966, which destroyed much of the city, killing hundreds of people and directly affecting over a million, was initially reported as a minor tremor:

> Journalists on the scene accepted the apparent decision to play down the disaster... But the central radio in Moscow then announced that a major disaster had in fact occurred and that Brezhnev and Kosygin were flying to Tashkent to assess the damage... Journalists on the spot [only] now used information they already possessed. ...The system was designed to have instructions poured in at the top end. It cannot easily be re-programmed to take in news at the opposite end (Tunstall, 1977, p. 14).

The availability of reporters and access to international news services will bias the coverage of news even before conscious 'distortions' are applied. Goodey (1974) mapped the distribution of BBC foreign correspondents, implying that their limited numbers and usually relatively 'safe' locations act as a major filter on incoming news stories, biasing the ranging of spatial information transmitted to the British public.

Summary and conclusions

This paper has undertaken a brief survey of some of the interlocutions of geography and politics, and has attempted to present them within a framework tentatively providing a perspective on the concept of a geography of propaganda. Exploratory in nature, the paper has also tried to emphasize those spatially expressed facets of propaganda which may benefit the political geographer through further and more detailed examination. In conclusion, it can be simply stated that through a conceptual focus on propaganda, political geographers at least might more readily appreciate some of the value-laden depths of 'objective reality'.

References

Alonso, W. (1970). 'What are new towns for?', *Urban Studies,* 7, 37-55.

Andrews, J. H. (1960). 'The 'Morning Post' line', *Irish Geographer,* 4, 99-106.

Anon (1979). 'Listening to voices in Potemkin land', *The Observer,* 7 Oct.

Bailey, J. (1975). *Social Theory for Planning* (Routledge & Kegan Paul, London).

Balfour, M. (1979). *Propaganda in War 1939-1945* (Routledge & Kegan Paul, London).

Board, C., and Taylor, R. M. (1977). 'Perception and maps: human factors in map design and interpretation', *Transactions of the Institute of British Geographers, NS,* 2, 19-36.

Brooks, E. (1977). *Geography and Public Policy,* D204 Unit 30 (Open University, Milton Keynes).

Clinard, M. B. (1978). *Cities with Little Crime* (Cambridge University Press, Cambridge).

Connell, J. (1971). 'The geography of development', *Area,* 3, 259-64.

Cresswell, P. (1974). 'The concept of community and urban planning', Paper, Urban Sociology Study Group, British Sociological Association, Stirling.

Davies, J. G. (1972). *The Evangelistic Bureaucrat* (Tavistock, London).

Dennis, N. (1970). *People and Planning* (Faber, London).

Dennis, N. (1972). *Public Participation and Planners' Blight* (Faber, London).

Ellul, J. (1965). *Propaganda: the Formation of Men's Attitudes* (Knopf, New York).

Evans, I. S. (1977). 'The selection of class intervals', *Transactions of the Institute of British Geographers, NS,* 2, 98-124.

Freeman, T. W. (1965). *Ireland* (Methuen, London).

Geis, G., and Meier, F. R. (eds.) (1977). *White-collar Crime* (Free Press, New York).

Goodey, B. (1974). *Where You're At* (Penguin, Harmondsworth).

Hall, A. R. (1955). 'Mackinder and the course of events' *Annals of the Association of American Geographers,* 45, 109-26.

Hall, D. R. (1975). 'Some developmental aspects of Albania's fifth 5-year plan 1971-5', *Geography,* 60, 129-32.

Hall, D. R. (1978). 'A geographical study of social divisions in Portsmouth' (unpublished PhD thesis, University of London).

Hall, D. R. (forthcoming). *Spatial Aspects of Urban Community Development Policy in India* (Research Studies Press, Letchworth).

Hall, D., and Howlett, A. (1976). 'Neither east nor west', *Geographical Magazine,* 48, 194-6.

Hamilton, F. E. I. (1971). 'Decision making and industrial location in Eastern Europe', *Transactions of the Institute of British Geographers,* 52, 77-94.

Hand, G. J. (1970). *The Report of the Irish Boundary Commission* (Irish University Press, Dublin).

Herbert, D. T. (1979). 'Urban crime: a geographical perspective', in Herbert, D. T., and Smith, D. M. (eds.), *Social Problems and the City*, pp. 117-38 (Oxford University Press, Oxford).

Hillery, G. (1955). 'Definitions of community — areas of agreement', *Rural Sociology*, **20**, 111-23.

Hodgkiss, A. (1977). 'The geographer as map maker', in *Man and Environment*, Units 1-3, pp. 91-135 (Open University, Milton Keynes).

Kettle, M. (1979). 'Arresting figures', *New Society*, 25 October.

Kirby, D. A. (1979). *Slum Housing and Residential Renewal* (Longman, London).

Kirk, W. (1963). 'Problems of geography', *Geography*, **48**, 357-71.

Leys, S. (1979). *Chinese Shadows* (Penguin, Harmondsworth).

Lisann, M. M. (1975). *Broadcasting to the Soviet Union: International Politics and radio* (Praeger, Boulder).

Lobeck, A. K. (1956). *Things Maps Don't Tell Us* (Macmillan, London).

Lyons, G. (ed.) (1977). *The Russian Version of the Second World War* (Leo Cooper, London).

Mazrui, A. (1979). 'The Garden of Eden in decay', *The Listener*, 8 November.

Mellor, R. E. H. (1978). *The Two Germanies* (Macmillan, London).

Mikhalyov, P. (1977). *Ulster! Violations of Human Rights in Northern Ireland* (Novosti).

Minghi, J. V. (1963). 'Boundary studies and national prejudices: the case of the South Tyrol', *Professional Geographer*, **15**, 4-8.

Muir, R. (1978). 'Radical geography or a new orthodoxy?', *Area*, **10**, 322-7.

Murray, R., and Boal, F. W. (1979). 'The social ecology of urban violence', in Herbert, D. T., and Smith, D. M. (eds.), *Social Problems and the City*, pp. 139-57 (Oxford University Press, Oxford).

Orwell, G. (1939/1970). 'Review: *Russia under Soviet Rule*, by N. de Basily', *New English Weekly*, 12 January. Reprinted in Orwell, S., and Argus, I. (eds.), *The Collected Essays, Journalism and Letters of George Orwell*, vol. I: *An Age Like This, 1920-1940*, pp. 416-19 (Penguin, Harmondsworth).

Orwell, G. (1946/1970). 'Politics and the English Language', *Horizon*, April. Reprinted in Orwell, S., and Argus, I. (eds.), *The Collected Essays; Journalism and letters of George Orwell*, vol. IV: *In Front of your Nose*, pp. 156-70 (Penguin, Harmondsworth).

Pahl, R. E. (1967). 'Sociological models in geography', in Chorley, R. J., and Haggett, P. (eds.), *Models in Geography*, pp. 217-42 (Methuen, London).

Panjabi, R. M. (1958). 'Chandigarh: India's newest city', *Geographical Magazine*, **31**, 401-14.

Peet, R. (ed.) (1978). *Radical Geography* (Methuen, London).

Pounds, N. J. G. (1962). *Divided Germany and Berlin* (Van Nostrand, Princeton).

Pounds, N. J. G. (1963). *The Economic Pattern of Modern Germany* (Murray, London).

Prescott, J. R. V. (1959). 'Functions and methods of electoral geography', *Annals of the Association of American Geographers*, **49**, 269-304.

Quam, L. O. (1943). 'The use of maps in propaganda', *Journal of Geography*, **42**, 21-32.

Quinney, R. (1970). *The Social Reality of Crime* (Little, Brown, Chicago).

Scholler, P. (1963). 'The division of Germany — based on historical geography?', *Erdkunde,* **19,** 161-4.

Sheane, M. (1978). *Ulster & the German Solution* (Highfield Press, Stockport).

Speier, H. (1941). 'Magic geography', *Social Research,* **8,** 310-30.

Spencer, J. C. (1968). 'A study of incarcerated white-collar offenders', in Geis, G. (ed.), *White-collar Criminal,* pp. 84-124 (Atherton, New York).

Thrower, N. J. W. (1972). *Maps and Man: an Examination of Cartography in Relation to Culture and Civilization* (Prentice Hall, Englewood Cliffs, NJ).

Tsfasman, R. (1979). 'Before a crime is committed', *Soviet Weekly,* 22 September.

Tunstall, J. (1977). 'The subversive media', *New Society,* 7 April.

Ungerson, C. (1971). *Moving Home* (Bell, London).

Watson, J. (1977). 'On the teaching of value geography', *Geography,* **62,** 198-204.

Websters (1973). *New Collegiate Dictionary* (Bell, London).

White, D. (1980). 'Bears, lions and doves', *New Society,* 17 January.

Wirsing, G. (1941). *The War in Maps* (German Library of Information, New York).

Wraith, R. E., and Lamb, G. B. (1971). *Public Inquiries as an Instrument of Government* (Allen & Unwin, London).

Wright, J. K. (1942). 'Map makers are human: comments on the subjective in maps', *Geographical Review,* **32,** 427-44.

Part 4

Applications

Introduction

Unlike many of the contributions in the previous parts, the focus in this section of the book is predominantly empirical. This does not mean that the chapters below are devoid of theory; in fact some — notably Hudson and Williams — have their own theoretical prefaces. Nor are the contributors necessarily applying, illustrating, or exemplifying the theories and models discussed earlier. It is possible, nonetheless, to discern links between the detailed case-studies presented here and some of the earlier papers. For example, the territorial processes described by Rowley and Paddison provide excellent illustrations of the concept of territoriality discussed by Sack. Likewise, despite differences in scale and emphasis, Clark, Dear, and now Hudson share a conviction in the efficacy of Marxist analysis. There is also considerable overlap in the contents of the papers by Burnett, Kirby, and Paddison since all three are concerned with spatial aspects of local politics and policy in the United Kingdom. Finally the voting studies presented by O'Loughlin and Lemon exemplify the massive output of Anglo-American electoral geography which was briefly discussed in the introduction to the orientation section.

Again there is enormous diversity in the subject-matter of the research being presented. The chapters include the following topics: political regionalism, voting behaviour, national transport policy, the establishment of neighbourhood organizations, and spatial aspects of international conflict. Whether this selection is a representative sample of the empirical political geography research being currently undertaken is difficult to assess. Notable omissions include electoral redistricting, maritime political control, and political participation between elections. Furthermore, themes pursued are at varying stages of the scale continuum, with the problem of neighbourhood definition and community council area delimitation in Glasgow at one end, and O'Loughlin's cross-national voting study at the other. Meanwhile conflict in Southern Africa is analysed by Brohman and Knight at three different scales. Although it is true that all the authors teach in North American or British institutions, nonetheless the fact that their studies are set in different parts of the world may help to redress the otherwise 'narrow' Anglo-American flavour of the book.

The chapters in this section fulfil one important function, and that is to remind us that, however urgent the need for theory-building in political geography, and however elegant the spatial models are, they have to be applied to the complex and confused reality of political life. It is not surprising — given the difficulty of this task — that some of the papers are exploratory and, as their authors admit, their findings and conclusions should be treated with caution.

While earlier political geography was, as Johnston has noted, excessively descriptive in its approach, nonetheless it left an empirical tradition which should not be disregarded. Well-documented case-studies, for example, by Augelli (1980), are at least as important in the long run as theoretical developments. For this reason, as well as for the intrinsic merits of the studies, this text is completed on an empirical note. Again a brief introduction to each chapter will attempt to put them in context, and précis their contents.

During the 1970s geographers have examined the areal bases of both representative and participatory democracy. With respect to the former Paddison (1976) has already evaluated the degree of bias inherent in the electoral system operating in the Republic of Ireland. Here, however, he is looking at (and indeed was involved in) the process of setting up and delimiting areas for community councils in Glasgow — Scotland's largest city. In recent years throughout the world there has been a great deal of experimentation in neighbourhood decentralization. Attempts have been made to give urban residents a greater say in influencing, if not deciding, the policies and public allocations which affect them (Hallman, 1974; Hill, 1978; Hambleton, 1978; Webster, 1980). In both American and European cities local neighbourhood organizations have been given official status and support as one way of making urban governments more responsive.

Paddison tells us why and how community councils were established in Scotland under local government reorganization, and what has been achieved in Glasgow. While neither he, nor indeed others (Knox, 1978; Cooper and Burdess, 1979), have concentrated entirely on the question of areal delimitation, nonetheless this is the focus of his paper. The advice given by central government was somewhat intuitive (Scottish Development Department, 1974; Hain, 1976). In the event steering committees set up by local activists played a crucial part in deciding what size and sort of areas would be best for them. Whether other areas could have been found which would have encouraged participation further cannot be proved (Herbert and Raine, 1976). As it turned out, in the lengthy process by which the hundred or so community councils in Glasgow were established, a definite element of territoriality was discernible in the conflicts which emerged within and between neighbourhoods. As Hall observed earlier, the term 'community' is a highly emotive one and perhaps it is not surprising that Glaswegians disagreed amongst themselves as to how to divide up their city. As far as effectiveness is concerned, the evidence appears to be contradictory, but if just a few more people are involved and public allocations are altered to reflect the preferences and demands of groups of citizens, then perhaps there *are* important lessons to be learnt from Glasgow (Burnett, 1976).

Contextual and spatial influences on voting behaviour have been thoroughly examined by geographers and political scientists who have employed both aggregate/quantitative and, more recently, behavioural research methods. O'Loughlin favours the former approach, and in previous publications has focused on the electoral geography of minority groups in cities in the United States. In his paper in this volume he has accomplished three tasks: first he has given us a thorough review of the literature — like Fitton, asking the questions (1971), *and* outlining major research findings; secondly, he has grappled with the technical problems associated with multi-collinearity and autocorrelation; and lastly the findings of his innovative cross-national study have made a valuable addition to electoral geography. By contrasting the significance of neighbourhood influences between voters in Indianapolis, Winnipeg, Detroit, and Dusseldorf he has reinforced the conclusion indicated recently by Wolfe and Burghardt (1978) that spatial models should be employed with caution and due consideration for scale and (national) circumstance.

Like Agnew in the previous section, the subject of Williams' paper is also political regionalism. The two authors agree that modernization has not eroded the strength of regional-ethnic political movements, and are at least in partial accord over some of the factors which may explain its incidence. Williams frames his analysis in terms of *requisites* and *preconditions* and illustrates models proposed by Hechter and Smith in relation to Quebec. His conclusions are that the uneven impact of modernization and the cultural division of labour are important structural determinants in Canada, but that the role of the ethnic intelligentsia should not be underestimated in shaping both the movements and the demands they make. It will be interesting to see future developments in Quebec following the majority NO vote to sovereignty/Association status in the May 1980 referendum. From a broader perspective the two papers in this volume provide a firm basis for the study of political regionalism whenever and wherever it arises.

Lemon's interest in the electoral politics of South Africa stems from his background as a specialist in the political geography of southern Africa. He points out that half a million whites (mainly non-South African citizens) were unenfranchised in the two elections he studied. The role of elections in the South African political system has also been discussed by Gudgin and Taylor (1979). It is interesting to speculate what would/will happen if and when a 'free and fair' Zimbabwean-style election is held in the future (races that play rugby together vote together!?).

Lemon shows that the elections that were held in South Africa in 1974 and 1977 were uneven contests between the traditionally Afrikaans-based National Party and a myriad of splintering minority parties. The background and outcomes of these two elections are carefully described, and changing patterns of support are analysed at both national and regional levels. It appears that the ethnic cleavage which has traditionally been the basis of party affiliation is weakening in that some voters in wealthy Afrikaans urban areas are less inclined to vote for the National Party even if its power base in rural and small towns remains as firm as ever. Meanwhile a substantial number of English-speaking, white, South Africans register their tacit support for apartheid by voting for National Party candidates. Lemon's paper will be of interest to electoral geographers and students of South Africa. The author suggests that it be followed up by behavioural studies which may verify the conclusions drawn.

Rowley has in recent years published articles on a wide variety of topics (Rowley, 1975, 1976). In an academic dialogue on conflict in the Middle East (1976) he has asserted that the Palestinian refugee problem will have to be solved if a lasting peace is to be found in the region. The formation of the state of Israel has been variously interpreted by geographers with De Blij, for example, using it to illustrate Jones' unified field theory (De Blij, 1967). Other aspects of the political geography of the state have also been recently studied (Waterman, 1980). In this article Rowley traces the colonization and settlement of Palestine by Zionists, and concentrates on the religious belief systems which have underpinned their territorial expansion. He argues that an appreciation of fundamental Hebrew attitudes to *Land* is necessary to understand the actions of Jewish settlers and Israeli governments. Certainly it cannot be disputed that land is of great symbolic value and that holy places — especially in the old walled city of Jerusalem — are revered. Of course land in the West Bank and Jerusalem also means olive groves, minerals, strategic military positions, homes, and building sites. Given the strength of religious/national feeling on the part of Jews *and* Palestinian Arabs (Rodinson, 1968; Nijim, 1969) there appear few grounds for optimism in the search for a just and lasting solution to their conflicting claims.

During the 1970s the radical/Marxist paradigm has increasingly found favour with human geographers and indeed in social science as a whole. Many studies have been purely theoretical. Not so the paper by Hudson on state transport policy in the United Kingdom, or indeed his previous research on regional problems and policies with special reference to the northeast of England. Why has British transport policy since the war been characterized by road investment and rail disinvestment? Certainly a number of public agencies have been involved — the Department of Transport and British Rail for example. There are also key personalities to be considered — Beeching, Marsh, and Marples. Likewise changing technology and consumer choice may have also played a part. The author, however, favours an explanation which emphasizes the constraints and conflicting pressures arising from a capitalist economy. A dual role has been forced on the state — to sustain the growth of private capital and simultaneously take account of social costs, and this has led to a rationality and legitimacy crisis. Government reports and ministerial autobiographies are cited in this thorough survey of the changing policies pursued by Conservative and Labour governments. The author recognizes that there is a need for further analyses into the causal links between capitalist dynamics and spatial policies of governments. The onus is on geographers who are convinced of the utility of this type of adisciplinary analysis — and there are a growing number — to spell out these relationships conceptually and empirically. There are surely plenty of examples where the policies of western governments reflect the interests and pressure of private capital at all scales, including at the international level outlined by Taylor earlier in this volume.

The final paper is concerned with the power vacuum in South-West Africa. It was originally conceived by Uren and has been written by two specialists on southern Africa. Brohman and Knight adopt an explicitly spatial perspective on the conflicts in Namibia. World powers are competing for influence over an area which is strategically located and rich in valuable minerals. From a regional perspective South Africa, and the black states to the north, are concerned to reduce and encourage, respectively, the possibility of a SWAPO nationalist government being installed or elected. Lastly the struggle is between blacks and whites in the country itself. At all these levels there are background locational and environmental factors which are important in a contest for power waged by military and propaganda means. Its outcome will significantly affect the relative well-being of blacks and whites both inside and outside South-West Africa.

Political and territorial conflict is certainly a feature of many parts of the developing world, and there has in the past been no shortage of spatial political studies in such areas. What is needed in future is not only regional political geographies such as that by Boateng (1978) but also case-studies which, as Darkoh has urged, illustrate and test recent theories and models, some of which are to be found in the earlier part of this text (Darkoh, 1980).

References and bibliography

Augelli, J. P. (1980). 'Nationalization of Dominican borderlands', *Geographical Review,* **70**(1), 19-36.

Boateng, E. A. (1978). *A Political Geography of Africa* (Cambridge University Press, Cambridge).

Burnett, A. D. (1976). 'Legislating for neighbourhood councils in England: the lessons from Scotland', *Local Government Studies,* **2**(4), 31-8.

Cooper, M., and Burdess, N. (1979). 'Community councils', *Area,* **11**(3), 31-8.

Darkoh, M. B. K. (1980). Review article. *Annals of the Association of American Geographers,* **70**(1), 117-18.

De Blij, H. (1967). *Systematic Political Geography* (Wiley, London).

Fitton, M. (1971). 'Neighbourhood voting: a sociometric examination', *British Journal of Political Science,* **3**, 445-72.

Gosenfeld, N. H. (1974). 'Spatial divisions within the city of Jerusalem 1948-67', *New Zealand Journal of Public Administration,* **36**(2), 77-102.

Gudgin, G., and Taylor, P. J. (1979). *Seats, Votes and the Spatial Organisation of Elections* (Pion, London).

Hain, P. (1976). 'Neighbourhood councils: the attitude of central authorities', *Community Development Journal,* **11**(1), 2-10.

Hallman, H. (1974). *Neighbourhood Government in a Metropolitan Setting* (Sage, Beverley Hills).

Hambleton, R. (1978). *Policy Planning and Local Government* (Hutchinson, London).

Herbert, D. T., and Raine, J. W. (1976). 'Defining communities in urban areas: an analysis of alternative approaches', *Town Planning Review*, **47**, 325-59.

Hill, D. (1978). 'Neighbourhood councils', *Planning and Administration*, **5**(1), 27-40.

Knox, P. L. (1978). 'Community councils, electoral districts and social geography', *Area*, **10**, 387-91.

Nijim, B. K. (1969). 'Israel and the potential for conflict', *Professional Geographer*, **21**, 319-23.

Paddison, R. (1976). 'Spatial bias and redistricting in proportional representation election systems: a case study of the Republic of Ireland', *Tijdshrift voor Economische en Sociale Geographie*, **67**, 230-41.

Rodinson, M. (1968). *Israel and the Arabs* (Penguin, Harmondsworth).

Rose, G. (1971). *Local Councils in Metropolitan Areas* (Fabian Research Series, 296).

Rowley, G. (1975). 'The redistribution of parliamentary seats in the United Kingdom: themes and opinions', *Area*, **7**, 16-21.

Rowley, G. (1976). 'Urbanization and development in Latin America: recurring trends and problems', *Geoforum*, **7**, 74-9.

Rowley, G. (1977). 'Israel and the Palestinian refugees: background and present realities', *Area*, **9**(2), 81-9.

Scottish Development Department (1974). *Community Councils: Some Alternatives for Community Council Schemes* (HMSO, London).

Waterman, S. (1980). 'The dilemma of electoral districting for Israel', *Tijdshrift voor Economische en Sociale Geographie*, **71**(2), 88-98.

Webster, B. A. (1980). Policy making and responsive local government: the experience of area management in England (unpublished paper given to the American-European conference on neighbourhood level government. Florence, Italy).

Wolfe, J. S. and Burghardt, A. F. (1978). 'The neighbourhood effect in a local election', *Canadian Geographer*, **22**(4), 298-305.

Yates, D. (1974). *Neighbourhood Democracy* (Lexington Books, Lexington, Mass.).

Political studies from spatial perspectives
Edited by A.D. Burnett and P.J. Taylor
© 1981 John Wiley & Sons Ltd

_____ *16*__

Identifying the local political community: a case-study of Glasgow

Ronan Paddison

One of the more intractable problems in the organizing of governments within industrial societies is how to equate the quest for technical and administrative efficiency with the popularly expressed demands for local democratic control (Hill, 1974). In the modern industrial state (it is argued) the population is too large and matters of state frequently too complex to allow of direct democracy, at least in the form espoused by the classical political theorists. Among developed countries, then, direct democracy is restricted to a few apparently anachronistic cases of local government, the New England town meeting and the *landsgemeinde* of central Swiss cantons. The more general case, whether at the level of national or subnational government, is representative democracy, the basis of which is the entrusting of the tasks of governing to elites popularly elected through the ballot box.

Representative forms of democracy, however more viable they may be for the industrial state, inevitably distance the citizen from the decision-making process. It is this sense of alienation and relative powerlessness, even within the level of local government, which more than any other factor helps explain the demand for greater citizen participation, a movement which to varying degrees, and within a variety of ways, has been experienced in most of the advanced nations.

The process of local government reform, the revision of areas and boundaries, and the redistribution of functions to jurisdictions whose size is more suited to their technical requirements, has highlighted the need for direct forms of citizen participation. This is particularly the case in Britain in which the recent reforms have left local governments large by comparison with other West European countries and, even more markedly, with the United States. Compared with other West European countries in which the average population of the basic local government unit varied between 1320 in France (communes, 1968) and 29,527 in Sweden (communes, 1976), the figure for England and Wales, 122,740 (1972) in the reformed network of districts, is significantly higher.

Though based on a different system of local government, reform in Scotland was characterized by developments similar to those elsewhere in Britain. The reform legislation (of 1973) replaced the map of over 400 local authorities, distinguishing 'small' and 'large' burghs, rural districts and the county, with a less complex two-tier structure of 65 units based on nine regional and 53 district authorities, together with three separate all-purpose councils serving the peripheral island populations. Regional councils were given responsibility for a number of strategic functions — notably education, physical planning, and the social services — while the most important responsibilities left to the district council were housing and local planning.

As elsewhere in Britain, the wholesale reduction in the number of jurisdictions in Scotland served to reduce the 'local-ness' of local government. However, unlike England, reform in Scotland incorporated a statutory form of local participatory body, the community council, the origin of which was clearly traceable as a counterbalance to the reform process. This process would inevitably mean the loss of separate status by many of the smaller authorities and it was from these, and particularly the small burghs, that pressure for the community council was initially greatest. The community council idea allowed the small burghs to retain something of a separate political identity, and it was to this that the Royal Commission (1969) mainly confined application of the concept. Nevertheless, the idea was extended to cover all Scotland and by 1977, two years after reorganization into regions and districts, most of the country was also served by the community council. In this discussion our emphasis is on how the councils were established within a major urban area, Glasgow, though before turning to this some words on the main characteristics of the councils, as they were intended and have been in practice, will assist in seeing how they relate to the need for participation.

Community councils as citizen participation

Participation is a term which defies simple definition (Kasperson and Breitbart, 1974). At minimum it implies that the citizen is given a greater say in how political decisions are made, though as such this raises more questions than it answers. It says nothing of who is to participate, how important to the decision-making process is participation designed to be and what are the objectives to be sought for through participation.

The community council idea was poorly articulated in terms of such questions as it was initially discussed. The Royal Commission had talked of it in terms of it acting as the 'voice of the neighbourhood', while within the enabling legislation the role of the council was left very general. Its functions were:

> to ascertain, coordinate and express to the regional, district and island councils and other public bodies the views of the community about matters for which those bodies are responsible... [and]... to take such action in the interests of the community as appears to its members to be desirable and practicable.

Community councils were not considered to be a third tier of local government and in that sense were not given statutory responsibility for the delivery of services or the right to raise finance though the imposition of a property tax. Though their existence was to be given statutory backing they were otherwise not restricted in how they might operate.

Partly because of the imprecision as to their role it is difficult to classify the community council within any of the existing typologies of citizen participation. In one of the more influential of such typologies Arnstein (1969) categorized levels of participation arranged in the form of a ladder. To her model participation was seen as a means of redress to the 'have-nots' so that the highest rungs of the ladder, labelled 'citizen power', meant the delegation of sufficient responsibilities (and capabilities) so that local groups would be able to independently marshal resources to meet local preferences. Community councils fall short of having such power, nor was this really the intention behind their establishment. Insofar as one of the major roles of the councils is that they act as the local 'sounding-board' for district and regional government policies their function is closer to what Arnstein terms 'tokenism'. On the other hand the councils can also initiate proposals themselves to improve the local area, particularly within certain regions where financial grants are available for community projects.

In practice community councils have become involved in a wide range of activities (Scottish Office, 1978). These can be grouped under three major headings — monitoring and making representations to the district and regional governments over the provision of services; liaison with local governments, particularly over planning issues; and general problems (e.g. vandalism) affecting the community. Inasmuch as problems over the delivery of services, especially of housing, are an important concern, the councils are being used as a vehicle through which contact between the citizens and the local government can be maintained. It is in this capacity that district and regional governments are increasingly using the community council in spite of their misgivings that the councils have failed to adequately cultivate relations with the public.

It is axiomatic to the working of the community council that it act as an adequate mouthpiece of the community, yet this has proved an elusive objective. Membership of most councils is divided between representatives that are popularly elected and members nominated from local organizations. The emphasis on elections has tended to create a division between the councillors and the community at large. The elections themselves are based on a variety of methods — type, frequency, and duration all vary — though turnouts have characteristically been low (Masterson, 1978). In a sample of 29 district councils covering 266 community elections the average turnout was 19% though it was argued that the low polls may be 'the result not of public indifference to community councils so much as the electorate's lack of knowledge of community councils and acquaintance with the candidates' (Scottish Development Department, 1974a). (In those elections based on a postal ballot — where, in other words the candidates would be known — turnouts were substantially higher.)

While low electoral turnouts do not necessarily imply community apathy the problem of adequately representing community opinion through reliance on elections is more apparent in the social composition of the councils. In common with the pattern for local government in Britain generally there are marked biases apparent in the recruitment of representatives. Thus in Strathclyde community councillors are disproportionately male, older, represented by professional workers and, in terms of housing tenure, owner-occupiers. These biases have in some cases raised suspicions that the council is not a faithful reflection of community opinion, particularly in areas where there is a socially mixed population.

As one of the prime functions of the community council is to act as a communications link between the citizen and the local authorities, ensuring an efficient flow of information is essential. To this end Glasgow district council has devised a Code of Conduct itemizing what information councils will receive as of right; this includes the minutes of the district and regional councils, planning applications which affect the community, and prior notificaiton of any proposals which impinge on the community. The community councils for their part have adopted a number of strategies to overcome the communications problem, from the use of questionnaires and public meetings to newsletters; each of the strategies has its disadvantages from the viewpoint of eliciting community opinion. Larger councils, in terms of population and/or area, have found the task of communication with their electorate more burdensome. Despite this, within Glasgow the adoption of the strategy of subdividing the council's area for representational purposes is not one that correlates significantly with the size of the community's electoral roll.

   While the information flow from the local authorities has helped in informing the community and providing the governments with feedback, it is clear that not all proposals affecting the community stem from the district and regional councils. Other public agencies are under less pressure to cooperate, which inevitably tends to erode the efficacy of the community council to act as a local 'environmental watchdog'. For example, one such case arose through the activities of an *ad hoc* agency (GEAR) charged with renewal of the city's east end. One of GEAR's proposals was the resiting of a noxious industry to an alternative, more peripheral site. The host community was not informed of the proposal, at least until it was effectively too late to suggest alternative sites, and as the area had previously been zoned industrial objections on planning grounds could not carry weight with the city council.

   The question of working relationships is an important one in that one of the primary functions of the councils is to ascertain, coordinate, and express the view of the community. Yet the efficiency of the councils in this respect partly depends on the cohesives of the community, which in turn is related to how the community is spatially defined.

The approach to delimitation

Formally the task of spatially delimiting the community councils was delegated to the new district councils. The task was to frame a scheme for community councils covering the entire district, the scheme to embrace the issues of area and constitution. It is permissible that in an area it might be thought inappropriate to establish a council — where, for example, there was insufficient demand — though in practice few such cases have arisen. Within Glasgow only one of the 98 councils is not operating, in an area which local opinion considered that the existing resident's associations served satisfactorily.

Within much of the country the issue of defining the community area was not a politically contentious one. This was the case where previous jurisdictions could be utilized and, indeed, where to propose otherwise would encounter local opposition. In such areas, notably in the more rural parts but also the small burghs, the community had a separate political tradition so that there was less reason to question whether the community area could function meaningfully for community council purposes. Such areas were likely, as an official advisory report had expressed it, 'to fulfil their role more effectively as the areas correspond to local communities, that is places to which people feel they belong and in which they have an interest' (Scottish Development Department, 1974b).

It was in the more urbanized areas, and particularly the major cities, that the problems of defining the political community were likely to be greater. Two reasons help explain the difference. In the cities there was no, or at most only rudimentary, formal network of geographically defined participatory bodies by which the entire urban area was subdivided. What did exist was an incomplete patchwork of local political organizations — ratepayers' groups particularly in middle-class areas, and residents and tenant's groups, the latter in working-class areas — and a number of environmental interest and pressure groups. Their existence relates to the second reason why designation of the councils in the urban area was more politicized, that because of the heterogeneity of interests, and their spatial density, the stakes of participation in the city are higher. If participation is to affect how public goods are to be distributed then the community council would potentially be a beneficial institution to the community; because of the greater mix of classes within the city the fixing of boundaries, and decisions as to which areas were to have separate councils and which were to be joined to existing ones were issues which were likely to be the more contentious. Further, in the cities there was a denser network of existing political groups whose *raison d'être* was potentially threatened by the community council and who, therefore, would tend to resist the innovation or modify it to meet its own requirements, arguments which in practice have proved largely fallacious. Nevertheless, the existence of these organizations was, according to Edinburgh district councillors, sufficient to obviate the need for the community council. That is, the city had an existing network of 30 community associations; 13 city-wide associations;

and 120 street, residents' and tenant groups; and these adequately met the need for participation.

The district council, and particularly its elected members, occupied a central role in the process of delimitation, though they were not the only actors. In Glasgow local steering committees were established to formulate proposals on boundaries and constitutions, and besides these there were the existing community groups.

How the political communities were defined within the city and the final configuration of boundaries reflected the different roles played by these actors. Of fundamental importance was how the district councillors foresaw the process of delimitation, particularly as ultimate responsibility lay with them. Given a blank map of the city, councillors could either draw the areas and boundaries themselves, aided by their technical officers, or they could rely more on 'grass-roots' delimitation. Imposition from above, a technique not of course unfamiliar in the history of local boundary reform, would probably result in administrative neatness (for example, the councils could be based on the then recently reapportioned electoral districts), though it would strike against the spirit of the legislation, besides which it would encounter local opposition. Devolving the task, while retaining the rights of sanction and arbitration, would not only enlist grass-roots support but also contribute to the transference of the problem to a more local level. Equally, the decision by the district councils to encourage local steering committees to define their own community — definition, that is, 'from below' — reflected the ruling Labour Party's support for the concept of neighbourhood participation in general, while for the individual councillor to advocate otherwise might be harmful to their re-election chances.

Even though district councillors do have sub-city connections they also identify at the city-wide level, in contrast to the steering committee member. Problems arising from the clash of interests between levels of government are frequent, and over the community council arose over differing perceptions as to its role and composition. Thus one conflict arose from the fundamental point as to who constitutes the community for the purposes of the community council. As one steering group proposed this could be all of the residents of the community area, rather than the generally accepted notion that elected representatives would act as the council. It was because the latter offered the tidier solution administratively and, more importantly, conformed to the 'elective tradition' of local government that the alternative proposal was vehemently opposed by the district council even though the idea embodied more closely the ideals of participatory democracy.

Reliance on grass-roots definition as the approach also allowed for differing interpretations of community locally. As it is commonly suggested, one advantage of decentralizing the task is that local differences will be catered for, and this more than offset the problem of differing perceptions of what constituted the spatial community.

Issues in identifying the political community

Few terms have occasioned so much debate as has that of community. An early but still frequently quoted article enumerated 94 different definitions, though it found common ground among a number of these in the terms area, common ties, and social interaction (Hillery, 1955). These can be viewed as the primary criteria by which communities can be defined; secondary factors would include the extent to which the area is self-sufficient for mundane needs and what kinds of institutions and commercial facilities it has. To the local steering groups minimal advice was given on how to define the community so that in effect, in the absence of 'technical expertise', this relied on the perceived community. Beyond this there were several issues which steering groups discussed, notably the nature of the community, the question of size and social balance (Table 16.1).

Table 16.1   Some issues involved in the spatial definition of the local political community

---

1. How relevant is the community as defined for community council purposes?

2. What are the implications of 'small' and 'large' community council areas in political terms?

3. What significance as a delimiting factor is class, and what is the desirability of 'socially mixed' community councils?

According to some students of community the existence of such a social institution defined within discrete boundaries is illusory. In highly mobile societies, as Webber (1963) has suggested, interests are diffused widely throughout the city rather than being closely tied to a single area. Without arguing the validity of this hypothesis or otherwise — and clearly this will vary between and within cities according to differences in mobility — the argument has relevance to the process of defining community councils, not only in whether

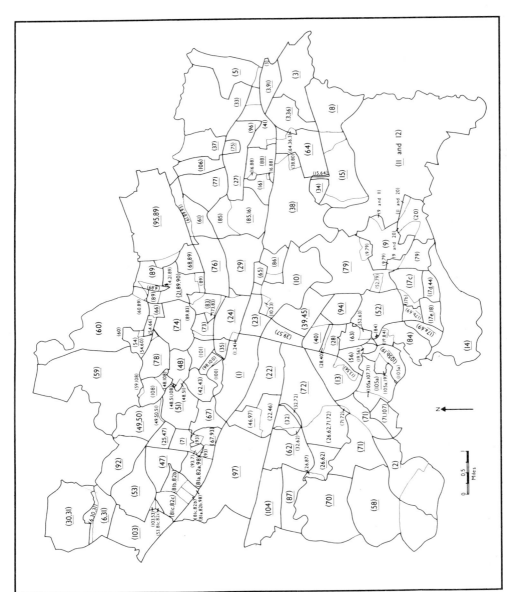

FIGURE 16.1 Political communities. Numbers in parentheses refer to individual steering committees representing and/or competing for particular territories. Final network of councils shown in bolder outline and by the underlined number

boundaries can be meaningfully delimited, but also whether political rights — of voting and standing for election, for instance — should be restricted to residents or be extended to 'temporary in-migrants', such as those only working in the area. From the submissions by the local steering groups, support for the idea of a spatial political community being meaningful was universal and, not unexpectedly, political rights were confined to residents. To do so was the better strategy from the viewpoint of neighbourhood defence, particularly in areas of mixed land-use. Thus in the CBD, despite the small size of the resident population and the apparent logic (to some) in extending membership rights to other groups the restriction has ensured that residents' interests are heard against the powerful economic and other interest groups which speak for the central area through other bodies.

The question of the appropriate (population) size for the community council, as had been apparent elsewhere in the wider debate on local government reform, was a contentious issue. It was divided between those who advocated the 'small' neighbourhood and the 'large' locality approach to community council definition. An official survey of Glasgow identified 176 neighbourhood areas defined on the basis of housing type, 'reasonably distinct' physical boundaries, and the occurrence of community facilities such as a primary school and a shopping centre catering for low-order goods (Scottish Development Department, 1974b). Populations varied between 600 and 20,000 with a median of 1200. Proponents of the small council argued that they would engender a high degree of local political consciousness, more than half of the 176 already having some form of voluntary locally based organization. A small council would also, therefore, enhance the likelihood of participation in that it would be closer in size to the 'home area' defined by several surveys as that locale with which citizens most immediately identify and in which they have an interest in its well-being. The alleged disadvantages of the small council were that they would be politically impotent — lacking leadership and other resources because of their smallness — while their large number would mean that the district council tasks of coordination and overseeing would be more difficult.

The alternative district scheme in Glasgow could be served by 35 community councils based on the major shopping centres, secondary schools, physically bounded areas, and similar housing and social class structure. Most would have populations of between 20,000 and 40,000. It was assumed that councils of this size would have command over greater resources and potentially a greater power base. This at least would be advantageous given that the community council was to be so dependent upon the actions of the district and regional level governments; a 'large' council would be in a better position to challenge local governments. Offsetting this was the difficulty that the large council would experience in attracting widespread participation and in ensuring that its representations faithfully mirrored community opinion.

As has been suggested, seeking an optimum (or even single appropriate) population size for the community council proved a largely fruitless exercise, except that it provided a framework for discussion of different 'types' of community council. Even in this respect terms such as 'power', and 'resources' were being used loosely — there is (for instance) no evidence to suggest that size correlates with leadership resources. In practice both types of community council are to be found in the city, several having populations larger than 20,000 while slightly less than half (48) have a population of less than 10,000. What experience there has been tends to favour the smaller council — not only has it been able to 'reach' its community more effectively and hence claim to be able to speak for the majority of the community, but this has, in the eyes of the district council, given greater legitimacy to its claims.

Class is another issue around which the process of delimitation focused. It is of importance for two main reasons. Firstly, in Britain it acts as *the* political cleavage as expressed through support for the national political parties. Secondly, many of the issues over which participation within the city focus involve externalities whose positive or negative incidence is class-related. To the extent that residential areas can be socioeconomically defined, then community councils serving homogeneous areas would be better suited to 'defending' the community. Steering committees were aware of the possible advantages and otherwise of the socially balanced community and in some cases, though only a small number, this was given physical expression. In most cases because communities were perceived as small areas and because they were being defined within areas seen as having common values and ideologies the tendency was for homogeneity. Using 1971 Census Small Area data Cosgrove (1978) investigated the social homogeneity of the councils in Glasgow showing that social classes I, II, and III (viz. professional, managerial, and non-manual workers) had formed their own communities, excluding large numbers of the manually occupied.

Boundary conflicts

Though communities can be defined in several ways, in general there was a high degree of agreement between adjacent steering committees as to what constituted the core area of their community. Where conflict developed was either over the precise delimitation of boundaries or, more unusually, over the appropriate size of councils. Conflict of the first kind was the more common because in many communities, though the core was distinct, its limits were more fuzzy (Figure 16.1). In these cases arbitration, by the district council, provided a solution often based on a poll seeking local preferences.

Conflicts of the second type were the more far-reaching in that they involved whole areas of one or more steering groups being claimed by another. This situation arose where there was an already existing political body serving the former pattern of wards. The 37 wards of the city were considerably larger than the average steering committee, though in three main cases in the city the ward committee strove to secure community council status over their area. Figure 16.2 illustrates one case from the southern boundary of the city in which the entire area, with a population of 24,000, was competed for between a ward committee and six steering groups. Four of the six were only concerned with peripheral parts of the territory while the remaining two effectively dismembered the larger area claimed by the ward committee. Though the debate between the two types of committee centred on the alleged advantages of the 'large' versus 'small' community council, in essence the problem arose because, as is typical to any reform of local government, there are powerful inertia forces. In this case, as on the northern perimeter of the city where a similar situation arose, the smaller units were favoured by the district council largely because they were perceived as being closer to local preferences. It was only in the case of the ward committee covering a part of the eastern edge of the central city that the larger approach was adopted, because there were no strong counter-claims. Significantly, though, the area is now one of the few under review because of its size.

Conclusions

The final pattern of community councils in Glasgow, largely because of the process of definition being developed 'from below', attests to the difficulty in generating meaningful generalizations

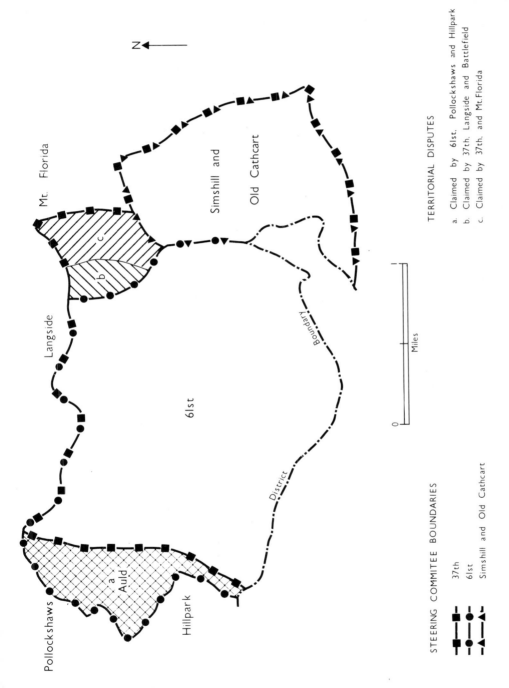

STEERING COMMITTEE BOUNDARIES

37th
61st
Simshill and Old Cathcart

TERRITORIAL DISPUTES

a. Claimed by 61st, Pollockshaws and Hillpark
b. Claimed by 37th, Langside and Battlefield
c. Claimed by 37th, and Mt. Florida

FIGURE 16.2   Sample case from southern boundary of Glasgow; details in text

about the term 'community'. Hence, in terms of size the smallest council with a population of 390 contrasts markedly with the largest, 34,032. The size frequency distribution is bimodal with peaks occurring in the ranges 5000-7500 and 10,000-15,000. Indeed most of the largest and smallest councils have been formed in spite of their size. Of the 12 smallest, with a median population of 1500, eight have been formed principally because of their clear definition by physical features, notably motorways, railways, or open spaces. Similarly a number of the largest councils have been defined by factors such as their previous administrative status or their homogeneity as public-sector housing areas.

Delegation of the task to the local level ensured that there would be differing interpretations as to the role of the community council. In all but one of the four peripheral post-war public housing schemes (for instance), with populations of 40,000-50,000, the areas were subdivided into five or six councils. However, in the exception, otherwise very similar in terms of housing and social composition and in the networks of existing tenants' associations, a single community council was adopted because its role was to be a coordinating one between the existing political groups.

Identifying the local political community within the city, where there was at most only a rudimentary precedent upon which the exercise could be based, encounters problems typical to those defining communities in general, and also specific administrative and political hurdles. Following their establishment there have been only four minor boundary changes, most councils being willing to develop community participation within their defined territories.

References and bibliography

Arnstein, S. R. (1969). 'A ladder of citizen participation', *Journal of the American Institute of Planners,* **35**(4), 216-24.

Burnett, A. D. (1976). 'Legislating for neighbourhood councils in England', *Local Government Studies,* **2**(4), 31-8.

Clarke, C. (1977). 'Community councils: power to the people?', *British Political Sociology Yearbook,* **3,** 110-42.

Cosgrove, D. F. (1978). Unpublished research finding — Forthcoming, in 'Report on Community Councils in the Strathclyde Region' (Paisley College of Technology).

Hill, D. M. (1974). *Democratic Theory and Local Government* (Allen and Unwin, London).

Hillery, G. A. (1955). 'Definitions of community: areas of agreement', *Rural Sociology,* **XX,** 111-23.

Kasperson, R. E. & Breitbart, M. (1974). *Participation, Decentralization and Advocacy Planning,* Commission on College Geography Resource Paper No. 25 (Association of American Geographers, Washington, DC).

Masterson, M. P. (1978). 'Forming community councils — East Kilbride', *Local Government Studies,* **4**(4), 67-79.

Rowe, A. (1975). *Democracy Renewed* (Sheldon Press, London).

Royal Commission on Local Government in Scotland, 1966-1969, Cmnd. 4150 (HMSO, London).

Scottish Development Department (1974a). *Community Councils* (HMSO, Edinburgh).

Scottish Development Department (1974b). *Steering Group on Community Councils, Glasgow District Report,* Part I (HMSO, Edinburgh).

Scottish Office (1978). *'Community Councils Research Projects — Interim Reports'* (Central Research Unit, Scottish Office, Edinburgh).

Silk, P., Fyfe, A., and Gillon, S. (1978), *Community Councils in Glasgow* (Strathclyde Area Survey Paper, Strathclyde University).

Webber, M. M. (1963) "Order in diversity: community without propinquity', in Wingo, L. (ed.), *Cities and Space,* pp. 23-56. (Johns Hopkins University Press, Baltimore).

Political studies from spatial perspectives
Edited by A.D. Burnett and P.J. Taylor
© 1981 John Wiley & Sons Ltd

_____ 17__

The neighbourhood effect in urban voting surfaces: a cross-national analysis

John O'Loughlin

Contextual effects in vote preferences based on social interactions are well known, but not totally accepted, within electoral geography. The contextual effect is often equated to the 'community' or 'neighbourhood' effect, implying that after social, economic, ideological, cultural, and campaign factors are controlled, the choice of candidate is determined to some extent by the voter's interactions with other members of the community in which he or she lives. Given early impetus by V. O. Key (1949) in American electoral studies and introduced into electoral geography by Cox (1968) and Reynolds (1974), the neighbourhood effect has produced more discussion in the discipline than any other, because it is the core of a traditional definition of electoral geography — that a geographical influence on voting behaviour exists in addition to the predictor variables considered by other social scientists.

The purpose of this paper is to propose a method for isolating the contextual dimension, by removing its effects from predictive models of voting choice based on aggregate data. It attempts to update the approach of Reynolds and Archer (1969) by incorporating recent methodological innovations in geography.

Measuring the contextual effect

Efforts to measure the contextual effect can be equated with the respective disciplines. Political scientists have used survey data first to determine the individual causes of vote choice and then,

357

using aggregate data, to measure the community effect. As a counter to studies relying exclusively on survey data, a growing number of political scientists are attempting to 'put the context back' into electoral choice models. Early evidence for the contextual effect by Lazarsfeld *et al.* (1944) and Berelson *et al.* (1954), through the use of repeated surveys before presidential elections, was complemented by researchers who found an ethnic influence in voting, after social status was controlled (Wolfinger, 1965). Recent papers by Blake (1978) and Wright (1977) following Ennis (1962) have combined individual and aggregate data analysis. In a typical example of this method, Blake (1978) calculated the probability of finding Liberal voters among social categories using Canadian survey data. Shifting to aggregate analysis, he then computed the expected Liberal vote in each constituency based on its demographic composition and the calculated probabilities. The difference between expected and actual votes was then analysed for a contextual effect, resulting from minor party activity, campaigning, and other local elements. Finally, a regional effect was demonstrated.

In contrast to political scientists, geographers have generally manipulated aggregate election statistics and census data to isolate the neighbourhood component of voting choice. Two exceptions exist. Cox (1969a, 1971, 1972), in a series of papers, used an approach similar to Ennis (1962) to point to the presence of a neighbourhood element, by first determining the expected vote proportions in a precinct based on survey data. Recently, Wolfe and Burghardt (1978), in a micro-level study in Guelph, Ontario, concluded that neighbours operated as one of several informal local channels, and they concluded that neighbourhood-effect models need to be applied with caution and with due consideration for scale and local circumstance.

While general agreement exists that survey methods are preferable when examining the contextual effect, two objections to their use persist. First, because of the prohibitive cost and time involved in such surveys, those voters sampled are necessarily from a local population. Major national surveys, as yet, pay little attention to the contextual element apart from asking the kind or size of community the respondent lives in. When other information (such as the income or ideological context) is generated, greater use of national and state surveys by political geographers can be expected (see Epstein, 1979 for an example of possible future studies). Second, there is undoubtedly some contextual influence present in survey data, as is shown by the consistent finding that Labour support from the lower class varies between the regions of

Britain (P. J. Taylor and Johnston, 1979, chap. 5). Electoral geographers will continue to rely on aggregate data to explain voting choice and contextual influences. Therefore it is necessary to re-examine present aggregate approaches and modify them to eliminate persistent biases. We also need accurate measurement of the components (social, geographical, or otherwise) of voting choice.

Previous aggregate analyses of voting context have generated controversy, as for example, about Cox's (1968) study of Conservative support in the London area. Using a causal modelling approach, he argued that the effects of the suburban environment on voting choice are significant, after socioeconomic causes are removed from the equation. Criticisms of Cox's results by P. J. Taylor (1969) and Kasperson (1969), focused both on the interpretation of the model and on the causes of the suburban effect. Using a two-stage factor analysis approach, using only those variables which load highest on the initial factors as input data to the second factor analysis, Biel (1972) tested the separate effect of the suburban-central city dimension on voting behaviour. His conclusion, in line with Cox's original assertions, was that 'suburbanism' operated, both through the socioeconomic context and through effects of its own, to influence party choice.

In another aggregate study, Reynolds and Archer (1969) focused on the residuals from a multiple regression of votes and principal components scores of socioeconomic variables, in their examination of the neighbourhood effect in Republican voting in Indianapolis. They used Geary's (1968) approach arguing that if the residuals from regression are not significantly autocorrelated while the original observations were, then the independent variables completely 'explain' the phenomenon. They estimated the effects of the social variables ($R^2 = 0.82$) but were unable to remove auto-correlation in the residuals. They concluded that significant evidence of spatial contamination in the voting surface remained, after the social effects had been removed. This autocorrelation of residuals was viewed as suggestive of a contextual effect but no further evidence was presented on this point.

Cox (1971) has said that if a contextual effect exists it is not detectable at the scale commonly used (census tract), while Scanlan (1977) has argued that to equate spatial contiguity of residuals from regression with contagion, based on neighbourhood interaction, is not defensible. Scanlan's study of Brisbane, and those of Johnston and his associates of New Zealand local elections (Johnston, 1974; Forrest et al., 1977; Johnston, 1977) have indicated the existence of strong personal voting after socioeconomic factors are controlled, as well as 'friends and neighbours' voting based on distance from the candidates' homes. However, there is undoubtedly some overlap between 'friends and neighbours' voting and community-based voting, especially in local elections when party labels are frequently not presented on the ballot. Nevertheless, Johnston (1977) found evidence of contagion in Christchurch elections, but a strong candidate-based influence confounded the relationship between votes and community support, independent of social status, and based on intra-neighbourhood contacts.

The contextual effect is not confined to Anglo-Saxon nations but in Western democracies is strongly related to urban-rural and other cleavages. Thus in Germany, Laux and Simms (1973) found support for the Social Democratic Party lower among Protestant populations in rural areas than among similar groups in urban areas. Non-social cleavages are generally not considered in election studies but as Rokkan (1970) has indicated, national, religious, rural-urban, and social class divisions operate simultaneously to determine party choice. While these cleavages are evident on a national scale, elements of each one may be present within a single metropolitan area Electoral geographers who have considered only social and neighbourhood effects as determinants of vote choice run the risk of ignoring other major, independently operating, causal factors.

The determinants of voting choice and a simple model

Previous research in electoral geography has examined variations of voting proportions as dependent upon a series of overlapping causes. Most researchers focus on one or two causes, while trying to control the remainder. We can propose a simple model of voting behaviour as:

Vote % = f (social/economic status, social context, relative space, campaign effort, other electoral cleavages, random elements)

Each cause is considered in turn before we move to a consideration of the methodology to be used in this present research report.

The argument that social class indicators influence party choice and, consequently, the voting decision is well documented for the Western democracies. The party system of most nations (the United States, Ireland, and Canada being noteworthy complications) is founded on the distinction between those who work and those who manage (Rose, 1974). This basic relationship has not been of great interest to electoral geographers; most have been concerned with analysing the complications in the link produced by local circumstances and community contexts (Taylor and Johnston, 1979). Although the strength of the relationship varies (related to political culture and socialization, the presence of other cleavages, the historical development of parties and other national-level influences), social effects persist as the most significant determinant of voting behaviour (Dogan and Rose, 1971; Rose, 1974; Taylor and Johnston, 1979). An important element in the social status/party choice link is the social context in which it is set. To view the individual voter in isolation from the rest of the community is a mistake: a counter-trend to the individual-level view of voting is now evident in North American political science, partly a reflection of the influence of the European ecological approach.

While general agreement on strength of the social class/vote choice relationship exists, the importance of the second determinant of voting behaviour, contextual effects, is subject to debate. The key issue is the influence of any contextual effects, after other effects are controlled. Thus, in order to test Key's hypothesis that the context (black population concentration) exerted a significant influence on support for racist candidates, Wright (1977) was forced to control for regional division, education, urbanization, and the 'friends and neighbours' effect in order to reach the conclusion that southern white support for George Wallace increased with the relative size of the black population in the county and state. Parallel results from Britain, United States, Canada, Belgium, and other nations (Rose, 1974) indicate that voters are often influenced in their choice of candidate by the community in which they live. For example, working-class voters in Britain display a greater likelihood of giving their vote to Labour candidates in predominantly Labour areas than their fellow-workers who live in Conservative areas (Taylor and Johnston, 1979).

R. J. Johnston (1976) has suggested that the relationship between the percentages supporting a party at two time-periods will approximate an S-shaped curve. In the absence of a contextual effect (without contact between individuals), we would expect a linear relationship. It is assumed that people will, in general, adopt the norms of the neighbourhood in which they live, through the personal influence of their neighbours, through conversation and example. Consequently, support for the majority party will be magnified and that for the minority party eroded. While this model is appealing in the abstract, efforts to test it have met only partial success. Obviously survey data for neighbourhoods are needed at different time-periods. Cox (1969a) showed that greatest conversion took place not in neighbourhood conversation but within the realm of formal-social groups, often not place-specific, and that newest immigrants and those of moderate political involvement were susceptible to conversion by long-time residents and the politically committed. In a complementary analysis, Cox (1971) also showed that deviations from a predicted vote proportion (based on a transition probability matrix from a survey of voters) were indicators of a neighbourhood effect and were magnified in towns of larger size. An assumption of a uniform swing to or from a party is present, which for American communities is often not valid.

A third possible cause of electoral behaviour is the location of the voter with respect to stimuli from the candidate or the community. This influence, termed the 'relative space' or 'friends and neighbours' effect, is based on the assumption that people residing close to a candidate will receive more information regarding that person through local communication networks. It was identified by Key (1949) in the American South and measured by Reynolds (1974) for gubernatorial candidates in Georgia, and Tatalovich (1975) for primary candidates in Mississippi. In New Zealand, R. J. Johnston (1974) and Forrest et al. (1977) have shown that it is a significant factor in at-large local elections. This 'friends and neighbours' effect will be greatest in non-partisan ballots, where party labels do not provide a voting cue, and in at-large or multi-member contests, where deviations from a partisan trend suggest some local circumstances, often loyalty to the neighbourhood candidate.

Non-partisan elections in American cities have been characterized by ethnic-based voting, where attraction to a candidate of the same ethnic group persists across social classes (Wolfinger, 1965; Weed, 1973). Because ethnic groups have well-defined neighbourhood spaces, the ethnic factor is also a 'friends and neighbours' factor. Nomination of balanced ethnic tickets is designed to appeal to all segments of the heterogeneous voting population. In addition, a distance factor is present in referenda (such as the vote on siting of public housing projects, line of a motorway, or open housing) and in elections where candidate's appeal is related to the local social geography. Thus, candidates making environmental or racial appeals may gain votes from those voters who feel themselves threatened by a governmental or court decision, related to distance from the perceived threat. A linear measure of distance is normally used to determine this relational effect; however, there is no guarantee that the proportion of voters perceiving the threat or supporting the candidates declines in this manner. Until all other possible factors governing the voting decision are controlled, it is difficult to fit distance-decay equations to residuals from regressions of vote proportion and previously defined causal variables.

Three other possible sets of influences upon the voter are generally recognized. First, the influence of campaign efforts in changing a voter's preference or in swinging undecided voters has not been well documented. Based on British and American studies, we can conclude that only a small proportion of the voters are influenced by the campaign efforts, somewhere between 1 and 5% (Katz and Eldersveld, 1961; Crotty, 1971; A. H. Taylor, 1972; Price and Lupfer, 1973). The efforts examined have been personally oriented campaigning such as door-to-door, literature mailing, and telephone contact. Greatest response was seen in precincts where the campaigning party already had a comfortable majority. Undoubtedly the major impact of a voter canvas is on turnout (getting apathetic supporters to the polls), and it may not significantly affect the vote proportions in a sub-area, although it has important effects for the final result in a closely contested election. The variable effects of mass media campaign efforts are much more difficult to document. Recently, Minghi and Rumley (1978), in an intensive study of three local areas in Vancouver, documented the party campaign effort but were unable to make a definitive connection between party activity and voting behaviour, although they seemed to be positively related.

Second, the effects of national cleavages on vote choice are often transferred to the local level. In many nations rural and urban voters behave quite differently, Catholic and Protestant voters support different parties, regional divisions are evident, or ideological conflict based on a historical event is reflected in the vote totals. We can readily think of examples from Britain, West Germany, United States or Canada, and Ireland to match each of these suggested effects. One possibility of measuring the influence of national cleavages is to incorporate additional independent variables (often of the dummy variety) into the equation. An examination of the relative size of the regression weights will give an estimation of the importance of these divisions, relative to the social status variables.

Finally, truly local (for aggregate data) or personal (for individual data) deviations from voting trends, predicted on the basis of variables listed above, are difficult to isolate and incorporate into predictive models. Examination of the deviations (residuals) may suggest additional predictor variables but more often they are assigned to the error term or residual component. Ideally, the residual component will contain only errors in measurement but realistically we cannot expect to incorporate all influences into our vote choice models. From both a geographical and statistical perspective, it is important that the residuals meet the independence assumption so that we can be fairly confident that our model has accounted for any systematic variation in the residuals. Such systematic variation may be the result of an explanatory variable not included in the model and produce autocorrelation among the residuals. If we have taken all possible explanations into account, then we are faced with two choices: either eliminate the autocorrelation or measure it. Gould (1970) has argued that it is the interdependence of spatial units that makes them interesting in geographical analysis, and we should allow for its presence in our studies. In electoral geography, Reynolds and Archer (1969) have equated autocorrelation with contagion (a contextual effect). Unfortunately, we do not know how much of the positive autocorrelation is attributable to contagion processes, how much is caused by the exclusion of an independent variable, or how much is caused by other autocorrelated disturbances. Alternatively, we can modify the regression to remove the autocorrelation by transforming the original data. Cliff and Ord (1973), following on J. Johnston (1963), have shown that positive autocorrelation of the error terms in regression will result in an inflated value of the coefficient of multiple correlation, while negative autocorrelation leads to under-statement of the significance of the relationship. In the present problem, it was decided to attempt to remove the autocorrelation from the residuals as the only practical method available, since that would enable us to isolate the other causes of the contextual effect and by comparison of the first and recalibrated equations, we can obtain some measure of its significance from city to city.

Method of analysis

The choice of elections to be analysed was dictated by four considerations. First, cities were selected in more than one nation; second, partisan elections with candidates running for single-member seats were included, as well as a referendum and a partisan election with only a party choice; third, small area data had to be available for both election and census variables; and fourth, elections close to the census year, to minimize the temporal gap between the dates, were selected. To minimize differences due to size considerations (such as Cox's variable contextual effect as a function of city size), large cities were chosen. The cities and elections were Indianapolis (1970 population 792,299), 1970 State Senate elections; Detroit (1970 population 1,511,482), 1970 Private School Aid Referendum; Winnipeg (1971 population 540,262), 1973 Provincial Legislature elections; and Düsseldorf (1970 population 663,000), 1972 Bundestag elections. Two of these choices need explanation. The Detroit referendum asked voters to vote Yes or No on a state-wide proposal to prohibit financial aid from the state to private schools, mostly Catholic parochial institutions. This election was controversial and it divided the voters along religious and racial lines as few blacks attend private schools. Overall the proposition was upheld in Detroit by 196,960 to 187,676. The Bundestag election results analysed were for the Zweitestimmen or party vote. In German elections the voter chooses twice; the first is for a candidate in a single-member seat, while the second is for a party list. Thus, the personal vote effect is not a factor in the party list elections.

Since precincts are smaller than census tracts, they were agglomerated to match the larger divisions. A necessary assumption for boundaries that do not match is that the population is evenly distributed within precincts. In North America, electoral and census tract limits usually coincide and allocations can be computed for non-matching divisions, although some data errors are unavoidable. In Düsseldorf, census block data were agglomerated to *stimmbezirke* or voting districts with no boundary problems. The independent variables are the Republican percentage in Indianapolis, the Yes percentage (agreement to prohibit public aid to private schools) in Detroit, the New Democratic Party (NDP) percentage in Winnipeg and the Christian Democratic Union (CDU) percentage in Düsseldorf.

To provide a basis for an analysis, the independent variables were first tested for autocorrelation. In this test and in subsequent analyses, Moran's I coefficient was used, calculated from

$$I = \frac{n}{W} \left(\sum_i \sum_j w_{ij}\, z_i\, z_j \Big/ \sum_i z_i^2 \right) \tag{1}$$

where w_{ij} is a weight denoting the influence that the ith observation had on the jth, and z_i are deviations from the mean. The choice of weights for W, the weight matrix, is an important issue. Often the distances between the cell centroids are used; in this study, a 1-0 matrix was used, with contiguity being defined according to the rook's case. The autocorrelation coefficient *I* can be converted into a standard normal deviate using

$$z = \frac{I - E_I}{\sigma_I}$$

(2)

where the expected value of *I* is:

$$E_I = -\frac{1}{n - 1}$$

(3)

and

$$\sigma_I = $$

(4)

$$\frac{n[(n^2 - 3n + 3)S_1 + 3W^2 - nS_2] - k[(n^2 - n)S_1 - 2nS_2 + 6W^2]}{(n - 1)(n - 2)(n - 3)W^2}$$

where *k* is the kurtosis of the variable, S_1 is the distance between x_i and x_j, and S_2 is the distance from x_i to all neighbours. The significance of the standard normal deviate can be measured by reference to a table of critical values (Cliff and Ord, 1973).

The null hypothesis tested is that of randomization; given this set of x values, what is the probability that they could have been arranged in this way by chance? The significance level is $\alpha = 0.01$ in every instance, and with a two-tailed test the critical value of z at $\alpha = 0.01$ is 2.576 (-2.576). When testing the regression residuals for autocorrelation, a modified statistic based on a recomputed variance of *I* is necessary (Haggett et al., 1977, pp. 360-1).

To idenfity social, demographic, and cultural effects on voting, the independent variables were selected from the respective census reports. Rather than pick one measure for each effect, it was decided to use the principal components approach to collapse the variable sets into orthogonal dimensions. Only measures directly related to voting behaviour in past studies were selected: indirect measures, such as distance to nearest ghetto and distance to city centre, were not included since it is not clear on what conceptual grounds their relationship with voting behaviour is based. The selection of variables, identical for Indianapolis and Detroit and very similar for Winnipeg, was constrained by the narrower range available in the German census. Nevertheless all hypothesized effects were measured for each city (Tables 17.1-17.4). All variables were transformed to meet the requirements of normality and then standardized. The principal components scores were tested for autocorrelation before being entered into a multiple regression with the dependent variable. In each city, a cut-off of five

Table 17.1   Indianapolis principal axis factor solution

Variable	Loadings[a]					Communality
	PC 1	PC 2	PC 3	PC 4	PC 5	
Black percentage	−0.54		0.44			0.55
Old population	−0.44	0.69		0.35		0.81
Young population		−0.85				0.83
Single percentage			0.77			0.72
Married percentage	0.58	−0.51	−0.55			0.88
Foreign born	0.40	0.44				0.49
Foreign stock	0.56	0.49			0.44	0.65
German percentage	0.43	0.45			0.34	0.53
Hispanic percentage	−0.32					0.20
School children	0.38	−0.59	0.34	0.44		0.74
College population	0.64		0.40		−0.30	0.75
Fertility	−0.45	−0.30				0.55
Migration		−0.57				0.52
Unemployed percentage			−0.48	0.55		0.48
Women in labour force	−0.79					0.69
On Social Security	0.80					0.87
Professional employed	0.55				−0.37	0.37
Poor families	−0.58	−0.57				0.78
Medium education	−0.64	0.35				0.60
Medium income	0.91					0.90
Eigenvalue	7.01	3.39	2.35	1.54	1.20	
Cumulative percentage of total variance	33.4	49.5	60.7	68.1	73.8	
Autocorrelation coefficient *I*	1.97	1.19	0.954	0.632	0.647	
Standard normal deviate	16.36*	9.91*	7.99*	5.32*	5.45*	

[a]*Only those loadings* >0.30 *are shown.*
*Significant at $\alpha = 0.01$ level (two-tailed test).

components was suggested by eigenvalue (1.0) and variance explained (5%) thresholds, and account for 72-83% of the variance in the original data set (Tables 17.1-17.4).

   The linear regression model is appropriate since all requirements of the method were met, except the independence of residuals assumption. Since the values are standardized, no intercept value is present and the standardized regression coefficients indicate the relative strength of each independent variable. For Indianapolis and Winnipeg a distance measure (the square of the inverse of the straight-line distance from the centre of the census tract to the home of the candidate) was added to the independent variables, and in Detroit a measure of Catholic ethnicity (percentage of the population of foreign stock from the European Catholic nations)

Table 17.2   Detroit principal axis factor solution

Variable	Loadings[a]					Communality
	PC 1	PC 2	PC 3	PC 4	PC 5	
Black percentage	−0.81	−0.32				0.85
Old population		0.74	0.33		0.35	0.85
Young population	−0.58	−0.38	−0.56	0.38		0.97
Single percentage		0.42	0.75	0.40		0.96
Married percentage		0.43	0.58	0.47		0.79
Foreign born	0.73	0.38				0.76
Foreign stock	0.86	0.37	−0.30			1.0
Polish percentage	0.53		−0.38			0.52
Canadian percentage	0.64					0.53
School children		−0.31		0.65		0.61
College population	0.58			0.40		0.44
Fertility	−0.41					0.18
Migration			−0.31			0.47
Unemployed percentage	−0.68					0.82
Women in labour force		−0.59	0.35			0.25
On Social Security	0.34		−0.30			0.79
Professional employed	0.70		0.31		0.34	0.73
Poor families	−0.80					0.92
Medium education	0.64	−0.58	0.32			0.74
Medium income	0.75	−0.33				
Eigenvalue	6.68	2.90	2.54	1.72	1.09	
Cumulative percentage of total variance	33.4	47.9	60.7	69.3	74.8	
Autocorrelation coefficient *I*	1.712	1.210	1.563	1.037	0.802	
Standard normal deviate	22.16*	15.68*	20.34*	13.45*	10.41*	

[a]Only those loadings >0.30 are shown.
*Significant at $\alpha = 0.01$ level (two-tailed test).

was incorporated. A low level of multicollinearity existed between these and the previously defined dimensions. The size of the standard error of each independent variable was noted, and although we are not concerned with inferences to a population, the standard errors indicate the level of dispersion around the partial regression line and thus provide an indication of the goodness of fit.

The residuals from the regression equations were tested for autocorrelation. While the R^2 value may indicate a high level of explanation, autocorrelation among the residuals may indicate the deletion of an important independent variable or the operation of a contagious process between the data units. If autocorrelation is still present after analysis of the residuals and the addition of other variables to the equation, we must assume a contextual effect, a function of the grouping of the census tracts into communities.

Table 17.3 Winnipeg principal axis factor solution

Variable	Loadings[a]					Communality
	PC 1	PC 2	PC 3	PC 4	PC 5	
French percentage			−0.50		0.68	0.89
Old population	0.76	0.35				0.89
Young population	−0.70	0.32	−0.51			0.91
Single percentage	0.71	−0.52				0.90
Married percentage	0.39	0.53				0.76
Foreign born percentage	0.54	0.75				0.92
British Isles percentage	−0.35	0.69	0.47			0.87
German percentage		0.73				0.60
Ukrainian percentage		0.63	−0.41			0.77
Catholic percentage	0.31	0.34	−0.67			0.84
Jewish percentage					−0.41	0.58
School children	0.56					0.41
College population	0.70					0.50
Fertility	−0.75		−0.42	−0.46		0.87
Migration					0.42	0.62
Unemployed percentage	0.70		−0.34			0.64
Women in labour force		0.48	0.49	−0.71		0.99
Professional employed	−0.45		0.51	0.43		0.86
Family income	−0.76		0.34			0.98
Eigenvalue	5.18	4.11	3.10	2.53	1.62	
Cumulative percentage of total variance	22.5	40.4	53.9	64.9	72.0	
Autocorrelation coefficient I	0.929	0.492	0.987	0.358	1.12	
Standard normal deviate	5.83*	3.15*	6.18*	2.34*	7.00*	

[a]Only those loadings >0.30 are shown.
*Significant at $\alpha = 0.01$ level (two-tailed test).

Unlike the Reynolds and Archer (1969) study, rather than stopping at this point and suggesting the existence of a neighbourhood effect, we move to an alternative modelling approach, which involved the use of an autoregressive model.

With an autoregressive model, the value of the ith residual is predicted from the values of the residuals of the surrounding cells. Rather than using more predictor variables to reduce unexplained variance in the model, we use the neighbours of each cell in the equation

$$\epsilon_i = \varrho L \epsilon_i + \mu_i \qquad (5)$$

where $L\epsilon_i$ is a spatial lag operator and μ_i is a vector of residuals. ϱ (rho) is a measure of autocorrelation that can then be used to

Table 17.4 Düsseldorf principal axis factor solution

Variable	Loadings[a] PC 1	PC 2	PC 3	PC 4	PC 5	Communality
Foreign percentage	0.39		0.53			0.44
Young population	0.31	0.92				0.95
Old population	0.68	−0.30		−0.45		0.77
Single percentage	0.74	−0.44				0.88
Married percentage			0.74			0.66
Catholic percentage	0.70	0.60				0.89
School children		0.64	0.46	−0.36		0.79
College population					0.32	0.12
Fertility		0.96				0.95
Sex ratio	0.85	0.49				0.97
Professional employed	0.55		−0.67			0.86
On pension	0.64			−0.54		0.68
Subrenter percentage	0.32		0.36		0.30	0.35
Women in labour force	0.74					0.73
Eigenvalue	4.19	4.02	2.14	1.13	1.00	
Cumulative percentage of total variance	28.0	54.8	69.1	76.7	83.4	
Autocorrelation coefficient *I*	0.615	0.732	0.948	0.558	0.653	
Standard normal deviate	8.17*	9.69*	12.55*	7.41*	8.66*	

[a]Only those loadings >0.30 are shown.
*Significant at $\alpha = 0.01$ level (two-tailed test).

reconstruct the original variables. We must specify the lagged values. In time-series analysis the problem is confined to one dimension, but in spatial analyses it is very difficult to calculate the lagged values for other than a square lattice. In this study the average of the cell's neighbours was used as an estimate of the autocovariance, so that:

$$L\epsilon_i = \sum_j w_{ij} \overline{\epsilon_j} \qquad (6)$$

It is realized that some information is lost by this procedure, but given the data constraints it is a realistic method for calculating the neighbouring influence. As Johnston (1963) points out, estimates of ϱ through the use of ordinary least-squares will be biased because of autocorrelation of the error terms and correlation between the lagged dependent variable and the error terms. A maximum likelihood approach to estimate ϱ must be used. Frequently ϱ is equated to unity, but this procedure tends to over-adjust for autocorrelation and the subsequent β estimates, while unbiased, are inefficient (Cliff and Ord, 1973, pp. 102-4). In time-series analysis, ϱ is readily computed from the lagged values of the residuals and in any case lies between $+1$ and -1. Thus, making $\varrho = 1$, is a maximum estimate for the presence of autocorrelation (Hu, 1973, pp. 79-82). If the researcher has valid grounds to suspect a strong contagious process working to produce an electoral pattern, either in conjunction with or independent of the social effect, this unity estimate of ϱ would compensate (probably over-compensate) for the process.

A non-linear estimation procedure of the parameters in the model of equation (5) was computed using the P3R procedure, available in the BMDP-77, (*BMDP-77*, pp. 461-83). The parameters are estimated using an iterative algorithm. When the solution converges (within three iterations in each instance), the estimate of ϱ was then substituted into the original equation using the Cochrane-Orcott procedure (Mather, 1976, pp. 89-93). Thus, the original equation

$$\gamma_i = \beta_1 x_{1i} + \beta_2 x_{2i} + \ldots \beta_5 x_{5i} + \epsilon_i \tag{7}$$

becomes

$$\gamma_i - \varrho L \gamma i = \beta_1 (x_{1i} - \varrho L x_{1i}) + \beta_2 (x_{2i} - \varrho L x_{2i}) + \ldots$$
$$\beta_5 (x_{5i} - \varrho L x_{5i}) + \mu_i \tag{8}$$

Each of the independent and the dependent variables is also lagged using the average values of the contiguous cells. No statistics or tests are given for the significance of this fit since this averaging method may distort the distribution. However, the standard errors for the regression coefficients of the recalibrated model should be lower than those of the original equation if the autocorrelation that was present is not filtered through the use of ϱ. Furthermore, we can test the residuals from this final model for autocorrelation to see if it has been removed. We would expect a reduction in the R^2 value since the OLS line is, by definition, the best fit line (Mather, 1976, p. 93).

By this rather long procedure, our original model which included measures of social, demographic, cultural, and relative distance effects on voting behaviour is now a more accurate estimation of these effects because any contextual effects have been eliminated through the autoregressive procedure. Returning to our original voting model, we have not taken campaign efforts into the equation but, given the elections under study here, they are not expected to exert a significant variable influence between census tracts. Obviously we cannot be certain that we have included all the necessary predictor variables in the regression equation and, thus, cannot be sure that our regression coefficients are unbiased estimates of the true effect of the respective variables. Nevertheless, the method goes a long way towards elimination of a major complicating factor, that produced by interdependence between the aggregate units.

Analysis

After the initial selection of the independent variables, they were inserted into a principal components model with no rotation. The component scores were then regressed against the dependent voting variable and the residuals from these equations mapped. Based on the residual patterns, additional variables were included in the principal components analysis so that all possible explanatory factors of voting behaviour would be included in the analysis, the results shown in Tables 17.1-17.4 are those from the recomputations after the variables addition.

   The principal components, as expected, are dimensions of social, demographic, and ethnic composition, similar from city to city and to previous results for the same cities (Reynolds and Archer, 1969; R. J. Johnston, 1971; Herbert, 1972). Each set of component scores was tested for spatial autocorrelation under the assumptions outlined above. All were significantly autocorrelated, an expected result since the social and economic processes governing the residential location of individuals in capitalist cities produce consistent patterns of segregation (Johnston, 1971; Eyles, 1978). The size of the standard normal deviate (z value) gives a measure of the intensity of the segregation. Not unexpectedly the components for Detroit show higher autocorrelation than those in other cities, since its historical development has been characterized by strong neighbourhood identification, intense segregation of racial and ethnic groups, and an evident inner/outer-city social and economic cleavage (Sinclair and Thompson, 1976). Both Winnipeg and Düsseldorf have lower z values, a reflection of the absence of non-white populations, the inclusion of suburbs within the city and a more active governmental role in city development. It must be remembered that contiguity measures are strongly affected by scale: the finer the scale, the larger the index or z value (Reynolds and Archer, 1969). In this study the census tracts for Detroit, Winnipeg, and Indianapolis are approximately equal in size (about

3500-5000) but the Düsseldorf voting districts are much smaller (average size 1438 people). Thus, the size of the spatial autocorrelation in the Düsseldorf dimensions is probably magnified compared to the other cities.

The level of explanation of the vote percentages due to the five components (and distance variables for Winnipeg and Indianapolis) varied significantly. In voting studies, referenda returns are easier to predict because they are not complicated by personality, party or (often) campaign efforts. With the addition of a variable measuring ethnicity to the Detroit equation, the R^2 rose from 0.631 to 0.662, although there is some multicollinearity between this additional predictor and principal components 1 and 3 (0.669 and -0.272 simple correlation coefficients, respectively). Because the assumption of orthogonality assumption was violated, no further analysis with this ethnic variable was pursued. Much of its independent effect on the vote for public aid to private schools was incorporated into principal component 1, and including this variable in further analyses is redundant (Gordon, 1968).

The successes of the models for Detroit and Indianapolis are in line with other studies of this kind for American cities (Reynolds and Archer, 1969; Brunn and Hoffman, 1970; McPhail, 1971) but the low R^2 values for Winnipeg and Düsseldorf require some consideration. Numerous studies of Canadian voting behaviour have shown that social class plays a less important role in determining voting choice there than in other parliamentary democracies. Region, religion, and ethnicity significantly alter the basic social class-vote choice relationship (Alford, 1963; Scarrow, 1965; Anderson, 1966; Gagne and Regenstreif, 1967; Schwartz, 1974). The urban working-class vote is split between the NDP and the Liberals. A combination of factors (including the absence of policy conflict, non-partisan posture of organized interest groups, dominance of non-economic correlates of partisan preference, low image differential, low party identification, low policy polarization among respective supporters and wide swings of the electoral pendulum) all contribute to low levels of explanation when using aggregate data. Recently, the NDP has become more class-based, leading to the strange phenomenon of a 'class-based party in what is not a class-voting system' (Van Loom and Whittington, 1976, p. 266). The party's support is greatest in the western cities of Canada, particularly in Winnipeg, where it is the strongest party. Winnipeg itself has been characterized by strong ethnic-based voting for members of the same group, a function of the presence of large numbers of economically and socially competitive immigrants. In elections with few issues (particularly local and provincial races) the ethnic factor becomes more important *vis-à-vis* the class factor (K. W. Taylor and Wiseman, 1974, 1977). The results of this Winnipeg analysis closely match those for Simmons (1967) for London, Ontario, in the directions of the regression coefficients and approximate strength of the relationship.

Few comparative studies of the aggregate election results of German elections have been completed: the vast majority are of national survey results (Liepelt, 1971; Urwin, 1974; Kaase, 1976). Two aggregate studies of election district and census data confirm the general results for Düsseldorf (Table 17.5). In both Marburg (a small university city) and Munich, the CDU/CSU was strongest in areas of high Catholic population, middle-income and middle-level employees, and older populations. They compete with the SPD for the worker vote and with the FDP for the high income vote (Ganzer, 1966; Eichler and Stäblein, 1975). The R^2 values for these two studies are much higher than that given here (0.309) but both studies violate many of the assumptions of multiple regression, particularly multicollinearity among the independent variables. Party choice in West Germany is strongly related to nine cleavages (class, religion, education, income, trade union membership, urban-rural divisions, region, sex, and age) with church attendance, the single most important influence (Laux and Simms, 1973; Urwin, 1974). Our measure of religion, Catholic percentage of the population, is not adequate to measure the church-attendance factor, which is more important than religious denomination or socioeconomic status. Unlike North American maps of voting returns, characterized by large homogeneous voting regions within cities, similar displays for German cities show highly localized patterns corresponding, in part, to housing estates of different social status (Ganzer, 1966; Maier et al., 1977). This pattern is reflected in the z values of the autocorrelation coefficient in the voting data (Table 17.5), which is lower than the two American cities but higher than Winnipeg, a probable reflection of *stimmbezirk* (voting district) size. The absence of strong social segregation in German cities, in turn reflected in the absence of strong electoral segregation, would seem to lessen a neighbourhood effect and produce a weaker relationship between social status and electoral choice.

Although the regression coefficients for all variables are shown in Table 17.5, only those with a *t* value ratio (beta weight/standard error) greater than 2 are discussed. All of the partial regressions are in the hypothesized direction, such that for Detroit, the Yes vote to prohibit public aid to private schools is negatively related to socioeconomic status (PC 1), family status (PC 2), positively related

Table 17.5   Calibration of multiple regression model (component scores with vote proportions)

(i) Component scores with vote proportions

City	Dependent	Independent						R^2
		PC 1	PC 2	PC 3	PC 4	PC 5	Inverse of distance	
Indianapolis	Rep. percentage	0.517 (0.05)*	0.216 (0.05)*	−0.297 (0.07)*	−0.079 (0.08)	0.126 (0.08)	0.361 (0.06)*	0.550
Detroit	'Yes' percentage	−0.395 (0.03)*	−0.413 (0.03)*	0.478 (0.03)*	−0.126 (0.03)*	0.137 (0.03)*	—	0.631
Winnipeg	NDP percentage	0.277 (0.10)*	0.149 (0.44)	−0.115 (0.12)	0.154 (0.31)	0.353 (0.26)	0.068 (0.32)	0.195
Düsseldorf	CDU percentage	0.286 (0.04)*	−0.257 (0.04)*	−0.215 (0.04)*	0.276 (0.04)*	0.234 (0.05)	—	0.309

Figures in parentheses are the standard errors of the regression coefficients.
*Significant at $\alpha = 0.05$ level (one-tailed test).

(ii) Autocorrelation in dependent variable

	Autocorrelation coefficient	Standard normal deviate	Number of cases
Indianapolis	1.271	10.597*	183
Detroit	1.666	21.564*	420
Winnipeg	1.334	8.298*	106
Düsseldorf	0.849	11.244*	438

*Significant at $\alpha = 0.05$ level (one-tailed test).

to racial status (PC 3), and negatively related to the ethnic percentage. The influence of the 'friends and neighbours' variable, the inverse of distance to the candidate's home, differed strongly in strength between Indianapolis and Winnipeg, reflecting the fact that many candidates do not live in their districts in the Canadian city, and the greater role of party as a factor in voting there. In local and state races in American cities, personality of the candidates gains in importance against party label. Socioeconomic status provides the most important relationship in each city, asserting to its influence on voting in Western cities regardless of the nature of the election.

Based on the size of the standard errors, the Winnipeg model stands out as a particularly poor fit. The reason for this was not apparent from an examination of the intercorrelations between the component scores but a map of the regression residuals showed clustering within legislative district boundaries. Obviously there is a candidate effect in operation based on differential appeal above or below that of their party. One possible explanation is the division of the 106 census tracts into 27 legislative districts, or an average of 3.9 district. Many of the census tracts are split by legislative boundaries so that, while in reality there may be a strong relationship between NDP candidate percentage and social variables, it will be diluted because the votes of two or more NDP candidates are averaged to compute the NDP percentage for the census tract. Given the nature of this study (Manitoba provincial legislature elections), it is difficult to take differential candidate appeal between legislative districts into consideration. However, it might be informative to recompute the regression equation using data for elections based on larger districts, such as the Federal constituencies.

The residuals from the multiple regressions are significantly autocorrelated for each city, with the standard normal deviates (z

Table 17.6   Autocorrelation of residuals from multiple regressions

City	Autocorrelation coefficient	Standard normal deviate	Rho (ϱ) estimate
Indianapolis	0.9778	8.18*	0.230
Detroit	0.6518	8.48*	0.707
			0.787
Winnipeg	1.2912	8.03*	0.892
Düsseldorf	0.5782	7.68*	0.431

*Significant at $\alpha = 0.01$ level (two-tailed test).

values) clustering around 8.0 (Table 17.6). These are reduced for each city from the original z values of the dependent variables, except for Winnipeg. The better the fit of the regression equation, the greater the reduction in the autocorrelation. One of the requirements of the multiple regression model, randomness among the error terms, is still violated. The addition of the ethnic variable to the Detroit regression reduced the standard normal deviate (z) to 7.53, still showing significantly autocorrelated residuals. To remove this element of interdependence between the data units, an autoregression approach was used to calculate ϱ, the auto-correlation function which could then be used to recalibrate the multiple regression equation and to produce a less biased estimate of the effects of these social components on voting choice.

The autoregression approach

The estimate of ϱ, an autocorrelation index, was derived using the procedure outlined above. Detroit differed from the other cities in that it required two iterations of the Cochrane-Orcott method before a result that did not indicate autocorrelated residuals was obtained. Thus, the initial ϱ estimate of 0.707 became 0.787 after the revised procedure. The ϱ values were then used to calibrate the least-squares equation (8) and the final model parameters are shown in Table 17.7.

  As expected, the R^2 values dropped in three of the cities but rose in the case of Winnipeg. While not uncommon in recalibrations of this type (Cliff and Ord, 1973, p. 128), this increase indicates the presence of a substantial disturbance among the independent variables in Winnipeg, so that when this disturbance is removed through the elimination of autocorrelation, the multiple-regression model provides a better fit. This explanation is substantiated by the above comments on the effect of election boundaries in the census tract database. Because the lack of correspondence between the two sets of lines has the effect of splitting homogeneous electoral groups into different data-calls and the autoregression approach uses the cell's neighbours to compute the interdependence effect, evidence of a neighbourhood or contextual effect is suggested. In other cities we would expect the autoregression method to remove a contextual effect and generally to reduce the R^2 values. In Detroit, Indianapolis, and Düsseldorf, the vote totals in a district are not only caused by the characteristic of the individuals living there but also are affected by the populations of the surrounding districts, a common occurrence in cities where electoral districts

Table 17.7   Calibration of the multiple regressions using rho (ϱ) estimates

City	Dependent	Independent variables						R^2
		PC 1	PC 2	PC 3	PC 4	PC 5	Inverse of distance	
Indianapolis	Rep. percentage	0.013 (0.06)	0.198 (0.06)*	−0.007 (0.07)	0.069 (0.06)	−0.356 (0.07)*	0.184 (0.06)*	0.215
Detroit	'Yes' percentage	−0.411 (0.03)*	−0.390 (0.03)*	0.481 (0.03)*	−0.150 (0.03)*	0.125 (0.03)*	—	0.549
Winnipeg	NDP percentage	0.346 (0.10)*	−0.306 (0.09)*	−0.916 (0.12)	−0.361 (0.06)*	0.070 (0.21)	0.170 (0.01)*	0.298
Düsseldorf	CDU percentage	0.279 (0.04)*	−0.246 (0.05)*	−0.116 (0.05)*	0.217 (0.04)*	0.152 (0.05)*	—	0.104

Figures in parentheses are the standard errors of the regression coefficients.
* Significant at $\alpha = 0.05$ level (one-tailed test).

Table 17.8   Autocorrelation of residuals from modified multiple regressions

City	Autocorrelation coefficient	Standard normal deviate
Indianapolis	−0.0098	−0.034
Detroit	0.4581	5.978*
	0.0081	1.343
Winnipeg	−0.2921	−1.637
Düsseldorf	−0.1150	−1.439

*Significant at $\alpha = 0.01$ level (two-tailed test).

are simply convenient data-gathering subunits of a larger socio-spatial group.

The estimation of the effects of the explanatory variables on the vote proportions using the ϱ estimation is significantly better. For Winnipeg, the standard errors are greatly reduced, confirming previous statements on neighbouring effects. In the other cities, while the beta weights are generally smaller, the associated standard errors are smaller or the same. The directions of the relationships remain stable, except in Winnipeg. An examination of the residuals revealed those for Detroit to be significantly positively autocorrelated while those for the other three cities did not differ significantly from the null hypothesis of zero autocorrelation (Table 17.8). It is now assumed that the parameters provided unbiased estimates of the effects of these components on voting proportions since the model now meets all of the requirements of the linear regression model (Poole and O'Farrell, 1971). To calculate the unbiased estimates for Detroit, the autoregression-substitution procedure was repeated, again using the residuals from the neighbours of a cell in the maximum likelihood estimation of ϱ. The final calibration of the Detroit model is shown in Table 17.7 with the two sets of autocorrelation coefficients shown in Table 17.8. (The beta weights hardly changed between the two iterations.)

Discussion

This long procedure, repeated for four large data sets, yielded initial and unbiased estimates of the effects of two sets of variables (social and 'friends and neighbours') on voting behaviour. It does not provide a quantitative index of a contextual effect, nor does it provide a reliable estimate of any campaign efforts and other local, especially pre-election, trends. What then is its value to electoral geographers?

This study has shown that regression models of voting behaviour that ignore interdependence among the data units will probably produce biased and inaccurate reflections on the true relationships between vote choice and predictor variables. If some previous aggregate studies of voting behaviour were to be reworked, we might see quite different results. Cliff and Ord (1969) have provided an easily computed estimate of ϱ that does not require the use of lengthy maximum-likelihood methods. At a minimum we should recalibrate our models using the autocorrelation coefficient (Moran's I statistic) as ϱ to remove the effects of interaction between the data-cells. Since ϱ comprises all interaction effects, it includes, in voting studies, contextual and other effects. If we could derive some method of partitioning ϱ into contextual and other causes, we could obtain an approximation of the proportion of spatial autocorrelation due to interactions between the aggregate units; that due to such factors as data errors, or aggregation adjustments; and that due to random causes.

Regardless of the sophistication of our methods, we must continue to question and modify our basic theoretical assumptions. One of the most immediate considerations is our near-exclusive use of linear models. As Gould (1970) suggested, we transform our data so that they meet the requirements of linear models without examining the relationships for underlying structure and theoretical significance in their non-linear state. The relationship between class and party is often non-linear, such as that for the CDU support and social status in West Germany — an inverted U relationship. Political scientists have shown that, in certain electoral situations, power relationships of the multiplicative form give better predictions of vote choice than linear models of the additive form (Soares and Hamblin, 1967). For controversial candidates such as George Wallace (and in controversial referenda), voters move away from the stable social infrastructure of the established parties to vote in blocs which cut across social structures and party alignments (Burnham and Sprague, 1970). In elections of this kind, Czudnowski (1976, p. 98) suggests that feelings of hostility and threat are related to interactions with individuals and groups who are perceived as objects of hostility or sources of threat. We should expect a larger role for contextual effects, relative to social or historical determinants, as a result of the interaction of 'threatening' and 'threatened' group.

As pointed out earlier, variables measuring social class provide the most consistent predictors of party choice. If our goal is to maximize the R^2 value and gain easier interpretation of the relationship, we should probably use the individual predictor variables rather than composite indices based on the results of a principal components analysis. The choice of these predictor variables may be derived from their consistency in a factor analysis or, preferably, based on some model of national electoral behaviour. The studies reported in Dogan and Rose (1971), Rose (1974) and Budge *et al.* (1976) provide excellent starting points for the selection of predictors. However, use of single variables produces complications that may preclude their use. First, multicollinearity is undoubtedly a major problem. Second, a concept such as social status is not readily measured by a single index. Social class is multi-dimensional and should be measured as such (Sartori, 1969). Third, any index of social class we produce from aggregate data is unlikely to be totally representative of the subjective self-classification of the voters (Thompson, 1970). Alford (1963) hypothesized that deviations from the social class/party relationship are a function of party orientation, class structure, and party historical development. Without survey data these complications cannot be adequately tested for their importance between nations.

Calculation of spatial autocorrelation coefficients in electoral geography also raises a number of conceptual issues. As Cliff and Ord (1973) have emphasized, the choice of weights measuring the neighbouring effect is very important. In this study they were considered a function of contact: 1 if cells were contiguous and 0 otherwise. An isotrophic surface (distance is irrelevant) was assumed. We know, however, that interaction over distance is not isotrophic but declines in a fairly regular manner. In urban neighbourhoods interaction is not only a function of distance but also of life-style, ethnicity, and neighbourhood stability (Keller, 1968; Bell and Newby, 1976). We should give thought to our choice of weight in the light of these results. Perhaps a combination of boundary contact and distance, such as the Dacey statistic (Dacey, 1965) should be our weight, modified by a value indicating the probability of contact as a function of the social composition of the census tract. Although this would require detailed calculations of the autocorrelation weights, it is justified by their importance, especially in a situation where interaction is assumed to occur. As Gattrell (1979) has shown, we might accept the null hypothesis of zero autocorrelation with one set of weights but not with another. In contrast to weight selection, there appears to be no strong rationale for second-order lagging in autoregressive procedures since, as researchers such as Cox (1971) have argued, even the census tract itself may be too large a unit to detect contagion between voters living in different cells.

As well as methodological questions, a number of important conceptual issues are raised by the present approaches now used to analyse election returns. Undoubtedly the 'sitting member' effect is an important determinant of the size of the residual from the regression fit. In Australian and New Zealand elections, incumbents tend to benefit from name recognition and receive a vote greater than that predicted for their party (Forrest *et al.*, 1977). As Ferejohn (1977) has shown, incumbency is growing in the United States: a measure of the candidate's tenure in public office could easily be incorporated into an explanatory model and might reduce auto-correlation, leaving only a true contextual effect and not that partly caused by the grouping of a candidate's personal votes or by name recognition because of the absence of other voting cues (as in non-partisan ballots). In this study this incumbent factor was particularly important in Winnipeg and the addition of a dummy variable (incumbent or not) raised the R^2 value of the first model from 0.195 to 0.365.

The identification of a clear contextual effect using only aggregate data still eludes electoral geographers. Various possibilities using regression models come to mind, but all suffer from conceptual or methodological defects. If contiguity of residuals from a regression model is not contagion, indicative of a neighbourhood effect, then what can cause it? Exclusion of predictor variables and mis-specification of the nature of the relationship (linear instead of non-linear) provide possible answers. Experimentation with variable selection and model form could reduce these problems. Conceptually, we would expect suburban areas to show high levels of interaction and consequently, conversion. However, R. J. Johnston (1977) found no relationship of family status to the residuals from a social model of voting behaviour. In general, we will not discover such relationships because the predictor variables will include measures of life-cycle status, and in regression, there is no relationship between the residuals and the independent variables. Mapping the residuals, while strongly suggestive of a neighbourhood effect if high positive values cluster, does not provide an adequate measure of the phenomenon (see Scanlan, 1977 and R. J. Johnston, 1977).

A method suggests itself in our effort to detect contextual effects. In this study variables were standardized in the belief that it was important to show their relative strength. If they are not standardized and the intercept value derived, it represents an important value in electoral geographical research. Assuming careful selection of the variables to eliminate social, incumbent, distance, and party effects, the α value represents something of an initial advantage or disadvantage for a party. The city could be divided into community areas (groups of census tracts) and the model calibrated for each community. The null hypothesis is no significant difference in the α values between the regions. Neighbourhoods characterised by positive α values may experience a contextual effect and could be examined in that light for evidence of social and political interaction.

A conceptual problem in using aggregate data to study political context is that the contextual effect itself is essentially the product of a group effort on an individual. We put the affected individuals into groups, making what should be an individual focus, an aggregate examination. We then have possible aggregation bias, produced by differences between the specification bias of aggregate and individual level estimation. This aggregation bias may change the relative variances of dependent and independent variables and affects the expected values of standardized measures, like correlation coefficients and beta weights (see Langbein and Lichtman, 1978, p. 33ff.). Additionally, we assume that individuals living in heterogeneous census tracts behave in a similar fashion and are subject to similar influences as voters living in homogeneous neighbourhoods. Yet all the evidence points to the opposite, different interaction intensity and pattern (Keller, 1968). One possibility of identifying the effect of heterogeneity, presumably a function of scale, would be to calibrate the same model at a different scale, which should consist of small units such as census tracts and precincts. As Reynolds and Archer (1969) showed, autocorrelation coefficients are magnified as the size of the data-cell is reduced. Unfortunately, we cannot get complete census data for units smaller than census tracts to calibrate the model — but complete census data for German cities, for example, are available for blocks. We should expect a higher level of explanation of the variance in the dependent variable since heterogeneity is minimized, but the autocorrelation among the residuals should not be unduly affected by the independent variables, allowing a comparison of its value between the two scales. If contagion is present as a result of political interaction, we would expect it to be greater at the larger scale (smaller data-cells) since cell interaction will be more evident.

About a decade ago, Cox (1969a, 1971, 1972) found 11% of the vote explained by contextual effects but other studies of this sort have not been completed in sufficient numbers to verify this result. Burstein (1976) and Wolfe and Burghardt (1978), have recently attempted to verify the flow of political information between individuals over space and how it varies with the characteristics of the candidates concerned. Within the whole voting population, the contextual effect may not be very important in determining the outcome since a contextual vote in one part of the city (say, in Democratic strongholds) may be counterbalanced by a similar vote in Republican areas. Nevertheless, if we wish to understand fully why people choose candidates as they do, we must isolate and measure a possible contextual effect.

Acknowledgements

I am indebted to the Alexander von Humboldt-Stiftung for support during the 1978-9 academic year at the University of Düsseldorf, and to Professor G. Glebe of the Geographisches Institut for his assistance in providing a stimulating and profitable work environment. The initial research was supported by a travel grant from the Center for International Comparative Studies of the University of Illinois. Thanks are also due to Marc Armstrong for his assistance with computer programming.

References and bibliography

Aiken, M. (1976). 'Urban social structure and political competition: a comparative study of local politics in four European nations', in Walton, J., and Massotti, L. H. (eds.), *The City in Comparative Perspective,* pp. 119-53 (Sage, New York).

Alford, R. (1963). *Party and Society: The Anglo-American Democracies* (Rand McNally, Chicago).

Anderson, G. (1966). 'Voting behavior and ethnic and religious variables', *Canadian Journal of Economics and Political Science,* **32,** 27-37.

Bell, C., and Newby, A. (1976). 'Community, communion, class and community action: the society sources of the new urban politics', in *Social Areas in Cities,* vol. 2 *(Spatial Perspectives on Problems and Policies),* pp. 189-207 (Wiley, New York).

Berelson, B. R., Lazarsfeld, P. F., and McPhee, W. (1954). *Voting* (University of Chicago Press, Chicago).

Biel, H. S. (1972). 'Suburbia and voting behavior in the London metropolitan area: an alternative perspective', *Tijdschrift voor Economische en Sociale Geographie,* **63,** 39-43.

Blake, D. E. (1978). 'Constituency contexts and Canadian elections', *Canadian Journal of Political Science,* **11,** 279-305.

Blydenburgh, J. C. (1971). 'A controlled experiment to measure the effects of personal contact campaigning', *Midwest Journal of Political Science.* **15,** 365-81.

BMDP-77 Biomedical Computer Programs (1977). (University of California, Berkeley).

Brunn, S. D., and Hoffman, W. L. (1970). 'The spatial response of Negroes and Whites toward open housing: the Flint referendum', *Annals of the Association of American Geographers,* **60,** 18-36.

Budge, I., Crewe, I., and Fairlie, D. (eds.) (1976). *Party Identification and Beyond: Representations of Voting and Party Competition* (Wiley, London).

Burnham, W. D., and Sprague, J. (1970). 'Additive and multiplicative models of the voting universe: the case of Pennsylvania, 1960-1968', *American Political Science Review,* **64,** 471-90.

Burstein, P. (1976). 'Social networks and voting: some Israeli data'. *Social Forces,* **54,** 833-47.

Cliff, A. D., and Ord, J. K. (1969). 'The problem of spatial autocorrelation', in Scott, A. J. (ed.), *London Papers in Regional Science,* pp. 25-55 (Pion, London).

Cliff, A. D., and Ord, J. K. (1973). *Spatial Autocorrelation* (Pion, London).

Cliff, A. D., and Ord, J. K. (1975). 'The comparison of means when samples consist of spatially autocorrelated observations', *Environment and Planning, A,* **7,** 725-34.

Cox, K. R. (1968). 'Suburbia and voting behavior in the London metropolitan area', *Annals of the Association of American Geographers,* **58,** 111-27.

Cox, K. R. (1969a). 'The spatial structuring of information flows and partisan attitudes', in Dogan, M., and Rokkan, S. (eds.), *Quantitative Ecological Analysis in the Social Sciences,* pp. 157-85 (MIT Press, Cambridge, Mass.).

Cox, K. R. (1969b). 'The voting decision in a spatial context', *Progress in Geography,* **1,** 81-117.

Cox, K. R. (1971). 'The spatial components of urban voting response surfaces', *Economic Geography,* **47,** 27-35.

Cox, K. R. (1972). 'The neighborhood effect in urban voting response surfaces', in Sweet, D. C. (ed.), *Models of Urban Structure,* pp. 159-76 (D. C. Heath & Co., Lexington, Mass.).

Crotty, W. J. (1971). 'Party effort and its impact on the vote', *American Political Science Review,* **65,** 439-50.

Czudnowski, M. M. (1976). *Comparing Political Behavior* (Sage, Beverley Hills).

Dacey, M. F. (1965). 'A review of measures of contiguity for two and K-color maps', in *Technical Report No. 2, Spatial Diffusion Study* (Department of Geography, Northwestern University, Evanston, Ill.).

Dogan, M., and Rose, R. (eds.) (1971). *European Politics: A Reader* (Little, Brown, Boston).

Eichler, G., and Stäblein, G. (1975). 'Quantitativ-geographische Analyse des Wahlverhaltens am Beispiel der Universitätsstadt Marburg', *Geographische Zeitschrift,* **63,** 81-103.

Ennis, P. (1962). 'The contextual dimension in voting', in McPhee, W., and Glaser, W. (eds.), *Public Opinion and Congressional Elections,* pp. 180-211 (Free Press, New York).

Epstein, L. K. (1979). 'Individual and contextual effects on partisanship', *Social Science Quarterly,* **60,** 314-22.

Eyles, J. (1978). 'Social geography and the study of the capitalist city; a review', *Tijdschrift voor Economische en Sociale Geographie,* **69,** 296-305.

Ferejohn, J. A. (1977). 'On the decline of competition in congressional elections', *American Political Science Review,* **71,** 166-76.

Forrest, J., Marjoribanks, E., and Johnston, R. J. (1977). 'Local effects at New Zealand local elections', in Johnston, R. J. (ed.), *People, Places and Votes: Essays on the Electoral Geography of Australia and New Zealand,* pp. 35-50 (University of New England, Department of Geography, Armidale, NSW).

Gagne, W., and Regenstreif, P. (1967). 'Some aspects of New Democratic Party urban support in 1965', *Canadian Journal of Economic and Political Science,* **33,** 529-50.

Ganzer, K. (1966). *Sozialgeographische Gliederung der Stadt München aufgrund der Verhaltensweisen der Bevölkerung bei politischen Wahlen,* (Geographische Hefte, Universität München, No. 28, Munich).

Gattrell, A. C. (1979). 'Autocorrelation in spaces', *Environment and Planning, A,* **11,** 507-16.

Geary, R. C. (1968). 'The contiguity ratio and statistical mapping', in Berry, B. J. L., and Marble, D. F. (eds.), *Spatial Analysis,* pp. 461-78 (Prentice-Hall, Englewood Cliffs, NJ).

Gordon, R. A. (1968). 'Issues in multiple regression', *American Journal of Sociology,* **73,** 592-616.

Gould, P. (1970). 'Is Statistix Inferens the geographical name for a wild goose', *Economic Geography* (Supplement), **46,** 439-48.

Haggett, P., Cliff, A. D., and Frey, A. (1977). *Locational Analysis in Human Geography,* vol. 2 *(Locational Methods)* (Edward Arnold, London).

Herbert, D. (1972). *Urban Geography: A Social Perspective* (Praeger, New York).

Hu, T. W. (1973). *Econometrics: An Introductory Analysis* (University Park Press, Baltimore).

Irvine, W. P. (1972). 'The measurement of regionalism in Canadian voting patterns', *Canadian Journal of Political Science,* **5,** 55-81.

Johnston, J. (1963). *Econometric Methods* (McGraw-Hill, New York).

Johnston, R. J. (1971). *Urban Residential Patterns: An Introductory Review* (Bell, London).

Johnston, R. J. (1974). 'Local effects in voting at a local election', *Annals of the Association of American Geographers,* **64,** 418-29.

Johnston, R. J. (1976). 'Contagion in neighborhoods: a note on problems of modelling and analysis', *Environment and Planning, A,* **8,** 581-6.

Johnston, R. J. (1976). 'Political behavior and the residential mosaic', in Herbert, D. T., and Johnston, R. J. (eds.), *Social Areas in Cities,* vol. 2 *(Spatial Perspectives on Problems and Policies),* pp. 65-88 (Wiley, New York).

Johnston, R. J. (1977). 'Congatious processes and voting patterns: Christchurch, 1969-1972', in Johnston, R. J. (ed.), *People, Places and Votes: Essays on the Electoral Geography of Australia and New Zealand,* pp. 11-34 (University of New England, Department of Geography, Armidale, NSW).

Johnston, R. J., and White, P. E. (1977). 'Reactions to foreign workers in Switzerland: an essay in electoral geography', *Tijdschrift voor Economische en Sociale Geographie,* **68,** 341-54.

Kaase, M. (1976). 'Party identification and voting behavior in the West German election of 1969', in Budge, I., Grave, I., and Fairlie, D. (eds.), *Party Identification and Beyond: Representations of Voting and Party Competition,* pp. 81-102 (Wiley, London).

Kasperson, R. (1969). 'On suburbia and voting behavior', *Annals of the Association of American Geographers,* **59,** 405-11.

Katz, D., and Eldersveld, S. (1961). 'The impact of local party activity upon the electorate', *Public Opinion Quarterly,* **25,** 1-24.

Keller, S. (1968). *The Urban Neighborhood: A Sociological Perspective* (Random House, New York).

Key, V. O., Jr. (1949). *Southern Politics in State and Nation* (Alfred P. Knopf, New York).

Langbein, L. I., and Lichtman, A. J. (1978). *Ecological Inference,* Sage University Paper series on Quantitative Applications in the Social Sciences 07-010 (Sage, Beverly Hills).

Laux, H. D., and Simms, A. (1973). 'Parliamentary elections in West Germany: the geography of political choice', *Area,* **5,** 166-71.

Lazarsfeld, P. F., Berelson, B. R., and Gaudet, H. (1944). *The People's Choice* (Columbia University Press, New York).

Liepelt, K. (1971). 'The infra-structure of party support in Germany and Austria', in Dogan, M., and Rose, R. (eds.), *European Politics: A Reader,* pp. 183-201 (Little, Brown, Boston).

Maier, J., Paesler, P., Ruppert, K., and Schaffer, F. (1977). *Sozialgeographie* (Westermann, Braunschweig).

Mather, P. M. (1976). *Computational Methods of Multivariate Analysis in Physical Geography* (Wiley, London).

McPhail, I. R. (1971). 'The vote for Mayor of Los Angeles in 1969', *Annals of the Association of American Geographers,* **61,** 744-58.

Minghi, J. V., and Rumley, D. (1978). 'Toward a geography of campaigning: some evidence from a provincial election in Vancouver, British Columbia', *Canadian Geographer,* **22,** 145-62.

Poole, M. A., and O'Farrell, P. N. (1971). 'The assumptions of the linear regression model', *Transactions of the Institute of British Geographers,* **52,** 73-98.

Price, D. E., and Lupfer, M. (1973). 'Volunteers for Gore: the impact of a precinct-level canvass in three Tennessee cities', *Journal of Politics,* **35,** 410-38.

Reynolds, D. R. (1974). 'Spatial contagion in political influence processes', in Cox, K. R., Reynolds, D. R., and Rokkan, S. (eds.), *Locational Approaches to Power and Conflict,* pp. 233-73 (Halsted, New York).

Reynolds, D. R., and Archer, J. C. (1969). *An Inquiry into the Spatial Basis of Electoral Geography,* Discussin Paper 11 (University of Iowa, Department of Geography).

Rokkan, S. (1970). *Citizens, Elections, Parties* (David McKay, New York).

Rose, R. (ed.). (1974). *Electoral Behavior: A Comparative Handbook* (Free Press, New York).

Rumley, D., and Minghi, J. V. (1977). 'A geographical framework for the study of stability and change of urban electoral patterns', *Tijdschrift voor Economische en Sociale Geographie,* **68,** 177-82.

Sartori, G. (1969). 'From the politics of sociology to political sociology', in Lipset, S. M. (ed.), *Politics and the Social Sciences,* pp. 65-100 (Oxford University Press, New York).

Scanlan, P. M. (1977). 'Spatial variations in electoral behavior in urban Brisbane, 1972', *Australian Geographical Studies,* **15,** 22-41.

Scarrow, H. (1965). 'Distinguishing between political parties: the case of Canada', *Midwest Journal of Political Science,* **9,** 61-76.

Schwartz, M. A. (1974). 'Canadian voting behavior', in Rose, R. (ed.), *Electoral Behavior: A Comparative Handbook*, pp. 543-618 (Free Press, New York).

Simmons, J. W. (1967). 'Voting behavior and socio-economic characteristics', *Canadian Journal of Economics and Political Science*, **33**, 389-400.

Sinclair, R., and Thompson, B. (1976). 'Detroit', in Adams, J. S. (ed.), *Contemporary Metropolitan American*, vol. 3, pp. 285-354 (Ballinger, Cambridge, Mass.).

Soares, G., and Hamblin, R. (1967). 'Socio-economic variables and voting for the radical Left; Chile, 1952', *American Political Science Review*, **61**, 1053-66.

Tatalovich, R. (1975). 'Friends and neighbors' voting: Mississippi, 1943-73', *Journal of Politics*, **37**, 807-14.

Taylor, A. H. (1972). 'The effect of party organization: correspondence between campaign expenditure and voting in the 1970 election', *Political Studies*, **20**, 328-31.

Taylor, A. H. (1973). 'Variations in the relationship between class and voting in England, 1950 to 1970', *Tijdschrift voor Economische en Sociale Geographie*, **64**, 164-8.

Taylor, K. W., and Wiseman, N. (1974). 'Ethnic v class voting: the case of Winnipeg, 1945', *Canadian Journal of Political Science*, **7**, 314-28.

Taylor, K. W., and Wiseman, N. (1977). 'Class and ethnic voting in Winnipeg: the case of 1941', *Canadian Review of Sociology and Anthropology*, **14**, 174-87.

Taylor, P. J. (1969). 'Causal models in geographic research', *Annals of the Association of American Geographers*, **59**, 402-4.

Taylor, P. J., and Johnston, R. J. (1979). *The Geography of Elections* (Penguin, Harmondsworth).

Thompson, K. (1970). *Cross-National Voting Behavior Research: An Example of Computer-Assisted Multivariate Analysis of Attribute Data*, Sage Professional Papers in Comparative Politics 01-003 (Sage, Beverley Hills).

Urwin, D. W. (1974). 'Germany: continuity and change in electoral politics', in Rose, R. (ed.), *Electoral Behavior: A Comparative Handbook*, pp. 109-70 (Free Press, New York).

Van Loom, R. J., and Whittington, M. S. (1976). *The Canadian Political System: Environment, Structure and Process*, 2nd edn. (McGraw-Hill Ryerson Ltd, Toronto).

Weed, P. (1973). *The White Ethnic Movement and Ethnic Politics* (Praeger, New York).

Wolfe, J. S. and Burghardt, A. F. (1978). 'The neighbourhood effect in a local election'. *Canadian Geographer*, **22**, 298-305.

Wolfinger, R. E. (1965). 'The development and persistence of ethnic voting', *American Political Science Review*, **59**, 896-908.

Wright, G. C., Jr. (1977). 'Contextual models of electoral behavior: The southern Wallace vote', *American Political Review*, **71**, 497-508.

Political studies from spatial perspectives
Edited by A.D. Burnett and P.J. Taylor
© 1981 John Wiley & Sons Ltd

_____ 18__

Identity through autonomy: ethnic separatism in Québec

Colin H. Williams

Minority dissatisfaction is a central problem of our time, and a dominant theme in the historic development of the uniformly organized modern state. A number of states are currently faced with the task of maintaining the delicate balance between the interests of their constituent ethnolinguistic groups whilst also governing as if ethnicity *per se* were not a major determinant of state policy. This is because, until recently, most states conceived of ethnicity as an expression of a pre-modern and pre-rational form of social and political organization. From this standpoint, one would anticipate that the incidence of ethnic conflict and ethnic identification in political spheres would decline as societies modernize. However, the simple developmental model of social class predominating in advanced industrial states, and thereby eclipsing ethnic identification, has been called into question as an inadequate explanation of social development (Williams, 1979b). Ethnic minorities in such diverse Western states as the United Kingdom, Canada, Spain, Belgium, France, the United States of America, and Italy share certain characteristics. First, linguistic and cultural differences in particular regions have persisted over several generations and have survived despite strong pressures towards the assimilation of the minorities in question. Secondly, new political leaders have emerged among these ethnic groups who seek more political power and varying degrees of regional autonomy. They reject the tacit historic alliances which co-opted previous generations of ethnic leaders into the central government and they challenge the legitimacy of an alien state, claiming a moral right to national self-determination. Thirdly, in all cases there is evidence of long-standing economic inequality, in which, individually and collectively, members of the subjugated minority have received a less than proportionate share of power and wealth. Closely allied to the question of economic inequality is that of social status and group rights. When economic and social inequalities coincide with linguistic and/or cultural differences a system of ethnic stratification is created. Class conflict and ethnic conflict reinforce each other to provide a dynamic impetus to change. Where such divisions correspond with territorial boundaries this force is likely to take the form of a nationalist movement which aims at total independence from the dominant majority. The latter is perceived both as an exploiting class and as a threat to the minority's linguistic and cultural heritage.

In what follows I shall argue that separatism is one form of challenging the inevitability of ethnic assimilation. It is a powerful expression of ethnic identity and of social regeneration among culturally distinct peripheral collectivities. Moreover, it is also an instrumental ideology capable of providing new opportunities and a path for upward social mobility for members of a strata hitherto excluded from political power and privilege. My particular concern is to examine two alternative theories designed to account for ethnic political resurgence (Hechter, 1975; Smith, 1979) and to apply both in an examination of ethnic separatism in Québec. The essay will demonstrate the manner in which a nationalist francophone elite has attempted to develop a Québécois national consciousness, and has, since the early 1970s, been attempting to mobilize that consciousness as the driving force for the separatist challenge to the Canadian Federation. The issues discussed should alert us to the fact that the attributes of nations are hardly ever 'given' in any case, and that the process of nationality formation and ethnic assertion remain salient features of the advanced industrial states, despite the predictions of earlier modernization theorists.

The salience of ethnic resurgence cannot be ignored (Williams, 1979a). It is evident from Table 18.1 that most West European states, as well as Canada, are experiencing serious ethnoregional challenges. Earlier work (Williams, 1980) has outlined the characteristics of ethnic secession in Western Europe. A number of factors were identified which served to transform 'regional autonomist' movements into outright 'ethnic regional movements', chief of which were the historical circumstances which determined the nature of the minority's incorporation into the now dominant centralized state, the tolerance of the state towards politicized ethnic sentiments, the skill and industriousness of the mobilizing nationalist elite, and the international dimension of ethnonationalism. Lest it be forgotten, the majority of small nation-states were created in the aftermath of major continental warfare and revolution, as in the 1840s, 1920s, and 1940s. These micro-states were hardly ever established in response to domestic claims for administrative and constitutionally devolved territories. More often the new states and their boundaries conformed more to the realities of super-power hegemony than to the satisfaction of ethnic claims to territorial homogeneity. Under such circumstances nationalist leaders faced a paradox, in that the boundaries of the political unit within which they were to operate did not correspond to the territorial dominance of the ethnic group on whose behalf the claim of independence had been made. Europe has since witnessed a succession of claims to remedy this discrepancy between state and nation. Both state nationalism and ethnic nationalism compete for the loyalty of their target population, with state nationalism attempting to make state and nation co-extensive at the expense of minority nationalities in most cases. Canada also is attempting to forge a new 'national' identification which will correspond with the Canadian state, and at a sub-federal level Québec is currently engaged in a process of nationality formation, spearheaded by the government of the Parti Québécois, pledged to bring about the self-government of the 'Québécois nation'.

Territorial and ethnic separatism

An important analytical distinction exists between 'territorial' and 'ethnic' separatism. The former rests its case primarily on the spatial distinctiveness of the potentially independent unit. Distance, relative isolation, and a perception of an unfulfilled resource potential can be powerful mobilizing influences in the development of a separatist movement, especially when allied to a regional distinctiveness which may encompass other variables such as language, religion, or a common shared history of exploitation (Whebell, 1973; Smith, 1979). The history of European imperialism abounds with cases of ex-colonial territories who, having seceded from their Metropolitan cores, commonly trace a particular epoch in their experience when the 'materials' of their uniqueness were moulded by geographical isolation, despite the many apparent similarities in the racial origin, culture system, and settlement pattern between metropole and colony (Young, 1976).

The main characteristics of the process of territorial separatism have been outlined by Whebell (1973), who defines it as an attempt

Table 18.1   Québécois separatism in comparative perspective

Ethnoregional group	Major ethnonational linkage(s)	Degree of institutionalization
Québécois (6.0 million in Québec, Canada).	*Parti Québécois* — Governing party of Québec Province since November 1976.	High; successive transfer of power from Ottawa to Québec City; P.Q. of a referendum on Sovereignty-Association defeated in June 1980.
Scots (5.2 million in Scotland, UK).	*Scottish National Party* — 17.24% of the Scottish vote in May 1979 British general election.	Medium but diminishing; despite narrow majority in devolution referendum the promise of legislative devolution to an elected Scottish Assembly shelved by Tory government.
Welsh (2.7 million in Wales, UK).	*Plaid Cymru* — 8.1% of Welsh vote in May 1979 British general election; *Cymdeithas yr Iaith Cymraeg*, an active, non-violent interest group committed to preserving the Welsh culture.	Low; outright rejection of Labour's devolution proposals for an elected Assembly in March 1979 referendum.
Flemish (5+ million in Flanders and bilingual Brussels in Belgium).	*Volksunie* — (Flemish People's Party) — 11.3% of Flemish Belgium's vote in December 1978 general election.	Extensive institutionalization in the 'regionalized' Belgian state created by the 1970 revision of the constitution, including Cultural Councils inside the Belgian parliament, advisory regional assemblies for Flanders, Wallonia, and Brussels-Brabant, strong possibility of Belgium moving toward a federal structure.
Francophone Belgium composed of the Walloons (3+ million in Wallonia and the nearly 1 million Bruxellois).	*Rassemblement Wallon Party*, with 9.2% of Wallonia's vote in 1978, and the *Front démocratique des francophones bruxellois*, with 27.98% of Brussels' total vote in 1978.	
Jura Francophones (60,000 citizens of northernmost part of Switzerland's German-speaking canton of Bern).	*Rassemblement Jurassien*, system-participatory party now eclipsing earlier protest movements seeking a separate canton for the region's Francophones.	By referenda, area separated from Bern canton, separate status as the Republic of Jura within the Swiss Confederation.
South Tyroleans (220,000 + German-speaking inhabitants in Italy's Alto Adige region).	*Süd-Tiroler Volks Partei* — 30% of the vote in the Trento-Bolzano region of the 1972 Italian general election.	Limited implementation of the 1969 *Pakage* designed to guarantee political and cultural autonomy of region; 1971, the creation of autonomous regions of Trentino-Alto Adige, subdivided into German province with some local autonomy.

Group	Movements	Concessions / Status
Alsaciens (1.3 million inhabitants of France's Alsace-Lorraine region).	Several quasi-political associations with an interest group hue seeking to preserve area's dialect and language, including the *Alsacian Party of Progress*.	Virtually none; however since the Summer violence of 1975 and 1979 France has instituted a re-evaluation of its regional policies *vis-à-vis* its ethnoregional minorities.
Corsicans (150,000 nationals in an island population of 250,000).	*Action pour la renaissance de la Corse*, and *Union de Peuple Corse* seeking regional autonomy and independence.	Since 1975 Corsicans have gained some limited concessions, e.g. right to teach Corsican in schools, a promised reopening of a university and the appointment of Corsica's first Corsican prefect since 1870; extra grant of 446 million francs in the 1978/9 budget.
Bretons (nearly 2.4 million inhabitants in the Brittany region of France).	Three banned, paramilitary, clandestine organizations, each with a limited following and commitment to regional autonomy.	Minimal, as above; however, Giscard d'Estaing's Minister of Education in 1975 announced a programme of state subsidies for teaching Breton in schools; more recently a Cultural Charter has allowed additional time on radio and television for Breton-medium programmes and finance for Breton societies.
Northern Ireland's (essentially) Celtic-descended 'Catholics', (35% of the regional population).	The *Provisional* wing of the *Irish Republican Army*, a clandestine terrorist organization seeking an end to British rule, and the 'Protestant' domination, drawing a wider but spasmodic following among the inhabitants than either the official IRA or its political auxiliaries.	Non-functional. Northern Ireland has possessed a regional assembly since its partition from the rest of Ireland; for most of the half-century before its suspension Stormont was dominated by a 'Protestant' majority largely insensitive to the needs of the Catholic minority and overtly discriminatory. Efforts to re-establish civilian government since 1973 have focused on a power-sharing committee system scheme designed to replace the former cabinet-government, majority-rule system with shared authority; so far, efforts to create this system have been thwarted by the Protestant community's principal linkages to the shared-power concept.
Northern Ireland's (essentially) English-Scottish-descended 'Protestant' majority (65% of the regional population).	*United Ulster Unionist Council*, a party committed to Loyalist-Protestant cause which won 46 of the 78 seats in the regional constituent assembly elected in June 1975; several clandestine Protestant terrorist movements.	

Table 18.1 contd.

Ethnoregional group	Major ethnonational linkage(s)	Degree of institutionalization
Frisians (The Netherlands' northern-most province).	*Frisian National Party*, since 1962 demanding local autonomy for Friesland; since 1979 has one seat in council of Warkum, four seats in Doanjewerstal, two seats in Sloten and two representatives in the States.	Virtually none; essentially a catalyst for reforming measures which other parties adopt and threaten to deflate the Frisian claim to autonomy.
Catalonians (8 million in northeastern Spain).	*Esquerra Democratica* and *Llige* — leftist- and rightist-oriented parties seeking to promote regional political autonomy.	Very limited. Some cultural autonomy developed from the 1976 recognition by the government of the region's unique identity, gradualist devolution proposals likely.
Basques (nearly 2 million in the four provinces of northern Spain and the three of southern France).	*Euzkadi 'Ta Askatasuna* (ETA — 'Basque Homeland and Liberty'), an outlawed, clandestine and violent irredentist group seeking a free Basque state in a 'European Federation of Races'; PNV (Basques Nationalist Party) *Partido Nacionalists Vasco* founded in 1895 has been the traditional voice of Basque regional autonomy. *Enbata*, a Basque association of cultural and political pro-autonomy groups in Basque France, also outlawed.	Developing; after decades of neglect and persecution, and following a violent campaign of bomb attacks and political assassinations, the Spanish state is offering a form of Home Rule to the Basque country and has legalized the use of Euskera, the Basque language. It remains to be seen whether the recent measures will placate the demands of the *'polismilis'* who have always insisted on complete sovereignty.

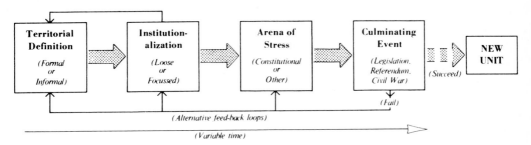

FIGURE 18.1   A simple model of territorial separatism

by territorially defined formal or informal organizations to achieve increased autonomy. It is a process which can be observed at all territorial scales and includes both economic and cultural components. In differentiating territorial separatism as a specific category of organizational separatism Whebell noted that the separatist unit was defined initially, either formally (hierarchic type) or through some functionally or socially differentiated area not coincident with a formal division of territory (non-hierarchy). Figure 18.1 provides a summary of the main stages in this process.

The motivation of such separatism is most often linked with some attribute of the land

> in terms of an environmental hazard to be mitigated or some developmental potential to be realized; these are considered to be inadequately provided for by the superior establishment. The separatist group thus conceives itself to be in an unsatisfactory dependency-status and this essentially economic factor may be coupled with racial/cultural and social factors as well (Whebell, 1973).

This dependency status may in turn arise as a result of two alternative responses of the respective political system:

1. the inability of the political unit to meet the demands and absorb the aspirations of the dependent territory; or
2. the refusal on behalf of the competing elites to provide the framework within which the developmental potential of the dependent territory may be fulfilled.

When either of these two conditions obtain, and when there is no other institutionalized channel of redress through which the grievances of the dependent group may be expressed, one is likely to find the potential for a separatist movement. Such movements have as their rationale the establishment of an alternative centre or hierarchy with a new territorial framework, one which in turn both sanctions the legitimate development of the new unit and is also capable of sustaining such development. Thus inherent in national territorial separatism we have two complementary forces:

1. the consciousness of deprivation and unfulfilled potential; and
2. the desire for independence, coupled with the perceived capability of achieving and maintaining such independence.

In contrast 'ethnic' separatism rests its case on the cultural distinctiveness of the community pressing for independence. Frequently, but not necessarily so, they are 'renewal movements' seeking to recover the cultural identity of a formally independent unit. For nationalist leaders, imbued with the uniqueness of their destiny and contribution to the common fund of world civilization, the incorporation of their group into a multi-national state is inherently contrary to nature and a severe impediment to the full realization of that group's developmental potential. As Smith (1979) has demonstrated

> the watchwords of ethnic separatism are identity, authenticity and diversity... it seeks through separation the restoration of a degraded community to its rightful status and dignity, yet it also sees in the status of a separate political existence the goal of that restoration and the social embodiment of that dignity.

It follows that for independence to be achieved the primary function is to translate the goal of separate ethnic identity into a political ideology which will animate a movement for national freedom. The remarkable feature of many contemporary separatist movements in advanced industrial states is that both types of separatism, the territorial and the ethnic, are increasingly being combined to produce 'ethnic-regional' movements which seek to liberate their respective peoples firmly settled in distinct, if subservient, territories.

The materials of separateness

We have identified ethnicity and territory as the key materials of separateness. We may elaborate upon ethnic separatism, the primary concern of this chapter, as a powerful, if somewhat vague, sentiment. It would incorporate descent as a basis of group and of individual status, and of spiritual confirmation. We need to know to whom else we belong; ethnic separatism can thus provide a 'myth of origin'. It can also provide an historic explanation for the tragic events of past conquest and subordination, and a rationale for group superiority achieved through the pain of suffering, a 'myth of development'. Underlying all of this is the question of isolation, of self-sufficiency, of the relative infrequency of sustained inter-cultural contact giving rise to ethnocentrism, a 'myth of uniqueness'.

Cultural separateness reinforces the sense of unique descent and provides a 'mission/destiny' view of historical development. It operates through three salient markers, the meanings of which can vary in different social settings within the ethnic territory. The first are group customs and institutions which serve as group boundaries, as modes of exclusion and as sustainers of special routines and distinctive procedures. A second important variable is language, for not only is it a functional means of communication, but it is also an instrument for cultural division. Often it provides the most tangible barrier to assimilation because of its pervasive influence in social interaction (Williams, 1978). A third material of culture distinctiveness is religion; a phenomenon, like language, which is capable both of uniting and dividing populations at a local and universal scale.

The politicization of national identity

The materials of separateness have to be translated into a self-conscious group identity before they can become politically relevant to the drive for national independence. This process of nationality formation is one in which objective differences between peoples acquire subjective and symbolic significance, are transformed into group consciousness, and become the basis for political demands. There are two main stages in the development of a politicized nation. In the first stage the thwarted intelligentsia attaches symbolic value to certain objective characteristics, creates a nationalist reinterpretation of past history and future glory, and attempts to communicate their vision of social development to the defined population, especially to the socially mobilizing elements. Four interactive requisites are essential for the successful transformation of an objectively differentiated group into a subjectively conscious community, namely:

1. the existence of a pool of symbols of distinctiveness to draw upon;

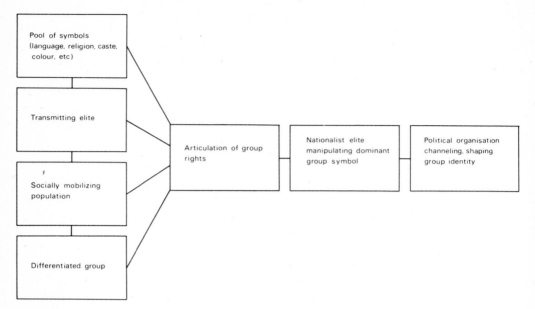

FIGURE 18.2   Factors in the process of nationality formation

2. an elite willing to select, transmit, and standardize these
   symbols for the group;
3. a socially mobilizing population to whom the symbols of
   group identity can be transmitted;
4. the existence of one or more other groups from whom the
   formative group is to be differentiated (Figure 18.2).

Of central importance is the relationship between the rates of
social mobilization and assimilation of an ethnic group in relation
to another dominant or competitive group. The leading hypothesis
is that the conditions for the differentiation of a culturally distinct
ethnic group from a rival group with which it must interact and
communicate, occur when the rates of social mobilization within
the group move faster than the rates of assimilation of that group
into the language and culture of its rival.

The second stage in nationality formation involves the
articulation and acquisition of political rights for members as a
group and not as individual representatives of the state's citizenry;
that is, the promotion of group rights over individual rights
(Williams, 1977). Political demands may be articulated by an elite
even before a group acquires cohesion. They may even be

conceded in the absence of group cohesion. But the clearest proof of the existence of a nationality is the achievement and maintenance of group rights through political mobilization. This movement from communal consciousness to political action requires two preconditions:

1. a perception of inequality in the distribution of, and competition for, the allocation of scarce resources and material rewards between groups; and
2. a political organization to articulate group demands.

Government policies may intensify or moderate group conflicts, but the kinds of political demands made are likely to depend more upon calculations relating to the relative power of competing elites in a political system than to the adequacy of government policies in satisfying ethnic demands. The willingness of competing communal elites to share political power is of greater importance in maintaining the cohesion of multi-national societies than almost any other factor. Where that willingness is in evidence, communal conflicts can be accommodated; where it is absent, separatist demands and overt violence and civil war are to be expected.

In our discussion of nationality formation we should take due cognizance of two caveats. Firstly, it is intended that the objective markers of group identity, such as language and religion, are not givens from which national identity naturally springs. Rather they are themselves subject to variation and manipulation. Secondly, not all symbols of group identity are of equal value in a functional sense. Often nationalists tend to emphasize one symbol above all others and strive to bring other symbols into congruence with it. We shall be arguing that in the cases under consideration here, language has been accorded primary group-defining significance.

However, two types of structural constraint must first be overcome by the nationalist movement in order to expand its social base. It must challenge the politically established 'colonial-type' elite who control the means of violence in the ethnic territory. In addition, because of the constraints inherent in a particularistic and traditional culture, it must attack the social control of long-established institutions and discredit the political rationalization of alien rule.

This leads the nationalist movement into its third, offensive phase, simultaneously challenging the legitimacy of the state's exclusive exercise of power and the legitimacy of the basic values underpinning indigenous, traditional social structures. At times the attack on tradition in the name of modernization and economic development may cause ambivalence, as certain portions of the native culture must be preserved, and even exalted, for the sake of ethnic continuity.

The fourth and final stage of a successful nationalist movement is to create a new consensus in support of the new nation-state. This involves the elaboration of a new set of priorities, the socialization of new generations by strict control of the schools, the mass media, etc., and the tightening of bureaucratic control over the entire territory to avoid the centrifugal tendencies inevitable in the initial establishment of a new state. Control of the communication media and of education are essential in such circumstances, a feature of which nationalist elites are eminently aware.

Ethnic resurgence

A satisfactory understanding of ethnic separatism necessitates a clear formulation of state development and of ethnic group formation. Of the many interesting accounts advanced in recent years this chapter will focus on two which promise to assist in the comparative analysis of ethnic regionalism, namely Hechter's internal colonialism and Smith's work on the seminal role of the ethnic intelligentsia.

Internal colonialism

In Hechter's (1975) work *Internal Colonialism* it was argued that ethnic solidarity among any objectively defined set of individuals is due primarily to the existence of a hierarchical cultural division of labour which promotes reactive group formation. This cultural division of labour is typically to be found in regions that have developed as internal colonies; that is, as ethnic enclaves of advanced nation-states. As capitalist expansion, from the late eighteenth century onwards, follows ethnic cleavages and promotes cultural assimilation into the core area, industrial development must always disadvantage peripheral ethnic collectivities. The result of continued economic exploitation of the periphery by the core elite created a clear-cut division of labour on predominantly cultural lines, creating 'a system of stratification where objective distinctions are superimposed upon class lines' (Hechter, 1975, p. 30). Economic progress was instrumental in delaying the development of the Celtic periphery, and this facilitated the main-tenance of distinct ethnic identities until well into the late twentieth century. In addition, by encouraging core-periphery interaction, industrialization has further reinforced the dependence of the Celtic periphery and its consequent cultural stratification. On realizing their condition, the ethnic leadership must advocate separatism if they are ever to avoid the inevitability of economic development as a perpetual dependency of the state's core region. The initial thesis has attracted more attention than almost any other explanation for the rise of Celtic nationalism, and has been subjected to extensive scrutiny and criticism by a number of scholars (Sloan, 1979; Nairn, 1977; Smith, 1979b; Page, 1977; Williams, 1979a). Whilst Hechter argues that most ethnic-regional movements appear to have emerged in marginal, peripheral areas, there are notable exceptions (among them Scotland, Catalonia, and Euskadi) which necessitate a reinterpretation of the original thesis. In his more recent work (Hechter, 1977, Hechter and Levi, 1979) a second, segmented division of labour was identified which leads to interactive as opposed to reactive group formation, being largely determined by the ethnic group itself.

How do these mechanisms explain why specific groups and regions are able to maintain their ethnic identity despite modernization and state centralization? The crucial distinction between the original (hierarchical) and revised (segmental) division of labour appears to relate to the power and vitality of the ethnic group's interaction with the international economic order, and the residual strength of the customs and institutions which the peripheral region was allowed to maintain after its initial integration into the developing state. As Hechter and Levi (1979) explain, the hierarchical mechanism contributing to the group formation 'is the extent to which group membership determines individual life chances. The greater this is, the greater the psychic significance of ethnicity for the individual — and by extension, for the group as a whole'. Thus in Western European peripheral regions, where individuals are not assigned to occupations solely on ascriptive criteria, ethnic identity tends to be strongest among those groups at the lower end of the stratification system.

In contrast the segmental mechanism contributing to the formation of ethnic solidarity is the extent to which members interact wholly within the boundaries of their own group.

> The most critical locus of this interaction is the work site, and the best single indicator of it is the degree to which group members monopolize certain niches in the occupational structure. Occupational specialization of this kind contribute to group solidarity by establishing settings for personal contact that strengthen ties between individuals with a set of

common material interests that serve to reinforce informal social ties (Hechter and Levi, 1979).

If we translate these socio-structural characteristics into regional characteristics we find that in 'hierarchical' cases, individuals avowing the importance of their culture in peripheral regions (e.g. those with a distinctive language or religion such as in Wales, Brittany, and Corsica) are primarily found in the lower-ranking positions of the regional class structure. However, in 'segmental' cases, individuals adhering to the peripheral culture have succeeded in monopolizing key occupations and in maintaining a separate set of 'national' institutions. Both types of situation structure the respective interaction with the centralizing Western European state. The former, where the peripheral culture remained beyond, or tangential to, the interests of the ruling elite of the state, produces a reactive response; the latter, where the peripheral culture was protected by the existence of distinctive regional institutions, promotes interactive formation.

Two further factors determine the relative rates of ethnic incorporation, namely the strength of the respective cores and the institutional completeness of the peripheries. In general, if the periphery had a state apparatus of its own prior to its incorporation, the nature of its integration into an expanding neighbouring core would be determined by the relative strength of the core. In some cases, for example Scotland, diplomatic means such as the Act of Union (1707) guaranteed the functional survival of a separate Scottish legal, educational, and ecclesiastical system. Such institutional autonomy permits the development of occupational niches for incumbents who adhere to the peripheral culture. They in turn articulate the main threads of Scottish cultural distinctiveness and help maintain a continuity of ethnic identification, initially amongst the bourgeoisie, but as other strata of the population habitually come to interact with their own 'national' institutions, they too develop a sense of ethnic group identity. Thus the social base of ethnic-regionalism will tend to be relatively widespread in such cases.

Alternatively, in situations where peripheries were annexed outright by their respective cores (Wales, Brittany, Corsica, Galicia, and Friesland) little heed was given to the rights of the conquered minority to maintain their respective governmental institutions. All formal administrative, legal, and ecclesiastical institutions were disbanded and for all intents and purposes the periphery ceased to maintain a distinctive governmental identity. What did survive were the elements of a primordial, peasant, and particularistic society, a minority language or an outmoded agriculturally based sense of community identification, which could be expected to disappear as the process of state integration heralded the dawn of a new cultural epoch, based on rational, modern, and universalistic elements, the all-powerful, all-civilizing modern bureaucratic state. According to Hechter, what determines the rate of cultural absorption is not the transactions between core and periphery as two distinct aggregate units, but the patterns of contact between representatives of the core group and the peripheral masses within the *periphery* itself. A key variable influencing the extent of such inter-cultural contact is the onset of industrialization and the exploitation of the periphery's resources.

The implication is that in times of acute social dislocation (industrialization, for example) the ethnic minority is hampered by the lack of a set of national institutions which can help it adjust to the new demands, and which, in time, could have provided an alternative focus for group mobilization to resist the more onerous effects of capitalist development and core exploitation.

The ethnic intelligentsia

An alternative perspective is provided by Smith (1979) who seeks to explain the politicization of ethnic consciousness primarily in terms of the rise of scientific bureaucracies and secular education. Modern bureaucracies, unlike previous forms of state administration, are not only more complex, more centralized and more interventionist, they are also more 'scientific'; that is they incorporate into their organizations the latest techniques and methods of scientific technology. This innovation not only requires a new type of personnel as bureaucrat, but also assists the effective penetration of the state apparatus to the farthest part of the state territory. This new kind of bureaucracy demanded a more secular, utilitarian, and rational perspective and relied more on experimental and methodical techniques. Rational education began to displace the classical/clerical education and the secularization of society began to undermine the cosmic myths which had formed the close traditional bond between state and church. State modernization and its pattern of uneven development began to erode the established agrarian norms and roles, favouring the centre at the expense of the periphery and the educated intelligentsia at the expense of the landed classes.

> Since the new bureaucracies, often situated in the capitals, tended to command many of the avenues to wealth and

power, ambitious and qualified professionals clamoured for admission. Hence the rise of scientific bureaucracy and critical education spurred a whole wave of elite mobility, and paved the way for a potentially dissident stratum, and one more dangerous than any predecessor on account of their education and ability to organise into factions and movements (Smith, 1979).

Discontent was deepened amongst the ambitious and qualified professionals from peripheral areas and minority ethnic groups because of the many discriminatory barriers erected against them by the imperial and colonial administration which restricted coveted positions to the elite of the dominant group.

As a second stage, Smith argues that increased state intervention in the present century has produced an aggravated crisis for the thwarted intelligentsia in ex-imperial medium-sized states, such as Great Britain and Spain, because the traditional overseas outlets for talented professionals are withering away. The effect, he claims, is worse for the ethnic elites of Wales, Scotland, and Corsica, because the increased competition in the domestic sector means they can no longer be accommodated, nor can their aspirations be fulfilled. Struggling under their 'double burden' of exclusion and ambition the intelligentsia turn inward to reach a deeper understanding of their own ethnic community. In such a milieu nationalism is embraced for it seeks to offer an historical vision of man in society, and because it is especially concerned with the formation of identity through autonomy it promises to provide a respected place for the committed intelligentsia which bureaucracy helped to create. Nationalism from this perspective is a meaning- and role-seeking movement.

Government policies become the decisive determinant as to which direction the politicized ethnoregional movement will take. Insensitive bureaucratic policies or benign neglect will tend to evoke a separatist challenge; while an accommodating system participatory approach will tend to blunt the separatists' grievances and lead to communalist options. Ultimately, of course, the success of the separatist movements in the West will be heavily influenced by the unfavourable international climate as sub-state dissolution in any one medium-sized state might herald the beginning of wider fragmentation within the international political system.

Québec

> I know of no national distinctions marking and continuing a
> more hopeless inferiority... if they prefer remaining
> stationary, the greater of them must be labourers in the
> employ of English capitalists. In either case it would appear
> that the great mass of French Canadians are doomed, in some
> measure, to occupy an inferior position, and to be dependent
> on the English for employment. The evils of poverty and
> dependence would merely be aggravated in a ten-fold degree,
> by a spirit of jealous and resentful nationality which should
> separate the working class of the community from the
> possessors of wealth and the employers of labour (Lord
> Durham, 1838).

How did separatism develop amongst this 'jealous and resentful
nationality'? Four problems confront us in the application of
Hechter's and Smith's discussion of ethnic resurgence to the
province of Québec. The first of these is the choice of Québec as
the politico-spatial unit of analysis. Nationalist leaders face the
difficult task of making state and nation coterminous. The basis of
separatism in French Canada is a reinvigorated ethnic
consciousness. But rather than undertake the dangerous and
politically suicidal task of redrawing Québec's boundaries to
coincide with the distribution of the ethnic majority — the
Francophone nation — separatist ideology attempts to convince
the non-Francophone minorities that the Parti Québécois (PQ)
government's conception of nationalism is territorial and state-
based, hence pluralistic and liberal. The second problem is that no
theory, when grounded in the reality of other examples, can do
more than point to the complex structural conditions which
engender separatist movements. One should be wary, then, of
asking a particular theory to explain too much. The third problem is
that aggregate-level theories often fail to take account of the
significant, if at times ephemeral, nature of leading personalities,
the charismatic leader and the myriad interpersonal contacts which
contribute to the development of political cultures. Finally the
interpretation of contemporary history is a notoriously difficult and
humbling task, the details of which we all too often misrepresent in
order to be theoretically consistent.
    The history of Québec's post-Conquest development reveals
much in the relations between the French-speaking majority and the
English-speaking minority which supports Hechter's cultural
division of labour. By the nineteenth century French-Canadian

society was essentially rural, consisting of a loosely integrated set of expanding parishes (Cartwright, 1977). Within this context the development of supra-parochial institutions gave rise to an ethnic elite composed primarily of the clergy and seigneurs who, when faced with a surplus population on a rapidly diminishing land resource base needed 'structural relief' to maintain their dominance. Guindon (1968) argues that structural relief in that milieu could only consist in industrialization, the very reform the traditional elite could not ensure, since it was not, and had not been, primarily an entrepreneurial bourgeoisie and hence lacked the requisite capital. McRoberts (1979) has demonstrated that during the earlier period of New France, French-Canadians did in fact possess an entrepreneurial capacity based on the fur trade. Their failure to accumulate capital in post-Conquest Québec was due to a major structural change within the Québec economy and to a reorientation of Canada's trade resulting from the replacement of France by Great Britain and the USA as the main market, thereby disadvantaging French-Canadian entrepreneurs, many of whom ceased to trade as a result. Whilst successive French-Canadian economic ventures remained small and limited, English-Canadian ventures in Québec developed as a consequence of the expanded international market afforded by the Empire and the industrialization of Canada and her southern neighbour.

Hierarchical structures developed relatively late in Québéc, becoming prominent only in the early decades of the twentieth century as a result of increased inter-ethnic contact. Large scale rural-urban migration and industrialization had created an occupational system where French-Canadians were disproportionately concentrated in blue-collar positions and underrepresented in managerial and technical positions within the overwhelmingly Anglophone-owned enterprises. The evidence points to an established and widely recognized cultural division of labour.

However, it is incorrect, I believe, to explain this situation as being a direct reflection of the value system of the two contending ethnic groups. The orthodox explanation implies a deterministic subordination of French-Canadians, culture-bound and unable to compete with the more innovative, rational, and business-orientated English-Canadian character type (Langlois, 1960). As a counter-argument two structural explanations are offered (McRoberts, 1979). One concentrates on ethnic discrimination as the primary instrument delaying the social advancement of the French-Canadian work-force. English-Canadian 'bosses' showed a clear preference towards appointing personnel from within the

Anglophone community. The other explanation stresses the role of language as a 'sorting device' in the allocation of English and French occupations. Given that few, until recently, were functionally bilingual, Québec's Anglophones had a distinct advantage in aspiring for top managerial positions. Also the language barrier might stifle not only the performance of French-Canadians, but also the capacity of Anglophone managers to recognize and promote talent. Given such behavioural circumstances language discrimination need not necessarily be a conscious ploy by an ethnic elite, but an inbuilt operating mechanism reflecting the dominance of English in the business world.

Had Québec's linguistic particularism been maintained in both private and public occupations, with English predominating, Hechter's theory would undoubtedly remain unchallenged. However, since the early 1960s the rapid expansion of the provincial public sector gave rise to new bureaucratic elites, whose occupational promotion depended upon their linguistic competence in French, and not in both French *and* English. In addition, the persistence of linguistically differentiated educational institutions, the development of an aggressive and innovative French-language mass media and the expansion of the provincially financed social-welfare services had, by the mid-1960s, created a comprehensive arrangement of French-medium institutions, in short, a unilingual public domain. Thus linguistic and cultural differences in Québec have persisted, not so much because of their instrumentality in operating the cultural division of labour (although significant in this respect), but because they have become embedded in a distinct French-medium network of public and semi-public institutions which have a relevance for the everyday needs of the Québéçois people.

The cultural division of labour is intimately connected to Hechter's interpretation of core-periphery relations. By relating ethnic identity and territorial autonomism to the economic inequality of disadvantaged peripheral regions, the internal colonial theory attempts to link them to a central mechanism of international capitalism, the uneven development of regions. We may accept the operation of a cultural division of labour in Québec, without necessarily accepting Québec as a dependent periphery, and this for a number of reasons. Firstly, as the core-periphery model is essentially a regional level type explanation, it in no way accounts for differential development amongst individuals (Williams, 1980). Thus some members of the periphery will undoubtedly gain from the extension of the core's political and commercial activity e.g. the entrepreneurial classes and the intermediaries of regional administration and commerce. Others will often lose; e.g. the traditional political elite and the landed classes. Similarly in the core, some may lose out as a result of peripheral incorporation, e.g. manual and semi-skilled labourers, whose competitiveness may be undercut by cheaper labour costs in the periphery. In addition after integration, many in the periphery may experience an absolute rise in their standard of living and welcome closer economic ties to the core, even though relative to the core's population they are still disadvantaged. Secondly, there are likely to be clear spatial differences between different subregions in the periphery which confuse its categorization as either core or periphery. Thus whilst eastern Québec remained underdeveloped, Montreal continued to be the financial centre of Canada long after Ontario had emerged as the industrial and manufacturing centre. A region may at the same time be both a core and a periphery, depending upon which regions one is comparing. Whilst Québec exhibits many of the characteristic traits of a periphery in relation to southwestern Ontario, she is undoubtedly a core area in her relations with the Atlantic provinces and (until very recently) with the West. Even if we limit the comparison to Ontario, the model is further weakened by the fact that Québec has a provincial government which of late has done much to erode the cultural division of labour by political means, irrespective of core interests. Hence, historically, it must be concluded that Québec's decline owes more to her geographical location, her resource underdevelopment and the relative advance of other Canadian regions, rather than to the specific role which cultural factors played in determining economic opportunity and performance. We must perforce turn to other explanations for the emergence of separatism, ones which, while not denying the importance of inter-regional inequalities, do not focus on the regional level to the exclusion of analysing the role of key actors in the nationalist struggle, the ethnic intelligentsia.

We have accepted Hechter's revised account of the cultural division of labour without acceding to its predicted relationship with the core-periphery model. It is possible, *a priori,* to assume that the grievances which arise from the occupational discrimination which underlies the cultural division of labour, will be translated into a political movement pledged to redress such grievances. This does not, however, imply that the resultant movement will necessarily be separatist in character as Hechter assumes. It could be, and in fact was, in Québec, a Social Credit or a Liberal Party, neither of which challenged the legitimacy of the federal system;

merely its operation when it seemed to threaten Québéçois interests. Although feelings of disadvantage are common within the French-Canadian population, only some translate these grievances into a preference for the independence option. The difference between the general electorate and the more committed PQ supporters appears to derive from different estimates of the chances of improvement coming with independence. The touchstone of the separatist case in Québec is that they alone can offer a better future through good government *('vrai')* to replace the discredited federalist parties. The question of independence would be decided at a later time and only after a public commendation through a province-wide referendum. It is not that nationalism is a new element in the situation. Nationalist ideology has long been a prominent feature of Québec politics ever since the Patriotes movement of the 1820s and 1830s (Wade, 1968; Quin, 1963; Berger, 1969). Previously, however, it has always been accommodated within the federal structure, within a broad philosophy of elite cooperation. What Québec has witnessed of late is a reformulation of the basic principles of self-determination; one in which a radical and reforming ethnic bureaucratic and technological elite have played a leading role, both in the development of a separatist ideology and in the establishment of an effective, interventionist state apparatus which had become the prime instrument for separation.

Québec modernization

From Confederation to the present the pattern of ethnic accommodation between French and English in Québec developed within the context of rapid industrialization. Historically, ethnic accommodation has been based on Québec's segmented character, with separate ethnic schools, religious organizations, social communication networks, residential differentiation, and trade unions providing a self-perpetuating institutional separation serving both linguistic communities. What disturbed this arrangement and fuelled the separatist case was provincial modernization and its attendant new actors, the 'scientific bureaucrats'. In the immediate post-war period, the growing discontent with the character and policies of the Duplessis regime (Nish, 1970) as evidenced by the asbestos workers' strike of 1949, hardened the split between the secularizing intelligentsia and the defensive clerico-nationalist ideology which had underpinned Church-State relations since Confederation days. The attack on church-dominated education, health, and welfare services which the Quiet Revolution heralded

was spearheaded by the expanding provincial bureaucracy created
by Premier Paul Sauve (Guindon, 1978). Henceforward, it was the
provincial state apparatus which was to be used as the reforming
instrument capable of allowing Québec to 'catch up' with
neighbouring Ontario as a modern society, and of providing
employment, status, and a future political role for the ambitious
ethnic bureaucrats within a framework of Francophone public and
parapublic institutions. 'The aspirations of the new middle class
and the growth and development of the institutions they staffed
were to become the political priorities of the provincial state'
(Guindon, 1978, p. 214). Having replaced the church as the main
source of authority, the new elite now successfully challenged the
leadership of the traditional, conservative Francophone elite, by
restricting the management prerogatives of the authorities of such
institutions as local school boards and hospital administrations.
They espoused a politically centralized bureaucratic model of
social modernization, which apart from curtailing the authority of
French institutional managers, also transformed the Anglophone
institutional, managerial elite into a minority dependent upon the
state and its dictates. Modernization pointed to the pivotal role of
the state as the focus of reform, initiative, and enterprise. State-
financed ventures such as Hydro Québec, the Sidbec steel complex
and the pension and investment fund represented instruments for
extending Québécois control over economic development also. But
increasingly the leaders of the Lesage and successive governments
recognized that Québec's drive towards autonomy would clash
with federal priorities, especially as the federal government was
itself playing a more aggressive role in regional development and
cultural affairs, policies which did not always accord with Québec's
interests (Meekison, 1971; Crepeau and Macpherson, 1968).

Social mobilization and state modernization created a brand of
nationalism quite distinct from previous expressions of Québécois
self-assertion in several important respects. As we have seen, the
new nationalism embraces the logic of social and economic
modernization as the *key* to a dynamic and prosperous future.
Whilst traditional nationalism has been conservative and engaged
in the politics of cultural defence, the new nationalism is activist
and interventionist, engaged in the politics of cultural promotion.
Where the old nationalism was content to maintain the ethnic
institutional separation, even if this meant that Anglophones had
the upper hand in certain sectors, the new nationalism now sought
to penetrate all sectors developing new forms of competition with
the English. Where the old nationalism had challenged the
legitimacy of federal jurisdiction only when it infringed on

Québec's legal rights, the new nationalism called into question the basis of Confederation, challenging Ottawa's right to determine revenue levels and resource allocation. Finally, the traditional nationalism's suspicion of the state as an instrument of reform was displaced by an ideological commitment to state intervention and planning, such that it became the key sector in the struggle for ethnic survival and the springboard for group development (De Wilde, 1977).

We have argued that the ethnic bureaucratic elite played a decisive role in shaping Québec modernization, but what of separatism and ethnic promotion? To many outsiders, language and cultural questions seem to have received a disproportionate share of government attention, which has increased since the election of the PQ government in November 1976. Many obsrvers fail to appreciate the pervasive role which language plays in almost all aspects of public life; most notably in education, the work-place, and government. Given the overriding concern to preserve the 'French fact in North America' (2.5% of the total population), it is not surprising that language, the essence of French-Canadian identity, should be a prime political concern of the new nationalists. This concern with *'survivance'* is related to the fact that in time the language of the business elite will come to dominate the language of the passive majority, if the state does not intervene. Elite-mass differences could be managed so long as Québec's birthrate remained high. The 'revenge of the cradle' would in time undo the Conquest. However, the province's birth-rate has changed from one of the world's highest to one of the world's lowest, being lower than all other Canadian provinces now. The recent trend of immigrants to assimilate into the Anglophone community has led to emotional assertions that, without restrictive language policies, only a tiny proportion of immigrants and their children would opt for the French immersion classes offered by education boards. Demographic forecasts predict that the French proportion would fall from 79.0% to about 70.0% if such trends continue in the 1980s. There is one qualification, however, which Pinard and Hamilton (in press) have shown which makes all the difference. The non-French population are disproportionately concentrated in the Montreal metropolitan area. Within this area (containing 45.5% of Québec's population) the French versus Others proportion is 5:3. Demographers argue that if the current trends continue the metropolis would lose its French majority within two decades, the heart of the nation would be lost, and provincial, rural Québec would provide only a partial defence of Francophone culture in an increasingly urban age.

One explanation for the centrality of language policies today relates to the growth of the public sector. The new middle class is overwhelmingly concentrated in the public sector as a consequence of the expansion of French-medium municipal and provincial civil service departments which required and recruited Francophone social science, engineering and business graduates. Unlike the private sector, the public sector did not insist on bilingualism as a criterion of employment. However, once the state sector began to be adequately manned in the mid- to late-1960s, language became a political issue as the aspiring middle classes, blocked in their attempts to swell the state bureaucracy, looked to the Anglophone-dominated private sector for employment. Disadvantaged linguistically, and experiencing blocked mobility in both sectors, the thwarted intelligentsia reinforced its determination to seek in separatism a collective, and then political, solution to its dilemma. Only in a separate, independent nation-state could the full aspirations of the Francophones be realized. 'Maitre chez nous' was to become a reality; Le Parti Québécois its champion.

We are all members of minorities, but with what rights?

The separatist case is based on the premise that ethnic majorities within a multi-ethnic polity have the right to constitute national governments in their own sovereign states. This of course is the right of national self-determination. Initially such claims appear to be framed in majoritarian terms and hence inherently democratic. Closer examination suggests much ambiguity in the justification of majoritarian independence. Despite clear victories in the 1976 election (Tables 18.2 and 18.3) the PQ government have opted for a referendum to endorse their mandate for Sovereignty-Association. Opponents of separatism have argued that given the importance of the issue to Québec and Canada a minimum of 50-55% voting to separate is an inadequate endorsement. From the PQ perspective, however, a 55% vote suggests acceptance of the principle by a 'huge majority' of Francophones, somewhere around 65%. The implication is that a genuine victory of the majority of Francophones is assured. Note that this interpretation defines the majority, not in terms of a collection of individuals, but by cultural groupings. What this suggests is that it is not the majority which ought to rule, but the majority of the dominant culture which should rule. This represents a claim to rule on behalf of a certain group within society, not simply by virtue of its being the majority, but by virtue of its cultural characteristics.

Table 18.2   Popular vote: Québec provincial election 1976 (1973 results in parentheses)

	Vote	Percentage of votes	Seats
PQ	1,390,363	41.4 (30.3)	71 (6)
Lib.	1,134,997	33.8 (54.8)	26 (102)
UN	611,678	18.2 (4.9)	11 (0)
PC	155,508	4.6 (9.9)	1 (2)
Other	67,681	2.0	1 (0)

Source: Rapport Préliminaire: Elections Générales du 15 Novembre 1976.

Table 18.3   Popular vote by region, 1976

Region	Total vote	Percentages					Seats
		Lib.	PQ	UN	PC	Other	
Montreal Region	750,603	31.3	45.1	19.7	3.83	0.24	21
Montreal East	591,370	33.0	52.0	11.2	2.35	1.36	18
Montreal West	502,768	43.7	26.3	22.0	1.26	6.59	16
Québec City	155,474	37.3	48.4	10.2	3.56	0.36	5
Québec Region	330,450	35.3	36.8	17.3	4.86	5.66	11
Three Rivers	169,071	29.2	39.9	24.0	5.79	0.52	6
Eastern Townships	295,699	27.0	33.4	31.3	7.81	0.41	11
Ottawa Region and North West	186,773	33.8	33.6	15.5	16.41	0.56	7
Saguenay-Lac St Jean	208,715	27.8	54.3	11.1	5.70	0.92	7
Lower St Lawrence-Gaspé	169,304	35.3	42.2	16.6	5.61	0.24	8

Source: Rapport Préliminaire: Elections Générales du 15 Novembre 1976.

Historically, it has always been argued that it is the special responsibility of the Québec state to represent the interests not simply of individuals *per se*, but of the French culture; the corollary of this is that it is the Francophone nation which has the right to separate if it so chooses. Now this is a right which is claimed irrespective of majoritarian status, for if we change the spatial context and consider Canada rather than Québec, the culture which is said to have this right is clearly a minority one. Majority-minority rights are determined by the political context; analytically they are quite distinct from the collective claims to independence as a right *per se*. This emphasis on the appropriate political context provides further illustration of the tensions inherent in the separatist ideal. In the past the PQ leadership, Camille Laurin, in particular, have pressed the claim of the Francophone nation to independence because it is the *only nation* in Québec (implying that only territorially defined majorities have rights to constitute nations);

other ethnic groups have a responsibility to participate and cooperate to develop the national culture of Québec. However, Laurin also uses the term nation in a way which is synonymous with the state, and not the ethnie. Separatist rhetoric refers to Québec as a nation struggling for political independence. In order to do so this argument must maintain that the Québec state represents not only the embodiment of the French nation (as used to be argued), but of all the people within it. The 'national culture' of Québec, though decidedly French, is the common inheritance of all its citizens. The extension of this nationalist doctrine is that the state, primarily responsible for the promotion of national culture, has the responsibility to ensure that every citizen learn the single official language. Thus the preamble of the original version of the Language Charter declared that 'the French language has always been the language of the Québec people, that it is, indeed the very instrument by which they have articulated their identity'. To maintain this identity throughout the province the language was to be used as an instrument of French cultural promotion. Québec's non-Francophone population saw in this formulation the establishment of an official state culture, with the implication that they would become disadvantaged citizens even within their own province. Recognizing this fear, the preamble to the new bill, Bill 101, was modified, referring to French as 'the distinctive language of a people that is in the majority French-speaking… the instrument by which that people has articulated its identity'. This awkward reformulation does not remove the inherent ambiguity which gave rise to the legal enforcement of French culture in Québec, and forces the nationalists to embrace a majoritarianism which negates a fundamental premise of nationalism, namely that nations and states should be coextensive.

The dilemma facing the Québécois government is that the rationale behind the separatist upsurge since the late 1960s is ethnic nationalism. But rather than re-define Québec's boundaries so that they coincide with the Francophone nation (possibly incorporating elements of the French language zone such as Madawaska, Acadia, northeastern Ontario and parts of the USA; see Figure 18.3), the PQ prefer to avoid this dilemma by refering to the *Québécois nation's right to self-government,* thereby converting an ethnic nationalism into a territorial nationalism. It hopes to persuade non-Francophones that its conception of nationalism is territorial and state-based, one in which they may partake if they will but choose to exercise their newly acquired right to assimilate into the 'national culture' and become Québécois citizens rather than hyphenated ethnic Canadians, e.g. Italian-Canadians.

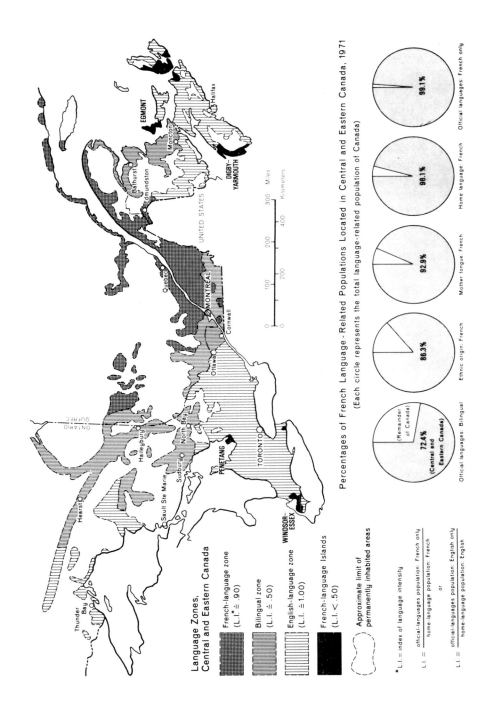

FIGURE 18.3   Language zones and regional concentration of French language populations, central and eastern Canada, 1971

The Québécois case demonstrates many of the classic issues which constitute the subject-matter of political geography. Inherent in the case-study is the abiding tension of Federal-Provincial relations, that is the problem of establishing acceptable conditions of political authority/dependency for the respective units in the territorial hierarchy to which they belong. A second feature is the conflict of 'nationalisms'. The tension between 'ethnic' and 'territorial' nationalism is a common characteristic of separatist situations. Other examples suggest that unless these twin bases of national identification can be united then the seeds for disintegration and fragmentation along ethnic/racial lines will remain a persistent obstacle to inter-ethnic harmony and to Federal-Provincial relations. For example, the Biafran secessionist attempt failed in large part due to the Ibo military elite's inability to convince the non-Ibo minority groups within Biafra that Ibo ethnic nationalism was but the spearhead of a larger Eastern Region territorial separatism. Similarly the failure of Plaid Cymru to extend its electoral base outward from the Welsh-speaking western heartland is due in main to its inability to convince the 79% non-Welsh-speakers that its nationalism is at least as territorially motivated as it is culturally motivated (Williams, 1977, 1978). If the PQ can arrive at a programme which can reconcile both ethnic and territorial-state nationalism then the separatist option of Sovereignty-Association will be both more democratic and more likely to provide a surer foundation for an independent Québec (Québec Government, 1979). However, the current attempt at nationality formation, identity through autonomy, is not without its inherent ambiguities, as we have seen; thus there is no necessary expectation that the pronouncements of the Québécois elite will be translated into the establishment of a sovereign Québécois state.

Conclusion

This chapter has demonstrated that the uneven spatial impact of modernization, coupled with the cultural division of labour, are important structural determinants of ethnic relations within Québec. However, in order to explain the timing and political character of separatism one must perforce turn to the role of the ethnic intelligentsia in shaping the nature of separatist demands, in articulating Québécois group rights as essentially majoritarian and hence liberal and democratic in their conception, and in providing the political philosophy which animates the current Québécois government programme of Sovereignty-Association. It remains to be seen to what extent Québec's experience of nationality formation, of achieving identity through independence, will be endorsed by the general electorate of this most distinctive Canadian province.

Acknowledgements

This chapter is based in part on research conducted by the author while at Harvard University, the Research Centre for French-Canadian Studies, McGill University, and the University of Western Ontario. I am grateful to Professor Don Cartwright, UWO for his permission to reproduce Figure 18.3 and to Mrs Jane Perks for preparing the diagrams.

References and bibliography

Berger, C. (1969). *Imperialism and Nationalism, 1884-1914* (Copp Clark, Toronto).

Cartwright, D. G. (1977). 'Institutions on the frontier: French-Canadian settlement in eastern Ontario in the nineteenth century', *Canadian Geographer,* **21**(1), 1-21.

Crepeau, P-A., and Macpherson, C. B. (eds.) (1965). *The Future of Canadian Federalism* (University of Toronto Press, Toronto).

Day, G. (1979). 'The sociology of Wales: issues and prospects', *Sociological Review,* **27**(3), 447-74.

De Wilde, J. (1977). 'The Parti Québécois in power', in Simeon, R. (ed.), *Must Canada Fail?* (McGill-Queen's University Press, Montreal).

Guindon, H. (1978). 'The modernization of Québec and the legitimacy of the Canadian state', In Glenday, D. *et al.* (eds.), *Modernization and the Canadian State* (Macmillan, Toronto).

Hechter, M. (1975). *Internal Colonialism* (Routledge & Kegan Paul, London).

Hechter, M. (1977). 'Language loyalty in theoretical perspective', *Language Problems and Language Planning,* **1**(1), 1-9.

Hechter, M. and Levi, M. (1979). 'The comparative analysis of ethnoregional movements', *Ethnic and Racial Studies,* **2**(3), 206-74.

Langlois, G. (1960). 'Cultural reasons given for the French-Canadian lag in economic progress', *Culture,* **21**(2), 152-70.

McRoberts, K. (1979). 'Internal colonialism: the case of Québec', *Ethnic and Racial Studies,* **2**(3), 293-318.

McWhinney, E. (1979). *Québec and the Constitution* (University of Toronto Press, Toronto).

Meekison, J. P. (ed.) (1971), *Canadian Federalism: Myth or Reality* (Methuen, Toronto).

Morgan, K. O. (1980). *Wales in British Politics* (University of Wales Press, Cardiff).

Nairn, T. (1977). *The Break Up of Britain* (New Left Books, London).

Nish, C. (1970). *Québec in the Duplessis Era, 1935-1959* (Cobb Clark, Toronto).

Page, E. (1977). 'Michael Hechter's internal colonial model of political development in the British Isles'. Paper presented to the PSA meeting, Aberystwyth.

Pinard, M. and Hamilton, R. (in press). 'The Québec independence movement'. In Williams, C. H. (ed.), *National Separatism* (University of Wales Press, Cardiff).

Québec Government (1979). *Québec-Canada: A New Deal* (Québec City).

Quinn, H. (1963). *The Union Nationale* (University of Toronto Press, Toronto).

Simeon, R. (ed.). (1977). *Must Canada Fail?* McGill-Queen's University Press, Montreal.

Sloan, W. N. (1979). 'Ethnicity or imperialism?' *Comparative Studies in Society and History,* **21,** 113-25.

Smith, A. D. (ed.) (1976). *Nationalist Movements* (Macmillan, London).

Smith, A. D. (1979). 'Towards a theory of ethnic separatism', *Ethnic and Racial Studies,* **2**(1), 21-37.

Thomas, C. J., and Williams, C. H. (1978). 'Language and nationalism in Wales', *Ethnic and Racial Studies,* **1**(2), 235-58.

Thompson, D. C. (ed). (1973). *Québec Society and Politics: Views from the Inside* (McClelland and Stewart, Toronto).

Wade, M. (1968). *The French Canadians, 1760-1967,* 2 vols (Macmillan, Toronto).

Whebell, C. F. J. (1973). 'A model of territorial separatism', *Proceedings of the Association of American Geographers,* **5,** 295-8.

Williams, C. H. (1974). 'Quebec after the elections', *Planet,* **21,** 5-16.

Williams, C. H. (1976). 'Cultural nationalism in Wales', *Canadian Review of Studies in Nationalism,* **4**(1), 15-38.

Williams, C. H. (1977). 'Non-violence and the development of the Welsh Language Society', *Welsh History Review,* **8**(4), 426-55.

Williams, C. H. (1978). 'Language decline and nationalist resurgence in Wales' (unpublished Ph.D. thesis, The University of Wales).

Williams, C. H. (1979a). 'Ethnic resurgence in the periphery', *Area,* **11**(4), 279-83.

Williams, C. H. (1979b). 'An ecological and behavioural analysis of ethnolinguistic change in Wales', In Giles, H. and Saint-Jacques, B. (eds.), *Language and Ethnic Relations* (Pergamon, Oxford).

Williams, C H. (1980). 'Ethnic separatism in Western Europe', *Tijdschrift voor Economische en Sociale Geografie,* **71**(3), 142-58.

Young, C. (1976). *The Politics of Cultural Pluralism* (University of Wisconsin Press, Madison).

19

The geography of voting patterns in South African general elections, 1974-77

Anthony Lemon

The rapid growth of electoral geography is reflected in both micro- and macro-studies in most English-speaking countries (Johnston, 1979). That South Africa is a notable exception is perhaps reflective of the general weakness of political geography in that country (Nel, 1979). English-speaking South African geographers have, more than their colleagues in other social sciences, tended to eschew studies with political implications. Afrikaans interest in political geography has been largely restricted to Black 'homelands' and other spatial aspects of government policy.

Geographical analysis of voting at the macro-scale was until recently limited to Williams' (1976) survey of the changing distribution of seats in General Elections since 1943. A more analytical approach is adopted by Taylor and Johnston (1979, pp. 306-8) and by Gudgin and Taylor (1980, pp. 34-41), who in the course of general works on electoral geography devote consideration to particular aspects of South African electoral contests, including the number of seats uncontested by major parties. Significant geographical content does appear in the major political study of Heard (1974), but forms a minor and somewhat concealed part of the overall analysis and lacks cartographic support. The General Elections of 1974 and 1977 have been analysed politically by Stadler (1975) and Midlane (1979) respectively, but both refer only fleetingly and by implication to the spatial dimension. Serious analysis has been made of political parties (Kleynhans, 1975), White attitudes (Schlemmer, 1973, 1978), the sociology of voting behaviour (Lever 1972a, b) and its ethnic basis (Peel and Morse, 1974). Lever's micro-scale study of the Jeppe and Johannesburg West constituencies in the 1966 and 1970 elections,

419

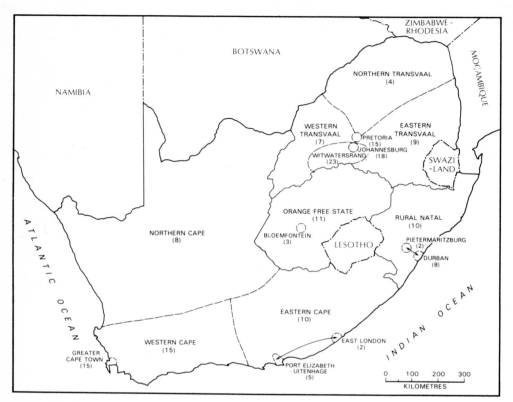

FIGURE 19.1   Electoral regions used in this study. Numbers in parentheses denote the number of seats in each region

together with the work of Peel and Morse in three Cape Town constituencies in 1970 provides the nearest approach to the methods advocated by the behaviouralist school of electoral geographers (Cox, 1969) so far applied to South Africa.

The present study aims to remedy the deficiency of macro-scale analysis rather than to attempt behavioural study of spatial processes. In addition to the valid criticisms of behavioural approaches levelled by Prescott (1972, pp. 86-7), such work is inevitably restricted to the micro-scale, given its dependence on questionnaire methods. The regionalization of voting patterns adopted here is similar to that of Heard (1974), but with some further subdivision (Figure 19.1); the major urban areas are considered as distinct regions, but smaller towns are considered as part of 'rural' regions. The regions remain identical for the 1974 and 1977 elections, as the Thirteenth Delimitation of constituency boundaries was used for both. An attempt is made to extend the more geographical elements of Heard's work to these elections, and party fortunes are examined in terms of effective, excess, and wasted votes in a single-member plurality system (Johnston, 1979, pp. 63-7).

A complicating feature is the large number of uncontested seats (43 in 1974, 44 in 1977). Reasons advanced for this distinctive characteristic of South African elections include the polarization of the White electorate between sections which are also spatially segregated (Taylor and Johnston, 1979, pp. 306-7). For present purposes uncontested seats constitute a technical problem of electoral analysis, in terms of both meaningful estimation of overall regional and national strength of the major parties and comparison of different elections. A method of estimating the strength of Government and opposition parties in uncontested seats, based partly on Heard (1974), is applied, and should prove capable of wider application.

Long-term voting trends and the 1970 general election

Ethnic identification of voters appears much stronger in its hold over people's loyalties than the basis of party identifications elsewhere, such as those of socioeconomic class in Britain. Peel and Morse (1974, p. 1526) make the important observation that:

> If we can tell better how a person is going to vote on the basis of his father's occupation rather than his own, and on the basis of the language he spoke in childhood rather than the language he speaks now, then it is his *ethnic background* rather than his *current status in society,* that most strongly determines his party preference.

This appeared to be very largely the case for Afrikaners in Cape Town, apart from those who now spoke English as their home language, many of them 'ambiguous Afrikaners' who regarded themselves as English, and over half of whom voted for the United Party (UP) (Peel and Morse, 1974. pp. 1528-9). Had their investigation included rural areas of the Cape it is probable that Peel and Morse would also have identified a significant 'Bloedsap' element amongst older Afrikaners: those who have traditionally supported the UP because they regard the National Party (NP) as destructive of White unity in South Africa. Otherwise the UP has drawn its support from English-speakers, although Peel and Morse note that both socioeconomic status and area of residence, as well as ethnicity, influence English voting behaviour.

The 1970 election was the first since the NP was returned to power in 1948 in which the Nationalists lost ground, losing eight seats to the UP. This result surprised most observers, but the swing to the UP was markedly concentrated in the Johannesburg area and the predominantly urban areas of Natal; elsewhere it was minimal or non-existent (Vosloo, 1970, pp. 4-5). The seats lost by the Nationalists were those gained by them in 1966, and ones where the English-speaking vote played a major part. Nevertheless the reduction of Nationalist majorities in the Orange Free State and the northern Cape, *platteland* (rural) areas where the English-speaking vote is negligible, indicated at least some Afrikaans support, probably of a protest variety, for the UP.

It was widely assumed that the Government called an election in April 1970 in order to rout the recently formed Herstigte Nasionale Party (HNP), an extreme right-wing breakaway from the NP and thus a threat to the tribal unity of Afrikanerdom. In this the Government succeeded; all four MPs who had crossed the floor lost their seats, and the party gained a derisory total of 53,000 votes. It was, however, undoubtedly responsible for the conservative line taken by a NP fearful of losing right-wing support, and this may in turn explain the return of English-speaking Nationalist voters of 1966 to their normal allegiances, as well as the loss of small numbers of *verligte* (enlightened) Afrikaner and immigrant votes. In addition many English voters may well have regarded sentiments voiced by the HNP, including its policy of relegating English to the second language, as confirmation of their worst fears about the true nature of the Nationalists themselves.

Political background to the 1974 general election

The General Election of 24 April 1974 was announced early in February on the grounds that 'the next 3-5 years... would be decisive for the continued existence of South Africa and her people' (Vorster, 1974), and that in these circumstances the Government must be assured of its people's confidence. Most observers saw the Government as taking advantage of the divisions which were racking the UP. After the 1970 election it seemed that the UP could, if it pursued a consistently *verligte* line, hold its new voters and, with improved organization, add to them (Kleynhans and Labuschagne, 1970, p. 8). In the event it failed to follow such a line, with the reformists or 'Young Turks' arousing fierce and unconcealed opposition, which led to unseemly struggles over the nomination of candidates in 1974. Nevertheless Kleynhans (1974) predicted continuing Nationalist losses on the basis of by-elections and opinion polls, arguing that as long as the NP maintained its exclusive cultural and political character, it would not attract the English voter.

Although all parties professed to view the election as 'crucial to the country's future', the campaign was unremarkable, even sterile; few major issues emerged. The Nationalist appeal stressed the need for White unity in the face of uncertainty, demanding 'a clear and unequivocal mandate to carry on protecting South Africa from onslaughts from within and without' (Mulder, 1974): in other words, a blank cheque. *'Swart gevaar'* ('Black danger') tactics were used by both sides, the Nationalists concentrating on the dangers of the UP's federal policy, and the UP stressing the issue of White land needed for the Government's intended 'homeland' consolidation. It thus failed to provide concerted *verligte* opposition, despite the abundance of ammunition available: South Africa's increasing international isolation; her growing internal divisions and deteriorating race relations; the impracticability of *apartheid* as evidenced by continued increase in numbers of urban Blacks, the negligible economic advance of the 'homelands', and the paralysis of government policy in relation to the Asian and Coloured communities; violation and diminution of democratic rights; the often inhuman application of ideology; and widespread administrative incompetence.

National voting patterns: 1974

In the event, the UP gained only one seat, Randburg, from the Nationalists, and lost four, including two Natal seats which had been badly delimited for the UP. The Progressive Party (PP) provided the major surprise, winning five seats from the UP (two in Cape Town and three in Johannesburg) in addition to Houghton, for long its sole parliamentary seat. Reference to two available maps of socioeconomic status (Hart, undated, p. 52, and University of Stellenbosch, 1977, p. 80), both of which recognize five status categories, reveals that these victories all occurred in areas belonging to the two highest categories. A similar correlation between relatively 'liberal' voting and high-income suburbs has been noted in Salisbury, Zimbabwe (Lemon, 1978). Such voting behaviour may be viewed as reflecting either the enlightenment of the better-educated, or more cynically the remoteness of the better-off from any threat to their jobs or life-style. Differences between the results of Parliamentary and Provincial Council contests

Table 19.1   Seats and votes, 1974

				Un-		Seats by PR	Votes for
						Of	each
		Per-	Total	contested	Of	contested	contested
Party	Votes	centage	seats	seats	total	seats	seat won
NF	619,154	55.3	117	30	91	70	7,117
UP	362,716	32.3	41	13	53	41	11,318
PP	77,400	6.9	7*	0	12	9	11,057
HNP	44,235	3.9	0	0	6	5	—
DP	12,053	1.1	0	0	2	1	—
Others	5,369	0.5	0	0	1	0	—
	1,120,387	100.0	165	43	165	122	8,892

*Includes Pinelands, a Cape seat where the contest was postponed until June owing to the death of the UP candidate after nomination day. The by-election result has been incorporated in all tables.

appeared to indicate support for reformist UP candidates rather than 'old guard' or 'verkrampte' elements, although personal factors were also involved. The varying performance of UP candidates in relation to their known position in the political spectrum tended to confirm the pattern of stronger support for *verligte* candidates.

The Nationalists 55.3% of all votes (Table 19.1) was 2.4% down on their peak achievement of 1966, but the UP lost 5.0%. The HNP, despite four years to organize, suffered a decline in its total vote, but this was viewed by the English-language press as a mixed blessing:

> The pathetic showing of the H.N.P. is a measure of the reactionary extremists who prefer to influence the National Party's direction from within. Their inhibiting effect on Government policy is a growing source of concern to more realistic Nationalist thinkers (*Eastern Province Herald, 1974*).

The Democratic Party, recently founded by a former Nationalist cabinet minister, performed creditably and came close to winning Pietermaritzburg North. Its policies, which are discussed elsewhere (Lemon, 1976, pp. 225-6) presented a fresh alternative to the tired uncertainties of the UP.

The NP won a disproportionate number of seats in relation to votes (Table 19.1), even if only contested seats are taken into account. Prior to 1966 this phenomenon was attributable mainly to the geographical concentration of UP support in urban areas, which produced larger average majorities than those of the NP (Heard,

Table 19.2   Distribution of party majorities according to size, 1974

	Cape			Transvaal			Orange Free State	Natal		S.A.		
	NP	UP	PP	NP	UP	PP	NP	NP	UP	NP	UP	PP
8000-8999										2		
7000-7999	2											
6000-6999	1			5	1		2			8	1	
5000-5999	1			11			2	1		15		
4000-4999	3			13	1		3		1	19	2	
3000-3999	7	4	1	19	2	1	2	1	2	29	8	2
2000-2999	2	2		3	1			1	4	6	7	
1000-1999	3	4	1	1	1	1			1	4	6	2
500-999				1	1	1			1	1	2	1
1-499		1	1	1		1		2	1	3	2	2
Uncontested	18	4		7	4		5	5			30	13

Table 19.3   Effective, excess and wasted votes, 1974

		Effective	Excess	Wasted
Cape	NP	43,604	77,200	24,949
	UP	34,415	27,426	54,043
	PP	15,802	2,348	14,185
Orange Free State	NP	11,953	45,050	—
	UP	—	—	7,903
	PP	—	—	1,388
Natal	NP	17,080	11,636	9,297
	UP	27,637	22,737	16,257
	PP	—	—	14,410
Transvaal	NP	126,484	227,787	17,324
	UP	20,833	21,899	123,215
	PP	18,824	6,495	3,948
Total	NP	199,121	361,673	51,570
	UP	82,885	72,062	201,418
	PP	34,626	8,843	33,936

1974), and hence large numbers of excess votes (i.e. votes additional to those needed to win). By 1966 the pattern was already changing (Heard, 1974, p. 177) and by 1974 it had been transformed, with 84% of Nationalist majorities but only 39% of UP majorities exceeding 3000 (Table 19.2).

The reason for the UP's relatively high ratio of votes to seats was to be found in *wasted* votes, i.e. those received in seats which the party failed to win (Table 19.3). It had four times as many wasted votes as the NP, and nearly twice as many even in its strongest province, Natal. The *effective* vote of the NP (the minimum required to win each seat) totalled more than twice that of the UP. The slender majorities of successful Progressive candidates are reflected in a very small excess vote, whilst the wasted votes accruing to PP candidates were cast mainly in the Cape and Natal. In the latter, the party's substantial support was insufficient to capture a single seat, reflecting the disadvantageous position of any minority party in a 'first-past-the-post' electoral system.

The HNP fought only seats where Nationalists also stood, whilst the PP contested only two seats in the absence of UP candidates: these small parties clearly aimed to draw support primarily from Government and Opposition respectively. The NP received over 130,000 excess votes in 24 straight fights with the HNP, compared with just over 200,000 in 58 seats where UP candidates stood unsuccessfully.

To obtain a more complete picture, an attempt was made to estimate party support in uncontested seats. Following Heard (1974, pp. 174-5) each unopposed candidate was deemed to have the support of a percentage of voters equal to the average percentage support received by victorious candidates of his party in the electoral region concerned. The number of votes was calculated on the basis of the average percentage poll for the electoral region. Support for hypothetical unsuccessful UP or NP candidates in uncontested seats was calculated as equivalent to the same proportion of the estimated vote for unsuccessful candidates as they obtained in unsuccessfully contested seats in the relevant electoral region. This may slightly underestimate true UP support, as it makes no allowance for potential UP voters in the relatively large number of contested constituencies where the party failed to field a candidate. On the other hand, the UP would presumably have done less well in seats it chose not to contest.

The overall results of these calculations give the NP 833,225 votes (56.6%) and the UP 483,281 (32.9%), thus slightly widening the gap between them compared with actual voting (Table 19.1). In relation to the total electorate, NP strength is reduced to 38.7% compared with 22.4% for the UP. Whilst the former figure is not unduly low given an average abstention rate, it does suggest that the UP position was not hopeless in 1974. Given improved organization and clearer direction, the large untapped voting potential could do much to close the gap. The percentage poll in 1974 was 69.1, a 4.4% decrease relative to 1970, thus continuing a decline which had characterized every election since 1960. It is probable that most of the additional abstentions represented potential UP voters discouraged by the party's lack of clear purpose.

Many immigrants to South Africa, some of long standing, have not become South African citizens, and are thus ineligible to vote — a factor shown to be of major significance in Rhodesian elections (Lemon, 1978, p. 513). Accordingly the total White population aged 18 and over was calculated from the 1970 census and found to be 2,381,287: this would leave 226,203 people unenfranchised in 1974. If, however, allowance is made for annual growth of the White population of 1.0%, the number of unenfranchised Whites rises to 322,651. Given a growth rate of 1.5% p.a. (still conservative in relation to a known White growth rate of almost 1.9% p.a. in the 1960s) the figure increases to 372,327. This represents 45% more than the gap between total Nationalist and UP votes in contested seats, and marginally more than the difference in overall estimated strength of the two parties. Whilst it obviously cannot be assumed either that all unenfranchised voters would support the UP, or that their percentage poll would exceed the average, the size of the unenfranchised group, of whom few can be Afrikaans speakers, is clearly of considerable significance.

Regional voting patterns: 1974

For the purpose of mapping seats a cartogram (Figure 19.2) was preferred, as a simple map would give little visual evidence of opposition strength owing to its urban concentration. Nationalists won 65 out of 74 seats in rural/small town regions. The UP won five rural seats in Natal, whose English character owes much to the aftermath of British annexation in 1843, including the Byrne settlement of the late 1840s. The Eastern Cape, home of the greatest single incursion of 5000 British settlers in 1820, was the scene of three rural UP victories. The Nationalists also possessed three urban strongholds, winning all seats in Pretoria and Bloemfontein and 20 out of 23 on the Witwatersrand. Administrative functions, in which Afrikaans employees predominate, are very important in Pretoria, the administrative capital, and Bloemfontein, the judicial capital and provincial capital of the Orange Free State. Many Witwatersrand constituencies include large concentrations of mining workers, as well as lower-paid industrial and railway workers; such groups are highly conservative owing to their vulnerability, actual or perceived, to any removal of restrictions on Black occupational and residential mobility.

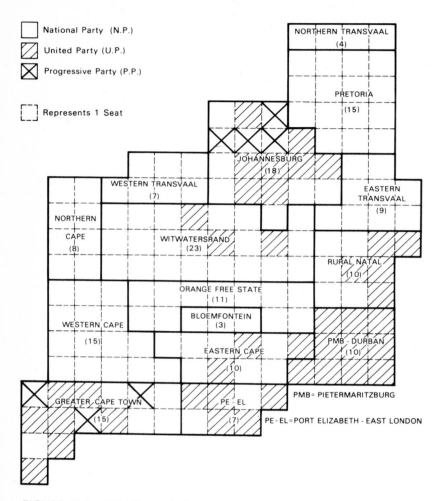

☐ National Party (N.P.)

▨ United Party (U.P.)

▨ Progressive Party (P.P.)

⌐¬
⌊_⌋ Represents 1 Seat

NORTHERN TRANSVAAL
(4)

PRETORIA
(15)

JOHANNESBURG
(18)

WESTERN TRANSVAAL
(7)

EASTERN
TRANSVAAL
(9)

NORTHERN
CAPE
(8)

WITWATERSRAND
(23)

RURAL NATAL
(10)

ORANGE FREE STATE
(11)

WESTERN CAPE
(15)

BLOEMFONTEIN
(3)

EASTERN CAPE
(10)

PMB - DURBAN
(10)

GREATER CAPE TOWN
(15)

PE - EL
(7)

PMB = PIETERMARITZBURG

PE - EL = PORT ELIZABETH - EAST LONDON

FIGURE 19.2   1974 General Election results by seats won

Opposition parties held 12 of the 18 Johannesburg seats and nine out of 15 seats in Cape Town. In both cities the UP continued to hold several higher-income seats, although Progressive support exceeded 25% in three such UP seats in Cape Town. The real UP strongholds were in the cities of the Eastern Cape and especially Natal, where the Party made a clean sweep of the Durban-Pietermaritzburg seats.

The UP contested only 34 rural seats leaving the HNP, which fought 26, to provide opposition in many others, notably in the Transvaal. In the Cape, where the HNP has less support, 17 rural seats were unopposed, all but one going to the NP. The PP fought only five rural seats, performing best (29.4%) in the Natal seat of Umhlanga, which includes many holiday and retirement homes. The HNP fought only 19 urban seats, 11 of them in Pretoria, indicating its limited basis of urban support. Uncontested urban seats were predictably divided between the respective strongholds of the NP and UP.

Regional voting figures (Table 19.4) show the NP facing little rural challenge outside the Eastern Cape and Natal. The concentration of the HNP's rural support in the Transvaal and the Orange Free State is obvious, whilst its urban support was even more strongly concentrated in Pretoria. Support for the Progressives rose to around 20% in Johannesburg, Durban-Pietermaritzburg and Cape Town, but in each of these areas the UP was more than twice as strong. The Nationalists' three urban strongholds stand out clearly, but even in other urban areas, apart from Natal, they attracted about one-third of votes cast. Their largest majorities were achieved in Pretoria, the Orange Free State, and the small number of contested seats in the Western Cape.

The major discrepancies between seats and votes occurred in the Northern Cape, Eastern and Northern Transvaal, where the UP's share of around one-fifth of the vote was widely scattered and nowhere constituted a majority. A similar fate befell the PP in Durban-Pietermaritzburg and the HNP in the Northern Transvaal, where it achieved 22.3% of votes cast in straight fights with Nationalists. In Johannesburg the PP won the same proportion of seats as the UP (26.7%) with only 18.3% of votes cast compared with the UP's 43.6%. This striking contrast reflects the Progressives' far more cautious selection of contests. In the Witwatersrand too, for similar reasons, the UP's share of the votes was more than twice its share of seats. Its compensation was in Durban-Pietermaritzburg, where it won all 10 seats with only 57.2% of votes cast, a highly satisfactory result in the short term but one which exposed the party's vulnerability in its major stronghold.

Political background to the 1977 general election

The announcement in September of a General Election to be held on 30 November, 18 months before one was due, surprised almost everyone. Even the voters' rolls were in disorder because the Department of the Interior was in the process of switching to a computerized system. Mr Vorster's stated reasons for calling the election were threefold (Vorster, 1977): first, to allow the electorate

Table 19.4 Regional voting patterns, 1974 (numbers of seats contested in parentheses)

	NP		Percentage	UP		Percentage	PP		Percentage	HNP		Percentage
Rural												
Orange Free State	45,113	(7)	81.5	4,926	(3)	8.9	1,388	(1)	2.5	3,937	(6)	7.1
Natal	31,265	(6)	41.8	36,279	(8)	48.4	3,450	(2)	4.6	816	(1)	1.1
Eastern Cape	26,016	(5)	52.7	21,206	(5)	43.0	1,761	(1)	3.6	–		–
Western Cape	35,798	(5)	77.3	7,488	(2)	16.2	1,703	(1)	3.7	722	(2)	1.6
North Cape	28,969	(5)	74.0	8,557	(3)	21.9	–		–	1,612	(2)	4.1
Eastern Transvaal	52,680	(9)	69.0	17,116	(8)	22.4	–		–	6,532	(6)	8.6
Western Transvaal	39,998	(6)	71.4	10,529	(5)	18.8	–		–	5,435	(4)	9.7
Northern Transvaal	24,398	(4)	77.7	–		–	–		–	7,003	(4)	22.3
Urban												
Pretoria	82,558	(12)	74.0	12,634	(5)	11.3	1,870	(1)	1.7	11,534	(11)	10.3
Johannesburg	45,837	(7)	33.1	62,460	(14)	45.1	27,397	(5)	19.8	613	(1)	0.4
Witwatersrand	132,914	(20)	64.1	69,029	(17)	33.3	–		–	4,807	(6)	2.3
Durban-Pietermaritzburg	6,748	(2)	12.7	30,352	(6)	57.2	10,960	(4)	20.6	–		–
Cape Town	44,208	(9)	32.4	63,954	(13)	46.9	25,258	(7)	18.5	716	(1)	0.5
Port Elizabeth-East London	10,762	(2)	37.0	14,697	(3)	50.5	3,613	(2)	12.4	–		–
Bloemfontein	11,890	(2)	76.7	2,977	(1)	19.2	–		–	–		–

'to add its voice to Government protests against international "meddling" in South African affairs'; secondly, to obtain a verdict on the Government's proposed constitutional changes, which involved the creation of Coloured and Indian parliaments and an executive Presidency (Vosloo, 1979); and thirdly, because of the 'unreal' situation created by the disintegration of the UP.

To most observers it appeared that the Prime Minister had once more chosen the moment of maximum disarray for the opposition. The UP had collapsed in two stages. Its reformists had first departed to form the Reform Party, which soon merged with the Progressives to become the Progressive Reform Party (PRP). More recently the UP formally dissolved itself, splitting into three fragments. Those on the left joined the PRP, which again changed its name to the Progressive Federal Party (PFP). The 'hardliners' formed the South African Party (SAP), whilst the residual and largest element of the UP reconstituted itself as the New Republic Party (NRP). Whilst these developments might be viewed as healthy for the long-term growth of White opposition, the new parties were in no position to face an election in 1977; none had finalized its policy.

It was further suggested that Mr Vorster wanted his 'mandate' for constitutional change quickly, before the electorate understood the new proposals. Retrospectively, it also seems likely that he was anxious to secure a large majority before the full extent of the 'Information scandal' was revealed.

In other respects electoral circumstances were hardly propitious for the Government. A year after the Soweto riots there appeared to be no clear policy for urban Blacks. The Black education system had partially collapsed, with many schools closed, boycotts of classes, and resignation of teachers. The Coloured Labour Party and Coloured Representative Council, and even the moderate Indian Council, had all rejected the new constitutional proposals. More important perhaps for White voters, South Africa had followed Western Europe into a long and deep recession: just when some signs of recovery appeared, the Government's clampdown in October on the Black newspaper, *The World*, on two editors and 18 organizations, had provoked an intensely adverse overseas reaction. So too had the death in detention, under suspicious circumstances, of the founder of the Black Consciousness movement, Steve Biko, and the subsequent insensitivity displayed by the Minister of Justice, Police and Prisons, Mr Kruger. Meanwhile the African détente policy had collapsed entirely, and relations with the West were the worst ever, as the absence of a veto against the UN Security Council mandatory arms embargo

Table 19.5   Candidates in the 1977 General Election.

	Contested seats						Uncontested seats	
	NP	NRP	PFP	HNP	SAP	Others	NP	PFP
Urban	58	35	48	23	4	3	16	2
Rural	47	11	9	33	3	2	26	0
Total	105	46	57	56	7	5	42	2

against South Africa had demonstrated. The head of the South African Defence Force had warned that South Africa must go over to 'an economy of survival' in the face of deepening domestic problems and isolation abroad. Not surprisingly, in such circumstances, Mr Vorster was accused of going to the country 'before the going gets tough' in an attempt 'to batten down the hatches' (*Rand Daily Mail,* 1977a).

Paradoxically, the very seriousness of the situation created by Government policies could rebound to the advantage of the NP. In the words of the *Rand Daily Mail* (1977b): 'Spectacular all-round failure has created a national crisis — and the resultant public anxiety is causing some people to respond to the Government's emotional appeal to patriotism.' The parallel with Rhodesia is striking: the critical situation in that land had in the July 1977 election led people to close ranks behind the Government of Mr Ian Smith, which had itself led Rhodesia into crisis (Lemon, 1978, pp. 527-9). The 1977 General Election in South Africa was to demonstrate that White South Africans had either not yet realized the dangers of such a syndrome, or had failed to perceive these dangers as applicable to themselves.

National voting patterns: 1977

For the first time since the Nationalists were elected in 1948, no opposition party contested sufficient seats to win (Table 19.5). The Nationalists were unopposed in 42 seats and faced only HNP opposition in 49 more. In 15 seats only 'intra-opposition' contests took place amongst the other three parties. The NRP clearly had neither hope nor expectation of inheriting the scale of support formerly enjoyed by the UP, at least in the short term: it virtually abandoned the rural areas and fought less than half the urban seats. The PFP contested over half the urban seats, compared with the 20% fought by the Progressives in 1974, and was unopposed in two Johannesburg seats.

The inevitability of NP victory almost certainly contributed to a further decline in the poll to 64.4%. Other probable factors included the 'homelessness' of many former UP supporters and the lack of enthusiasm of the NP rank and file for the proposed constitutional changes.

Total opposition strength declined from 48 to 30 seats, and the PFP not unexpectedly became the official Opposition with 17 seats, including all six won by the PP in 1974. The NRP won only 10 seats, all except one (East London North) in Natal. SAP victories were limited to three of the seven seats held at the end of the old Parliament: Simonstown (Cape peninsula), where the MP had strong personal support, and two Port Elizabeth seats held by slender majorities over the PFP. The HNP vote declined by a further 10,000 votes, despite the fielding of 11 more candidates than in 1974.

The PFP seats included the Progressives' first Natal victory in a General Election at Musgrave (Durban), but the party lost Durban North, which it had won in a three-cornered by-election contest in 1976, to the NRP, and Pinelands, whose UP Member had joined the PFP, to the Nationalists. PFP strength was again clearly concentrated in Cape Town (four more seats) and Johannesburg (five). The new seats included several high-income constituencies where Progressive support had been rising in 1974, but also others of more mixed socioeconomic composition including Groote Schuur and Wynberg. It seemed, therefore, as if PFP support was beginning to diffuse geographically from the concentrated pockets of high-income population to which it was largely confined in 1974.

The Nationalists increased their share of the vote by 10% to a record level (Table 19.6), whilst the PFP vote equalled the combined NRP, SAP and HNP total. The discrepancy between votes and seats widened slightly in favour of the NP at the expense of both major opposition parties, a reflection of their high proportion of unsuccessful contests. The SAP's favourable ratio of votes and seats merely reflects its very selective entry into the electoral arena.

The size distribution of NP majorities confirms Nationalist invincibility: they included all 66 of the seats with majorities of over 5000, 54 of them in the Transvaal and the Orange Free State. The NRP had no majorities of more than 3000. Some of the Progressive seats of 1974 were now relatively safe, but seven PFP seats were held with majorities of under 500.

Such large NP majorities piled up over half a million excess votes (Table 19.7), mostly in the Transvaal, although in relative terms the Nationalists also received a vast excess vote in the Orange Free State. As in 1974, they wasted far fewer votes than their opponents.

Table 19.6   Seats and votes, 1977

Party	Votes	Per-centage	Total seats	Un-contested seats	Seats by PR Of total	Seats by PR Of contested seats	Votes for each contested seat won
NP	690,384	65.3	135*	42	108	80	7,423
PFP	181,049	17.1	17	2	28	21	12,070
NRP	127,335	12.0	10	0	20	15	12,733
SAP	19,308	1.8	3	0	3	2	6,436
HNP	34,161	3.2	0	0	5	4	—
Others	6,271	0.6	0	0	1	0	—
	1,058,508	100.0	165	44	165	122	8,676

*Includes Springs, a Witwatersrand seat where the contest was postponed until April 1978 after the murder of the NP candidate after nomination day. The by-election has been incorporated in all tables.

Table 19.7   Effective, excess and wasted votes, 1977

		Effective	Excess	Wasted
Cape	NP	30,924	77,400	5,609
	NRP	2,929	2,226	33,480
	PFP	24,894	9,101	34,213
Orange Free State	NP	6,464	65,867	—
	NRP	—	—	827
	PFP	—	—	2,423
Natal	NP	26,702	26,317	14,639
	NRP	28,479	12,136	27,264
	PFP	4,391	140	26,548
Transvaal	NP	75,691	335,282	25,429
	NRP	—	—	19,994
	PFP	25,436	15,176	38,278
Total	NP	139,781	504,866	45,677
	NRP	31,408	14,362	81,565
	PFP	50,330	24,417	101,912

The PFP's heightened ambitions produced three times as many wasted votes as in 1974, divided fairly evenly between the Transvaal (37.6%), the Cape (33.6%), and Natal (26.0%). Again it was Natal where substantial PFP support was largely unrewarded. Its slender majorities in many of the seats won are reflected in a very small excess vote; the vulnerability of the NRP, even in Natal, is similarly reflected.

The strength of support for Government and Opposition in uncontested seats was again estimated. In the absence of any PFP candidates in the Northern Cape, the Party's support was calculated using its lowest regional share of total opposition votes elsewhere (in the Western Transvaal). Total estimated support for the NP was 974,753 (68.2%), compared with 227,497 (15.9%) for the PFP. In relation to the total electorate these figures represent 43.2% (NP) and 14.0% (PFP). The low turnout almost certainly concealed even greater untapped opposition voting potential than in 1974, however, given that this was the second consecutive General Election fought in the worst possible circumstances for the opposition parties.

The unenfranchised population, calculated in the same manner as for 1977, amounted to 358,266, allowing a 1% p.a. increase in the White population, or 448,807 assuming a 1.5% increase. The latter figure, whilst no longer sufficient to bridge the gap between Government and official Opposition votes, still represents 17.5% more than the gap between NP and combined PRP/NRP votes, and marginally more than the estimated total support gap between the NP and combined PFP/NRP. Theoretically the opposition parties might attempt to persuade unenfranchised persons to become South African citizens and so qualify for the vote. In practice current circumstances are highly unpropitious for such a campaign, given the uncertainty felt by many Whites about their future in South Africa.

Nor can it any longer be assumed that a large majority of non-Afrikaans speakers would necessarily vote against the NP. Indeed, the major feature of the 1977 election might well be seen as the high level of English support for the Nationalists. From an estimated trough of just over 10% in 1972 this rose, according to opinion polls, to 13-15% in 1973 and over 20% by 1975; by late 1976 it verged on 30%, a level maintained in the 1977 General Election (Schlemmer, 1978, p. 77). The election produced four English-speaking Nationalist MPs, and the NP emerged ahead of the NRP in several PFP seats with largely English-speaking electorates. It seems possible, therefore, that erosion of traditional South African voting along lines of ethnic identification is accelerating. In 1977 this was very largely in favour of the NP; a survey carried out by the Afrikaans newspaper *Rapport* shortly before the election showed that more than 86% of Afrikaans-speaking voters backed the NP.

Regional voting patterns: 1977 (Figure 19.3)

The Nationalist grasp on rural areas and small towns was virtually complete. Of 74 seats, the NRP won only three (in Natal) and the

National Party (N.P.)

Progressive Federal Party (P.F.P.)

New Republic Party (N.R.P.)

South African Party (S.A.P.)

Represents 1 Seat

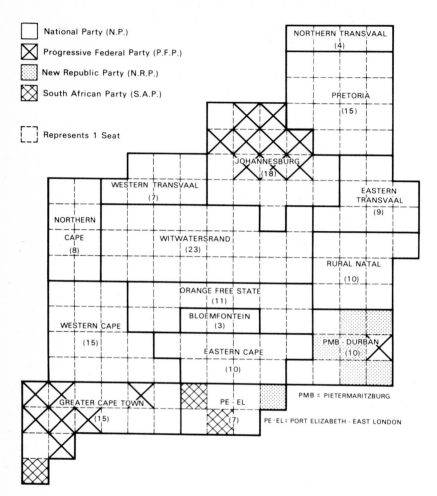

NORTHERN TRANSVAAL
(4)

PRETORIA
(15)

JOHANNESBURG
(18)

WESTERN TRANSVAAL
(7)

EASTERN
TRANSVAAL
(9)

NORTHERN
CAPE
(8)

WITWATERSRAND
(23)

RURAL NATAL
(10)

ORANGE FREE STATE
(11)

BLOEMFONTEIN
(3)

WESTERN CAPE
(15)

EASTERN CAPE
(10)

PMB - DURBAN
(10)

GREATER CAPE TOWN
(15)

PE - EL
(7)

PMB = PIETERMARITZBURG

PE - EL = PORT ELIZABETH - EAST LONDON

FIGURE 19.3   1977 General Election results by seats won

PFP none. The NP won all 23 Witwatersrand seats for the first time, together with three more seats in Johannesburg where it gained equality with the PFP. The Nationalists also gained three seats in Durban-Pietermaritzburg, thus threatening the NRP in its only stronghold, although two of the NP victories (Pietermaritzburg North and Pinetown) were won on minority votes in three- and four-cornered contests respectively. Two Cape Town seats fell to the Nationalists and one seat each in Port Elizabeth and East London.

Regional voting figures (Table 19.8) show that the NP had consolidated still further its grip on rural regions, winning a

Table 19.8   Regional voting patterns, 1977 (number of seats contested in parentheses)

	NP		Percentage	NRP		Percentage	PFP		Percentage	SAP		Percentage	HNP		Percentage
Rural															
Orange Free State	65,403	(9)	93.2	827	(1)	1.2	750	(1)	1.1	—		—	3,204	(7)	4.6
Natal	46,601	(9)	57.0	26,652	(7)	32.6	7,142	(2)	8.7	—		—	863	(2)	1.1
Eastern Cape	13,678	(3)	53.0	7,376	(3)	28.6	3,257	(1)	12.6	1,507	(1)	5.8	—		—
Western Cape	37,601	(5)	88.6	—		—	3,564	(2)	8.4	—		—	1,270	(3)	3.0
North Cape	16,191	(3)	91.8	—		—	—		—	—		—	1,466	(3)	8.2
Eastern Transvaal	55,622	(9)	83.9	—		—	—		—	—		—	6,277	(9)	9.5
Western Transvaal	37,251	(5)	88.1	—		—	414	(1)	1.0	—		—	4,605	(5)	10.9
Northern Transvaal	26,279	(4)	88.3	—		—	—		—	—		—	3,477	(4)	11.7
Urban															
Pretoria	109,323	(14)	85.0	4,202	(3)	3.3	6,959	(4)	5.4	—		—	8,027	(13)	6.2
Johannesburg	82,524	(15)	57.1	9,311	(7)	6.4	51,757	(14)	35.8	—		—	924	(2)	0.6
Witwatersrand	125,403	(16)	79.8	6,481	(3)	4.4	20,210	(7)	12.9	—		—	3,701	(7)	2.4
Durban-Pietermaritzburg	21,057	(5)	24.4	41,227	(10)	47.7	23,937	(7)	27.7	160	(1)	0.2	—		—
Cape Town	36,097	(7)	31.9	23,781	(9)	21.0	44,971	(11)	39.7	7,990	(2)	7.1	367	(1)	0.3
Port Elizabeth-East London	10,366	(2)	24.6	7,478	(3)	17.8	16,416	(5)	39.0	7,815	(2)	18.6	—		—
Bloemfontein	6,928	(1)	80.5	—		—	1,673	(1)	19.5	—		—	—		—

majority of votes even in rural Natal. In the Eastern Cape it was lucky to win all the seats with only 53% of the votes; it was aided here by a four-cornered contest in Albany, normally an opposition stronghold which includes the university city of Grahamstown. The halving of HNP support from 22.3% to 11.7% in the northern Transvaal left it without strong support in the rural regions. In urban areas HNP support was negligible outside Pretoria, and even there it mustered a mere 8027 votes (6.2%) for 13 candidates. Nationalist support increased in most urban areas, most dramatically in Johannesburg and Durban-Pietermaritzburg at the expense of the NRP. In Cape Town and Port Elizabeth-East London the effectiveness of the PFP challenge held back further Nationalist advance, the NP share of the vote actually decreasing in the latter in the face of the relatively strong showing of the SAP. This suggests that the SAP may serve to reduce the English-speaking Nationalist vote by appealing to the conservative English voter who wishes to retain the *status quo*. As such, according to the main Port Elizabeth daily newspaper, it has 'a greater claim to exist nationally than the New Republic Party' (*Eastern Province Herald*, 1977).

Much more important, however, is the advance of the PFP to the position of leading party in both Cape Town and Port Elizabeth-East London. In the latter it was unlucky to win no seats, coming a close second in three constituencies. The PFP also won over one-third of all Johannesburg votes and over one-quarter of those in Durban-Pietermaritzburg; in both it could well become the largest party if it enters the next General Election better equipped. These observations remain substantially unaltered if allowance is made for estimated support in uncontested seats; the PFP falls somewhat relative to the NP in Cape Town, but the gap closes a little in Johannesburg.

By-elections in 1979

Only one by-election contest took place in the 18 months after the General Election, although four Nationalists were returned unopposed. The Springs by-election was really an extension of the General Election (see footnote to Table 19.6); the low turnout was seen as reflecting the response of Nationalist voters to the 'Information scandal'.

Subsequent by-elections produced dramatic results. Nationalist majorities were drastically reduced, largely in the face of HNP opposition: in three contests the HNP won some 40% of the votes cast. Such results were achieved in 'blue-collar' constituencies (Koedoespoort, Rustenburg, and Germiston) characterized by large numbers of mining and/or railway workers, and represented a protest against proposed liberalization of labour legislation following the Wiehahn Report. Three out of four October by-elections produced polls of only 23-32%, levels of voting which are almost unknown in South African by-elections and must be interpreted as deliberate large-scale abstention by Nationalist voters unhappy about the Prime Minister's plans to carry out what constitute, by Nationalist standards, radical reforms in major areas of policy. Such voters clearly cannot, as yet, bring themselves to vote for another party: this is an undoubted strength of the NP when compared with the opposition parties, many of whose supporters more easily change their allegiance.

The PFP more than doubled its 1977 vote in Johannesburg West, and increased its vote in Brentwood, another Johannesburg constituency, despite a very low turnout. Again there is a suggestion of diffusion, as Johannesburg voters outside the wealthy suburbs are beginning to view the PFP as an acceptable replacement for the UP, which formerly held Johannesburg West and enjoyed substantial support in Brentwood.

But it appears that the PFP can make no impact on traditional Nationalist strongholds. Thus it came a poor fourth in Randfontein, and a disastrous third in the Swellendam Provincial Council by-election in June, where it managed only 3.9% compared with the 27.2% of the NRP. This might be regarded as a test of the PFP in the kind of rural constituency it seldom contests in a General Election: indeed the Parliamentary seat of Swellendam has been uncontested since 1970. The NRP naturally seized upon these failures, making much of its own July success in winning back the Natal South Coast Provincial seat from the NP in the absence of a PFP candidate to divide the opposition. Its 2750-vote majority was assisted by an influx of new registrations and the transfer of 2200 voters from the Kokstad area, previously in the Griqualand East constituency, when the district of East Griqualand was transferred from the Cape to Natal. To many observers the logic of these results is an electoral pact between NRP and PFP, but this appears to have been ruled out; certainly there are fundamental policy differences, and the PFP has an international credibility wholly denied to the NRP. The latter regards the 1977 election as a 'phoney election' because of its unpreparedness. Whilst this clearly has an element of truth, the PFP appears to have a greater chance of actually winning seats, except in Natal. It demonstrated this in November 1979 by winning its first Witwatersrand seat in a three-cornered contest at Edenvale.

Conclusion

The two General Elections studied clearly demonstrate the geographical polarization of electoral support in South Africa, with Nationalists having an almost unchallenged grip on rural areas and small towns outside the English-speaking areas of Natal, and to some extent the Eastern Cape. In the urban areas of Pretoria, the Witwatersrand and Bloemfontein Nationalists are also supreme. The new divisions of the opposition find equally strong geographical expression: urban Natal is the main NRP stronghold, whilst PFP support shows signs of diffusing from its established concentrations in high-income suburbs of Johannesburg and Cape Town. HNP support was minimal in all areas by 1977, but has increased dramatically since in 'blue-collar' Nationalist constituencies, in the face of more *verligte* Government policies.

The single-member plurality system of voting inevitably produced large numbers of wasted votes for the relatively small opposition parties. Equally, it produced a massive excess vote for the NP in its major strongholds, where these were contested. The percentage poll continued its long-term decline in 1974 and 1977, with the result that only 43.2% of the electorate supported the NP in 1977, when allowance is made for uncontested seats. In addition some 450,000 Whites of voting age are unenfranchised, as they are not South African citizens.

The 1977 General Election was notable for the strong support given to the NP by English voters. This may be interpreted as a closing of ranks in the face of international pressures reminiscent of that which occurred in Rhodesia in the 1970s. It represents a major departure from the hitherto strongly ethnic behaviour of White South African voters, but there is little evidence that this can be a two-way process. Schlemmer (1978, p. 72) has found the concerns of Afrikaans voters to be those of Whites, with issues related to Afrikaner culture accorded a low priority. For many Afrikaners it appears that the NP is not, as the orthodox view would have it, primarily a matter of language, culture, and history; rather it is a matter of good wages, good jobs, and good contacts from association with the party. Thus although Schlemmer found Afrikaans university graduates, businessmen, and a surprisingly substantial proportion of civil servants to have relatively progressive views on certain subjects, it appears much more likely that most will express their views within the NP rather than outside it. The current *'verligte'* directions of Government policy, whilst they may cost votes and even perhaps some seats to the HNP, make significant defection of Afrikaners to the PFP or NRP less likely.

These conclusions indicate the need for further research at the micro-scale. It should focus particularly upon the relationship between high socioeconomic status and PFP voting, the areas where this relationship is absent, and the apparent diffusion of PFP voting to lower-status areas. It is also important to explore the possibility of generation change in voting patterns, particularly amongst young urban Afrikaners. In the absence of such change the National Party, with its fundamental commitment to dividing power on its own terms but not sharing power with other race groups, is unassailable through the ballot box.

Acknowledgements

I am grateful to Professor Calvin Woodward of New Brunswick University, Richard Bouch and Christopher de Wet of Rhodes University for valuable comments on an earlier version of this paper. Dr F. Van Zyl Slabbert, Leader of the PFP, Mr Vause Raw, Leader of the NRP, and Mr Ray Swart, PFP, MP for Musgrave, generously gave up time to be interviewed.

References and bibliography

Cox, K. R. (1969). 'The voting decision in a spatial context', in Board, C., Chorley, R. J., and Haggett, P. (eds.), *Progress in Geography*, **1**, 81-117 (Edward Arnold, London).

Eastern Province Herald (1974). Leader on 26 April.

Eastern Province Herald (1977). Leader on 2 December.

Gudgin, P. J., and Taylor, P. J. (1980). *Seats, Votes and the Spatial Organization of Elections* (Pion, London).

Hart, T. (undated). *The Factorial Ecology of Johannesburg*. Occasional Paper 5, Urban and Regional Research Unit, University of the Witwatersrand, Johannesburg.

Heard, K. A. (1974). *General Elections in South Africa, 1943-1970* (Oxford University Press, London).

Johnston, R. J. (1979). *Political, Electoral and Spatial Systems* (Clarendon Press, Oxford).

Kleynhans, W. A. (1974). Comments reported in the *Eastern Province Herald*, 23 April.

Kleynhans, W. A. (1975). 'Political parties in South Africa', *Politikon*, **2**(1), 6-32.

Kleynhans, W. A., and Labuschagne, G. (1970). Contributions to a discussion entitled 'The 1970 election analysed', *New Nation* (June 1970), 2-8 and 20.

Lemon, A. (1976). *Apartheid: a Geography of Separation* (Saxon House, Farnborough).

Lemon, A. (1978). 'Electoral machinery and voting patterns in Rhodesia, 1962-1977', *African Affairs*, **77**, 511-30.

Lever, H. (1972a). *The South African Voter* (Juta, Cape Town).

Lever, H. (1972b). 'Factors underlying change in the South African general election of 1970', *British Journal of Sociology,* **23,** 236-43.

Midlane, M. (1979). 'The South African General Election of 1977', *African Affairs,* **78,** 371-87.

Mulder, C. P. (1974). Speech reported in the *Rand Daily Mail,* 24 April.

Nel, D. E. (1979). 'Perspectief op geografiese navorsing. (14). Politieke Geografie', *Die Suid-Afrikaanse Geograaf,* **7,** 49-63.

Peel, S., and Morse, S. J. (1974). 'Ethnic voting and political change in South Africa', *American Political Science Review,* **68,** 1520-41.

Prescott, J. R. V. (1972). *Political Geography* (Methuen, London).,

Rand Daily Mail (1977a). Leader on 21 September.

Rand Daily Mail (1977b). Leader on 29 November.

Schlemmer, L. (1973). *Privilege, Prejudice and Parties: a Study of Patterns of Political Motivation among White Voters in Durban* (South African Institute of Race Relations, Johannesburg).

Schlemmer, L. (1977). Quoted in the *Rand Daily Mail,* 30 November.

Schlemmer, L. (1978). 'White voters and change in South Africa: constraints and opportunities', *Optima,* **27**(4), 62-83.

Stadler, A. W. (1977). 'The 1974 General Election in South Africa', *African Affairs,* **74,** 209-218.

Taylor, P. J., and Johnston, R. J. (1979). *Geography of Elections* (Penguin, Harmondsworth).

University of Stellenbosch (1977). *Sosiale Atlas van die Kaapstad Metropolitaanse Gebied* (Institute for Cartography).

Vorster, B. J. (1974). Speech reported in the *Eastern Province Herald,* 5 April.

Vorster, B. J. (1977). Speech reported in the *Rand Daily Mail,* 21 September.

Vosloo, W. B. (1970). 'The election of 1970 (or who really won?)', *New Nation* (August) 4-7.

Vosloo, W. B. (1979). 'Consociational democracy as a means to accomplish peaceful political change in South Africa: an evaluation of the constutitional change proposed by the National Party in 1977', *Politikon,* **6**(1), 13-28.

Williams, O. (1976). 'The White voter: a spatial analysis of voting patterns in general elections, 1943-74', in Lemon (1976), pp. 91-101.

Political studies from spatial perspectives
Edited by A.D. Burnett and P.J. Taylor
© 1981 John Wiley & Sons Ltd

_____ *20*__

The land *in Israel*

Gwyn Rowley

The central thesis of this essay is that any understanding of the recent colonization and settlement of the Holy Land by Zionists must be based not only upon an appraisal of the simple territorial aspirations of the colonists but also upon a deeper appreciation of the fundamental Hebrew system of beliefs in which *land,* the Promised Land, plays a central and crucial role. The modern development of Zionism is viewed as an outgrowth of this latent nationalism which for long had remained as an enshrined and symbolical yearning for place; a yearning that is now receiving renewed general attention (Berger, 1973; Hall, 1966; Leighley, 1963; Tournier, 1968; Tuan, 1976, 1977).

Maier (1975), combining Jungian psychological and Lorenzian ethnological concepts, considers Jewish history in terms of territorial symbolism, suggesting that the Torah became the conceptual substitute for the Promised Land as a type of movable territory. However, this paper emphasizes that Torah was never and never could be a substitute for land. Rather it must be seen as a deed of title between Israel and God with solemn obligations on behalf of both parties (Newman, 1962, pp. 29-38); von Waldov, 1974). In essence we will seek to show that no real understanding of the development of historical Israel, nor of the modern state of Israel, is possible without an appreciation of land, God-given land as *storied place.*

The initial sections of the paper form not simply the backcloth but the guiding principles against which to consider the establishment of the modern state of Israel, together with the continuing Israeli occupation and progressive settlement of the occupied territories, particularly the West Bank, including East Jerusalem.

The first section focuses upon the Jewish notion of covenant and land which derives from a specific development of a homeless and

443

wandering people, followed by the occupation of the land and culminating in the construction of King Solomon's temple in Jerusalem (960-930 BC). Throughout the Babylonian exile, the return, and further exile into the Diaspora the land-covenant tradition continues.

The second part provides not only the link into the third and final section but considers the continuing Jewish nationalism, with its rewakening and politicalization in the latter part of the nineteenth century. While this incipient nationalism reached its particular climax with the creation of the State of Israel in 1948 the land theme continued to find expression, and weaves like a thread through these modern developments.

The final section considers the progressive and continuing settlement of the occupied territories, particularly the West Bank and East Jerusalem. Here again the notion of the Promised Land, *Eretz Yisrael,* suggests not the occupation of an erstwhile Palestinian homeland but rather the basic philosophy and justification for *liberating* those territories occupied following the Six-Day War in 1967.

The covenantal dimension

The sojourn in Egypt, the exodus and the related covenant are of particular significance to any understanding of the subsequent development of Israel. A wandering group of Hebrew people, led by Moses, miraculously escapes Egyptian bondage with the help of God — Yahweh. In the Sinai wilderness at Kadesh-Barnea in the first half of the thirteenth century BC these Hebrews enter into a solemn covenant with Yahweh. A brief quote summarizes the basic belief:

> A Syrian ready to perish was my father, and he went down into Egypt, and sojourned there with a few, and became there a nation, great, mighty and populous: and the Egyptian evil en- treated us, and afflicted us, and laid upon us hard bondage.... And the lord brought us forth out of Egypt with a mighty hand.... And he brought us into this place and hath given us this land (Deuteronomy 26: 5-9).

Each of the Old Testament traditions on the covenant specifically indicates that the Hebrews left Sinai and travelled towards Palestine for the explicit purpose of invading and possessing it (Alt, 1959).

Indeed Brueggemann (1977) suggests that 'The Bible is addressed to the central human problem of homelessness *(anomie)* and seeks to respond to that agenda in terms of grasp and gift' (p. 187). It is contended that no real understanding of the development of Israel can be forthcoming without an appreciation of the impact of the covenantal dimension of the land question to a lost, displaced, and homeless people wandering in a wilderness (Davies, 1974, p. 194).

Thus Maier's suggestion that 'Before they had land the Israelites became a people identified with a Divine Law around which they rallied in peace and war' is incorrect and quite unacceptable (Maier, 1975). For the Israelites, in essence, to become or rather to accept the position as 'a people identified with a Divine Law' was conditional upon God's offer of land. These two aspects, chosen people and land, are not separate issues but intimately and irrefutably connected.

Exodus 34:10 clarifies the issue. God says 'Behold, I make a covenant: before all thy people I will do marvels', continuing later: 'Observe then that which I command thee this day: behold I drive out before thee the Amorite, and the Canaanite, and the Hittite, and the Perizzite, and the Hivite, and the Jebusite' (Exodus 34:11).

This is briefly God's side of the bargain; while in exchange it is later stressed that 'thou [Israel] shalt worship no other God: for the Lord, whose name is Jealous, is a jealous God' (Exodus 34:14). There follows, in the subsequent nine verses of Exodus, the specific covenantal details and duties that the Iraelites must undertake. Later again God reassures Israel that acceptance and adherence to these strictures will earn for Israel its desired result, that is land. 'For I will cast out the nations before thee, and enlarge they borders' (Exodus 34:24). Thus Brueggemann emphasizes that:

> The covenant is characteristically about land, about the promise of land not given, about retention of land now possessed, and about land-loss because of covenant breaking. Israel never had a desire for a relation with Yahweh in a vacuum but only in land (Brueggemann, 1977, p. 188).

Perhaps the most telling passage in this context concerns the passage over the Jordan into the Promised Land. Pausing, prior to this momentous event, the Wilderness behind them, the land before them, God unequivocably relates to the Israelites:

> See, I have set before thee this day life and good, and death and evil, in that I command thee this day to love the Lord thy God, to walk in his ways, and to keep his commandments and

his statutes and his judgements, that thou mayest live and multiply: and the Lord thy God shall bless thee in the land whither thou goest to possess it. But if thine heart turn away, so that thou wilt not hear, but shall be drawn away, and worship other gods, and serve them; I denounce unto you this day, that ye shall surely perish, and that ye shall not prolong your days upon the land, whither thou passest over Jordan to go to possess it (Deuteronomy 30:15-18).

The position is clear. Possession of the land is and must always be conditional.

Eretz Yisrael

The actual territorial extent of *Eretz Yisrael,* the land of Israel, this Promised Land, is considered in a number of verses within the Old Testament. Scripture is generally less precise concerning the specific boundaries of this homeland.

One of the earliest references concerning the earlier covenant with Abraham, relates that: 'In the same day the Lord made a covenant with Abram, saying, Unto thy seed have I given this land, from the river of Egypt unto the great river, the river Euphrates' (Genesis, 15:18). The river of Egypt referred to is probably not the Nile but rather the Wadi el Arish in Sinai (Rowley, 1977). Other passages are equally expansive. Moses, according to Numbers 34:3-12, inherited a land that included much of present-day Israel and parts of Egypt, Iraq, Jordan, Lebanon, and Syria. A fundamental point here, however, is that the notion of the Promised Land has always included Samaria and Judea, the presently so-called West Bank, the areas being firmly embedded in the twelfth-century BC lands of the Twelve Tribes, with Israel reaching its maximum extent during the reign of King Solomon in the tenth century BC (Figure 20.1).

The conquest/colonization of Palestine by what Newman (1962) terms the Joseph tribes, commencing about 1250 BC, did not aim simply at an occupation of the Promised Land alongside the native inhabitants, rather the land was seen to be unclean: 'The land, unto which ye go to possess it is an unclean land with the filthiness of the people of the lands, with their abominations, which have filled it from one end to another with their uncleanliness' (Ezra 9 : 11). The purification of the land thus required an alternative separatist consciousness. Those who had entered into marriages with non-sectarian Israelites were admonished and instructed by God to 'separate yourselves from the people of the land, and from strange

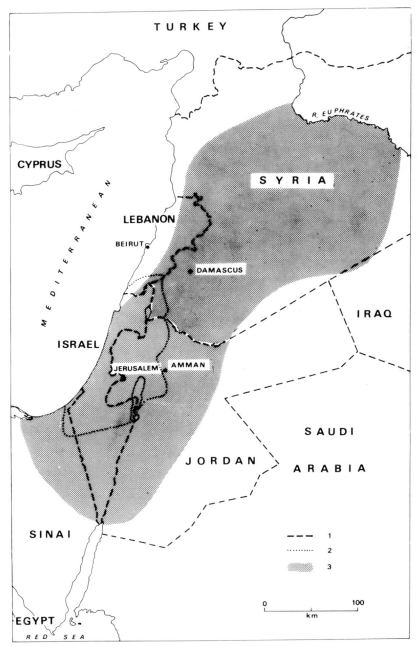

FIGURE 20.1   Territorial extents of Israel: (1) present-day boundaries; (2)
twelve tribes of Israel, twelfth century BC; (3) Kingdom of David and
Solomon, tenth century BC. Sources of data: Martin (1974) and *I Chronicles*,
18:5-14

wives' (Ezra 10:11), so 'that ye may be strong, and eat the good of the land, and leave *it* for an inheritance to your children for ever' (Ezra 10:12). That is, those who had intermarried with non-sectarian Israelites had to separate.

Storied place

While the first five books of the Bible, the Torah, present an essentially ethnocentric viewpoint, they nonetheless establish and pledge allegiance not to land or a land but to *the* land. Thus, in the Torah or Pentateuch, there is no timeless space nor is there spaceless time. Rather there is *storied place,* that is a place which has meaning because of the history lodged there. In essence, the unbreakable dialectic between a people and a place increases the burden of awareness (Hall, 1966; Tuan, 1977). 'It is briefly', in the words of J.Z. Smith, 'history that makes a land mine' (Smith, 1969, p. 109). Indeed Brueggemann (1977) suggests that:

> It is land that provides the central assurance to Israel of its historicality, that it will be and always must be concerned with actual rootage in a place which is a repository for commitment and therefore identity. Biblical faith is surely about the life of a people with God as has been shown by all the current and recent emphases on covenant in an historical place. And if God has to do with Israel in a special way, as surely he does, he has to do with land as an historical place in a special way. It will no longer do to talk about Yahweh and his people but we must speak about Yahweh, his people *and his land* (pp. 5-6).

There are, it is true, problems concerning the factual nature, *Tatcharakter,* the precise historicism, and interpretation of these historical events, which are discussed in part by Eichrodt (1961, vol. 1, p. 37) and Newman (1962, pp. 29-38). However it should be realized that here:

> We are dealing with traditions cherished and handed down by people transmitting in the most solemn way *their* view of *their* own origins, not with history as such. *What is important is what remained engraved on the national memory* (Daiches, 1975, p. 7); italics mine.

These early attempts to order intellectually the world of experience led on, in time, to the subsequent incorporation of myths and symbolisms, together with ritual re-enactments, into mainstream systems of beliefs. Any understanding of such systems, it is suggested, cannot be accomplished without an appreciation of the notion of wilderness and of a wandering people without land, and the conditional gift of land, grasp, and continual fear of land-loss.

Jerusalem

Jerusalem is of particular importance in this general development. David chose Jerusalem, then a Canaanite enclave occupied by the Jebusites, as his capital in the first quarter of the tenth century BC.

This was a particularly astute and imaginative move as it, together with the later Davidic innovation of centring Israel on the city, brought the northern and southern Hebrew tribes together. The theological-sectarian differences separating the north and south, arising in part from differing interpretations of the covenant, were assuaged and under David Jerusalem became the centre of a great empire (Newman, 1962, pp. 18-19; Noth, 1960, p. 197). At this time, it should be noted, Egypt was weak, the Hittite Kingdom was beset by large and unsettling migrations of people, and the Assyrians and Babylonians were troubled by the Aramite ascent.

Within Jerusalem the wanderers can be said to have come to rest. 'He shall build an house for my name, and I will establish the throne of his kingdom for ever' (II Samuel 7:13). A house, not a tent, and a throne were established; the Hebrews had finally arrived, and in the tenth century BC the Ark of the Covenant itself was brought to King Solomon's temple which, as Bright points out, was not only a royal chapel but also *the* national shrine of the Israelites (Bright, 1959, p. 197). Likewise the arborescent tabernacle menorah, for long a part of the cultic tradition of the wilderness period, was apparently no longer needed 'Once a fixed location for YHWH's shrine was established on God's holy mountain in Jerusalem, a grove of living trees replaced the menorah as the vehicle for that part of the cosmic imagery of the santuary' (Meyers, 1976, p. 185). Real vegetation, like real land, had replaced the symbolism of the tabernacle menorah.

While the death of Solomon, who had endeavoured to manage the land outside of covenant, in 922 BC heralded the break-up of the Kingdom, the city of David and the Temple were firmly established as the focal point, the pure physical manifestation of this longing for homeland and unity in, with, and of the land (I Kings 12:16).

Exile and promise

The Kingdom of Judah was conquered in 586 BC by the Babylonians, followed by exile of a large part of the population in Babylon (II Kings). In 516 BC, following the defeat of the Babylonian empire by the Persians, the land of Israel also came under Persian rule. King Cyrus allowed the Jews to return to the land and rebuild the Temple. In 63 BC Judah came within the Roman Empire. Following the Jewish revolt against the Romans, which began in AD 66, most of the Jewish population was driven into exile. Yet again Israel was to be cast in the role of wanderer, dispersed. But important changes had occurred since those never-forgotten wanderings in Sinai.

The tradition of Jeremiah emphasizes that any new history must finally be history that leads to Zion; W. D. Davies showing that the land theme is centrally expressed in the Jerusalem temple (Davies, 1974, pp. 130-54). In this poetic vision destroyed Jerusalem is not only restored but it is established as the centre of a coherent, well-ordered place-based communal life, the very antithesis of exile, in which there is satisfaction, rest, and renewal.

Thus, while Israel is condemned to wander again it is now steadfast in the belief, knowledge, and strength that exile will end and a return to the *land* will come about. Again it is its being in land which is both the destiny of Israel and the mark of Yahweh's lordship:

> Behold, O my people, I will open your graves, and cause you to come out of your graves, and bring you into the land of Israel.
>
> And shall put my spirit in you, and ye shall live, and I shall place you in your own land: then shall ye know that I the Lord have spoken it, and performed it, saith the Lord (Ezekiel 37:12, 14).

Ezekiel thus envisages the history beyond exile that would permit the exiles, both in Babylon and later the Diaspora, to live as Israel, the people of the Covenant, in the sure belief that Yahweh and his people are sacramentally bound together to share a common future and destiny in the land, not conceptual space alone but, in time, real physical space.

The modern development of Zionism

While the modern development of Zionism, a movement 'looking toward the segregation of Jewish people upon a national basis and in a particular home of its own' (Singer, 1939, p. 666), by Theodor Herzl in the last decade of the nineteenth century, provided the critical impetus towards the development of the modern state, it must be clearly understood that throughout the centuries of the Diaspora there existed a vital Jewish nationalism which implied the eventual recolonization of the Holy Land (Haddad, 1973). For example, the Shabbatai Zevi movement in the mid-seventeenth century called for a massive return to the land, while a relay of emissaries, *Shelichim,* maintained contact between the land and the communities of the Diaspora.

This nationalism had its roots and its hopes embedded deeply in storied earth, which in turn formed the central driving force of its uncompromising ethical faith. Indeed some Jewish immigration into the Holy Land had taken place throughout the nineteenth century and earlier, although this increased quite markedly, particularly after 1880 in response to persecution in much of eastern Europe (Rowley, 1970). It was, however, Herzl who provided the format for the specific agenda concerning the Jewish state, *Judenstaat,* which rapidly became the classic of the Zionist movement which Herzl inaugurated (Herzl, 1946). The first Zionist Congress was held in Basle in August 1897.

The foundation of the modern state and aftermath

In brief five interconnected features provide the background against which to consider the creation of the State of Israel in 1948. Firstly, the dissolution of the Ottoman Empire following the First World War (Hurewitz, 1979). Secondly, the failure of Arab nationalism (Amin, 1978; Flapan, 1979). Thirdly, British attempts to continue their imperialistic intentions in Palestine, despite the decline of Britain as a world power (Monroe, 1963). Fourthly, the increasing Jewish immigration, both willing and coerced, into Palestine (Kimche and Kimche, 1954, pp. 23 and 60-1; Mardor, 1957, pp. 89-90). Fifthly, the growth of US influence in the Middle East together with the UN proposals, under direct pressure from the US, to effect the partition of Palestine. This latter point, concerning the UN proposals, is of importance for on 19 March 1948 the US requested the UN Security Council to suspend action on the partition plan, a plan which would have resulted in a Jewish state with a population half Jewish and half Arab, a Palestinian state almost entirely Arab in population, and a separate Jerusalem.

But civil war had already broken out in Palestine. The better-armed Jewish underground forces, particularly because of the massive defeat wreaked upon the Palestinian Arabs by the British occupying forces in 1936-9, understandably seized the opportunity and occupied not only the territory allotted to the Jewish state, as envisaged by the UN, but also more than half of that earmarked for the proposed Arab state. The opportunist Hashemite-Jordanian and Egyptian forces occupied the remainder of this stillborn Arab state (Figure 20.2).

As with the earlier occupation of the Promised Land by the Joseph tribes, which commenced c. 1250 BC, the general sentiment, clearly and unequivocably expressed by Joseph Weitz as early as 1940, emphasized the separatist consciousness:

> Among ourselves it must be clear that there is no place in the country for both peoples together... with the Arabs we shall not achieve our aim of being an independent people in this little country... there is no other way but to transfer the Arabs, from here to neighbouring countries (Weitz, 1967, p. 4).

Thus violence, as within any colonization which attempts to take possession of an occupied territory, is viewed by David Hirst as being implicit within Zionism (Hirst, 1977). This is as true of the early occupation of Canaan by the Joseph tribes as of the recent twentieth-century Zionist recolonization of the Promised Land. Maier again is quite off-target in suggesting that:

> The identification of modern Israel is with land; the Torah does not dominate the life of the [Jewish] people. Apparently real territory is better suited to rally the people than the 'movable territory' *which did well enough* for two thousand years (Maier, 1975, p. 23); italics mine.

The important point here is that 'movable territory' *never* did 'well enough'. There never was, nor could there ever be, a substitute for *real* land (Newman, 1962, pp. 37-8). Basically no matter how much the land theme has been spiritualized it is seen that the image is never robbed of its original, historical referent (Brueggemann, 1977, pp. 189-92). Likewise Ardrey's assertion, in accordance with what he terms the 'amity-enmity complex', that in the twentieth century the Arabs have made Israel by uniting its polyglot peoples in a constant need to attend to its borders, derives from a most

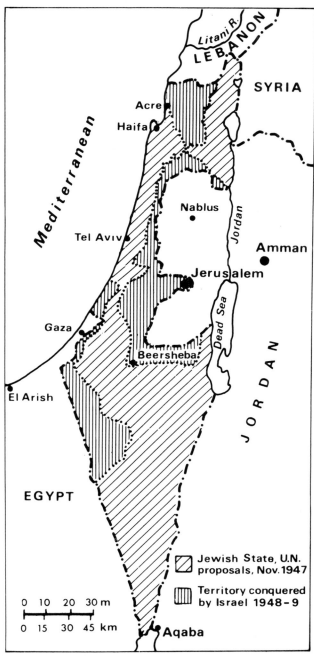

FIGURE 20.2   The UN proposals for the partition of
Palestine, November 1947

superficial and essentially ahistorical, and thus unacceptable consideration of Israel (Ardrey, 1966, pp. 305-12).

As has been seen, the end of exile and return to *the* land is at the core of the covenantal dimension, the prophetic poetry of Ezekial envisaging this history beyond exile (Ezekial 37:12,14; Martens, 1972, pp. 170-90). By contrast, the dispossessed Palestinians continue to emphasize their right to return and seek the creation of an independent Palestinian entity (United Nations, 1978).

The occupied territories

Following the Six-Day War in 1967 a victorious Israel occupied the West Bank, including East Jerusalem, the Gaza strip, and the Golan Heights. Particular attention will be focused upon the continuing Israeli settlement of Samaria and Judea, the so-called West Bank, including Jerusalem, as this area is considered to be of crucial importance for any political development of an Arab-Palestinian homeland. However the West Bank and Jerusalem are viewed by Israel as integral parts of *Eretz Yisrael*, in other words covenantal land. Here again the modern manifestation of the ancient land problem emerges as a central theme in the unfolding saga.

The settlements

Three main types of colonial settlement have been utilized to settle the West Bank: outpost villages, religious settlements, and residential suburbs (Figure 20.3). As a background it is to be noted that the colonization process of rural Israel, following independence in 1948, included both the communal kibbutz and the private enterprise moshava (Sharon, 1955). Several sub-varieties of the moshavim, transitional in character and adapted to local conditions, were developed.

Outpost villages are one such sub-variety, and occur when settlement is seen as the best way to 'improve the security situation but when farming can become profitable only after years of thorough reclamation work' (Orni, 1963, p. 178; Orni and Effrat, 1964, pp. 196-216). In the outpost village Nahal units, the Pioneer Settlement Corps of the Israeli army, undertake site preparations, construct the villages, sink a well, provide mobile power supply and power cables, sanitation and sewerage facilities, etc., with certain of the soldiers, whose demobilization is imminent, being posted in as permanent settlers, to remain after their demobilization.

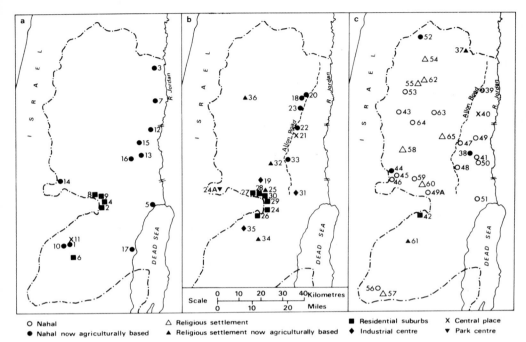

FIGURE 20.3   The progression of Israeli settlement in Judea and Samaria, 1967-78: (a) 1967-70;
(b) 1971-75; (c) 1976-78. Sources of data: Jewish National Fund (1978) and Leach (1978)

Two examples will demonstrate certain of the impacts of the colonial settlement upon the established order. It should be noted here that a dunum, referred to in the following examples, equals 0.25 acre or 0.101 hectare. Mehola (3 on Figure 20.3a), on a strategic site covering the road to Tubas, was the first nahal established in the Jordan valley, in February 1968, with 1689 dunums of land being expropriated from Bardala village together with further lands from Ain al Beida. Whereas the Mehola well had seriously depleted the water supply in the two proximate Arab villages, by December 1978 Mehola had a population of 137 persons with an established commercial agricultural economy, including field crops, grapefruit, and turkeys, together with a small metal-fabrication plant. Salit Nahal (53 on Figure 20.3a), established in September 1977 between Tulkarm and Kaddum, expropriated 1268 dunums of land from Kufr Sahr village, and, with additional lands earmarked, was to become a moshav by December 1979. By December 1978, 17 houses had been completed and the village contained a residential population of 46.

The nahal settlement form has been the prime settlement type introduced to colonize the West Bank. The years of 'thorough reclamation work', both in the physical and human environments, prior to agricultural profitability here includes particularly sequestration and purchase of lands and consolidation of holdings into viable economic units.

Such nahal settlements in the West Bank are seen by the Palestinians and others as in direct violation of the Geneva convention of 1949, which states that 'an occupying power shall not deport or transfer parts of its own civilian population into the territory it occupies' (United Nations, 1976, paras. 1-2). The counter-claim by Israel suggests that Samaria and Judea, that is the entire West Bank, including Jerusalem, as traditionally with Eretz Yisrael, is then an integral part of the modern state. What is more, the Israeli government is not strictly posting in 'parts of its own civilian population'. Thus the Israeli government is adhering to the word if not the spirit of the Geneva convention.

The second major type of Israeli rural settlement within the West Bank is the religious village, particularly by Gush Emunim, Group of the Faithful. Here an initial settlement is established by the group and, in various ways, lands are assembled to facilitate the transition from the initial colonial settlement form to an integrated village community with related rural-farming structures. Within the initial stages such settlements are often 'illegal', in the sense that they are not recognized by the Israeli government for allocations of various fundings for health, education, welfare, social services, etc., although external funding is obtained from, for example, the Jewish National Fund, Youth Aliyah and Keren Hayesod.

As of February 1979 all of those settlements established in the West Bank prior to December 1978 had been 'regularized', that is legalized, recognized, and accepted by the Israeli Government. It is of interest to note that in the period since the Conservative Likud government attained power in 1977 to December 1978, 17 colonial settlements were established in the West Bank, eight of these being founded by religious groups. Ofra (32 on Figure 20.3b), east of Ramallah, on the east-west road to Jericho, was established by Gush Emunim in May 1975 and 'regularized' in July 1977. The village site was formerly a Jordanian army base with 180 and 250 dunums of land having been expropriated from, respectively, Ain Yabrud and Silwad. As of December 1978 there were 360 dunums of agricultural lands, with additional pastures and plans for further major land acquisitions; Ofra having a population of 302, and possessing several workshops in addition to the agricultural enterprises. It should be noted that during the later stages of development both the considered military and religious rural settlements are quite comparable, and both may become either moshav or kibbutz, although moshavin are now by far the dominant type.

The third general type of Israeli settlement within the West Bank is the residential suburb usually established directly by the Israeli government. Such settlements have been located particularly along the northern and eastern edges of Jerusalem, which will be considered later, but also adjacent to smaller urban centres such as Bethlehem and Hebron.

Qiryat Arba (6 on Figure 20.3a), begun as an 'illegal' settlement in April 1968 and recognized by the Israeli government in February 1970, is a large urban settlement for religious Jews adjacent to Hebron in Judea. Upon establishment 1620 dunums of agricultural land were expropriated from individuals in Hebron and Halhal. Qiryat Arba had an estimated population of 1677 (December 1978) and factories, fabrication units, various services with certain individuals commuting to work in Jerusalem.

The spatial pattern

The initial Israeli settlements in the West Bank, following the occupation after the 1967 war, were established along the eastern slopes of the Samarian mountains, the Jordan Rift Valley and about the Jerusalem-Latrun salient (Figure 20.3a). Between 1971 and 1975 developments occurred particularly along the eastern slopes but to the west of the earlier settlements, and also in a concentration to the north and east of Jerusalem, and to the west of Jericho and about Bethlehem (Figure 20.3b). These settlements have now been

Table 20.1   Present status of West Bank settlements established since 1967

Settlement type	1967-70	1971-5	1976-8
Nahal (established)	11	5	4
Nahal (initial)	—	—	14
Religious (established)	—	4	2
(initial)	—	—	7
Residential suburbs	5	6	1
Central places	1	1	1
Industrial centre	—	3	1
Park centre	—	1	1
Total in period	17	20	29

Sources: Jewish National Fund, 1978; Leach, 1978.

linked by a new military highway, the Allon road, that ostensibly defines the area which Israel intends to hold.

Figures 20.3a-c and Table 20.1 present data on the progression and general type of Israeli settlement established in the West Bank since 1967, the numbering of the settlements within Figures 20.3a-c relating to the temporal ordering of settlement foundation. The period between 1976 and 1978 witnessed a marked increase in the number of such foundations. A general locational map of the West Bank is provided to facilitate comprehension (Figure 20.4).

Samaria and Jerusalem

Samaria and Jerusalem will be considered in some detail here, for both are seen as representing core areas of any envisaged Palestinian political entity; Samaria in terms of its agricultural importance and Jerusalem in terms of its historico-political status.

The earlier patterning of Israeli settlements and land acquisitions in the West Bank took place along two prime axes, firstly west-east from Latrum to Jerusalem to the west of Jericho and, secondly, north-northeast to south-southwest from Mehola to Hebron meeting near Ma'ale Adumin (Figure 20.3a). Since mid-1977 the Likud Government has placed the greater emphasis on settling the central hills and western slopes of Samaria, in particular the central agricultural area northwest and southeast of Nablus (Figure 20.3c). This extends settlement away from the two aforementioned prime axes to the Samarian agricultural core, with agricultural land in those areas being acquired 'at a most favourable rate' (Jewish National Fund, 1978, p. 17).

As a background it is important to note the specific physical qualities of Samaria and contrasts with Judea. A differentiating feature of the fold structures between Judea and Samaria is the occurrence of wide fault basins in the latter. Samaria thus is composed of a group of isolated mountain blocks with intervening basins. Whereas the Samaritan *rendzina* soils, developed on chalk and soft limestones, are somewhat less fertile than the *terra-rossa* type soils, developed on dolomites and limestones in Judea, they are deeper, less rocky, and consequently easier to work.

Therefore, together with its greater reliability of rainfall, Samaria has traditionally possessed a denser population than Judea and can be generally characterized as a prosperous agricultural area centring upon Nablus (Karmon, 1971, pp. 316-17).

Thus, while the settlement along the eastern slopes of the Samarian mountains and in the Jordan valley itself can be viewed

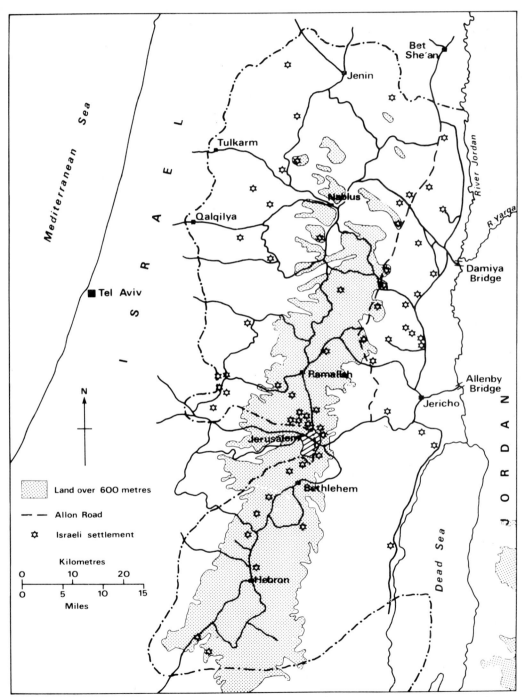

FIGURE 20.4   Samaria and Judea, the West Bank, December 1978

as being motivated by strategic considerations, the continuing and increasing rate of settlement of the Samarian heartland is considered to be particularly important for the general Israelization of the entire West Bank. It is of interest to note that much of this Israeli colonization of the Samarian agricultural heartland has been by the religious settlements (Figure 20.3c).

Furthermore the recently publicized Weitzman plan calls for the construction of six 'large' new towns on the West Bank in the next 5-10 years (Figure 20.5). The creation of such structures, together with the settlements considered above, would further reinforce Israeli control and possession of the West Bank by integration into a re-modelled urban network.

Jerusalem

The importance of Jerusalem to Israel, both ancient and modern, as briefly considered above, cannot be over-emphasized. It should now be appreciated that while the *land* is covenantal this is nowhere more so than within Jerusalem itself.

Since the time of David it has been the Jewish ambition to lay particular claim to this single symbolic place 'because the Temple and the City are inextricable in Judaism... and serve as the quintessence of the land' (Davies, 1974, p. 194; see also Zecharia, 1:14-17 and 8:2-3). The words of Ben Gurion in 1949 still represent the prevailing Israeli sentiment concerning the Holy City and the symbolic attachment to land as place with meaning and soul:

> [Jerusalem] is an integral part of Israeli history in her faith and in the depths of her soul. Jerusalem is the 'heart of hearts' of Israel.... A Nation which over 2,500 years has always maintained the pledge vowed by the banished people on the rivers of Babylon not to forget Jerusalem — this nation will never sanction its separation. [Moreover], Jewish Jerusalem will never accept foreign rule after thousands of her sons and daughters have freed, for the third time, their historic homeland and delivered Jerusalem from destruction (Divrei Ha-Knesset, 1949, p. 221).

By contrast the special significance of Jerusalem and the international status accorded to the city was provided for in the UN General Assembly resolution 181, and also by specific assurances and undertakings, regarding the *corpus separatum* of the Holy City, entered into by Israel upon its admittance to the UN in May 1949 (Hirst, 1973-4). The political reality, however, is that following the

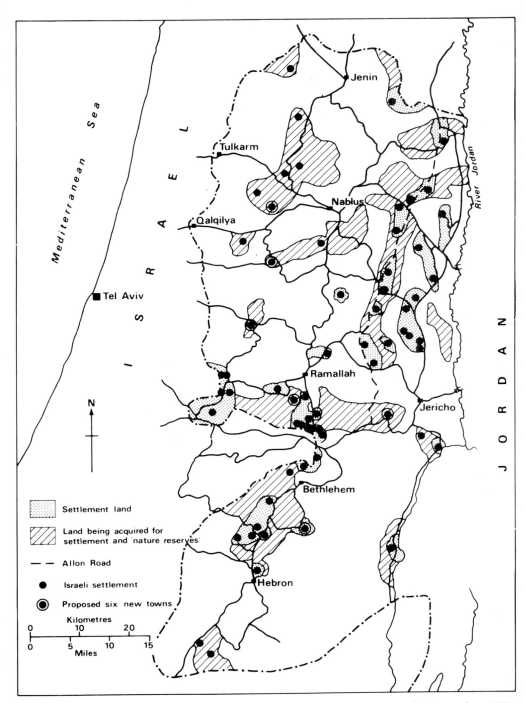

FIGURE 20.5   Israeli settlements and land-holdings within the West Bank, December 1978.
Sources of data: Jewish National Fund (1978) and Leach (1978)

Six-Day War in 1967 Jerusalem became united under Israeli control, and the Israelization of East Jerusalem has proceeded apace.

Since 1967, 12 Israeli suburbs have been constructed on Arab lands. For example French Hill, a recently constructed Israeli residential suburb at the northern edge of Jerusalem, strategically overlooks the road to Ramallah. In 1968-9 3500 dunums, and in August 1970 a further 11,680 dunums, of land were expropriated and purchased from Arab owners. By December 1978 French Hill contained 2400 new housing units with an estimated population of 9350.

Such suburban developments as French Hill and related smaller undertakings within the Old City are proceeding to modify the established spatial dispositions of the various communities considered by Ben-Arieh (1975). While Benevistri (1976) has provided a succinct review of the alternative ideas to resolve the conflict over Jerusalem he assumes that the city will remain politically united and under Israeli control (see also Cohen, 1977). This *status quo* is likely to be resisted by the Palestinians.

Concluding remarks

In any consideration of such a contentious subject bias is an omnipresent threat. The aim here has been to recognize this bias and to seek to remove, or at least endeavour to balance, the presentation, however impossible that may have been (Kaplan, 1964, pp. 373-7; Swan, 1978). The historical emphasis, focusing upon the conceptual development relating to the central issue of land, has facilitated the consideration and has revealed certain of the complexities and problems inherent within the study.

The consideration in some detail of the philosophical notions of covenant and land has enabled us to more fully appreciate the historical base of the modern state of Israel and the crucial importance of Judea and Samaria, but particularly of Jerusalem, to any Jewish state. Indeed Jerusalem has been seen to represent the veritable 'quintessence of the land' theme.

The movement towards the development of the modern state of Israel from the later nineteenth century is viewed as the logical progression and outgrowth not only of pre-existing 'real world' conditions but also of enshrined beliefs relating to land, gift, and covenant. The recurring progression of this land theme through the essay in promise, possession, loss, promise, etc. is crucial, with the present attempt to arrest this sequential development at the present state of possession. Elizabeth Monroe has suggested that:

'Since 1967 the hard core of the Palestinian problem has never changed: the Israelis are unwilling to surrender enough territory to get the peace they want' (Monroe, 1977, p. 397). However it should now be appreciated that Israel is quite unable to surrender any territory of *Eretz Yisrael* for it is not simply Israeli land to give, but is perceived as holy and *storied place,* covenantal land that is seen to be held in trust from God for his people for all time. Thus, even for those supposedly non-religious Jews, the recognition of Israel as storied place and historical referent remains, despite an erosion of the fundamental beliefs that initially gave rise to the basic philosophy. Many would emphasize, nonetheless, that this gift of land to Israel, as we have seen, is not absolute; it is and always has been conditional, requiring obedience to Yahweh. Without such obedience, integrity, and righteousness from Israel no other guarantee can keep the land; otherwise land can and will be lost.

Acknowledgements

I thank Mr D. J. A. Clines and Dr E. M. Jacobs for insightful comments on an initial draft of this paper.

References and bibliography

Alt, A. (1959). 'Der gott der väter', *Kleine Schriften Gesellschaft Volkes Israel,* **1,** 1-78.
Amin, S. (1978). *The Arab Nation: Nationalism and Class Struggles* (Zed Press, London).
Ardrey, R. (1966). *The Territorial Imperative* (Atheneum, New York).
Ben-Arieh, Y. (1975). 'The growth of Jerusalem in the nineteenth century', *Annals of the Association of American Geographers,* **65,** 252-69.
Benevistri, M. (1976). *Jerusalem: the Torn City* (Isratypeset, Jerusalem).
Berger, P. (1973). *The Homeless Mind: Modernization and Conscientiousness* (Random House, New York).
Bright, J. (1959). *A History of Israel* (The Westminster Press, Philadelphia).
Brueggemann, W. (1977). *The Land: Place as Gift, Promise and Challenge* (Fortress Press, Philadelphia).
Cohen, S. B. (1977). *Jerusalem: Bridging the Four Walls; A Geographical Perspective* (Herzl Press, New York).
Daiches, D. (1975). *Moses* (Weidenfeld, London).
Davies, W. D. (1974). *The Gospel and the Land* (University of California Press, Los Angeles).
Divrei Ha-Knesset, *Official Records of the Knesset* (1949). Quoted from Brecher, M. (1978). 'Jerusalem: Israel's political decisions, 1947-1977', *Middle East Journal,* **32,** 13-34.

Eichrodt, W. (1961). *Theology and the Old Testament* (The Westminster Press, Philadelphia).

Flapan, S. (1979). *Zionism and the Palestinians* (Croom Helm, London).

Haddad, H. A. (1973). 'The biblical bases of Zionist colonialism', *Journal of Palestinian Studies*, **3**, 97-113.

Hall, E. T. (1966). *The Hidden Dimension* (Doubleday, New York).

Herzl, T. (1946). *The Jewish State: An Attempt at a Modern Solution to the Jewish Question*, 4th edn (Rita Searl, London).

Hirst, D. (1973-4). 'Rush to annexation: Israel in Jerusalem', *Journal of Palestinian Studies*, **3**, 3-31.

Hirst, D. (1977). *The Gun and the Olive Branch: The Roots of Violence in the Middle East* (Faber & Faber, London).

Hurewitz, J. C. (1979). *The Middle East and North Africa in World Politics: A Documentary Record* (Yale University Press, Newhaven, Conn.).

Jewish National Fund (1978). *Annual Report and Statistical Abstract* (Jewish National Fund, Jerusalem).

Kaplan, A. (1964). *The Conduct of Inquiry: Methodology for Behavioral Science* (Chandler, San Francisco).

Karmon, Y. (1971). *Israel: A Regional Geography* (Wiley, New York).

Kimche, J., and Kimche, D. (1954). *The Secret Roads: The 'Illegal' Migration of a People* (Secker & Warburg, London).

Leach, A. M. (1978). 'Israeli settlements in the occupied territories', *Journal of Palestinian Studies*, **8**, 100-17.

Leighley, J. (ed.) (1963). *Land and Life: A Selection from the Writings of Carl Ortwin Sauer* (University of California Press, Berkeley).

Maier, E. (1975). 'Torah as movable territory', *Annals of the Association of American Geographers*, **65**, 18-23.

Mardor, M. M. (1957). *Strictly Illegal* (Robert Hale, New York).

Martens, E. (1972). *Motivations for the Promises of Israel's Restoration to the Land in Jeremiah and Ezekiel* (University Microfilms, Ann Arbor, Michigan).

Martin, G. (1974). *The Arab-Israel Conflict: Its History in Maps* (Weidenfeld & Nicolson, London).

Meyers, C. L., and Nicholson, D. (1976). *The Tabernacle Menorah: A Synthetic Study of a Symbol from the Biblical Cult* (Scholars Press, Missoula, Montana).

Monroe, E. (1963). *Britain's Moment in The Middle East* (Chatto & Windus, London).

Monroe, E. (1977). 'The west bank: Palestine or Israel', *Middle East Journal*, **31**, 397-412.

Newman, M. L. (1962). *The People of the Covenant: A Study of Israel from Moses to the Monarchy* (Abingdon Press, New York).

Noth, M. (1960). *The History of Israel* (Harper & Brothers, New York).

Orni, E. (1963). *Forms of Rural Settlement* (Jewish National Fund, Jerusalem).

Orni, E., and Effrat, E. (1964). *Geography of Israel* (Israel Program for Scientific Translations, Jerusalem).

Rowley, G. (1970). 'Israel and the potential for conflict: a rejoinder', *Professional Geographer*, **22**, 248-51.

Rowley, G. (1977). 'Israel and the Palestinian refugees: background and present realities', *Area*, **9**, 81-9.

Sharon, A. (1955). 'Collective settlements in Israel', *Town Planning Review*, **25**, 255-70.

Singer, I. (ed.) (1939). *The Jewish Encyclopaedia* (Funk & Wagnalls, New York).

Smith, J. Z. (1969). 'Earth and the gods', *Journal of Religions, 49,* 107-21.

Swan, B. (1978). 'Geography: heyday, mayday?', *Northern University Quarterly, 33,* 97-106.

Tournier, P. (1968). *A Place for You: Psychology and Religion* (trans. E. Hudson) (SCM Press, London).

Tuan, Y. F. (1976). 'Humanistic geography', *Annals of the Association of American Geographers, 66,* 266-76.

Tuan, Y. F. (1977). *Space and Place: The Perspective of Experience* (University of Minneapolis).

United Nations (1976). *General Assembly Records: Thirty-First Session,* Supplement 13 (United Nations, New York).

United Nations (1978). *The Committee on the Exercise of the Inalienable Rights of the Palestinian People* (United Nations, New York).

Von Waldov, H. E. (1974). 'Israel and her land: some theological considerations', in Breamond, H. N., and Moore, C. A. (eds.), *A Light Unto My Path,* pp. 493-508. (Temple University Press, Philadelphia).

Weitz, J. (1967). 'A solution to the refugee problem: an Israeli state with a small Arab minority', *Davar* (29 September), p. 4. Quoted in Davis, U. (1973-4). 'Palestine into Israel', *Journal of Palestinian Studies, 3,* 88-105.

Political studies from spatial perspectives
Edited by A.D. Burnett and P.J. Taylor
© 1981 John Wiley & Sons Ltd

_____ 21__

State policies and changing transport networks: the case of post-war Great Britain

Ray Hudson

Introduction

The history of post-war transport in Britain appears in many ways as a series of paradoxes. Of these, perhaps the most dramatic was the reduction of the rail network in the 1960s (from 17,830 route-miles in 1962 to 11,600 in 1972), the writing-off of considerable quantities of fixed capital, at the same time as considerable investment took place in the road system, particularly in the form of new motorways (of which there were some 700 miles by 1970). These were momentous changes, which were to have widespread socioeconomic and environmental implications. That both road investment and disinvestment from the rail system reflected decisions originating within the state apparatus served to emphasize their paradoxical character.

Geographers have long been interested in the growth and decline of transport networks, although generally approaching this topic in a way which abstracts such changes from their social context and which, in particular, pays scant regard to the state. In the 1960s, reflecting wider changes within the discipline, the issue of network change came to be approached from within the new locational analysis paradigm. Attempts were made to explain network growth and structure via statistical analyses and models (for example Black, 1967; Kansky, 1963; Taffe, et al., 1963). However, the limits to such an approach were soon identified (see Eliot Hurst, 1974, p. 517). These limits arise because locational analysis is rooted within the confines of 'traditional theory' (Horkheimer, 1972). Lewis and Melville (1978) have demonstrated the limits of this as a mode of explanation within regional science in particular and social science in general.[1] At the same time, they point out the possibilities of reconstructing social science as critical theory, which 'allows for the fact that hypotheses about society are "tested" by the development of the class struggle rather than by statistical methods and in offering alternative theories... to those of the dominant ideology, sees itself as a moment in their validation' (p. 198). Clearly, given its central role in the reproduction of advanced capitalist societies, an analysis of the scope and character of state involvement must be central to realizing the goal of reconstructing social science in the mould of critical theory. More modestly, in the context of this paper, such an analysis is a necessary step in further understanding the paradoxical changes that took place in British transport networks in the post-1945 period.

   This, in turn, necessarily implies an examination of theses on the capitalist state and modes of state intervention, something that is largely absent from the geographical literature (although see Dear and Clarke, 1978, for a rare exception to this general trend). While there are a variety of possible theoretical approaches that could be investigated (for example, Althusser, 1971; Miliband, 1973; Poulantzas, 1975, 1976; and those summarized in Holloway and Picciotto, 1978), emphasis will be given here to the work of Offe (1975) and, particularly, Habermas (1976), which lays considerable stress on qualitative changes in the nature of state intervention and on its inherently problem-prone and contradictory character (see also Krieger, 1977). Habermas' theses are developed at a high level of abstraction — that of the capitalist state in general — without reference to the peculiar characteristics of the development of the state in a particular social formation. This is of some importance in relation to the British state, for as Nairn (1975) has correctly argued, because of its unique developmental history, this remains locked in a transitional form, never undergoing the modernizing 'second bourgeois revolution' and becoming a truly modern capitalist state. However, from another point of view, this is of less significance as Nairn concludes that the British state is structurally incapable of fulfilling the various roles ascribed to it — essentially Habermas' conclusion concerning the capitalist state in general, although arrived at from a very different starting point.

The changing logic of the capitalist state: from liberal to interventionist state

At its most general level, the rationale for the development of the capitalist state is to ensure the reproduction of capitalist relations of production. However, the mechanisms through which this goal has been attained have changed qualitatively through time. This qualitative transition may be summarized as that from the liberal to interventionist state (see Offe, 1975; Habermas, 1976).

The liberal state

This was formally constituted within a political sphere. In so far as it intervened within the economic sphere, it did so via an allocative mode, intended to provide the necessary general conditions for capital accumulation and economic growth and rectify market imbalances — for example, via legislation. Indeed, state intervention of this sort preceded the rise of industrial capitalism, dating back, in the case of transport in Britain, to an Act of Parliament of 1546 that placed responsibility for road maintenance on the parishes (for a general account of the character of the British state around this time see Anderson, 1974). Such allocative intervention increased in scale with economic growth, not only with respect to roads but also in relation to providing the legislative preconditions and legal framework within which turnpike roads, canals, and later railway investment and network growth could occur (for concise accounts of the relationship between transport investment and economic growth in this period, see Aldcroft and Dyos, 1974; Hobsbawm, 1968; Savage, 1970).

In essence, then, the role of the liberal state was to guarantee, where necessary, the preconditions for continuing capital accumulation. To do this, however, the state did not directly replace market mechanisms or engage in production. The scope and extent of state intervention was controlled by a normative acceptance of market rationality — that is, of free and fair exchange in the market — as the organizing principle of economic relations and as the overall steering mechanism of the economy. State interventions were thus limited to facilitating the control of economic processes by the invisible hand of the market, characteristically by legislation (Holloway and Picciotto, 1977, p. 90).

At an ideological level, this character of state intervention necessarily required the development of a view that depoliticizes class relations and the public realm — the sphere of nongovernmental opinion-making. The economic and political spheres are presented as more or less distinct. Crises grounded in the conflict between capital and wage labour thus emerged directly as conflict between classes within the relations of production, as economic crises at the systemic level, as interruptions in the process of accumulation.

The interventionist state

This was first born in response to the requirements of accumulation and legitimation in the late nineteenth and early twentieth centuries. It is defined by the inclusion of a productive mode of intervention (to supplement the allocative mode). State intervention and involvement comes to embrace economic planning and public ownership of (parts of) the means of production and transport. Public ownership becomes necessary because certain branches of production (for example, energy and raw materials) and transport cease to offer a sufficiently high rate of return to remain attractive as spheres of investment to individual units of capital, yet investment in these is crucial to profitable production in other branches and indeed to the reproduction of capital in general. This is particularly so in the case of transport, which influences the circulation time of all commodities and hence has a generalized effect on capital (see Marx, 1971).

Therefore, rather than merely supplementing market mechanisms, the state of necessity comes to replace these. Thus, by definition, the state acts imperatively to counter economic crises. Consequently, the boundary of state activities and involvement is greatly extended and the apparent separation of economic and political spheres dissolves. This implies, to a degree, the repoliticization of the relations of production (and hence leads to fresh demands for their legitimation).

However, the state is unable to abolish economic crises; rather, these are displaced elsewhere. As Habermas (1976, p. 46) puts it: 'the activity of the State cannot compensate for the tendency of the falling rate of profit. It can at best mediate it, that is, itself consummate it by political means.' However, the fact that crises are consummated in this way implies that state interventions and actions in planning and production have

> to fulfil functions that can be neither explained with reference to prerequisites of the continued existence of the mode of production, nor derived from the imminent movement of capital. This movement is no longer realised through a market

> mechanism that can be comprehended in the theory of value, but is a result of the still effective economic driving forces and a political counter control in which *a displacement of the relations of production* finds expression (Habermas, 1976, pp. 52-3; emphasis in original).

No longer, then, is capital movement simply realized through a market mechanism that can be justified by a principle of fair exchange, grounded in formally democratic processes. Rather this movement is now a result of economic forces in conjunction with countervailing political forces. As a result, class conflict tends to appear in fresh forms. The fundamental economic crisis tendency finds expression in political and cultural crises, which may be categorized as rationality crises, legitimation crises, and motivation crises (see Habermas, 1976, pp. 45-94 especially). Schroyer (1975, p. 116) neatly summarizes the point:

> a crisis that originates in the economic system can also be displaced to the political-administrative system (as a rationality crisis), or the crisis of either economic or political systems can coincide with a sociocultural crisis (a crisis of legitimation and/or motivation)... [C]apitalist crisis can originate in different societal components and lead to either crisis of system reproduction (economy or rationality) and/or social integration (legitimation and/or motivation). Economic crisis (resulting from an economic 'output' crisis) may not, as Marx expected, lead through social crises to political crises but may be displaced into different, but developmentally related, crisis tendencies.

Of these, rationality crisis — which 'we can speak of... in the strict sense only if it takes the place of economic crisis' (Habermas, 1976, p. 47) — is of most direct relevance to understanding the changing transport network of post-war Britain.[2]

Rationality crises and the interventionist state

The origins of rationality crises are situated in the fact that the state administrative system, operating by criteria of Weberian purposive rationality, is unable, by its sovereignly executed administrative decisions, to reconcile and fulfil imperatives defined by the economic system (imperatives which themselves may be competitive), given the sociopolitical constraints that bind its scope for manoeuvre. As Habermas (1976, p. 47) has put it:

> While the State compensates for the weakness of self-blocking economic system and takes over tasks complementary to the market, it is forced by the logic of its means of control to admit more and more foreign elements into the system. The problems of an economic system controlled by the imperatives of capital realisation cannot be taken over into the administratively controlled domain, and processed there, without the spread of orientations alien to the structure.

The thesis of rationality crisis is thus based upon two fundamental premises concerning the development of the capitalist mode of production. First, capitalism *inevitably* generates contradictions. Put another way, the process of the development of a particular mode of production is, simultaneously, the process of the destruction of the preconditions necessary for the reproduction of society by this mode. Offe (1975, p. 246) has clearly and succinctly expressed that point: 'Contradictions become manifest in situations where... a collision occurs between constituent pre-conditions and the results of a specific mode of production, or where *the necessary becomes impossible and the impossible becomes necessary...*' (emphasis added).

Second, state activities operate by a logic that diverges from that of individual units of capital. Efficiency criteria or those of Weberian purposive rationality cannot be applied to state activities. The operational rationality of state agencies is quite different from that of individual units of capital and is much less easily specified.

The tendency towards rationality crisis reflects the joint impact upon the state administrative apparatus of these two sets of processes. Habermas (1976, p. 63) argues that: 'Rationality deficits are the *unavoidable* result of a snare of relations into which the advanced capitalist state fumbles and in which its contradictory activities *must* become more and more muddled' (emphasis added). The contradictions of capitalist production are thus displaced into the state apparatus in such a way as to make it 'unavoidable' that state agencies, through their administrative decisions, cannot reconcile socio political demands with the imperatives of accumulation. Necessary policy decisions become impossible; impossible decisions necessary. This contradiction in the logic of governance appears in the articulation of policies which seem to be the natural outcome of the competing demands of the political system and those of efficient management of resources under direct state control (and so of capitalist accumulation).

Aspects of transport network change in post-war Britain

The above categories of modes of state intervention and of possible crisis tendencies within late capitalism that arise as a consequence of the transition from a liberal to interventionist state can be used to illuminate changes in British transport networks in the post-war period: in particular, the decline of the rail network and growth of the motorway system. In order to demonstrate this, I shall draw mainly upon central Government[3] policies with regard to transport, particularly railways, in the post-war period, examining competing imperatives at two related levels: first, competition between rail and road-based transport; second, the choice between criteria of economic efficiency and sociopolitical criteria within rail transport. To some extent, the struggle between these competing imperatives appears as a choice between competing party political ideologies: for example, in general terms, criteria of competition and economic efficiency are consonant with a Conservative rather than Labour Party ideology (although such differences have increasingly been diminished and become matters of emphasis rather than substance at the level of both ideology and practice). Furthermore, the question of how the class interest of capital is secured and legitimated in the context of parliamentary democracy is one of some importance (see also McEachern, 1979). However, in fact these contradictory imperatives are much more deeply situated, inherent to the structure of the interventionist state, their existence there, and their expression at the level of ideology, both reflecting their grounding in the nature of the accumulation process itself.

The Labour Government, 1945-51

Aldcroft (1968, pp. 105-6) has argued that, in the case of the railways, nationalization was nearly a dead issue by 1945 since some form of public ownership or control was largely inevitable, whatever the political party in power at the time. Thus nationalization in 1948 reflected the formation of a broad consensus as to the desirability of such a measure, the convergence of very different interests on a common goal. First, at a political level there were pressures resulting from the return to power of a Labour government with a reforming mandate and a long-standing commitment to socialize the means of production and transport. Moreover, state involvement in and control over transport was well established (see Savage, 1970) and the wartime Transport Minister, Lord Reith, had drawn up a scheme for nationalization 'remarkably similar to that executed by Labour in 1947' (Donoghue and Jones, 1973, p. 355). Second, at an economic level, there were pressures for an unprofitable, technically backward industry (see Brown, 1963, p. 75) to be taken into public ownership, for this was central to the smooth functioning of the economy and to continuing accumulation.

However, a precondition for the formation and maintenance of a consensus favouring railway nationalization was an agreement that railway company shareholders be generously compensated on a scale that bore little relation to the value of railway assets — namely, Stock Exchange quotations for railway shares. Thornhill (1968, p. 105) argues that if the compensation terms had been pitched any lower, the political controversies about nationalization could have been more vicious and Chester (1975, pp. 264ff.) suggests that considerable pressure was exerted to extract even more favourable compensation terms. However, the method and scale — beyond the dreams of avarice — of compensation were to have serious negative consequences for the future nationalized railway industry:

> when the railways were nationalised, the former owners received £927m. of 3% gilt-edged securities, with guaranteed annual dividends no matter what the results were and *no matter what borrowings had to be made* in order to make good the scrap heap that was nationalised (Brown, 1963, p. 76; emphasis added).

From the outset, then, an albatross of debt encumbrance was hung around the neck of the nationalized railway industry.

However, within the ideology of then-contemporary Labourism it was not this future financial millstone that was emphasized — indeed, its existence was implicitly denied — but rather the positive, social reformist aspects of the public ownership of transport. In *Let us Face the Future: A Declaration of Labour Policy for the Consideration of the Nation* (quoted by Chester, 1975, p. 2) it was argued that:

> Co-ordination of transport services by rail, road, air and canal cannot be achieved without unification. And unification without public ownership means a steady struggle with

sectional interests or the enthronement of a private monopoly which would be a menace to the rest of the industry... These socialised industries, taken over on the basis of fair compensation, are to be conducted efficiently in the interests of consumers, coupled with proper status and conditions for the workers employed in them.

To achieve these ends, the British Transport Commission (BTC) was set up in 1948. The key issue to be faced concerned the criteria for deciding 'efficiency' and by which coordination could be achieved between different transport media (that these might be incompatible objectives is not the point at issue here). Broadly speaking, were these to be those of market forces or more general political and social guidelines?

Some prominent figures within the Labour movement argued that these two sets of factors were, in fact, compatible and that no conflict existed. For example, Herbert Morrison believed that the administrative form through which nationalization was to be pursued, the Public Corporation, stood 'the tests of being both ethically and economically sound... It was a device of socialism and a sound business proposition' (Donoghue and Jones, 1973, p. 145; see also pp. 355-6). Morrison, in a speech to Labour's national conference at Blackpool in June 1949 (in part reproduced in Donoghue and Jones, 1973, p. 446) later elaborated on this view, identifying: '... a new application of socialism and socialist doctrine. It is called competitive public enterprise... aiming at total economic efficiency... within a proper field of competition between private and public enterprise which will be good for both the public and private sectors of industry.'

However, within the ideology of Labourism in the late 1940s, the dominant emphasis was upon the nationalized industries being guided by broad political/social objectives. To some extent this was translated into practice in establishing criteria for running these industries: for example, in the decisive area of pricing policy, they were merely required to break even over a period of years. But at another, deeper level, the conflict between economic efficiency and broader sociopolitical criteria continued to exist. Although denied and temporarily hidden it remained inherent in this particular mode of state intervention and the specific form through which it was mediated, the Public Corporation. Indeed, although there were attempts (e.g. by Morrison) to deny the existence of such a conflict, its existence had been clearly recognized at an early stage by those civil servants responsible for drafting the transport nationalization legislation. A Minute (dated 8 January 1946) put to the Permanent Secretary in the Ministry of Transport by the civil servant generally responsible for handling the emerging transport nationalization Bill put the point clearly and succinctly, and it is worth quoting this and the Permanent Secretary's response to it at some length (see Chester, 1975, pp. 395-6):

> In the preparation of the Bill there are emerging two fairly well defined, although partly subconscious, points of view. The first envisages the N.T.C. (National Transport Commission) acting as an instrument of the will of the Government expressed in the Statutes but more fully and from time to time by general and particular directions of the Minister. The second regards the N.T.C. as an independent public utility with wide Statutory rights and obligations, interpreted as necessary by independent tribunals, but subject to these interpretations the N.T.C. would largely follow its own policies in the light of its own conception of the public interest. The Minister would have remote control and his directives would be of a general character.
>
> The first point of view accepts any disadvantages which may result from political control in order to provide opportunity for the settlement and variations of principle as the public interest expressed through Parliament may from time to time require. The second point of view aims at removing transport as far as possible from political control and keeping the business element predominant.

The Permanent Secretary minuted in reply, in a way which attempted to minimize the distance between these two viewpoints, to the effect that:

1. N.T.C. will be the organ through which unification and co-ordination of a socialised transport system is to be secured with full powers of direction and control over the major activities of the Executives (i.e. the operating bodies), subject to acceptance of guidance or general directions from the Minister on broad aspects of public policy. The conception is therefore the second of those mentioned above, but the Minister's control would not be remote as there would be close contact between him and the N.T.C. What is not to be envisaged is the superimposition on N.T.C. of a detailed and constant supervision by a Department.

However, to attempt to paper over the cracks in this way did nothing to abolish the existence of fundamentally contradictory imperatives and settle the issue of the criteria upon which the nationalized railways were to operate.

The Conservative Government, 1951-64

Brown (1963, p. 75) argues that for the Conservative government, the choice of operating criteria was clear-cut: 'Was transport to be developed into a genuine and prosperous public service or was it to serve the interests of private profit?' Regardless of whether one accepts the implications of Brown's question as to subjective motivations shaping policy to serve particular interests, the guiding principles of transport policy under the Conservative government undoubtedly swung far towards economic efficiency and competition between modes. This was to have serious implications for the rail system, particularly given the burden of debt encumbrance that resulted from the character of the nationalization measures.

In the early 1950s, despite an increasing burden of dept repayment, railway losses were small. In the first six years of nationalization, interest payments to former railway shareholders amounted to £297.6 million. Of this, £266 million was met from revenues earned — most of the rest being borrowed and thus adding further to future debt repayments (Brown, 1963, p. 76). Nevertheless, by 1955 the total cumulative railway deficit was only £70 million, and would have been less had it not been for Ministerial interference holding down price rises in 1952 and 1956 to below those desired by the BTC (Reid and Allen, 1970, p. 115).

To some extent, railway losses had been offset by cross-subsidization from other BTC activities, mainly road haulage (Brown, 1963, p. 77). However, with the hiving-off of profitable road haulage activities under the 1953 Transport Act, the possibilities of such cross-subsidization were removed. Moreover, the 1953 Act, emphasizing greater efficiency, introduced the possibility that both passenger and rail-freight services could be withdrawn if they were no longer operating efficiently.

In 1955 an ambitious Railway Modernization Plan was launched, supposedly to put the railways on a viable basis and enable them to compete fairly with road transport. Given the antiquated character of much of the fixed capital taken over on nationalization, this Plan involved heavy investment in modern track, signalling, and other equipment, the abandonment of steam and its general replacement by diesel traction or electric traction on selected routes (Thornhill, 1968, p. 220). The estimated costs of the Plan were considerable.

Originally estimated at £1200 million over 15 years, these were
raised to £1660 million in 1957 (Reid and Allan, 1970, p. 115). The
financing of this modernization programme, together with the
requirement to repay interest to holders of compensation stock
issued on nationalization, imposed a tremendous burden on the
railways. Further legislation in succeeding years (the Transport
(Railway Finances) Act, 1957 and the Transport (Borrowing Powers)
Act, 1959) enabled the BTC to borrow money (up to £400 million) to
cover revenue deficits and the interest on capital borrowed to
finance the investment programme. By 1962 the accumulated
railway deficit had risen to £935 million, of which £707 million was
made up of revenue deficits (see Thornhill, 1968, pp. 220-3 for
further details). Some (for example, Morrison — quoted in
Donoghue and Jones, 1973, pp. 551 and 557-8; Brown, 1963, p. 79)
have gone so far as to suggest that the railways were *deliberately*
run into debt to further the interests of the 'road lobby'[4] by
providing a pretext for a simultaneous reduction of the rail network
and expansion of the road-building programme.

It was against this background of sharply rising debt that, in 1960,
a White Paper on the *Reorganisation of the Nationalised Transport
Undertakings* (Cmnd. 1248) was published while, in the same year,
the House of Commons Select Committee on Nationalized
Industries reported on British Railways *(House of Commons Paper,
No. 254)*. The White Paper argued that the practical test for the
railways, as for other transport modes, was how far users were
prepared to pay economic prices for the services provided —
broadly, this would settle the size and pattern of the railway
system. More generally, but in similar vein, the Select Committee
suggested that efficiency criteria, in terms of a target rate of return
on capital, be established for the nationalized industries. This
proposal became incorporated into a subsequent (1961) White
Paper, *The Financial and Economic Obligations of the Nationalised
Industries* (Cmnd. 1337), and into the 1962 Transport Act which also
reformed the capital structure of British Railways, writing off £480
million of debt, in an attempt to make possible a positive rate of
return. Thornhill (1968, p. 109) has argued that the target rate of
return was seen as a solution to two problems. It simultaneously
provided an index against which the worth of new capital
investment could be measured and effectively, if implicitly, set a
floor to price levels in so far as these had to include provision for a
surplus.

The intention and effect of the 1962 Transport Act, which
abolished the BTC and established discrete operating authorities
for different transport modes, was to abandon attempts at a

coordinated inland transport system, except in so far as this could be said to arise from a market allocation of resources. Efficiency had triumphed over coordination, both between and within different modes of transport. For the 1962 Act set the scene for the establishment of the Beeching inquiry, which, given the dominant political climate of the time, proposed drastic reductions of the rail network to at least reduce, if not eliminate, British Railway's deficit (by 1970) and make the operation of the railways conform to criteria of economic efficiency. The Beeching 'proposals for reshaping the railways are all directed towards... [making] the field which they cover one in which their merits predominate and *in which they can be competitive'* (British Railways Board, 1963, p. 58). Put rather more baldly, the basic philosophy underlying the Beeching proposals was 'to shape and operate the railways so as to make them pay' (British Railways Board, 1963, p. 2), this being seen as synonymous with the nation's best interests.

However, despite the recurrent emphasis on profitability in these various documents, this was regarded as the main rather than the sole criterion. The Select Committee, in 1960, qualified this basic test of profitability by arguing that, while in general the railways should be bound by it, decisions in relation to opening or closure on grounds relating to the requirements of the national economy or social needs should be taken by the Minister — implying the necessity for subsidies from the Government to British Railways for lines to be kept open for sociopolitical reasons. This clear definition of responsibilities was seen by the Committee as essential to any proper accounting, in both financial and political senses, for decisions to continue operating railway lines that could no longer be justified by their profitability (Thornhill, 1968, p. 41). Thus the Committee suggested that the competing imperatives, which the nationalized industry was required to satisfy, be met by categorizing lines into one of two types: those on which normal commercial criteria would operate, which would be the responsibility of British Railways; those to which political and social criteria would apply, for which central Government would be responsible. This distinction was reproduced in the 1963 Beeching Report in which it was recognized that the direct measurement of profitability was not the only criterion to be used in determining the size of the rail network, and that other social and political criteria must be given due weight where appropriate (British Railways Board, 1963, pp. 55-7). In effect, the Select Committee and later Beeching were suggesting that the latent rationality crisis within the railway industry be contained and concealed by means of this categorization of routes. In fact, it served to bring it into the open.

One should not, however, as the views of Brown and Morrison cited above make clear, view these plans for a sharp reduction in the railway network out of the broader context of changes in transport and, indeed, the national and international economies. To some extent this was recognized in the Beeching Report: 'The profitability or otherwise of a railway system is dependent on a number of external influences which may change markedly from time to time, important among them being decisions which affect the freedom of use, cost of use, and availability of roads' (British Railways Board, 1963, p. 2). Furthermore, at the same time as plans were emerging for a sharp reduction in the network — a reduction that nevertheless was seen as 'conservative' by those who proposed it (British Railways Board, 1963, p. 2) — so too were other plans being formulated to begin an extensive motorway system to cope with the actual and forecast expansion of road transport, both personal travel and freight movement. Thus the deepening of the state's allocative mode of intervention with respect to road transport was intimately related to the character of its productive mode of intervention in relation to railways. In addition, the expansion of road transport was linked to state fuel policies at a national level, a switch in emphasis from a predominantly single- to multi-fuel economy and, in particular, from coal to oil. Moreover, given the key role of motor-vehicle production as a growth sector in the domestic economy and as a major export sector, there were powerful objective pressures acting upon the state to foster the growth of road transport. Regardless of whether one is prepared to go as far as those, such as Brown and Morrison, in imputing collusion and intent, what is undeniably clear is that policies were being moulded to reflect the interests of a 'road lobby'. In any case, in the final analysis it is such objective pressures, originating within the dynamic of the dominant mode of production, rather than the subjective intentions of policy-makers (which are constrained within limits imposed by the former), which are decisive.

Thus, for a variety of reasons, a formidable consensus emerged favouring road transport, legitimated by an ideology of fair competition between transport modes as the most efficient method of resource allocation and therefore as being in the national interest. State policies were increasingly cast in such a way as to satisfy this consensus, one consequence of this being to establish more rigid criteria of efficiency for the rail system. However, such policies and criteria did not pass unopposed and, while shelving certain short-term problems, the adoption of a rate of return criterion sowed the seeds of others. In turn, this was to act as a precondition for the blossoming of a fully blown rationality crisis in the running of the railways in the later 1960s, one consequence of which was that the full Beeching cuts were never implemented so that the fiscal crisis of the railways, which itself precipitated the Beeching proposals, continued.

The Labour Government, 1964-70

While an emphasis on competition and efficiency as organizing principles in transport was compatible with the wider ideology of Conservative politics, this was not traditionally so in the case of the politics of Labourism. The return of a Labour government which took over part of this ideology encompassing the attainment of efficiency through technological progress, but which continued to adhere to a belief in social reform, presaged the emergence, more or less into the open, of the rationality crisis which had been inherent — although largely hidden — within the structure of the nationalized railway industry since 1948.

In part, the adoption by the Labour government of rate of return criteria for the nationalized industries reflected concern over the financing of investment within these, since a commitment to modernization and technological advance implied a substantial investment programme. However, the adoption of such criteria created fresh problems, particularly for a Labour government. As Thornhill (1968, p. 47) points out, the post-war nationalization legislation tacitly assumed that over the medium to long term, nationalized industries would have neither deficit nor surplus. He continues:

> The railways... have... in their own way proved the futility of this proposition. The problems of recurring deficits and surpluses have been aggravated by the problems of capital financing of the public corporations, whether as internal economic questions for the individual industries or as part of the national economic complex. The result has been a gradual swing of opinion — *irrespective of party political attitudes* — to the measurement of a public corporation's performance by the rate of return on capital employed. This has implied the acceptance of the idea that a surplus should be earned — but a surplus has to be disposed of either as a contribution to new capital expenditure or to the Exchequer. A third and traditionally socialist method of disposing of a surplus, by a reduction in prices or an increase in wages, is *inconsistent with the rate-of-return on capital target itself* (emphasis added).

The internal inconsistencies within the attitudes to the nationalized industries in general and transport in particular, and in the transport policies of the Labour government, were soon to emerge. In 1966 a White Paper on *Transport Policy* (Cmnd. 3057) argued that (para. 14) 'The touchstone of a sound railways policy is the extent to which it meets the country's overall needs. Commercial viability is important but secondary...' The White Paper continued, claiming that Beeching had been given (para. 15)

> no proper yardstick, statutory or otherwise, for measuring the effectiveness of the rail system against the real national requirement. Too little account was taken in the (1962) Act of the interrelation of the railways with other forms of transport and of economic and environmental needs, whether national or regional.

The point at issue was how (indeed, whether) these objectives could be translated into consistently applicable policies, whether these various sociopolitical criteria were compatible with those of efficiency and a specified rate of return on investment.

At a technical level, this reconciliation was attempted through cost-benefit analysis (see below). At a political level, it became clear that this was impossible and decisions as to the size and shape of the rail network emerged in a muddled fashion, political and social forces modifying the logic of economic efficiency but in a way that was neither predetermined nor predictable. Decisions necessary for efficient management had become impossible. Commenting on the inability of British Rail to reduce its deficit over the period 1962-67, Allen and Reid (1970, p. 122) comment that the industry was not able to make all the cuts in the system size which it desired or that were required under the Beeching proposals. Successive Ministers of Transport recognized that a commercially viable system was not politically acceptable nor socially desirable. A similar point is made by Dodgson (1977, pp. 151-2), specifically in relation to Labour government policies, arguing that in 1967 (as set out in the White Paper on Railway Policy), a political decision was made to stabilize the rail network at 11,000 miles outlined in the joint British Rail/Ministry of Transport maps known as the 'Network for Development'. This mileage was not based on any rational calculations but was 'a shot in the dark, more closely related to political targets than economic reality' (Munby, 1968, p. 161). In effect, it was a compromise, giving British Rail management some stability after the rapid changes of the Beeching era, but nevertheless providing the Ministry of Transport with a substantial number of services still to be withdrawn.

This ambiguity as to the basis of the criteria on which the size and shape of the railway network was to be decided in fact reflected a deeper, more widespread indecision among the members of the Labour government as to the criteria upon which the nationalized industries were to be run. Crossman[5] (1976, p. 524) demonstrates this vividly in his account of an exchange in Cabinet between Callaghan and himself over the 1967 White Paper on the financial obligations of the nationalized industries:

> The paper on nationalised industries was [very] disconcerting. This has been a paper which the Chancellor has been struggling to produce, really revising the 1961 decision that the nationalised industries should be run strictly commercially, and *defining where prices were to be fixed by purely financial targets and where they were to be socially costed.* We had exactly twenty minutes to consider it. Having rung Harold [Wilson] beforehand and prepared a number of amendments with Tommy [Balogh] I insisted on tabling them, much to the annoyance of my colleagues. As I got up from the table, I said to Callaghan, 'This is a very poor paper.' 'What does it matter?', he said, 'It's only read by a few dons and experts.' 'Well, I'm one don', I said, and he replied, 'You're a don who knows nothing about the subject. Personally as Chancellor, I couldn't care less and I took no part in composing it.' Here was a key issue of socialist strategy and the Chancellor of the Exchequer washes his hands of it (emphasis added).

The confused and weak treatment of this central issue of government concern — the relationship between the social/political and economic imperatives by which to govern the nationalized industries — reflects the emergence of a rationality crisis in this sphere of governmental responsibility. This contradiction in the logic of governance was expressed *(inter alia)* in decisions as to the size and shape of the rail network that appear as both haphazard and inevitable, natural outcomes of a struggle between essentially incompatible imperatives.

In the 1968 Transport Act, the Government attempted to manage this contradictory situation by reproducing the categorization of railway lines, which distinguished those to be judged on normal commercial criteria from those deemed socially necessary and/or desirable (on the basis of cost-benefit analysis). In any case:

As John Morris, M.P., the Chairman of the Joint (B.R. and Government) Steering Group explained, the grants for socially necessary passenger services were also intended partly as a political compromise: the quid pro quo (for these grants) was that no more would the begging bowl be presented for more money. B.R. would put its house in order and, in particular, it would tackle its loss-making wagon-load traffic (Dodgson, 1977, p. 152).

However, as Dodgson (1977, pp. 162-6) has made clear, the distinction between commercial and social lines has in practice subsequently proved unworkable and the criteria established under the 1968 Act have to a degree been ignored by successive Governments, both Labour and Conservative. He points out (p. 162) that withdrawal of services failing to generate social benefits sufficient to cover specific costs would have involved the complete closure of 910 route-miles in 1971; the deterioration between 1971 and 1974 implies withdrawal of all passenger services from a further 175 miles of route. He further points out (p. 166) that the failure to implement a closure policy stemmed not so much from the technical limitations of cost-benefit analysis but from the context in which it had been applied (i.e. the machinery set up under the 1968 Act). Within this administrative system, the pressures on the Minister to refuse closure (even though the original stimulus to consider withdrawal came from the Government) tend to be stronger than those to accept closure. Proposals to withdraw services generally excite opposition both from rail-users and local authorities, particularly since the financial costs of any such services are usually not borne locally. Since rail closures are unpopular, there may also be more direct political pressure on the Minister both from local Members of Parliament and from local politicians of his own party.

Again, there is evidence from Crossman (1977, pp. 602-3) which is consistent with such an interpretation. Describing a meeting which he describes as 'something like' a Cabinet Steering Committee on Strategic Economic Planning, he writes:

> The final item was the proposal to close down at long last the Central Wales Railway Line which has in winter only 100 people travelling on its ninety miles, 200 in summer and only six regular passengers. This is a parody of a railway and there is an overwhelming case for permanent closure next January, because otherwise we will have to pay a £300,000 subsidy.
> Dick Marsh moved this proposal and the Chancellor

supported him. I barged in and said, 'Look, if you're going to start playing politics with this, you mustn't do it', but they did. Roy [Jenkins] half-heartedly stood out, I stood out with Dick Marsh, but round the table the others were in favour of the £300,000 subsidy, because three seats were in danger in central Wales.

This failure by the central state apparatus even to operate rules and procedures which it itself establishes is further evidence of the manifest rationality crisis within the sphere of state intervention in transport and more generally of the limits to the effectiveness of the state in governance.

Concluding remarks

The intention of this paper was to give a preliminary account of aspects of change in the inland transport network of Great Britain in the post-war period. Two related purposes lay behind this aim: first, to explore the validity of certain theses concerning modes of state intervention and crisis tendencies in late capitalism; second, to seek an alternative framework of explanation of network change to those situated within traditional theory. In so far as it has been possible to offer a tentative, albeit at this stage still somewhat speculative, account that links these theses with empirical material on network change, the original intention may be said to have been realized. It remains to emphasize that this has been merely a preliminary exposition and that what is required is further concrete analyses to enable the further elaboration of theory.

In essence, the argument has revolved around the proposition that what seems paradoxical in terms of policies as to the size and shape of transport networks reflects basic contradictions of capitalism displaced from the economic sphere into the state administrative apparatus. This basic contradiction reappears as state policies that cannot fulfil the incompatible imperatives of accumulation and legitimation. When efficient management is necessary, concern with social costs must be abandoned. When concern with social costs prevails, efficient management must be sacrificed. It is also evident that the attempt to reconcile these inevitably incompatible imperatives has been an important proximate cause of the fiscal crisis of the state (on this general thesis, see O'Connor, 1973), which in turn has implications for network change. In this way, the changing transport network reflects new crisis tendencies within the state in late capitalism.

Notes

1. Rather than attempting to produce a critique of 'positivism', Lewis and
    Melville prefer the category 'traditional theory'. This is because, as they
    correctly point out, citing the example of the debate between Popper,
    Albert and Habermas in Adorno (1976), there is considerable
    ambivalence in what is denoted by the term to the point where
    'definitions of positivism are so divergent as to make communication
    almost impossible' (p. 84).
2. Although in the present context of less direct and immediate relevance,
    Habermas' categories of legitimation and motivation crises are briefly
    sketched out here. Legitimation crises arise because the system of
    social will formation in the public realm fails to maintain required
    levels of mass loyalty while imperatives from the economic system are
    fulfilled. The implementation of state planning tends to repoliticize the
    public realm, hence to question the formally democratic securing and
    disposal of the means of production: the invisible hand of the market is
    seen to be replaced by the perfectly visible hand of the state, casting
    doubt as to the class neutrality of the state as formally democratically
    constituted.
         Motivation crises owe their origin to changes in the sociocultural
    system such that it becomes dysfunctional for the state and the
    dominant mode of social labour. Civic and familial privatism —
    motivational patterns crucial to the continuance of the political and
    economic systems — are eroded. Motivational conditions appropriate
    to limited civic participation in a depoliticized public realm, on the one
    hand, and a family and career/work orientation suitable to the
    consumption, socialization, and labour needs of capitalism on the
    other hand are systematically undermined. At an empirical level the
    crisis emerges in changed attitudes towards work and career. (For a
    fuller consideration, see Habermas, 1976.) Although the notion of
    rationality crisis is of most immediate relevance to the issue under
    consideration here, in terms of social progress the crucial crisis tendency
    is that of legitimation crisis since only here 'is the crisis of system
    reproduction and social identity thematised together, this is the
    logically necessary condition for a revolutionary situation' (Schroyer,
    1975, p. 117).
3. This is not to imply an equation of central government with the state.
    Rather the latter embraces the former as one of its constituent parts.
    Furthermore, as Habermas (1976, p. 33) points out, the relationship of
    empirical evidence to theoretical categories of possible crisis
    tendencies is itself problematic: 'It is not easy to determine empirically
    the probability of boundary conditions under which the *possible* crisis
    tendencies *actually* set in and prevail. The empirical indicators we have
    at our disposal are as yet inadequate.' This qualification only serves to
    reinforce the point that the present paper is to be regarded as a
    preliminary exposition.
4. More generally, the existence of a very powerful and persuasive 'road
    lobby', influencing the course of state transport policies, has been
    documented by Hamer (1974). Habermas (1976, p. 60) argues, at a
    theoretical level, that particular interest groups 'capturing' parts of the
    state apparatus for a time is unavoidable, given the mode of operation

of the state in late capitalism: 'The various [state] bureaucracies are, moreover, incompletely co-ordinated and, because of their deficient capacity for perceiving and planning, dependent on the influence of their clients. *It is precisely this deficient rationality of governmental administration that guarantees the success of organised special interests'* (emphasis added).

5. While in general one must exercise caution in interpreting the evidence contained in Crossman's diaries — particularly his tendency to emphasize his own role — the direction of his comments cited here is quite clear.

Acknowledgements

This is a slightly revised version of a paper presented to a Symposium on 'Geography, Political Economy, and the State', held at the Institute of British Geographers Annual Conference, Hull, 5 January 1977. In preparing the original version a series of discussions with Jim Lewis, Joel Krieger, and John Carney on the work of Habermas were invaluable. However, the author alone is responsible for what appears here.

References and bibliography

Adorno, T. W. (ed.) (1976). *The Positivist Dispute in German Sociology* (Heinemann London).

Aldcroft, D. H. (1968). *British Railways in Transition* (Macmillan, London).

Aldcroft, D. H., and Dyos, H. J. (1974). *British Transport* (Penguin, Harmondsworth).

Althusser, L. (1971). 'Ideology and Ideological State Apparatuses', in Althusser, L. (ed.), *Lenin and Philosophy and Other Essays* (New Left Books, London).

Anderson, P. (1974). *Lineages of the Absolutist State* (New Left Books, London).

Black, W. R. (1967). 'Growth of the railway network of Maine: a multivariate approach', *University of Iowa, Department of Geography Discussion Papers, No. 5.*

British Railways Board (1963). *The Reshaping of British Railways* (HMSO, London).

Brown, A. (1963). *The Tory Years, 1951-62* (Lawrence & Wishart, London).

Chester, Sir Norman (1975). *The Nationalisation of British Industry, 1945-51* (HMSO, London).

Crossman, R. (1976). *The Diaries of a Cabinet Minister*, vol. 2 (Hamish Hamilton, London).

Crossman, R. (1977). *The Diaries of a Cabinet Minister*, Vol. 3 (Hamish Hamilton, London).

Dear, M., and Clark, G. (1978). 'The state and geographic process: a critical review', *Environment and Planning,* **10**, 173-83.

Dodgson, J. (1977). 'Cost-benefit analysis, Government policy and the British Railway Network', *Transportation,* **6**, 149-70.

Donoghue, B., and Jones, G. W. (1973). *Herbert Morrison: Portrait of a Politician* (Weidenfeld & Nicolson, London).

Eliot Hurst, M. E. (ed.) (1974). *Transportation Geography* (McGraw Hill, New York).

Habermas, J. (1976). *Legitimation Crisis* (translated by T. McCarthy) (Heinemann, London).

Hamer, M. (1974). *Wheels within Wheels* (Friends of the Earth, London).

Hobsbawm, E. (1968). *Industry and Empire* (Penguin, Harmondsworth).

Holloway, J., and Picciotto, S. (1977). 'Capital, crisis, and the state', *Capital and Class,* **1**(2), 76-101

Holloway, J., and Picciotto, S. (eds.), (1978). *State and Capital: a Marxist Debate* (Edward Arnold, London).

Horkheimer, M. (1972). *Critical Theory* (Herder & Herder, New York).

Kansky, K. J. (1963). 'The structure of transportation networks, *University of Chicago Department of Geography Research Paper, No. 84.*

Krieger, J. (1977). 'British coal closure programmes in the north east: from paradox to contradiction'. Paper read to Regional Science Association Tenth Annual Conference, London; forthcoming in Cullen, I. (ed.), *London Papers in Regional Science,* **10** (Pion, London).

Lewis, J., and Melville, B. (1978), 'The politics of epistemology in regional science', in Batey, P. (ed.), *London Papers in Regional Science,* **9**, 82-100 (Pion, London).

McEachern, D. (1979). 'Party government and the class interest of capital: Conflict over the steel industry' in *Capital and Class,* **8**, 125-43.

Marx, K. (1971). *Capital* (vol II) (Lawrence & Wishart, London).

Miliband, R. (1973). *The State in Capitalist Society* (Quartet Books, London).

Ministry of Transport (1966). *Transport Policy* (Cmnd. 3057; HMSO, London).

Munby, D. (1968). 'Mrs. Castle's transport policy', *Journal of Transport Economics and Policy,* **2**, 135-73.

Nairn, T. (1975). *The Break-up of Britain: Crisis and Neo-nationalism* (New Left Books, London).

O'Connor, J. (1973). *The Fiscal Crisis of the State* (St Martins Press, New York).

Offe, C. (1975), in Lindberg, L. N., Alford, R., Crouch, C., and Offe, C. (eds.), *Stress and Contradiction in Modern Capitalism,* pp. 125-44 and 245-9 (D.C. Heath, Boston).

Poulantzas, N. (1975). *Classes in Contemporary Capitalism* (New Left Books, London).

Poulantzas, N. (1976). 'The capitalist state: a reply to Miliband and Laclau', *New Left Review,* **95**, 84-114.

Reid, G. L. and Allen, K. (1970). *Nationalised Industries* (Penguin, Harmondsworth).

Savage, C. I. (1970). *An Economic History of Transport* (Hutchinson, London).

Schroyer, T. (1975). 'The Re-politicisation of the relations of production: An interpretation of Jürgen Habermas' analytic theory of late capitalist development', *New German Critique,* **5**, 107-28.

Taafe, E. J., Morrill, R. L., and Gould, P. R. (1963). 'Transport expansion in underdeveloped countries: a comparative analysis', *Geographical Review,* **53**, 503-29.

Thornhill, W. (1968). *The Nationalised Industries* (Nelson, London).

Political studies from spatial perspectives
Edited by A.D. Burnett and P.J. Taylor
© 1981 John Wiley & Sons Ltd

_____ *22*__

Some geopolitical aspects of the conflict in Namibia/South West Africa*

John A. Brohman & David B. Knight

Following a prolonged period of virtual neglect, the territory of Namibia/South-West Africa has, in recent years, begun to command more attention from the world community. The problems associated with the conflict in Namibia have taken on a special significance when viewed in conjunction with the global superpower rivalry and the racial struggle in southern Africa. On a world scale, Namibia's mineral wealth and strategic location have provided a sufficient incentive for the involvement of the great powers in Namibian affairs. On a regional scale, Namibia represents the only remaining territory in South Africa's traditional 'buffer zone' between herself and Black Africa.

The Namibian problem today has been made all the more intractable because of anomalies springing from its protracted colonial history and the profound heterogeneity of the territory. The tremendous diversity presented by the ethnic composition, socioeconomic structure, and physical characteristics of contemporary Namibia has had far-reaching spatial consequences for the Namibian conflict. The shape and structure of Namibian boundaries reflect its status as a colonial relic from a bygone era. Strategically important territorial enclaves have acted to compound the problem. Before Namibia can confidently take its place among the world's independent sovereign states, solutions

---

* The authors dedicate this paper to the memory of Dr Philip E. Uren, of the Department of Geography, Carleton University, Ottawa, Canada. Although our views sometimes differed, he was a man to be admired both for his bountiful knowledge of southern Africa and for the courage of his convictions. Phil. had a deep and abiding interest in the resolution of conflict within southern Africa. His devotion to humanitarian concerns and his scholarly intellect serve as a continuing inspiration to all of us.

must be found for the spatial contradictions which stem from inherent anomalies within Namibian society. As the attention of African states and the world community becomes increasingly focused on the Namibian conflict, this task is made ever more urgent.

The notion of scale is, of course, basic to an understanding of geography. The idea that relationships and perceptions change as we narrow or widen our focus is particularly true in political geography. Local problems, within Namibia, have assumed an added importance as their regional and global ramifications are taken into consideration. Perceptions of the Namibian situation have been radically divergent, depending upon one's ideological orientation and spatial perspective. That which is vitally important to the black Namibian peasant may seem trivial or inconsequential to the European diplomat. In order to gain a realistic understanding of the geopolitical aspects of the Namibian conflict, it is necessary to view the problem from its global, regional, and local perspectives.

Global perspectives

In recent years, emerging states within the Third World have acquired added significance in the international geopolitical configuration. Many strategists argue that the potential for many areas of the Third World to flash into a situation where international military escalation would be manifested is greater today than that of the traditional 'flash-points' of central Europe (Luttwak, 1978, p. 1). Several factors in the present international politico-economic environment seem to give credence to this judgement. In a world growing increasingly short of vital resources, the major metropolitan powers have become dangerously reliant on raw materials from potentially volatile areas of the Third World. For a variety of reasons, many North American and European-based multinational firms have invested heavily in the Third World, not least to increase their profits, and their activities often arouse resentment. As the maintenance of stability in Third World states has become ever more vital to the economic performance of the industrialized West, an array of increasingly sophisticated and lethal weaponry has been supplied to certain areas of the Third World to protect Western interests. This flow of armaments has been matched by an equally devastating supply of Communist weaponry to the Third World client states of the Eastern bloc. In addition, certain states outside the industrialized core areas of

Europe and North America have established modern indigenous armaments industries, often with the tacit support of the great powers. From a global perspective, the present volatility of the southern African geopolitical situation reflects an intermingling of all of these factors.

At present, the Western industrial nations are less than 65% self-sufficient in non-fuel raw materials (Schneider, 1978, p. 43). The Republic of South Africa and Namibia contains 30% of the non-Communist world's reserves of uranium oxide, 60% of its diamonds, 70% of its gold, 74% of its chromite (with Zimbabwe/Rhodesia, 96%), 60% of its manganese, 70% of its platinum, and virtually all of its amosite and asbestos (Vanneman and James, 1976, p. 96). Namibia has substantial deposits of diamonds, copper, lead, zinc, cadmium, silver, vanadium, germanium, and uranium oxide. In 1980 it is estimated that the United States of America will import 98% of its cobalt, 80% of its platinum, 99% of its manganese, 91% of its chromite, and 36% of its vanadium from South Africa and Namibia (Cas de Villiers, 1978, p. 12). In 1979 both Britain and France were still directly importing shipments of uranium and other minerals from Namibia in direct defiance of United Nations sanctions.

The West has invested heavily in both South Africa and Namibia. In 1977 British investments in the two countries amounted to more than £5 billion sterling, while West German and American figures were about half this amount (Legum, 1978, p. A25). The Namibian mining industry is almost totally owned by foreign corporations. These include a large concentration of South African concerns (de Beers, JCI, General Mining, ISCOR), but the British (Rio Tinto), Americans (Newmont, Amax), and Canadians (Falconbridge) have also invested heavily in the mining industry. Almost all of these foreign firms have continued to invest in Namibian mining operations in direct violation of UN imposed sanctions *(New African Yearbook,* 1979, p. 236).

In addition to this increased dependence on supplies of raw materials from southern Africa, the West has become vitally dependent on the continued operations of the sea lanes around the Cape of Good Hope. Traffic along the Cape sea route has increased more than 20-fold since 1965. Currently, 90% of Eurpean NATO oil, 40% of US oil, and 70% of all NATO strategic minerals pass through the Cape route (Cas de Villiers, 1978, p. 12). More than 2300 vessels per month pass around the Cape of Good Hope, including 600 oil tankers (Schuettinger, 1976, p. 72). If the Cape 'choke point' was effectively closed off to the free flow of international shipping by unfriendly governments in either Namibia or South Africa, the

economic and political capabilities of the West would be severely
curtailed. Since 1959, when the Simonstown Agreement was
abrogated by Britain, South Africa has been given *de facto* control
over the maintenance of stability along the Cape sea route. Walvis
Bay, on the Namibian coast, is the only deep-water port suitable for
military purposes along more than 2500 km of coastline from Cape
Town, South Africa, to Moçâmedes, Angola. As such, it could be
used by a hostile power to constrict movement in the international
sea lanes of much of the south-eastern Atlantic Ocean.

As the great powers have begun to realize the strategic
importance of southern Africa, an ever-increasing supply of modern
armaments has been introduced into the region. Angola has been
the recipient of a vast array of Soviet weaponry, including Mig-21
fighter-bombers, T-54 tanks, and BM-21 multiple rocket launchers
(nicknamed 'Stalin organs'). In addition, there are thought to be
15,000-23,000 Eastern bloc and Cuban military advisers and combat
troops in Angola at present. Despite a UN arms embargo since 1972,
South Africa has managed to remain equipped with an impressive
variety of modern Western weaponry, including Mirage III fighter-
bombers, Alouette III helicopter gunships, Centurion tanks, and
Daphne-class submarines. This has been achieved by embargo
contraventions and the development of an indigenous arms
manufacturing industry (ARMSCOR) with covert Western support
(Gann and Duignan, 1978, p. 30). South Africa is also widely
believed to have developed a tactical nuclear capability with the
assistance of Western Germany and Israel *(African Contemporary
Record,* 1977-78: pp. B920, B959). Moreover, there are currently an
estimated 50,000 South African troops within a short distance of the
Angola/Namibia border, deployed against the 6000-10,000 guerillas
of the South-West African People's Organization (SWAPO). The
latter are supported by an unknown number of Eastern bloc, Cuban,
and Angolan military personnel *(New African Yearbook,* 1979, p.
233).

In recent years, the West has mounted a major diplomatic effort
to encourage peaceful change in both Zimbabwe and Namibia. The
success of the British-sponsored ceasefire and subsequent elections
in Zimbabwe may pave the way for a similar chain of events in
Namibia. However, it is questionable whether South Africa would
acquiesce in the near future to the probable installation in Namibia
of yet another Marxist-Leninist government on her northern border
until the intentions of the newly-elected Mugabe government in
Zimbabwe are more fully known. The Western emphasis on diplomatic
initiatives to the exclusion of direct military involvement in southern
Africa has been severely criticized in many quarters. It is felt that the

failure of the West, and particularly the US, to project its military power into the region has created a vacuum, which the Soviets and their surrogates have been quick to fill. Angola is pointed to as an example of the lack of resolve on the part of the West to stand up to Soviet military adventures in the Third World. However, in order to successfully intervene militarily in southern Africa, it is essential to articulate an ideological stance which will be compatible with the wishes of the people. As the debacle of Vietnam has shown, naked military aggression will not be sufficient in the long run to consolidate a territory. The recent elections in Zimbabwe have shown that the large rural Black population of southern African states demand sweeping land reform as a vehicle for the attenuation of widespread socioeconomic inequality. Support will be given to the organization best able to articulate the 'ideology' of agrarian reform, whether or not this group is backed by the West, the Soviets, or the Chinese. If the West is to revitalize its influence in southern Africa, and more particularly Namibia, more support will have to be given to political organizations of a socialist orientation, such as SWAPO, which advocate an egalitarian redistribution of rural land.

While the West has maintained its distance from African nationalist organizations of any socialist hue, the Soviets have seized the initiative. At the Khartoum Conference of January 1969, organized by the Soviet-controlled World Peace Conference and the Afro-Asian Peoples' Solidarity Organization, the Soviets closely associated themselves with the ANC (South Africa), ZAPU (Zimbabwe), MPLA (Angola), FRELIMO (Mozambique), PAIGU (Guinea-Bissau), and SWAPO (Namibia). In post-revolutionary African states, only ZAPU has failed to achieve power and it lost the Zimbabwe election to ZANU, an organization which advocated more fundamental and sweeping land reforms. According to French and Spanish intelligence, the Soviets devised a master plan in the 1960s, called 'Oran', for their operations in southern Africa. The strategic objective of this plan was to capture Portuguese Africa as a base to be used for the rest of the region (Moss, 1978, p. 78). In the face of Western inconsistency and indecision in formulating a clear and coherent policy with respect to southern Africa, the Soviet strategy seems to have worked admirably. SWAPO guerillas, trained and armed by the Soviets or their surrogates, are presently using southern Angola as a base from which to attack Namibia on a regular basis. As the West has procrastinated, fearing for the stability of their interests in southern Africa, the Soviets have seized the initiative with their offers of unfailing military support to African nationalist organizations, including SWAPO, whose ideology closely articulates the wishes of the large majority of rural Blacks in the respective regions in southern Africa. The Soviets, by this means, have all but ensured that at least their short-term strategic objectives will be met.

Regional perspectives

When one contracts one's view to a more regional perspective, it is discovered that the conflict in southern Africa has devolved into a bi-polar struggle between South Africa and the Black African states of the Organization of African Unity (OAU). As South Africa's 'buffer zone' has been gradually diminished by the installation of Marxist-Leninist governments either on or near its northern border, White South Africans have become increasingly fearful for the survival of their *apartheid* political and socioeconomic systems. Despite having sophisticated and highly mobile armed forces, as

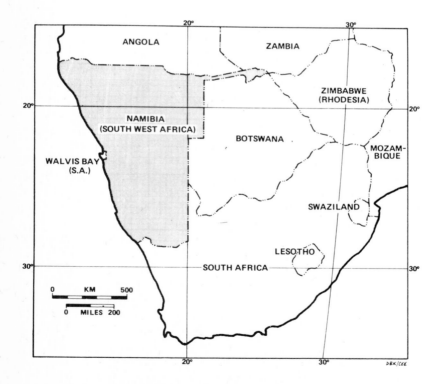

FIGURE 22.1   Namibia/South-West Africa and its regional setting

well as an effective internal policy for the suppression of dissent, it is improbable that South Africa can continue to deny basic human rights to the majority of its citizens, without confronting an unavoidable crisis in the near future.

On the other hand, the confidence of Black African states in their dealings with South Africa has grown with the installation of each Black-ruled government near the northern border of South Africa. Moreover, the socialist orientation of the states that ring South Africa and Namibia (Angola, Zambia, Tanzania, Zimbabwe, and Mozambique; Figure 22.1) make them ideologically incompatible with South Africa's capitalist, minority-controlled socioeconomic system. Botswana, with its non-racialist policy (Knight, 1974), despite being economically dependent upon South Africa, refuses to exchange diplomatic missions with it (Dale, in Potholm and Dale, 1972, pp. 110-24; Knight, 1969). Although many Black African states have declared their preference for the maintenance of a non-aligned Africa free from foreign intervention, some of these states have felt it necessary to accept military assistance from the Eastern bloc, Cuba, or China in order to combat White-supremacy-generated conflict. With the installation of a Black-ruled government in Zimbabwe, the focus of Black Africa's attention seems destined to be directed to the continuing conflict in Namibia. As both world opinion and the force of time are clearly on the side of Black Africa, it appears unlikely that South Africa will be able to persist in the postponement of free elections for Namibia. With the probable ascendancy of yet another radical, Marxist-Leninist government on its northern border, the dismantlement of South Africa's former 'buffer zone' will have been completed.

As the West has increasingly distanced itself from South Africa, at least diplomatically, the South Africans have grown ever more disillusioned with Western policy. Most South Africans regard their gravest threat as coming not from Black Africa, but from Communists and their surrogates near their northern borders. They cannot understand the failure of the West, and particularly the US, to forcefully oppose any intervention by Communist countries in southern Africa. As one frustrated South African commentator writes about American policy in southern Africa: 'Congress, for whatever mix of reasons, is pursuing a near-sighted, short-term, and selfish internal political power struggle which prevents the U.S. from formulating an objective, coherent, and effective foreign policy' (*Rand Daily Mail*, 8 March 1976).

In the face of increasing international pressure to find a suitable solution to the Namibian conflict, South Africa has resorted to delaying tactics in order to postpone the inevitable. Fearing the installation of a hostile government in Namibia, but at the same time feeling the pressure of international condemnation, South Africa has adopted what Donald McHenry (present American Ambassador to the UN) has termed a 'two-track strategy'. One track promotes the internal security of Namibia through actions such as the deployment of South African forces in northern Namibia and the election of a moderate government in South African-sponsored elections. The other track leads to international acceptability through the undertaking of meaningful negotiations with SWAPO and others, which may lead to free UN-sponsored Namibian elections. However, South Africa is presently caught in a dilemma — whether the probable electoral victory of a radical, unfriendly organization in Namibia is worth the price of international short-term acceptablity. Thus far, it appears that it is not. The Prime Minister of South Africa, P. W. Botha, recently stated: 'If we are presented with a choice, either the internal stability of South-West Africa as against international recognition, we prefer to have internal stability in South-West Africa' (Johannesburg foreign radio broadcast, 15 November 1979).

According to military experts, however, the loss of Namibian territory, by itself, would have very little effect on South Africa's strategic vulnerability to attack from the north (Gann and Duignan, 1978, p. 53). Namibia has only a few north-south transportation links for troop movements (see Figure 22.2), which could easily be disrupted in wartime. The huge expanse of sparsely vegetated desert on either side of the South African/Namibian border enhances the mobility of a highly mechanized conventional army such as that of South Africa. The lack of vegetation would also seriously hamper the likelihood of successful guerilla infiltration from the Namibian side. Moreover, the Orange River, which forms the major section of the South African/Namibian border, acts as a natural barrier to any attack from South Africa. Even if the improbable scenario that all of these factors may be overcome by an invading army, the north-western section of South Africa offers the defender hundreds of kilometres of thinly populated semi-desert through which to retreat before the more densely populated sectors of South Africa would be imperilled. The tactical nuclear capability which South Africa is believed to have achieved would further impair the chances of success in a frontal assault on north-western South Africa. Most tacticians feel that if the South African armed forces are to be defeated, an attack would have to be carried out in the mountainous, thickly forested region of north-east South Africa in concert with coordinated insurrection in the populated areas of the country (Gann and Duignan, 1978, pp. 53-4).

FIGURE 22.2   Namibia, showing major economic nodes and linkages, and
the location of the reserves/homelands

South Africa has attempted to forestall the possibility of this
'worst-case' scenario by promoting the mutual benefits of a
proposed regional economic integration of southern Africa. Prior to
the disruptions of the 1960s, southern Africa had an excellent
railway network which had enabled an embryonic intra-regional
specialization of labour to take place (Schneider, 1978, p. 44).
Southern Africa has long been recognized as a potentially viable
economic unit, capable of integration (Green and Fair, 1962). Flows
of labour have linked most of the southern African countries to
South Africa for decades. The industrial power of South Africa
could be combined in a new relationship of mutual benefit with the
agricultural potential of many of the Black African states. By the
creation of an expanded regional economy of scale through

economic integration, an attractive environment for capital formation and investment could be fostered. Further, through the development of such linkages a *cordon sanitaire* could be created if the Black African states developed critical attitudes towards 'liberation' forces. However, unless fundamental political and socioeconomic changes are made within South Africa itself, it is highly unlikely that the Black-ruled states of southern Africa will have any sympathy with the newly articulated South African dream of a regional 'constellation of states', despite the economic benefits that might accrue from such a plan. (There is still some confusion, even within South Africa, over just what Prime Minister Botha and his ministers mean by this phrase which was first used late in 1979; Thomas, 1980.)

The economies of all of the Black southern African states are presently in a shambles. Unemployment is rampant, capital formation for investment is almost non-existent, skilled manpower and technical expertise are sorely lacking, and basic foodstuffs and commodities are in short supply. Out of economic necessity, these states have presently been forced to enter into economic relationships with South Africa (despite their advocacy of UN economic sanctions against South Africa). Mozambique still sends thousands of its citizens to work in South African mines under clearly exploitative conditions. Zambia, after having redirected its economic linkages away from South Africa, recently accepted South African emergency supplies of medicine, grain, and fertilizer. Angola has entered into negotiations with South Africa concerning the maintenance of stability for economic investment in the Namibian/Angolan border area. Botswana, while oriented to the north in spirit, remains almost totally dependent on South Africa for its economic livelihood, despite the recent development of major diamond and copper-nickel finds (Knight, 1975). Some argue that if South Africa were to release its military grip on Namibia and instigate meaningful changes within its own society, Black African states would welcome more economic integration. Recent signs of economic pragmatism in the policies of Black African states give credence to this point of view. However, South Africa's leaders first need to convince the powerful *verkrampte* (arch-conservative) faction of the ruling National Party that these types of changes would be in their long-term best interests. Until this happens, the present mutually destructive stalemate between South Africa and the states of Black Africa will continue.

In addition to economic reasons, many Black African states would like to see an end to the conflict in southern Africa so that the Soviet military presence could be removed from the area. The

Lusaka Manifesto of April 1969 was signed by thirteen Black African states and declared:

> We have always preferred, and will prefer, to achieve [the right to independence] without physical violence. We would prefer to negotiate rather than destroy, to talk rather than kill. We do not advocate violence; we advocate an end to the violence against human dignity that is now being perpetrated by the oppressors of Africa. If peaceful progress to emancipation were possible, or if changed circumstances were to make it possible in the future, we should urge our brothers in the resistance movements to use peaceful methods of struggle even at the cost of some compromise on the timing of change (quoted in Charles, 1976, p. 14).

Following the Soviet-backed MPLA victory in Angola, President Kenneth Kaunda of Zambia was prompted to comment:

> Our failure to find a solution here [in Angola] confirms that the Organization of African Unity has no power to shape the destiny of Africa. Power is in the hands of the superpowers, to whom we are handing Africa by our failure (Legum, 1976, p. A3).

In 1978, Nigerian President Obasanjo reiterated the widespread African disillusionment with both the West and the East for their meddling in African affairs:

> We need in Africa massive economic assistance to make up for the lost ground of the colonial era and not military hardware for self-destruction, and sterile ideological slogans which have no relevance to our African society. Africa is not about to throw off one colonial yoke for another... We totally reject as an instrument of neocolonialism any collective security scheme for Africa fashioned and teleguided from outside Africa for the economic, political, or military interest of any superpower bloc (Lagos foreign radio broadcast, 27 July 1978).

The underdevelopment of the armed forces in Black southern African states *vis-à-vis* South Africa forced them to look elsewhere for the military hardware they felt was needed to combat white supremacy in southern Africa. The steadfast refusal of the West to give military support to the Black liberation movements caused them to seek military aid from the Eastern bloc, Cuba, and to a lesser extent China. There is, however, ample evidence to suggest that Black Africa desires both an end to the conflict and the removal of the foreign military presence in southern Africa. Beginning in 1975, the OAU Liberation Committee has attempted to channel all arms shipments to the liberation movements through its offices as a way of contravening direct foreign involvement in the individual organizations. Furthermore, several times during the Zimbabwe negotiation process, and especially at the London talks of 1979, the 'Front Line States' put heavy pressure on both ZANU and ZAPU to accept Western peace proposals, against Soviet wishes. Throughout 1978 and 1979, both the OAU and the Front Line States have attempted to pressure SWAPO to enter into Western-sponsored negotiations with South Africa and other Namibian political parties. Even Angola, which remains almost totally dependent on Soviet and Cuban military support, has recently entered into secret negotiations on several occasions with the West, Zaire, and South Africa to try to end the conflict and achieve a negotiated settlement in Namibia *(Rand Daily Mail,* 4 July 1978 and *Africa Confidential,* 1 August 1979). Indeed, the Soviets perceive themselves as being left on the sidelines by all of these Western diplomatic initiatives. The only major influence which they have been able to project into southern Africa has been through overt military involvement. The Soviet press has regularly castigated efforts to find peaceful negotiated settlements in both Zimbabwe and Namibia, going so far as to dub the Western 'Contact Group' (Britain, United States, West Germany, France, and Canada) which is negotiating to find a settlement in Namibia by way of internationally supervised elections, the 'gang of five'.

It is probable that, if a peaceful solution could be found for the conflict in southern Africa, most of the Black states in southern Africa would move to distance themselves from the military objectives of the Soviet Union. Only Angola presently finds itself in a highly dependent relationship with the Soviets and the ongoing Angolan civil war is testament to the unpopularity of this subservient role among Angolans. The primary goal of the Black African states is to rebuild their shattered economies. The power of Western economies *vis-à-vis* their Communist counterparts gives the West an advantageous edge in any offers of aid to Black African states. However, any process of rapprochement of the West with Black Africa must await an equitable solution to the problems of white supremacy in southern Africa. A ceasefire and UN-sponsored elections in Namibia would be an important first step in this direction. But neither Black Africa nor the people of Namibia will be satisfied with elections which exclude SWAPO from active participation.

Local perspectives

As we narrow our perspectives more locally to Namibia itself, the geopolitical aspects of the Namibian conflict come more sharply into focus. Contemporary Namibia is perceived by most observers as a colonial relic. The UN and particularly the five Western nations of the 'Contact Group', have in recent years sought a solution to this problem which, once solved, would allow Namibia to join the world community as a sovereign, independent state. As noted earlier, the mineral wealth and the strategic importance of enclaves, plus the tremendous diversity of ethnic groups, help make the Namibian situation intractable. Until recently South Africa seemed intent on finding its own 'internal solution' to the Namibian problem. However, in the face of increasing pressure from both indigenous Namibian political parties and the world community, South Africa has of late begun to soften its opposition toward the eventual independence of Namibia.

European contact with the Namibian desert coast began in the late 1400s, but the Portuguese and later the Dutch made no attempt to establish permanent settlements. Late in the 1700s and early to mid-1800s European settlers, traders, and missionaries gradually moved into the region north of the Orange River. In 1878 Walvis Bay was claimed by the British and then was incorporated into the Cape Colony in 1884. Because of British inattention to the region, however, Germany claimed the remainder of the coast, from the Cunene River in the north, south to the Orange River, and inland to 20° East latitude, with the added finger-like proruption in the northeast which extended as far east as the Zambezi River. The boundaries were established by agreement with Portugal in 1886 and with Britain in 1890.

The Germans first occupied the port of Lüderitz, and then Windhoek in the interior highland became a focus for settlement. Aided by railway construction and government-sponsored land schemes, German settlement spread both north and south from Windhoek. Conflict occurred between the incoming Europeans and the Africans. The Germans suppressed an uprising by the Swartbooi Hottentots in 1897 and one by the Bondelswartz Hottentots in 1903 (Figure 22.3). The worst suppression followed a great Herero rebellion in 1904 when the German forces slaughtered thousands of people and cattle. A major Hottentot uprising occurred in the south in 1904-06. The colony was finally 'pacified' in 1907, but the results were far-reaching. Thousands of Africans were dead, few cattle remained, lands were confiscated by the Germans (including 10 million hectares from the Hereros and 100 million hectares from the rebel Hottentot tribes — Wellington, 1967, pp. 213-14), and the European population grew as immigration increased and farms were created. In 1908 diamonds were discovered in the Namib near Lüderitz, with copper having earlier been discovered and mined near Tsumeb.

From 1884 to 1915 *Südwestafrika* was a German colony. The First World War brought Namibia a different colonial master when South African military forces compelled a German surrender of Namibia on 9 July 1915. Later, the Treaty of Versailles confirmed the South African occupation of Namibia under a 'C-class mandate' of the League of Nations. Article 22 of the Covenant of the League of Nations required Namibia to be governed as an integral part of the territory of the mandatory power (South Africa). The mandate contained no sanctions but included some vaguely worded obligations for the mandatory power to promote the material and moral well-being and social progress of the inhabitants of the territory. With the creation of the UN, following the Second World War, trusteeship for Namibia was transferred to the UN from the League of Nations. However, Namibia continued to be governed under international mandate by South Africa, according to Article 76 of the UN Charter.

Since the start of the mandate period, the South African Parliament has been the highest legislative authority for Namibia. In 1925, the South-West Africa Constitution Act conferred limited self-government on the territory and in 1949, the South-West Africa Affairs Amendment Act provided for direct representation of Namibia in the South African Parliament. All existing constitutional provisions were replaced in 1968 by a consolidating act, including a provision for the transfer of further legislative functions from Namibian authorities to the Parliament in South Africa. But in 1960, Ethiopia and Liberia instituted proceedings in the International Court of Justice against continued South African administration of Namibia. In 1966, the Court ruled that Ethiopia and Liberia did not possess the legal right to proceed further with the matter. However, in 1971 an advisory opinion of the International Court stated that South Africa was indeed in illegal occupation of Namibia and was under an obligation to withdraw its administration. Furthermore, UN members were obliged to recognize the illegality of the South African presence in Namibia.

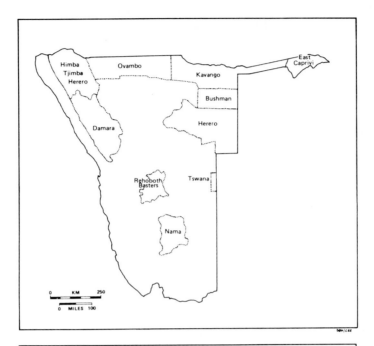

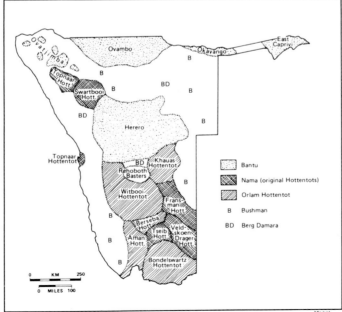

FIGURE 22.3   Location of tribal groups in Namibia: above, present-day; below, at around 1900. (After First (1963), Wellington (1967), Fraenkel (1974), and several South African official maps)

Since the 1950s there have been several UN agencies concerned with the situation in Namibia: the *ad hoc* Committee on South West Africa (1950), the Committee on South-West Africa (1953), the Good Offices Committee (1957), the *ad hoc* Committee for South-West Africa (1966), the United Nations Council for South-West Africa (1967), and the United Nations Council for Namibia (1968). In 1976 the United Nations Institute for Namibia was opened in Lusaka, Zambia. Presently the *de jure* internationally recognized representative of Namibia is the UN Council for Namibia, assisted by an executive commissioner for Namibia. However, the *de facto* government of Namibia continues to be administered by South Africa through an Administrator-General appointed by the South African Parliament. Many public functions in Namibia, such as the armed forces, police, and foreign affairs, are directly controlled by South Africa.

In 1960, the UN General Assembly instructed the Committee on South-West Africa to investigate and propose 'conditions for restoring a climate of peace and security' to the territory and to take 'steps to enable the indigenous inhabitants of South-West Africa to lead them to complete independence as soon as possible' (in First, 1963, p. 217). A UN resolution was passed in 1962 which called for the establishment of a UN Special Committee of Seven to oversee the progress toward independence of Namibia. But it was not until 1977 that the UN-sponsored 'Contact Group' was established. In 1970, the UN Security Council voted 13 to nil, with Britain and France abstaining, to withhold both credit and investments from Namibia. The UN General Assembly endorsed a decree in 1974 which stated that it was illegal to either exploit or export resources from Namibia without the express approval of the UN Council for Namibia. Therefore, in the eyes of most of the world community, and particularly those of Black Africa, continued Western exploitation and investment in Namibian resources has been illegal.

For the past several years, the Western 'Contact Group' has been negotiating with South Africa and Namibian political parties to try to set into motion a process which would allow for a ceasefire and subsequent UN-sponsored elections to take place in Namibia. On several occasions the negotiations have seemed close to a satisfactory conclusion, which would have set the election process in motion. Unfortunately, in each instance, the negotiations have ultimately collapsed because of the mutual distrust between the parties involved. Currently there are a number of contentious issues which have not yet been resolved. Despite American promises to construct an electronic monitoring system along the northern

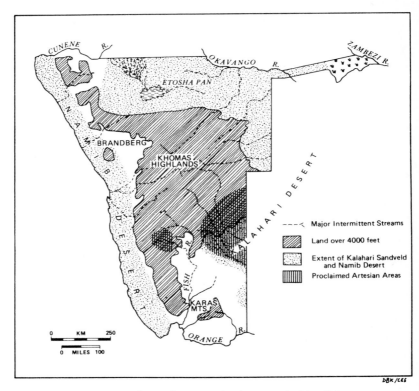

FIGURE 22.4   Major physical geography features in Namibia

Namibian border, South Africa and moderate Namibian political
parties fear that this alone will not deter widespread SWAPO
infiltration into Namibia after a ceasefire is arranged. South Africa
has requested direct UN supervision of SWAPO forces in Angola
and Zambia, but this demand has been termed unacceptable by
Angola, Zambia, and SWAPO. SWAPO wants its forces to be openly
present in Namibia at the time of the ceasefire, by being collected
into base camps reflecting the spatial extent of SWAPO operations
in Namibia. South Africa has not yet accepted this principle which
would thus allow the establishment of UN-supervised SWAPO
camps within the very territory South African forces have worked
so hard to keep clear. It is indeed ironic that the peace negotiations
have hitherto led only to an escalation of the Namibian conflict, for
South Africa has intensified its bombing of SWAPO base camps in
Angola and Zambia, while SWAPO has sent terrorist squads ever
deeper into Namibian territory.

Topographically, Namibia may be divided into four distinct natural regions. The diversity of the physical geography of Namibia has important implications pertaining to the suitability of different types of warfare in each region. The northern sector, from Ovamboland eastwards to the Caprivi Strip, has a woodland and dry forest vegetation akin to that in southern Angola and in Zimbabwe. Shallow watercourses run through the woodlands. This type of environment has proven to be amenable to guerilla warfare tactics and has hindered the mobility of more conventional armed forces. The arid coastal Namib Desert extends from the southern to the northern border of the country (Figure 22.4). For the most part it is composed of moving sands and rocky, barren plains, and it is very difficult to traverse. To the east of the desert is the Great Escarpment with the Central Plateau beyond. The latter has a diversified landscape of undulating plains, sand-filled valleys, and some high rocky outcrops. This sub-desert steppe has scattered low shrubs and grasses, with portions of the plateau sustaining reasonably good grazing lands when it rains. The Kalahari Belt, to the east and north-east of the plateau, is largely a wooded steppe and savannah, with sand dunes in the east. The Central Plateau and the Kalahari are thus sparsely vegetated with very little forest cover. An environment such as this is not too conducive to the successful launching of guerilla operations and instead favours more conventional warfare techniques. Some higher and remoter areas of the Central Plateau proved to be good locations for guerilla-like fighting by the Hottentots in 1904-06, but today's South African ground forces, supported by helicopter gunships, would make a formidable foe even in that terrain.

The irregular shape of Namibian boundaries has also had important strategic implications for the territory. The South African Government has shown an increasing understanding of the strategic advantages offered by maintaining military control of the Caprivi Strip and Walvis Bay. Since the days of Count Caprivi, the German Chancellor who seized the area for his country in 1890, the Caprivi Strip in north-east Namibia has been described as a 'dagger pointing to the heart of Africa' (Figure 22.1). Bases in the Caprivi Strip are able to project military power over wide areas of Angola, Zambia, Zimbabwe, and Botswana. The South Africans have recently constructed military bases at Mpacha, Kamenga, and Katina Mulilo in the Caprivi Strip for this purpose.

Walvis Bay has great military importance as a port, as noted earlier, because of its location. Also, the pattern of Namibia's transportation infrastructure makes Walvis Bay the only major outlet to the sea for Namibia. As Namibia's only deep-water port, control over Walvis Bay is vital for both the country's economy and security. South Africa claims that Walvis Bay has been an integral part of the Cape Province of South Africa since the Cape Colony legislature passed the 'Walvis Bay and St John's River Territories Annexation Act' in 1884. However, it has somewhat compromised its position by administering Walvis Bay from Windhoek (the capital of Namibia) since 1922, only transferring administration back to the Cape Province on 1 September 1977. The fate of the future status of Walvis Bay has been left for a future independent government of Namibia to negotiate.

Any geopolitical study of Namibia must also take into account problems posed by the tremendous ethnic diversity of the population. In 1979 Namibia's total population was estimated to be 961,522 (SWA/Namibia Information Service, 1979 p. 13). Broken down this is: Ovambo, 442,936 (46%); White, 110,271 (11.5%); Damara, 85,518 (8.9%); Kavango, 65,254 (6.8%); Herero, 61,988 (6.4%); Nama, 42,865 (4.5%); Coloured, 36,571 (3.8%); East Caprivi, 33,205 (3.4%); Bushman, 29,343 (3.1%); Rehoboth Baster, 22,256 (2.3%); Koakolander, 7459 (0.8%); Tswana, 4937 (0.5%); and others, 18,919 (2.0%).

Namibia has been inhabited since prehistoric times by the Bushman, Nama, and Damara ethnic groups. In the sixteenth and seventeenth centuries the Herero and Ovambo migrated to what is now Namibian territory. The Basters, Coloureds, Orlam Hottentots, and Whites followed in the eighteenth and nineteenth centuries. Namibian tribal societies have traditionally been nomadic, stateless, and patriarchically organized according to clans. In the far north, where cultivation and stock-raising were possible, strong monarchies developed in the larger population clusters. Most Namibian tribal societies have traditionally subdivided their land in a communal fashion according to the established usufruct rights of the tribe. Roman-Dutch territorial law has proven to be foreign and unintelligible to most of Namibia's tribal inhabitants. Many of these peoples have been dislocated from their traditionally settled areas by incoming Whites and persons of mixed blood. In 1922 African reserves were established for native settlement, but many of these reserves were located on land which is dry or otherwise unusable. Since the arrival of Whites in Namibia, the natives have gradually been removed from most of the best agricultural land in the territory, often through trickery or simply outright force.

Currently, the White population, which comprises but 11.5% of the total population, is located on more than two-thirds of the viable agricultural land in the country. Put another way, in per capita terms, the white population has ten times more land than the

Africans, although it has been suggested that if water availability (including artesian supplies) is considered then the ratio could be as much as fifty times more (Wellington, 1967; Best and de Blij, 1977, p. 376). Water availability is critical for most activities for only the north-east quarter of the country receives more than 12 in. (305 mm) average annual precipitation, but even in those areas which receive more than this there are problems caused by high evaporation rates. Most of the White farming areas are located in sections of the country which receive less than 12 in. of rain each year.

Today 60% of the Africans are located in the northern areas. Almost all of the non-Whites have been crowded into the reserves, or 'homelands' (Figures 22.2 and 22.3), unable to leave without official government passes for employment on the outside. Those who have received permission to be within White areas are restricted in their movements and are denied both free access to jobs and many fundamental human rights (Fraenkel, 1974). Widespread socioeconomic inequality has become one of the cornerstones of Namibian society. In 1977, according to UN calculations, White salary income was set at 2000 rand per capita, while the combined Black wage and subsistence income was only 113 rand per capita (UN Institute for Namibia, 1978). The denial of adequate public amenities has turned the reserves into pockets of squalor, disease, and poverty. In 1973 there was one doctor for every 900 Whites in Namibia, but in the northern reserves the ratio was one to 30,000 *(New African Yearbook,* 1979, p. 239). With this level of inequality in Namibian society, it is little wonder that Namibian Blacks have increasingly focused their attention on the question of land reform.

Until recently, South Africa has vigorously attempted to forestall the possibility of free elections in Namibia involving all political parties. Only since 1977 have South African leaders admitted publicly that UN-sponsored elections are the only vehicle which will bring about an end to the conflict in Namibia. Until the early 1970s, South Africa attempted to promote the division of Namibia into seven or eight 'Bantustans' which would be given severely limited powers under the overall authority of the South African appointed Administrator-General. When it became apparent that the division of Namibia into 'Bantustans' was unacceptable to the world community, Black Africa, and the majority of Namibians themselves, South Africa began to support the idea of an 'internal settlement' involving elections among moderate Namibian parties. In 1977 the South African-sponsored elections were finally held. SWAPO and several other radical parties did not participate, and the elections did not serve to defuse the atmosphere of conflict.

At present, the 50,000 South African troops in Namibia are mostly stationed in the northern sector in a string of base camps stretching from the Atlantic Ocean to the Caprivi Strip. All inhabitants have been forcibly removed from within 50 km of the Angolan/Namibian border and a fence has been constructed along the border in an attempt to prevent guerilla infiltration. In addition, South Africa has conducted numerous air strikes on SWAPO base camps in Angola and Zambia and has formed a covert alliance with the Angolan guerilla faction UNITA against SWAPO and their supporters.

Despite a heavy commitment of sophisticated equipment and manpower into the war effort, the South Africans have been unable to halt SWAPO guerilla incursions into Namibia. Until recently, South African troops were successful in preventing guerilla infiltration beyond the 'Red Line' into the southern 'Police Zone' where the country's resource wealth, development technology, and White population are located (Figure 22.3). However, in 1979 several roads and railway lines in the southern sector were sabotaged and guerilla bands were reported to be operating in several areas of White-owned farms. Endeavouring to combat guerilla incursions into the 'Police Zone', vigilance squads of White farmers have been formed in the Tsumeb, Grootfontein, and Outjo districts which border the northern African sector. But, so far, these and other anti-terrorist measures have failed to prevent an increase in the intensity or spatial extent of SWAPO operations.

It appears from any analysis of the situation that only free, UN-sponsored elections involving all Namibian political parties will decrease the tensions and conflict in Namibia. Most observers feel that SWAPO will handily win such elections. Although SWAPO has traditionally received its greatest support from Ovamboland (it began as the Ovamboland Peoples' Organization in 1957), recent indicators show that it has greatly expanded its appeal with other Namibian ethnic groups, including the Hereros, Namas, Tswanas, and Caprivians. Other Namibian political parties have as yet been unable to gain any broad ethnic support and have suffered from a perceived closeness to the South African administration. If the recent Zimbabwean election is a sound guide, the majority of Black African voters will support the party which has most intently carried on the guerilla struggle against White supremacy and which can best articulate the philosophy of land reform. SWAPO has been the only Namibian political party to wage a guerilla struggle against South African authority. It has spread its operations from the Caprivi Strip, in the 1960s, to almost the entire northern sector, in the final half of the 1970s. In the last two years, guerilla infiltration has spread south of the 'Red Line'. This persistent effort against South African domination, combined with SWAPO's strong stand on land reform, will undoubtedly be remembered at the polls if ever free elections are held.

Conclusion

With the ascendancy of a Black-ruled government to power in Zimbabwe, more attention will surely be focused on the continuing conflict in Namibia. A peaceful solution to the Namibian problem would have important ramifications on a local, regional, and world scale. The lives of the people of Namibia would, hopefully, be returned to a state of normalcy once the disruptive effects of the war are removed. A Black government in Namibia could institute fundamental rural and land reforms as a vehicle for the narrowing of widespread socioeconomic inequalities which now plague Namibian society. Rather than have racial and ethnic distinctivenesses continue to be stressed, as has been the case under South African rule, the disparate tribal groupings would have to be welded together in order to create a sense of national spirit that would serve to unite peoples and regions. A positive 'Black' African *raison d'être* for their country will have to be formulated that will have continuing importance after the 'anti-South African/for independence' excitement has passed. The *raison d'être* as developed by the elites will have to be related to traditional ways of doing things and should find expression in a 'developmental framework' for the people to work within (Knight, 1974).

Black rule in itself will not solve all of the country's problems, for many reconstructions will be necessary (and it will be interesting to trace how these happen; Knight, 1971). However, a Namibian solution to the present situation would promote the establishment of an atmosphere of mutual trust and understanding between the states of Black Africa and South Africa. If such an atmosphere could prevail new economic relationships and a meaningful dialogue could be established. The benefits which could accrue to both Black Africa and South Africa would far out-reach any strategic consequences which a change in power in Namibia might entail. Finally, an end to the Namibian conflict would remove the immediate necessity of Soviet military intervention in southern Africa. Black African states could move to distance themselves from military dependency on any of the great powers. There will remain, of course, the immense issue of the future *within* the

Republic of South Africa. For the moment, however, if the conflict can be removed from Namibia, it will certainly have significant repercussions not only for the people of Namibia, but for the region of southern Africa and, indeed, the world community itself.

Acknowledgements

Mr Sam S. Aryeetey-Attoh assisted Knight with the compilation of the figures which were drafted by Miss Chris Earl, Cartographer, Department of Geography, Carleton University.

References

Arkhurst, F. S. (ed.) (1975). *United States Policy Toward Africa* (Praeger, New York).

Best, A. C. G., and de Blij, H. (1977). *African Survey* (Wiley, New York).

Boateng, E. A. (1978). *A Political Geography of Africa* (Cambridge University Press, Cambridge).

Bruwer, J. P. van S. (1966). *South West Africa: The Disputed Land* (Nasionale Boekhandel, Cape Town).

Charles, B. (1976). 'The impossible dialogue with 'White' southern Africa', *International Perspectives* (Canada), July/August, pp. 11-16.

Cline, R. S. (1978). 'The geo-politics of Southern Africa', in de Villiers, C. (ed.), *The United States of America and Southern Africa*, pp. 30-41 (Foreign Affairs Association, Pretoria).

Daniels, G. M. (ed.) (1969). *Southern Africa: A Time for Change* (Friendship Press, New York).

de Villiers, C. (ed.) (1977). *Southern Africa: The Politics of Raw Materials* (Foreign Affairs Association, Pretoria).

de Villiers, C. (ed.) (1978). *The United States of America and Southern Africa* (Foreign Affairs Association, Pretoria).

du Plessis, J. (1976). *Soviet Strategy Towards Southern Africa* (Foreign Affairs Association, Pretoria).

du Plessis, J. (1977a). *The Brezhnev Doctrine and South Africa* (Foreign Affairs Association, Pretoria).

du Plessis, J. (1977b). *South Africa: The Link of Terror* (Foreign Affairs Association, Pretoria).

First, R. (1963). *South West Africa* (Penguin, Harmondsworth).

Fraenkel, P. (1974). *The Namibians of South West Africa* (Minority Rights Group, London).

Gann, L. H., and Duignan, P. (1978). *South Africa: War, Revolution, or Peace* (Hoover Institution, Stanford).

Green, L. P., and Fair, T. J. D. (1962). *Development in Africa: A Study in Regional Analysis with Special Reference to Southern Africa* (Witwatersrand University Press, Johannesburg).

Knight, D. B. (1969). 'Botswana: external politico-economic problems', *Focus*, **XX**(3), 9-12.

Knight, D. B. (1971). 'Impress of authority and ideology on landscape: a review of some unanswered questions', *Tijdschrift voor Economische en Sociale Geografie,* **LXII**(6), 383-7.

Knight, D. B. (1974). 'Racism and reaction: the development of a Botswana 'raison d'etre' for the country', in Evenden, L. J., and Cunninghams, F. F. (eds.), *Cultural Discord in the Modern World: Geographical Themes,* pp. 111-26 (Tantalus, Vancouver).

Knight, D. B. (1975). 'Botswana at the developmental threshold', *Focus,* **XXVI**(2), 9-13.

Legum, C. (1976). 'Foreign intervention in Angola', *African Contemporary Record* (1975-76), pp. A3-A38.

Legum, C. (1977). 'Southern Africa: the year of the whirlwind', *African Contemporary Record* (1976-77) pp. A3-A58.

Legum, C. (1978). 'The southern African crisis', *African Contemporary Record* (1977-78), pp. A3-A32.

Luttwak, E. N. (1978). *The Third World: Premises of US Policy* (Institute of Contemporary Studies, San Francisco).

Morris, M. (1974). *Armed Conflict in Southern Africa* (Jeremy Spence, Cape Town).

Moss, R. (1978). 'Response to Soviet expansion', in de Villiers, C. (ed.), *The United States of America and Southern Africa,* pp. 77-85 (Foreign Affairs Association, Pretoria).

Potholm, C. P., and Dale, R. (eds.) (1972). *Southern Africa in Perspective* (The Free Press, New York).

Prinsloo, D. S. (1976). *The Turnhalle and Independence* (Foreign Affairs Association, Pretoria).

Prinsloo, D. S. (1977). *Walvis Bay and the Penguin Islands* (Foreign Affairs Association, Pretoria).

Prinsloo, D. S. (1977). *South West Africa/Namibia: Towards a Negotiated Settlement* (Foreign Affairs Association, Pretoria).

Rikhye, I. J. (1978). *Negotiating the End of Conflicts: Namibia and Zimbabwe* (Bourne Press, Bournemouth, England).

Schieber, M. T. (1976). 'Apartheid under pressure: South Africa's military strength in a changing political context', *Africa Today,* **23,** 27-46.

Schneider, W. (1978). 'Southern Africa and the politics of raw materials', in de Villiers, C. (ed.), *The United States of America and Southern Africa,* pp. 42-52 (Foreign Affairs Association, Pretoria).

Schuettinger, R. L. (1976). *South Africa: The Vital Link* (Council on American Affairs, Washington).

Spence, J. E. (1970). *The Strategic Significance of Southern Africa* (Royal United Services Institution, London).

SWA/Namibia Information Service. (1979). *SWA/Namibia Today* (Creda Press, Cape Town).

Thomas, W. H. (1980). 'A Southern African 'constellation of states': challenge or myth', *South Africa International,* **X**(3), 113-28.

Vanneman, P., and James, M. (1976). 'The Soviet intervention in Angola: intentions and implications', *Strategic Review* (Summer 1976), pp. 92-103.

Wellington, J. H. (1967). *South West Africa and Its Human Issues* (Clarendon Press, London).

Whitaker, J. S. (1978). *Africa and the United States* (New York University Press, New York).

Africa Confidential (Miramoor, London).

African Contemporary Record (Africana, New York).

Facts and Reports on Southern Africa (Committee on Southern Africa, Amsterdam).

Military Balance, 1977-78 (International Institute of Strategic Studies, London).

New African Yearbook (IC Magazines, London).

Index

Authors whose models are debated in the text are referred to in this index; other authors whose publications are mentioned are listed at the end of each introduction and chapter.

515